Rural India Perspective 2017

Rural India Perspective 2017

NABARD

OXFORD

UNIVERSITY PRESS

Oxford University Press is a department of the University of Oxford.
It furthers the University's objective of excellence in research, scholarship,
and education by publishing worldwide. Oxford is a registered trademark of
Oxford University Press in the UK and in certain other countries.

Published in India by
Oxford University Press
2/11 Ground Floor, Ansari Road, Daryaganj, New Delhi 110 002, India

ISBN-13: 978-0-19-949146-9
ISBN-10: 0-19-949146-1

Typeset in 10.5/12.7 Minion Pro
by Tranistics Data Technologies, Kolkata 700 091
Printed in India by Rakmo Press, New Delhi 110 020

Contents

Tables, Figures, and Boxes

FIGURES

BOXES

Foreword

I have immense pleasure in presenting *Rural India Perspective 2017*, a report by the National Bank for Agriculture and Rural Development (NABARD). The report is, in a way, a reiteration of our commitment to address the issues and challenges, both at policy and operational levels, in the achievement of sustainable agriculture and rural prosperity in India.

The report is a compilation of insightful and scholarly research papers by eminent researchers, practitioners, and experts in the field of agriculture and rural development. It highlights the importance of agriculture and the rural sector in India's growth story, along with its various problems and challenges, and prescribes suitable policy interventions to address the same.

Agriculture provides employment to about 48.9 per cent of the total workforce in India, but contributes only 15 per cent to the country's gross value added (GVA). With 85 per cent of operational agricultural land holdings belonging to the category of small and marginal, the average size of holding is a minuscule 1.15 hectares, thereby preventing the majority of farmers from crossing the poverty line. In this context, the Government of India's mission of 'Doubling of Farmers' Income by 2022' is expected to lead to a significant increase in the income of farmers through enhancement in agricultural production and productivity, reduction in cost of cultivation, crop diversification, promotion of allied and off-farm activities, efficient agri-value chain management, and marketing of produce through electronic National Agriculture Market (e-NAM). This would entail massive investments in irrigation, high value agriculture and horticulture, dairy, poultry and other allied sectors, agri-value chains, and rural infrastructure. This report prescribes that in order to make agriculture more profitable, productive, and sustainable, there is a need to carry out innovations all along the agri-value chains.

The report examines regional variations in agricultural performance and growth pattern across Indian states. There is also an analysis of the growth and trends in major agricultural inputs, including land, labour, water, fertilizers, seeds, pesticides, farm power/machinery, and electricity.

The importance of the dairy sector in enhancing rural income is widely acknowledged. This report includes an assessment of opportunities and challenges in smallholder livestock production systems, and the role of public policy for faster and sustainable development of the livestock sector.

Access to credit from formal sources at affordable rates of interest is essential to improve productivity and income in agriculture, allied, and off-farm sectors. This report makes an in-depth analysis of agriculture credit, financial inclusion and microfinance in the country.

The report also covers analysis of other areas of importance to the rural economy, namely, rural infrastructure, reforms in rural development policies of the government, social sector development, agri-value chains, farmer producer organizations, and the MSME sector.

Rural India Perspective 2017 is a comprehensive document covering a gamut of policy and operational issues related to agriculture and rural development. I hope this report will be very useful, while generating significant interest among policymakers, bankers, financial institutions, academicians, researchers, and practitioners in the area of agriculture and rural development.

DR HARSH KUMAR BHANWALA
Chairman, NABARD
Mumbai, India

Acknowledgements

At the outset, we wish to express our sincere gratitude to Dr Harsh Kumar Bhanwala, chairman, National Bank for Agriculture and Rural Development (NABARD), for being the inspiration and the driving force behind the preparation and publication of *Rural India Perspective 2017*. His inspiring leadership, unstinted support, and guidance have motivated us to successfully accomplish the task of editing this first-of-its-kind report by NABARD.

We wish to express our sincere thanks to Mr H.R. Dave and Mr R. Amalorpavanathan, deputy managing directors at NABARD, not only for being our guides and master strategists, but also for contributing two thought-provoking chapters in this report.

We are grateful to all the contributors in this report. It has indeed been a great honour for us to receive chapters from eminent academicians and policymakers such as Prof. Ramesh Chand, member, NITI Aayog, New Delhi, India; Dr Ashok Gulati, Infosys chair professor of agriculture, Indian Council of Research on International Economic Relations (ICRIER), New Delhi; Dr G. Raghuram, director, Indian Institute of Management Bangalore, India; Mr Jugal K. Mohapatra, ex-secretary, Government of India, Ministry of Rural Development; Dr Santhosh Mathew, chairperson, National Council for Teacher Education, Ministry of Human Resource Development, Government of India; Prof. Vasant Gandhi, NABARD chair professor, Indian Institute of Management Ahmedabad, India; Dr Pratap S. Birthal, ICAR national professor, National Institute of Agricultural Economics and Policy Research, New Delhi; Dr Gopal Naik, professor and chairperson of economics and social sciences, Indian Institute of Management Bangalore; Dr Amar K.J.R. Nayak, NABARD chair professor, Xavier Institute of Management Bhubaneswar, India; Dr J. Dennis Rajakumar, director, EPW Research Foundation, Mumbai, India; Dr P.M. Mathew, senior fellow and director, Institute of Small Enterprises and Development, Cochin, India; Prof. R. Ramakumar, NABARD chair professor and dean, School of Development Studies, Tata Institute of Social Sciences, Mumbai; and Dr C. Hazarika, director, postgraduate studies, Assam Agricultural University, Jorhat, India.

We also thank other accomplished authors and co-authors, Dr Shivendra Kumar Srivastava, researcher, and Ms Jaya Jumrani, scientist, at ICAR-National Institute of Agricultural Economics and Policy Research, New Delhi; Ms Shweta Saini, senior external consultant at ICRIER; Ms Ashwini Baje, research associate at Indian Institute of Managment Bangalore; Dr Indrajit Barman, assistant professor at Assam Agriculture University; and Dr Tulsi Lingareddy, an independent economist.

We are grateful to Mr M.V. Ashok, chief general manager (retired), Department of Economic Analysis and Research (DEAR), NABARD, Mumbai, for his constant encouragement since the conception of the idea of the report till the finalization of the draft document, before his retirement. We also thank Dr U.S. Saha, chief general manager, DEAR, NABARD, for his encouragement and keen interest in the publication of the report.

Thanks are due to our colleagues Mr B.V.S. Prasad and Dr K.J.S. Satyasai, general managers, DEAR, NABARD, for their encouragement. We also thank our other colleagues for their support: Ms Asavari Amlekar, Mr Greville Kharlukhi, Swati Ranadive, and Deblina Patra, managers at DEAR, NABARD.

Finally, we wish to express our gratitude to Oxford University Press and its excellent editorial and other teams involved in the publication of *Rural India Perspective 2017*.

We would like to emphasize that the views expressed by the authors in this report are personal and do not necessarily reflect the views of NABARD.

DEBESH ROY
GOPAKUMARAN NAIR
GYANENDRA MANI
(Editorial Team*)

* Debesh Roy and Gopakumaran Nair are Deputy General Managers and Gyanendra Mani is General Manager at the National Bank for Agriculture and Rural Development (NABARD), Mumbai, Thiruvananthapuram, and Itanagar (respectively), India.

Abbreviations

AABY	Aam Aadmi Bima Yojana
AAGR	average annual growth rate
ABEP	Annual Branch Expansion Plan
ACD	Agricultural Credit Department
AF	Adaptation Fund
AFB	Adaptation Fund Board
AIBP	Accelerated Irrigation Benefits Programme
AIC	Agriculture Insurance Company of India Limited
AIDIS	All India Debt & Investment Surveys
AISES	All India School Education Survey
ANBC	adjusted net bank credit
ANM	auxiliary nurse midwives
APEDA	Agricultural & Processed Food Products Export Development Authority
API	Application Programming Interfaces
APMC	Agricultural Produce Marketing Committee
ARDC	Agricultural Refinance and Development Corporation
ARWSP	Accelerated Rural Water Supply Programme
ASER	Annual Survey of Education Report
ASHA	Accredited Social Health Activists
ASI	Annual Survey of Industries
AWS	automated weather station
AYUSH	Ayurveda, Yoga and Naturopathy, Unani, Siddha and Homoeopathy
BAU	business as usual
BBNL	Bharat Broadband Network Limited
BC	banking correspondent
BDS	business development services
BE	biennial ending
BIS	Bureau of Indian Standards
BIT	Behavioural Insights Team
BPL	below poverty line
BPO	business process outsourcing

BQ	Black Quarter
BRICS	Brazil, Russia, India, China, and South Africa
BRLF	Bharat Rural Livelihoods Foundation
BSBDA	Basic Savings Bank Deposit Accounts
CAG	comptroller and auditor general
CAGR	compounded annual growth rate
CASP	Central Assistance to State Plan
CBGA	Centre for Budget and Governance Accountability
CBLO	Collateralized Borrowing and Lending Obligation
CBO	community based institution
CBR	crude birth rate
CCA	Controller of Certifying Authorities
CD	credit to deposit
CDC	Centres for Disease Control and Prevention
CDR	crude death rate
CE	consumption expenditure
CEA	chief economic adviser
CFMP	Citizen Feedback Monitoring Programme
CGARD	Centre for Geo-Informatics Application in Rural Development
CGTMSE	Credit Guarantee Fund Trust for Micro and Small Enterprises
CHC	community health centre
CIG	common interest group
CISS	competitiveness, inclusiveness, sustainability and scalability
CLTS	Community-Led Total Sanitation
CMC	collateral management services
CPI	consumer price index
CRAFICARD	Committee to Review Arrangements for Institutional Credit for Agriculture & Rural Development
CS	central sector
CSC	common service centre
CSO	Central Statistical Organization
CSR	corporate social responsibility
CSS	Centrally Sponsored Scheme
CUG	closed user group
DAE	Direct Access Entity
DAR	debt to asset ratio
DBT	Direct Benefit Transfer
DCCB	District Central Cooperative Bank
DDUGJY	Deen Dayal Upadhyay Gram Jyoti Yojana
DDU-GKY	Deen Dayal Upadhyay Grammen Kaushalya Yojana
DEAR	Department of Economic Analysis and Research
DES	Directorate of Economics and Statistics
DFS	Department of Financial Services
DME	Directory Manufacturing Establishment
DoRD	Department of Rural Development
DPEP	District Primary Education Programme
ECCE	Early Childhood Care and Education
EDII	Entrepreneurship Development Institute of India
EDP	Entrepreneurship Development Program
e-NAM	electronic National Agriculture Market
EPoD	Evidence for Policy Design
EPWRF	Economic & Political Weekly Research Foundation

ES	Enterprise Survey
EU	European Union
EUS	Employment & Unemployment Survey
FAO	Food and Agriculture Organization
FDI	Foreign Direct Investment
FIF	Financial Inclusion Fund
FIP	Financial Inclusion Plan
FITF	Financial Inclusion Technology Fund
FM	finance minister
FMC	Forward Markets Commission
FMD	Foot and mouth disease
FPC	farmer producer company
FPF	Food Processing Fund
FPO	farmer producer organization
FSS	Farmers' Service Society
FSSAI	Food Safety and Standards Authority of India
FY	financial year
GCA	gross cropped area
GCC	General Purpose Credit Card
GCF	Green Climate Fund
GCFA	gross capital formation in agriculture
GDP	gross domestic product
GER	gross enrollment ratio
GHI	Global Hunger Index
GHP	good hygienic practice
GIZ	Deutsche Gesellschaft für Internationale Zusammenarbeit GmbH
GJRHFS	Golden Jubilee Rural Housing Finance Scheme
GLC	general line of credit/ground level credit
GMP	good manufacturing practice
GP	gram panchayat
GPI	Gender Parity Index
GPS	global positioning system
GSDP	gross state domestic product
GSM	global system for mobile communications
GST	Goods and Services Tax
GSTN	Goods and Services Tax Network
GTI	gross trading income
GVA	gross value added
HACCP	hazard analysis and critical control points
HDI	Human Development Index
HFC	housing finance company
HYV	high yielding variety
IAP	Integrated Action Plan
IAY	Indira Awaas Yojana
ICAR	Indian Council of Agricultural Research
ICDS	Integrated Child Development Services
ICRIER	Indian Council for Research on International Economic Relations
ICT	information communication technology
IEC	information, education, and communication
IFAD	International Fund for Agricultural Development
IGNDPS	Indira Gandhi National Disability Pension Scheme

IGNOAPS	Indira Gandhi National Old Age Pension Scheme
IGNWPS	Indira Gandhi National Widow Pension Scheme
IMD	India Meteorological Department
IMF	International Monetary Fund
IMR	infant mortality rate
IOI	incidence of indebtedness
IoT	Internet of Things
IPA	Innovations for Poverty Action
IPBB	India Post Payments Bank
IPCC	Intergovernmental Panel on Climate Change
IPO	initial public offering
IRC	Indian Roads Congress
IRCTC	Indian Railway Catering and Tourism Corporation
IRDP	Integrated Rural Development Programme
ISDN	Integrated Services Digital Network
ISOPOM	Integrated Scheme for Oilseeds, Pulses, Oilpalm and Maize
ISRO	Indian Space Research Organisation
IT	information technology
IWMP	Integrated Watershed Management Programme
JLG	joint liability group
JMP	Joint Monitoring Programme
JPAL	Abdul Latif Jameel Poverty Action Lab
JRY	Jawahar Rozgar Yojana
JSSK	Janani Shishu Suraksha Karyakarm
JSY	Janani Suraksha Yojana
KCC	Kisan Credit Card
KFC	Kerala Financial Corporation
KfW	Kreditanstalt für Wiederaufbau
KIS	knowledge-intensive services
KVIC	Khadi Village Industries Commission
KVK	Krishi Vigyan Kendra
KVVES	Kerala Vyapaari Vyvasaayi Ekopana Samithi
KYC	Know Your Customer
LAMPS	Large-sized Adivasi Multi-Purpose Societies
LCM	life cycle management
LED	local economic development
LEDP	Livelihood and Enterprise Development Programme
LFPR	labour force participation rate
LTIF	Long-Term Irrigation Fund
MACS	Mutually Aided Cooperative Societies Act
MCTS	Mother and Child Tracking System
MCX	Multi Commodity Exchange of India Limited
MDG	millennium development goals
MDMS	Mid-Day Meal Scheme
MDWS	Ministry of Drinking Water and Sanitation
MFI	microfinance institution
MGNREGA	Mahatma Gandhi National Rural Employment Guarantee Act
MGNREGS	Mahatma Gandhi National Rural Employment Guarantee Scheme
MIS	Management Information System
MMR	maternal mortality rate
MMT	million metric tonne

MNEW	National Mission for Empowerment of Women
MNRE	Ministry of New and Renewable Energy
MoDWS	Ministry of Drinking Water and Sanitation
MoFPI	Ministry of Food Processing Industries
MoHFW	Ministry of Health and Family Welfare
MoRD	Ministry of Rural Development
MoSPI	Ministry of Statistics and Programme Implementation
MoUD	Ministry of Urban Development
MoWR	Ministry of Water Resources
MPCE	monthly per capita consumption expenditure
MSE	micro and small enterprises
MSME	micro, small, and medium enterprises
MSP	minimum support price
MT	million tonne
MUDRA	Micro Units Development and Refinance Agency
NABARD	National Bank for Agriculture and Rural Development
NABFINS	NABARD Financial Services Ltd
NAFCC	National Adaptation Fund for Climate Change
NAIS	National Agricultural Insurance Scheme
NAS	National Accounts Statistics
NASSCOM	National Association of Software and Services Companies
NBA	Nirmal Bharat Abhiyan
NBFC	Non-banking Finance Companies
NBOT	National Board of Trade
NCDEX	National Commodity & Derivatives Exchange Limited
NCIP	National Crop Insurance Programme
NCTE	National Council for Teacher Education
NDME	non-directory manufacturing establishment
NDP	net domestic product
NDWM	National Drinking Water Mission
NER	North Eastern Region
NFBS	National Family Benefit Scheme
NFPDC	National Food Processing Development Council
NFS	non-farm sector
NFSA	National Food Security Act
NFSM	National Food Security Mission
NGO	Non-Governmental Organization
NGP	Nirmal Gram Puruskar
NHB	National Housing Bank
NHM	National Health Mission
NICRA	National Initiative on Climate Resilient Agriculture
NIDA	NABARD Infrastructure Development Assistance
NIE	National Implementing Entity
NIRD	National Institute of Rural Development
NITI Aayog	National Institution for Transforming India Aayog
NLEDF	National Local Economic Development Fund
NLM	National Literacy Mission
NMCE	National Multi Commodity Exchange
NMEW	National Mission for Empowerment of Women
NMFP	National Mission on Food Processing
NMSA	National Mission on Sustainable Agriculture

NNMB	National Nutrition Monitoring Bureau
NOFN	National Optical Fibre Network
NPA	non-performing asset
NPCI	National Payments Corporation of India
NPE	National Policy on Education
NPS	National Pension System
NPV	net present value
NRC (LTO)	National Rural Credit (Long-Term Operations)
NREP	National Rural Employment Programme
NRHM	National Rural Health Mission
NRLM	National Rural Livelihoods Mission
NRRDA	National Rural Road Development Agency
NSAP	National Social Assistance Programme
NSS	National Sample Survey
NSSO	National Sample Survey Office
NUEPA	National University of Educational Planning and Administration
NWM	National Water Mission
NWR	negotiable warehouse receipt
OAE	own account enterprises
OAME	own account manufacturing enterprise
OBC	Other Backward Classes
OBE	off-balance sheet exposure
ODF	open defecation free
OECD	Organisation for Economic Co-operation and Development
OG	outgrowth
OMMAS	Online Management, Monitoring and Accounting System
OTS	one time settlement
PACS	Primary Agricultural Credit Societies
PC	producer company
PCARDB	Primary Cooperative Agriculture and Rural Development Bank
PDS	public distribution system
PE	private equity
PFA	Project Facilitation Agency
PFMS	Public Financial Management System
PFRDA	Pension Fund Regulatory and Development Authority
PHC	primary health centre
PHIRA	Productive Housing in Rural Areas
PIM	Participatory irrigation management
PITB	Punjab Information Technology Board
PLP	Potential Linked Credit Plan
PMAY-G	Pradhan Mantri Awas Yojana - Gramin
PMEGP	Prime Minister's Employment Generation Programme
PMFBY	Pradhan Mantri Fasal Bima Yojana
PMGSY	Pradhan Mantri Gram Sadak Yojana
PMJDY	Pradhan Mantri Jan Dhan Yojana
PMKSY	Pradhan Mantri Krishi Sinchai Yojana
PMSBY	Pradhan Mantri Swasthya Bima Yojana
PODF	Producer Organization Development Fund
POPI	Producer Organization Promoting Institution
PPP	public–private partnership
PPR	peste des petits ruminant

PRODUCE	Producers Organization Development and Upliftment Corpus
PSK	Poorna Shakti Kendra
PSL	priority sector lending
PTR	pupil-to-teacher ratio
QR	quantitative restriction
R&D	research and development
RBI	Reserve Bank of India
RBSK	Rashtriya Bal Swasthya Karyakram
RCM	Rotary Club of Madras
RE	revised estimates
REDP	Rural Entrepreneurship Development Programme
ReMS	Rashtriya Electronic Market Scheme
RFI	Rural Financial Institution
RGGVY	Rajiv Gandhi Gram Vidyutikaran Yojana
RHF	Rural Housing Fund
RIDF	Rural Infrastructure Development Fund
RKVY	Rashtriya Krishi Vikas Yojana
RLEGP	Rural Landless Employment Guarantee Programme
RMSA	Rashtriya Madhyamik Shiksha Abhiyan
RNF	rural non-farm
RPCC	Rural Planning and Credit Cell
RRB	regional rural bank
RSBY	Rashtriya Swasthya Bima Yojana
RSETI	Rural Self-Employment Training Institute
RTD	Round Table Discussion
RUDSETI	Rural Development and Self Employment Training Institute
SAGY	Sansad Adarsh Gram Yojana
SAS	Situation Assessment Survey
SBA	Swachh Bharat Abhiyan
SBI	State Bank of India
SBLP	SHG–Bank Linkage Programme
SBMO	Small Business Membership Organization
SC	Scheduled Caste
SCARDB	State Cooperative Agriculture and Rural Development Bank
SCB	Scheduled Commercial Bank
SDG	sustainable development goal
SDI	skill development initiative
SDP	skill development programme
SEBI	Securities and Exchange Board of India
SECC	Socio Economic and Caste Census
SFAC	Small Farmer Agribusiness Consortium
SFC	State Finance Corporation
SFHE	Small Farmers Horticulture Estate
SFPDC	State Food Processing Development Council
SGSY	Swarnajayanti Gram Swarojgar Yojana
SHG	self-help group
SIDBI	Small Industries Development Bank of India
SLBC	State Level Bankers Committee
SPV	special purpose vehicle
SSA	Sarva Shiksha Abhiyan
ST	Scheduled Tribe

StCB	state cooperative bank
STCCS	Short Term Co-operative Credit Structure
STCRC	Short Term Cooperative Rural Credit
STMPCP	Short Term Multipurpose Credit Product
TRAI	Telecom Regulatory Authority of India
TReDS	Trade Receivables Discounting System
TQM	Total Quality Management
UC	Utilisation Certificate
UCB	Urban Co-operative Banks
U-DISE	Unified District Information System for Education
UIDAI	Unique Identity Authority of India
UIS	UNESCO Institute of Statistics
UNCSD	United Nations Conference on Sustainable Development
UNDP	United Nations Development Programme
UNFCCC	United Nations Framework Convention on Climate Change
UPNRM	Umbrella Programme for Natural Resource Management
URP	Uniform Recall Period
URR	Unit Rejection Rate
USOF	Universal Service Obligation Fund
UT	Union Territory
VHSNC	Village Health Sanitation and Nutrition Committee
WDRA	Warehousing Development and Regulatory Authority
WDT	water-point data transmitter
WFPR	workforce and workforce participation rate
WIF	Warehouse Infrastructure Fund
WOTR	Watershed Organisation Trust
WSP	warehouse service provider

About the Contributors and Editors

CONTRIBUTORS

R. Amalorpavanathan, currently Deputy Managing Director of NABARD, is a graduate in agricultural engineering and a postgraduate in management from Indian Institute of Management Bangalore, India. He also holds a Master's degree in development management from Asian Institute of Management, Philippines. He is a fellow in engineering and a chartered engineer from Institution of Engineers (India), Kolkata, India, apart from having secured distinction in the Certified Associate of Indian Institute of Bankers (CAIIB) examinations. He is also chairman of NABKISAN Finance Limited, a subsidiary of NABARD. He has been with NABARD for more than 31 years and has worked in major states of the country such as Karnataka, Gujarat, Andhra Pradesh, and Kerala. He has had varied experience in the areas of project finance, banking, institutional development, training, and financial management. He was a member of the Asia-Pacific Policy forum. He was a professional consulting in treasury and fund management. He has provided consultancy services to several organizations, developed optimal business solutions, and worked on development strategies in diverse fields. He served as a director on the boards of regional rural banks, cooperative banks, and the Multi Commodity Exchange Ltd, New Delhi, India. Under his guidance, NABARD obtained the approval for six climate change adaptation projects from the Adaptation Fund Board, secured as National Implementing Entity of the Green Climate Fund.

Ashwini Baje is a Research Associate at the Centre for Public Policy, Indian Institute of Management Bangalore, India. She holds a Master's degree in international business management from ESC Rennes School of Business, France, and a Bachelor's degree in information technology from School of Engineering, Cochin University of Science and Technology, Kochi, India. Her research interests include the application of information technology in the fields of agriculture, education, and rural development.

Indrajit Barman is Assistant Professor at the Department of Extension Education, B.N. College of Agriculture, Assam Agriculture University, India.

Pratap S. Birthal is currently ICAR National Professor at the National Institute of Agricultural Economics and Policy Research, New Delhi, India. He holds a Master's degree and a PhD in agricultural economics from the Indian Agricultural Research Institute, New Delhi. Earlier he was Principal Economist at the International Crops Research Institute for the Semi-Arid Tropics, Hyderabad, India. His research concentrates on understanding the role of high-value crops and animal production in fostering rapid and sustainable growth in the agricultural sector and its impact on food security and poverty; market linkages and value chains in smallholder production systems; and resilience of agriculture to climate change and extreme climatic events. He is Fellow of the National Academy of Agricultural Sciences (NAAS), New Delhi, India; a recipient of the 'Young Scientist' award from the Indian Council of Agricultural Research, New Delhi, India; the D.K. Desai Prize Award from the Indian Society of Agricultural Economics, Mumbai, India; and the Dr R.T. Doshi Award from the Agricultural Economics Research Association (India), New Delhi. Birthal has published more than a hundred research papers in international and national peer-reviewed journals, in addition to several books and policy papers.

Ramesh Chand is currently member of NITI Aayog in the rank and status of Union Minister of State. He has a PhD in agricultural economics from the Indian Agricultural Research Institute (IARI), New Delhi, India. He is also a member of the Board of Trustees of International the Maize and Wheat Improvement Center (CIMMYT), Mexico; the Policy Advisory Council of the Australian Centre for International Agricultural Research, Australia; and the World Economic Forum's Global Future Council on the Future of Food Security and Agriculture. Ramesh Chand has authored seven books and more than a hundred research papers in reputed national and international journals in the areas of agriculture. He has been bestowed with the Jawaharlal Nehru Award and the Rafi Ahmed Kidwai Award of the Indian Council of Agricultural Research (ICAR), New Delhi, India.

H.R. Dave is Deputy Managing Director, NABARD. He did his postgraduate diploma in management from Indian Institute of Management Ahmedabad, India, in 1983. H.R. Dave has held various positions in NABARD, including that of Director of Bankers Institute of Rural Development (BIRD), Lucknow, India, and Chief General Manager of Corporate Planning Department at the NABARD Head Office. He has successfully steered NABARD's engagements in rural development in the states of Gujarat, New Delhi, and Arunachal Pradesh in the capacity of Regional Office In-Charge. He has extensively worked on reforms in the cooperative credit system. He has also worked as member of the secretariat to the RBI Committee on Enhancing Flow of Credit to Agriculture, besides executing advisory services assignments for national and international agencies such as Deutsche Gesellschaft für Internationale Zusammenarbeit (GIZ) GmbH, Germany, and International Fund for Agricultural Development, Italy. He has represented NABARD in several international fora including Micro Credit Summit, APRACA, and Green Climate Fund and has also negotiated collaborations with multilateral and bilateral funding agencies. He is currently Chairman on the board of NABSAMRUDDHI Finance Ltd, besides being a Director on the board of NABARD Consultancy Services Ltd (NABCONS) and the Vice-Chairman of the Governing Council Members of BIRD.

Vasant Gandhi is NABARD Chair Professor and Chairman of the Centre for Management in Agriculture, Indian Institute of Management Ahmedabad, India. He has a PhD from Stanford University, California, USA, and has worked with the World Bank and the International Food Policy Research Institute (IFPRI) in Washington, USA. He has been a Consultant to the Food and Agriculture Organization, World Bank, and the Government of India, and is a part of several company boards. He has published extensively on agriculture policies, institutions and technology in agriculture, food security, as well as markets and agribusiness. He is currently Chairman of the editorial board of the *Indian Journal of Agricultural Economics*.

Ashok Gulati is Infosys Chair Professor for Agriculture at the Indian Council for Research on International Economic Relations, New Delhi, India. He was Chairman of the Commission for Agricultural Costs and Prices, Government of India (2011–14); Director at the International Food Policy Research Institute, New Delhi, India (2001–11); NABARD Chair Professor at the Institute of Economic Growth (1998–2000); and Chief Economist at the National Council of Applied Economic Research, New Delhi, India (1991–7). He was the youngest member of the Economic Advisory Council to Prime Minister Atal Bihari Vajpayee. Currently, Gulati is a member of the Chief Minister's Task Force on Agriculture for the governments of Madhya Pradesh and Rajasthan; a member of the Board of Directors of several institutions including the Reserve Bank of India, NABARD, National Commodity and Derivatives Exchange, Mumbai, India, TERI University, New Delhi, India, and IDFC Foundation, New Delhi, India. He was awarded the Padma Shri in 2015.

C. Hazarika is Director of Postgraduate Studies, Assam Agricultural University, Jorhat, India. Earlier he was a Professor of Agricultural Economics and was involved in the teaching, research, and extension activities of the university. He is an accomplished academic with more than 28 years of distinguished performance and has contributed to institutional growth through a combination of creativity, initiative, and strong leadership. After completing his M.Sc. from Assam Agricultural University in 1987, he completed his PhD from the Tamil Nadu Agricultural University, India, in 1996. Hazarika has published more than 45 research papers, 20 abstracts, 1 book, and 14 book chapters and has also completed 13 externally funded research projects. He is a life member of various professional societies and presently is the Vice-President of the Indian Society of Agricultural Economics, Mumbai, India. He has also served as a member of the NABARD Expert Committee on Research for two years.

Jaya Jumrani is Scientist at the National Institute of Agricultural Economics and Policy Research, New Delhi, India. Her broad areas of research include food and nutritional security, agricultural credit, and agricultural growth and modelling. She holds a Master's degree in economics from the Delhi School of Economics, University of Delhi, India.

Tulsi Lingareddy is an Economist with over 15 years of research experience in the areas of macroeconomics, commodity, currency, and bond markets. She has a PhD in agricultural economics from Acharya N.G. Ranga Agricultural University, Hyderabad, India. She was awarded the University Gold Medal during postgraduation. Lingareddy has diverseed research experience working in various reputed institutes including National Academy for Agricultural Research Management, Hyderabad, EPW Research Foundation, Mumbai, India, CNBC TV18 Group, Mumbai, and Clearing Corporation of India Ltd, Mumbai. She has published numerous research articles in refereed journals and presented papers at national and international conferences.

P.M. Mathew is Senior Fellow and Director at the Institute of Small Enterprises and Development, Cochin, India. Mathew completed his studies and training in India, the UK, and the Netherlands. A development economist by training, he specializes on industrial policy, local economic development, and responsible business strategies. Mathew has been working as Consultant to the United Nations, the Government of India, and to several international organizations. A Chevening Fellow in Economic Governance at the Foreign and Commonwealth Office, UK, Mathew is also a recipient of the Oshikawa International Award, presented by the Asian Productivity Organization, Tokyo, Japan. He has written widely on public policy, enterprise development, and local economic development, and is the Editor of the India Micro, Small and Medium Enterprise Report series, published by the Government of India. P.M. Mathew is the founder of the 'ISED Small Enterprise Observatory', as also of the 'India MSME Communication Programme', India's largest stakeholder network on micro, small, and medium enterprises. As a senior fellow of the Indian Council of Social Science Research, New Delhi, India, Mathew is currently working on a project on the 'Comparative Experience of SME Policy in Developed and Emerging Economies, with Special Focus on India and the United Kingdom'.

Santhosh Mathew is a Political Economist with extensive experience as a civil servant. With a PhD from the Institute of Development Studies, Sussex, UK, an MSc from the University of Sussex, UK, and an MA from the Delhi School of Economics, India, he combines teaching and research with his assignments in the civil service. He is currently Chairperson of the National Council for Teacher Education in the Ministry of Human Resource Development, Government of India. He has previously taught at India's civil service college in Mussoorie (1994–2000) and was Country Director (2000–3) of the Leadership for Environment and Development (LEAD) programme in India. A member of the Indian Administrative Service for over 31 years, he has worked in the departments of Social Welfare, Labour, Rural Development, Finance, Health, Agriculture, and Education in Bihar. He was district magistrate of Palamau (now in Jharkhand) from 1992 to 1994.

Jugal Mohapatra, a postgraduate from Delhi School of Economics, India, joined the Indian Administrative Services (Odisha Cadre) in 1979. Later, he also obtained a Master's degree in economics from Boston University, USA, in 1992. During his career in civil service spanning over 37 years, he served as Secretary to the Chief Minister; Principal Secretary, Finance; and Development-Commissioner-cum-Additional-Chief Secretary and Chief Secretary, Government of Odisha. He was Secretary in the Department of Fertilisers and Rural Development of the Government of India during

2014–16. Currently, he is Chairman of NABARD Financial Services Ltd (NABFINS)—a subsidiary of NABARD. He was also a member of the Third Pay Revision Committee constituted by the Government of India for the central public sector enterprises.

Gopal Naik is Dean (Faculty) at the Indian Institute of Management Bangalore, India. He completed his PhD in agricultural economics at the University of Illinois at Urbana–Champaign, USA, and was a Faculty Member at Indian Institute of Management Ahmedabad, India, during 1988–2003. At the Indian Institute of Management Bangalore, which he joined in 2003, he has been teaching graduate courses on research methodology, public policy, econometrics, and managerial economics. He received Awards for Professional Excellence in recognition of superior achievement in agricultural economics in 2007 from The American Agricultural Economics Association. His co-authored paper was awarded the Title of Meritorious Paper for its contribution to the Practice of Electronic Governance in the 4th International Conference on the Theory and Practice of Electronic Governance held on 25–8 October 2010 at Beijing, China.

Amar K.J.R. Nayak is Professor of Strategic Management at the Xavier Institute of Management, Xavier University Bhubaneswar, India, where he also holds the position of NABARD Chair Professor. Nayak engages in research, teaching, and policy advice on transition strategies for rebuilding sustainable community systems. He uses both deductive and contextually rich inductive methods of research in his analysis and adopts action research in rural communities from a systems perspective to test his hypothesis and theories on specific ecosystems. He has published 4 books, 2 monographs, and over 70 cases and research articles.

G. Raghuram has been Director, Indian Institute of Management Bangalore, India, since February 2017. He was Dean (Faculty) at the Indian Institute of Management Ahmedabad, India, from September 2013 to December 2015. He was the Vice-Chancellor of the Indian Maritime University, Chennai, India, from July 2012 to March 2013. He was the Indian Railways Chair Professor from January 2008 to August 2010. Raghuram specializes in infrastructure and transport systems, and logistics and supply chain management. He conducts research on the railway, port, shipping, aviation, and road sectors. He has published over 35 refereed papers in journals and written over 155 case studies. He has also co-authored six books. He was awarded the M.C. Puri Memorial Award for contribution to operational research in India in 2016; the 'Lifetime Achievement Award' for contribution to logistics and infrastructure by EXIM News in 2014; and the 'Academician of the Year' award by the Chartered Institute of Logistics and Transport (CILT), UK, in 2012. He is a fellow of the Operational Research Society of India, Kolkata, India, and CILT. He has taught in universities in India, the USA, Canada, Yugoslavia, Singapore, Tanzania and the UAE. He is a member of the Global Future Council on Mobility of the World Economic Forum, Executive Council of the National Aviation University, and of the Board of Directors of six companies in the fields of infrastructure, logistics, and education.

J. Dennis Rajakumar is the Director of Economic and Political Weekly Research Foundation, Mumbai, India. He received his PhD in economics and M.Phil in applied economics from Jawaharlal Nehru University, New Delhi, India, through the Centre for Development Studies, Thiruvananthapuram, India. He was Charles Wallace India Trust Visiting Research Fellow at The Management School, The University of Edinburgh, Edinburgh, UK (February–April 2005). His research interests include applied macroeconomics, applied financial economics and studies of corporate sector in India. He has published several research papers.

R. Ramakumar is a Development Economist with research interests in agricultural economics, agrarian studies, and public finance. He has a PhD in quantitative economics from the Indian Statistical Institute, Kolkata, India. Currently, he is NABARD Chair Professor and Dean at the School of Development Studies, Tata Institute of Social Sciences, Mumbai, India. He is also deeply interested in the study of the economy and society of Kerala. He was previously a visiting fellow at the Centre for Development Studies, Thiruvananthapuram, India. From September 2016, he is also serving as a Non-ministerial Member in the Kerala State Planning Board.

Shweta Saini is Senior External Consultant at Indian Council for Research on International Economic Relations, New Delhi, India.

Shivendra Kumar Srivastava is a Researcher at ICAR-National Institute of Agricultural Economics and Policy Research, New Delhi, India. He has a PhD in agricultural economics from the Indian Agricultural Research Institute (IARI), New Delhi, India. His research areas include sustainable agriculture production, food and nutritional security, and policy analysis. He is Faculty Member of the Division of Agriculture Economics, ICAR-IARI.

EDITORS

Debesh Roy is currently Deputy General Manager in the Department of Economic Analysis and Research, NABARD Head Office, Mumbai, India. He is a PhD in economics from Utkal University, Bhubaneswar, India. He joined NABARD in 1988 and has been involved in several important and varied assignments in the areas of economic research, rural infrastructure development (Rural Infrastructure Development Fund and NABARD Infrastructure Development Assistance), microfinance, rural credit planning, rural non-farm sector, and institutional development of rural cooperative banks. Debesh Roy is the author of *Dynamics of Bank Deposits: The Developing States in India* (2003), four book chapters, and several research papers and articles published in journals or presented at various national and international conferences.

Gopakumaran Nair is currently Deputy General Manager, NABARD, Kerala Regional Office, Thiruvananthapuram, India. Nair joined NABARD as an economist in 1996. A native of Thiruvananthapuram, he completed his postgraduation in economics from University of Kerala, Thiruvananthapuram. He got his doctorate in economics for his study entitled 'Micro Level Planning of Health Services in Kerala' from University of Kerala. He also holds a CA degree from the Indian Institute of Banking and Finance, Mumbai, India. He had a long tenure in the Department of Economic Analysis and Research, NABARD, Head Office, Mumbai, as economist before joining the Kerala Regional Office in 2017. He has conducted more than 85 studies (many of them being all-India studies) for NABARD on various subjects including agriculture credit, interest subvention scheme of Government of India, self-help groups, joint liability groups, agriculture commodities, agriculture investment, and rural infrastructure. NABARD has published ten of his study reports and many other reports have been used as input for policy changes by the Government of India, especially in the area of agriculture credit. He was also associated with various committees as part of task forces set up by the Government of India. He has executed various consultancy assignments of the Government of India as well as Government of Kerala on behalf of NABCONS, the consultancy wing of NABARD. He has published several papers with reputed journals and presented papers at various national and international seminars.

Gyanendra Mani is currently General Manager and Officer in Charge, NABARD, Arunachal Pradesh Regional Office, India. He is a PhD in agricultural economics from G.B. Pant University of Agriculture and Technology, Pantnagar, India. He has conducted around 40 studies on behalf of NABARD and published numerous articles and research papers in Indian and international journals. Mani conceived the idea of and launched the *The Microfinance Review* journal on behalf of the Bankers Institute of Rural Development (BIRD), Lucknow, India, and managed it from 2009 to 2015 in the capacity of Managing Editor. As a faculty member of BIRD, he conducted two exposure visits of senior bankers to Israel and the Netherlands. He is also a national resource person for the 'Design of Training' programme being conducted by the Department of Personnel and Training, Government of India. He is also the Lead Editor of the recently published book *Financing Agriculture Value Chains: Challenges and Opportunities*.

Agriculture Performance in India
Main Trends, Commercialization, and Regional Disparities

Ramesh Chand* and S.K. Srivastava**

ABSTRACT

The chapter examines long-run trend in agricultural growth at disaggregated level, and assesses resilience and stability in the sector. Further, the study analyses agriculture performance across regions and delineates disadvantaged districts in the country based on selected indicators. The results suggest a cyclical pattern of growth in agricultural sector around a long-run average annual growth rate of 2.75 per cent. The year to year fluctuation in growth points out the risky nature of agricultural activities in the country. However, the sector is becoming resilient mainly because of stable growth in livestock output and broadening of production base. Although there is clear and strong evidence of rising commercialization in agriculture, efficiency, and profitability from crop cultivation have emerged as important issues that necessitate a much faster growth in productivity through application of improved technology. Agricultural growth in the last decade has narrowed down the regional disparity in agricultural productivity but large variation still persists. Future strategy of development of agriculture must focus on location-specific and regionally differentiated approach centred on resource endowment at disaggregated level.

JEL Classification: Q10, Q16, Q17, Q18, R11

Keywords: agriculture performance, commercialization, regional disparities

1.1 INTRODUCTION

Agriculture sector continues to occupy a central place in overall economic growth and development in India. Although, its contribution in total gross domestic product has declined from 51.8 per cent in 1950–1 to 17.4 per cent in 2014–15, agriculture sector still remains the largest sector of Indian economy in terms of value added output and in terms of source of livelihood. The sector provides employment to 48.9 per cent of the total workforce of the country. Besides, it sustains food and

*Member, NITI Aayog, New Delhi, India.

**Scientist, ICAR-National Institute of Agricultural Economics and Policy Research (on deputation to NITI Aayog), New Delhi, India. Views expressed in the paper are personal.

nutrition security of the large and rising population of the country. In the course of development, the sector has moved through different phases of growth following various technological interventions, institutional changes, and policy regimes (Rao 1996; Chand and Parappurathu 2012; Deokar and Shetty 2014). Significant changes have been witnessed in input use pattern and in cropping pattern in favour of commercial crops. These changes have transformed a large segment of agriculture from subsistence to a commercial enterprise. However, these changes have not been uniform across states and there exists wide regional variations and temporal fluctuation in agricultural performance.

The present chapter examines long-run trend in agriculture GDP and output at disaggregated level, and assesses resilience and stability in the sector. Using the concept of cost and return, the study evaluates changing economic viability of farm enterprises and provides empirical evidences on spatial variations in technological adoption in crop cultivation. While analysing the transition from subsistence to commercialized agriculture, we have estimated the additional returns which could be generated by the farmers if they diversify towards commercial crops. A glimpse of increasing commercialization of agriculture is also captured through achievement in international trade of agricultural products. The chapter also examines regional variations in agriculture performance and tests whether growth pattern across Indian states is leading to convergence in agricultural income or not. Lastly, disadvantaged districts in the country were delineated based on indicators of natural resources endowment, infrastructural development, input use, agricultural productivity, and demographic pressures.

1.2 TRENDS IN GROSS DOMESTIC PRODUCT–AGRICULTURE AND ALLIED SECTOR

The performance of agriculture depends on a variety of institutional, technological, and policy interventions. In the course of development, effects of such changes are aptly captured by growth in gross domestic product—agriculture and allied sectors (GDP–Ag). In the present analysis, growth trajectory of agriculture sector is examined by estimating decadal trend-growth rate in GDP–Ag. The GDP–Ag series (at 2011–12 prices) was first smoothened by taking two-year moving averages to moderate the effects of weather aberrations and other supply shocks. The trend growth rates were estimated for the 10-year period starting from the decade 1971–2 to 1980–1 and extended to the latest decade covering the period 2005–6 to 2014–15. The estimated growth rates for the decadal periods ending with 1980–1 to 2014–15 are presented in Figure 1.1.

The growth trajectory of GDP–Ag shows that agriculture sector has undergone different phases of growth since 1970–1. During 1971–2 to 1980–1 the agriculture sector witnessed 1.94 per cent annual growth, which gradually accelerated to 3.0 per cent during the 1980s. This was followed by a short spell of stagnation in agriculture growth at 3 per cent during the initial years of the 1990s. The subsequent period from 1992–3 onwards witnessed acceleration in growth rate up to 3.6 per cent

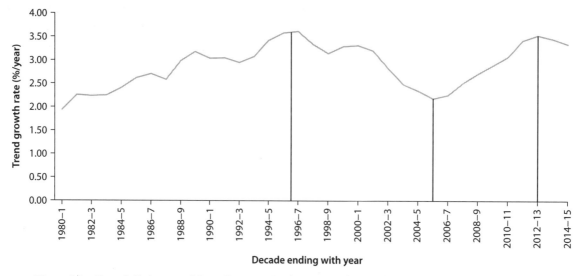

Figure 1.1   Growth Trajectory of Gross Domestic Product–Agriculture and Allied Sectors (at 2011–12 Prices)

Source: Authors' estimates based on data from National Accounts Statistics, Central Statistical Office (CSO), Ministry of Statistics and Programme Implementation, Government of India.

during the decade ending in year 1996–7. But, the tempo of growth could not be sustained for a longer time and the later half of the 1990s witnessed deceleration in agriculture growth, which continued up to the middle of the 2000s. After 2005–6 a quick recovery was registered. This took agriculture growth rate to the peak level similar to the earlier peak level. Like in the past, agriculture growth showed a tendency to move downward after 2012–13. Based on these evidences, growth trajectory of agriculture sector during the past four decades can be divided into three distinct phases. These are (*a*) 1971–2 to 1996–7; (*b*) 1996–7 to 2004–5; and (*c*): 2004–5 to 2014–15. The first period is termed as pre-liberalization period as India started liberalization of external trade following a World trade Organization (WTO) agreement in the year 1996. The second phase is termed as post-liberalization period and the third phase as the period of recovery.

The trend growth rates in GDP–Ag at constant prices during the three sub-periods are presented in Figure 1.2. The results show that Indian agriculture moved on a growth trajectory of 2.89 per cent per annum during the pre-reform period (1971–2 to 1996–7), which dropped to below 2 per cent during the next nine years. The deceleration in agriculture growth during post-reform period had a very adverse effect on farm incomes, and the country witnessed spread of agrarian distress and a big increase in the number of farmer suicides in this period. The *Mid-Term Appraisal of the Eleventh Five Year Plan* reviewed the depressing trend in agriculture and proposed multi-pronged steps to revive agriculture (Deokar and Shetty 2014). As a consequence, several policy initiatives were taken after 2004–5. Agriculture growth accelerated to 3.33 per cent during 2004–5 to

2014–15. Thus, the post-2004–5 period can be termed as the period of recovery when agriculture sector moved back to the long-term growth trajectory. However, agricultural growth trend in the last three years has moved downward. This raises doubts about sustaining the recovery of growth which began in 2004–5. The growth rates observed in recent years signal a possibility of cyclical growth pattern as witnessed after 1996–7.

1.2.1 Instability in Growth

Due to high dependency on rainfall and other vagaries of nature, growth in agricultural output faces year on year fluctuations and often witnessed decline and negative growth. During the 10-year period from 1975–6 to 1984–5, GDP–Ag witnessed a negative growth in three years (Table 1.1). The subsequent two decades also witnessed three and four years of negative growth respectively. However, it is interesting to note that during the recent decade since 2005–6, not a single year has witnessed negative growth in GDP except 2014–15. Amidst severe drought in 2009–10 and adverse effects of climate change, positive growth in GDP implies improved resilience in agriculture sector in the country. Broadening of base in favour of livestock activities also contributed to lower frequency of negative growth in the GDP (Chand 2014). The estimation of instability index further revealed decline in instability in GDP–Ag during the recent decade as compared to earlier period. These results clearly indicate improved resilience and stability in agriculture sector. The reasons underlying this stability are expansion of irrigation, technology for drought proofing, contingency plans for each district to face monsoon aberrations, development of alternative crops and varieties suitable for seasonal variations, and broadening of production base in the country (Chand 2014).

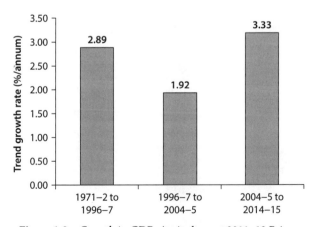

Figure 1.2 Growth in GDP–Agriculture at 2011–12 Prices
Source: Authors' estimates based on data from National Accounts Statistics, Central Statistical Office (CSO), Ministry of Statistics and Programme Implementation, Government of India.

Table 1.1 Decade-wise Frequency of Negative Growth (Year-on-Year) and Instability in Gross Domestic Product–Agriculture in India

Period	Frequency of Negative Growth	Instability Index (%)*
1975–6 to 1984–5	3	7.76
1985–6 to 1994–5	3	4.98
1995–6 to 2004–5	4	5.17
2005–6 to 2014–15	1 (2014–15)	2.51

Note: *Instability index was estimated as [Standard deviation $\{\ln(Y_{t+1}/Y_t)\}$] ×100.
Source: Authors' estimates based on data from National Accounts Statistics, Central Statistical Office (CSO), Ministry of Statistics and Programme Implementation, Government of India.

As pointed out earlier, acceleration in growth rate in agriculture that started after 2004–5 reached peak level around 2012–13 and show downward movement after that. If this downward trend continues for some more years then the recovery in growth, post 2004–5, will characterize presence of cyclical growth in the sector rather than a permanent shift in growth trajectory. It is also pertinent to point out that after 2004, as agriculture growth accelerated, the number of farmer suicides started declining and fell from 18,241 in year 2004 to 11,772 in year 2012 (Chand et al. 2015). Further, when as agriculture growth turned adverse after 2012–13, the number of suicides in farming sector increased—from 11,772 in 2013 to 12,360 in 2014 and 12,602 in 2015.

1.2.2 Agriculture Performance at Disaggregated Level

Agriculture performance at disaggregated level was seen from progress in physical output of group of commodities as well as individual commodities. Between biennium ending (BE) 1995–6 and BE2004–5, foodgrain production increased from 186 million tonnes (mt) to 206 mt, with annual growth rate of 0.55 per cent (Table 1.2). In the subsequent period between 2004–5 and 2014–15, foodgrain production accelerated at 2.72 per cent per annum and reached 259 mt by BE2014–15. Similarly, cereal production increased by 49 mt during BE2004–5 to BE2014–15 as compared to increment of only 19 mt during the previous 10 years.

Pulse production was almost stagnant at around 13 mt during BE1995–6 to BE2004–5. But the subsequent period witnessed impressive annual growth of 3.78 per cent in pulse production and output reached 18 mt by BE2014–5. Almost similar trend was noticed in case of oilseeds whose production increased by 5 mt during the recent decade as compared to addition of only 3 mt during the 10 years between BE1995–6 and BE2004–5.

The horticulture crops like fruit and vegetables witnessed impressive growth rate of more than 5 per cent during 2004–5 to 2014–15, which is significantly higher than the growth obtained during the previous period. Consequently, production of fruit and vegetables increased to 88 mt and 165 mt by BE2014–15 respectively. Within the crop sector, cotton production witnessed highest annual growth of 8.28 per cent during 2004–5 to 2014–15. The impressive growth in cotton production is primarily attributed to successful adoption of Bt technology by the cotton growers (Srivastava and Kolady 2016). Within a decade of commercial release in 2002–3, Bt hybrids occupied 91 per cent of the total cotton area in the country. The post–Bt cotton period witnessed doubling of cotton production and a transition from net importer to net exporter of cotton.

The production of all livestock products has been rising steadily for a long time and it has further picked pace after 2004–5. Presently, India is producing 142 mt of milk, 77 billion eggs, 10 mt of fish (inland and marine), and 6 mt of meat, including poultry meat. During 2004–5 to 2014–15, milk, eggs, fish, and meat

Table 1.2   Production Performance of Selected Crops/Groups

Groups/ Crops	Production (Million Tonnes)			Growth in Total Production (%/Year)		Growth in Per Capita Production (%/Year)	
	BE1995–6	BE2004–5	BE2014–15	1995–6 to 2004–5	2004–5 to 2014–15	1995–6 to 2004–5	2004–5 to 2013–14
Foodgrains	185.96	205.78	258.86	0.55	2.72	−1.23	1.36
Cereals	172.79	191.76	240.64	0.61	2.64	−1.18	1.28
Pulses	13.18	14.02	18.22	−0.23	3.78	−2.01	2.41
Oilseeds	21.73	24.77	29.71	−0.83	1.81	−2.59	0.46
Fruit	40.06	48.00	87.63	1.72	5.48	−0.09	4.08
Vegetables	69.44	94.79	164.98	3.14	5.20	1.31	3.81
Cotton*	12.38	15.08	35.69	−0.01	8.28	−1.78	6.84
Milk	65.00	90.30	142.00	3.69	4.53	1.84	3.15
Fish	4.87	6.35	10.03	2.76	4.95	0.93	3.56
Eggs[#]	26.59	42.80	76.65	6.19	5.80	4.30	4.40
Meat	1.90	2.15	6.46	2.68	12.72	0.93	11.22

Notes: *Production in million bales of 170 kg; #Production in billion numbers.
Source: Authors' estimates based on data from 'Agricultural Statistics at a Glance', Directorate of Economics and Statistics (DES), Ministry of Agriculture and Farmers' Welfare, Government of India.

grew at annual growth rates of 4.53, 5.80, 4.95, and 12.72 per cent respectively—these growth rates are higher than the earlier period except for egg. These results indicate that acceleration in agricultural output during the recent period is across all crop-groups and livestock products.

From food security point of view, increase in production should be adequate to feed the growing population in the country. During 1995–6 to 2004–5, rate of increase in production of all the food groups except vegetables and livestock products was less than the growth in population (1.81 per cent) (Table 1.2). This resulted in decline in per capita production during this period. But, the subsequent period after 2004–5 witnessed significantly higher growth in per capita production across all crop groups and livestock product due to acceleration in growth of output and deceleration in growth of population in the country.

We examined sources of recent growth in production by decomposing production of crop groups into area effect, yield effect, and interaction effect of area and yield. The results revealed that growth in crop output during 2004–5 and 2014–15 is primarily contributed by improvement in crop productivity (Table 1.3). About 88 per cent of the increase in foodgrain production was attributed to increase in yield. Similarly in cereals, pulses, oilseeds, and cotton crops, increase in yield contributed 92 per cent, 76 per cent, 67 per cent, and 45 per cent share in increase in production respectively. The higher area effect in pulses and oilseeds than in cereals could be due to relatively higher increase in area under these crops as a result of various government schemes like National Food Security Mission-Pulses (NFSM-Pulses), Integrated Scheme for Oilseeds, Pulses, Oilpalm and Maize (ISOPOM), and Accelerated Pulses Production Programme (A_3P). In case of cotton, Bt hybrids not only replaced area under *desi* cotton but also incentivized farmers to bring additional area under its cultivation. Between 2004–5 and 2014–15, area under cotton increased by 2.9 million hectares, which contributed 31 per cent in total increase in cotton production. From the preceding discussion it can be concluded that improvement in yield has emerged as a primary contributor to agricultural growth in the country.

1.3 ECONOMICS OF CROP CULTIVATION (COSTS AND RETURNS)

Economic viability of farm enterprise assumes an importance in sustaining the interest of farming community. We have examined long-term changes in real cost of production and net return from crop cultivation in India. The time-series data on cost of cultivation was collected for 10 crops across 19 major producing states for the period 1990–1 to 2014–15. The selected crops were paddy, wheat, cotton, gram, arhar, sugarcane, rapeseed and mustard, groundnut, maize, and jowar. These crops covered 66 per cent of gross cropped area (GCA) of the country in 2014–15. Thus, the estimates generated in the study represent two-thirds of the GCA of the country. The nominal values of input cost and return were expressed in real term using consumer price index for agricultural labour (CPI–AL). Further, cost and returns of selected crops across the states were aggregated into a single representative series by calculating weighted average. For this purpose, crop area in given state was taken as weight. For cost calculations, concept of A_1^1 + imputed value of family labour (Cost A_1 + FL) was taken

[1] Cost A_1 comprises of all paid out cost components such as value of hired human labour, hired bullock labour, maintenance and upkeep charges on owned bullock labour, upkeep charges of owned machines, hired machine charges, seed cost, pesticide cost, manure cost, fertilizer cost, canal irrigation charges, depreciation of implements and farm buildings, land revenue cess and other taxes, interest on working capital, and miscellaneous expenses on other inputs. Imputed value of family labour was estimated by multiplying working hours of family labour with prevailing wage rate.

Table 1.3 Growth Rate in Production of Selected Crop Groups and Its Decomposition: 2004–5 to 2014–15

Crop/Group	Growth Rate (Per Cent)			Decomposition of Production Change (Per Cent)		
	Area	Yield	Production	Area Effect	Yield Effect	Interaction Effect
Foodgrains	0.15	2.57	2.72	9	88	3
Cereals	0.01	2.63	2.64	6	92	2
Pulses	0.73	3.03	3.78	18	76	6
Oilseeds	−0.32	2.14	1.81	26	67	7
Cotton	4.44	3.68	8.28	31	45	24

Source: Authors' estimates based on data from 'Agricultural Statistics at a Glance', Directorate of Economics and Statistics (DES), Ministry of Agriculture & Farmers' Welfare, Government of India.

into account. The long-run trend in cost of cultivation (CoC:Rs/hectare), cost per Rs 100 output (Rs/Rs 100 output), and return (Rs/hectare) are plotted in Figure 1.3.

The results revealed that the real average CoC of field crops witnessed varying trends during the past three decades. During 1990–1 to 2002–3, real CoC increased at annual growth rate of 2.06 per cent. Thereafter, CoC increased at a moderate rate till the year 2007–8. The period after 2007–8 witnessed acceleration in growth in real CoC to 3.22 per cent per annum till the year 2014–15. The recent increase in CoC is primarily attributed to rising input prices, particularly labour wages (Srivastava et al. 2017). Labour constitutes close to 50 per cent share in total cost of cultivation and since 2005–6 the real daily

wages of agricultural labour has increased at the rate of 4.96 per cent per annum, which is very high (Chand and Srivastava 2014).

The rising CoC poses financial challenges to farmers and necessitates commensurate increase in crop output to absorb financial burden. We examined trend in cost per Rs 100 output over the years to know the changes in profitability in crop production. During the two decades between 1990–1 and 2002–3, increase in CoC was higher than increase in output per hectare (Figure 1.3, Panel 1). This also resulted in shrinkage in crop profitability (Figure 1.3, Panel 2). A similar result was reported by Narayanamoorthy (2007) who attributed the decline in profit from crop production to lower change in output

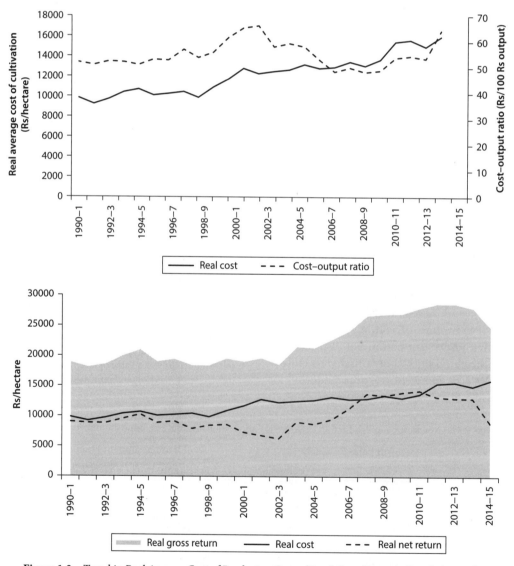

Figure 1.3   Trend in Real Average Cost of Producing Crops (Panel 1) and Return (Panel 2) in India

Source: Authors' estimates based on data from 'Agricultural Statistics at a Glance', Directorate of Economics and Statistics (DES), Ministry of Agriculture and Farmers' Welfare, Government of India.

prices as compared to the cost of production. The subsequent period between 2002–3 and 2007–8 witnessed positive growth in real output against a moderate increase in real CoC. Consequently, crop profitability witnessed substantial improvement during this period. However, in the recent period since 2007–8 the rate of increase in real CoC turned out to be significantly high as compared to stagnation in real output leading to decline in net returns from crop production in the country.

Since 2007–8, CoC is increasing at annual rate of 3.22 per cent as compared to −0.14 per cent growth in real gross return of selected crops. This implies that marginal returns from investment in crop enterprises are declining, leading to lowering down of crop profitability in the recent years (Figure 1.3, Panel 2). For economic viability of farm enterprises, there should be commensurate increase in output prices to cover production cost and sustain reasonable profit margin to the farmers. However, such cost-push inflationary trend is not desirable for the economy and hence serious efforts are needed to check rising CoC and to absorb the cost rise, if any, by accelerating crop yield improvement.

There exists wide variation in CoC across crops. Among selected crops, average CoC varied from Rs 19,983 for gram to Rs 53,318 for cotton during 2014–15 (Table 1.4). The inter-crop variation in CoC arises due to varying levels of input requirement by different crops. Besides inter-crop variations, there also exist wide inter-state variations in CoC of the same crop in the country. For instance, CoC for paddy was Rs 24,900 in Jharkhand and Rs 55,587 in Tamil Nadu during 2014–15. Thus, cultivation of paddy in Tamil Nadu involves 2.23 times the investment in paddy cultivation in Jharkhand. In India crops are grown across varied agro-climatic and geographical locations. Therefore, production technology for cultivating a crop may not be similar across different regions. The inter-state variation in CoC of crops might be the result of varying levels of technological adoption by the farmers across producing states. Apart from varying levels of technological adoption, variation in CoC

Table 1.4 Variation in Cost of Cultivation (Cost A_1+FL) across Crops and Producing States in 2014–15 (Rs/hectare)

State	Cost A_1+Family Labour (Rs/ha)							Net Returns (Rs/ha)						
	Paddy	Wheat	Maize	Arhar	Gram	R&M	Cotton	Paddy	Wheat	Maize	Arhar	Gram	R&M	Cotton
Andhra Pradesh*	52,033		41,495				56,551	31,939		33,632				9,617
Assam	36,952					27,449		−133					−2,649	
Bihar	26,862	27,472	30,414		16,039			16,621	18,582	13,233		22,544		
Chhattisgarh	31,681				15,972			13,622				7751		
Gujarat		31,163	31,736			26,193	55,606		23,067	12,522			34,526	24,348
Haryana	46,033	33,649			17,993	24,941	45,095	73,944	37,905			23019	25,833	2,183
Himachal Pradesh		22,823	22,390						5,496	1,694				
Jharkhand	24,900	20,859	32,602	13,487				18,529	1,998	14,990	29930			
Karnataka	48,704	21,189	30,761		20,886		42,892	32,867	−3,682	6,782		22845		15,615
Kerala	53,392							36,535						
Madhya Pradesh	29,281	26,221	24,803	20,303	21,377	18,674	59,275	8,211	29,014	10,064	15,928	18675	29,592	−8,340
Maharashtra		34,275	59,231	42,313			54,888		7,836	−1,014	13,958			6,532
Odisha	43,013		39,792	13,009			35,655	4,140		−1,228	9,763			−7,164
Punjab	34,347	24,119	35,704				45,470	72,479	46,367	14,057				35,136
Rajasthan		35,566	33,711		16,872	23,925	49,320		27,429	13,962		9679	22,008	34,008
Tamil Nadu	55,587						69,913	20,707						25,864
Uttar Pradesh	40,381	31,569	21,951	17,707	22,456	25,065		10,036	15,020	−463	26,509	972	9,754	
Uttarakhand	30,735	21,766						31,380	21,670					
West Bengal	55,164							3,792						
Overall	40,731	29,863	33,884	32,348	19,983	23,558	53,318	18,701	24,449	8,392	15,023	15691	20,990	13,412

Note: *Includes Telangana.
Source: Unit level data from 'Cost of Cultivation of Principal Crops', Directorate of Economics and Statistics (DES), Ministry of Agriculture and Farmers' Welfare, Government of India.

might also be due to difference in prices of inputs used for crop production across different states.

The variation in technological adoption along with varied agro-climatic conditions results in differential yield levels. Consequently, net returns varied across the states (Table 1.4). Interestingly, net returns of the selected crops were found to be higher in the states incurring higher cost of cultivation. This implies that in low productive states, there exists great scope to increase the net returns by increasing the input use.

1.3.1 Commercialization and Diversification

Increasing production, evolving modern supply chains, institutional changes, and policy reforms are driving Indian agriculture on the path of commercialization. The degree of commercialization in agriculture sector can be captured from both product-side and factor-side. Product commercialization maybe understood from increased surplus production over and above self-consumption or from changing composition of product basket towards cash crops. From factor-side, commercialization may be understood as adoption of modern inputs such as quality seeds, fertilizers, pesticides, irrigation, and power use in agriculture, most of which are purchased from market (Satyasai and Viswanathan 1997). Few indicators reflecting increasing commercialization of Indian agriculture are given in Table 1.5.

Over the years, use of purchased inputs except pesticides has increased many folds in the country. The distribution of certified/quality seeds and per hectare use of power in agriculture sector increased by more than five times between BE1984–5 and BE2014–15. Similarly, total and per hectare fertilizer consumption registered 195 per cent and 171 per cent increase respectively during the same period. Moreover, irrigation infrastructure in the country has improved considerably bringing more stability in crop production. These evidences provide a fairly good idea about the increasing pace of commercialization in Indian agriculture.

The product-side evidences of increasing commercialization of Indian agriculture are increasing share of non-foodgrains crops in GCA and total value of crop output (VoP) over the years. The share of non-foodgrains crops in GCA and total VoP increased by 10 percentage points and 16 percentage points during BE1984–5 to

Table 1.5 Indicators of Commercialization in Agriculture in India

Indicators	BE1984–5	BE1994–5	BE2004–5	BE2014–15
Factor Side				
Distribution of certified/quality seeds (lakh qtls)	46.72	64.03	123.50	302.55
Fertilizer use				
Total NPK (lakh tonnes)	84.74	129.65	175.99	250.29
Per ha GCA (kg/ha)	47.48	73.07	92.42	128.75
Pesticide use (technical grade 000 tonnes)	55.50	62.51	40.84	58.82
Irrigation coverage (%)	30.45	37.07	41.79	47.62
Power use in agriculture (Kwh/ha)	110.21	400.29	461.29	739.55
Product Side				
Share of non-foodgrains cash crops in GCA (%)	27.38	33.06	34.95	37.46
Share of non-foodgrains commodities in total value of crop output (%)*	41.00	46.19	52.50	57.30
Marketed surplus ratio (%)				
Rice	–	–	73.28	81.76
Wheat	–	–	65.51	75.30
Maize	–	–	74.74	85.65
Barley	–	–	49.72	74.01
Arhar	–	–	69.89	85.66
Lentil	–	–	76.96	89.49

Note: *Non-foodgrains commodities include oilseeds, sugarcane, fibres, condiments and spices, fruit and vegetables, flowers, rubber, indigo, dying and tanning material, and drugs and narcotics.

Source: Authors' estimates based on data from 'Agricultural Statistics at a Glance', Directorate of Economics and Statistics (DES), Ministry of Agriculture & Farmers' Welfare, Government of India.

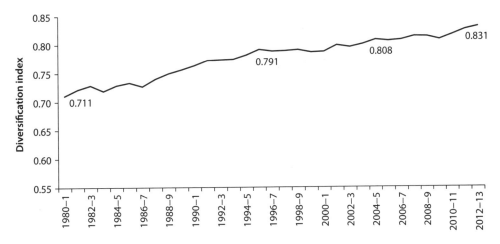

Figure 1.4 Modified Entropy Index of Crop Diversification

Source: Authors' estimates based on data from 'Agricultural Statistics at a Glance', Directorate of Economics and Statistics (DES), Ministry of Agriculture & Farmers' Welfare, Government of India.

BE2014–15 respectively. Apart from shifting cropping pattern and increasing diversification towards commercial crops, staple food crops are also heading towards commercialization. This is evident from the increasing ratio of total market arrival to production of staple food crops (Table 1.5). The available data shows that between BE2004–5 and BE2014–15, marketed surplus for rice, wheat, maize, barley, arhar, and lentil increased by 8, 10, 11, 24, 16, and 13 percentage points respectively.

The estimation of modified entropy index[2] revealed an increasing rate of diversification over the years (Figure 1.4). Diversification towards commercial crops (oilseeds, fibres, sugarcane, condiments and spices, fruit, and vegetables) offers great scope to improve farmers' income (Birthal et al. 2007 and Chand 2016). The staple crops (cereals and pulses) that occupy 64.32 per cent of GCA produced only 33.40 per cent of total agriculture output in 2013–14 (Table 1.6). On the other hand, commercial crops contributed 48.78 per cent to total crop output from only 33.75 per cent of GCA. Average productivity of commercial crops after adjusting for cropping intensity was estimated as Rs 99,402 per hectare as compared to Rs 40,109 per hectare in case of foodgrains. Thus, average productivity of commercial crops is 2.48 times higher than productivity in foodgrains, and diversification towards these crops has potential to generate additional revenue of Rs 59,293 per hectare.

Although Indian agriculture is gradually diversifying towards commercial crops, the pace of diversification is slow and cropping pattern is still dominated by staple crops. There exists several impediments hindering acceleration in diversification. First, family consumption remains the foremost criteria for choice of cropping pattern by majority of farmers and it take precedence over commercial sale. This prevents farmers from diversifying completely towards commercial crops and commercial production. Second, cultivation of commercial crops is risky and capital intensive. Lack of financial resources prevents poor small and marginal farmers from cultivating those crops. Third, even if the farmer manages financial resources, lack of market infrastructure and high price volatility are real impediments for growing commercial crops. Finally, most of the commercial crops being perishable in nature require value addition and processing facilities. The lack of skills for value addition and poor processing infrastructure in rural areas restrict adoption of commercial crops by the farmers. A systematic effort to identify and remove existing bottlenecks in marketing channels and improve marketing infrastructure will accelerate commercialization and crop diversification.

The ongoing changes in consumption pattern support diversification towards fruit, vegetables, and livestock products. Fear is sometimes expressed about the effect of large-scale diversification on supply of staple food and food security. There is a large gap between attainable yield and actual yield of staple food crops in most of the states. This indicates reasonable scope to raise production of staple food crops even

[2] Modified Entropy Index (MEI) $= -\sum_{i=1}^{n} P_i \times log_n P_i$, where 'P' is the proportion of area under i'th crop group in GCA and 'n' is number of groups (cereals, pulses, oilseeds, sugarcane, condiments and spices, fruit and vegetables, and fibres) taken into consideration.

Table 1.6 Per Hectare Value of Output of Major Crops in 2013–14

SL	Crop	Value (in Rs Crore)	Area (in Mha)	Productivity (in Rs/ha)	Adjusted Productivity* (in Rs/ha)	Share (%) In Total Output	Share (%) In Total Area
1	Pulses	62,135	25.21	24,647	24,647	4.14	12.97
2	Cereals	439,383	99.83	44,013	44,013	29.26	51.35
A	**Foodgrains**	**501,518**	**125.04**	**40,109**	**40,109**	**33.40**	**64.32**
3	Oilseeds	116,181	28.05	41,419	41,419	7.74	14.43
4	Fibre crops	95,993	12.80	75,037	75,037	6.39	6.58
5	Sugarcane	76,295	4.99	152,896	109,997	5.08	2.57
6	Condiments and spices	54,163	3.16	171,239	123,194	3.61	1.63
7	Fruit	155,547	7.22	215,558	155,078	10.36	3.71
8	Vegetables	234,219	9.40	249,275	249,275	15.60	4.83
B	**Commercial crops**	**620,558**	**65.61**	**111,633**	**99,402**	**48.78**	**33.75**
C	**All crops**	**1,501,464**	**194.4**	**77,236**	**61,503**	**100**	**100**

Note: *Productivity for annual crops such as sugarcane, fruit, and condiments and spices has been adjusted with present cropping intensity of 139 per cent.

Source: Authors' estimates from sources as in Figure 1.1 and Table 1.2.

with reduced area. Therefore, moderate shift in area towards commercial crops is not seen as a threat to supply of staple foods.

1.3.2 Performance of Agriculture Trade

After liberalization of external trade India's export basket has diversified and the country has emerged as a large exporter of some agricultural commodities. The recent years have witnessed an impressive achievement in agricultural trade in the country. The total volume of agricultural export increased from US$ 2.65 billion in 1990–1 to US$ 9.43 billion in 2004–5 at an annual growth rate of 8.26 per cent (Figure 1.5). In the subsequent period after 2004–5, agricultural exports witnessed 17.14 per cent annual growth and reached US$ 37.33 billion in 2014–5. Presently, major exported agricultural products are marine products, meat products, and basmati rice with their respective share of 14.07 per cent, 12.58 per cent, and 11.53 per cent in total export value.

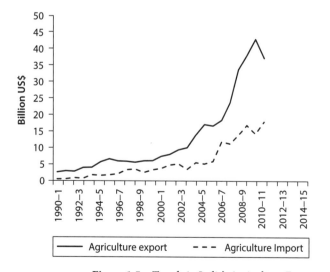
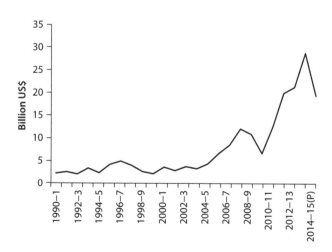

Figure 1.5 Trends in India's Agriculture Export and Import (Panel 1) and Net Trade Surplus (Panel 2)

Source: Authors' estimates based on data from 'Agricultural Statistics at a Glance', Directorate of Economics and Statistics (DES), Ministry of Agriculture & Farmers' Welfare, Government of India.

Total value of export has remained higher than import value throughout the period under consideration.

A perusal of Panel 1 of Figure 1.5 reveals that both export and import increased at an exponential rate after the mid-2000s. The net trade surplus from agriculture, which remained below US$ 5 billion till 2004–5, turned more than US$ 19 billion after 2010–11.

1.4 REGIONAL DISPARITIES IN AGRICULTURE

There exists wide spatial variation in agriculture performance in India. The regional disparities in agriculture were examined on the basis of growth in net state domestic product from agriculture (NSDP–Ag) during 2004–5 to 2014–15. State-wise estimated growth rate in NSDP–Ag along with per hectare agriculture income during base year (2004–5) is presented in Table 1.7. Among the states, Jharkhand, Madhya Pradesh, Chhattisgarh, and Rajasthan registered impressive growth of more than 6 per cent per annum during the past decade. In Gujarat, Bihar, Tamil

Nadu, and Odisha, growth in agriculture income was higher than the targeted level of 4 per cent. On the other hand, Kerala witnessed negative growth in agriculture income during the period under consideration. In an agriculturally developed state like Punjab, growth in agricultural income was far less than other states.

It was interesting to note that states which had lower agricultural income (in terms of per ha NSDP), witnessed significantly higher growth in NSDP–Ag than relatively developed states. Relatively higher growth in underdeveloped states implies that they are moving towards convergence in agriculture income over the time. The existence of convergence in per ha NSDP–Ag among states was tested using the concept of β-convergence, in which growth in per ha NSDP–Ag across states is regressed with logarithmic of initial level of per ha NSDP–Ag. The coefficient of per ha NSDP–Ag in initial year (2004–5) was negative (−3.47), which indicates that states with lower income from agriculture grew faster than states with high level of income

Table 1.7   Level and Growth in Net State Domestic Product-Agriculture (Per Hectare and Total) during 2004–5 to 2014–15

State	NSDP–Ag/ha NSA during 2004–5 (at 2011–12 Prices)	Trend Growth Rate in NSDP–Ag/ha NSA during 2004–5 to 2014–15	NSDP–Ag/ha NSA during 2014–15 (at 2011–12 Prices)	Trend Growth Rate in NSDP–Ag (at 2011–12 Prices) during 2004–5 to 2014–5
Jharkhand	61,194	9.27	133,663	8.10
Madhya Pradesh	34,469	7.24	67,822	7.67
Chhattisgarh	22,898	7.21	48,977	6.97
Rajasthan	37,819	5.98	61,246	6.65
Gujarat	56,938	4.16	96,673	4.85
Bihar	64,046	5.24	89,437	4.71
Tamil nadu	98,096	5.90	190,094	4.42
Odisha	39,836	5.04	63,742	4.27
Maharashtra	45,001	4.00	65,015	3.90
Karnataka	42,850	4.27	66,740	3.53
Andhra Pradesh	60,606	2.58	77,695	3.40
Haryana	120,755	3.35	160,703	3.18
Assam	61,654	2.78	78,762	3.06
Uttar Pradesh	77,142	2.68	97,137	2.65
Uttarakhand	109,748	2.71	130,479	1.65
Himachal Pradesh	120,727	1.23	142,445	1.29
Punjab	146,146	1.40	165,049	1.26
Jammu and Kashmir	109,751	0.81	109,899	0.85
Kerala	168,536	−1.80	140,561	−2.29

Note: Estimation could not be done for West Bengal because of non-availability of data on NSDP–Agriculture. Further, state-wise data on net sown area (NSA) for the years 2013–14 and 2014–15 is not available. Therefore, per ha NSDP–Ag is estimated using NSA for the year 2012–13.
Source: Authors' estimates from sources as in Figure 1.1 and Table 1.2.

(Figure 1.6). The speed of convergence in NSDP–Ag among states was 3.47 per cent during the period under consideration.

Regional variations in agricultural performance are the result of the interplay of many factors such as natural resource endowments, agro-ecological conditions, irrigation development, level of policy support, institutional factors, historical factors, and demographic features (Somasekharan et al. 2011; Srivastava et al. 2014). Chand and Srivastava (2016) have classified 487 districts (covering 94 per cent of net sown area of the country) into six homogenous regions exhibiting similarity in determinants of agricultural

performance using the k-means cluster (multivariate) analysis. The variables used for clustering are cropping intensity, irrigation coverage, fertilizer use, rainfall, problem soil, groundwater development, agricultural productivity, and worker per unit land. The number of districts in each cluster and mean value of clustering variables are presented in Table 1.8.

Interestingly, out of a total 487 districts covered in the study, only 35 appeared as highly advantaged based on the clustering variables. The highly advantaged districts record highest per hectare agricultural productivity, cropping intensity, irrigation coverage, fertilizer use, and

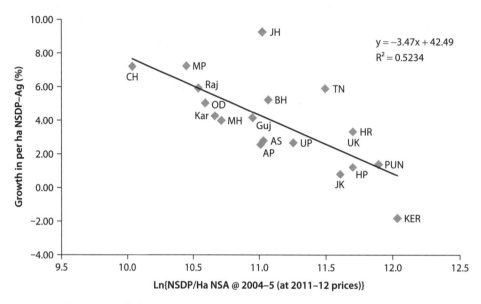

Figure 1.6 β-Convergence in Per ha NSDP–Ag during 2004–5 to 2014–15

Source: Authors' estimates based on data from 'Agricultural Statistics at a Glance', Directorate of Economics and Statistics (DES), Ministry of Agriculture & Farmers' Welfare, Government of India.

Table 1.8 Homogenous Regions and Mean Value of Clustering Variables

Clustering Variables	First Stage Clustering				Second Stage Clustering	
	Highly Advantaged	Moderately Advantaged	Less Advantaged	Disadvantaged	Less Disadvantaged	Highly Disadvantaged
Crop intensity (%)	188	156	144	135	137	132
Irrigation coverage (%)	74	65	49	29	33	21
Fertilizer use (Kg/ha)	236	209	148	107	130	60
Rainfall (mm)	632	918	1,056	1,148	1,206	1,032
Problem soil (%)	16	35	41	41	39	44
Groundwater development (%)	138	74	65	51	51	52
Agricultural productivity (Rs/ha)	119,345	72,570	45,257	26,477	30,524	18,443
Agricultural worker per sq km	156	222	240	304	312	288
No. of districts	**35**	**88**	**158**	**206**	**137**	**69**

Source: Chand and Srivastava (2016).

Table 1.9   Within State Distribution of Net Sown Area among Homogenous Regions (%)

State	Advantaged Region			Disadvantaged Region			Net Sown Area (Thousand Hectares)
	Highly Advantaged	Moderately Advantaged	Less Advantaged	Less Disadvantaged	Highly Disadvantaged	Total Disadvantaged	
Andhra Pradesh	–	28.80	37.71	23.86	9.63	33.49	11,170
Assam	–	–	32.86	63.28	3.86	67.14	2,590
Bihar	8.49	–	47.95	43.56	0.00	43.56	5,327
Chhattisgarh	–	–	11.23	58.96	29.81	88.77	3,373
Gujarat	5.76	23.55	57.52	9.59	3.58	13.17	9,402
Haryana	57.32	38.15	4.53	–	–	–	3,293
Himachal Pradesh	33.05	–	–	32.38	34.57	66.95	117
Jharkhand	–	2.74	3.36	24.88	69.02	93.90	1,102
Karnataka	–	18.84	17.47	45.52	18.18	63.70	9,880
Kerala	–	43.03	28.48	28.49	0.00	28.49	726
Madhya Pradesh	–	1.23	18.59	51.51	28.68	80.18	15,178
Maharashtra	2.48	14.32	52.09	31.11	0.00	31.11	17,396
Odisha	–	–	16.08	38.71	45.21	83.92	5,357
Punjab	79.94	20.06	–	–	–	–	3,946
Rajasthan	–	–	34.25	17.97	47.78	65.75	18,192
Tamil Nadu	–	47.78	35.82	16.40	0.00	16.40	4,709
Uttar Pradesh	3.60	41.41	44.14	5.19	5.66	10.85	16,075
Uttarakhand	–	74.77	25.23	–	–	–	347
West Bengal	4.23	80.82	14.95	–	–	–	5,009
Total	5.48	19.20	33.12	26.06	16.14	42.20	133,190

Source: Chand and Srivastava (2016).

level of groundwater development among all the regions. At the same time, these districts have least problematic soil as well as workforce pressure on agriculture land. On the other hand, 206 districts were found to be disadvantaged. Total disadvantaged area in the country has been estimated as 56.2 Mha, which is about 42 per cent of NSA (Table 1.9). The state-wise list of disadvantaged districts is given in the Appendix. The disadvantaged regions are characterized with low cropping intensity, poor irrigation coverage and groundwater use, low fertilizer use, and large area under problematic soils. Further, the poor irrigation and water storage infrastructure in this region resulted in sub-optimal utilization of rainfall. The expansion of water storage capacity and irrigation network would go a long way in improving agricultural productivity in the region.

Within states, distribution of NSA among identified homogenous regions revealed a glaringly unequal picture (Table 1.9). In some of the states like Jharkhand, Chattishgarh, Odisha, and Madhya Pradesh, more than 80 per cent of NSA is found to be disadvantaged based on the selected indicators. On the other hand, in a few states like Punjab, Haryana, West Bengal, and Uttarakhand,

none of the districts was found disadvantaged in the present context. This indicates inequality in the agricultural development across the geographical regions.

1.5 CONCLUSIONS

India's agriculture sector shows cyclical pattern of growth around long-term average of 2.75 per cent annual growth rate. The deviation from long-term growth rate on either side lasted for a short period. The growth rate is marred by year to year fluctuations pointing to the risky nature of agricultural activities in the country. However, the sector is becoming resilient mainly because of stable growth in livestock output and broadening of production base. The growth rate is predominantly driven by increase in productivity. As the country has very low crop intensity, there is large scope for increase in crop output through vertical expansion in the area under cultivation. The growth rate in output was below the growth rate in population in majority of the crops during the mid-1990s to mid-2000s. This trend got reversed after 2004–5, which shows moderate to high growth in per capita production in output of all food groups. This has contributed to improvement in food security in the country and also substantial increase in agricultural exports. The sector has generated trade surplus of more than US$ 19 billion each year after 2010–11. There is clear and strong evidence of rising commercialization in agriculture. Though requirement for family consumption still has strong influence on cropping pattern, overall resource allocation has fast moved towards market-based input use and crop pattern. As a result, input mix is changing, dependence on external funding (credit) is rising. This has also led to emergence of efficiency and profitability as important concerns for the sector. The ratios of input to output in financial terms indicate sharp deterioration after 2000–1. Though there is small improvement after 2006–7 due to fast growth in productivity, both efficiency as well as profitability require much faster growth in productivity through application of improved technology for healthy growth of the sector. Almost all dimensions of agriculture show significant variation across states. These variations become starker at district level. Agricultural growth in the last decade has narrowed down the regional disparity in agricultural productivity to some extent but large variation still persists. Future strategy of development of agriculture must focus on location-specific and regionally differentiated approach centred on resource endowment at disaggregate level.

APPENDIX

Table 1A.1   State-wise List of Disadvantaged Districts in India during BE2011–12

State	Less Disadvantaged Districts	Highly Disadvantaged Districts
Andhra Pradesh	Adilabad, Cuddapah, Mahabubnagar, Rangareddy, Srikakulam, Visakhapatnam	Anantapur
Bihar	Arwal, Aurangabad, Begusarai, Bhagalpur, Darbanga, Gaya, Jamui, Katihar, Khagaria, Kishangunj, Madhubani, Mungair, Muzaffarpur, Nalanda, Purnea, Saran, Supaul	–
Gujarat	Baroda, Bulsar, Dahod	Dangs, Panch, Mahals
Karnataka	Bangalore (rural), Bidar, Bijapur, Chamarajanagara, Chickballapur, Chickmagalur, Chitradurga, Gadag, Haveri, Koppal, North Kannara, Raichur, Udupi, Yadgir	Gulbarga, Kolar, Ramanagar, Tumkur
Madhya Pradesh	Ashoknagar, Betul, Bhind, Burhanpur, Damoh, Datia, Dhar, Guna, Gwalior, Indore, Jabalpur, Khargone, Mandsaur, Neemuch, Raisen, Rajgarh, Ratlam, Sagar, Ahjapur, Sheopur Kalan, Shivpuri, Tikamgarh, Vidisha	Alirajpur, Anuppur, Balaghat, Barwani, Chhatarpur, Dindori, Jhabua, Katni, Khandwa, Mandla, Panna, Rewa, Satna, Seoni, Shahdol, Sidhi, Singrauli, Umaria
Maharashtra	Amravati, Beed, Chandrapur, Gadchiroli, Jalna, Nagpur, Nanded, Thane, Wardha, Yeotmal	–
Odisha	Bhadrak, Dhenkanal, Gajapati, Jajapur, Kalahandi, Kendrapara, Khordha, Mayurbhanj, Nabarangapur, Puri, Rayagada, Sambalpur	Koraput, Bolangir, Angul, Baudh, Deogarh, Ganjam, Jharsuguda, Keonjhar, Malkangiri, Nayagarh, Nuapada, Phulbani, Sundergarh
Rajasthan	Ajmer, Banswara, Bhilwara, Jalore, Jhunjhunu, Pratapgarh, Rajsamand, Sikar, Udaipur	Barmer, Bikaner, Churu, Dungarpur, Jaisalmer, Jodhpur, Nagaur, Pali
Tamil Nadu	Coimbatore, Kamarajar, Karur, P. Mutthuramalingam, Ramanthapuram, the Nilgiris	–
Uttar Pradesh	Hamirpur, Jalaun, Mirzapur	Banda, Chitrakut, Mahoba, Sonabadra
Chhattisgarh	Bijapur, Bilaspur, Janjgir (Champa), Kanker, Koriya, Narayanpur, Raipur, Rajnandgoan, Surguja	Dantewada, Kawardha (Kabirdham), Korba, Mahasamund, Raigarh
Jharkhand	Chatra, Devghar, Dhanbad, Godda, Hazaribagh, Khodrama, Santhal Paragana, Sariakela/Kharsawan	Bokaro, Gadva/Garhwa, Giridih, Gumla, Latehar, Pakund/Pakur, Palamu, Ranchi, Sahebganj, Simdega, Singhbhum East, Singhbhum West
Assam	Barpeta, Bongalgaon, Chirang, Darrang, Dhemaji, Dhubri, Dibrugarh, Jorhat, Karbi-Anglong, Karimganj, Marigaon, N.C. Hills, Nagaon, Sibsagar, Tinsukia	Udalguri
Himachal Pradesh	Solan	Shirmaur
Kerala	Idukki	–

Source: Chand and Srivastava (2016).

REFERENCES

Birthal, P.S., P.K. Joshi, D. Roy, and A. Thorat. 2007. 'Diversification in Indian Agriculture towards High Value Crops: The Role of Smallholders'. IFPRI Discussion Paper 00727, Markets, Trade and Institutions Division.

Chand, R. 2014. 'From Slow Down to Fast Track: Indian Agriculture since 1995'. Working Paper 01/2014, ICAR-National Centre for Agricultural Economics and Policy Research, New Delhi.

———. 2016. Doubling Farmers' Income: Prospects and Strategy. Presidential Address, Seventy Sixth Annual Conference of *Indian Society of Agricultural Economics*, 21–23 November at Assam Agricultural University, Jorhat.

Chand, R., R. Saxena, and S. Rana. 2015. 'Estimates and Analysis of Farm Income in India: 1983–84 to 2011–12'. *Economic and Political Weekly* 50(22): 139–45.

Chand, R. and Shinoj P. 2012. 'Temporal and Spatial Variations in Agricultural Growth and Its Determinants'. *Economic and Political Weekly* 47(26 and 27): 55–64.

Chand, R. and S.K. Srivastava. 2014. 'Changes in Rural Labour Market and Its Implications for Indian Agriculture'. *Economic and Political Weekly* 49(10): 47–54.

———. 2016. 'Disadvantaged Agricultural Regions: Is There a Way Forward?' *Indian Journal of Agricultural Economics* 71(1): 36–48.

Deokar, B.K. and S.L. Shetty. 2014. 'Growth in Indian Agriculture: Responding to Policy Initiatives since 2004–05'. *Economic and Political Weekly* 49(26 and 27): 101–5.

Narayanamoorthy, A. 2007. 'Deceleration in Agricultural Growth: Technology Fatigue or Policy Fatigue?' *Economics and Political Weekly* 42(25): 2375–9.

Rao, V.M. 1996. 'Agricultural Development with a Human Face'. *Economic and Political Weekly* 31(26): A-50–A62.

Satyasai, K.J.S. and K.U. Viswanathan. 1997. 'Commercialisation and Diversification in Indian Agriculture'. Occasional Paper-5, National Bank for Agriculture and Rural Development, Mumbai.

Somasekharan, J., S. Prasad, and V.P.N. Roy. 2011. 'Convergence Hypothesis: Some Dynamics and Explanations of Agricultural Growth across Indian States'. *Agricultural Economics Research Review* 24(2): 211–16.

Srivastava, S.K., S. Ghosh, A. Kumar, and P.S.B. Anand. 2014. 'Unravelling the Spatio-temporal Pattern of Irrigation Development and Its Impact on Indian Agriculture'. *Irrigation and Drainage* 63(1): 1–11.

Srivastava, S.K., R. Chand, and J. Singh. 2017. 'Changing Crop Production Cost in India: Input Prices, Substitution and Technological Effects'. *Agricultural Economics Research Review*, 30: 171–82.

Srivastava, S.K. and D. Kolady. 2016. 'Agricultural Biotechnology and Crop Productivity: Macro-level Evidences on Contribution of Bt Cotton in India'. *Current Science* 110(3): 311–19.

2

Agricultural Inputs in India

Growth, Trends, and the Changing Scenario

*Vasant P. Gandhi**

ABSTRACT

Inputs form the backbone of India's agriculture, and the production and productivity of agriculture depend substantially on inputs. It was inputs which ushered in the green revolution in India, and the inputs of high yielding variety (HYV) seeds, fertilizers, and irrigation played a huge role in boosting food production. It is difficult to envision feeding the world today without the vital contribution of agricultural inputs. The study examines the recent trends and changes in agricultural input use in India, covering land, labour, water, fertilizers, seeds, pesticides, farm power/machinery, and electricity. Overall, the study finds a declining trend in the recent years in a number of agricultural inputs, and this is a cause of considerable concern. The contribution of land input to agricultural production growth is declining and frequently negative. Fertilizers are showing a decline and the growth of certified seeds is also showing a slowdown. Farm machinery showed good growth in the past but a substantial slowdown in the recent years. An exception is water, which, in terms of irrigated area, is showing a relatively good growth mainly due to expansion of groundwater tubewell irrigation and better management. However, the growing scarcity of the resource calls for strong promotion of conservation of water and its sound and efficient use. Decline of land availability will require emphasis on boosting yields and productivity. Reduction in the agricultural workforce calls for enhancing labour productivity through appropriate mechanization. Decline in fertilizer use may lead to a soil fertility/nutrient crisis, and calls for urgent reforms of the fertilizer policy and subsidy regime. New advances are required on the seed front including through biotechnology. A major shift is evident in consumer demand and agriculture towards high-value products including vegetables, fruit, livestock, edible oils, pulses, and processed products and this needs to be recognized in technology and input research and policy.

JEL Classification: Q15, Q16, Q18

Keywords: agriculture, technology, inputs, resources, productivity, India

*NABARD Chair Professor, Indian Institute of Management Ahmedabad, India. The author wishes to thank Nicky Johnson and Kishor Jadav for their assistance.

2.1 INTRODUCTION

Inputs form the backbone of Indian agriculture, and the production and productivity of India's agriculture depend substantially on the kinds and levels of inputs used. Numerous studies have shown that modern technology and inputs have played a huge role in the growth of India's agricultural production (see Mellor 1988; Sarma and Gandhi 1990; Gandhi, Zhou, and Mullen 2004; Ganesh-Kumar et al. 2012). It was inputs that brought about the Green Revolution, and studies show that the inputs, particularly HYV seeds, fertilizers, and irrigation played a huge role in increasing yields and productivity, thereby boosting food production. In the process, their use also expanded greatly: for example, fertilizer use in wheat increased from less than 2 kg/ha to 137 kg/ha between 1950–1 and 1998–9; HYVs which were non-existent between 1950–1 and 1960–1 now cover 88 per cent of the area; and irrigation has risen from 34 per cent to 89 per cent in wheat.

Increasing demand due to rising population and incomes, coupled with the scarcity of basic natural resources such as land and water, has been the major driver for the modernization of agriculture in India in the recent decades (Gandhi 2014). The constraint of land area as a source of production growth has led to substantial dependence on yield increase for raising agricultural production. This has led to an intense focus on advances in science and technology to increase crop yields, and this has resulted in the discovery or development of numerous new technologies and inputs for raising yields and production. These include:

- Better genetics/HYV seeds
- Better plant nutrition through fertilizers and micronutrient supplements
- Better water provision through water sourcing technology and management
- Better pest control through pesticides
- Farm power and machinery for better physical and time efficiency

Both public and private efforts have been involved in the above developments. Urgent needs of food security and the need to boost rural employment and incomes (and alleviate poverty) have pushed governments and international development organizations to join hands and make huge efforts and investment for improving yields and productivity. In recent times, the efforts have included not only government systems and institutions but also the development of private sector industries and businesses that invest in, innovate, and contribute to agricultural growth. This has galvanized the development of various new agro-industries and agribusinesses.

These include the seed industry, fertilizer industry, irrigation equipment and construction industry, agro-chemical industry, farm machinery industry, and others. These are now making huge contributions to overcoming the land and resource constraints in agriculture. It is unthinkable now to envision feeding the world today and in the future without the significant contribution of these vital industries. As farmers see advantages in using new technologies for raising production and profits, there is a growing demand for the latest and state-of-the-art technology, including the harnessing of the potential of biotechnology. This chapter examines the growth and trends in the major agricultural inputs including land, labour, water, fertilizers, seeds, pesticides, farm power/machinery and electricity, which constitute some of the most important inputs in Indian agriculture.

Table 2.1 provides a quick picture of the growth in some of the major agricultural inputs in the recent decades—from early 1980s to 2014–15 (or the latest year). It shows that the seed business has grown by 6.7 times from 45.0 to 301.4 lakh quintals. The fertilizer business has grown 4.2 times from 60.6 lakh tonnes to 255.8 lakh tonnes. Groundwater irrigation and its equipment business have more than doubled in coverage from 187.4 to 412.6 lakh hectares. The tractor business representing farm machinery has increased the most—by over 8 times from 74.3 to 626.8 thousand tractors. Only the pesticide business has not grown much—it grew from 47.0 to 72.1 thousand tonnes from the early 1980s to early 1990s but declined to 39.8 by 2005–6, and grew again to 58.2 thousand tonnes.

2.2 LAND INPUT

Land is the most basic input in agriculture and Table 2.2 shows the trends in land from 1980–1 to 2012–13. The table indicates that the geographic area of the country is 328 million hectares, of which only about 55 per cent is cultivable, that is, about 182 million hectares. It also shows that there is a small declining trend of −0.06 per cent over the years in cultivable areas. The cultivated land is about 85 per cent of the cultivable land, that is, 155 million hectares, and in this there is a very small negative trend of −0.01 per cent but the decline is at a faster rate of −0.20 per cent since 2010–11. The net cropped area in 2012–13 is about 90 per cent of the cultivated land, that is, 140 million hectares and this shows a small decline at −0.02 per cent over the whole period, an increase at 0.16 per cent between 2000–1 and 2010–11, and a decline at

Table 2.1   Recent Growth in Selected Agricultural Inputs

Years	Certified Quality Seeds Sales (in Lakh Quintals)	Fertilizer Consumption in Nutrients (in Lakh Tonnes)	Pesticides Technical Grade Material Sales (in Thousand Tonnes)	Groundwater Irrigation (Wells and Tubewells) Net Irrigated Area (in Lakh Hectares)	Tractors Sales Number (in Thousands)
1981–2	na	60.6	47.0	187.4	na
1983–4	45.0	77.1	55.0	193.9	74.3
1991–2	57.5	127.3	72.1	260.4	150.6
2001–2	91.8	173.6	47.0	351.8	225.3
2005–6	126.8	203.4	39.8	360.7	296.1
2006–7	155.0	216.5	41.5	376.4	352.8
2007–8	179.1	225.7	43.6	384.0	346.5
2008–9	215.8	249.1	43.9	388.0	342.8
2009–10	257.1	264.9	41.8	390.4	393.8
2010–11	277.3	281.2	55.5	390.6	545.1
2011–12	294.9	277.9	53.0	405.4	607.7
2012–13	313.4	258.0	45.6	412.6	590.7
2013–14	301.4	239.6	58.2	NA	696.8
2014–15	NA	255.8	NA	NA	626.8
Increase (multiple)	× 6.7	× 4.2	× 1.2	× 2.2	× 8.4

Note: 'NA' refers to 'not available'.

Sources: Gandhi (2014); Directorate of Economics and Statistics, Ministry of Agriculture and Farmers Welfare, Government of India (2014); and Fertiliser Association of India (2013).

Table 2.2   Trends in Land Area in Agriculture in India (1980–1 to 2012–13) (Area in Thousand Hectares)

Years	Geographical Area	Cultivable Land	Cultivated Land	Net Cropped Area	Gross Cropped Area	Area Sown More Than Once	Gross Irrigated Area
1980–1	328,726	185,156	155,114	140,288	172,630	32,342	49,775
1985–6	328,726	185,127	155,795	140,901	176,330	37,563	54,281
1990–1	328,726	185,187	156,710	142,870	185,742	42,872	63,203
1995–6	328,726	183,623	156,028	142,197	180,053	45,274	71,352
2000–1	328,726	183,455	156,113	141,336	185,340	44,005	76,187
2005–6	328,726	182,686	155,375	141,162	192,756	51,575	84,280
2010–11	328,726	182,012	155,839	141,563	198,969	56,000	88,887
2011–12	328,726	181,959	155,488	140,974	195,632	54,658	91,729
2012–13	328,726	181,950	155,214	139,932	194,399	54,467	92,575
Annual Growth Rate							
1980–1 to 2012–13	–	−0.06	−0.01	−0.02	0.37	1.59	1.97
1980–1 to 1990–1	–	0.005	0.05	−0.02	0.50	2.52	2.33
1990–1 to 2000–1	–	−0.09	−0.04	−0.07	0.28	1.22	2.26
2000–1 to 2010–11	–	−0.09	0.01	0.16	0.61	2.19	1.83
2010–11 to 2012–13	–	−0.02	−0.20	−0.58	−1.16	−1.38	2.05

Source: Calculations based on information from Ministry of Agriculture (2014 and various years), Government of India.

−0.58 per cent from 2010–11. The overall decline and the sharper recent fall indicates the increasing diversion of land from agricultural to non-agricultural uses, and as a result the land constraint in agriculture is becoming more severe, and the contribution of land to agricultural growth is becoming negative. This will also require further focus on yield increase.

The gross cropped area is considerably more than the net sown area, that is, 194 million hectares due to multiple cropping on the same land (Figure 2.1). The gross cropped area shows an increasing trend at 0.37 per cent from 1980–1 to 2012–13, but a decline at −1.16 per cent after 2010–11, which is a matter of concern. The area that is sown more than once shows an increasing trend of 1.59 per cent over the whole period, but a decline at −1.38 per cent after 2010–11, which is a matter of concern. The growth in the gross cropped area and area sown more than once is expected to be closely related to increase in irrigation, and Table 2.2 shows that the gross irrigated area has grown substantially throughout all the periods at a rate of about 2 per cent per year to reach 47 per cent, that is to 93 million hectares by 2012–13. In comparison, however, the gross cropped area shows a growth of only 0.37 per cent during 1980−1 to 2012–13, at 0.61 per cent between 2000–1 and 2010–11, but a decline at −1.16 per cent since 2010–11. It is a matter of concern that growth in irrigated area is not translating to a comparable growth in gross cropped area. Due to this, land is making an even smaller contribution to

production growth overall, and a negative contribution in the recent years.

Table 2.3 presents the use of land area under major crop groups. Of the total area of 194 million hectares under crops, 139 million hectares is under food crops and 55 million hectares is under non-food crops in 2012–13. The bulk of the area under food crops is under foodgrains, that is, 120 million hectares (Figure 2.2). After 1980–1, the area under foodgrains is showing decline at a rate of −0.16 per cent and the area under food crops is showing a slow increase at a rate of 0.09 per cent. However, the area under non-food crops is growing at a rate of 1.29 per cent per year. After 2010–11, the growth rate is even faster at 2.36 per cent, when the food crop area is showing a decline at −2.45 per cent. Thus, there is a clear shift from food crops to non-food crops. In the years after 2010–11, the rice area is showing a small decline at −0.13 per cent but the wheat area shows increase at 1.59 per cent. The area under pulses is showing a sharp decline at −6.14 per cent after 2010–11 and the area under oilseeds also shows a decline at −1.37 per cent. Therefore, overall, even though the total cropped area is growing at 0.37 per cent the composition of cropped areas is undergoing a significant transition, especially towards non-food crops, but also towards wheat, among foodgrains. The negative area trend in food crops, and especially in some crops such as rice, pulses, and oilseeds, is of considerable concern. The reasons for these trends appear to be relatively poor profitability of rice, pulses, and oilseeds, due

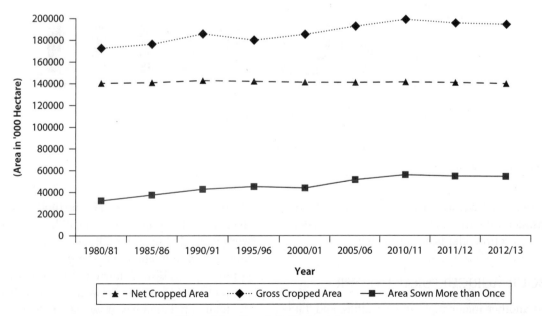

Figure 2.1   Growth in Cropped Area

Source: Courtesy of the author.

Table 2.3 Land Area under Different Crops (in Thousand Hectares)

Year	Rice	Wheat	Total Cereals	Total Pulses	Total Foodgrains	Total Food Crops	Total Oilseeds	Total Non-food Crops	Gross Cropped Area
1980–1	40,237	22,225	100,867	22,708	127,608	137,591	15,698	34,955	172,630
1985–6	41,220	23,179	101,121	24,437	128,756	139,932	19,435	38,521	176,330
1990–1	42,744	24,046	100,693	24,883	127,948	141,031	25,152	44,711	185,742
1995–6	43,016	25,105	98,040	23,637	123,463	138,276	27,943	49,195	180,053
2000–1	44,761	25,797	99,905	21,325	122,680	138,493	24,625	47,327	185,340
2005–6	43,660	26,484	99,208	22,391	121,599	141,172	27,863	51,584	192,756
2010–11	42,862	29,069	100,269	26,402	126,771	146,265	27,224	52,705	198,969
2011–12	44,006	29,865	100,293	24,462	124,755	142,306	26,308	53,326	195,632
2012–13	42,754	30,003	97,519	23,257	120,776	139,174	26,484	55,225	194,399
Annual Growth Rate									
1980–1 to 2012–13	0.27	0.82	−0.16	0.00	−0.16	0.09	1.34	1.29	0.37
1980–1 to 1990–1	0.51	0.54	−0.21	0.18	−0.18	0.04	4.43	2.17	0.50
1990–1 to 2000–1	0.68	1.35	−0.01	−0.67	−0.08	0.13	−0.07	0.79	0.28
2000–1 to 2010–11	−0.05	1.36	−0.16	1.12	0.24	0.28	1.31	1.24	0.61
2010–11 to 2012–13	−0.13	1.59	−1.60	−6.14	−2.39	−2.45	−1.37	2.36	−1.16

Sources: Calculations based on information from Ministry of Agriculture (2014 and various years), Government of India.

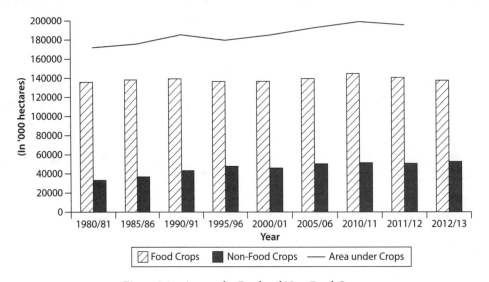

Figure 2.2 Area under Food and Non-Food Crops

Source: Courtesy of the author.

to weak price incentives as well as technology limitations in increasing productivity. On the other hand, non-food crops such as cotton offer better profitability.

2.3 LABOUR: AGRICULTURAL LABOUR

Labour is another major input in agriculture and Table 2.4 provides a profile of the changes in agricultural labour. India's total population reached 1,210 million in 2011 and

of this, 833 million was rural, constituting 69 per cent of the total. Of this population, 263 million were agricultural workers, including 118 million cultivators and 144 million agricultural labourers. The growth rate of the total population has slowed down over the decades, from 2.16 per cent to 1.64 per cent. Between 2001 and 2011, whereas the total population has grown at 1.64 per cent the rural population has grown far more slowly at 1.16 per cent. This is substantially due to migration from rural to urban areas. The number of agricultural workers is growing at 1.17 per cent per year. However, the number of cultivators is showing a decline at –0.70 per cent, whereas the number of agricultural labourers is increasing at 3.06 per cent. The data, therefore, indicates a slowing growth in rural population but a growing population of agricultural labourers in the country (Figure 2.3). The trend may be due to fragmentation of land holdings leading to increasing number of non-viable farms resulting in farm sales and increasing number of agricultural labourers.

Table 2.5 provides a break-up of the total workforce into agricultural and non-agricultural workforce. The table indicates that whereas the total workforce stood at 467 million in the year 2011–12, the agricultural workforce stood at 228 million, constituting 48.8 per cent of the workforce. The table indicates that the share of the agriculture workforce has been declining from 59.9 per cent in 1999–2000 to 48.8 per cent in 2011–12. The rate of growth was positive at 0.26 per cent between 1999–2000 and 2009–10, but turned negative at –2.9 per cent between 2009–10 and 2011–12. The share

of agricultural workforce has shown a decline and the rate of decline accelerated from –1.09 per cent between 1999–2000 and 2009–10 to about –2.90 per cent between 2009–10 and 2011–12. Thus, even though the

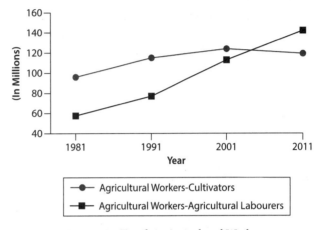

Figure 2.3 Trends in Agricultural Workers
Source: Courtesy of the author.

Table 2.4 Population and Agricultural Workers in India (in Millions)

Year	Total Population	Rural Population	Agricultural Workers– Cultivators	Agricultural Workers– Agricultural Labourers	Total Agricultural Workers
1981	683.3	526	93	56	148
1991	846.4	631	111	75	185
2001	1,028.7	743	127	107	234
2011	1,210.6	834	119	144	263
Annual Growth Rate					
1981–2011	1.92	1.55	0.83	3.24	1.93
1981–91	2.16	1.84	1.81	3.00	2.27
1991–01	1.97	1.65	1.41	3.65	2.37
2001–11	1.64	1.16	–0.70	3.06	1.17

Sources: Calculations based on information from Ministry of Agriculture (2014 and various years), Government of India.

Table 2.5 Agricultural and Non-Agricultural Workforce (in Millions)

Years	Total Workforce	Agri Workforce	Non-agri Workforce	Share Agri Labour Force
1999–2000	397	238	159	59.9
2004–5	457	259	198	56.7
2009–10	460	245	215	53.3
2011–12	467	228	239	48.8
Annual Growth Rate				
1999–2000 to 2011–12	1.26	–0.33	3.18	–1.56
1999–2000 to 2009–10	1.35	0.26	2.78	–1.06
2009–10 to 2011–12	0.50	–2.37	3.59	–2.90

Source: Calculations based on information from Ministry of Agriculture (2014 and various years), Government of India.

total workforce has been growing in the country, the share of the agricultural workforce is showing a decline. This shows a movement of the workforce away from agriculture to non-agriculture. The absolute number for agricultural workforce is also showing a decline from 2004–5 to 2011–12 (Figure 2.4). This shows a decreasing workforce availability in agriculture. The reason for this trend may be the increasing and relatively better formal and informal employment opportunities in the non-agriculture sector.

2.4 WATER: IRRIGATION

Water is a major input for agriculture and Table 2.6 indicates the trends in water use in agriculture in terms of irrigated area. The net irrigated area has increased substantially from 38 million hectares in 1980–1 to 66 million hectares in 2012–13. The growth in net irrigated area has been fairly steady over the years and has actually accelerated a little to 1.90 per cent per year after 2010–11. The gross irrigated area has increased from 49 million hectares in 1980–1 to 92 million hectares in 2012–13 (Figure 2.5).

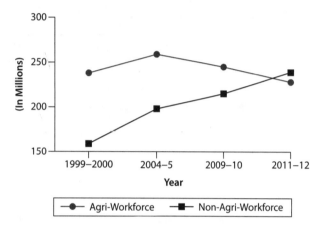

Figure 2.4   Agricultural and Non-Agricultural Workforce
Source: Courtesy of the author.

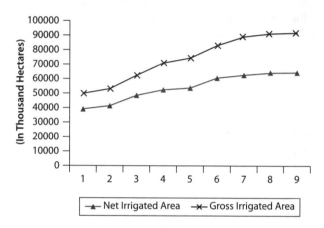

Figure 2.5   Trends in Net and Gross Irrigated Area
Source: Courtesy of the author.

Table 2.6   Water: Progress in Area Irrigated (in Thousand Hectares)

Years	Net Area Sown	Gross Cropped Area	Cropping Intensity (%)	Net Irrigated Area	Gross Irrigated Area	Irrigation Intensity (%)	Percentage Area Irrigated	
							Net	Gross
1980–1	140,288	172,630	123.1	38,720	49,775	128.6	27.6	28.8
1985–6	140,901	178,464	126.7	41,865	54,283	129.7	29.7	30.4
1990–1	142,870	185,742	130.0	48,023	63,204	131.6	33.6	34.0
1995–6	142,197	187,471	131.8	53,402	71,352	133.6	37.6	38.1
2000–1	141,336	185,340	131.1	55,205	76,187	138.0	39.1	41.1
2005–6	141,162	192,737	136.5	60,837	84,280	138.5	43.1	43.7
2010–11	141,563	197,563	139.6	63,657	88,887	139.6	45.0	45.0
2011–12	140,974	195,632	138.8	65,693	91,729	139.6	46.6	46.9
2012–13	139,932	194,399	138.9	66,103	92,575	140.0	47.2	47.6
			Annual Growth Rate					
1980/81–2012/13	−0.02	0.36	0.38	1.66	1.97	0.30	1.68	1.61
1980/81–1990/91	−0.02	0.50	0.52	1.91	2.33	0.41	1.93	1.82
1990/91–2000/01	−0.07	0.24	0.31	1.70	2.26	0.55	1.77	2.01
2000/01–2010/11	0.16	0.69	0.52	1.66	1.83	0.17	1.49	1.14
2010/11–2012/13	−0.58	−0.80	−0.25	1.90	2.05	0.15	2.50	2.88

Sources: Calculations based on information from Ministry of Agriculture (2014 and various years), Government of India.

Table 2.7   Irrigated Area by Sources of Irrigation (in Thousand Hectares)

Year	Government Canals	Private Canals	Total Canals	Tanks	Tubewells	Other Wells	Total Wells	Other Sources	Net Irrigated Area
1980–1	14,450	842	15,292	3,182	9,531	8,164	17,695	2,551	38,720
1985–6	15,715	465	16,180	2,765	11,903	8,515	20,418	2,502	41,865
1990–1	16,973	481	17,453	2,944	14,257	10,438	24,695	2,932	48,023
1995–6	16,561	559	17,120	3,118	17,910	11,787	29,697	3,467	53,402
2000–1	15,809	203	16,012	2,466	22,566	11,252	33,818	2,909	55,205
2005–6	16,490	227	16,718	2,083	26,026	10,044	36,070	5,966	60,837
2010–11	15,476	171	15,647	1,980	28,544	10,630	39,175	6,855	63,657
2011–12	15,838	172	16,010	1,918	29,942	10,595	40,537	7,228	65,693
2012–13	15,462	165	15,628	1,748	30,497	10,764	41,261	7,466	66,103
Share in Total Irrigated (2012–13)	23.39	0.25	23.64	2.64	46.14	16.28	62.42	11.30	100.00
Annual Growth Rate									
1980–1 to 2012–13	−0.06	−4.26	−0.15	−2.02	3.84	0.69	2.73	3.84	1.66
1980–1 to 1990–1	1.06	−2.70	0.91	−1.51	4.09	1.99	3.18	2.20	1.91
1990–1 to 2000–1	−0.18	−10.92	−0.39	−2.23	4.82	1.48	3.53	−0.32	1.70
2000–1 to 2010–11	0.76	−1.17	0.74	−1.70	2.27	−0.34	1.48	7.71	1.66
2010–11 to 2012–13	−0.05	−1.69	−0.06	−6.04	3.36	0.63	2.63	4.36	1.90

Sources: Calculations based on information from Ministry of Agriculture (2014 and various years), Government of India.

During the 1980s and 1990s, the growth had been quite rapid at about 2.3 per cent per year, but in the 2000s this had decelerated to about 1.8 per cent per year, but accelerated again to 2.05 after 2010–11. The gross irrigated area had increased substantially from 28.8 per cent to 47.6 per cent during the period 1980–1 to 2012–13. However, the period 2000–1 to 2010–11 experienced a deceleration in the growth of irrigated area to 1.14 per cent. But, post-2010–11 there has been acceleration to 2.88 per cent, indicating a revival of growth in irrigation, which is a positive sign. This could be due to considerable efforts made in recent years to improve the conservation of water resources and in the efficiency of water use, including promotion of participatory irrigation management (PIM), watershed development, and the use of water conservation technologies such as drip and sprinkler irrigation.

Table 2.7 presents the sources of irrigation and the trends over the years. The table shows that currently only about 24 per cent of the irrigated area is irrigated through canals, whereas about 62 per cent is irrigated through wells. The canal-irrigated areas show a negative trend of −0.15 per cent during the period 1980–1 to 2012–13. While a positive growth of 0.74 per cent was observed during 2000–1 and 2010–11, the growth was −0.06 during the period 2010–11 to 2012–13. On the other hand, the area irrigated through wells (groundwater) had expanded rapidly at the rate of more than 3 per cent in the 1980s and 1990s, followed by a sharp deceleration to 1.5 per cent between 2000–1 and 2010–11, and an acceleration to 2.63 per cent. The major engine of growth has been tubewell irrigation, which has expanded rapidly at more than 4 per cent in the 1980s and 1990s, followed by a deceleration to 2.27 per cent during the period 2000–1 to 2010–11, which was followed by an acceleration to 3.36 per cent during 2010–11 to 2012–13 (Figure 2.6). The findings indicate that there has been a sharp increase in the dependence on ground water irrigation in the recent decades. Some deceleration was evident between 2000–1 and 2010–11, indicating emerging constraints. But the growth of ground water irrigation again accelerated after 2010–11, perhaps indicating better management and more efficient use of the groundwater. The reasons appear to be the special efforts that have been made towards this, including increasing groundwater recharge through check-dams in some areas, watershed development activities in other areas, and the use of efficient irrigation methods such as drip and sprinkler irrigation.

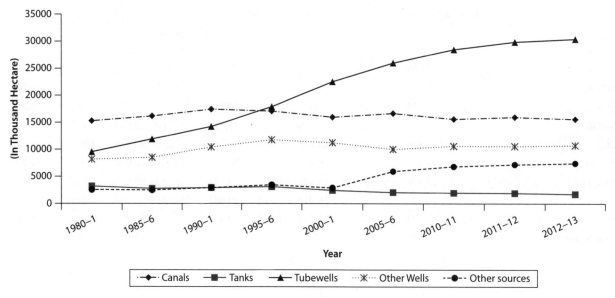

Figure 2.6   Irrigated Area by Source

Source: Courtesy of the author.

2.5 FERTILIZERS

Fertilizer is a very important modern input for agriculture since it addresses the problem of soil fertility, which is critical for yields. Table 2.8 below shows that fertilizer use has grown quite rapidly at the rate of about 4.5 per cent from 55 million tonnes to 255 million tonnes between 1980–1 and 2014–15. However, the 1980s saw a much faster increase in fertilizer use at over 8 per cent per year, which has subsequently decelerated to about 4 per cent per year in the 1990s followed by some acceleration

Table 2.8   Fertilizer Consumption in India in Nutrients (in Lakh Tonnes)

Year	Nitrogenous Fertilizers (N)	Phosphatic Fertilizers (P)	Potassic Fertilizers (K)	Total Fertilizer
1980–1	36.78	12.14	6.24	55.16
1985–6	56.61	20.05	8.08	84.74
1990–1	79.97	32.21	13.28	125.46
1995–6	98.23	28.98	11.56	138.77
2000–1	109.20	42.15	15.67	167.02
2005–6	127.23	52.04	24.13	203.40
2010–11	165.58	80.50	35.14	281.22
2011–12	173.00	79.14	25.76	277.90
2012–13	180.36	59.55	18.13	258.04
2013–14	165.25	54.58	19.76	239.59
2014–15 (P)	169.45	60.98	25.32	255.76
Annual Growth Rate				
1980/81–2014/15	4.32	4.87	4.54	4.49
1980/81–1990/91	7.66	10.17	6.96	8.18
1990/91–2000/01	4.10	4.37	3.36	4.08
2000/01–2010/11	4.79	7.03	9.98	5.95
2010/11–2014/15	1.31	−6.44	−10.50	−2.06

Note: 'P' refers to 'Provisional'.

Source: Fertilizers Association of India (2015).

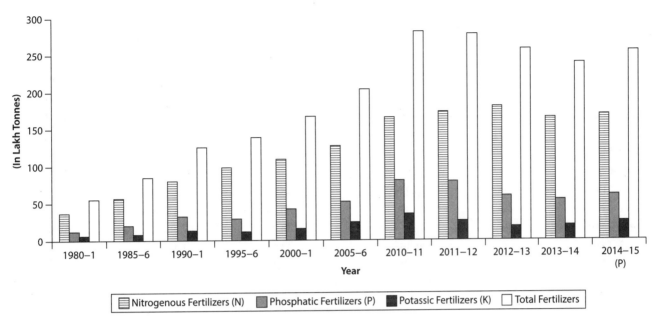

Figure 2.7 Fertilizer Consumption

Source: Courtesy of the author.

to about 6 per cent between 2000–1 and 2010–11. However, after 2010–11 there is a negative trend and a considerable decline in the fertilizer use. The rate of growth falls to –2.06 per cent, with phosphatic fertilizers declining at –6.44 per cent and potassic fertilizers at –10.50 per cent. Even the growth of nitrogenous fertilizers slows down to just 1.31 per cent (see Figure 2.7). The changes appear to be related to changes in the fertilizer subsidy and pricing policies. With the shift to nutrient based subsidy (NPS) policy, the quantum of subsidy on phosphatic (P) fertilizers as well as potassic (K) fertilizers has been substantially reduced. At the same time, their prices have been decontrolled and these changes have resulted in a sharp rise in the prices of P and K fertilizers. Due to this P and K fertilizer use has reduced sharply, and the resulting imbalance has also influenced the productivity of N fertilizers, thereby decreasing its use. Due to this, Indian agriculture may be headed for a major nutrient and soil fertility crisis that may seriously impact agricultural production. There is great need for reform in the fertilizer policy regime.

Fertilizer use needs to be assessed on a per hectare basis and Table 2.9 gives the results. The table shows that fertilizer consumption per hectare has grown substantially from 32 kg per hectare in 1980–1 to 131 kg per hectare. However, the growth rates show a similar picture as the total fertilizer consumption. The growth rate was much higher during the 1980s at 7.6 per cent and this has decelerated to 3.8 per cent in the 1990s and 5.2 per cent

in the first decade of 2000s. However, after 2010–11, the growth rates drop substantially, turning to 0.67 per cent for N, –8.08 per cent for P_2O_5 and –7.74 per cent for K_2O (see Figure 2.8). Thus, a substantial drop in fertilizer use is evident in the recent years, which would have consequences for agricultural production. The major reason as described earlier is the change in the fertilizer subsidy regime as well as the lack of a clear fertilizer industry and subsidy policy on each nutrient, taking into account soil fertility and nutrient needs of agriculture.

2.6 SEEDS

The input of quality certified seeds is of significant importance for increasing agricultural production. Table 2.10 shows the trend in the use of quality seeds in India. The distribution of the seeds reached a high of 313 lakh quintals in the year 2012–13 and the major share was that of cereals, which constituted 204 lakh quintals. Overall, between 1990–1 and 2013–14, seed use has grown at a rapid pace of 8.4 per cent per year. There is particularly rapid growth between 2000–1 and 2010–11 at 13 per cent overall, in pulses at 17 per cent and in oilseeds at 16 per cent (see Figure 2.9). However, there is a decline in quantity in the case of fibres at –0.93 per cent in this period, perhaps because of the transition to Bt cotton seeds which are expensive. After 2010–11 the overall growth rate fell to 3.15 per cent from 13.13 per cent mainly on the account of much slower growth in pulses and

Table 2.9   Consumption of Fertilizers per Hectare

Year		Gross Cropped Area (in Thousand Hectares)		Consumption in Kilogram per Hectare	
		N	P₂O₅	K₂O	Total
1980–1	172,630	21.31	7.03	3.61	31.95
1985–6	178,464	31.72	11.24	4.53	47.48
1990–1	185,742	43.06	17.34	7.15	67.55
1995–6	187,471	52.40	15.46	6.17	74.02
2000–1	185,340	58.92	22.74	8.46	90.12
2005–6	192,737	66.01	27.00	12.52	105.53
2010–11 (P)	197,563	83.22	40.46	17.66	142.35
2011–12 (P)	195,632	88.43	40.46	13.16	142.05
2012–13 (P)	194,399	86.53	34.23	10.36	131.36
2013–14 (P)	194,399	86.16	28.98	10.80	125.94
2014–15 (P)	194,399	87.17	31.37	13.03	131.57
Growth Rate					
1980/81–2014/15	0.34	3.94	4.57	4.25	4.14
1980/81–1990/91	0.50	7.11	9.63	6.42	7.63
1990/91–2000/01	0.24	3.86	4.12	3.11	3.83
2000/01–2010/11	0.69	4.04	6.26	9.18	5.23
2010/11–2014/15	−0.39	0.67	−8.08	−7.74	−2.74

Note: Abbreviations: N: Nitrogen; P₂O₅: Phosphate; K₂O: Potash; (P): Provisional; Figures of consumption and gross cropped area refer to the same year except the last three years, where gross cropped area is taken for the year 2012–13 due to lack of data.
Source: Fertiliser Association of India (2015).

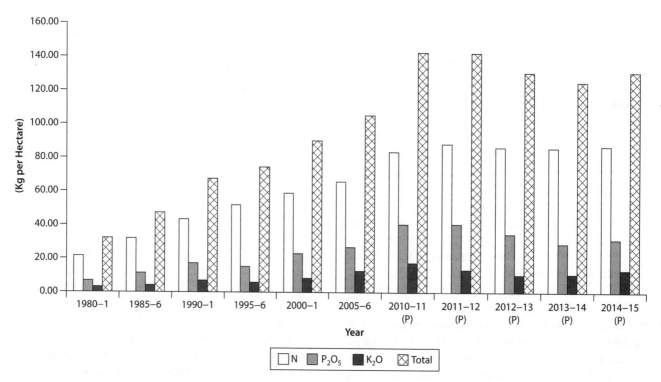

Figure 2.8   Fertilizer Consumption in Nutrients per Hectare

Source: Courtesy of the author.

Table 2.10   Crop-wise Distribution of Certified Quality Seeds Used in India (in Lakh Quintals)

Year	Cereals	Pulses	Nine Oilseeds	Fibres	Potato	Others	Total
1990–1	34.70	3.41	8.59	2.16	7.97	0.27	57.10
1995–6	44.03	3.58	12.64	2.58	6.85	0.24	69.92
2000–1	59.47	3.85	12.54	2.91	7.23	0.27	86.27
2005–6	86.73	7.37	24.35	2.89	5.08	0.33	126.75
2010–11	182.62	20.83	50.61	2.64	20.08	0.55	277.34
2011–12	189.69	22.26	61.49	3.09	18.32	1.64	294.85
2012–13	204.37	24.51	58.41	2.95	23.20	1.73	313.44
2013–14	183.03	27.80	61.09	2.87	26.60	1.97	301.39
			Growth Rate				
1990/91–2013/14	8.69	10.51	9.29	1.14	4.61	8.56	8.40
1990/91–2000/01	6.49	1.91	3.81	4.90	−0.35	−6.91	5.00
2000/01–2010/11	12.64	17.42	16.69	−0.93	9.59	8.66	13.13
2010/11–2013/14	0.82	10.10	5.27	2.06	11.40	47.42	3.15

Sources: Calculations based on information from Ministry of Agriculture (2014 and various years), Government of India.

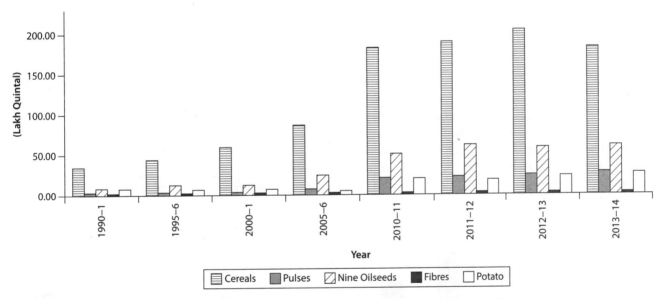

Figure 2.9   Use of Certified Quality Seeds

Source: Courtesy of the author.

oilseeds, but the use of other seeds, which would include vegetables, even though the quantities are small, show a huge growth indicating a buoyant demand for them. On the whole, the use of certified seeds shows a healthy growth except during 2010–11 to 2013–14 when there is a slowdown. The growth appears to be on account of farmers increasingly eager to use latest technology and the best seeds. The recent slowdown may be largely on account of cereals and this may be due to poor rains and low profitability.

2.7 PESTICIDES

The use of pesticides is important to protect the crops from damage by pests, and it can be seen from Table 2.11 that the consumption of pesticides has increased from 45,000 tonnes in 1980–1 to 75,000 tonnes in 1990–1 but has fallen to 40,000 tonnes by 2005–6. Since then it has risen to 58,000 tonnes in 2013–14 (see Figure 2.10). Overall, the growth rate is negative at −0.82 per cent and is slightly negative even after 2010–11. This appears

Table 2.11 Consumption of Pesticides (in Thousand Tonnes)

Year	Consumption
1980–1	45.00
1985–6	52.00
1990–1	75.00
1995–6	61.26
2000–1	43.58
2005–6	39.77
2010–11	55.54
2011–12	52.98
2012–13	45.62
2013–14	58.21
Annual Growth Rate	
1980/81–2013/14	−0.82
1980/81–1990/91	5.41
1990/91–2000/01	−5.37
2000/01–2010/11	0.55
2010/11–2013/14	−0.09

Sources: All India Report on Input Survey, Department of Agriculture Cooperation & Farmers' Welfare; Ministry of Agriculture & Farmers' Welfare (2012).

to be due to environmental concerns about pesticides and the development of pest-resistant varieties such as Bt cotton, which do not require much use of pesticides. Besides, more effective less bulky pesticides are now available.

Table 2.12 shows recent trends in different kinds of pesticides. It shows that whereas insecticides are showing a significant negative growth rate of −3.39 per cent, fungicides are showing a strong positive growth rate of 12.40 per cent and herbicides/weedicides are also showing an uptrend between 2006–7 and 2013–14 (see Figure 2.11). The negative trend in insecticide use appears to be due to environmental concerns and their highly toxic nature, as well as the development of pest-resistant varieties, particularly Bt cotton. Fungicide use appears to be growing due to the increasing importance of plant diseases for which resistant varieties are not available, and weedicide use is growing due to high labour cost of weeding.

Table 2.12 Consumption of Pesticides by Type in India (2006–7 to 2013–14) (in Thousand MT)

Year	Insecticide	Fungicide	Weedicide
2006–7	38.23	23.12	11.14
2007–8	39.19	26.99	12.91
2008–9	38.2	35.32	12.43
2009–10	34.65	31.55	8.66
2010–11	45.75	26.74	10.01
2011–12	39.36	44.38	7.92
2012–13	32.78	45.72	6.59
2013–14	29.02	58.88	12.05
Annual Growth Rate			
2006/07–2013/14	−3.39	12.40	0.99

Source: Ministry of Chemical and Fertilizer.

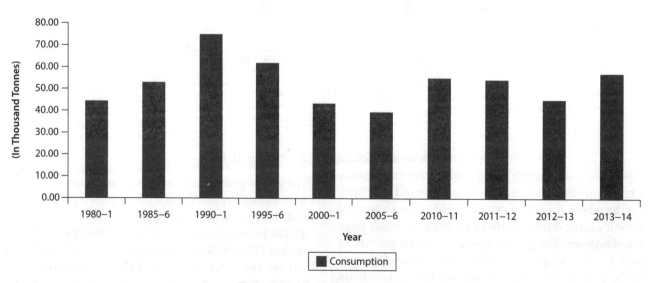

Figure 2.10 Pesticide Consumption

Source: Courtesy of the author.

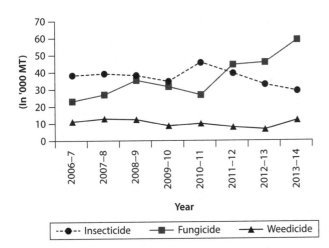

Figure 2.11   Product-wise Consumption of Pesticides

Source: Courtesy of the author.

Table 2.13   Production and Sale of Tractors in India

Year	Tractors Number	
	Production	Sale
1980–1	71,024	72,012
1985–6	75,550	76,886
1990–1	139,233	139,828
1995–6	191,311	191,329
2000–1	235,602	251,939
2005–6	296,080	291,680
2010–11	530,303	545,128
2011–12	625,946	607,658
2012–13	578,112	590,672
2013–14	707,898	696,828
2014–15	612,994	626,839
Annual Growth Rate		
1980/81–2014/15	6.79	6.87
1980/81–1990/91	6.41	6.73
1990/91–2000/01	7.87	8.10
2000/01–2010/11	10.38	9.93
2010/11–2014/15	4.21	4.25

Note: Sale includes Exports.
Source: Agricultural Research Data Book.

2.8 FARM MACHINERY AND EQUIPMENT

Farm machinery and equipment are becoming increasingly important inputs for agriculture. Table 2.13 shows the growth in the production and sale of tractors in India. The number of tractors sold has increased almost 10 times from 71,024 in 1980–1 to almost 707,898 in 2013–14. The growth rate during the period 1980–1 to 2014–15 was 6.87 per cent. There was an acceleration to 9.93 per cent during 2000–1 to 2010–11, but a deceleration to less than half of this, that is, 4.25 per cent was evident after 2010–11 (see Table 2.12). Thus, the recent years are showing a considerable slowdown in the growth of tractor sales (see Figure 2.12). The declines in 2012 and 2014 are partly due to poor monsoon

rains in both these years, which also resulted in credit constraints.

Table 2.14 shows the number of operational holdings using different important items of agricultural machinery. The table indicates that the holdings using diesel pumpsets are showing a relatively steady growth at about 7 per cent,

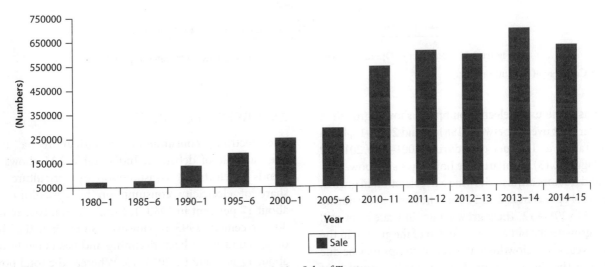

Figure 2.12   Sale of Tractors

Source: Courtesy of the author.

Table 2.14   Estimated Number of Operational Holdings Using Agricultural Machinery (in Thousands)

	Power Operated Equipment			
Year	Diesel Engine Pumpset	Electric Pumpset	Power Tiller	Agricultural Tractors
1981–2	3,353	3,977	273	489
1986–7	5,968	6,349	701	1,580
1991–2	6,892	9,324	1,071	3,764
1996–7	8,890	9,160	1,671	6,797
2001–2	14,261	18,448	3,261	15,463
2006–7	13,180	12,714	2,895	31,279
2011–12	30,082	22,761	7,954	61,133
	Annual Growth Rate			
1981/82–2011/12	7.33	5.79	11.49	16.85
1981/82–1991/92	6.77	8.05	13.23	20.39
1991/92–2001/02	6.83	6.40	10.65	13.71
2001/02–2011/12	7.02	1.93	8.44	13.31

Sources: All India Report on Input Survey, Department of Agriculture Cooperation and Farmers Welfare; Ministry of Agriculture and Farmers Welfare (2012).

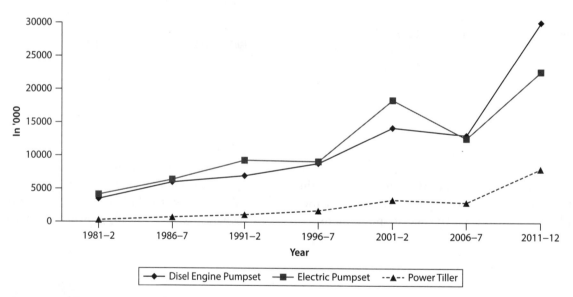

Figure 2.13   Number of Operational Holdings with Different Power Operated Equipment
Source: Courtesy of the author.

whereas those using electric pumpsets show a growth at 5.79 per cent overall between 1981–2 and 2011–12, but a deceleration to 1.93 per cent during 2001–2 to 2011/12 (see Figure 2.13). Similarly, the holdings using power tillers and tractors are also showing a deceleration in growth rate to 8.44 per cent and 13.31 per cent respectively during 2001–2 to 2011–12. These growth rates indicate an overall rapid growth rate but a slowing down of the growth in the recent years. The slowdown in electric pumps may be due to power shortages and supply problems in a number of states. The situation favours diesel pumpsets.

2.9 POWER: ELECTRICITY

The electricity consumption by agriculture has often been a topic of debate in India. Table 2.15 shows the trends in electricity consumption by agriculture. The share of electricity consumption by agriculture was about 17 per cent in 1980–1, from which it rose to over 30 per cent in 1995–6. However, since then the share of agriculture has been declining and has fallen to only about 17 per cent by 2014–15. Whereas the total power consumption has been growing at almost 9 per cent per

Table 2.15 Consumption of Electricity (in Gigawatt Hours)

Year	Consumption for Agricultural Purposes	Total Consumption	% Share of Agricultural Consumption to Total Consumption
1980–1	14,489	82,367	17.59
1985–6	23,422	122,999	19.04
1990–1	50,321	190,357	26.44
1995–6	85,732	277,029	30.95
2000–1	84,729	316,600	26.76
2005–6	90,292	411,887	21.92
2010–11	126,377	694,392	18.20
2011–12	140,960	785,194	17.95
2012–13	147,462	824,301	17.89
2013–14	152,744	874,209	17.47
2014–15(P)	168,913	948,328	17.81
Annual Growth Rate			
1980/81–2014/15	6.65	6.88	−0.21
1980/81–1990/91	14.07	8.80	4.84
1990/91–2000/01	5.82	5.33	0.46
2000/01–2010/11	0.04	0.08	−0.04
2010/11–2014/15	0.06	0.09	−0.03

Note: 'P' refers to 'Provisional'.

Source: Ministry of Statistics and Programme Implementation, Government of India (2014).

year from 2000–1 to 2014–15, the rate of growth is 5.5 per cent for agriculture (see Figure 2.14). The share of agricultural consumption shows a negative growth rate during both 2000–1 to 2010–11 and 2010–11 to 2014–15.

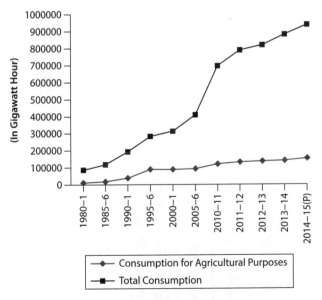

Figure 2.14 Consumption of Electricity

Source: Courtesy of the author.

Thus, power consumption by agriculture, which was a significant problem in the earlier years, is no longer a major contributor to the overall power consumption or its growth in India and its share is declining. The slowdown in overall growth may also be due to increasing consciousness about energy use.

2.10 VALUE OF INPUTS, OUTPUTS, AND GROSS DOMESTIC PRODUCT OF AGRICULTURE

The performance and growth of agricultural inputs in the aggregate can also be studied through the National Accounts Statistics where these are incorporated at the national level for the purpose of gross domestic product (GDP) calculation. Table 2.16 provides figures from this data in constant 2004–5 prices and examines the growth in the total input into agriculture in relation to the total value of output and the GDP. The table shows that the total value of output of agriculture grew at 2.95 per cent between 1980–1 and 2012–13 in constant prices. The growth rate accelerated somewhat to 3.30 per cent during 2000–1 to 2010–11, but there is a slight deceleration to 3.09 per cent after this during 2010–11 to 2012–13 (see Figure 2.15). The output of the livestock sector

Table 2.16 Value of Output, Inputs, and Gross Domestic Product of Agriculture and Allied Activities (Constant Prices, 2004–5) (in Rs Crore)

	1980–1	1985–6	1990–1	1995–6	2000–1	2005–6	2010–11	2011–12	2012–13
Total Value of Output	330,986	384,179	454,441	507,265	585,555	672,367	819,398	861,183	870,896
Agriculture	262,541	293,426	345,678	374,491	429,505	484,588	579,233	609,352	609,126
Livestock	68,093	90,505	108,489	132,629	156,050	187,779	240,166	251,831	261,771
Total Inputs	104,227	114,463	129,637	143,719	16,0380	183,797	224,281	233,638	237,692
Seed	9,744	10,514	12,113	12,746	12,593	13,151	14,224	14,254	14,318
Organic Manure	7,403	7,959	7,916	8,007	8,757	9,875	11,590	11,925	12,212
Chemical Fertilizers	7,361	12,056	16,875	20,828	22,535	26,436	35,983	36,755	32,911
Current Repairs, Maintenance of Fixed Assets, and Other Operational Costs	1,300	1,564	1,979	2,836	3,177	3,535	6,058	6,750	7,493
Feed of Livestock	65,998	65,486	66,810	70,010	78,774	87,450	93,789	95,366	96,765
Irrigation Charges	753	919	1,154	1,251	1,718	1,333	2,032	2,022	2,023
Market Charges	8,372	9445	11,465	11,183	13,896	16,882	18,743	19,717	19,714
Electricity	1,040	1,516	3,414	7,372	6,386	5,898	8,876	10,475	10,475
Pesticides and Insecticides	594	787	649	837	694	899	1,257	1,199	1,199
Diesel Oil	2,273	3,508	5,229	6,399	8,236	11,372	14,105	15,985	18,519
Financial Intermediation Services Indirectly Measured	442	932	2,351	3,228	3,613	6,965	17,624	19,190	22,064
Gross Domestic Product	238,172	280,788	336,202	376,285	439,479	502,996	610,905	643,543	649,424
Agriculture and Allied Activities	229,964	271,838	325,901	364,529	425,787	488,569	595,118	627,545	633,204
Operation of Government Irrigation System	8,208	8,950	10,301	11,756	13,692	14,427	15,787	15,998	16,220
Consumption of Fixed Capital	13,721	15,755	19,267	21,980	27,539	35,796	5,4046	55,103	60,948
Net Domestic Product	236,355	277,269	329,446	363,033	415,770	467,200	556,859	588,440	588,476

(Contd)

Table 2.16 (*Contd*)

			Annual Growth Rate			
	1980/81–2012/13	1980/81–1990/91	1990/91–2000/01	2000/01–2010/11	2010/11–2012/13
Total Value of Output	2.95	2.97	3.02	3.30	3.09
Agriculture	2.59	2.46	2.8	2.89	2.55
Livestock	4.02	4.76	3.71	4.35	4.40
Total Inputs	2.52	2.06	2.46	3.23	2.95
Seed	1.07	1.7	1.11	1.44	0.33
Organic Manure	1.39	0.62	0.86	3.19	2.65
Chemical Fertilizers	4.47	8.68	3.64	5.39	–4.36
Current Repairs, Maintenance of Fixed Assets & Other Operational Costs	5	4.11	5.5	6.70	11.21
Feed of Livestock	1.37	0.03	1.85	1.24	1.57
Irrigation Charges	2.57	4.42	2.47	0.27	–0.22
Market Charges	2.62	2.8	2.58	2.94	2.56
Electricity	6.9	13.77	8.02	3.54	8.63
Pesticides and Insecticides	1.53	1.74	–0.7	3.91	–2.33
Diesel Oil	5.98	8.13	4.6	5.04	14.58
Financial Intermediation Services Indirectly Measured	11.55	17.34	3.53	18.69	11.89
Gross Domestic Product	3.06	3.23	3.18	3.26	3.10
Agriculture and Allied Activities	3.09	3.26	3.21	3.31	3.15
Operation of Government Irrigation System	2.24	2.27	2.34	1.60	1.36
CFC	4.47	3.76	3.43	6.61	6.19
NDP	2.75	3.09	2.82	2.90	2.80

Source: Calculations based on Ministry of Statistics and Programme Implementation. 2014 and other years, New Delhi, India: MOSPI, Government of India.

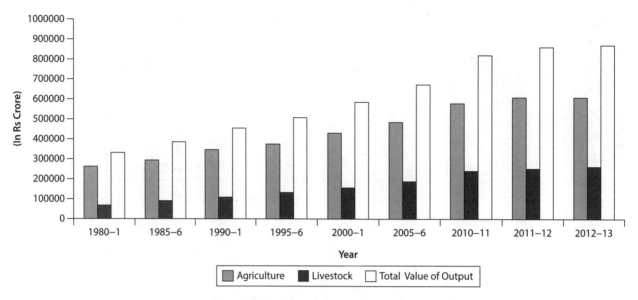

Figure 2.15   Value of Output of Agriculture

Source: Courtesy of the author.

within agriculture grew at a faster rate of 4.40 per cent and 4.35 per cent respectively in these periods. The total input in agriculture grew at 3.23 per cent during 2000–1 to 2010–11, but decelerated slightly to 2.95 per cent during 2010–11 to 2012–13.

Among the agricultural inputs, the largest appears to be feed of livestock, which constitutes almost 40 per cent of the total input. However, this grew at a slow rate of 1.24 per cent during 2000–1 to 2010–11 and 1.57 per cent in 2010–11 to 2012–13. Another major item is chemical fertilizers and this grew rapidly at 5.39 per cent in 2000–1 to 2010–11, but shows a decline at −4.36 per cent in 2010–11 to 2012–13. This is a matter of concern. Some of the other major inputs in value terms are market charges, diesel oil, and financial services. Diesel oil grew at 5.04 per cent in 2000–1 to 2010–11 and the growth substantially accelerated to 14.58 per cent in 2010–11 to 2012–13. Thus, diesel oil seems to be adding substantially to the input cost in recent years. Financial services cost grew even more rapidly at 18.69 per cent in 2000–1 to 2010–11 and 11.89 per cent during 2010–11 to 2012–13. Thus, financial service is a rapidly growing cost component. Market charges are not growing as rapidly at 2.94 in 2000–1 to 2010–11 and at 2.56 per cent during 2010–11 to 2012–13. Another rapidly growing input appears to be repairs and maintenance of fixed assets, which grew at 6.70 per cent in 2000–1 to 2010–11 and more rapidly 11.21 per cent during 2010–11 to 2012–13. The growth rates indicate that the structure of cost within the agricultural inputs is changing considerably over time, with diesel cost and a number of services such as financial services and repair and maintenance growing at a fast rate. The GDP of agriculture grew at 3.06 per cent over the entire period of 1980–1 and 2012–13, but the growth accelerated to 3.26 per cent during 2000–1 to 2010–11 but decelerated a little to 3.10 per cent during 2010–11 to 2012–13 (see Figure 2.16). It may be noted that the consumption of fixed capital, which represents use of capital in agriculture, has accelerated to over 6 per cent since 2010–11, leading to net domestic product (NDP) growth rate of 2.80 per cent during 2010–11 to 2012–13.

Table 2.17 shows the National Accounts Statistics break-up of the value of output of agriculture across different major crop groups and their growth rates. Table 2.17 shows that composition of the value of output has been changing considerably over the years. By 2012–13 fruit and vegetables have become greater in value than cereals as well as all other crop groups. The growth rate of value of cereals has been decreasing since 1980/81–1990/91, and drops to 1.87 per cent by 2010–11 to 2012–13, whereas the growth rate for fruit and vegetables has become higher and accelerated to 5.17 per cent by 2010–11 to 2012–13. The growth rate for pulses has accelerated to be higher than that of cereals, to be 2.74 per cent in 2000–1 to 2010–11, and the growth rate for oilseeds accelerated to 4.73 per cent in this period but became negative at −2.03 per cent during 2010–11 to 2012–13.

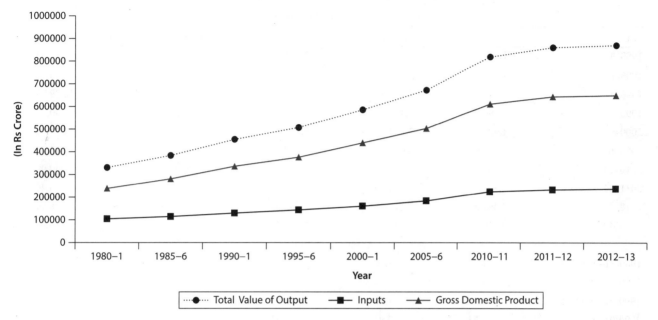

Figure 2.16   Value of Output, Inputs, and Gross Domestic Product of Agriculture and Allied Activities

Source: Courtesy of the author.

Table 2.17   Agriculture: Value of Output (at Constant Prices 2004–5) (Amount in Rs Crores)

Year	Cereals	Pulses	Oilseeds	Sugars	Fruit and Vegetables	Other Crops	Value of Output from Agriculture
1980–1	90,461	16,248	19,658	13,672	50,378	17,849	262,541
1985–6	104,137	19,492	22,100	14,547	57,891	15,914	293,426
1990–1	123,447	21,576	36,448	20,274	65,124	18,151	345,678
1995–6	128,103	18,568	42,425	22,787	80,762	17,687	374,491
2000–1	140,142	17,669	35,969	35,089	110,036	22,543	432,310
2005–6	145,068	20,627	52,786	31,269	121,981	28,568	484,588
2010–11	165,754	26,794	60,279	36,897	158,616	28,566	579,233
2011–12	178,689	26,165	57,534	38,482	169,637	29,500	609,352
2012–13	171,999	27,955	57,861	36,481	177,256	29,944	609,126
Share per cent 2012–13	28.24	4.59	9.50	5.99	29.10	4.92	100.00
Annual Growth Rate							
1980/81–2012/13	1.93	1.04	3.04	3.45	4.02	2.13	2.60
1980/81–1990/91	3.08	1.93	5.63	2.83	2.33	−0.43	2.46
1990/91–2000/01	1.91	−0.02	0.86	5.63	5.94	1.90	2.86
2000/01–2010/11	1.83	2.74	4.73	0.80	3.76	1.19	2.85
2010/11–2012/13	1.87	2.14	−2.03	−0.57	5.71	2.38	2.55

Source: Calculations based on information from Ministry of Agriculture (2014 and various years), Government of India.

2.11 INPUT PRODUCTIVITY IN TERMS OF YIELD

Yield per hectare of land is a very important measure of productivity of inputs in agriculture. Table 2.18 indicates the trends in the yields for foodgrains. It shows that during 1980–1 to 2013–14, the overall yield of foodgrains had risen by only 2.09 per cent per year. The growth rate for rice and wheat was about 1.75 per cent each and that of cereals as a whole was 2.21 per cent, indicating that the yields of other/coarse cereals

Table 2.18 Yield of Foodgrains (Kg/Hectare)

Year	Rice	Wheat	Total Cereals	Total Pulses	Total Foodgrains
1980–1	1,335.74	1,629.71	1,142.00	473.00	1,023.05
1985–6	1,551.53	2,045.65	1,323.00	547.00	1,175.13
1990–1	1,740.22	2,281.34	1,571.39	578.00	1,379.77
1995–6	1,796.92	2,483.01	1,702.65	552.00	1,490.95
2000–1	1,900.69	2,708.00	1,844.47	544.00	1,626.00
2005–6	2,102.00	2,619.00	1,967.75	596.93	1,715.00
2010–11	2,239.26	2,988.45	2,256.47	690.90	1,930.00
2011–12	2,392.84	3,176.99	2,414.93	698.59	2,078.40
2012–13	2,461.53	3,116.65	2,448.65	788.69	2,128.99
2013–14	2,416.30	3,145.38	2,462.11	763.61	2,119.63
Annual Growth Rate					
1980/81–2013/14	1.75	1.76	2.21	1.00	2.09
1980/81–1990/91	3.21	3.15	3.24	1.63	3.06
1990/91–2000/01	1.12	1.75	1.90	0.57	1.92
2000/01–2010/11	1.61	0.94	1.91	1.79	1.71
2010/11–2013/14	2.60	1.35	2.79	4.31	3.10

Source: Calculations based on information from Ministry of Agriculture (2014 and various years), Government of India.

have been growing faster, with perhaps an important contribution from maize. For pulses, the yield growth rate is very low at only 1.00 per cent (see Figure 2.17). However, in the final period of 2010–11 to 2013–14 there was an acceleration in the yield growth in most crop groups. The yield growth rate for rice accelerated to 2.60 per cent, total cereals to 2.79 per cent, pulses to 4.31 per cent, and foodgrains to 3.10 per cent. Only the growth in respect of wheat decelerated to 1.35 per cent.

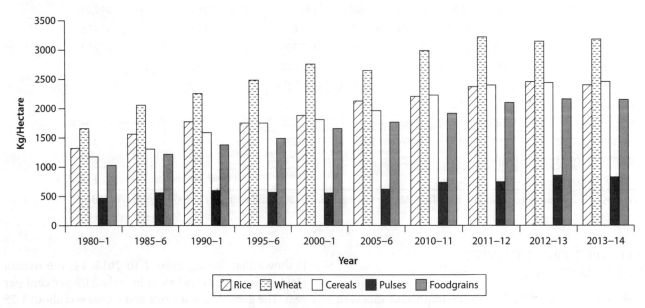

Figure 2.17 Yield of Foodgrains

Source: Courtesy of the author.

Table 2.19 shows the yields and their growth rates for other crops including oilseeds, cotton, sugarcane, and fruit and vegetables. Oilseeds show an overall growth rate of 2.05 per cent during 1980–1 to 2013/14, cotton 3.46 per cent, and sugarcane 0.57 per cent (see Figure 2.18). During 2000–1 to 2010–11, cotton experienced a tremendous acceleration to 10.81 per cent and oilseeds grew by 3.13 per cent. However, subsequently,

Table 2.19   Yield of Nine Oilseeds, Cotton, Sugarcane, and Fruit and Vegetables (Kg/Hectare)

Year	Nine Oilseeds	Cotton (Lint)	Sugarcane	Fruit	Vegetables
1980–1	532.00	152.00	57,844.00	–	–
1985–6	570.00	197.00	59,889.00	–	–
1994–5	843.00	225.00	71,254.00	11.89	13.42
1999–00	853.75	242.00	70,933.95	11.98	15.16
2004–5	884.83	189.63	64,751.71	10.07	15.01
2009–10	958.50	362.43	70,019.79	11.3	16.75
2010–11	1,193.01	499.33	70,090.80	11.73	17.25
2011–12	1,132.68	491.38	71,668.00	11.4	17.39
2012–13	1,168.23	485.71	68,254.43	11.64	17.62
2013–14	1,167.52	510.31	70,522.19	12.33	17.34
Annual Rate Growth					
1980/81–2013/14	2.05	3.46	0.57	–	–
1980/81–1990/91	3.06	4.15	1.37	–	–
1990/91–2000/01	1.41	1.30	0.82	0.63	2.58
2000/01–2010/11	3.13	10.81	0.61	0.86	2.24
2010/11–2013/14	−0.34	0.54	−0.30	1.72	0.29

Note: (–): not available.

Source: Calculations based on information from Ministry of Agriculture (2014 and various years), Government of India.

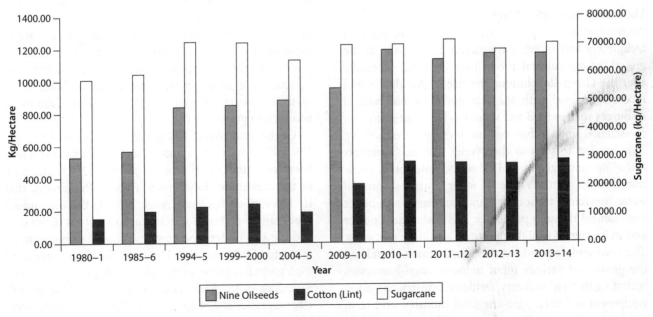

Figure 2.18   Trend in Yields of Nine Oilseeds, Cotton, and Sugarcane

Source: Courtesy of the author.

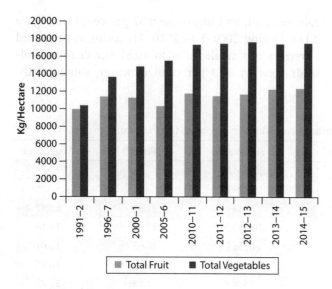

Figure 2.19   Trend in Yields in Fruit and Vegetables

Source: Courtesy of the author.

in 2010–11 to 2013–14, the yield growth rate for cotton dropped substantially to 0.54 per cent and it turned negative for oilseeds to –0.34 per cent and for sugarcane to –0.30 per cent. Only fruit shows a little acceleration to 1.72 per cent (Figure 2.19). Thus, non-foodgrain crops are generally showing a deceleration in yield growth in the recent years.

2.12 SUMMARY AND CONCLUSIONS

The level and kinds of inputs substantially determine the production and productivity of agriculture. Modern technology and inputs have played a huge role in the growth of agricultural production in India, especially after the Green Revolution. The rise in population and incomes coupled with the scarcity of various natural resources such as land and water has led to intense focus on science and technology to increase productivity. This has led to various discoveries and developments including better genetics/HYV seeds, better plant nutrition through fertilizers, better water provision through water sourcing technology and management, better pest control through pesticides, and better farm power and machinery for higher physical and time efficiency. The need and demand for these inputs have stimulated the growth of various input industries/agri-businesses including the seed industry, fertilizer industry, irrigation equipment industry, agro-chemical industry, and farm machinery industry. These are now making huge contributions to agriculture.

From the early 1980s to 2010–11, the seed business has grown in size by over 6 times, the fertilizer business about 5 times, the groundwater irrigation and its equipment business has doubled, and the tractor business representing farm machinery has increased by over seven times. The pesticide business shows a rise and subsequent fall. This chapter examines the recent trends and changes in the agricultural input use in India, covering land, labour, water, fertilizers, seeds, pesticides, farm power/machinery, and electricity.

Land is the most basic input in agriculture, but of India's 328 million hectare geographic area only about 55 per cent or 182 million hectares is cultivable. The net cropped area is only about 140 million hectares and this shows a small decline at –0.02 per cent over 1980–1 to 2012–13, but sharper decline to –0.58 per cent during 2010–11 to 2012–13. This appears to be due to loss of land to non-agricultural uses such as housing and industry. The gross cropped area is considerably more than the net sown area, that is, 194 million hectares and shows an increasing trend at 0.37 per cent from 1980–1 to 2012–13, but a decline at –1.16 per cent after 2010–11. The area that is sown more than once shows an increasing trend of 1.59 per cent over the whole period but a decline at –1.38 per cent after 2010–11. These trends indicate considerable loss of land in agriculture and calls for stricter land use policies if further diversion is to be prevented. The gross irrigated area has shown a fairly steady growth at a rate of about 2 per cent per year, but the gross cropped area, which should be related, has shown a growth of only 0.37 per cent from 1980–1 to 2012–13, and a decline at –1.16 per cent during 2010–11 and 2012–13. Thus, growth in irrigated area is not translating to a comparable growth in gross cropped area perhaps indicating poor resource utilization. Land resource available for agriculture is getting more constrained and land, on its own, is making a negative contribution to agricultural production growth in the recent years.

Of the total area of 194 million hectares under crops, 139 million hectares is under food crops and 55 million hectares is under non-food crops in 2012–13. The bulk of the area under food crops is under foodgrains, that is, 120 million hectares. After 1980–1, the area under foodgrains has shown a decline at a rate of –0.16 per cent and the area under food crops has shown a slow increase at a rate of 0.09 per cent. However, the area under non-food crops has grown at the rate of 1.29 per cent per year, including in the years after 2010–11 when the growth rate was faster at 2.36 per cent, while the area under food crop showed a decline at –2.45 per cent. Thus, overall there was a clear shift from food crops to non-food crops. In the years after 2010–11, the rice area showed a small decline by −0.13 per cent but the area under wheat increased by 1.59 per cent. The area under pulses showed a sharp decline of −6.14 per cent after 2010–11 and the area under oilseed also declined at −1.37 per cent, perhaps showing poor incentive environment in these crops. At the policy level, there is a need to reassess the distribution of crop areas in relation to the need and demand for different foods and output in the country. Price and other incentives need to be reviewed and adjusted so as to achieve a better balance between supply and demand.

Labour is another major input in agriculture and of the total population of 1,210 million (in 2011), 69 per cent or 833 million were rural, and of these, 263 million or 32 per cent were agricultural workers. This included 118 million cultivators and 144 million agricultural labourers. Between 2001 and 2011 while the total population grew by 1.64 per cent the rural population grew at a far slower rate of 1.16 per cent, and the number of agricultural workers grew at 1.17 per cent. However, whereas the number of cultivators had declined by −0.70 per cent, the number of agricultural labourers had increased by 3.06 per cent, indicating a growing proportion of agricultural labourers. This would increase the incidence of unemployment and poverty unless new employment opportunities are created.

In another break-up, of the total workforce of 467 million in the country in 2011–12, the agricultural workforce stands at 228 million or 48.8 per cent. Even though the total workforce is growing, the share of agricultural workforce is declining and the rate of decline is accelerated from −1.09 per cent between 1999–2000 and 2009–10 to −2.90 per cent between 2009–10 and 2011–12. Thus, there is a movement of workforce away from agriculture to non-agriculture, and even the absolute number of agricultural workforce is declining between 2009–10 and 2011–12. This indicates that the labour supply to agriculture is reducing in the recent years. This calls for inputs and technology that enhance the productivity per labour if the production of agriculture is to be maintained or increased.

Water is another major input for agriculture and shows significant change and development. The net irrigated area has increased from 38 million hectares in 1980–1 to 66 million hectares in 2012–13 and the gross irrigated area has increased from 49 million hectares to 92 million hectares. The per cent gross area irrigated has increased substantially from 28.8 per cent to 47.6 per cent from 1980–1 to 2012–13. However, the period from 2000–1 to 2010–11 shows a deceleration in the growth of per cent area irrigated to 1.14 per cent but after 2010–11 there is

an acceleration to 2.88 per cent. This perhaps indicates that the water management problems and constraints faced during 2000–1 to 2010–11 have been overcome to some extent, and the efforts for conservation of water and enhancing its use efficiency such as rainwater harvesting through check-dams, watershed development, drip and sprinkler irrigation, and other methods are yielding results.

The sources of irrigation show substantial change. The canal-irrigated area shows a negative trend of −0.15 per cent overall but a reversal between 2000–1 and 2010–11 to positive 0.74 per cent. Groundwater irrigation has expanded rapidly at more than 3 per cent in the 1980s and 1990s but shows a sharp deceleration to 1.5 per cent between 2000–1 and 2010–11 followed by an acceleration to 2.63 per cent during 2010/11 to 2012–13. The major driver has been tubewell irrigation, which has expanded rapidly at more than 4 per cent in the 1980s and 1990s but decelerated to 2.27 per cent between 2000–1 and 2010–11, and accelerated again to 3.36 per cent during 2010/11 to 2012–13. The findings indicate that there is a sharp increase in the dependence on ground water irrigation in the recent decades and currently about 62 per cent is irrigated through wells. Some deceleration in groundwater irrigation growth is evident between 2000–1 and 2010–11 indicating emerging constraints, but the growth has again accelerated subsequently, perhaps indicating improvement in management and more efficient use of water, perhaps due to various programmes undertaken to improve water conservation and water use efficiency.

Fertilizer use has grown quite rapidly at the rate of about 4.5 per cent from 55 million tonnes to 255 million tonnes between 1980–1 and 2014–15. However, the 1980s saw a much faster increase in fertilizer use at over 8 per cent per year, which has subsequently decelerated to about 4 per cent per year in the 1990s followed by some acceleration to about 6 per cent between 2000–1 and 2010–11. However, after 2010–11 there is a substantial decline in fertilizer use—the rate of growth falls to −2.06 per cent for all, with phosphatic fertilizers declining at −6.44 per cent and potassic fertilizers at −10.50 per cent, and even nitrogenous fertilizers slow to just 1.31 per cent. Fertilizer consumption per hectare grew substantially from 32 kg per hectare in 1980–1 to 131 kg per hectare in 2014–15. However, after 2010–11, the growth rates drop substantially, turning to 0.67 per cent for N, −8.08 per cent for P and −7.74 per cent for K. This appears to be due to the major changes in the fertilizer subsidy policies where there is shift to nutrient-based subsidies leading to sharp rise in prices of P and K fertilizers leading to a decline in their use and the imbalance also affecting N.

Given this, agriculture may be headed for a soil nutrient and fertility crisis that could considerably affect agricultural production, unless policies are substantially reformed keeping in view the nutrient requirements for soil fertility and sound agriculture.

The use of quality certified seeds is of significant importance for increasing agricultural production. Overall, between 1990–1 and 2013–14, the seed use has grown at a rapid pace of 8.4 per cent per year, and reached a high of 313 lakh quintals in the year 2012–13 in which cereals constituted 204 lakh quintals. There is particularly rapid growth between 2000–1 and 2010–11 at 13 per cent including pulses at 17 per cent and oilseeds at 16 per cent but fibres at −0.93 per cent (perhaps due to expensive Bt cotton seeds). After 2010–11 the overall growth rate fell sharply to 3.15 per cent but the use of other seeds which would include vegetables shows a large acceleration. There is great need to revive the use of good seeds which are fundamental to a productive agriculture.

The use of pesticides, important to protect the crops, increased from 45,000 tonnes in 1980–1 to 75,000 tonnes in 1990–1. It then fell to 40,000 tonnes by 2005–6, but rose again to 58,000 tonnes by 2013–14. Overall the growth rate is negative at −0.82 per cent. This appears to be due to environmental concerns about pesticides, the development of pest-resistant varieties such as Bt cotton that require much less use of pesticides, and the use of more effective less bulky pesticides. Trends across different kinds of pesticides shows that whereas insecticides are showing a significant negative growth rate of −3.39 per cent, fungicides are showing a strong positive growth rate of 12.40 per cent and herbicides are also showing an uptrend from 2006–7 and 2013–14. The trend appears positive for the environment but continuous innovation and research is required since pests become resistant and new problems arise.

Farm machinery and equipment are becoming increasingly important inputs for agriculture. The number of tractors sold has increased from about 70,000 in 1980–1 to almost 700,000 in 2013–14, a growth rate of 6.87 per cent. The growth accelerates to 9.93 per cent in 2000/01–2010/11 but decelerates to 4.25 per cent evident after 2010–11. Thus, the recent years show a considerable slowdown in tractor sales growth. On the number of operational holdings using different important items of agricultural machinery, diesel pumpsets are showing a relatively steady growth of about 7 per cent, whereas electric pumpsets show a growth at 5.79 per cent overall between 1981/82–2000/01 but a deceleration to 1.93 per cent during 2001/02–2011/12. Similarly, the holdings using power tillers and tractors are also showing a

deceleration in growth rates during 2001/02–2011/12. These growth rates indicate an overall rapid growth but a slowing down in the recent years, which may be due to credit constraints and poor rainfall in a few recent years. Providing appropriate mechanization would be very important for enhancing labour productivity as less labour becomes available in agriculture.

Electricity is another important input and the share of electricity consumed by agriculture rose from 17 per cent in 1980–1 to 30 per cent in 1995–6. However, since then the share has been falling and stands at only 17 per cent by 2014–15. Whereas the total power consumption has been growing at almost 9 per cent per year from 2000/01 to 2014/15, the rate of growth is 5.5 per cent for agriculture. The share of agricultural consumption shows a negative growth rate during both 2000/01–2010/11 and 2010/11–2014/15. Thus, power consumption by agriculture, which was a significant concern in the 1990s, is no longer a major issue since its share has sharply declined. This can be further reduced if solar power is harnessed.

Study of the value of agricultural inputs and output in the aggregate at constant 2004/05 prices through the National Accounts Statistics used in GDP calculation indicates that the total value of output of agriculture grew at 2.95 per cent between 1980–1 and 2012–13. The growth rate was higher at 3.30 per cent during 2000/01–2010/11 but fell to 3.09 per cent after this during 2010/11–2012/13. The output of the livestock sector within agriculture grew at a faster rate of 4.40 and 4.35 per cent respectively in these periods. The total input in agriculture grew at 3.23 per cent during 2000/01–2010/11 but decelerated slightly to 2.95 per cent during 2010/11–2012/13. The trends indicate no decline but a slight increase in the input–output efficiencies in the aggregate in agriculture, which is positive,

Among the agricultural inputs, the largest is reported to be feed of livestock, which constitutes almost 40 per cent of the total input. Chemical fertilizers grew rapidly at 5.39 per cent in 2000/01–2010/11 but declined at −4.36 per cent in 2010/11–2012/13. Diesel oil grew at 5.04 per cent in 2000/01–2010/11 but substantially accelerated in growth to 14.58 per cent in 2010/11–2012/13. Financial services cost grew even more rapidly at 18.69 per cent in 2000/01–2010/11 and 11.89 per cent during 2010/11–2012/13. Repairs and maintenance of fixed assets grew at 6.70 per cent in 2000/01–2010/11 and more rapidly at 11.21 per cent during 2010/11–2012/13. The growth rates indicate that the structure of cost within the agricultural inputs is changing considerably over time, with diesel cost, financial services, and repair and maintenance growing at a fast rate. Overall, the GDP of agriculture grew at 3.06 per cent over 1980-1 to 2012-13. The growth accelerated to 3.26 per cent during 2000/01–2010/11 but decelerated a little to 3.10 per cent during 2010/11–2012/13. In terms of GDP, the growth performance of agriculture is fairly stable at slightly over 3 per cent over the long run.

The study of the National Accounts Statistics breakup of the value of output of agriculture across different major crop groups shows that composition of the value of output has been changing considerably over the years. The growth rate of value of cereals has been decreasing since 1980/81–1990/91, and drops to 1.87 per cent by 2010/11–2012/13, whereas the growth rate for fruit and vegetables has become higher and accelerates to 5.17 per cent by 2010/11–2012/13. The growth rate for pulses accelerates to be higher than that of cereals at 2.74 per cent in 2000/01–2010/11, and the growth rate for oilseeds also accelerates to 4.73 per cent in this period but becomes negative as –2.03 per cent in 2010/11–2012/13. By 2012–13, fruit and vegetables have become larger in output value than cereals as well as all other crop groups. This shows a fundamental shift on the value front in agriculture towards higher-value products, particularly fruit and vegetables.

The yield per hectare of land is a very important measure of productivity of inputs in agriculture. During 1980/81–2013/14 the yield of foodgrains grew at only 2.09 per cent per year. The growth rate for rice and wheat is about 1.75 each and that of cereals as a whole is 2.21, indicating that the yields of other/coarse cereals have been growing faster, perhaps with an important contribution from maize. For pulses, the yield growth rate is very low at only 1.00 per cent. However, in the final period of 2010/11–2013/14 there is an acceleration in the yield growth in most crop groups. The yield growth rate for rice accelerates to 2.60 per cent, total cereals to 2.79 per cent, pulses to 4.31 per cent and foodgrains to 3.10 per cent. Only wheat decelerates to 1.35 per cent. Oilseeds show an overall growth rate of 2.05 per cent during 1980/81–2013/14, cotton at 3.46 per cent and sugarcane at 0.57 per cent. During 2000/01–2010/11, cotton shows a tremendous acceleration to 10.81 per cent and oilseeds to 3.13 per cent. However, subsequently, in 2010/11–2013/14, the yield growth rate for cotton drops to only 0.54 per cent and it turns negative for oilseeds to –0.34 per cent and for sugarcane to –0.30 per cent. Only fruit shows a little acceleration to 1.72 per cent. Thus, whereas yield growth of a number of food crops show acceleration, non-foodgrain crops are generally showing

a deceleration in yield growth in the recent years. This may be related to the high food price inflation during this period improving incentives for food production.

Overall, the study finds that a number of agricultural inputs are showing decline in recent years. The contribution of land input to agricultural production growth is on the decline and even negative in the recent years. The net cropped area shows decline and the gross cropped area, though rising since the 1980s, shows decline in the recent years. There is a substantial shift of area from food to non-food crops. On labour, the agricultural workforce is showing a decline in numbers since 2004–5, though by another estimate, the agricultural labourers are showing an increase over 2001–11. Water in terms of irrigated area is one input which is showing a relatively healthy growth trend at 1.7 to 2.0 per cent and this is mainly due to tubewell groundwater irrigation, which is growing at 3.0 to 4.0 per cent. Fertilizers are showing a decline in the recent years and the growth of certified seeds is also showing a slowdown. Farm machinery shows good growth since 1980s but a substantial slowdown in the recent years. In terms of National Accounts values in constant prices, agricultural output, agricultural input, and agricultural GDP are all growing at about 3.0 per cent in the recent years. In the agricultural output value, the share of livestock products has risen substantially, and the output value of fruit and vegetables has crossed that of cereals. Productivity or yields of pulses and rice are growing faster in the recent years, thereby raising the foodgrain yield growth rate to about 3.0 per cent. Yields of oilseeds, cotton, sugarcane, and vegetables are not showing good growth in the recent years, but that of fruit is showing an increase. Better conversion of irrigated area growth to gross cropped area growth is strongly called for, and the reversal of the poor/declining trends in fertilizers, seeds, and farm machinery is urgently required if healthy agricultural production growth is to be achieved.

Policy changes are urgently required to monitor land use, else diversion of agricultural land will further constrain agricultural growth. This also calls for further emphasis on yield and productivity increase. The sector will also need to deal with a decline in the agricultural workforce, calling for different means of enhancing labour productivity such as through appropriate machines and mechanization. Improvement is evident on the irrigation front but the growing scarcity of the resource calls for continuing efforts to promote conservation of water and its sound and judicious use. The recent decline in fertilizer use may lead to a soil fertility and nutrient crisis, and calls for urgent reform of the fertilizer policy and subsidy regime. On the seed front, new technology is strongly needed and new advances including from biotechnology can provide many solutions and play a major role. Overall, the major shift in agriculture as well as demand towards high-value output including vegetables, fruit, and livestock products needs to be seriously recognized and special policies developed to support the needs of these sub-sectors.

REFERENCES

Fertiliser Association of India. 2013. *Fertiliser Statistics*. New Delhi, India: FAI.

Gandhi, Vasant P. 2014. 'Growth and Transformation of the Agribusiness Sector: Drivers, Models, and Challenges'. *Indian Journal of Agricultural Economics* 69(1): 44–74.

Gandhi, Vasant P., Zhang-yue Zhou, and John Mullen. 2004. 'Wheat Economy of India: Will Demand Be a Constraint or Supply?'. *Economic and Political Weekly* 39(43): 4737–46.

Ganesh-Kumar, Anand, Rajesh Mehta, Hemant Pullabhotla, Sanjay K. Prasad, Kavery Ganguly, and Ashok Gulati. 2012. *Demand and Supply of Cereals in India 2010–2025*. IFPRI Discussion Paper 01158. Washington, DC: International Food Policy Research Institute.

Mellor, J.W. 1988. 'Food Production, Consumption and Development Strategy'. In *The Indian Economy: Recent Developments and Future Prospects* edited by R.E.B. Lucas and G.P. Papanek, pp. 53–76. Boulder, CO: Westview.

Ministry of Agriculture. 2012. *All India Report on Input Survey*. New Delhi, India: Ministry of Agriculture and Farmers Welfare.

Ministry of Agriculture. 2014 and various years. *Agricultural Statistics at a Glance*. New Delhi, India: Ministry of Agriculture.

Ministry of Statistics and Programme Implementation. 2014 and other years. New Delhi, India: MOSPI, Government of India.

Sarma, J.S. and Vasant P. Gandhi. 1990. *Production and Consumption of Foodgrains in India: Implications of Accelerated Economic Growth and Poverty Alleviation*. IFPRI Research Report no. 81. Washington, DC: IFPRI.

3

Livestock Development in India
Opportunities, Challenges, and Public Policy

Pratap S. Birthal* and Jaya Jumrani**

ABSTRACT

Sustained economic and income growth and a fast-growing urban population have been fuelling rapid growth in demand for foods of animal origin. On the supply side, livestock generate a continuous stream of outputs that can be consumed within the owning households to improve nutritional security of the family members, and sold for cash to purchase daily consumption needs or to meet other household expenditures. Livestock can be raised with a small start-up capital, and being a form of reproducible asset they can be easily multiplied to enhance income and accumulate wealth. Livestock production is less prone to climatic shocks and thus acts as insurance when crops fail. Livestock production in India has been growing faster and provides a cushion to agricultural growth, and contributes to poverty reduction. Nonetheless, productivity of India's livestock is low; and is constrained by low level of adoption of technologies, scarcity of feed and fodder, and poor animal health services. Institutional and policy support to livestock sector in terms of investment, credit, insurance, extension, and markets is not commensurate with its economic contribution. The extent to which pro-poor growth potential can be harnessed would depend on how research, institutions, and policies together address the constraints that the livestock sector is confronting.

JEL Classification: Q10, O20, Q51, I32

Keywords: livestock, agricultural growth, poverty, challenges, policies

3.1 INTRODUCTION

Since time immemorial, livestock have been an integral component of India's rural economy and have contributed to the welfare of rural people in several ways. They provide nutrient-rich foods, such as milk, meat, and eggs; dung for fuel and manure; draught power for rural transportation and cropping activities; and hides, skins, and bones for use in industries. They are an important source of wealth and income for farmers, and also serve

*ICAR National Professor at the National Institute of Agricultural Economics and Policy Research, New Delhi, India.

** Scientist at the National Institute of Agricultural Economics and Policy Research, New Delhi, India.

as a financial institution for them—a living bank with offspring as interest and insurance during the crisis. Their non-food functions, however, have been dwindling due to the declining landholding size accompanied by increasing mechanization of agricultural operations, availability of alternative and faster means of rural transportation, growing use of chemical fertilizers, and emergence of formal financial institutions.

Livestock are now valued more for their food production function. The sustained economic and income growth and a fast-growing urban population, increasing participation of women in workforce, improvements in transport, and rise of supermarkets have been fuelling rapid growth in demand for animal food products (Delgado et al. 1999; Kumar and Birthal 2004; Parthasarathy Rao and Birthal 2008; Joshi and Kumar 2012). On the supply side, livestock produce a continuous stream of outputs on daily basis or at very short intervals which can be consumed within the owning households to improve nutritional security of the family members, and sold for cash to purchase daily consumption needs and meet other household expenditures. They can be raised with a small start-up capital, and being a form of a reproducible asset they can be easily multiplied to generate income and accumulate wealth. Livestock production is less prone to external shocks such as droughts, heat waves, and so on (Birthal and Negi 2012), and thus livestock act as self-insurance for farmers. Livestock production is also labour-intensive and has potential to absorb surplus labour from agriculture.

Indian agriculture is dominated by small landholders. Farm households cultivating less than or equal to one hectare of land comprise two-thirds of the total farm households, but agriculture is not the sole source of livelihood for a majority of them (Birthal et al. 2014). A majority of such households have a higher endowment of family labour in relation to land they own. Therefore, the characteristics of livestock production match with the resource endowments and income requirements of small landholders.

With regard to this background, we assess opportunities and challenges in smallholder livestock production systems and the role of public policy for faster and sustainable development of the livestock sector. Specifically, we focus on the following issues.

- Opportunities for growth of livestock sector
- Potential of livestock in enhancing agricultural growth, food, and nutrition security; in reducing poverty and gender disparities; and in conserving natural resources

- Role of technology, institutions, and policies in converting the challenges into opportunities for rural prosperity.

The chapter is organized as follows. In the next section, we examine changes in the consumption pattern and the potential demand for animal food products. Section 3.3 highlights prominent trends in livestock production. In section 3.4, we discuss the contribution of livestock to agricultural growth; and it is followed by a discussion on the effect of demand-driven growth on rural poverty, human nutrition, and women empowerment. Section 3.6 discusses environmental contributions of livestock. Role of public policies in harnessing the potential of livestock in socio-economic development is discussed in section 3.7. Concluding remarks are made in the final section.

3.2 OPPORTUNITIES FOR GROWTH

3.2.1 Domestic Demand

In the past two decades, the food baskets of Indian consumers have undergone a significant shift away from cereals towards horticultural and animal products. The share of cereals in total food expenditure declined in both rural as well as urban India (Table 3.1). On the other hand, the expenditure share of animal products (milk, meat, eggs, and fish) remained almost constant in rural areas and declined marginally in urban areas.

The changes in food consumption pattern are better revealed in the quantities consumed. During this period, in rural areas the per capita consumption of cereals declined and that of milk increased by 11 per cent, meat and fish by 33 per cent, and eggs by 83 per cent. The consumption of animal products also increased in urban areas. Milk is the most preferred animal product in the diet of Indians. A sizeable proportion of India's population though is non-vegetarian, yet meat, eggs, and fish do not for a part of its regular diet (Kumar and Birthal 2004). The observed changes in their consumption show rural consumption catching up with the urban consumption. Not only that, this change is not specific to a socioeconomic group but is quite extensive. Although the poor consume less, the proportionate increase in the consumption is much larger for them as compared to that for the rich (Kumar and Birthal 2004; Joshi and Kumar 2012).

These changes in the food basket are as expected. Compared to staple foodgrains, the consumption of animal products is more responsive to income changes (Joshi and Kumar 2012), and the response is bigger for

Table 3.1 Changes in Food Consumption Patterns in India, 1993–4 to 2011–12

Commodity Groups	Rural		Urban	
	1993–4	2011–12	1993–4	2011–12
Share of Food Expenditure (%)				
Cereals	24.3	12.1	14.1	7.4
Pulses	4.0	3.3	3.2	2.2
Edible oils	4.4	3.8	4.4	2.7
Sugar	3.1	1.8	2.4	1.2
Fruit, vegetables and nuts	7.7	6.7	8.2	5.7
Milk and milk products	9.5	9.1	9.8	7.8
Meat, fish, and eggs	3.3	3.6	3.4	2.8
Others	6.9	8.2	9.2	8.8
Food	63.2	48.6	54.7	38.6
Per Capita Consumption (Kg/Month)				
Cereals	13.4	11.2	10.6	9.3
Pulses	0.8	0.7	0.9	0.8
Edible oils	0.4	0.7	0.6	0.9
Sugar	0.8	0.8	1.0	0.9
Fruit, vegetables, and nuts	5.8	5.9	10.1	9.0
Milk and milk products	4.0	4.4	5.0	5.5
Eggs (no.)	0.6	1.1	1.5	1.7
Meat and fish, and so on	0.3	0.4	0.4	0.5

Source: Authors' estimates based on National Sample Survey unit-level data.

Table 3.2 Demand for Livestock Products, 2010 to 2030

	2010	2030
Milk	112.0	185.0
Meat	5.3	9.3
Eggs	3.5	5.8
Fish	6.4	11.2

Source: Joshi and Kumar (2012).

rural and for poor consumers. This implies that the poor and rural consumers allocate more of their food budgets to animal food products when their incomes rise.

These changes in consumption pattern have been driven by sustained economic and income growth, and a fast-growing urban population. Since 1991–2, India's economy has been growing at an annual rate of close to 7 per cent, and the per capita income at 5.2 per cent. The urban population has been increasing fast—at an annual rate of 2.8 per cent (compared to an annual growth of 1.8 per cent in the total population), raising its share in the total population from 25.7 per cent in 1991 to 31.2 per cent in 2011. These trends are considered quite robust, and are unlikely to subside in near future. Projections indicate that if the current economic and demographic trends continue to 2030 the demand for milk will increase to 185 million tonnes, of meat to 9.3 million tonnes, of eggs to 5.8 million tonnes, and of fish to 11.2 million tonnes (Table 3.2).

3.2.2 Export Demand

The global market for animal food products is also expanding fast, especially in the developing countries. The per capita consumption of almost all animal food products has been increasing throughout the world but faster in Asia and Africa (Table 3.3). This is an opportunity for India to increase its exports. At present, India accounts for 0.5 per cent of the global exports of dairy products and 2.5 per cent of meat and meat products.

Since the early 1980s, India has experienced significant growth in milk production, turning it self-sufficient and even an occasional exporter of dairy products from

Table 3.3 Global Consumption of Animal Food Products (Kg/Capita/Annum)

	Milk		Meat		Eggs		Fish	
	2001	2011	2001	2011	2001	2011	2001	2011
World	78.82	90.73	37.23	42.36	8.12	8.95	16.13	18.93
Africa	38.51	46.17	15.27	18.62	2.14	2.47	8.32	10.86
North America	254.7	252.95	119.00	115.11	14.34	13.7	21.83	21.71
South America	115.81	140.12	65.65	78.38	7.01	9.23	8.64	10.24
Asia	41.39	58.74	24.59	31.31	7.93	9.11	17.48	21.28
Europe	209.75	219.06	71.14	76.01	12.33	12.87	19.92	21.76
Oceania	183.11	202.87	101.23	116.24	6.23	7.36	23.42	26.48

Source: FAO-FAOSTAT.

Table 3.4   Trends in Export of Dairy and Meat Products

	India			World		
	Quantity (in Thousand Tonnes)	Value (US$ in Million)	Unit Value (in US$/ Tonne)	Quantity in Thousand Tonne	Value (US$ in Million)	Unit Value (in US$/t)
Dairy Products						
1991–3	14	4	266	53,924	22,690	421
2001–3	121	30	243	73,020	28,260	387
2011–13	572	270	472	11,1395	76,169	684
Total Meat						
1991–3	97	100	1,028	15,663	36,837	2,352
2001–3	308	302	979	26,488	46,898	1,771
2011–3	1,217	3,471	2,853	43,047	1,28,836	2,993
Bovine Meat						
1991–3	88	83	941	6,544	16,077	2,457
2001–3	296	285	964	7,481	15,575	2,082
2011–3	1,193	3,380	2,832	10,466	43,319	4,139

Source: FAO-FAOSTAT.

a chronic importer until the late 1980s (Table 3.4, Figure 3.1). So far domestic production has managed to keep balance with demand. Recently, India has imported dairy products in large quantities, and there is an apprehension that even if the current production trends continue, the fast-growing demand for dairy products may not be met from domestic production.

India's livestock-based exports comprise mainly of bovine meat, that is, buffalo meat.[1] It accounts for over

85 per cent of the total earnings from exports of livestock products. In 2011–13, the country, on an average, exported 1.2 million tonnes of buffalo meat (almost three-fourths of the total production) valued at US$ 3,380 million on average. This is equivalent to 9.1 per cent of the total value of exports of agricultural products and almost three times larger than its share in the late 1990s. It may be noted that in recent years India has emerged as one of the largest exporters of bovine meat. In 2011–13, it accounted for 11.3 per cent of the global exports of bovine meat. India's main export destinations include Vietnam, Malaysia, Thailand, Egypt, Philippines,

[1] Cattle slaughtering in India is banned; hence, it is mostly buffalo meat that is exported by the country.

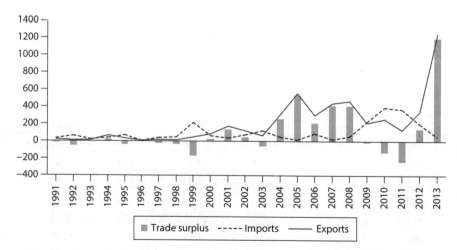

Figure 3.1   India's Trade in Dairy Products (Milk Equivalent in Thousand Tonnes)

Source: FAO-FAOSTAT.

Kuwait, Saudi Arabia, and United Arab Emirates. Malaysia, Philippines, the UAE, Jordan, Oman, Kuwait, and Iran have been India's traditional export markets, while Vietnam, Thailand, Angola, Congo, and Egypt have emerged as the new markets.

Several factors have contributed to India's rise as one of the largest exporters of bovine meat. First, India's existing export markets (mainly in Southeast Asian and Middle Eastern countries) were until recently served by the European Union (EU), but with reduction in the subsidy support there, the cost of beef production increased, making imports from EU costlier for the poor countries. Buffalo meat is a close substitute of cattle meat. It blends well with other value-added products, and is much cheaper than beef. Second, India is closer to the countries that import from it; hence the cost of transport is lower. Third, the Islamic countries prefer halal meat, and India produces and supplies halal meat. Note that India also realized a greater value of its exports in recent years, almost thrice of that in 2001–3. Though, global beef prices have been increasing, yet it is at a slower rate compared to that of buffalo meat.

India has considerable potential to export buffalo meat. Buffalo meat is low in fat and cholesterol, and free from radiation. India does not use hormones, antibiotics, and chemicals for fattening of animals and/or processing of meat. It utilizes primarily male buffaloes that are of little use for agricultural purposes for meat production. In 2012, males comprised only 15 per cent of the total buffalo population. Note that though majority of the Hindu population considers the cow as a sacred animal and its slaughtering is banned in most Indian states, no such religious sentiments are attached to buffaloes. However, the main problems in harnessing the potential of buffaloes for meat are the lack of incentives for farmers to raise buffalo calves to an optimum slaughter age,[2] and the poor institutional arrangements linking them to markets.

[2] Most slaughtered buffalo males are of less than one year of age.

3.3 SUPPLY OF LIVESTOCK PRODUCTS

India has a huge population of different livestock species. In 2012, it had 191 million cattle, 109 million buffaloes, 135 million goats, 65 million sheep, 10 million pigs, and 729 million poultry birds (Table 3.5). Except that of cattle, populations of other species have increased over time. Cattle population shows no definite trend on account of several reasons. Historically, Indian farmers have raised indigenous cattle primarily to produce males for draught power. However, with increasing mechanization of agricultural operations, the utility of male cattle has declined. The indigenous cows also possess no advantage in milk production over buffaloes and crossbred cows. The average milk yield of an indigenous cow is only about 2.5 kg/day—one-third of the yield of a crossbred cow and half of that of a buffalo. On the other hand, the rising demand for animal food products has led to a substantial increase in the number of buffaloes for milk; and sheep, goats, and poultry for meat.

India experienced a tremendous growth in milk production in the past three decades. This is termed as 'white revolution' and in the development literature is as celebrated as the 'green revolution'. Milk production that hardly exceeded 20 million tonnes during the 1960s gradually increased to 36 million tonnes in 1982–3 and further to 132 million tonnes in 2012–13 (Table 3.6). In 1997, India overtook the United States of America as the largest producer of milk, and since then it has retained its position. Milk is now the largest agricultural commodity, in physical as well as value terms (Birthal and Negi 2012).

The revolutionary progress in milk production can be attributed to the spread of dairy cooperatives that improved farmers' access to urban demand centres. The number of dairy cooperatives increased from a little over 13,000 in 1980–1 to more than 1.65 lakhs in 2014–15 (Table 3.7). During this period, milk procured by these cooperatives increased 15-fold, from less than 1 million tonne to 13.9 million tonnes, equivalent to about 10 per cent of the total milk produced in the country. The spread

Table 3.5 Trends in Livestock Population in India (in Millions)

Year	Cattle	Buffalo	Sheep	Goat	Horses and Ponies	Camels	Pigs	Mules	Donkeys	Yaks	Poultry
1982	192.45	69.78	48.76	95.25	0.90	1.08	10.07	0.13	1.02	0.13	207.74
1992	204.58	84.21	50.78	115.28	0.82	1.03	12.79	0.19	0.97	0.06	307.07
2003	185.18	97.92	61.47	124.36	0.75	0.63	13.52	0.18	0.65	0.06	489.01
2012	190.90	108.7	65.07	135.17	0.63	0.4	10.29	0.20	0.32	0.08	729.21

Source: GoI (2014).

Table 3.6   Trends in Livestock Production in India

	Milk	Total Meat	Poultry Meat	Eggs
Production (Million Tonnes)				
1982–3	35.8	3.0	0.13	0.6
1992–3	58.0	3.9	0.51	1.3
2002–3	86.2	4.7	1.09	2.2
2012–13	132.4	6.3	2.33	3.6
Per Capita Availability (Kg/Annum)				
1982–3	50.56	4.17		0.89
1992–3	65.07	4.48		1.41
2002–3	81.63	4.45		2.09
2012–13	109.24	5.19		2.97

Source: GoI (2015); FAO-FAOSTAT.

Table 3.7   Progress in Dairy Cooperatives in India

	1980–1	1990–1	2000–1	2014–15
Dairy cooperatives organized (no.)	13,284	63,415	96,206	1,65,835
Farmer members (in thousands)	1,747	7,482	10,738	15,399
Milk procured (in million tonnes)	0.94	3.54	6.02	13.85

Source: NDDB (2015).

of dairy cooperatives, however, remains uneven across states. Gujarat, Karnataka, Maharashtra, and Tamil Nadu account for more than 70 per cent to the total milk procured by cooperatives.

The other notable factor in the success of the 'white revolution' has been the increasing adoption of crossbreeding technology. Since the early 1960s, the Government of India has been pursuing the policy of genetic enhancement of indigenous cows through artificial insemination (AI) using semen of high-yielding indigenous and exotic breeds. As a result, the share of crossbred cows in the population of total in-milk bovines increased from 9.3 per cent in 1999–2000 to 15 per cent in 2014–15 and now these contribute to one-fourth of the total milk production (GoI 2015a). Adoption of crossbreeding technology has been uneven—higher in states like Kerala and Punjab, and much less in the eastern states of Bihar, West Bengal, and Odisha.

India also experienced a revolution in poultry production. Egg production increased from a mere 0.6 million tonnes in 1982–3 to 3.6 million tonnes in 2012–13 (Table 3.6). Likewise, there was a significant increase in broiler meat production, from 0.13 million tonnes to 2.33 million tonnes. The revolution in poultry was steered by the private sector. It made huge investments in the integrated value chains linking farmers to markets through contract farming, which enabled them to easily access improved technologies, quality inputs, and veterinary services; and to share market and price risk (Ramaswami et al. 2005).

The growing production lifted the per capita availability of animal food products despite a rapid increase in human population. The availability of milk more than doubled from 50.6 kg/capita/annum in 1982–3 to 109.2 kg/capita/annum in 2012–13, and that of eggs more than trebled from 0.9 kg/capita/annum to 3.0 kg/capita/annum.

3.4 LIVESTOCK AND AGRICULTURAL GROWTH

India's policymakers have been targeting 4 per cent growth for the agricultural sector (including crops, livestock, fisheries, and forestry) since the ninth five-year plan (1997–2002); the target, however, has remained elusive. The realized rate of growth remained around 3 per cent, except during the eleventh plan (2007–11), when it improved to 3.8 per cent. The twelfth five-year plan (2012–17) has also set a target of 4 per cent growth for agricultural sector. Though the share of agriculture in gross domestic product (GDP) has been declining fast (less than 15 per cent in 2014–15), enhancing agricultural growth remains a major challenge.

There has been a significant increase in the contribution of livestock to the gross value of output of the agricultural sector: from 20.9 per cent in 1982–3 to 30.1 per cent in 2012–13 (Figure 3.2). In absolute terms, the value of output of livestock increased from Rs 724 billion to Rs 2,618 billion at the annual rate of 3.9 per cent, which is almost 1.3 times of the annual growth in agriculture (Table 3.8). The rate of growth has been at an all-time high in the recent decade. Further, it is interesting to note that except wool and hair, production of milk, meat, and eggs has grown faster compared to the overall growth of agriculture. These trends clearly bring out the importance of livestock in generating agricultural growth. Birthal and Negi (2012) have noted a rise in the contribution of livestock to overall agricultural growth, from 31 per cent during the 1990s to 36 per cent during the 2000s. In most states too, we find growth in livestock sector to be higher than the growth in crop sector (Table 3A.1 in the Appendix).

With a share of one-fifth in the gross value of output of agricultural sector, dairying has emerged as the largest

Table 3.8   Annual Growth (%) in the Value of Output

	Agriculture and Allied Activities	Agriculture	Total Livestock	Milk	Meat	Eggs	Wool and Hair
1983–4 to 1992–3	2.87	2.58	3.86	4.32	4.05	4.86	2.39
1993–4 to 2002–3	2.42	2.12	3.52	4.02	2.64	3.71	3.05
2003–4 to 2012–13	3.80	3.39	4.87	4.39	5.71	5.77	0.71
1983–4 to 2012–3	2.96	2.61	3.93	4.10	4.17	4.87	1.76

Source: GoI (various years).

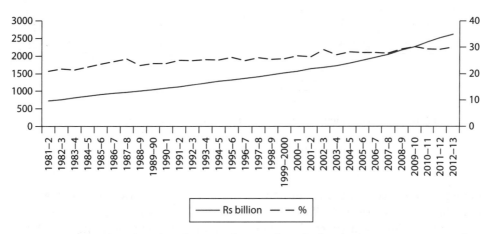

Figure 3.2   Trends in the Value of Output of Livestock in Absolute (at Constant 2004–5 Prices) and as Proportion of the Total Value of Output of Agricultural Sector

Source: GoI (various years).

agricultural enterprise in rural India. Figure 3.3 shows trends in its economic contribution vis-à-vis cereals. In the early 1980s, the value of milk was half of that of cereals, which by 2009–10 became almost equivalent to that of cereals.

An important contribution of livestock that has often been overlooked in the empirical literature is their role

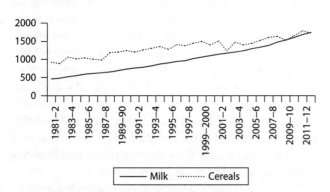

Figure 3.3   Trend in the Value of Milk vis-à-vis Cereals (Rs in Billion at 2004–5 Prices)

Source: GoI (various years).

in improving farm households' capacity to cope with climatic risks. During crises caused by extreme climatic shocks, such as droughts, the earnings from sale of livestock and livestock products smoothen household consumption. At the macro level, this translates into a cushion for agricultural growth. Livestock are raised as part of the mixed farming systems extracting their energy requirements from crop residues and by-products. In the event of a climatic shock, though the production of both crops and livestock experiences a shortfall, the extent of shortfall is small in livestock production, because when crops fail to produce grains, their by-products remain available as fodder for livestock. Figure 3.4, which shows deviations in the value of output of livestock vis-à-vis crops from their trends, provides credence to this observation.

3.5 LIVESTOCK, POVERTY, NUTRITION, AND GENDER

Several studies have shown that growth in agricultural sector, of which livestock comprise an important

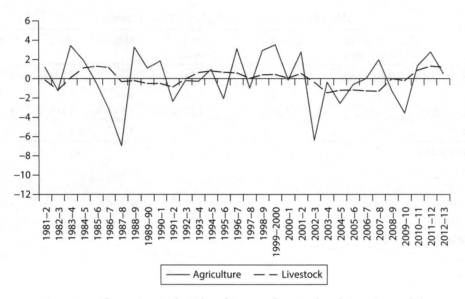

Figure 3.4 Fluctuations in the Value of Output of Livestock and Crop Sectors (%)

Source: GoI (various years).

component, is more pro-poor than the growth in non-agricultural sectors (Ravallion and Datt 1996; Warr 2003; Ravallion and Chen 2004; Christiaensen et al. 2006; Cervantes-Godoy and Dewbre 2010). In India too, agricultural growth has been more pro-poor, but its effect has weakened over time (Datt et al. 2016), possibly due to declining farm size and tardy shift of labour from farm to non-farm sectors.

In India, the empirical evidence on the effect of livestock on poverty is scarce and mostly anecdotal, largely based on the distribution of livestock across land classes. Birthal and Negi (2012) found livestock as a more important source of income at the lower-end of land distribution and having an equalizing effect on income distribution. Akter et al. (2008) found households at the bottom quintile of income distribution obtaining a higher share of their income from livestock as compared to those belonging to the richest quintile. Birthal and Taneja (2006) plotted the changes in the incidence of headcount rural poverty against rates of growth in value of output of crops and livestock for Indian states and found poverty reduction more responsive to the growth in livestock sector than the growth in crop sector. Based on a survey of rural households, Ojha (2007) reported livestock as an important pathway for escaping poverty for about 25 per cent of the households.

Evidence from many other developing countries also finds livestock an important means for poverty reduction. From a study in South Asia, Dolberg (2003) concluded that livestock can be an entry point for landless and near-landless households to escape poverty. In Nepal, households owning livestock are reported to be less poor (Maltsoglou and Taniguchi 2004). Kristjanson et al. (2004) also provide similar evidence from Kenya. From a review of a number of studies in Africa, Asia, and Latin America, Delgado et al. (1999) have concluded that the poor households have a higher contribution of livestock in their incomes compared to the rich.

The extent to which poor benefit from demand-driven growth depends on the distribution of livestock across rural households. At least two-thirds of the farm households in India are associated with livestock production (Birthal 2008). From Table 3.9, which presents distribution of different livestock species across landholding classes, it is evident that animal husbandry is pervasive across farm categories but is concentrated among smallholders—the households cultivating less than or equal to 1.0 hectare of land comprise three-fourths of the rural households and control 68 per cent of cattle, 57 per cent of buffaloes, and 70 per cent of other species as against their share of 30 per cent in the land. Birthal and Negi (2012) examined changes in livestock distribution over time and found that marginal farm households have consolidated their position in livestock sector. These findings clearly show that distribution of livestock is more equitable compared to that of land.

This pattern in the distribution of livestock has implications for poverty reduction. In Table 3.10 we reproduce the results from Birthal and Negi (2012), and these clearly show that the probability of escaping poverty is

Table 3.9   Distribution of Land and Livestock Holdings in India (%), 2012–13

	Landless (Less Than or Equal to 0.002 ha)	Marginal (0.002 to 1.0 ha)	Small (1.0 to 2.0 ha)	Semi-medium (2.0 to 4.0 ha)	Medium (4.0 to 10.0 ha)	Large (More Than 10.0 ha)	Total
% of households	7.41	75.42	10.00	5.01	1.93	0.24	100.00
% share in land	0.01	29.75	23.54	22.07	18.83	5.81	100.00
% Share in Livestock							
Cattle	3.43	67.98	14.69	8.47	4.44	0.99	100.00
Buffalo	12.37	56.86	13.88	10.52	5.36	1.00	100.00
Sheep and goat	4.49	70.68	10.45	5.72	8.04	0.62	100.00
Pig	0.00	72.87	18.91	7.11	1.03	0.07	100.00
Poultry	7.48	69.97	14.55	6.40	1.55	0.06	100.00

Source: GoI (2015b).

Table 3.10   Poverty Regressions

Explanatory Variables	Logistic Regression			Truncated Regression	
	Dependent Variable: Poor = 1; Otherwise = 0			Dependent Variable: Log Absolute Poverty Gap	
	Coefficient	t–stat	Marginal Effect	Coefficient	t–stat
Log per capita income	−1.272	−45.660	−0.265	−0.319	−15.520
Proportion of income from crops	−1.214	−22.480	−0.253	−0.333	−9.400
Proportion of income from livestock	−1.726	−20.210	−0.360	−0.448	−6.990

Source: Birthal and Negi (2012).

higher among those earning more from livestock—the estimated marginal effect of livestock income is 1.4 times more compared to that of crop income. This study also reports higher livestock income closing the poverty gap, that is, the difference between actual expenditure and poverty line expenditure. In other words, at a similar rate of growth, livestock production would have a larger impact on poverty reduction than crop production. Note that consumption of livestock products is income elastic, and with increase in their demand the poverty-reducing effect of livestock is expected to be stronger.

The other dimension of livestock production is its effect on gender disparity and child nutrition. In India, livestock production is subsistence-oriented being largely in the domain of women. Women comprise three-fourths of the labour force in livestock production. Livestock development, thus, can be an important factor in their empowerment. It may be noted that like land, livestock ownership is not bounded by property rights and can be owned by women to consolidate their bargaining power within the household. Livestock can impact a household's nutritional status via the family member(s) who controls the income generated from sale of livestock and livestock products. Women are primary caretakers

of household food security and, therefore, with a greater control over income they allocate more of it to improving nutrition, health, and education of the children (Das et al. 2013; Jumrani and Birthal 2015). Okike et al. (2005) and Ayele and Peacock (2003) have reported that in Africa ownership of livestock by women could lead to higher consumption of animal products, and higher income from the sale of animal products leads to an improvement in dietary diversity, and children's health and nutritional status. In another study from Ethiopia, cow ownership has been reported to improve children's milk consumption and reduce their stunting rates (Hoddinott et al. 2014). In Nepal, Malapit et al. (2013) have found improvement in maternal and children nutrition where women had a control over income from livestock. Jumrani and Birthal (2015) argue that it is important that all livestock-related interventions that directly contribute to children's nutrition should be analysed through a gendered lens.

3.6 LIVESTOCK AND ENVIRONMENT

Livestock, despite their significant contributions towards enhancing food and nutrition security and reducing poverty, are criticized for the negative externalities they cause to the environment through emission of greenhouse gases, overgrazing/deforestation, and water pollution. A number of studies in the past have quantified methane emissions from livestock production in India, and the estimates range from 8.5 to 10.5 million tonnes (see Dikshit and Birthal 2013).

In mixed farming systems as in India, animals draw their energy requirements from by-products of crops, cultivated green fodder and grazing, and in turn return that energy in the form of food (milk, meat, eggs), draught power, fuel, and manure. This process of energy exchange is associated with a number of environmental externalities, negative as well as positive. While the negative externalities are well-documented and quantified, positive externalities are not. Some of the positive externalities of livestock production include prevention of carbon dioxide release due to use of animal energy in place of fossil fuels, saving of natural resources, mainly land, due to use of agricultural by-products and residues as animal feed, and use of dung as domestic fuel in place of wood and as manure in place of chemical fertilizers.

Dikshit and Birthal (2013) estimated that if the feed energy that animals draw from consumption of agricultural residues were to be obtained from the cultivated green fodders, India would have needed an additional 40 million hectares of land to produce that much energy. Likewise, Indian households use about half of the dung for domestic fuel, and if the equivalent energy were to be obtained from fuel wood, the country would have to use 1.6 million hectares for fuel wood plantation. Use of dung as manure saves about 1.2 million tons of chemical fertilizers (NPK); and if the existing stock of draught animals were to be replaced by tractors it would have needed 13 million tons additional diesels to run the tractors. It may be noted that India imports huge quantities of chemical fertilizers and diesel, and livestock make significant contributions towards saving the precious foreign exchange reserves.

3.7 CHALLENGES AND PUBLIC POLICY

Livestock production faces numerous challenges. These need to be overcome to harness the pro-poor opportunities in livestock sector. India has huge livestock population, but of low productivity. The average milk yield of a cow in India is 1,350 kg/annum as compared to the world average of 2,347 kg/annum. Not only that, the growth in livestock production has largely been driven by numbers and not much by yield improvements (Birthal and Negi 2012). The yield growth has also been decelerating.

These are serious concerns as the number-driven growth, given the scarcity of feed resources, cannot be sustained for long.

Nevertheless, there exists a scope for growth. There is a huge gap between the potential and the actual yields of most species. Birthal and Jha (2005) have reported a gap of 25–75 per cent between the potential and the actual milk yield, and attribute it to inadequate supplies of feed and fodder, and poor breeding and health services. The livestock policy should focus on bridging the yield gap and stabilization of livestock population commensurate with the available resources. Some of the policy issues that merit attention are discussed below.

3.7.1 Genetic Enhancement of Low-Producing Animals

Crossbreeding of indigenous breeds through AI using semen of exotic breeds has been pursued as an important strategy to enhance the genetic potential. It has been successful to some extent. In 2012, the country had 21 per cent of the cattle, 24 per cent of the pigs, and 6 per cent of the sheep as crossbred. But, there is a wide regional variation in the adoption of the crossbreeding technology. Crossbreds comprise more than 70 per cent of the total cattle population in states like Kerala, Punjab, and Tamil Nadu. At the other extreme, there are states, such as Assam, Chhattisgarh, Jharkhand, and Madhya Pradesh where their adoption hardly exceeds 5 per cent because of poor breeding infrastructure.

A major problem with AI is its low conception rate (around 40 per cent) that discourages farmers from adopting it. Availability of semen is inadequate and delivery of breeding services is poor. There are 57 semen stations in the country supplying 50 million doses through 84,000 AI centres (GoI 2015a). Further, crossbreeds are not high yielding in themselves; they require better feeds and health services to produce more. In order to enhance acceptability and efficiency of AI, there is a need to identify quality bulls for semen production or import semen and improve semen collection, storage infrastructure, and delivery of services.

3.7.2 Feed and Fodder Supplies

In India, feed and fodder supplies have always remained short of their requirements. The deficit is estimated to the extent of 11 per cent in dry fodder, 35 per cent in green fodder, and 28 per cent in concentrate feed (Ramachandra et al. 2007). Area under food-feed-fodder crops, such as pearl-millet and sorghum, has declined considerably in the past three decades. Rice straw, though available in large quantity, is considered inferior as fodder. The deficit in concentrate feed, to some extent, is on account of export of soybean cakes. Area under green fodder crops is limited to about 10 million hectares and more than 55 per cent of it is concentrated in Punjab, Haryana, and Rajasthan. Common grazing lands that comprise 3 per cent of the geographical area have been deteriorating quantitatively as well as qualitatively.

There is a need to focus on improving production and dissemination of quality fodder seeds and rejuvenating and managing pastures and grazing lands. Note that feed and fodder scarcity is not universal. There are states, for example, Punjab and Haryana, that are surplus in fodder and there it is wasted due to mechanical harvesting. The wastage can be avoided if the surpluses can be processed and compacted into feed blocks. In the predominantly rice-growing states, adoption of nutritional technologies (for example, urea treatment) that improve quality of rice straws may help addressing fodder scarcity.

3.7.3 Animal Health Infrastructure and Services

There has been considerable improvement in animal health infrastructure in the country. In 2014, there were about 55,000 veterinary institutions (polyclinics, hospitals, veterinary aid centres) and more than 60,000 veterinarians, mostly in the public sector (Table 3.11). However, there is considerable regional variation in animal health infrastructure and manpower. Livestock units per veterinary institution are higher in states such as Jharkhand, Bihar, Madhya Pradesh, and Chhattisgarh as compared to Punjab and Haryana as against the national average of about 7,000 livestock units. Many diseases like foot and mouth disease (FMD), black quarter (BQ), peste des petits ruminant (PPR), influenza, and so on are frequently reported from one or another region. The policy should emphasize on prophylactic measures to manage diseases and on improving efficiency of health services.

3.7.4 Animal Science Research and Extension

Veterinary research, education, and extension are critical to the generation and diffusion of technologies. These activities, however, have remained underinvested—their share in the total livestock expenditure has hardly ever exceeded 3 per cent. Allocation of research resources within the livestock sector too has not been in congruence with the relative economic contribution of different species (Birthal et al. 2002). Cattle and buffalo research receives less than what it deserves. It may be noted that animal science research is capital-intensive and has a larger gestation period; hence it requires more investment to achieve technological breakthroughs.

Animal breeding research should also reorient its focus considering changing functions of livestock and climate risks. For example, with increasing mechanization of cropping activities there is now little demand for draught cattle. This implies a greater focus of research on breeding for milk. In recent years, the research has produced technologies, for example, 'sexed-semen technology', that offer producers a choice to select between male and female based on their economic utility for them.

Potential gains from research may remain undermined in absence of effective delivery mechanisms. Livestock extension system is almost absent, as only 5 per cent of the farm households have access to livestock related information (Adhiguru et al. 2009). In order to enhance livestock production, it is critical that farmers are provided livestock services at the right time.

3.7.5 Institutional Credit

Credit plays an important role in the adoption of improved technologies, use of quality inputs, and accumulation

Table 3.11   Veterinary Infrastructure and Manpower in India

Year	No. of Veterinary Institutions	No. of Veterinarians	Cattle Equivalent Units per Veterinary Institution	Cattle Equivalent Units per Veterinarian
1982	33,323	18,000	8,394	15,540
1992	40,586	33,600	7,632	9,219
1997	50,846	37,200	6,129	8,377
2003	51,973	38,100	5,926	8,084
2007	52,757	40,421	6,310	8,236
2014	53,896	60,112	6,375	5,823

Source: GoI (2015a); available at http://www.oie.int/wahis_2/public/wahid.php.

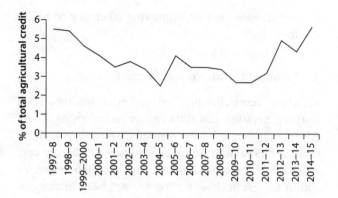

Figure 3.5 Share of Animal Husbandry and Dairying Institutional Credit

Source: Compiled from the annual reports of NABARD.

of livestock wealth. Unfortunately, livestock has not received much financial support from commercial banks and other financial institutions. The share of livestock in the total advances to agricultural sector has hardly ever exceeded 5 per cent (Figure 3.5). This is due to the fact that commercial banks treat credit to animal husbandry as investment credit, that is, for purchase of animals and equipment, and construction of cattle sheds. Securing investment credit requires collateral; but the poor lack assets that can serve as collateral. The poor also need short-term credit to purchase feed, fodder, medicines, and other inputs (Birthal et al. 2016). Further, animal husbandry remains excluded from the innovative and less cumbersome credit delivery schemes such as Kisan (farmer) Credit Card. There are also regional imbalances—about two-thirds of the total refinances by the National Bank for Agriculture and Rural Development (NABARD) for livestock development is concentrated in Punjab, Haryana, and Uttar Pradesh. If livestock

development has to be poverty-focused, the need for enhancing credit flow to the poor livestock keepers cannot be undermined.

3.7.6 Livestock Insurance

Institutional mechanisms to protect animals against biotic and abiotic risks are not developed enough to provide a cushion to the livelihoods of poor livestock producers. The central government initiated a subsidized livestock insurance scheme in 2006 in 100 districts, which is now operational in almost all the districts. The scheme is applicable to all the animals and the subsidy is restricted to five animals per beneficiary. The performance of this scheme, however, has not been encouraging. The number of animals covered under the scheme is miniscule (Figure 3.6) as compared to the total livestock population.

3.7.7 Markets and Value Addition

Lack of access to markets acts as a disincentive to farmers to adopt improved technologies and quality inputs. Except for poultry and to some extent for milk, markets for livestock and livestock products are thin, underdeveloped, and dominated by informal intermediaries. Markets for live animals are irregular and uncertain, and lack basic infrastructure and facilities. Likewise, slaughtering facilities are also inadequate. About half of the total meat production comes from un-registered slaughterhouses. Marketing and transaction costs associated with sale of livestock products are high, guzzling 15–20 per cent of the sale price (Birthal 2008).

Dairy cooperatives though have played an important role in providing market access to the producers,

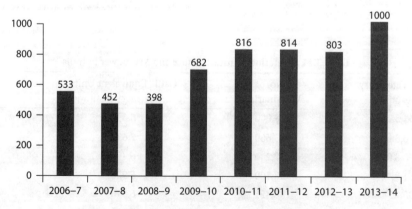

Figure 3.6 Number of Animals Insured (in Thousands)

Source: GoI (2015a).

but their spread has been highly unequal across states. Eastern and north-eastern states have by and large been bypassed by the cooperative movement.

India liberalized dairy markets in 1991 for private sector participation. Assuming that cooperatives and private processors procure milk in proportion of their processing capacity, the private processors procure about 15 per cent of the total milk produced in the country (Birthal et al. 2016). About 90 per cent of their processing capacity is concentrated in Uttar Pradesh, Maharashtra, Andhra Pradesh, Punjab, Haryana, Tamil Nadu, Madhya Pradesh, and Rajasthan. Most private processors procure milk from producers through informal contracts. Like cooperatives, contract farming has also been reported to reduce price uncertainty, marketing and transaction costs, and provide farmers an easy access to inputs, technology, credit, and services (Birthal and Joshi 2009).

Contract farming has been quite successful in poultry, and now a considerable proportion of broiler production in the country comes through contracts. Contract farming has also aided scaling up of the production systems (Birthal 2008). The growing demand for animal food products is an opportunity for agribusiness firms to scale out such institutional arrangements, particularly in the states that have potential for production but are constrained by poor market infrastructure. The level of processing or value addition to livestock products has remained low. Only about 6 per cent of the poultry meat, 21 per cent of the buffalo meat, and 35 per cent of the milk undergoes value addition (22 per cent in the organized

sector). Bulk of the poultry and buffalo meat is processed in the organized sector; the share of the organized sector in total milk processed is 63 per cent.

3.7.8 Investment Priorities

The livestock sector has remained under-invested; presently it receives 4 per cent of the total public expenditure on agriculture and allied sectors, which is disproportionately lower than its contribution to agricultural GDP (Table 3.12). It is interesting to note that despite its increasing share in agricultural income, the share of livestock in the total agricultural investment has been falling.

Dairy development has remained the main focus. In recent years the share of animal health and veterinary services in the total livestock expenditure has improved. Small ruminants, pigs, fodder development, and veterinary education, research, and training have received trivial investment, not even 3 per cent each of the total investment. The corollary to this is that there is a need to target efforts and investments towards development of feed and fodder, pro-poor small animals, and education and training.

3.8 CONCLUDING REMARKS

The expanding market of animal food products is creating significant opportunities for enhancing agricultural growth and reducing rural poverty through livestock

Table 3.12   Public Spending on Livestock Sector in India

	1991–3	1999–2001	2009–11
Total spending (Rs million at 2004–5 prices)	37,396	41,561	53,928
Public spending % of total agricultural spending	13.6	9.9	3.9
Public spending as % of livestock VOP	3.6	2.8	3.1
Composition of Public Spending (%)			
Dairy development	41.5	38.6	23.3
Veterinary services and animal health	23.7	24.1	27.8
Cattle and buffalo development	14.0	11.7	12.3
Sheep and wool development	2.7	2.4	1.7
Piggery development	1.8	0.5	0.4
Poultry development	3.1	2.4	2.4
Fodder development	0.9	1.0	1.4
Direction and administration	4.2	8.7	16.6
Research, education, extension and training	2.2	3.0	2.9
Others	5.8	7.6	11.2

Source: Birthal and Negi (2012).

development route. Productivity of India's livestock, however, is low; and is constrained by poor adoption of technologies, scarcity of feed and fodder, and poor animal health services. Institutional and policy support to livestock sector in terms of investment, credit, insurance, extension, and markets is not commensurate with its social and economic contribution.

In the past, growth in livestock production was largely number-driven, and this may not be sustainable for long. Future growth, therefore, should come from improve-

ments in productivity. This will require enhancing feed and fodder supplies and improvements in delivery of animal health and breeding services. Technology will be a key driver of growth and concerted efforts will be needed to generate and disseminate yield-enhancing and/or yield-saving technologies.

The extent to which the pro-poor growth opportunities in the livestock sector can be harnessed would depend on how research, institutions, and policies address the constraints that livestock producers are confronting.

APPENDIX

Table 3A.1 Share of Livestock in Gross Value of Output and Growth of Agricultural Sector (at 2004–5 Prices)

State	% Share of Livestock in Value of Output of Agricultural Sector		% Annual Growth in Livestock Sector		% Annual Growth in Agricultural Sector		% Share of Livestock in Agricultural Growth	
	1991–3	2007–9	1990s	2000s	1990s	2000s	1990s	2000s
Andhra Pradesh	22.5	30.2	6.3	5.3	3.0	4.6	46.7	35.4
Assam	10.6	13.0	1.2	3.5	1.9	0.1	6.7	–
Bihar[a]	28.7	36.8	6.2	7.4	6.6	3.9	27.3	69.1
Gujarat	19.6	25.4	5.3	6.2	3.4	5.0	30.0	31.4
Haryana	27.8	32.0	3.6	3.8	2.9	2.9	34.9	41.1
Himachal Pradesh	27.3	28.3	3.7	3.3	3.3	3.5	30.3	26.2
Jammu and Kashmir	25.4	33.3	8.5	4.0	3.1	4.5	68.4	29.8
Karnataka	17.5	20.6	5.4	0.9	3.0	1.1	31.1	16.7
Kerala	19.5	21.0	2.9	0.7	2.5	0.6	23.2	25.8
Madhya Pradesh[b]	26.8	27.0	3.1	3.2	3.3	2.9	25.5	29.9
Maharashtra	22.1	20.1	4.0	3.1	3.9	4.1	22.9	15.0
Northeastern states[c]	22.3	23.1	4.5	4.5	3.9	2.7	25.5	38.3
Odisha	10.2	18.6	4.2	7.7	0.4	3.4	104.3	42.3
Punjab	26.2	33.1	4.1	2.5	2.0	1.7	52.8	17.2
Rajasthan	33.9	38.5	5.2	1.7	3.3	2.3	53.2	29.3
Tamil Nadu	27.4	29.0	1.9	3.5	2.4	1.8	21.6	57.4
Uttar Pradesh[d]	21.0	28.2	4.5	3.6	3.0	1.5	31.8	69.7
West Bengal	21.6	20.9	2.5	2.1	3.5	1.5	15.4	29.4
All India	23.3	26.8	3.9	3.6	2.9	2.7	31.1	36.3

Note: [a]includes Jharkhand; [b]includes Chhattisgarh; [c]excludes Assam; [d]includes Uttarakhand.
Source: Birthal and Negi (2012).

REFERENCES

Adhiguru, P., P.S. Birthal, and B. Ganesh Kumar. 2009. 'Strengthening Pluralistic Agricultural Information Delivery System in India'. *Agricultural Economics Research Review* 22(1): 71–9.

Akter, S., J. Farrington, P. Deshingkar, and A. Freeman. 2008. *Livestock, Vulnerability, and Poverty Dynamics in India*. Nairobi, Kenya: International Livestock Research Institute.

Ayele, Z. and C. Peacock. 2003. 'Improving Access to and Consumption of Animal Source Foods in Rural

Households: The Experiences of a Woman-Focused Goat Development Program in the Highlands of Ethiopia'. *The Journal of Nutrition* 133: 3981S–6S.

Birthal, P.S. 2008. 'Linking Smallholder Livestock Producers to Markets: Issues and Approaches'. *Indian Journal of Agricultural Economics* 63(1):19–37.

Birthal, P.S., R. Chand, P.K. Joshi, and others. 2016. *Formal versus Informal: Efficiency, Inclusiveness and Financing of Dairy Value Chains in India*. Discussion Paper 01513. Washington, DC: International Food Policy Research Institute.

Birthal, P.S. and A.K. Jha. 2005. 'Economic Losses Due to Various Constraints in Dairy Production in India'. *Indian Journal of Animal Sciences* 75(12): 1470–5.

Birthal, P.S. and P.K. Joshi. 2009. 'Efficiency and Equity in Contract Farming: Evidence from a Case Study of Dairying in India'. *Quarterly Journal of International Agriculture* 48 (4): 363–78.

Birthal, P.S., P.K. Joshi, and A. Kumar. 2002. *Assessment of Research Priorities in Livestock Sector*. Policy Paper 15. New Delhi, India: National Centre for Agricultural Economics and Policy Research.

Birthal, P.S. and D.S. Negi. 2012. 'Livestock for Higher, Sustainable and Inclusive Agricultural Growth'. *Economic and Political Weekly* 47(26/27): 89–99.

Birthal, P.S., D.S. Negi, A.K. Jha, and D. Singh. 2014. 'Income Sources of Farm Households in India: Determinants, Distributional Consequences and Policy Implications'. *Agricultural Economics Research Review* 27(1): 37–48.

Birthal, P.S. and V.K. Taneja. 2006. 'Livestock Sector in India: Opportunities and Challenges for Smallholders'. In *Smallholder Livestock Production in India: Opportunities and Challenges* edited by P.S. Birthal, V.K. Taneja, and W. Thorpe. National Centre for Agricultural Economics and Policy Research (NCAP), New Delhi (India), and the International Livestock Research Institute (ILRI), Nairobi (Kenya).

Cervantes-Godoy, D. and J. Dewbre. 2010. 'Economic Importance of Agriculture in Poverty Reduction'. OECD Food, Agriculture and Fisheries Working Paper 23. OECD Publishing. Available at http://www.oecd-ilibrary. org/agriculture-and-food/economic-importance-of-agriculture-for-poverty-reduction_5kmmv9s20944-en.

Christiaensen, L., L. Demery, and J. Kuhl. 2006. 'The Role of Agriculture in Poverty Reduction: An Empirical Perspective'. World Bank Policy Research Working Paper 4013. The World Bank, Washington DC, USA.

Das, N., R. Yasmin, M. Kamruzzaman, P. Davis, J. Behrman, S. Roy, and A. Quisumbing. 2013. *How Do Intra-household Dynamics Change When Assets Are Transferred to Women?* Discussion Paper No. 1317. International Food Policy Research Institute, Washington, DC, USA.

Datt, G., M. Ravallion, and R. Murgai. 2016. 'Growth, Urbanization and Poverty Reduction in India'. World Bank Policy Working Paper 7568. The World Bank, Washington DC, USA.

Delgado, C., M. Rosegrant, H. Steinfeld, S. Ehui, and C. Courbois. 1999. *Livestock to 2020: The Next Food Revolution*. Agriculture and Environment Discussion Paper 28. International Food Policy Research Institute, Washington, DC, USA.

Dikshit, A.K. and P.S. Birthal. 2013. 'Positive Environmental Externalities of Livestock in Mixed Framing Systems of India'. *Agricultural Economics Research Review* 26(1): 21–30.

Dolberg, F. 2003. 'Review of Household Poultry Production as a Tool in Poverty Reduction in Bangladesh and India'. PPLPI Working Paper 6. Rome, Italy: Pro-Poor Livestock Policy Initiative, FAO.

FAO-FAOSTAT. Food and Agriculture Organization, Rome, http://faostat.fao.org/default.aspx

GoI (Government of India). 2015a. *Basic Animal Husbandry Statistics 2014*. Department of Animal Husbandry and Dairying, Ministry of Agriculture, New Delhi.

———. 2015b. *Livestock Ownership across Operational Land Holding Classes*. National Sample Survey Office, Ministry of Statistics and Programme Implementation, New Delhi.

———. Various years. *National Accounts Statistics*. Central Statistical Organization, Ministry of Statistics and Programme Implementation, New Delhi.

Hoddinott, J., D. Headey, and M. Dereje. 2014. 'Cows, Missing Milk Markets and Nutrition in Rural Ethiopia'. ESSP II Working Paper No. 63. International Food Policy Research Institute, Washington, DC, USA.

Joshi, P.K. and P. Kumar. 2012. *Food Demand and Supply Projections for India*. Mimeo. International Food Policy Research Institute New Delhi Office, New Delhi.

Jumrani, J. and P.S. Birthal. 2015. 'Livestock, Women and Child Nutrition in Rural India'. *Agricultural Economics Research Review* 28(2): 223–46.

Kumar, P. and P.S. Birthal. 2004. 'Changes in Demand for Livestock and Poultry Products in India'. *Indian Journal of Agricultural Marketing* 18(3): 110–23.

Kristjanson, P., A. Krishna, M. Radney, and W. Nindo. 2004. 'Pathways Out of Poverty in Western Kenya and the Role of Livestock'. PPLPI Working Paper 14. Pro-Poor Livestock Policy Initiative, FAO, Rome.

Malapit, H., S. Kadiyala, A. Quisumbing, K. Cunningham, and P. Tyagi. 2013. *Women's Empowerment in Agriculture, Production Diversity and Nutrition*. Discussion Paper No. 01313. International Food Policy Research Institute. Washington, DC.

Maltsoglou, I. and K. Taniguchi. 2004. 'Poverty, Livestock and Household Typologies in Nepal'. PPLPI Working Paper 13. Pro-Poor Livestock Policy Initiative, FAO, Rome.

NABARD. Various years. *Annual Reports*. National Bank for Agriculture and Rural Development, Mumbai.

NDDB. 2015. *Annual Report 2014–15*. National Dairy Development Board, Anand, Gujarat.

Ojha, R.K. 2007. 'Poverty Dynamics in Rural Uttar Pradesh'. *Economic and Political Weekly* 42(16): 1453–8.

Okike, I., M.A. Jabbar, G. Abate, and L. Ketema. 2005. 'Household and Environmental Factors Influencing Anthropometric Outcomes in Preschool Children in a Rural Ethiopian Community'. *Ecology of Food and Nutrition* 44: 167–7.

Parthasarathy Rao, P. and P.S. Birthal. 2008. *Livestock in Mixed Farming Systems in South Asia*. International Crops Research Institute for the Semi-Arid Tropics, Patancheru; and National Centre for Agricultural Economics and Policy Research, New Delhi.

Ramachandra, K.V., V.K. Taneja, K.T. Sampath, S. Anandan, and U.B. Angadi. 2007. *Livestock Feed Resources in Different Agroecosystems of India: Availability, Requirement and Their Management*. National Institute of Animal Nutrition and Physiology, Bangalore.

Ramaswami, B., P.S. Birthal, and P.K. Joshi. 2005. *Efficiency and Distribution in Contract Farming: The Case of Indian Poultry Growers*. MTID Discussion paper 91. International Food Policy Research Institute, Washington DC, USA.

Ravallion, M. and G. Datt. 1996. 'How Important to India's Poor Is the Sectoral Composition of Economic Growth?' *World Bank Economic Review* 10(1): 1–25.

Ravallion, M. and S. Chen. 2004. 'China's (Uneven) Progress Against Poverty'. Policy Research Working Paper 3408. The World Bank, Washington DC, USA.

Warr, P. 2003. Poverty and Economic Growth in India. In *Economic Reform and the Liberalization of the Indian Economy* edited by K. Kalirajan and U. Shankar. Cheltenham, and Northampton, MA: Edward Elgar.

4

Post-Harvest Value Chain Management in India

*Gopal Naik** and *Ashwini Baje***

ABSTRACT

Despite making significant improvements in terms of production, employment generation, and diversification, Indian agriculture continues to suffer due to inefficient value chain management. A significant share of the produce, with respect to both quantity and quality, is lost on its way from the farm to the fork. This is being reflected in the higher export rejection rates, greater presence of pesticides, and increasing imports. This chapter discusses the need for effective and streamlined post-harvest value chain management in India and roadblocks to achieving it. We also discuss how emerging trends like market reforms, infrastructure developments, technological innovations, farmer organizations, contract farming, and food processing can help transform the situation. There has also been ample support from the government in the form of various fiscal incentives and schemes aimed at boosting food processing in particular, and the agriculture sector in general. Few success stories in the areas of cooperatives, commodity exchanges, and farmer producer organizations (FPOs) are mentioned. Finally, some policy implications for streamlining agricultural value chain in India are also discussed.

JEL Classification: Q160, Q170, Q180, Q130

Keywords: agribusiness, agricultural markets, agricultural supply chain, farmer cooperatives, food quality and safety

4.1 INTRODUCTION

India, the world's second-largest country in terms of area under agriculture (157.35 million hectares) has the required agro-climatic conditions to be a leading agricultural producer. From being a nation crippled by food insecurity a few decades ago, it has decisively moved to become a food surplus nation, exporting around 10 per cent[1] of its total agricultural produce and providing

* Professor, Indian Institute of Management Bangalore, India.
** Research Associate, Indian Institute of Management Bangalore, India.

[1] IBEF, 'Indian Agriculture Industry Analysis', available at http://www.ibef.org/industry/agriculture-presentation, accessed on 24 September 2016.

employment to about 58 per cent[2] of its population. It has a major share in the world's production of wheat, rice, spices, pulses, milk, tea, cashew, jute, fruit and vegetables, sugarcane, cotton, and oilseeds.

Over the last few decades, owing to a number of factors such as changing lifestyles and consumption patterns, improved awareness at producer level, and development of markets and government policies, the composition of Indian agricultural production has also undergone changes. Farmers have begun to diversify production, and as a result, in 2015–16, the output of dairy, fruit, and vegetables (283.4 million tons) has surpassed that of food grains (252.2 million tons) (Bera 2016). Production for various agricultural, horticultural, poultry, and livestock produce over the last few years are depicted in Figure 4.1.

However, despite this growth in agricultural production, around one-sixth of the nation's total population of 1.2 billion remains undernourished.[3] Increasing

[2] IBEF, 'Indian Agriculture Industry: An Overview', available at http://www.ibef.org/industry/agriculture-india.aspx, accessed on 18 July 2016.

[3] India FoodBanking Network, 'Hunger in India', Available at https://www.indiafoodbanking.org/hunger, accessed on 22 September 2016.

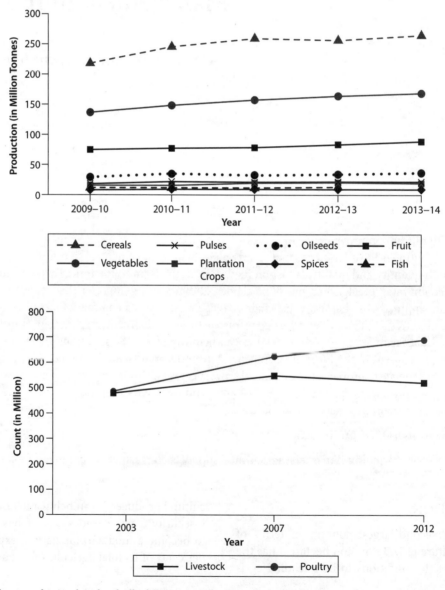

Figure 4.1 Production of Agricultural and Allied Sectors in India (between 2009–10 and 2013–14 in Million Tonnes or in Numbers)
Source: Figures created using data from *Indian Agricultural Statistics at a Glance 2014*, Ministry of Agriculture and Farmers Welfare, GoI.

agricultural production is an important requirement of fulfilling this food demand. Although measures such as expansion in irrigation facilities, availability of suitable crop varieties, mechanization, application of modern technologies, and increase in investment have been undertaken to improve agricultural productivity, they are constrained due to limitation with respect to land ownership structure and water availability as well as proper extension support. Often, what gets ignored is the amount of produce from agriculture and allied sectors that is lost (both in quality and quantity terms) on its way from the field to the consumer, which occurs due to various reasons—poor infrastructural facilities, poor management of value chains, lack of access to affordable credit facilities, market inefficiencies, low levels of food processing, and so on.

According to a study conducted by the ICAR-Central Institute of Post Harvest Engineering & Technology (CIPHET) on harvest and post-harvest losses in major crops and commodities in India, the total loss in agriculture, horticulture, and livestock sector sum up to Rs 917,870 million during 2012–13, as compared to Rs 628,750 million during 2005–6 (calculated using average wholesale prices of various commodities for 2014) (ICAR-CIPHET 2015 and Nanda 2012). Sectoral breakup of the losses in 2012–13 and its comparison with losses in a previous study conducted in 2005–6 are depicted in Figures 4.2 and 4.3. In terms of total loss, cereals have large amount of losses mainly due to its large size of production. Perishables such as livestock produce, vegetables, and fruit contribute significantly to the post-harvest losses primarily due to near absence of cold chains.

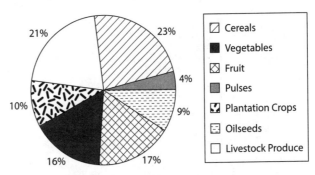

Figure 4.2   Post-Harvest Losses for Major Groups of Agricultural and Allied Produce (2012–13)

Source: Figure created using values of sectoral losses from ICAR-CIPHET Reports, *Assessment of Quantitative Harvest and Post-Harvest Losses of Major Crops and Commodities in India*, 2015.

Figure 4.3 also suggests that these losses are increasing over time. Sharper increase in the losses can be observed in livestock produce. Table 4.1 provides details on losses in individual products. Post-harvest losses are smaller (about 5 per cent) in the case of most cereals, oilseeds, and plantation crops, compared to other category of products. In the oilseed category, only soybean has high post-harvest loss mainly accounted for by the on-farm losses. Fruit and vegetables have high loss percentages mainly due to their perishability. In cases such as apple, guava, tomato, and marine fish, the losses exceed 10 per cent.

While the loss percentage may not look very high compared to other countries, what really takes place is the quality loss during post-harvest management. This is reflected in the rejection percentages in the international

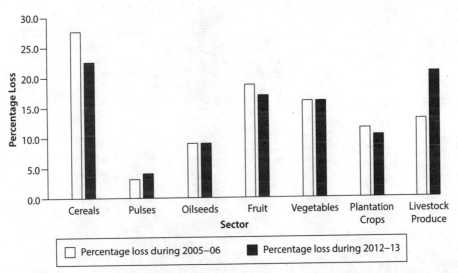

Figure 4.3   Comparison of Total Sectorial Losses during 2005–6 and 2012–13 (Calculated for 2014 Prices)

Source: Figure created using values for sectoral losses from ICAR-CIPHET Reports (ICAR-CIPHET 2015) and Nanda (2012).

Table 4.1 Harvest and Post-Harvest Losses of Various Agricultural Commodities in 2012–13 (in Percentage at National Level)

Commodity	Range of Loss in Farm Operations (in Percentage)	Where Do the Losses Majorly Occur?	Range of Loss in Storage Channels (in Percentage)	Where Do the Losses Majorly Occur?	Overall Total Loss (in Percentage)	Monetary Value of Total Total Sectorial Loss (in Crore)	Percentage of Total Sectorial Loss (%)
Cereals	3.9 (Maize) –4.78 (Sorghum)	Harvesting, Threshing	0.75 (Maize) –1.21 (Sorghum)	Farm Level, Wholesaler, Retailer and Processing Unit	Paddy 5.53 Wheat 4.93 Maize 4.65 Bajra 5.23 Sorghum 5.99	20,706	23
Pulses	4.69 (Pigeon Pea) –7.23 (Chick Pea)	Harvesting, Threshing, Collection, Winnowing/Cleaning	1.18 (Chick Pea/Black Gram) –1.67 (Pigeon Pea)	Farm Level, Wholesaler, Retailer and Processing Unit	Pigeon Pea 6.36 Chick Pea 8.41 Black Gram 7.07 Green Gram 6.61	3,877	4
Oilseeds	2.54 (Cottonseed) –8.95 (Soybean)	Harvesting, Threshing, Collection, Winnowing/Cleaning	0.22 (Mustard) –1.61 (Sunflower)	Farm Level, Wholesaler, Retailer and Processing Unit	Mustard 5.54 Cottonseed 3.08 Soybean 9.95 Safflower 3.24 Sunflower 5.26 Groundnut 6.04	8,275	9
Fruit	6.04 (Banana) –11.9 (Guava)	Harvesting, Sorting/Grading, Transportation	1.31 (Apple) –3.98 (Guava)	Wholesaler, Retailer, Processing	Apple 10.39 Banana 7.76 Citrus 9.69 Grapes 8.63 Guava 15.88 Mango 9.16	15,818	17

Category	Loss range (two columns)		Operations	Stakeholders	Commodity	Loss %	Value	No.
Vegetables	3.22 (Tapioca) –9.41 (Tomato)	0.78 (Potato) –3.03 (Tomato)	Harvesting, Sorting/Grading, Transportation	Farm-level Godown, Retailer, Wholesaler	Cabbage	9.37	14,845	16
					Cauliflower	9.55		
					Green Pea	7.45		
					Mushroom	9.51		
					Onion	8.21		
					Potato	7.32		
					Tomato	12.44		
					Tapioca	4.58		
Plantation Crops	0.99 (Black Pepper) –7.29 (Sugarcane)	0.2 (Black Pepper) –1.4 (Chilli)	Harvesting, Sorting/Grading, Drying, Winnowing/Cleaning	Wholesaler, Processing unit, Retailer	Arecanut	4.91	9,299	10
					Black Pepper	1.19		
					Cashew	4.17		
					Chilli	6.15		
					Coconut	4.77		
					Coriander	5.88		
					Sugarcane	7.89		
					Turmeric	4.44		
Livestock Produce	0.71 (Milk) –9.61 (Marine Fish)	0.21 (Milk) –4 (Poultry Meat)	Harvesting, Collection, Sorting/Grading, Packaging, Transportation	Processing unit, Wholesaler, Retailer	Egg	7.19	18,967	21
					Inland Fish	5.23		
					Marine Fish	10.52		
					Meat	2.71		
					Poultry Meat	6.74		
					Milk	0.92		
Total							91,787	

Source: Table created using results of post-harvest loss study conducted by ICAR-CIPHET: 'Assessment of Quantitative Harvest and Post-Harvest Losses of Major Crops and Commodities in India', ICAR-CIPHET 2015.

markets, extent of pesticide residues in agricultural products, and increasing imports of certain products and their high value compared to domestic produce. This is due to several factors such as poor post-handling practices, lack of proper knowledge, poor and inadequate infrastructure, and poor incentives for quality products in the markets.

4.2 IMPORTANCE OF POST-HARVEST MANAGEMENT

Efficient post-harvest management is critical to all stakeholders of the agricultural value chain (Figure 4.4). It helps in achieving food security, increasing value of exports, decreasing dependency on imports, and even reducing inflation at the national level. It helps consumers in terms of getting better-quality food at affordable price. Producers will have better returns with improved post-harvest management.

Post-harvest management helps address the following issues faced by various stakeholders of the agricultural value chain.

4.2.1 Difficulty in Achieving Food Security

Large amount of losses in agricultural produce suggests that improvement in post-harvest management is also important in achieving India's food security needs. A grain saved is equivalent to a grain produced, indeed!

4.2.2 Diminishing Value of Exports

Apart from the nation's food security needs, post-harvest management also impacts its exports and imports. According to APEDA, in 2015–16, the revenue from

Figure 4.4   Benefits of Post-Harvest Management to All Stakeholders
Source: Courtesy of the author.

Indian agricultural exports has fallen to a five-year low of US$ 32.09 billion. This is a sharp decline of about 17 per cent from the value of US$ 42.84 billion in 2014. This trend is evident in all commodities except sugar (including India's top exports of marine products, buffalo meat, and basmati rice). Although the quantity of our exports have grown, the income from these exports has not increased proportionately. This can be attributed to the lower prices of a few of our prominent agricultural export commodities (such as maize, soya meal, and wheat) in the global markets when compared to the domestic markets (Bhayani and Gera 2016).

Factors responsible for this fall in value are higher real effective exchange rate, collapse of global agri-commodity prices, and local scarcity of supply due to successive droughts (Bhayani and Gera 2016) and most importantly food safety and quality issues. For instance, according to Spices Board India, India's spices exports, which increased by 25 per cent in 2012–13, rose by only 9 per cent in 2014–15. This was because of adulteration and occurrence of pesticide residues in them (Dave 2016b).

A study conducted by the United Nations Industrial Development Organization (UNIDO) on the patterns and trends in border rejection of agricultural imports by the EU, the US, Japan, and Australia, during 2002–10, found that Indian imports figured in the list of exporters with largest number of rejections in all the four regions/countries (Figures 4.5 to 4.8). India's Unit Rejection Rate (URR) (the number of rejections per US$ 1 million of exports) from 2002 to 2010 is greater than the all-country average in most cases (Figures 4.9 to 4.12) (UNIDO 2015).

These values indicate substantive deficiencies in the compliance capacity of Indian exports and thus suggest a systemic issue in the agricultural and horticultural value chains that need urgent attention. However, there were significant variations in the patterns of rejections between the four regions/countries. For instance, while most EU and Japanese rejections were due to the presence of mycotoxins above a desired level, most US and Australian rejections were due to mismatch in labelling and company/processing registration requirements. A common reason for rejection in all regions/countries was microbial contamination (UNIDO, 2015). The major reasons for rejection of Indian agricultural exports in the four regions/countries are provided in Figure 4.13.

Although the regulatory framework governing food safety in India is gradually evolving with respect to inclusion of more commodities under its ambit,

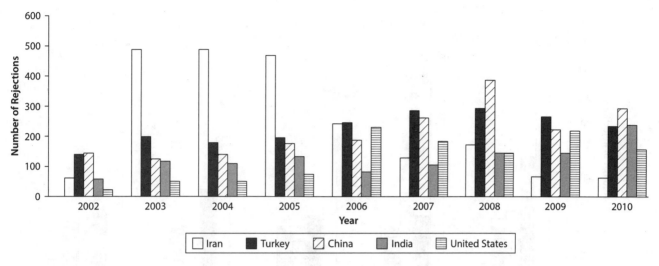

Figure 4.5 Top Exporters in EU Rejections

Source: Trade Standards Compliance Report 2015, UNIDO.

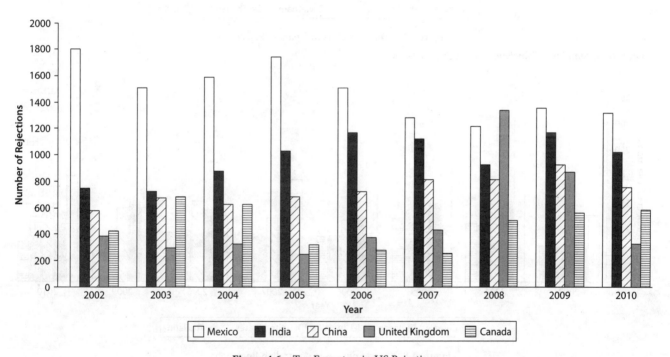

Figure 4.6 Top Exporters in US Rejections

Source: Trade Standards Compliance Report 2015, UNIDO.

and regarding the formation and harmonization of its standards with Codex standards, it has a long way to go. In developing countries such as India, which lack a well-organized, robust agribusiness value chain, issues of non-compliance can emerge at different stages of the value chain. For instance, most European countries expect a pre-shipment inspection for processed foods, but that is seldom done in India. Figure 4.14 depicts the potential pitfalls along the agribusiness value chain in India.

Consciousness about food safety and quality, and procedural measures to improve it need to be embedded right from the sourcing and production stages to transportation and marketing. Unless necessary measures are taken to improve the situation, winning in key export markets would continue to remain a challenge.

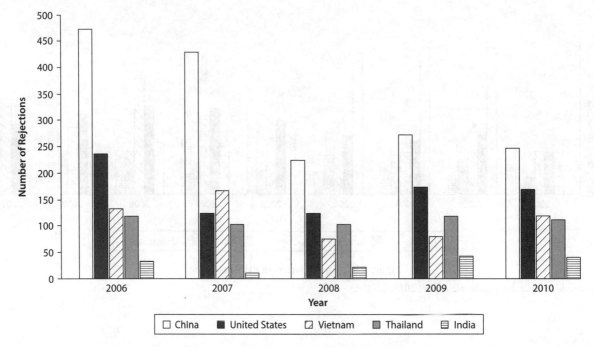

Figure 4.7   Top Exporters in Japanese Rejections

Source: *Trade Standards Compliance Report 2015*, UNIDO.

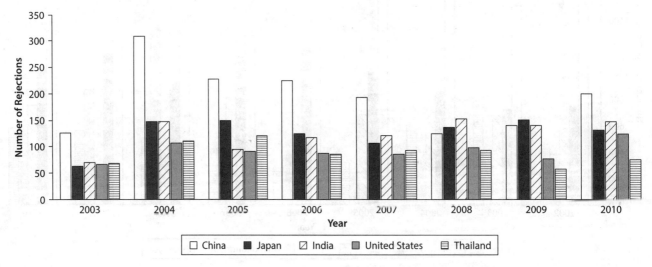

Figure 4.8   Top Exporters in Australian Rejections

Source: *Trade Standards Compliance Report 2015*, UNIDO.

4.2.3 Growing Dependency on Imports

India's agricultural imports basket is majorly constituted by oilseeds and pulses. Over the last few years, there has been a precipitous increase in their imports. The quantity of pulses imported increased from 3.6 million MT in 2013–14 to 5.8 million MT in 2015–16. Similarly, the quantity of edible oil imported increased from 10.5 million MT in 2013–14 to 15.7 million MT

in 2015–16.[4] Any reduction in their post-harvest losses can thus reduce dependency on imports and save foreign exchange.

[4] 'India Imports 57.97LT Pulses In 2015–16; 156.39 LT Of Edible Oil', available at http://www.commoditiescontrol.com/eagritrader/common/newsdetail.php?type=MKN&itemid=413729&comid=,1,2,&cid1=,2,&varietyid=,1,11,32,33,34,35,&varid=, accessed on 24 September 2016.

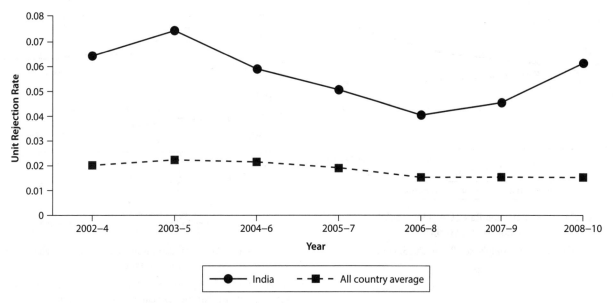

Figure 4.9   Unit Rejection Rate (URR) for EU Imports (India versus World)

Source: *Trade Standards Compliance Report 2015*, UNIDO.

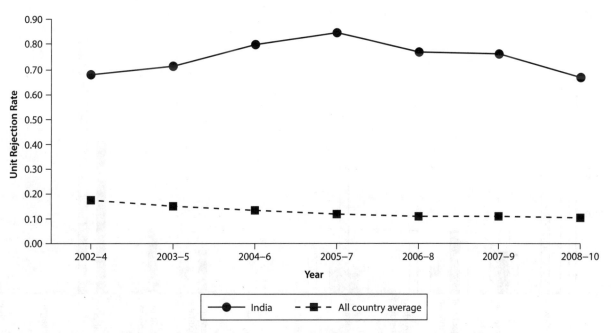

Figure 4.10   Unit Rejection Rate (URR) for US Imports (India versus World)

Source: *Trade Standards Compliance Report 2015*, UNIDO.

4.2.4 Varying Price Inflation

Food price inflation in India stood at 5.91 per cent in August 2016, in comparison with 2.2 per cent in August 2015. Between 2012 and 2016, it averaged at 8.46 per cent, with a maximum of 14.72 per cent in November 2013 and minimum of 2.15 per cent in July 2015.[5] These frequent and large variations in food prices (Figure 4.15) are worrisome.

[5] 'India Food Inflation', available at http://www.tradingeco-nomics.com/india/food-inflation, accessed on 24 September 2016.

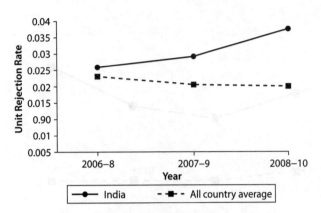

Figure 4.11 Unit Rejection Rate (URR) for Japanese Imports
(India versus World)

Source: *Trade Standards Compliance Report 2015*, UNIDO

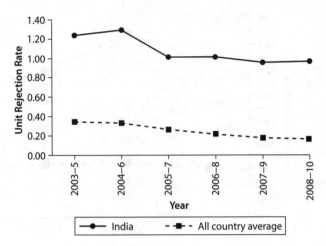

Figure 4.12 Unit Rejection Rate (URR) for Australian Imports
(India versus World)

Note: Here URR is presented as a three-year moving average to
smooth out any extraneous year-on-year variation.
Source: *Trade Standards Compliance Report 2015*, UNIDO.

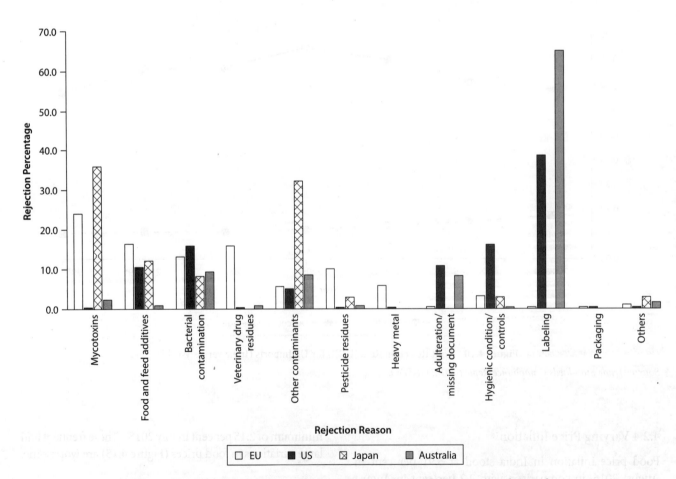

Figure 4.13 Reasons for Rejection of Indian Exports to the EU, the US, Japan, and Australia

Source: *Trade Standards Compliance Report 2015*, UNIDO.

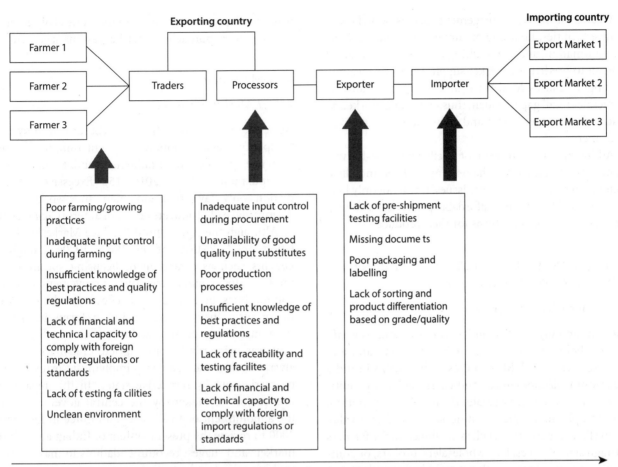

Figure 4.14   Potential Pitfalls along the Agribusiness Value Chain that Impact Food Safety and Quality

Source: Created by authors based on *Trade Standards Compliance Report 2015*, UNIDO.

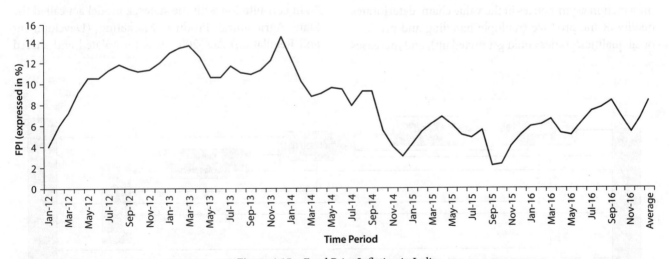

Figure 4.15   Food Price Inflation in India

Source: Figure created using the values for food price inflation from 'Trading Economics India Food Inflation', available at http://www.tradingeconomics.com/india/food-inflation, accessed on 24 September 2016.

Weak post-harvest management such as poor/lack of storage facilities, hoarding of supplies, insufficient market information, and the resulting large wastages make it difficult to predict the market supplies. This uncertainty in supplies causes food price inflation to rise and the wholesale–retail gap to widen, thus increasing marketing cost and consumer prices and reducing prices realized by farmers.

Addressing the problem of inefficient post-harvest management in the value chains of agriculture and allied sectors can help set right these issues. It will not only help consumers obtain food at affordable prices, but also help farmers receive better returns for their produce.

4.3 EXISTING BOTTLENECKS IN EFFICIENT POST-HARVEST MANAGEMENT

4.3.1 Value Chain Integration

The common saying 'A chain is only as strong as its weakest link' holds true for value chains of agricultural and allied sectors as well. Most of these value chains in India are traditional/unorganized and characterized by multiple intermediaries and a greater degree of fragmentation. For example, in a typical traditional horticultural value chain (Figure 4.16), the retailers are linked to the farmers through semi-wholesalers, wholesalers, brokers, or commission agents. At times, there could be more than one of these agents linked between the farmer and retailer for the same produce.

The presence of multiple intermediaries increases costs in the channel and increases prices to consumers, diminishes returns to farmers, exacerbates existing information asymmetries in the value chain, deteriorates quality of the produce (multiple handling and produce of all qualities/grades could get mixed up), and increases

wastage. Improving efficiency in the value chain requires an integrated approach to post-harvest management.

4.3.2 Marketing

4.2.6.1 Market Efficiency

Agricultural markets in India are characterized by poor competitiveness, monopoly, fragmentation, inefficiency, presence of excessive middlemen, and frequent price manipulations (Chand 2016, 15). Excessive intermediation only favours middlemen and works to the disadvantage of producers and consumers (Chand 2016).

Although the Agricultural Produce Marketing Regulation Act (APMRA) of the 1960s–1970s, brought in benefits such as scrapping of licensing specifications, limits on stocks, and restrictions on movement of certain commodities, by early 2000 its effects got diluted. Most importantly, they did not include reforms in agricultural marketing or transactions of farmers' produce. This was primarily because agricultural marketing has always been a state subject—implying reforms have to be carried out by respective states. In this regard, the first major step taken by the central government was the appointment of an Expert Committee in December 2000 to review the present system of Indian agricultural markets and suggest recommendations to make it more well-organized and effective. The answer to this was the amendment of the State Agricultural Produce Marketing Regulations Act and the Essential Commodities Act to remove restrictive provisions and the need to introduce a 'negotiable warehousing receipt system' in India (Chand 2016, 16).

In consultation with the states, a model act called the State Agricultural Produce Marketing (Development and Regulation) Act, 2003, was formulated and shared

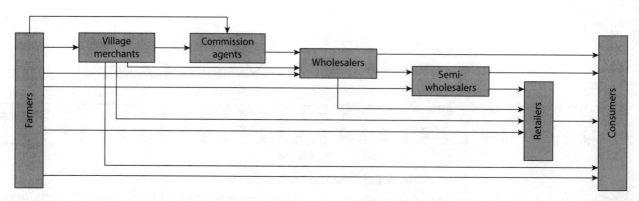

Figure 4.16   Typical Agricultural Value Chain

Source: Courtesy of the authors.

for implementation. Its provisions include permission to establish multiple markets in a particular market area; removal of mandatory selling of farmers' produce only through existing markets; adoption of contract farming; imposition of market fee only once upon the sale of notified agricultural commodities in a given area; direct purchase of agricultural produce from farmers, and so on. States were also provided investment subsidies to implement these provisions (Chand 2016).

Although many states have reported that they have adopted most of the key reforms suggested in the model act, the ground reality is stark. In most states, except Karnataka, reforms have been diluted, attached with new conditions, or partly implemented. Various central government orders during 2006–8 suspended the central government order of 2002 which liberalized trade in agricultural commodities. This brought back restrictions on licensing, storage, and movement of agricultural commodities with respect to their purchase, sale, supply, and distribution. In the meantime, unorganized functionaries such as commission agents and traders have also organized themselves into unions and been successful in foiling any attempts to amend market regulations and procedures (Chand 2016). Amidst this, various stakeholders of the value chain are frequently confused by conflicting objectives of the central and state government schemes. Therefore, a basic need for achieving effective post-harvest management is ensuring proper alignment of state and central government policies.

4.2.6.2 Distribution and Retail

In India, unorganized retail continues to be the most popular format to sell produce from agricultural and allied sectors. For instance, vendors with pushcarts sell fresh produce and small *kirana* stores mostly sell dry food products. Meat, poultry, and marine products are primarily sold by small retailers in wet markets. Unfortunately, produce sold in this format is more susceptible to quality deterioration due to low hygiene levels. Unlike in developed countries, in India, organized retailers are limited in number and are mostly regional players. They operate as convenience stores, supermarkets, hyper-markets, or cash and carry stores.

4.2.6.3 Market Information

In India, information pertaining to agricultural and allied sectors value chain is collated, built, and disseminated by an institutional framework consisting of various central/state government-run academic research, extension institutions, industry associations, and corporates. Most of the research institutions predominantly offer specialized information on a specific subject. Often, there is no one-stop source to obtain all the information pertaining to all value chains—market prices, supply and demand, weather forecasts, best farming practices, latest technological advancements, and government schemes/subsidies (Rabo India 2005). Currently, farmers access market information through television, mobile phones, or from local *mandis* (markets). ITC-enabled initiatives such as e-Choupal are also available. The need of the hour is to develop a demand-based model for production and market information.

4.3.3 Financing and Risk Management

Owing to the structural complexity of Indian agricultural and allied sectors, its actors, particularly farmers with smallholdings who do not possess any collateral, face immense difficulties in accessing timely, adequate, and affordable credit. They often rely on unorganized sources of credit that do not necessitate as much of documentation as banks do and are available on time. However, the cost of these funds is exorbitant due to their high interest rates.

In India, majority of the food processing firms are small or medium sized that carry out standalone operations with no linkages with farmers. They rely on retailers or other channels to undertake marketing of the processed products (Rabo India 2005). With large working capital requirements, they often find it difficult to access timely credit at reasonable costs.

Bankers express concerns over the following predicaments that could translate into huge risks for them (Rabo India 2005).

- Large section of the borrowers lack credit discipline. This is partly infused by the government's decision to waive outstanding loans of farmers in certain cases.
- Majority of the farmers lack tangible security and adequate insurance cover.
- Many a time, market information on topics such as supply and demand, price trends, and so on is unreliable. This impacts credit assessments carried out by banks.
- High operational/transaction costs in servicing small- and medium-sized processing firms.

Unfortunately, risk mitigation tools such as crop insurance schemes do not completely manage/cover risks. They face difficulties in assessing farmers' yields at various levels, calculating premium, and administrative hurdles in managing claims (Rabo India 2005).

4.3.4 Infrastructure and Technology

Post-harvest management infrastructure in India is inadequate in terms of both capacity and technology. This holds true across the value chain—with respect to farm-level collection centres, packing houses, ripening chambers, quality assurance labs, incubation centres, power supply, and transportation and cold chains.

Basic facilities Poor road connectivity in rural villages, inadequacy in cold storage incorporated transportation facilities, interrupted power supply, and so on damage the agricultural/horticultural/livestock produce on its way from farm to fork.

Support Facilities Farm-level collection centres, packing houses, quality assurance labs, incubation centres, ripening chambers, and processing units are inadequate and in most cases very far away from the farm gate. This results in low levels of processing and quality deterioration, thus leading to losses. For instance, out of India's total fruit and vegetables production of 227 million tonnes in 2013, only 1–2 per cent was processed. This also causes farmers and firms alike to export abroad low value-added products or bulk packaged commodities for re-processing and repackaging, where the real value addition takes place (Negi and Anand 2015).

Storage Studies indicate that around 7 per cent of foodgrains and as much as 30 per cent of fruit and vegetables are lost due to warehousing shortfall. Also around 10 per cent of valuable spices are lost during storage. It is estimated that there is a gap of 35 million metric tonnes between warehousing supply and demand from the agricultural sector. The current cold storage capacity in the country is only sufficient for 10 per cent of fruit and vegetables produced domestically (Sabharwal 2016).

Technology adoption At farm level, harvesting is mostly carried out manually. Most farmers and processors lack knowledge of latest advancements in technology. Even if available, they cannot afford them or do not receive adequate technical support services. Lack of suitable, standard machinery, use of obsolete technologies, lack of technical support services, and inadequate quality control systems are few of the difficulties faced by food processing firms when trying to adapt laboratory-scale technologies on a larger scale. This increases per unit cost of production and thus lowers the prospects of the end product in international markets. Further, due to low returns, processing firms find it difficult to maintain product quality or to invest in product marketing (Rabo India 2005).

The existing food testing laboratories are grossly insufficient in number and capacity. Most of them are not equipped with the minimum facilities to examine the presence of antibiotic remnants, or other toxic or heavy metal contaminants in the food sample. Testing manuals are also inept and do not outline the right testing procedures or parameters to be measured. Above all this, there is poor coordination between various laboratories (Rabo India 2005). Hence, there is inefficient utilization of the available food testing infrastructure. The services are also expensive and out of reach for small processing firms. Therefore, there is an urgent need to ramp up infrastructural facilities in India to improve the present state of post-harvest management.

4.3.5 Research and Development

Research and development is inevitable in post-harvest value chain management. It is essential to farmers, retailers, and consumers alike—in terms of products, processes, and inputs. However, owing to lack of infrastructure, credit facilities and human resources, innovation in the value chains of agriculture, horticulture, and livestock remain sporadic and low. This can be attributed to the separation of applied research and academics, restricted interaction with the industry, poor inclination to commercialize, dearth of adequate research personnel, and lack of collaboration with global peers. There is also poor coordination between the various Indian R&D institutes functioning in the area of food science and technology. Furthermore, in a majority of these institutes, the process for accepting new projects is tedious and time consuming. This hinders various stakeholders from seeking research knowledge from these institutes. (Rabo India 2005). For instance, in the case of fruit and vegetables, there is no connection between the research institutions that develop hybrid seeds or packaging material and nurseries or agencies that market the final product. In some cases, research bodies lack the infrastructure required to market the new crop species to growers. Even if available, they are unable to provide proper customer support on crop management or post-harvest practices. With respect to food processing, only firms with large investment are able to carry out significant market research (Rabo India 2005). There is a need to focus on innovation and develop comprehensive solutions that can compete at an international level and are also affordable to actors of the Indian agricultural value chain.

4.3.6 Human Resources Development

There is a gap in the capacity building of human resources employed across the value chains of agricultural and allied sectors. Farmers have limited knowledge regarding use of quality inputs; latest technologies in farming, harvesting, and post-harvest management of the produce; or international quality standards and certifications. Food entrepreneurs often lack technical knowledge about food sciences and technology. Small-scale retailers who run bakeries, fast food outlets, or sweet shops, or sell livestock in wet markets lack knowledge on practices to maintain hygiene and improve product quality (Rabo India 2005).

The reasons behind this are many—outdated syllabi for food sciences and technology in universities, which are not aligned with the needs of the industry; limited training programmes for upgrading skills of various stakeholders (even if offered they have poor follow-up support); and very few institutions offering programmes that cover both technological and managerial aspects of agribusiness or the food processing industry, or have the necessary business incubation facilities (Rabo India 2005). Addressing human resources development is vital to efficient post-harvest management.

4.4 EMERGING TRENDS AND FUTURE PROSPECTS

4.4.1 Market Reforms

As stated in the previous section (under 4.2.6.1 market efficiency), over the years, both the central and state governments in India have undertaken various reforms to improve the state of agricultural markets.

Few such reforms[6] include the following:

- Amendment to the State Agricultural Produce Marketing Regulation Act to facilitate competitive agricultural markets and emerging trends such as direct marketing, electronic trading, and contract farming;
- Amendment to the Essential Commodities Act to remove all restrictions on the production, transportation, storage, or trade of all agricultural commodities;
- Steps to provide farmers and agribusiness entrepreneurs easy access to institutional credit;
- Electronic weighment of goods;

- Establishment of proper grade standards, assaying processes, and facilities throughout the country;
- Introduction of negotiable warehousing receipt system for increasing the availability of warehousing services;
- Use of information and communication technology to streamline transaction processes.
- Steps to strengthen the State Agricultural Marketing Boards (AGMARK and AGMARKNET) and the Bureau of Indian Standards (BIS) with an aim to improve quality standards and marketing services;
- Steps to implement single registration/licence for trading in more than one state and thus levying market fee only once.

4.4.1.1 Unified Agricultural Market

A notable market reform brought about in recent times is the Unified Agricultural Market. National Agriculture Market (NAM) is an electronic trading portal that aims to create a unified national market for agricultural commodities across the country by networking the existing Agricultural Produce Market Committee (APMC) Act and other market yards. This implies that traders situated in outside states can also carry out transactions in the local markets. It enhances the strength of the local mandis and also allows farmers to sell their produce at the national level. It eliminates the need for farmers to possess multiple licences to trade in different market areas of the same state, lowers intermediation costs, retains quality, reduces wastage and end-prices, and boosts the income of farmers.[7]

Launched on 14 April 2016, it aims to connect up to 585 mandis by March 2018, and up to 585 mandis by March 2018. Currently, it aims to integrate 21 mandis in eight states—Gujarat (3), Telangana (5), Rajasthan (1), Madhya Pradesh (1), Uttar Pradesh (5), Haryana (2), Jharkhand (2), and Himachal Pradesh (2). The commodities traded are *channa* (gram), castor seed, paddy, wheat, maize, onion, mustard, and tamarind. Fruit and vegetables are yet to be included. It is basically a 'plug-in' provided free of cost to every mandi that agrees to join the national network. It can be customized to conform to the regulations of respective states (Das 2016[8]).

[6] 'Marketing Infrastructure & Agriculture Marketing Reforms' available at http://agmarknet.nic.in/amrscheme/markreform3.htm, accessed on 18 July 2016.

[7] Government of India, National Agricultural Market, available at http://www.enam.gov.in/NAM/home/about_nam.html, accessed on 18 July 2016.

[8] See also Government of India, National Agricultural Market, available at http://www.enam.gov.in/NAM/home/about_nam.html, accessed on 18 July 2016; Government of India, National Agricultural Market, available at http://www.enam.gov.in/NAM/home/implemented_progress.html, accessed on 18 July 2016.

A good example for unified market is the Rashtriya Electronic Market Scheme (ReMS), which was launched in the state of Karnataka in February 2014. Currently, out of 157 mandis in the state, almost 103 APMCs have been integrated into the system. About 1.4 million farmers have been registered with the system. Currently, an independent body outside the government (ReMSL) has been assigned the task of its unification. While electronic weighment and e-trading platform are introduced, other modules such as farmer registration, assaying, and direct payment have to take place on a larger scale. It has been an uphill task, since active participation from all stakeholders still eludes it (Vyasan 2016, Vijaykumar 2016).

Another popular example of market reform in the form of direct marketing is the farmers' markets organized in various states across the nation. The Rythu Bazaar in Andhra Pradesh and Telangana, Shetkari Bazaar in Maharashtra, and Uzhavar Sandhai in Tamil Nadu are a few of them. Smallholders, who generally have difficulties in selling their produce in the regular markets (due to small volume of produce) have benefited the most from such markets. It has helped them understand consumers' needs better and adopt necessary production and marketing strategies, for instance, including a larger variety of fruit and vegetables. Apart from these benefits, direct marketing also enables producers, processors, and bulk purchasers to reduce transportation costs, which in turn helps them realize better prices (Raju et al. 2016).

There is also a growth in the number of organized retailers entering the agribusiness sector. A few of them are Food World, Spencer, Reliance Fresh, and Heritage Fresh. Their value chains are shorter than those of traditional retailers, and hence bring about better profits for the farmers. This may be attributed to their advantage in terms of technical knowledge, high-quality inputs, and reduction in transaction costs. They are also a form of quality assurance to consumers (Negi and Anand 2015).

4.4.2 Infrastructural Improvements

4.4.2.1 Storage and Warehousing

There is a growing interest among both public and private enterprises to improve the condition of existing storage and warehousing facilities and develop new ones. They are amply supported by schemes introduced by the central government such as the National Mission on Food Processing (NMFP), launched in 2013, that includes three components: setting up mega food parks that contain state-of-the-art processing facilities; cold chain, value addition, and preservation infrastructure for poultry, meat, dairy, and fisheries; and setting up/modernization of abattoirs. Four mega food parks have been established at Haridwar (Uttarakhand), Chittoor (Andhra Pradesh), Tumkur (Karnataka), and Fazilka (Punjab) and are operational. The Scheme on Cold Chain, Value Addition, and Preservation Infrastructure, launched in 2008, aims to strengthen backward and forward linkages in the agricultural supply chain. It works to accomplish this by providing a package of cold chain facilities that are necessary across the value chain, such as pre-cooling at production site, reefer vans, and mobile processing. Value addition centres include facilities for minimal processing, sorting, grading, waxing, packing, retailing, collection, and so on. As on 31 October 2014, the scheme has been successful in developing 246,000 million MT of cold storage, controlled atmosphere (CA)/modified atmosphere (MA) storage, deep freezer, 59.513 MT per hour of individual quick freezing (IQF), 84.865 lakh litres per day (LLPD) milk storage, and 330 reefer carriers (MoFPI 2015).

Two main problems that throttle the Indian warehousing market are information asymmetry and inadequate nationwide regulation and enforcement. This negatively impacts trade and lending against commodities stored in warehouses. A few market-based solutions developed to resolve this are as follows:

4.4.2.1.1 COLLATERAL MANAGEMENT SERVICES

In collateral management services (CMCs), the service providers offer to protect and preserve the agricultural commodities stored in the warehouses. They take upon the responsibility of the lenders and also absorb any loss that occurs to the stored commodities on their balance sheet. A collateral manager, who either operates the warehouse or oversees its operations, plays the role of a 'mediator' between the warehouse provider and the lender. The presence of a collateral manager gives the lenders more confidence to participate in warehouse receipt-based lending (NIPFP 2015).

4.4.2.1.2 CLOSED USER GROUPS

Closed user groups (CUGs) of warehouse service providers (WSPs) generate and share relevant information within themselves. A good example would be the CUG operated by the National Commodity and Derivatives Exchange (NCDEX). It attempts to replicate the state regulatory interventions and thus resolve the problem of market failure. The CUG has its own monitoring and audit mechanisms that the member WSPs have to follow. Currently, the NCDEX-operated CUG has around 405 accredited warehouses with a holding capacity of 2 million metric tons (NIPFP 2015).

4.4.2.1.3 WAREHOUSE RECEIPT FINANCING

In this method farmers are provided with liquidity whenever they run out of cash. There is growing prominence of this form of financing because it smoothens the producer's cash flow. With the establishment of the Warehousing Development and Regulation (WDR) Act in 2007 and the Warehousing Development and Regulatory Authority (WRDA) in 2010, construction of warehouses, their regulation, and implementation of negotiability of warehouse receipts became easier. The negotiability of warehouse receipts allows the title to the goods to be transferred from one person to another (NIPFP 2015). It makes trading easier and also refinancing. They can be easily traded on secondary markets, such as commodity exchanges, and are also easily integrated with electronic trading. It also ensures that the quality of commodities is retained.

4.4.2.1.4 E-NWR

e-NWRs enable the seamless transfer of negotiable warehouse receipts (NWRs) and provide more information and transparency about the quality and services by WSPs. Few WSPs have adopted products and data management solutions such as SAP, that have helped improve internal control mechanisms (NIPFP 2015). However, adoption of such technologies is very expensive, time consuming, and brings about organizational change.

4.4.2.2 Food Safety and Quality Testing Laboratories

In the last few years, there has been an increase in the establishment or upgradation of existing food safety and quality testing infrastructure in India. However, they are more focused on prevention and detection of adulteration, rather than food inspections. Since 2012, the Food Safety and Standards Authority of India (FSSAI) has engaged external agencies to carry out inspections on its behalf. This has enabled it to cover more ground and, in the process, led to faster adoption of new-age testing techniques (Nadkarni, 2016).

The Bureau of Indian Standards has set up eight laboratories across the nation and also recognized independent laboratories that have complied with the IS/ISO/IEC 17025 quality standards for testing and calibration.[9]

APEDA has introduced IT-enabled traceability systems for agricultural and horticultural products, particularly organic products. It helps in co-opting all stakeholders of the value chain into a single system by maintaining their information. Peanut.net, Grapenet, Anarnet, and Meat.net are some of specific traceability systems developed for groundnuts, grapes, pomegranate, and meat respectively.[10] However, owing to the complex nature of the Indian market, although raw materials are mostly sourced locally, driving traceability through the value chain is a tedious process. An effective way to improve traceability would be to spread the infrastructure network of inspection deep into remote areas (Nadkarni 2016).

The task at hand is humongous and can only be achieved through collaborative responsibility. Players in the private sector are also expressing their interest to participate in this regard. For example, Nestle India, which in the year 2015, was hit by the controversy around its instant-noodle brand, Maggi, has expressed interest in partnering with the centre in setting up two food safety institutes (Verma 2016).

Traceability coupled with the right mix of lab infrastructure can help the nation respond more efficiently to the issues of food safety.

4.4.3 Technological Innovations

Of late, adoption of sustainable, productive, and remunerative technologies across the value chains of agricultural and allied sectors is garnering attention. They are summarized in the Appendix. However, adoption of many of these innovations remains low, partly due to absence of any significant advantage, convenience, awareness, availability, and so on.

4.4.4 Farmer Organizations

4.4.4.1 Farmer Producer Organization

Farmers are increasingly organizing themselves into farmer producer organizations (FPOs) to gain better access to information and services as well as take advantage of scale economies. FPOs offer a variety of services to its members, mostly end to end, covering almost all aspects of cultivation—financial services, input supply services, procurement and packaging services, marketing services, insurance services, technical services, and networking

---

[9] Bureau of Indian Standards, 'Product Certification', available at http://www.bis.org.in/home_product.asp, accessed on 18 July 2016.

[10] APEDA, available at apeda.gov.in/apedawebsite/miscellaneous/Apeda-April-June-2015.pdf, 2015, accessed on 14 February 2017.

facilities. Depending upon the changing needs, they also provide additional services (Ministry of Agriculture 2013).

NABARD and Small Farmers' Agribusiness Consortium (SFAC), and various other NGOs have extended comprehensive support to existing and emerging FPOs.[11] Today, there are around 694 SFAC-promoted FPOs and around 339 non-SFAC-promoted FPOs.[12]

4.4.4.2 Cooperatives

A common institutional model that has been successful in India is the producers' cooperatives. Similar to FPOs, it also enables farmers to organize themselves as collectives. They are registered with the Registrar of Cooperative Societies. A good example is the Amul Cooperative Model. Generally, cooperatives have a non-profit motive and are promoted by the state. However, many of them do not function profitably and are facing deep financial crisis. They mostly depend on state subsidies for their survival. Although, the Mutually Aided Cooperative Societies Act (MACS) was instituted with an objective to vanquish these limitations, many states did not adopt it. Also, it is not applicable to several commodities (Ministry of Agriculture 2013).

4.4.5 Contract Farming and Vertical Integration

In contract farming, a contractor enters into a contract with a farmer to plant a specific crop in the farmer's land. After harvest, the produce is delivered to the contractor at an price agreed upon earlier (Ajjan 2016; Murthy and Madhuri 2013).

It helps firms to optimize technological advantages through economies of scale to reduce transaction costs and fulfil market conditions. It provides a sense of security to producers by shifting production risk to the contracting company. It can lessen the burden on the procurement systems at the state and the centre levels, attract investments from the private sector, help diversify agriculture, provide access to latest agricultural technologies, generate a steady source of income for farmers, promote food processing, ensure uninterrupted regular flow of raw material, increase employment opportunities, and so on (Ajjan n.d.; Murthy and Madhuri 2013).

The tremendous growth of the poultry sector has created demand for maize (which forms feed for poultry) and changed its market economics. Maize farmers are able to fetch competitive prices for their produce and are thus encouraged to adopt improved varieties. One of the factors behind this phenomenal growth of poultry is contract farming via vertical integration. Vertical integration is the organizational design of a firm in which it owns two or more stages in the value chain and controls the decision making on product attributes and the logistics (Naik 2006b).

The difficulty lies in ensuring that the contracts are honoured. There is no credible enforcement mechanism or legal framework to ensure this. Other issues are the small size of land holdings and lack of comprehensive risk management techniques such as crop insurance (Murthy and Madhuri 2013).

4.4.6 Food Processing

Food processing is highly critical to effective post-harvest management. Its benefits include increase in shelf life of food, remunerative prices for farmers, greater employment opportunities, customer convenience, and diversification opportunities for agriculture (Rabo India 2005).

4.4.6.1 Current Growth, Exports, and Future Prospects

With a consistent, large agricultural production to bank upon, the Indian food processing industry has a huge advantage in terms of the input raw material supply. During 2011–12 to 2014–15, it grew at an average rate faster than even the agriculture sector (provided in Table 4.2). The average annual growth rate (AAGR) of the food processing industries sector is 2.26 per cent as compared to the agriculture sector's 1.69 per cent and manufacturing sector's 6.23 per cent (at 2011–12 prices). It is also fast emerging as an important segment of the nation's economy in terms of its contribution to GDP, employment, and investment. In 2014–15, it constituted about 1.6 per cent of the nation's GDP, and 9 per cent and 10 per cent of the GDP in the manufacturing and agriculture sectors respectively (MoFPI 2016). Data from the Annual Survey of Industries (ASI) for 2013–14 indicates that the food processing industry ranked fifth in the net value added (contributing around 6.7 per cent of the net value added by all industries put together).[13]

---

[11] 'How Do We Fund Our Farmer Producer Organizations?', *Swarajya*, available at http://swarajyamag.com/economy/how-do-we-fund-our-farmer-producer-organizations, accessed on 18 July 2016.

[12] FPO, http://sfacindia.com/List-of-FPO-Statewise.aspx, accessed on 23 January 2018.

[13] Central Statistics Office, Industrial Statistics Wing, available at www.csoisw.gov.in/cms/UploadedFiles/Table2PrincipalCharacteristicsbyMajorIndustryGroup_2013_2014.pdf, accessed on 27 January 2017.

Table 4.2   Contribution of the Food Processing Industry to the Nation's Gross Domestic Product (Calculated at 2011–12 Prices) (Rs in Crore)

Economic Activity	2011–12	2012–13	2013–14	2014–15
GDP–All India	8,195,546	8,599,224	9,169,787	9,827,089
GDP–Manufacturing	1,482,158	1,574,471	1,658,176	1,776,469
GDP–Agriculture, Forestry and Fishing	1,505,580	1,523,470	1,579,290	1,582,851
GDP–FPI	150,370	143,364	149,555	160,224
(%) Growth				
Economic Activity	2012–13	2013–14	2014–15	AAGR
GDP–All India	4.93	6.64	7.17	6.23
GDP–Manufacturing	6.23	5.32	7.13	6.23
GDP–Agriculture, Forestry, and Fishing	1.19	3.66	0.23	1.69
GDP–FPI	−4.66	4.32	7.13	2.26
(%) Share of FPI				
Economic Activity	2011–12	2012–13	2013–14	2014–15
GDP–All India	1.83	1.67	1.63	1.63
GDP–Manufacturing	10.15	9.11	9.02	9.02
GDP–Agriculture, Forestry, and Fishing	9.99	9.41	9.47	10.12

Source: MoFPI (2016).

Between the years 2000 and 2015, the food processing sector in India received foreign direct investment (FDI) worth US$ 6.70 billion.[14] A similar growth is also being witnessed by the organized food market and online food ordering business. Today, the organized food business in India is valued at around US$ 48 billion; of it, food delivery business is valued at around US$ 15 billion and is expected to grow bigger.[15]

APEDA's reports on export of processed food products (in terms of quantity and value), indicate that there is an increase in the export of cereal preparations, milled products, cocoa products, jaggery and confectionery, processed fruit and vegetables, and alcoholic beverages, and they are fetching greater returns (Figures 4.17 and 4.18). This could be due to changing lifestyles, growing number of nuclear families and working women, and rising income and consumer spending. However, in the last five years, exports of dairy products, prepared, dried, and preserved cucumber and gherkins, and mango pulp have witnessed a slight decline in the value fetched for same amount of exports (Figures 4.17 and 4.18), which

could be a result of poor quality and non-adherence to international standards as discussed in the earlier sections of this chapter. Thus, it is critical that the Indian food processing industry adopts international standards of food safety and quality assurance mechanisms such as Total Quality Management (TQM), ISO 9000, ISO 22000, Hazard Analysis and Critical Control Points (HACCP), Good Manufacturing Practices (GMPs), and Good Hygienic Practices (GHPs). It will safeguard consumer health and also enhance global competitiveness of firms.[16]

4.5 INSTITUTIONAL SUPPORT

4.5.1 Policy Support

4.5.1.1 Agricultural Insurance

The Government of India has replaced earlier crop insurance schemes of National Agricultural Insurance Scheme (NAIS) and Modified NAIS, with the Pradhan Mantri Fasal Bima Yojana (PMFBY). It covers both Kharif and Rabi crops—commercial and horticultural crops. The premium charged varies between crops and is a percentage

[14] IBEF, 'Indian Food Industry', available at http://www.ibef.org/industry/indian-food-industry.aspx, accessed on 18 July 2016.

[15] IBEF, 'Indian Food Industry', available at http://www.ibef.org/industry/indian-food-industry.aspx, accessed on 18 July 2016.

[16] IBEF, 'Indian Food Industry', available at http://www.ibef.org/industry/indian-food-industry.aspx, accessed on 18 July 2016.

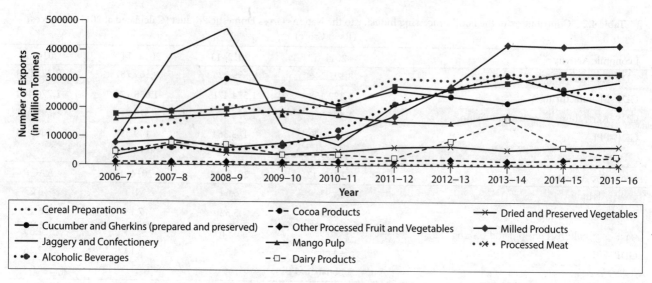

Figure 4.17 Exports of Processed Food Products from India (Quantity in Million Tonnes)

Source: APEDA, AgriXchange, available at http://agriexchange.apeda.gov.in/indexp/genReport_combined.aspx, accessed on 27 January 2017.

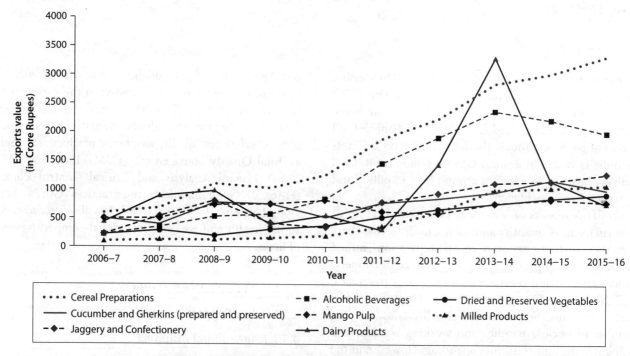

Figure 4.18 Exports of Processed Food Products from India (Value)

Source: APEDA, AgriXchange, available at http://agriexchange.apeda.gov.in/indexp/genReport_combined.aspx, accessed on 27 January 2017.

of the sum insured. For example, while in case of Kharif crops it can go up to 2 per cent, in case of Rabi crops, it can go up to 1.5 per cent. The central and the respective state governments bear the remaining share of the premium equally. This scheme also covers post-harvest losses. It also provides farm-level assessment for localized calamities including hailstorms, unseasonal rains, landslides and inundation.'[17] It has been implemented by the Agriculture Insurance Company of India (AIC), together with various other private firms. With an aim of expediting crop loss estimation and the claim settlement process, the scheme mandates the use of techniques such as remote sensing and equipment such as smartphones and drones.[18]

Krishonnati Yojana is an umbrella programme under the Ministry of Agriculture and includes all schemes related to crop husbandry such as the Rashtriya Krishi Vikas Yojana (RKVY), National Crop Insurance Programme (NCIP), National Food Security Mission (NFSM), and National Mission for Sustainable Agriculture (NMSA), and so on.[19]

4.5.1.2 Schemes for Food Processing

The Government of India, under the ambit of the Ministry of Agriculture and the Ministry of Food Processing, continues to offer financial and infrastructural support to the agricultural and the food processing sectors. They are stated in the XII Plan document and are as follows (MoFPI 2015):

- Setting up of the NMFP with an aim to involve the state governments and thus facilitate better coordination and quicker implementation of schemes.
- Modifying the current schemes pertaining to mega food parks and integrated cold chain, and expanding their reach.
- Establishing new abattoirs and modernizing existing ones.
- Developing new institutions and strengthening existing ones.
- Organizing food processing industry-oriented skill development programmes for the rural youth.
- Establishing a nationwide network of food testing labs (both public and private owned).

- Setting up new Codex Cells (in FSSAI offices) and strengthening existing ones.
- Setting up a fund for financing any innovation or venture capital in the area of food processing.

There are also existing schemes such as the scheme for Human Resource Development that aims to generate a large pool of well-qualified manpower which can serve all levels of the food processing sector. It aims to achieve this through the creation of infrastructure facilities in academic institutions, providing financial assistance, and providing entrepreneurship development programmes (MoFPI 2015).

During the 12th Plan (2012–13), the National Mission on Food Processing (NMFP), a centrally sponsored scheme (CSS), was launched. It aims to set up infrastructural facilities, build capacity, upgrade skills, raise food safety standards, and facilitate adoption of HACCP and ISO certification norms for post-harvest operations. On the lines of National Food Processing Development Councils (NFPDCs), State Food Processing Development Councils (SFPDCs) have also been set up in most states and union territories for effective supervision, monitoring, and implementation of NMFP at the state level (MoFPI 2015).

While these schemes have yielded some impact, significant impact is yet to be seen. This is due to poor implementation of schemes, absence of integration of various schemes as well as difficulty in aligning schemes with the state government policies.

4.5.1.3 Fiscal Incentives

A number of incentives have been given to the agro-processing sector. The significant ones are as follows.

4.5.1.3.1 FDI

Foreign direct investment is permissible in food processing sector up to 100 per cent on automatic route, subject to existing rules and regulations. It is not applicable on items reserved for micro and small enterprises (MSEs) (MoFPI 2015).

4.5.1.3.2 INCOME TAX

Deduction in expenditure Under Section 35-AD of the Income Tax Act 1961, deduction is permitted for expenditure incurred as part of investment in setting up or operating cold chain facilities, warehousing facilities,

[17] The Hans India, 'Indian government schemes', available at http://www.thehansindia.com/posts/index/Young-Hans/2016-07-10/Indiangovernment-schemes-/241138, accessed on 18 July 2016.

[18] The Hans India, 'Indian government schemes', available at http://www.thehansindia.com/posts/index/Young-Hans/2016-07-10/Indian-government-schemes-/241138, accessed on 18 July 2016.

[19] The Hans India, 'Indian government schemes', available at http://www.thehansindia.com/posts/index/Young-Hans/2016-07-10/Indian-government-schemes-/241138, accessed on 18 July 2016.

bee-keeping, and production of honey and beeswax, and so on (MoFPI 2015).

Deduction of tax from profit Any expenditure incurred when setting up or operating cold chain facilities, warehousing facilities, bee-keeping and production of honey and beeswax, and others can be claimed for deduction in expenditure. This comes under Section 35-AD of the Income Tax Act 1961 (MoFPI 2015).

4.5.1.3.3 SERVICE TAX

With a motive to promote the food processing sector, the Government of India has revised the service tax rate structure for various processed foods. Foodgrains and raw food items have been exempted from the goods and service tax (GST). Most processed foods prepared from fruit and vegetables or livestock such as pickles, sauces, ketchups, dairy products, or ready to fry meat attract lower taxes (12 per cent) than earlier rates (18 per cent) (Pinto 2017). This lowering of service taxes could help attract more players to enter the market. However, processed cocoa products like cocoa butter, chocolates, powder, aerated drinks, and sugar syrup will be liable to high service tax of 28 per cent.[20]

Interestingly, while the Government of India has exempted the storage and warehousing of agricultural produce from GST, the cost of constructing warehouses and cold storage will rise due to higher service tax (18 per cent) (Kaul 2017).

4.5.1.3.4 CUSTOMS DUTY

Any new business unit established in the area of food processing or related areas such as preservation and packaging (of any item fruit or vegetables, meat and meat product, poultry, marine, or dairy products) can claim income tax deduction. This comes under Section 80IB (11A) of the Income Tax Act, 1961. (MoFPI 2015).

4.5.1.3.5 CENTRAL EXCISE DUTY

On all food products such as milk, milk products (excluding condensed milk), vegetables, nuts, fruit, fresh and dried, and soya milk drinks, food processing machineries used in dairy, wine manufacturing, and others concessions on central excise duty are applicable (MoFPI 2015).

4.5.1.3.6 CREDIT ACCESS AND AVAILABILITY

Food processing units with an investment in plant and machinery not exceeding Rs 50 million are covered under priority sector lending. A NABARD has set up a special fund of Rs 20,000 million to provide affordable credit to the food processing sector. Under this fund, public and private entities can avail loans for establishing, expanding, or modernizing food processing plants (MoFPI 2015).

While these schemes have been there for some time now, there is no significant impact on the post-harvest management in the country.

4.5.2 'MAKE IN INDIA' Programme

The food processing sector has been identified as one of the preeminent sectors under the Government of India's ambitious 'Make in India' programme. It aims to construct mega food parks with common utility such as road, electricity, water supply, sewage facility and common processing facility such as pulping, packaging, cold storage, dry storage, and logistics across the nation. Entrepreneurs can take these facilities on rent or lease (MoFPI 2015).

4.5.3 Commodity Exchanges

Commodity markets are a platform for exchanging market information such as supply/demand and price trends. They are inexpensive, highly efficient and transparent.[23]

Today, there are around 25 commodity exchanges in operation in India carrying out futures trading in as many as 81 commodity items. They are mostly regional and commodity-specific exchanges. Commodity derivatives trading in India is regulated by the Forward Markets Commission (FMC), which was merged with the Securities and Exchange Board of India (SEBI) on 28 September 2015. National-level institutions such as NABARD have formed strategic partnerships with leading national-level commodity exchanges such as NCDEX and MCX. This will enable both NABARD and national-level commodity exchanges to establish an efficient and transparent agricultural market.[21] However, proper use of futures

---

[20] MOFPI. Product Wise GST Rates of Food Products, available at http://mofpi.nic.in/sites/default/files/product-wise_gst_rates.pdf, accessed on 23 January 2018.

[21] NABARD, Farm Sector Schemes, available at https://www.nabard.org/english/agri_com.aspx, accessed on 18 July 2016.

market for risk management and price discovery is still limited and proper spot market reforms are needed to enable the futures market to perform properly.

**

All these initiatives and institutional support provided by the government aims to provide operational, marketing, financial and risk management support for actors across the agricultural value chain—farmers to food processing firms. This in turn aids in the overall improvement of post-harvest value chain efficiency. However, the impact of these supports has been slow and limited due to issues of implementation as well as lack of comprehensive approach to improve post-harvest management.

4.6 SOME SUCCESS STORIES

With growth in the number of initiatives in the agricultural sector, there are some success stories that have helped to improve the efficiency of the agricultural value chain. A few of them are as follows:

4.6.1 Commodity Exchanges

A study conducted by UNCTAD on emerging commodity exchanges in India found that cardamom planters have benefited from the commodities futures market. They are able to secure better prices for their produce, as future prices are easily available for reference. Similarly, mentha farmers have also been able to acquire better price information, thus facilitating India to become a leading exporter of mentha oil (Ghosh 2014).

4.6.2 Cooperatives

Mahagrapes is a public–private partnership between the grapes producer associations and the state government agencies of Maharashtra. They have formed cooperatives across the state, which export grapes and other fresh produce to various parts of the world including high-quality standard European markets (Naik 2006a). They have succeeded in helping its member farmers earn higher incomes.

Each cooperative society is equipped with a pre-cooling and cold storage facility. Its quality control team monitors fruit quality at different stages of operation starting from cultivation to packing. Members of the association are frequently sent to study foreign markets in terms of export requirements and procedures. Fruit that do not meet quality specifications are rejected at source. It also

produces its own line of bio pesticides and bio fertilizers that are used by its member cooperatives and sold to other farmers as well. Whenever there is an acute shortage of water in the summer season, they use a cost-effective plastic reservoir film imported from Spain for storing water (Korde 2016). India has been able to compete effectively in the high-quality fresh produce market due to these efforts. This has been achieved through close collaboration with state government departments (Maharashtra State Agricultural Marketing Board), research organizations (ICAR's National Research Center for Grapes), FPOs (the Maharashtra State Grape Growers' Association), and infrastructural improvements (establishment of Grape Wine Parks and Agri-Export Zones) (Naik 2006a). The lessons learnt in this experiment are significant as meeting standards of high-quality markets requires change in the complete value chain right from inputs in the production process to packing and labelling. There has been some spill-over effect of this to other fruit crops such as pomegranate and mangoes, but it needs widespread adoption.

4.6.3 Farmer Producer Organizations

Maize farmers of Purnia district, Bihar, are now earning between 15 per cent and 20 per cent more than before through active participation on the futures platform, an effort initiated by FPOs such as Ram Rahim or Jeevika (Dave 2016a).

Currently, about 35 FPOs representing more than 25,000 farmers are actively engaged on the NCDEX. Ram Rahim Pragati Producer Company Limited (RRPPCL) operates in Madhya Pradesh and Rajasthan. It primarily trades on the forwards market and hedges commodities such as soybean, channa, and maize. In 2015, it earned a profit of Rs 600,000 (Dave 2016a).

4.7 WAY FORWARD

In today's global age, an efficient and effective agricultural value chain is characterized by reducing barriers to international trade (lower tariffs and prices, export subsidies, and so on), increasing consolidation of links due to advances in communication technologies, declining transactional and transportation costs, making available higher-quality products to consumers at affordable price, and, most importantly, better returns to the producer. However, for India, in spite of having a strong agricultural base, achieving this remains elusive.

Table 4.3 summarizes the various bottlenecks faced by agricultural, horticultural commodities, and livestock

Table 4.3 Post-Harvest Losses—Causes and Solutions

Commodity	Bottleneck	What Needs to Be Done?
Non-perishables such as cereals, pulses, oilseeds	Losses occur due to • Manual or inappropriate farm-level operations • Lack of/improper storage facilities • Weather calamities • Lack of timely and affordable credit • Inaccurate market information	• Encourage market reforms initiatives such as unified markets, producer organization, commodity exchanges and contract farming • Popularize warehouse receipt system • Proper assaying of agriculture commodities before transactions • Make farm equipment available at affordable rates and train farmers about mechanization of farm operations • Provide easy access to affordable and timely credit and risk mitigation tools such as crop insurance • Encourage agricultural research and development; adopt end-to-end ICT-based technologies, particularly in markets
Perishables such as fruit, vegetables and plantation crops	Losses occur due to • Lack of/improper cold storage facilities (at farm and market levels) • Poor quality/absence of infrastructural facilities (roads and transportation, waxing, grading, packaging and processing houses) • Weather calamities • Poor insect-pest management strategies • Inaccurate market information • Lack of product diversification through value addition • Poor access to markets where surplus produce can be sold	• Provide better infrastructural facilities (both farm and market levels) • Develop cold chains • Provide easy access to affordable and timely credit • Encourage agricultural research • Facilitate certification and portal-based transactions • Adopt end-to-end ICT-based technologies, particularly in markets
Livestock produce such as poultry egg, inland fish, marine fish, meat, and poultry meat	Losses occur due to • Lack of/improper cold storage/refrigerated display facilities (at farm/boat and market levels) • Poor quality/absence of infrastructural facilities (slaughter houses, sorting, grading, packaging centres, and so on) • Mixed farming (for example, inland fish and makhana) • Inaccurate market information • Lack of product diversification through value addition • Poor access to markets where surplus produce can be sold • Poor adoption of safety, hygiene and quality standards	• Encourage market reforms initiatives such as unified markets, cooperatives, commodity exchanges and contract farming • Train farmers about hygiene and quality standards • Animal identification to facilitate credit and insurance • Encourage agricultural research and development and the adoption of ICT-based technologies for database on animals and transactions

Source: Courtesy of the authors.

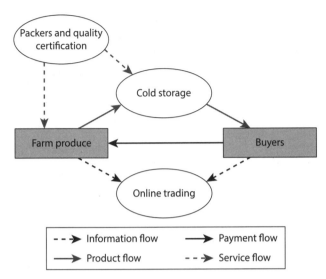

Figure 4.19   Integrated Approach to Post-Harvest Management for Perishable Produce

Source: Courtesy of the authors.

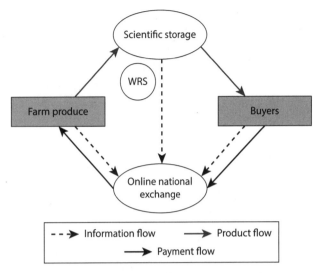

Figure 4.20   Integrated Approach to Post-Harvest Management for Non-Perishable Produce

Source: Courtesy of the authors.

that lead to post-harvest losses and what measures need to be taken to reduce this.

From the above table, it is clear that the solutions to post-harvest losses across various value chains are quite similar, with minor differences. However, there is a dire need to adopt an integrated approach to it. The key is to link and integrate various initiatives taken across the value chain to improve post-harvest management—farmers, commodity exchanges, food processing parks, packing houses, cold storage, terminal markets such as National Agricultural Market, and buyers.

For perishables, the value chain can be streamlined by having a pack house and quality certification at the block level and then on-line trading facilities to buy/sell the produce. The process is depicted in Figure 4.19. Such a system exists in the case of grapes in some of the main producing regions.

Here (Figure 4.19), produce from the farm is sent to packing houses, where it is cleaned, graded and quality certified. It is then kept in the cold storage. Buyers (retailers/wholesalers) can purchase produce through online trading platform or portals and choose required quality or grades and get it shipped to their location or pick it from cold storage. This can reduce the number of intermediaries and multiple handling, improve quality of produce and facilitate easy procurement. This can prove to be particularly useful in case of perishable commodities. The idea is to implement quality grading at the grassroots level, to prevent poor quality produce from

reaching the hands of consumer; and reduce intermediaries.

In case of non-perishables (given in Figure 4.20), scientific storage systems, particularly warehouse receipt systems should be linked to commodity exchanges, online trading platforms, farmers and buyers. Produce from the farm is collected, graded and stored in warehouses. Buyers (retailers/wholesalers) can purchase the produce through online trading platforms. Here, the warehouse receipt system serves as a guarantee for assuring quality of the produce. Such systems will reduce intermediaries, risk, marketing cost as well as wastage and improve the quality of produce and revenues of farmers.

4.8 CONCLUSION

Post-harvest management suffers from a number of inadequacies such as absence of appropriate infrastructure, trained manpower, information, standardization, investments, and appropriate policies. The key aspect is the lack of coordinated effort in streamlining the value chain. While streamlining of post-harvest management has taken place to a large extent in the export segment mostly through vertical integration, it is yet to take place in the domestic market. Proper streamlining of post-harvest management will not only save produce, enhance quality, and make the produce competitive, but it will also reduce the prices to the consumers and increase the revenues of the farmers.

Introducing proper pack-houses and quality systems will significantly streamline the post-harvest management for perishables. Similarly, moving towards proper assaying and popularizing warehouse receipt system along with e-trading is likely to revolutionize the post-harvest management for storable commodities. These require coordinated efforts of central and state governments in spearheading a movement to involve the stakeholders in transitioning to more modern post-harvest management in the country.

APPENDIX

4A.1 List of Technological Innovations Adopted across the Agricultural Value Chain in India

Stage of the Value Chain	Innovation
Farming	**Development of hybrid seed varieties** that have an extended shelf-life and do not need refrigeration or preservatives (Shankar and Vignesh 2016). **Use of precision farming**, which provides the precise amount of inputs such as water, fertilizers, pesticides, and so on to the crop, at the right time that helps increase yield and productivity. Using GPS technology, it also informs the farmer about the status of the crop and which part of the farm requires how much of input (Rajvanshi 2015). **Leasing mechanized equipment** such as drip irrigation systems on an hourly basis from agencies. This is mostly accompanied by trained manpower. Although it is still not prevalent, for farmers with small holdings and who face labour shortage, it is an attractive and economical concept (Rajvanshi 2015). Few other innovations include **vegetable fly trap, low-cost irrigation controller, and automated air-blast sprayers**, and **non-chemical-based alternatives for pesticides**. They are cheaper than foreign products, and easy to maintain and use (Shankar and Vignesh 2016).
Data Collection	Development and use of drones to collect farm-related data. A complex camera is attached to the drones to record information in real time (Shankar and Vignesh 2016).
Harvesting and Peeling	Application of **mechanical harvesters and peelers**. A few examples are as follows (Asian Productivity Organization 2005): **Mango Harvester** • Developed by the University of Agricultural Sciences, Bangalore • Prevents the flow of latex on to the fruit surface and thus prevents tissue damage. **Integrated Peeler** • Developed by the Indian Institute of Horticulture Research (IIHR) in Bangalore. • Can peel raw fruits such as mango, papaya, and others so that they can be easily processed into value-added products such as pickles, chutneys, and dry powder. • Can also deseed tamarind and chilli, and de-husk coconut. • Capacity of one metric ton/hour.
Maturity Standard Indices	Developed by the Bureau of Indian Standard (BIS), these **standards specify the ideal time (based on pulp–peel ratio, colour, and odour) and method for harvesting** various fruit and vegetables. For instance, bananas should be cut in bunches at the stalk end (Asian Productivity Organization 2005).
Sorting and Grading	Developed by the Bureau of Indian Standard (BIS), these **standards specify the parameters to be considered (maturity, size, shape, colour, weight, extent of decay due to insects/pests and pesticide residues), when sorting and grading** fruit and vegetables. For instance, mangoes are graded for export on a weight basis (Asian Productivity Organization 2005). Class A (200–350 g), Class B (351–550 g) or Class C (551–800 g). Vegetables are mostly graded on the basis of size, shape, weight, and maturity stage.
Market Information	ITC's **e-Choupal** provides information on market price, weather, risk management, best practices in farming, and latest technologies to the agricultural community in their local language. Facilitates the purchase of inputs and sale of produce (Sharma 2011). 'As a direct marketing channel, virtually linked to the mandi system for price discovery, 'e-Choupal' eliminates wasteful intermediation and thus reduces transaction costs' (Sahay and Sharma 2018, 113). Broadcasting market prices is through TV and sending SMS to individuals.

Storage	Development of low-cost, environment-friendly storage facilities **Zero Energy Cool Chamber** (Asian Productivity Organization 2005) • Developed by the ICAR, Delhi. • Can be employed on farm. • Made from locally available material. • Works on the principle of evaporative cooling. • Reduces the temperature within the chamber by as much as 17–18°C, and maintains a relative humidity of 90%, depending on the season (Asian Productivity Organization 2005). • Increases shelf-life of various fruits and vegetables such as gooseberries, bananas, mangoes, tomatoes, limes, grapes. **Control Atmosphere/Modified Atmosphere Storage** (Asian Productivity Organization 2005) • 'Involves adjustment of the atmospheric composition surrounding commodities by removal (mainly O_2) or addition (mainly CO_2) of gases from the environment' (Asian Productivity Organization 2005, 20). • Differs in the precision to which the concentrations of gases are controlled. • Enhances the shelf-life of fruit and vegetables, when combined with refrigeration. • Reduces the chances of chilling injury. • If not properly applied, it causes irregular ripening, off-flavour development and stimulates sprouting. **Solar-Powered Cold-Storage unit** (Shankar and Vignesh 2016) • Developed by start-ups • Prevents wastage and thus helps farmers attain greater price for their produce.
Drying, Ripening, and Processing	ICAR has developed various inexpensive innovations that can tackle post-harvest losses, are user-friendly, and easy on pocket. Few such examples are as follows (Indian Council of Agricultural Research 2015). **Solar biomass hot-dryer**, developed for drying soaked pigeon pea dal. **Set of equipment for ripening and giving hot-water treatment** to banana for increasing shelf-life. **Pre-harvest sprays** for onions, which reduce rotting and weight loss during storage. **Probiotic drinks** using exotic fruits such as bael and kokum. **Nutritious extruded snacks** from walnut kernels and rice.
Packaging	Few new packaging technologies that are inexpensive and environment friendly are as follows (Asian Productivity Organization 2005): **Corrugated Fibre Board** (CFB) Boxes • Used for packaging fixed number of uniformly sized produce such as mangoes or oranges. • Protect the produce by cushioning and immobilizing it. • Easy to handle and minimize the impact of rough handling. • Not suitable for storing produce at low temperatures. • Fabricated from kraft paper produced from bamboo, long grass, agricultural residues, and others. • Easy to recycle. **Window-type conical bamboo baskets** • Useful for transportation by rail. • Aid stacking and aeration of the produce. **Polyethylene film bags, plastic bags, plastic mesh, trays made of moulded pulp, paper board, plastic or foamed plastic** are used for wrapping during packaging.

Source: Courtesy of the authors.

REFERENCES

Ajjan, N. n.d. 'Contract Farming'. Available at http://www.fao.org/fileadmin/user_upload/contract_farming/presentations/Contract_farming_in_India_3.pdf, accessed on 18 July 2016.

Ambwani, Meenakshi Verma. 2016. 'Nestle's Helping Hand to Improve Food Safety'. *The Hindu Business Line*, 20 June. Available at http://www.thehindubusinessline.com/companies/nestles-helping-hand-to-improve-food-safety/article8752563.ece, accessed on 28 December 2017.

APEDA. 2015. 'e-APEX Update: Showcasing India Food Products'. Available at apeda.gov.in/apedawebsite/miscellaneous/Apeda-April-June-2015.pdf, accessed on 14 February 2017.

Asian Productivity Organization. 2005. *Postharvest Management of Fruit and Vegetables in the Asia-Pacific Region*. Available at http://www.apo-tokyo.org/00e-books/

AG-18_PostHarvest/AG-18_PostHarvest.pdf, accessed on 23 January 2018.

Bera, S. 2016. 'Horticulture Production Estimated at 283.36 Million Tonnes in 2015–16'. *livemint*, 6 September. Available at http://www.livemint.com/Politics/oMRlrRc-KLEqqqGjX23dqUM/Horticulture-production-estimated-at-28336-million-tonnes-i.html, accessed on 28 December 2017.

Bhayani, R. and K.A. Gera. 2016. 'Agri-exports Fall 17 Per cent to Five-year Low of $32.09 bn in FY16'. *Business Standard*, Mumbai.

Chand, Ramesh. 2016. 'e-Platform for National Agricultural Market'. *Economic and Political Weekly* 51(28). Available at http://www.epw.in/journal/2016/28/commentary/e-platform-national-agricultural-market.html?0=ip_login_no_cache%3D77d635c0ab549249afead53e27bec415, accessed on 18 July 2016.

Das, Sandip. 2016. 'Big Agriculture Reform: PM Modi's NAM to Electronically Integrate 585 Regulated Wholesale Market'. *The Financial Express*, 11 April. Available at http://www.financialexpress.com/economy/pm-narendra-modi-to-launch-national-agriculture-online-market-on-april-14/234832/, accessed on 28 December 2017.

Dave, Vimukt. 2016a. 'Better Returns Attract Farmers to Commodity Futures Platform'. *Business Standard*, 21 May. Available at http://www.business-standard.com/article/economy-policy/better-returns-attract-farmers-to-commodity-futures-platform-116052100402_1.html, accessed on 18 July 2016.

———. 2016b. 'Cleanliness Problem in Spice Export'. *Business Standard*, 15 June. Available at http://www.business-standard.com/article/markets/cleanliness-problem-in-spice-export-116061401005_1.html, accessed on 28 December 2017.

Ministry of Agriculture, Department of Agriculture and Cooperation. 2013. 'Policy and Process Guidelines for Farmer Producer Organizations'. Available at http://nhm.nic.in/Archive/FPO-Policy&Process-GuidelinesDAC2013.pdf, accessed on 18 July 2017.

Ghosh, Nilanjan. 2014. 'The Realities behind Myths in the Commodity Futures Market'. *The Hindu Business Line*, 17 April. Available at http://www.thehindubusinessline.com/markets/commodities/the-realities-behind-myths-in-the-commodity-futures-market/article5922800.ece, accessed on 28 December 2017.

ICAR-CIPHET. 2015. *Assessment of Quantitative Harvest and Post-Harvest Losses of Major Crops and Commodities in India*. Ludhiana: ICAR-CIPHET.

Indian Council of Agricultural Research. 2015. *DARE/ICAR Annual Report 2015–16*.

Kaul, Sanjay. 2017. 'GST Raises Cost of Agri Warehousing and Cold Chains; Amendments Are Need of the Hour'. *The Hindu Business Line*.

Korde, Sachin. 2016. 'MAHAGRAPES: A Success Story of Vision and Commitment'. Available at http://

www.commodityindia.com/templates/more_articles.aspx?gid=All&fn=DtGRAPES021016, accessed on 18 July 2016.

MoFPI. 2015. *Annual Report 2014–15*. New Delhi: Ministry of Food Processing Industries, Government of India.

———. 2016. *Annual Report 2015–16*. New Delhi: Ministry of Food Processing Industries, Government of India.

Murthy, M.R.K. and Bindu Madhuri. 2013. 'A Case Study on Suguna Poultry Production through Contract Farming in Andhra Pradesh'. *Asia Pacific Journal of Marketing & Management Review* 2: 58–68.

Nadkarni, Niranjan. 2016. 'Together, We Can Ensure that Food's Safe'. *The Hindu Business Line*, 17 June. Available at http://www.thehindubusinessline.com/opinion/together-we-can-ensure-that-foods-safe/article8742031.ece, accessed on 28 December 2017.

Naik, Gopal. 2006a. 'Bridging the Knowledge Gap in Competitive Agriculture: Grapes in India'. In *Technology, Adaptation and Exports*, edited by Vandana Chandra, pp. 243–74. Washington DC: The World Bank.

———. 2006b. 'Closing the Yield Gap: Maize in India'. In *Technology, Adaptation, and Exports*, edited by Vandana Chandra, pp. 275–300. Washington DC: The World Bank.

Nanda, S.K. 2012. 'Harvest and Post Harvest Losses of Major Crops and Livestock Produce in India. Ludhiana'. *All India Coordinated Research Project on Post Harvest Technology* (ICAR), 2012.

Negi, Saurav and Neeraj Anand. 2015. 'Issues and Challenges in the Supply Chain of Fruits and Vegetables Sector in India: A Review'. *International Journal of Managing Value and Supply Chains* 6(2). Available at https://pdfs.semanticscholar.org/6bd3/796d46faab2b3c000a873894844ccd6104b0.pdf, accessed on 28 December 2017.

NIPFP. 2015. 'Report on Warehousing in India: Study Commissioned by the Warehousing Development and Regulatory Authority'. National Institute of Public Finance and Policy.

Pinto, Viveat Susan. 2017. 'More Players Possible in Processed Foods after GST Cuts'. *Business Standard*.

Rabo India Finance Pvt. Ltd. 2005. Volume I, *Vision, Strategy and Action Plan for Food Processing Industries in India*. Rabo India Finance.

Raju, K.V., G. Naik, R. Ramseshan, T. Pandey, and P. Joshi. 2016. 'Transforming Agricultural Marketing in India: Linking Farmers to a National Gateway and E-Markets, Current Scenario and a Way Forward'. International Crops Research Institute for the Semi-Arid Tropics. Available at http://oar.icrisat.org/9746/, accessed on 28 December 2017.

Rajvanshi, Anil. 2015. 'Precision Agriculture Could Start a Green Revolution in India'. *Huffington Post*.

Sabharwal, Sandeep. 2016. 'Are We Ready for the Bumper Harvests?' *Business World*, 14 July. Available at http://businessworld.in/article/Are-We-Ready-For-The-Bumper-Harvests-/14-07-2016-100432/, accessed on 28 December 2017.

Sahay, Arun and V. Sharma. 2008. *Entrepreneurship and New Venture Creation*. New Delhi: Excel Books.

Shankar, Shashwati and J. Vignesh. 2016. 'How the Startup Boom Is Helping Farmers and Forcing Investors to Pay Attention to Agriculture'. *The Economic Times*.

Sharma, Arpita. 2011. 'ITC E-Choupal: Empowering Rural India'. Available at http://www.youthkiawaaz.com/2011/08/itc-e-choupal-empowering-rural-india-research/, accessed on 23 January 2018.

Tagat, Venkatesh and Anirudh Tagat. 2015. 'How Do We Fund Our Farmer Producer Organizations?'. *#Swarajya*, 2 June. Available at http://swarajyamag.com/economy/how-do-we-fund-our-farmer-producer-organizations, accessed on 18 July 2016.

UNIDO. 2015. *Meeting Standards, Winning Markets— Trade Standards Compliance Report 2015*. Available at https://www.unido.org/sites/default/files/2015-09/TSCR_2015_final_0.pdf, accessed on 23 January 2018.

Vijaykumar, Neeti. 2016. '1.4 Million Farmers in K'taka Are Selling Their Produce Online—without Worrying about Middlemen'. *The Better India*, 16 March. Available at https://www.thebetterindia.com/49314/ktaka-farmers-ump-trade-online/, accessed on 28 December 2017.

Vyasan, R. 2016. 'Lessons for Unifying Agricultural Markets'. *The Indian Express*, 16 April. Available at http://indianexpress.com/article/opinion/columns/lessons-for-unifying-agricultural-markets-2755464/, accessed on 28 December 2017.

5

Making Indian Agriculture Profitable, Productive, and Sustainable

Ashok Gulati* and *Shweta Saini***

ABSTRACT

'Doubling farmers' incomes in 5 years' has been mentioned by the Union finance minister in two successive budget speeches of FY17 and FY18. It reflects the good intentions and boldness of Government of India's (GoI) resolve to dramatically improve the financial situation of Indian peasantry. But to turn intentions into reality, one needs clarity in ambition, a solid strategy and ample resources to back it, and finally a champion to implement it and persevere till the goal is reached. Does GoI have that?

It is against this backdrop that the chapter delineates that the *real* incomes of farmers have increased only by 3.5 per cent per annum during FY03 to FY13. And to double farmers' incomes in five years, one requires a compound annual growth of at least 14 per cent. This cannot be achieved with the business-as-usual scenario. One has to undertake bold reforms in agriculture, starting with getting the incentive structures (prices and markets) right, rationalizing safety nets and input subsidies by moving towards direct benefit transfers (DBT) and using the savings in investments, institutional reforms in land and credit markets, and finally unleash several innovations all along the agri-value chain that can augment farmers' incomes as also make Indian agriculture more competitive, inclusive, and sustainable.

JEL Classification: Q01, Q13, Q16, Q18

Keywords: doubling farmers' incomes, intentions and reality, GoI agri-food-rural policy, safety nets, subsidies and investments, agri-reforms, innovations and way forward

5.1 BACKDROP

In his Budget speech of financial year (FY) 2017–18, the Union finance minister (FM) categorically stated that he has weaved his budget around 10 major themes, and farmers and rural people were accorded the top two priorities. He also reiterated his commitment of the previous year of doubling farmers' incomes within five years.

* Infosys Chair Professor for Agriculture at the Indian Council for Research on International Economic Relations (ICREIR).

** Senior Consultant at ICREIR.

This issue of doubling farmers' income was first raised by the prime minister (PM) in a farmers' rally in February 2016, where he called it as his 'dream' to double farmers' incomes by 2022. Thereafter it got mentioned in Union Budgets of FY17 as well as FY18. The Ministry of Agriculture also set up an expert committee in April 2016 under the then Additional Secretary, Ashok Dalwai, to look into this in detail and to see how best it can be achieved. Several other institutions, including the National Bank for Agriculture and Rural Development (NABARD), had held many meetings to discuss this issue.

At one level, this shows a high degree of good intentions of various stakeholders from the PM to FM to Ministry of Agriculture and NABARD to significantly raise farmers' incomes. It is, therefore, very heartening for those who have been trying to attract the attention of policymakers to the not-so-happy situation of farmers. But then one also needs to be realistic and analyse the situation as a professional, and point out various challenges to convert these good intentions into reality. However, as an optimist, one can always say that nothing is impossible, and where there is a will, there is a way. One hopes that these intentions are backed by solid strategy, ample resources, and a champion within the government to see that this dream of the PM is converted into reality and we see our farmers happy and prosperous over the next five years. That would surely incentivize them to give their best to the country by raising productivity of agriculture in a sustainable manner, and this will also help in alleviating poverty the fastest, as much of poverty (75 per cent) is concentrated in rural areas, where the main source of livelihood of the population is agriculture.

Making our peasantry prosperous is critical if one has to ensure that a population of 1.3 billion Indians is fed properly. Food security is likely to remain India's prime concern, especially so when India is likely to become the most populous country in the world, surpassing China, by 2024, as per UN population projections (revised, 2017). There are also projections by several multilateral institutions which state that for the next 10 years or so, Indian economy is likely to register an annual gross domestic product (GDP) growth of about 7–8 per cent. With an average Indian currently spending almost 45 per cent of his/her expenditure on food, rising incomes indicate tremendous pressures on limited land and water resources in the coming years. It is worth noting that India has 2 per cent of global area (though almost 10 per cent of gross cropped area) and 4 per cent of fresh water resources, but has to feed more than 17 per cent of the global population.

Higher incomes for farmers are also critical for the industry. Without a mass base for the demand for industrial products, industry faces demand constraint, which they experienced during back to back drought years of FY15 and FY16. So, a long-term healthy growth of industry also requires that farmers and farm wage workers all prosper, and they can prosper only when agriculture policies shift their focus from being just 'tonnage centric' to 'farmer centric'.

There could be various ways to raise farmers' incomes, but to do it in a manner that our agriculture remains globally competitive, inclusive of small holders, and environmentally and financially sustainable is a real challenge. Such a development model (and not a dole model), which satisfies these conditions of competitiveness, inclusiveness, sustainability, and scalability (CISS) has to draw on innovations all along the agri-value chains heavily, namely, innovations in policies, new technologies, farming practices, logistics, marketing, and even innovations in processing. And these innovations can be home grown, or brought in from different parts of the world as best practices, and then adapted to the local environment.

This chapter dwells on the issue of doubling farmers' incomes, the clarity needed, and challenges posed, but also goes further to explore various ways to make Indian agriculture more productive and sustainable. Accordingly, Section 5.2 dissects in brief the objective of doubling farmers' income in five years; Section 5.3 looks at the latest allocations of Union Budget FY18 across various schemes of GoI in the agri-food and rural space with a view to get a handle on what is the inherent strategy behind these budgets. In particular, we try to gauge whether it is a real development model or a dole model. In Sections 5.4 to 5.6, we talk about incentives, investments, and institutions that are impacting the performance of agriculture, and what changes are needed to bolster agri-growth and farmers' incomes in a sustainable manner. And finally, in Section 5.7 we talk of innovations and the way forward to achieve our multiple objectives.

5.2 DOUBLING FARMERS' INCOMES: THE OBJECTIVE AND ITS CHALLENGES

First and foremost is the need to clarify what one is talking about when one says 'doubling farmers' incomes in 5 years'. Is one talking of it in nominal terms or real terms? Whenever growth targets are set and talked about in the Union Budget, they are always in real terms (at constant prices). Initially, when the PM had expressed this as a 'dream', one was not sure whether he was talking of nominal incomes or real incomes. But the Dalwai Committee, which was set up in April 2016, has now come out with a report on doubling of farmers' income (DFI), and in that report it clearly states that the objective is to double farmers' real incomes and not nominal ones. Further, the report makes it clear that it is not within five years that the government is trying to double farmers' incomes, but the time horizon is seven years, with 2015–16 as the base year. So, in a seven years' time horizon, the compounded annual growth rate (CAGR) required to double farmers' real incomes is 10.4 per cent. The Dalwai Committee on DFI is slated to have prepared its report in 14 volumes. So far, as in January 2018, five volumes of 868 pages have been put in public domain with hundreds of recommendations. How many of those recommendations are likely to be accepted by the government is not yet clear. What is clear is that it would require stupendous effort to raise real incomes of farmers by 10.4 per cent per annum, almost three times faster than has been the case under business-as-usual (BAU) scenario during 2002–3 to 2012–13.

Since the latest year for which estimates for farmers' incomes are available is FY13 from the Situation Assessment Survey (SAS) of National Sample Survey Organization (NSSO), the Dalwai Committee projects these incomes to 2015–16 by using the growth rate in agri-GDP during FY13 to FY16. This gives a proximate income of farmers, but what is needed is a credible survey of farmers' incomes with a reasonably large size. We understand that NABARD has conducted such a survey with 2016–17 as the base year, which may throw better light on farmers' incomes.

In any case, let us see the magnitude of the challenge in achieving this target. A sense of this can only be gauged by looking at the past behaviour of farmers' incomes. The latest surveys (SAS of NSSO) that are available on this topic are of FY2003 and FY2013. We have computed the compound annual growth rates (CAGRs) of farmers' incomes between these two periods in nominal terms as well as in real terms (by deflating these nominal incomes by Consumer Price Index of Agricultural Labour [CPI–AL]) at the all-India level as well as for major states of India. Figure 5.1 presents these CAGRs in farmers' incomes.

The results indicate that the nominal incomes of farmers at the all-India level grew by 11.8 per cent per annum compound rate during this period, while the real incomes increased only by a CAGR of 3.5 per cent. There is no NSSO survey after FY13 on this subject and the survey by NABARD for FY17 is not yet out. However, if one projects real income growth by using the methodology adopted by the Dalwai Committee, we find that the CAGR of farmers' incomes actually came down during FY13 to FY18 to just 2.5 per cent, down from 3.5 per cent.

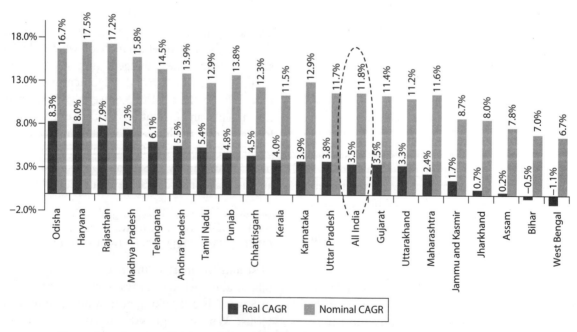

Figure 5.1   Compounded Annual Growth Rates of Farmer Incomes between 2002–3 and 2012–13

Source: Computed by authors based on data from Situation Assessment Survey (SAS), 59th and 70th Round, National Sample Survey Organization (NSSO) (2005 and 2014).

So, if the government is setting its target for doubling farmers' incomes in real terms even over a seven-year period (not five as is claimed in the Union Budget of FY18), it must realize that it requires raising this CAGR from 3.5 per cent during FY03 to FY13, or 2.5 per cent during FY13–FY18, to 10.4 per cent, which seems almost impossible to achieve under BAU scenario, or even with marginal changes in strategy. It would require complete overhauling of policies not only within agriculture but also in the non-agriculture sphere and massive infusion of investments; even then it is difficult to imagine, as on today, that such a dream can materialize. It does not inspire much confidence as nothing that dramatic has happened either in policies or in the budgets of the first three years of the National Democratic Alliance (NDA) government.

If one imagines that the remaining period of the NDA government ending in May 2019 will be most dramatic in terms of changing policies and commensurate investments in agriculture to achieve the objective of doubling real incomes of farmers by 2022, the question that will still arise is whether that much agri-produce can be absorbed within the system or can be competitively exported. In other words, would there be ready markets to absorb at least two to three times higher agri-production, if not more, without a collapse in their prices? The answer, most probably, is simply 'no'. We say this because even in this marketing season after the kharif harvest, during November 2016 to February 2017, farmers have been selling most of the fresh produce—especially vegetables, be it potatoes, tomatoes, onions, cauliflower, cabbage, green leafy vegetables, and so on—at less than Rs 5/kg in major *mandis* (markets), which does not even recover their costs fully. At places, farmers have discarded tomatoes and potatoes on roads as prices went as low as Re 1/kg. So, one can imagine where the prices would go if production doubles or triples, and how farmers' incomes would rise. This would be true even of those commodities that have been traditionally in short supply such as pulses, especially *tur* (pigeon pea) and urad, whose prices have tumbled with good harvest and have already gone below minimum support prices (MSPs). This surely cannot incentivize farmers to produce more of that commodity.

Many a times, government experts argue that to double farmers' incomes one should not look at the agri-GDP. Incomes can be enhanced through non-farm components of agri-households. In order to respond to this possibility, one has to first understand the structure of farmers' incomes and how it has changed during FY03 to FY13. Figure 5.2 gives this break-up at two points of time.

There are four components to farmers' incomes: (*a*) income from crop cultivation; (*b*) income from farming animals; (*c*) wages and salaries; and (*d*) income from non-farm businesses. It is interesting to see that while in FY03 almost 50 per cent of farmers' incomes came from crop cultivation and farming of animals, and the other half from wages, salaries, and non-farm-business, in FY13 the share of crops and animal husbandry increased to almost 60 per cent. The component of wages and salaries has wages coming from farming operations as well as non-farm. The Dalwai Committee projects that for doubling farmers' incomes by 2022, 69 to 80 per cent of incomes should come from within agriculture. That only shows that the opportunities for farmers to earn higher incomes from non-farm operations are very limited. The economy has not been growing in a manner that millions of farmers can move out of agriculture so easily in search of higher incomes. So, the larger focus of government policies in their endeavour to raise farmers' incomes has to be on agriculture, making it more profitable and productive in a sustainable manner. Is the system geared for that? Our answer, based on the reading of current situation, is 'only marginally'.

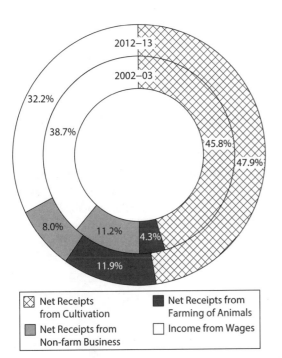

Figure 5.2   Changing Composition of Indian Farmer Incomes between 2002–3 and 2012–13

Source: Computed by authors from data in Situation Assessment Survey (SAS), 59th and 70th Round, National Sample Survey Organization (NSSO) (2005 and 2014).

5.3 UNION BUDGETARY ALLOCATIONS: A DOLE MODEL OR A DEVELOPMENT MODEL?

One critical area that has to be looked at in order to determine how serious the government is in terms of achieving its target of doubling farmers' incomes in seven years is the allocation of resources in the Union Budget. Does it allocate much higher resources to agriculture compared to previous years (BAU) or does it follow almost the same path with only marginal changes? Remember that the effort requires raising the CAGR of farmers' real incomes from 3.5 per cent during FY03 to FY13 to 10.4 per cent for the next seven years, with base year of FY16, as noted by the Dalwai Committee. This cannot be achieved without substantially raising the resources (at least doubling or tripling) going in as investments in agriculture.

Figure 5.3 gives the structure of allocations across major schemes of the Union government in the agri-food-rural space. We have organized these budgeted allocations into three categories: (*a*) safety nets; (*b*) input subsidies; and (*c*) investments that can propel growth in agriculture in a more efficient and sustainable manner.

It is clear from Figure 5.3 that much of the resources in agri-food-rural space go for safety nets, especially food subsidy and Mahatma Gandhi National Rural Employment Guarantee Act (MGNREGA), which together account for Rs 193,339 crore as against investments in and for agriculture (such as on agri-R&D and extension, rural roads, irrigation, rural power supplies, and so on), which add up to just Rs 32,103 crore. If one adds the pending bills of FCI on account of food subsidy (about Rs 50,000 crore), the resources flowing to safety nets increase further. However, in the agri-space, there is quite a substantial amount of resources (Rs 94,000 crore) that goes to subsidies on fertilizers, crop insurance, and interest subvention on agri-credit. The problem with this type of allocation—which is like putting the cart before the horse, that is, heavily tilting towards safety nets and subsidies instead of investments—is that it cannot change the trajectory of agri-growth in any significant manner than what has been going on for say the last 10 years or so under the BAU scenario. The agri-GDP growth during FY03 to FY13 has been 3.6 per cent per annum on average. And this certainly cannot help in doubling farmers' incomes by 2022.

One novel way that the Union Budget of FY18 has adopted with regard to raising investments in agriculture, however, is to allow NABARD to create a corpus

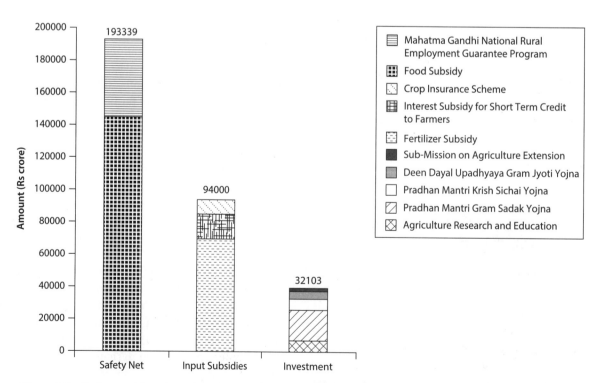

Figure 5.3   Budgetary Allocations across Major Safety Nets, Input Subsidies, and Agri-investments (FY18; in Rs Crore)
Source: Computed by the authors based on data from the Union Budget (expenditure statement).

of Rs 20,000 crore for faster completion of major and medium irrigation schemes. This is on top of last year's similar amount. Further, a corpus of another Rs 5,000 crore for micro irrigation and Rs 2,000 crore for milk processing plants (Rs 8,000 crore over three years) have been allowed with NABARD. This ingenious way of raising funds is commendable, as these non-budgetary resources, which will be given as loans to state governments, will surely help agriculture and thereby farmers. But will the state governments take these as loans, and are they large enough to push up growth rates in agriculture three times? One will have to wait and watch as to how far they help agriculture. However, the record of the first three years of the NDA government (FY15 to FY17) is that agri-GDP registered a growth of just 1.7 per cent per annum. This is dismally poor, even compared to the previous 10 years. It may be so partly because of back to back droughts in the first two years of NDA rule, but also because the price incentives that farmers are getting are too low, be it in the form of MSP from the government or market prices.

This brings us to the issue of incentives, which can power private investments in agriculture.

5.4 INCENTIVIZING FARMERS

Government policy tries to incentivize farmers primarily through output and input price policies. On the output side, GoI announces MSPs of 23 commodities, although effective support is provided through procurement primarily in case of wheat and rice, and very rarely for some other commodities.

It may be noted that the biggest crops in India, which occupy more than 70 million hectares (mha) of land, namely rice and wheat, are significantly impacted by the MSP regime in at least five to six states where procurement operations are significant (Punjab, Haryana, Andhra Pradesh, Madhya Pradesh, Chhattisgarh, and lately even Odisha). During the first three years of NDA rule, paddy and wheat MSP increases have been less than 5 per cent per year on average in nominal terms. With inflation rates averaging around the same, this indicates the rather stagnant position of real procurement prices.

Compared with some similar countries in terms of levels of MSPs, India's MSPs are way below those in other countries of south-east Asia, and certainly way below China. Figure 5.4 gives these prices for the year 2014–15, and the situation has not changed much since then. Indian price of rice, converted from MSP of paddy, is just US$ 330/MT compared to US$ 440/MT for Indica rice, and US$ 505/MT for Japonica rice, in China. Similarly, our wheat MSP (about US$ 227/MT) is way below China's US$ 385/MT and even that of Pakistan at US$ 320/MT. With such low MSPs, it is remarkable to see that Indian farmers still produce ample quantities of rice and

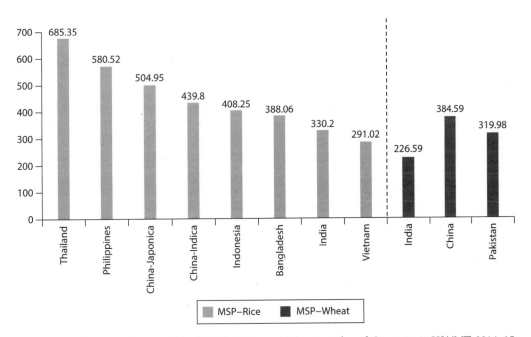

Figure 5.4   Minimum Support Price (MSP) of Rice and Wheat in Selected Countries in US$/MT, 2014–15

Source: Computed by authors from various country official sources.

wheat, so much so that India has been either the largest or second-largest exporter of rice in recent years.

It may be legitimate to argue that the government should not artificially jack up MSPs way beyond the global market prices as it may result in distorted cropping patterns that may not be sustainable in an open economy framework. What this means is that support prices should remain marginally below the normal trend of market prices. It also means that to incentivize farmers to invest and raise productivity, markets must be allowed to operate freely so that farmers can gain from those, especially when government is not able to give an effective floor price.

Let us take the case of pulses here. Pulses is an interesting case study which shows how government policy, despite having the best of intentions, failed over the last 25 years or so! And it is not likely to succeed unless drastic steps are taken to overhaul the policy framework for pulses.

It is well known that India is the largest producer, consumer, and importer of pulses. In a country where meat consumption is extremely low by international standards, partly because of religion and partly because of low incomes, pulses offer a good source of protein at a reasonably low cost, at least historically. Poor people's diets are colloquially called *dal-bhat* or *dal-roti* (pulses and rice or pulses and roti). No wonder the Government of India (GoI) always wanted to have self-sufficiency in pulses and adopted several schemes to do so, at least from 1990–1 onwards with a Mission on Pulses and Oilseeds. In 2007, pulses were merged with the National Food Security Mission. But despite these efforts for a long time, when India faced back to back droughts, in FY2015–16 prices of most of pulses increased astronomically, even becoming higher than the price of chicken! India had to import 5.8 MMT of pulses against a production of about 16.5 MMT. It was a clear failure of India's long-standing policy on pulses.

There were frantic efforts to revisit our strategy. The chief economic advisor (CEA) of the Government of India led a committee which concluded that pulse-growers must realize a price of at least Rs 6,000–7,000/quintal, if they have to switch from competing crops. The market prices in wholesale market were almost double of that, and in retail, almost triple of that level. So, Rs 6,000/quintal was considered as the rock bottom for farmers. The MSP for kharif pulses hovered between Rs 4,600–4,850/quintal at that time. But when MSPs for the marketing season 2016–17 were announced they were at Rs 5,050/quintal (including bonus) for tur and *urad* (black gram), and Rs 5,225/quintal for

moong (green gram). It was expected that market prices being much higher than MSPs will incentivize farmers to grow pulses anyway. The Government of India also decided to create a buffer stock of 2 MMT of pulses to stabilize their prices. It was envisioned that much of this stock will have to be created through imports as domestic production may remain under pressure. Accordingly, an MOU was signed with Mozambique for long-term import of pulses.

But what happened in 2016–17 is somewhat surprising. Farmers responded to high market price signals, and good rains helped to give a record output. The kharif pulses production increased dramatically. Tur, which had given sleepless nights to many just a few months back, registered a growth of 65 per cent, from 2.56 MMT to 4.23 MMT (see Figure 5.5)! As a result, tur prices started tumbling down despite some procurement by the government, and went even 15–20 per cent below MSP. Falling prices due to bumper domestic production, continued ban on international export, restrictions on private stockholding and futures' market, and uninterrupted import of pulses wiped out all profits of farmers, if there were any in the announced MSP. What would have happened in FY18 is anyone's guess. There is high probability that farmers will shift away from pulses and India will be back to imports! That in a nutshell speaks the story of incentives for farmers from output side.

What could have been done, and can still be done, to at least save chickpea from a similar impending crash (see Figure 5.5)? First, abolish stocking limits on private trade to hold stocks of any pulses; second, introduce all of them in futures markets; third, open up their exports; fourth, step up government procurement to build a buffer of 2 MMT; and fifth, impose import duty on pulses to ensure that landed prices of these pulses are not below their MSP. Unless these steps are taken up urgently, the pulses story will keep repeating year after year.

We must comment on one aspect of this policy, that is, government procurement of pulses to stabilize market prices through buffer stock operations. The Government of India has allocated Rs 500 crore for a Commodity Price Stabilization Fund. It should be noted that if the Government of India has to procure 2 MMT of pulses through its designated agencies, they will require not Rs 500 crore but Rs 10,000 crore as working capital. The Government of India should either set aside this amount in the budget or allow its procuring agencies to have a line of credit backed by government guarantee. Without this, it is not likely to take off. Further, it may be noted that the quality of pulses deteriorates fast, and it

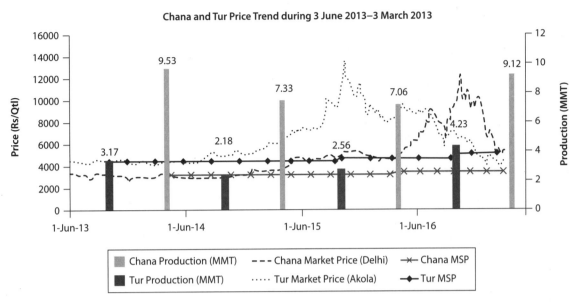

Figure 5.5   Tur and Chana Market Review

Source: Computed by authors from production and MSP data from Government of India and 'poll price' data from National Commodity and Derivatives Exchange.

needs specialized agencies to rotate them through open market operations rather quickly and on regular basis. Do the government agencies have that type of expertise? In this context, CEA's suggestion in its report of creating a new agency on public–private partnership may be worth giving a trial. But private agencies want quick disbursal of their due amounts, which the Government of India normally does not do, especially when open market operations incur losses. Even with the National Agricultural Cooperative Marketing Federation of India Ltd (NAFED) it has pending bills of more than Rs 1,000 crore. Third, the comptroller and auditor general (CAG) of India often comes down heavily on such operations that incur commercial losses, but this has to be treated as part of food subsidy for stabilization of prices. All this calls for institutional reforms, from the very basic thinking process to changes in several laws, especially the Essential Commodities Act of 1955.

But, before one talks of institutional reforms, one must also comment on the price incentives from the input side, especially fertilizer subsidies, power subsidies, credit subsidies, and lately subsidies on the premium for crop insurance. The problem with all these subsidies on the input front is that they lead to inefficient use of resources as also diversion of that resource to other countries and/or for non-agri purposes. There is ample literature on how low urea prices in India have led to its overuse in relation to P and K fertilizers, especially in certain pockets such as the Punjab–Haryana region. It has also led to its diversion to Nepal, as well as for non-agri purposes. Power subsidies are responsible for faster depletion of groundwater, and credit subsidies have also diverted agri-credit to non-agri uses. Our research also shows that a billion-dollar invested in agri-R&D, or rural roads, or irrigation, will give multiple times higher returns in terms of agri-GDP growth or poverty alleviation than the same amount being put in fertilizer or power or credit subsidies. This brings us to the topic of investments in and for agriculture.

5.5 INVESTMENTS IN AND FOR AGRICULTURE

Investments in agriculture are critical to improve productivity in a sustainable manner. As per standard United Nations (UN) system of national accounts, investments in agriculture, or also put as gross capital formation in agriculture (GCFA), comprise public and private sources. Public sources of GCFA primarily comprise investments in major and medium irrigation schemes, while private sources of GCFA comprise mainly investments by farmers for irrigation (tubewells, dug wells, and others) and farm machinery. It is interesting to see that in the early 1980s, the share of public and private sectors in overall GCFA was almost equal, as 50:50 (Figure 5.6). But since then, the share of the public sector has been consistently falling, and by early 2010s, it was only around 15 per cent. So, the real driver of investments in agriculture is primarily private-sector GCFA. And the private sector investments respond to profitability in agriculture. That's why price incentives for farmers are very critical if one is to see higher investments and thereby growth in agriculture. It may further be observed in Figure 5.6 that GCFA as per cent of agri-GDP had touched a rock bottom of about 8 per cent in the mid-1990s, but then it gradually improved and went all the way to more than 20 per cent in the early 2010s. However the latest data in *Economic Survey* show that in the last three years or so, it has come down to about 15–16 per cent, which should be a matter of concern to policymakers.

However, one limitation of this definition of investments in agriculture, as defined in standard UN system of accounts, is that it does not include many other investments which may have a strong influence on the performance of agriculture. For example, the expenditures on agri-R&D do not come under this definition, and so do not the investments in rural roads or rural power supplies. They are counted under separate heads, and many experts have included these under 'investments *for* agriculture' rather than 'investments *in* agriculture'. India's investments in rural roads have shown significant improvements, especially since the Pradhan Mantri Gram Sadak Yojana (PMGSY) has been launched. But expenditures on agri-R&D still languish way behind the norm of 1 per cent of agri-GDP for developing countries. The budgetary allocation for the Indian Council of Agricultural Research (ICAR), which is supposed to do research for a number of commodities for the whole country, normally hovers around Rs 6,000 crore (less than US$ 1 billion), while one company alone, Monsanto, spent more than US$ 1.7 billion on agri-R&D. So there is a case for raising resources for agri-R&D. But resources alone will not suffice. This must be coupled with institutional reforms of ICAR, where scientists will be incentivized and also made more accountable for their performance in terms of resources spent and outcomes achieved.

5.6 INSTITUTIONAL REFORMS NEEDED

Investments in any sector normally flourish when the main institutions (rules of the game) governing that sector are investment friendly. In case of agriculture, unfortunately, that is not the case. The ECA of 1955, under which one can impose stocking limits on private trade, discourages any significant investment in storage. Without much storage, prices of products remain volatile. Restrictive trade bans imposed in an ad-hoc and unpredictable manner further discourage the private sector and farmers as the profitability in the sector is adversely impacted. Agricultural produce market committees (APMCs) and associated high commissions and other charges have been another source of discouragement to various stakeholders to invest and add value. Restrictive land ceilings and land lease markets further add a depressing note. At least one third of farmers still do not have access to formal credit from banking and cooperative systems. They

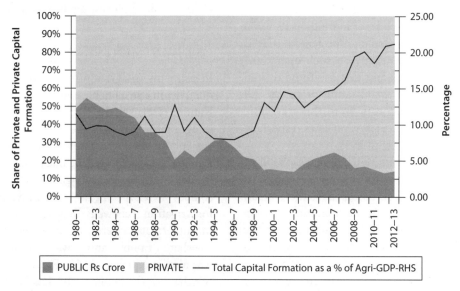

Figure 5.6 Investments in Indian Agriculture

Source: Computed by authors based on data from Ministry of Statistics and Programme Implementation, Government of India.

borrow from informal sources at double or even triple rates of interest, making agriculture an unviable proposition. The whole of this institutional framework needs a major overhauling as it is currently tilted more towards consumers, which goes against farmers' interests. Unless the Government of India, in association with state governments, has the vision and boldness to carry out this massive institutional change governing this sector, the chances that agri-growth and thereby farmers' incomes can double in seven years remains extremely low.

5.7 INNOVATIONS ARE THE WAY FORWARD

If we have to make our agriculture more profitable, productive, and sustainable, we will have to carry out innovations all along the agri-value chains.

First, there is a need to innovate in the sphere of agri-food policies. The policy of massively subsidizing food and fertilizers, for example, needs to be replaced with a direct benefit transfer (DBT) policy. In principle, the Government of India has already moved ahead putting at least 84 schemes under DBT, which the government claims has saved about Rs 50,000 crore. However, so far the biggest food and fertilizer subsidies have remained outside this move. The earlier one converts these into income support policy through DBT, the better it is for the country. Our estimates reveal that there could be savings of about Rs 50,000 crore annually as much of the leakages and diversions will be plugged, and these savings, if invested in irrigation and better water management, can ensure India's food security for the next two decades or even more.

Second, the requirement is for innovations in technology and moving from green to gene technology—India has seen how Bt cotton has benefited the country, making India the second-largest exporter of cotton. Our estimates reveal that India gained about US$ 55 billion during 2002–3 to 2014–15 with this new technology compared to the BAU scenario. But India has dithered in introducing Bt brinjal and GM mustard for commercial purposes. As there is a saying that justice delayed is justice denied, similarly in agriculture, if this new technology is delayed, it denies prosperity to farmers. The world is now moving towards high-zinc wheat and rice, iron-rich pearl millet, and so on under bio-fortified research. Most of them (except Golden Rice) are non-GMO. India can at least take a major leap in this, given the high incidence of iron deficiency in the country and high rates of stunting amongst children under five years of age.

Third, the revolution on the anvil is the 'Brown Revolution', which takes care of sustainability concerns with higher productivity and higher profitability. This revolution comprises precision agriculture, drips and sprinkler irrigation giving more crop for every drop of water, protected cultivation, tissue culture, use of sensors, drones, doves, robotics, putting up grid-connected solar panels on the field that could form the third crop for a farmer, solar-based cold storages in rural areas, digital dissemination of agri-information, and Internet of Things (IoT). Many of these are disruptive technologies being used in different parts of the world, including some pilots in India, which need to be scaled up to take Indian agriculture to version 2.0.

Fourth, the government needs to innovate in finding alternative sources of income for its farmers. While innovating to find ways to hedge the current income levels, government policymakers have to unearth ways for ensuring its sustainable growth too. The former can be done by introducing crop insurance schemes, by assuring deeper and wider physical markets, and by ensuring well-functioning, stable financial markets that reflect correct market signals to a farmer. Aggregation of producers across agri-sector through platforms like farmer producer organizations (FPOs) is an apt medium that has evolved in this regard. Visualizing integration of the spot and derivatives markets for farm produce under e-NAM (a pan-India electronic trading portal) will be a vital step too.

Further, to increase farmer incomes, the government can encourage the concept of a third crop, where apart from the two standard crops in a year, a farmer invests in sowing a third crop. Now, this third crop can be grid-connected solar panels that are put up at a height of 10–15 feet on farmers' fields. Without affecting crop yields, these panels will support the farmer's power needs and by selling the residual power to the grid will also help the farmer earn some extra money.

Diversifying to more remunerative and sustainable crops and animal husbandry is another way to augment farmers' incomes. Dairying and cultivating fruit and vegetables in particular offer a large scope. But in the absence of ample storage and processing facilities, they also bring in higher risks. Innovations in food processing such as dehydration of fruit and vegetables need to be given a much bigger push than has been the case so far. So is the case for dairy processing.

Finally, with farm labour becoming scarce and expensive, farm mechanization is inevitable. But given our small holding size, owning a large tractor, for example, may not be financially feasible for a farmer. It is, therefore, important to innovate and one such option is offered by extending the concept of Uber cars to farm machinery (popularly referred to as 'uberization' of farm machinery). Instead of buying machinery, if the farmers can rent it in exchange of a reasonable fee, farmers benefit in terms of lower costs of production (where machine replaces the more-expensive labour) and higher yields. Some companies like Mahindra and Mahindra, TAFE, EM3, and others have taken a lead in this, but to scale it up quickly, one has to do much more.

India's agri-growth has not been constrained by its policymakers' intents but by its inability to reform incentives for farmers, the nature of subsidies and investments in and for agriculture, and institutions dealing with the agri-food-rural space. If the Government of India can bite the bullet and overhaul these areas, a much prosperous India awaits, one that is competitive, inclusive, and sustainable. Else, we are afraid, Indian farmers and Indian agriculture will keep limping at a sub-optimal level, and big targets like doubling of farmers' incomes in seven years will remain only political slogans without much credibility.

6

Designing Farmer Producer Organizations for Sustainability of Smallholder Farmers

Amar K.J.R. Nayak*

ABSTRACT

This chapter discusses the five key design variables of a farmer producer organization (FPO) and their dynamic inter-relationships. The five key variables include Size, Scope, Technology, Ownership, and Management. It discusses the broad contours or optimal position of each design variable of an FPO such that it evolves as a sustainable community enterprise system and can serve as a single-window service centre to all farmers/producers in a cluster of village(s) or a Gram Panchayat (GP). The chapter also highlights the design issues of the externalities in terms of market landscape, institutional architecture of an FPO in a district, and convergence of development schemes that would be synergistic to the internal design of FPO and facilitate sustainability of an FPO and its producer members.

JEL Classification: Q01

Keywords: size, scope, technology, ownership and management

6.1 INTRODUCTION

Farmers and agriculture in India have been going through a very dynamic process of change during the last few decades. Smallholder farmers who constitute over 85 per cent of farmers in India seem to be under high risk in the recent years. In addition to the traditional 'monsters' of agriculture, namely, monsoon and markets, newer 'monsters' such as increasing cost of agricultural inputs, high cost of labour, and high health costs have been making farmers and agriculture increasingly vulnerable every season. With increasing risk among farmers; risk to banks and formal credit lending agencies has been high; reducing the credit access to smallholder farmers.

To deal with the numerous uncertainties in agriculture among smallholder farmers, organizing farmers to form producer cooperatives, collectives, and producer

*Professor of Strategic Management and NABARD Chair Professor, XIMB, Xavier University Bhubaneswar, India.

organizations have been well understood to be a solution globally and in India for a long time. Producer organizations, in the form of producer cooperatives, have existed for over a hundred years in India. The Primary Agricultural Cooperative Society (PACS) is one of the oldest forms of producer organizations in India. In addition to the cooperatives, there have been many other forms of producer organizations catering to specific or multiple function(s) such as self-help groups (SHGs), federation of SHGs, common interest groups (CIGs), joint liability groups (JLGs), farmers' club, producer organizations, and producer companies.

The Government of India, the National Bank for Agriculture and Rural Development (NABARD), Ministry of Rural Development, Ministry of Agriculture, Small Farmer Agribusiness Consortium (SFAC), and state governments have been investing largely in these organizations in the recent decades. NABARD started to support producer organizations through its Producer Organization Development Fund (PODF). Subsequently, with the Government of India special fund, namely, PRODUCE Fund, it has systematically deepened its support to establish producer companies (PCs) in the country.

International development agencies such as the World Bank, International Fund for Agricultural Development (IFAD), Food and Agriculture Organization (FAO) of the United Nations, United Nations Development Programme (UNDP), Rabobank Foundation, and others have been gradually investing in FPOs especially in the PCs. Some of the Indian banks such as Yes Bank and HDFC have given special focus to support FPOs and farmers' collectives. Many non-governmental organizations (NGOs) have been roped in to facilitate formation of producer organizations in the country.

An FPO is a generic name that represents different forms of community organizations/enterprises such as large cooperatives, PACS, SHG, federation of SHGs, CIGs, farmers clubs, producer companies, and so on. A producer company is a special case of producer enterprise that is registered under Section IXA of the Companies Act, 1956.

FPOs have existed both as formal legal entities and informal entities. They have also varied in size in terms of membership and geographic spread. While the objective of all these entities have been to improve the wellbeing of farmers, there has been no clarity on the design dimensions of such organizations in terms of their policies and practices. Design thinking and research on producer cooperatives have been limited to governance and management. PCs, as per Section IXA of the Companies Act, have considered ownership issues at the core

of their design. However, the dynamic interrelationships among the different design variables of FPOs have not been studied systematically.

This chapter discusses five key variables of an FPO and the dynamic interrelationships among these variables. Accordingly, it will provide the broad contours of each design variable such that the FPO evolves as a sustainable community enterprise system and can serve as a single-window service centre to all farmers/producers in a cluster of villages. So long as the internal design of an FPO is based on long-term sustainability, its legal identity—cooperative, society, or company—shall have little impact. The chapter also highlights the externalities that would be synergistic to the internal design and facilitate the sustainability of an FPO.

6.2 CONTEXT OF FARMERS AND AGRICULTURE IN INDIA

6.2.1 Rising Risk among Farmers

Distress among farmers has been a growing phenomenon over the years across the country. From a recent three-district sample study consisting of about 2,100 farmers (Nayak, Peppin, and Misra 2016), we find that the average net income of farmers in irrigated clusters is more negative than that of farmers in rain-fed clusters. However, the composite risk ratio[1] of farmers in irrigated clusters is lower as compared to that of farmers in rain-fed clusters. The relative risk ratios on different dimensions are, however, different in irrigated and rain-fed clusters. For instance, in irrigated clusters, land preparation, post-harvest, and value addition appear to be most risky, and in this order. In rain-fed clusters, marketing appears to be the most risky followed by on-farm crop and animal management and then credit. Among the different social (scheduled) groups, tribal farmers (ST) are most in risk; followed by Scheduled Caste (SC) farmers, Other Backward Classes (OBC) farmers, Brahmin farmers, and other farmers.

6.2.2 Risk of Banks and Lending Agencies

As the overall risk among farmers increasees, risk to bankers and credit-lending agencies also increases. From the recent three-district sample study we find that all formal banks are in risk, in the following order: cooperative banks, commercial banks, and regional rural banks (RRBs). The most risky lenders are the informal credit lenders namely, local *sahukar*s (creditors), family and

---

[1] Σ (average vulnerability/average capability)

friends, and local traders who charge an average interest rates in the range of 41–5 per cent. The most needy farmers usually seek such credit for emergency situations related to health and food requirements. Cross-country empirical data also show a rise in the share of credit lending from informal sources. A nuanced look at the category of moneylenders (local sahukars relatives/friends, local traders, SHGs, and money lenders) throws up more interesting features. Local sahukars who provide multiple services such as credit (agricultural production, consumption, and emergency credit) supply agricultural inputs including agricultural machinery on hire basis, and procure all marginal surplus produce of different grades have the highest share of lending among rural/agricultural credit lenders. Unfortunately, even now we do not have any government entity or community organization which provides such a single-window doorstep service to farmers and rural poor.

6.2.3 Non-adherence to the Science of Long-Term Efficiency in Agriculture

Agriculture is visibly a highly interconnected and inter-dependent system of production and its output is a result of deep and dynamic relationships among various living and non-living organisms in a micro ecosystem. More than the external industrial inputs of inorganic fertilizers, chemicals pesticides, and high-yielding terminator seeds, simultaneous management of local seed, soil, and moisture, mixed crops, and integration of agriculture with livestock and forestry can make agriculture safe, enjoyable, and prosperous. The global community's increasing acceptance of agricultural scientists focusing on agroecology as a way forward to sustainability in agriculture validates this point. *Diversity* is indeed the key to sustainability of agriculture and smallholder farmers (Lundgren and Scott 2015; Nayak, Nayak, and Panda 2016), and the best possible inbuilt insurance against climate and market risks. Violation of this principle only makes agriculture less efficient and farmers more vulnerable over time. Therefore, agricultural policy and research in India needs to seriously focus on diverse production systems at the farm and village level for sustainability of farmers and agriculture.

6.2.4 Lack of Convergence at the Local Level and Dysfunctional Signalling

In about the last four decades, both the national government and state governments have been rolling out a number of development schemes, and the average budgetary support at the GP level approximates to about Rs 20,000,000 per annum. Implementation of these schemes by multiple departments and agencies with little convergence and high information asymmetries at the grass-roots level has led to dysfunctional signalling. This process has led to opportunistic behaviour among people within the community, which disables the coordination process, making community organizations ineffective and inefficient. With poor coordination and lower social capital, the transaction cost of public service delivery has become expensive and sub-optimal (Nayak 2014b). Therefore, convergence of all development schemes at the GP-level FPO can indeed heal several contradictions that may exist in policy, technology, and markets, and make agricultural/rural communities sustainable in five to seven years.

6.2.5 Imperfect Institutions at the Local Level

In the agriculture sector, which is highly externality dependent, realization of net incomes by farmers appears to be heavily reliant on on the efficiency and effectiveness of local institutions that provide agricultural inputs, including credit, market agricultural surplus, and act as a single-window doorstep service provider for other services including health, basic entitlements, and basic infrastructure. Indeed with greater externalization of agricultural activities, the risk of credit lending to farmers now hinges heavily on either the presence or the absence of well-functioning institutions of farmers/producers at the community level. The critical need for such a last-mile well-functioning local institution for farmers has been highlighted by all major studies on agriculture in India, including the 12th Five Year Plan (2012–17).

6.2.6 Lack of Institutional Architecture to Balance Global Markets with Local Producers

During the last three centuries of industrial revolution, we have adopted *economies of scale* to resolve our large economic problems. Ironically, these have led to greater economic recession, market failures, climate change, food crises, and the growing un-sustainability of our ecosystem. While 'economies of scale' is an efficient means of industrial production; it does not seem to be so for agricultural production, which thrives on diversity. Therefore, the logic of *scale economies* of industrial product markets when applied to agricultural produce through a price signalling mechanism distorts the practice of agricultural production. Signalling of this logic has transformed the traditional diversified agricultural system to a mono-cropping system, which is no more efficient but survives on huge amounts of government subsidies across industrial countries. Empirical evidences from smallholder farmers and FPOs from across India show that adopting *economies of scope* in agriculture is not only more efficient for nutritious food production and better for the climate but also ensures sustainability of agricultural ecosystems and the overall socio-economic environment. In this context, the growing international trading of agricultural products and increasing food miles globally needs deeper review.

6.2.7 Credit-Intensive External Agri-inputs at the Root of Small Farmers' and Agricultural Crisis

From the overall analysis it appears that farmers suffer most from the externalities arising from either the production input side (seeds, manure, and water) or after crop harvest (value addition and marketing). However, the root cause of risk at the production phase is the gradual externalization of the internal capabilities of farmers whether it is in terms of seeds, manure, or farm labour. The greater dependency of farmers on external markets to procure these capabilities has made farmers more dependent on external credit. In other words, the *externalization of internal capabilities of farmers* is the root cause of increasing dependence on credit and rising vulnerability with every passing season (Nayak 2015c, 2016; Nayak, Peppin, and Misra 2016).

6.3 REVIEW OF LITERATURE

The present discussion on Farmer Collectives or FPOs is a continuation to the discourse, policy, and practice of cooperatives in India. Cooperative as a way of organization in India goes back to over a 110 years when the first cooperative act was legislated in British India in 1904. While the international principles of cooperation seem to have been adopted successfully by several great cooperators in this domain, design thinking has not been common. Shah (2015) explains this phenomenon and argues that the dominant thought among promoters and policy drivers of cooperatives in India has been more extrinsic than intrinsic. He argues that the promotional process of today's farmers' PCs provides little evidence of 'design thinking' towards 'transforming existing conditions into preferred ones' as conceived by Herbert Simon (1969) and later popularized by Rolf Faste in the 1980s.

Literature on design thinking in cooperatives in India until around 2010 has been quite limited. *Catalysing*

Cooperation: Design of Self-Governing Organisations by Shah (1996) seems to be the only significant work in India on the subject during these years. The model of an ideal cooperative is built on three key dimensions: member-user, governance structure, and operating systems. Shah refers to four design principles namely, choose an appropriate purpose central to members, get the right operating system, ensure patronage-cohesive governance, and secure, retain, and continually nurture member allegiance. These issues were also referred to as key areas of research in the 2015 Institute of Rural Management Anand (IRMA) producer collectives workshop (Malla and Singh 2015).

Till recently, research on cooperation in India has not extended much beyond the above design principles. However, since around 2010, research on cooperative design has picked up. In the global context, interestingly, after almost 300 years of the competitive logic of the Industrial Revolution, which apparently show signs of global un-sustainability, there has been a resurgence in research on cooperative logic, social enterprises, and solidarity economy from the beginning of the twenty-first century.

In the Indian context, the Department of Economic Analysis and Research (DEAR) of NABARD supported an action research project during 2009–11 on building a community-based, community-paced, community-owned, and community-managed enterprise system. The focus of this was to find the optimal design positions of key variables—size, scope, technology, management, and ownership—such that an FPO can be sustainable. Most importantly, this research took a systems view to community organization rather than as a mere independent entity that is concerned about its shareholders. Subsequently, DEAR supported an all-India study during 2011–13 on the status and performance of PCs. Based on these research studies, various design and policy issues of community enterprise systems, collectives, PCs, and FPOs have emerged in the recent years.

Nayak (2010a, 2011, 2013a, 2014, 2015a, 2015b; Nayak et al., 2012) discusses five internal organization design variables: size, scope, technology, management, and ownership. Figure 6.1 highlights the design issues that are relevant not only to producer organizations of farmers in the primary sector but also to industrial organizations in the secondary sector and service providers in the tertiary service sector.

Interestingly, the characteristics of the design variables seem to show a dynamic relationship with each other. As an illustration let us see how the five variables of organizational design, of size, scope, technology, ownership, and management, are dynamically interconnected with each other in the specific case of say an FPO (a cooperative or PC).

As we increase the organizational size in terms of membership and geographic spread, the scope of activities in the organization tends to get limited. In other words, as the size increases the organization tends to become specialized. As it tends to become specialized, it cannot but rely more on technologies, which leads to subsequent technology intensification in the organization. As the process and product technology intensifies or is required, it does not come free to the organization but does so through huge investments. These investments are brought in by some investors who would like to take ownership position in the organization either directly or indirectly through greater management control. With more capital inflow to the firm, ownership and management structure gradually gets modified and often shifts in favour of major investors. As the four variables shift towards one side of the spectrum (to far right as in Figure 6.1), that is, size increases, specialization increases, technology intensifies, and ownership-management is concentrated, the producer organization has to adopt a very complex management structure to reduce transaction costs. Interestingly, these interconnected changes could be initiated by a change in any one of these four variables; say a process or product technology intensification can lead to subsequent shift towards specialization and so on.

On the one hand; when the size grows, specialization increases, technology intensifies, ownership–management gets concentrated, and management gets complex, an organization often emerges to be a large multinational corporations. Unfortunately, large corporations seem to show signs of unsustainability. Several historical research studies (Schumpeter 1943; Vernon 1971, 1977, 2009; and Nayak 2011) on large multinational corporations around the world tend to make this point. Is the recent bankruptcy of Fagor, flagship unit of Mondragon Cooperative Group a result of such dynamics? Are the internal tensions in India's best cooperative, Amul, due to design flaws?

On the other hand, when these variable positions are at another end of the spectrum (to the far left, as in Figure 6.1), we get small informal organizations such as SHGs or small primary cooperatives in India. While SHGs have been good social units among economically backward women, they do not seem to be technically viable to undertake more than some limited functions. So it appears that one of the challenges to the sustainability of producer organizations has been to find optimal positions of the design variables. Small is indeed beautiful (Schumacher 1973); however, what would be an optimal organizational/community size in the current challenging context to facilitate the transition towards making a farmers' collective sustainable?

In addition to internal design variables, external design variables such as market landscape (Nayak 2012), institutional architecture of FPOs in a district for the stable relationship between small producers and large markets (Nayak 2013c, 2014b), and convergence of various development schemes of farmers and rural poor with optimal GP-level community enterprise system or an

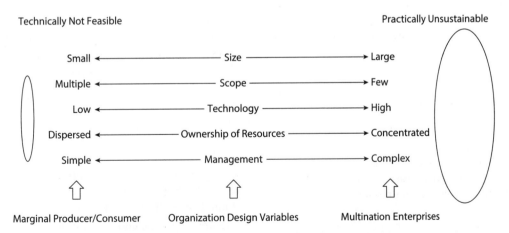

Figure 6.1 Factors of Organizational Design

Source: Nayak (2010).

FPO (Nayak 2013c; Nayak and Panda 2016) have also been highlighted from these previous studies supported by DEAR.

While the criticality of these internal and external variables are known, being discussed, and being implemented in bits and pieces in different cooperative and FPO experiments, the simultaneous optimization of these variables has not been attempted either in theory or in practice. While several larger dimensions of FPOs have become clearer over the years through soiling of hands by experts, donors, banks, and development agencies, there are a few macro-level dimensions and many micro-level issues of implementation which need to be clearly understood. Most importantly, clarity on the interconnected relationship among these dimensions is crucial to realize better outcomes from the collectives/producer organizations of the smallholder farmers.

All working in the domain of collectives, cooperatives, and community enterprise systems express the significance of member interest and their participation for success of these organizations. Among the various development schemes whether for drought proofing, poverty alleviation, or overall improvement of quality of life implemented by the Government in India, we find that the strongest factor for sustainability is that of people's participation (Nayak 2010b).

Participation can be further reduced to frequency of interactions in terms of business transactions and social transactions for a producer organization as seen in successful dairy cooperatives or in successful SHGs in the Indian experience. Nayak (2013b) highlights the significance of designing FPOs that facilitate greater frequency of interactions among members. Further, Nayak (2013b) describes the significance of relationship to sustainability as follows:

Sustainability is a dynamic state of deep relationships among the people and all the constituents both living and non-living within a micro ecological unit that strongly values the acts of sacrifice, reciprocity and love for each other; where the priority is to strengthen the weakest and the spirit of high external cooperation and high internal competition not only drives its own ecological unit to eternal peace, joy and happiness but also inspires other micro ecological units for such deeper inter relationships.

The foundation of people's participation in any collective, cooperative, community enterprise system, or producer organization, however, seems to rest on 'trust' or 'social capital'. This is common sense and has been brought out in a variety of literature across the world. From game theory analysis in competitive environments, to evolutionary biologists' perspectives on survival of life on earth (Nowak and Highfield 2011), to theological studies, all reiterate the significance of trust. Ostrom (1990) in *Governing the Commons* and Nayak (2010a, 2013b, 2014c, 2016a on recreating sustainable community enterprise systems emphasize the criticality of this dimension for self-governing cooperative systems. The criticality of trust for the long-term success of FPOs was expressed by many scholars and practitioners during the 2016 national Round Table Discussion (RTD) on optimal design of FPOs (Nayak and Panda 2016). On the whole, FPOs need to be designed to produce trust among members within a community, which in turn can sustainably produce financial capital, create wealth, and ensure well-being among people.

The internal design variables for the sustainability of FPOs include *size* of membership and geographic cluster, *scope* of product basket, services, and activities base, *technology* of agricultural production and processing, *management* systems, processes, and governance mechanisms, and *ownership* structure and sense of belongingness. The external design issues include *market landscape, institutional architecture* of cooperatives or farmer producer companies (FPCs) in a district, and *convergence* of various development schemes in a GP-level FPO.

Among these eight design issues, the issues of ownership and management have been discussed the most during the last about two decades. Alagh Committee, 2001, clarified *ownership* structure in farmers' producer companies. The dysfunctional managerial interference from local politicians in dairy cooperatives in Gujarat was the stimulant to the legislation of cooperatives as a PC. Section IXA of the Companies Act, 1956, provided equity participation of only producer members in a PC. The one member one vote policy was also introduced. Producers can include farmers, fishermen, forest produce gatherers, artisans, and craftspeople who engage directly with nature to produce or gather something.

In his writings, Alagh (2015)—and Nayak and Panda in the 2016 RTD on FPOs—however, laments that the spirit of ownership by producers and the interest of producer members as the basis of PCs seem to get diluted over the years. He expressed concern over the attempt of private enterprise to use these people's cooperatives for the sake of their own profit. That producer organizations or cooperatives are to be owned by the members, however, is clear among the various stakeholders in the sector. Further, the other design variables need to be optimized such that the members develop an increasing sense of ownership in the producer organization.

The issue of *management* has been raised the most by facilitators and promoters of PCs. The Vaidyanathan Committee on Primary Agricultural Cooperatives (2004) provides a detailed account on the issues of management in these primary cooperatives that are applicable to small FPOs. Vaidyanathan (2013) recommends the creation of sanctions and incentives to promote healthier management practices such as (a) training of personnel and (b) motivating and facilitating efficient and well-managed societies to introduce structural and managerial reforms to become models of true cooperatives that promote thrift, manage loans and repayments efficiently, and use surpluses for the collective benefit of their members. The significance of training and capacity building was reiterated by all the promoting agencies of FPOs and senior policy executives during the 2016 RTD on FPOs.

Nayak et al. (2012) critiqued the management methods as taught in schools of rural management that have contributed the maximum service to this sector in providing professionals to the cooperatives, and producer collectives and PCs in India. He argues that the language, logic, and values of paradigm of competition are contrary to the paradigm of cooperation and that these schools in their curriculum have not carefully segregated them and do not train the students accordingly. The tools, techniques, and business frameworks of traditional business schools are often taught in schools of rural management without much critique and modifications. Management @ Grassroots (Nayak et al. 2012) provides an alternative to the management curriculum, where individual courses are consistent with the language, logic, and values of the paradigm of cooperation.

The issue of size of organizations in general, that 'small is beautiful', goes back to the 1970s (Schumacher 1973). However, caution about the smaller size of cooperatives in India goes back to the early 1900s (Reserve Bank of India 1915) and was later repeated in the 1960s (Mehta 1960). These were recommendations of committees appointed to study the working of PACSs in India.

Nayak (2013c, 2014c, 2015a, 2015b) has argued for a member size of about 1,000 small and marginal producers within a geographic cluster size of 2–4 micro-watershed areas. The geographic cluster size will depend on whether the producer organization is in a well-irrigated cluster, a coastal region, a non-irrigated plain, or in a rain-fed hilly region. It is generally observed that only about 30–50 per cent members will actively participate in such cooperatives in the early years of its formation. To make matters simple for all stakeholders, Nayak argues for a GP-level producer organization to be optimal, as the boundary of a GP is somewhat coterminous with the desired conditions of size and that such a geographic boundary is also easily understandable and identifiable by most of the stakeholders. Nayak in the above-mentioned literature argues that this design feature is essentially a mechanism to balance social capital and financial capital for a producer organization. At this level of size, it is also possible for the local management to deal with the complex needs of small producer members. FPOs could begin small and gradually optimize their number of members (Nayak and Panda 2016).

The issue of *scope* can be assessed from the diversity of activities of a producer organization. Though diversity has been the basis of sustainability for agriculture and smallholder farmers, the logic of diversity is usually ignored when it comes to product basket choice of producer organizations that are primarily to serve the interest of small producers. The success of Amul has been reiterated to suggest the single-product strategy for a producer cooperative or company. The three principles of member interest, operating systems, and governance structure (Shah 1996, 2015) have indeed worked well for Amul and its financial performance has been good since its inception. However, recent data (Nayak 2014a) shows that nearly 10 per cent of members have withdrawn from Amul. More than 70 per cent of members have fewer than five cows, and Amul has been procuring milk from non-members within and outside Gujarat to meet its operational requirements.

Nayak (2013a, 2014c, 2016e) argues that *economies of scope* or *diversity of product basket* is the way out to design for greater frequency of interactions and larger number of business transactions among members for non-dairy-, non-fishery-, agriculture-based producer organizations. While there was not much dialogue on this issue for long, many executives and practitioners today appreciate the need for adopting the multiple product basket strategy for producer organizations. Interestingly, Amalsad, a 75-year-old cooperative working in just 17 contiguous villages in Gujarat with diversity in product basket and services has indeed shown success and resilience (Nayak 2014a, 2016).

This has a direct significance to the nature of agricultural production *technology*. The production technology that facilitates diversity is sustainable agricultural systems (Nayak, Nayak, and Panda 2016), which takes into account the synergy across soil health, in situ water conservation, genetically stable seeds, agricultural diversity, and ecology. The process technology also needs to be appropriate as high value addition in agriculture could lead to nutritional loss in case of agricultural produce.

For instance, polished rice and polished pulses have less nutrition than unpolished rice and whole pulses.

Now, we come to *market landscape*. Shah (2015) writes that Amul and the recently formed milk PCs by the National Dairy Development Board (NDDB) have done well because of their market-product approach. Based on the opportunity in the market, these FPOs developed their business plan and organized farmers accordingly. This sounds logical as the raw material collection for dairy-based PCs is only milk. However, should this mean that the priority of an FPO (with non-dairy and non-fishery produce) be the market over existing produce and capabilities of farmers, especially the small and marginal farmers who practise subsistence farming? Would such a market-oriented approach have a negative 'scale effect' on FPOs and would subsequent mono-cropping effect smallholder farmers through higher price signals for growing mono crops in any given cluster? How will such scale economies of product impact the market landscape strategy, associated transaction costs for an FPO, and overall net income to producer members in the medium to long run? More importantly, will this market-product strategy adversely impact the other design variables of an FPO, making it a product company rather than a PC? Empirical evidence does show that most producer organizations tend to become product companies over a period of—five to seven years and subsequently become unviable for the producer members.

Drawing on the experiences of several producer organizations across the country, Nayak (2012) argues that limiting market landscape is important for nascent FPOs including PCs and cooperatives to reduce the characteristic distance (Nayak 2013c) between small and marginal producers, and market to be able to reduce transaction costs and increase net income to the producers. Nayak (2012) also argues that for long-term sustainability, an FPO should not break the basic principle of sticking to the interest of the producer members and could avoid transforming itself to become a mere product company arising out of its efforts to comply with the needs of distant commodity markets.

Many practitioners and policy executives shared their experiences of optimal market landscape for small producers during the 2016 RTD on FPOs. Mulukanoor dairy cooperative and weaver cooperatives in Srikakulam have benefited by adopting nearby compact markets. Government policy in Odisha was to connect producer groups of *dal* (lentils) with local school consumption (Krishnagopal 2016; Nayak and Panda, 2016).

The three-tier *institutional architecture* of primary cooperatives in the Amul model is a live demonstration of successful institutional architecture of primary cooperatives. Similarly, the institutional architecture of credit delivery cooperatives, namely, PACS also has a similar working structure. A similar thought on institutional architecture for the GP-level FPOs is yet to be seriously discussed. Nayak (2013c, 2014c) suggests a three-tier architecture of PCs at GP level, which engages in multiple produce–service activities and basic value addition and local marketing. A block-level PC; formed with the membership of all the GP-level PCs in the respective block could engage in higher value addition of perishable produce. Finally, the district-level PC formed with the membership of all block-level PCs could undertake marketing of surplus produce from the district to large commodity buyers. This will also help adopt a saturation strategy of GP-level FPOs in a block and district subsequently. Some thoughts on this emerged during the 2016 RTD on FPOs. FPOs at GP level could be registered as a cooperative and its higher-level federation could be registered as PCs (Nayak and Panda 2016).

Lack of *convergence* in the development schemes appears to have been the main cause of ineffective coordination and poor efficiency in people's institutions, collectives, and producer organizations. Nayak (2014b) argues that despite huge funds being available for the development of rural agricultural communities, lack of convergence at the grass-roots level has a mixed and confusing signalling effect on the people, leading to opportunistic behaviour and distrust among them towards various schemes of the government. This phenomenon appears to be the biggest threat to any form of collective action by the weak, small, and marginal producers in today's context. Convergence of resources at the GP-level FPO and district-level saturation model through the three-tier institutional architecture may be a way out from the present *chakravyuha*[2] of smallholder farmers and Indian agriculture. Contradictions in individual policies of the government(s), if any, could be resolved if the development programmes were converged at a GP-level FPO and if people at this grass-roots level could decide on the process of implementation.

Some important observations were made during the 2016 RTD discussions (Nayak and Panda 2016). The efforts of putting up FPOs would be in vain if the government did not create an enabling environment for grass-root level decision-making. In addition to convergence in agriculture policy, there is a need for synchronization of programmes. Further, there is a need for

---

[2] It is a labyrinth, an ancient circular battle formation, or a circular trap as in Indian mythology.

district-level planning for making convergence feasible. Ostrom (1990) in other words argued that external agencies including government need to respect the norms set by the people of a community for better management of their common properties.

The complex interrelationships among the five internal variables and three external variables discussed earlier make the design for sustainability very challenging. Many, in this context would like to believe that 'one size does not fit all' and hence would pay little attention to the possibility of better organizational design. In the absence of a model with all these design features in place, it only appears theoretical to presume the sustainability of FPOs if these design issues are dealt with. Kanitkar (2016) accordingly considers FPOs, as of today, works in progress and would like them to evolve further before we can figure out what makes them most sustainable. It is also suggested that optimal designs be considered instead of optimal design of FPOs; a point that brings forth the significance of context and how the design features could vary for FPOs in different contexts (Figure 6.1, Nayak and Panda 2016).

In the context of the present dilemma on the usefulness of common design dimensions, it may be worthwhile to differentiate the variations that are visible at the phenomenon level from the existence of common principles at the core of these phenomena. In other words, it may be prudent to consider different sustainable design principles on size, scope, technology, management, ownership, market landscape, convergence, and institutional architecture from assigning specific numbers of each of these design variables. For practical purposes, each of the design variables could have a range, and its specificity may be determined in a given context.

I presume that our inability to optimally design the above-mentioned five internal and three external design variables simultaneously has been the hurdle in design thinking and policy support to develop sustainable FPOs and organizations in general. Nayak (2010a, 2013c, 2014c, 2015a), argues that the five internal organizational design issues, namely, size, scope, technology, management, and ownership, and the three external design variables of market landscape, institutional architecture, and convergence, when optimized simultaneously could enable trust, social capital, and social wealth to grow and make cooperatives sustainable community enterprise systems.

Interestingly, these issues of organizational design have great potential to inform scholarship on traditional industrial organizations in the secondary and tertiary sectors as we now find positive winds of change in the design of these traditional organizations. Given the global trends, I presume that the world will engage more in cooperative logic than competitive logic in the twenty-first century.

Though the organizational design issues are important for a medium- to long-term sustainability of FPOs, the burning issues faced by the PCs that needs immediate attention for short-term survival are managerial capacity, credit-related, taxation, legal provision, and budgetary support.

Since 2010, there have been many rounds of discussions in India on farmer producer companies by the Agricultural Finance Corporation, Access Development Services, Indian Institute of Management Bangalore, IRMA, NABARD, SFAC, FAO, National Rural Livelihood Mission (NRLM), and NABARD Chair Unit, XUB. There has been unanimity across all these rounds of discussions on the basic provisions on issues of managerial capacity, credit, legal, and budgetary provisions as part of facilitating an enabling external environment.[3] A summary of the recommendations on legal and budgetary provisions is given in later.

6.4 RECOMMENDATION ON LEGAL AND BUDGETARY PROVISIONS FOR FPOs IN INDIA

- The central government, state governments, and the Reserve Bank of India to legislate that the FPOs/production companies shall get all the financial and taxation and other benefits that are currently being extended to the societies, cooperatives, PACS, SHGs, and individual farmers and so on.
- The registration/processing fee for registering an FPO/production company with the Registrar of Companies shall not be charged by the Registrar of Companies.
- The FPOs/production companies need external professional help from NGOs/civil society organizations (CSOs) in the area in terms of community mobilization, stabilizing collation, processing, and marketing. As FPOs/production companies cannot generate funds for remuneration of professionals, the initial management should comprise a principal coordinator, a marketing professional, an accounting professional, and a social mobilization professional with remuneration ranging from Rs 30,000 to Rs 40,000 per

---

[3] See http://www.xub.edu.in/NABARD-Chair/activities.html.

month for principal coordinator and Rs 15,000 to Rs 25,000 per month for others. The central and state governments are to provide these professional expenses to the registered FPO directly.

- The FPOs (producer companies) need to be provided working capital at marginal interest rates without collateral or bank guarantees for the sanctioned limits. The central government, state government, Small Industries Development Bank of India (SIDBI), Nabard Financial Services Limited (NABFINS), and NABARD are to provide a one-time seed capital of Rs 5 million towards margin for capital and working capital directly to every registered FPO/production company.
- The registered FPO/production company must get all the tax holidays as applicable to societies, cooperatives, SHGs, and start-ups for the first 10 years, as most FPOs will take about five years to stabilize.
- Grants for capacity building, initial IT infrastructure, community radio, and physical infrastructure including two hectares of common village land, community office, storage, drying yard, and basic processing facility to be provided by the state and central governments. A provision of Rs 20 million per FPO/production company is to be made by the above-mentioned governments and other development agencies through convergence of various development schemes such as Mahatma Gandhi National Rural Employment Guarantee Act (MGNREGA), Rashtriya Krishi Vikas Yojana (RKVY), Watershed, NRLM, and so on and all district development programmes. All these are to be implemented within five years of formation of an FPO/ production company in a GP.
- SFAC guarantee cover and matching equity grant to be extended to all registered FPOs/FPCs.
- Government to notify that corporate social responsibility funds to be extended by companies to promote and stabilize FPOs/FPCs based anywhere in the respective states where the facilities of a company are located.

6.5 SUMMARY AND RECOMMENDATION ON POLICY MEASURES ON FPOS IN INDIA

Field observations, primary data analysis, focused group discussions, case studies and key findings thereof, and the root cause of risk to farmers are found to be the externalization of internal capabilities of farmers at the production stage (seeds, manure, water) or after harvest of crop (value addition and marketing). Lack of effective local-level farmer institutions that can timely and adequately address the possible risk at every stage of the value chain in agriculture, therefore, compounds the risk to farmers and credit lenders.

Optimal design of FPOs includes simultaneous optimization of size, scope, technology, ownership, and management. The optimal size would be around 1,000 producers in a geographic cluster of—two to four micro-watersheds that approximates one GP. The scope of activities of an FPO should ideally include multiple produce and services that are needed by the members. The technology of production has to be appropriate and farmer members need to adopt sustainable agricultural systems. The members are to be the sole owners and the management should be appropriate to match the needs and culture of the community, with the farmer members and their board having the last say in key decisions of the FPO. Further, convergence of government development schemes at GP-level FPOs, saturation of agricultural communities with FPOs through a three-tier institutional architecture from GP to block to district, and facilitation of deep local markets are critical externalities for the success of optimally designed FPOs.

In summary, based on the current context of smallholder farmers and agriculture, and internal design issues of FPOs and external requirements for the FPOs to be sustainable, the following recommendations on policy measures are suggested.

1. **Facilitate establishment of optimally designed and effective GP-level farmer institution and saturate a district with such FPOs**
   - Facilitate and fund establishment of GP-level multi-product, multi-service FPOs (farmer cooperatives or FPCs) as institutions of the farmers. This local institution can strengthen the capacity of farmers at all stages of agricultural value network/chain. District-level saturation of these FPOs through a three-tier system can stabilize the local diversity, result in higher value addition at block level, and connect to national/global markets to the district level.
   - Facilitate convergence of various agricultural extension services of the district/state at the GP-level FPO (farmer cooperative or FPC); which in turn can provide these services at the doorstep of farmers; minimizing transaction costs of all extension services.

2. **Redesign credit product for small and marginal farmers**
- Channel bank credit through GP-level FPO to farmers. The rate of interest charged to farmers can be marginally increased provided adequate credit for multiple needs and timely and speedy delivery are ensured. This will also reduce the cost of monitoring and follow-up cost on individual borrowers for the banks.
- Credit to small and marginal farmers may be delinked to specific agricultural activity but provided for multiple needs related to agriculture and allied activities, including credit for education of children and emergency credit for health care and food supplement. Institutional arrangement for repayment in installment may be introduced through the GP-level FPOs.

3. **Build capacity of farmers on sustainable agricultural system and implement it at village level**
- Provide systematic training to farmers on sustainable agricultural system and promote common cattle grazing at village level.
- Promote family farming among small and marginal farmers in order to facilitate diversity in agricultural production and timely care.

4. **Invest in basic and simple agricultural infrastructure**
- Invest in physical infrastructure for water harvesting and in situ water conservation in every village and on farmers' fields.
- Invest in kitchen garden, fodder cultivation, and cattle sheds at the farmer/village level.

REFERENCES

Alagh, Y.K. 2015. 'Organizing Social Enterprises'. National Round Table Discussions on Optimal Design of Farmer Producer Organizations, NABARD Chair Unit, Xavier University Bhubaneswar.

Kanitkar, A. 2016. 'The Logic of Farmer Enterprises'. *Occasional Publication 17*, IRMA.

Krishnagopal, G.V. 2016. 'Issues for FPOs, Access Livelihoods Consulting'. National Round Table Discussion on Optimal Design of FPOs. XIM Bhubaneswar.

Lundgren, Jonathan G. and Scott W. Fausti. 'Trading Biodiversity for Pest Problems'. *Science Advances* 1(6). DOI: 10.1126/sciadv.1500558.

Malla, M.A. and P.K. Singh. 2015. 'Producers Collectives and Livelihoods: Exploring Issues for Research and Policy'. *Workshop Report*. Centre for Sustainable Livelihoods, IRMA.

Mehta, V.L. 1960. Report of the Committee on Cooperative Credit, Government of India, New Delhi.

Naik, H.B. 2016. 'Pathway to Success of Amalsad Vibhag Vividh Karyakari Sahakari Khedut Mandali Ltd. Amalsad'. National Round Table Discussion on Optimal Design of FPOs. XIM Bhubaneswar.

Nayak, A.K.J.R. 2010a. 'Optimizing Asymmetries for Sustainability'. In *Global Conference of the Jesuit Higher Education*. Univesidad Ibero Americana (UIA), Mexico City, Mexico.

———. 2010b. 'Participation and Development Outcomes: Evidences from the Poor Districts of India'. *Journal of Management & Public Policy* 1(2): 6–27.

———. 2011. *Indian Multinationals: The Dynamics of Explosive Growth in Developing Country Context*. London, UK: Palgrave Macmillan.

———. 'Maximizing Net Incomes for Members of Farmer Producer Organization: Is There an Optimal Market Distance?' *Working Paper*, XIMB Sustainability Series 3.0.

———. 2013a. 'Economies of Scope: Context of Agricultural Science, Smallholder Farmers and Sustainability, Research Training Seminar Series, XIMB, Bhubaneswar, 15 November 2015 and National Livelihood Conference, New Delhi, 11 December 2013.

———. 2013b. 'Efficiency, Effectiveness and Sustainability: Basis of Competition and Cooperation'. *Proceedings of GLOGIFT 13*. 13–15 December 2013, Department of Management Studies, IIT Delhi.

———. 2013c. *Implementing Community Enterprise System for Sustainability of Rural Agricultural Communities—A Manual*. XIM Bhubaneswar.

———. 2014a. *All India Baseline Study on Producer Companies & Natural Farming Practices*. DEAR, National Bank for Agriculture & Rural Development, Mumbai.

———. 2014b. 'Asymmetries in Organizations, Institutions and Policy Signals in the Context of Sustainable Governance in India'. *The Administrator, Journal of LBSNAA* 55 (2). Available at https://www.researchgate.net/publication/279456420_Asymmetries_in_Organizations_Institutions_and_Policy_Signals_in_the_context_of_Sustainable_Governance_in_India, accessed on 2 January 2018.

———. 2014c. 'Logic, Language, and Values of Co-operation Versus Competition in the Context of Recreating Sustainable Community Systems'. *International Review of Sociology—Revue Internationale de Sociologie*. Available at http://dx.doi.org/10.1080/03906701.2014.894342.

———. 2015a. 'Farmer Producer Organizations in India: Policy, Performance, and Design Issues'. In *Organised*

Retailing and Agri-Business, edited by N.C. Rao, R. Radhakrishna, R.K. Mishra, and V.R. Kata, 289–303. New Delhi: Springer India.

———. 2015b. 'Size and Organizational Design Complexity for Sustainability: A Perspective'. *Vilakshan, XIMB Journal of Management* 12(1): 129–40.

———. 2015c. 'Reconnect with Thrift Essential'. *Odisha Post.* 4 December.

———. 2016. 'Smallholder Farmers and Agriculture in India: Challenges and Way Forward'. National Round Table Discussion on FPO & SAS, XIMB, Bhubaneswar.

Nayak, A.K.J.R., S. Nayak, and A. Panda. 2016. 'National Round Table Discussion on Sustainable Agricultural Systems'. *A Synthesis Report.* NABARD Chair Unit, Xavier University Bhubaneswar.

Nayak, A.K.J.R. and A. Panda. 2016. 'National Round Table Discussion on Optimal Design of Farmer Producer Organizations'. *A Synthesis Report.* NABARD Chair Unit, Xavier University Bhubaneswar.

Nayak, A.K.J.R., S. Peppin, and B.S. Misra. 2016. *Report on Ramification of Debt Waivers and the Need to Put in Place a Risk Mitigation Mechanism for Making Agriculture Sustainable in Odisha.* DEAR, National Bank for Agriculture and Rural Development, Mumbai, India.

Nayak, A.K.J.R., Laxmidhar Swain, S.K. Das, et al. 2012. *Management@Grassroots. Curriculum for Community Enterprise Systems (FPOs/POs/PCs).* SFAC-XIMB Publication.

Nowak, M. and R. Highfield. 2011. *Super Cooperators: Altruism, Evolution, and Why We Need Each Other to Succeed.* New York: Free Press.

Ostrom, E. 1990. *Governing the Commons: The Evolution of Collective Action.* Cambridge, UK: Cambridge University Press.

Reserve Bank of India. 1915. *Report of the Committee on Cooperation in India.* Mumbai: Reserve Bank of India.

Schumacher, E.F. 1973. *Small Is Beautiful: A Study of Economics As If People Mattered.* London: Bonde and Briggs.

Schumpeter, J.A. 1943. *Capitalism, Socialism and Democracy.* London: Routledge.

Shah, T. 1996. *Catalysing Co-operation: Design of Self-governing Organisations.* New Delhi: SAGE Publications.

———. 2015. *Making Farmers' Cooperatives Work: Design, Governance, and Management.* New Delhi, India: Sage Publications.

Simon, Herbert. 1969. *The Sciences of the Artificial.* Cambridge, Massachusetts: MIT Press.

Vaidyanathan, A. 2013. 'Future of Cooperatives in India'. *Economic & Political Weekly* 48(18): 30–4.

Vernon, R. 1971. *Sovereignty at Bay: The Multinational Spread of U.S. Enterprises.* New York: Basic Books.

———. 1977. *Storm over the Multinationals: The Real Issue.* London: Macmillan Press.

———. 2009. *In the Hurricane's Eye: The Troubled Prospects of Multinational Enterprises.* Cambridge, MA: Harvard University Press.

7

Agriculture and Rural Development in Disadvantaged Regions with Special Focus on the North Eastern Region

C. Hazarika* and I. Barman**

ABSTRACT

The North Eastern Region (NER) of India, comprising Arunachal Pradesh, Assam, Manipur, Meghalaya, Mizoram, Nagaland, Sikkim, and Tripura, is considered to be a backward enclave of a dynamic and progressing economy. The region, by and large, is characterized by fragility, marginality, inaccessibility, cultural heterogeneity, ethnicity, and rich biodiversity. In this chapter an attempt has been made to study the present status and characteristics of agriculture and allied sectors and to develop a few policy suggestions for the development of agriculture and rural economy of the NER. SWOT analysis was undertaken to identify the strengths and weaknesses of the region. Though rice is the main crop, in all the north eastern (NE) states, the production of fruit and vegetables has increased manifold indicating diversification. The annual area under shifting cultivation is 387,000 ha and 443,000 families are practising it. The region has almost 274 fish species, indicating potential for development of the fishery sector. The farmers of this region have rich indigenous technical knowledge for rearing a number of animals and birds, and the participation of women is also found to be very high. A strategy for the development of rural economy and employment in the region should include (*a*) a well-thought out plan for the development of rural infrastructure, agro-, horticulture-, and forest-based small-scale industries, floriculture and mushroom culture, and (*b*) the use of the export development fund to set up marketing infrastructure and to train the educated manpower for entrepreneurial activities.

JEL codes: O13, Q15, R14

Keywords: agriculture, North East India, policy, SWOT

* Director of Postgraduate Studies, Assam Agricultural University (AAU), Jorhat, India.
** Assistant Professor, Department of Extension Education, Biswanath College of Agriculture, AAU.
The authors are thankful to the anonymous reviewer for his comments on the earlier draft of the chapter.

7.1 INTRODUCTION

The North Eastern Region (NER) of India, comprising Arunachal Pradesh, Assam, Manipur, Meghalaya, Mizoram, Nagaland, Sikkim, and Tripura, is considered to be a backward enclave of a dynamic and progressing economy. For long, the backwardness of the NER has been an area of concern and various measures have been taken to improve its status. However, the region is still lagging behind on various counts. The NER has long international borders with Bangladesh, Bhutan, China, and Myanmar, and is close to Nepal. Notwithstanding its high potential for development through trade, the region has been faced with various challenges, both natural and man-made. A key area of concern for policy-makers is the huge difference between the potential and actual economic performance of the NER. It is a land where tea is an industry, handicrafts a major occupation, and martial arts a favoured sport (Hazarika 2006).

The NER has a total geographical area of 262,179 sq km, which is nearly 8 per cent of the total area of the country, and is inhabited by more than 45 million people (Census 2011). About 35 per cent area in the region is plain land, with a higher proportion (84 per cent) in Assam. The region receives an annual average rainfall of 2,000 mm. The soil of the region is acidic to strongly acidic in reaction. The region, by and large, is characterized by fragility, marginality, inaccessibility, cultural heterogeneity, ethnicity, and rich biodiversity. Though the NE reflects ecological and cultural contrasts between the hills and the plains, there are also significant elements of continuity. The NE is one of the most biodiverse regions in the world.

Strategic planning and implementation are necessary to develop agriculture and make the region marginally, if not significantly, surplus in rice, oilseed, fruit, and vegetable production by integrating research, extension, and education duly supported by time-bound reforms in the land tenure system. Harnessing agricultural potential would generate surplus to support the secondary sector, create demand for goods in the rural areas, increase disposable income that could enhance purchasing power of some 33 million people and bring socio-economic development. The impact of agricultural growth on farmers' income is evident from the fact that one incremental percentage growth, according to an estimate at the national level, leads to an additional income generation of Rs100 billion for the farmers and creates additional employment opportunities.

High growth of population with a large proportion of small and marginal farm households and traditional and low-input agricultural practices coupled with the problem of insurgency have adversely affected the agricultural economies in the region. As the pace of economic development in the NER is slow, a new regional model is needed, considering the past development deficiencies and the extreme diversities.

7.2 AGRICULTURE IN THE NORTH EAST

For 70 per cent of the NER's poor who live in rural areas, agriculture is the main source of income and employment. But depletion and degradation of land and water pose serious challenges to producing enough food and other agricultural products to sustain livelihoods here and meet the needs of urban populations.

The NER is a classic case of economic underdevelopment. The region is characterized by high dependence on agriculture, low levels of modern input use, traditional farming techniques, lack of farm mechanization, subsistence farming, low level of productivity, poor infrastructure, and so on. While the NE accounts for 3.4 per cent of the agricultural land of the country, it contributes only 2.8 per cent to total agricultural production, underscoring the low productivity of the region's agricultural sector. More than 70 per cent of total geographical area of the NER is covered by hills and about 3 million hectares suffer from soil erosion due to the practice of *jhum* (shifting) cultivation. The region offers scope for cultivation of a wide variety of agricultural crops because of its diversities in topography, altitude, and climatic conditions. The produce is mainly sold in the local markets, without any value addition.

Traditionally, agriculture has been the mainstay of people of this region but the agro-based economy fails to flourish, as it should have, due to lack of utilization of technological aids. As a result, the stamp of 'backwardness' has been attached to this region suffering from food scarcity, while the country moves ahead from its target of production to food surplus in different phases of the post-Independence era. Increasing the yield of crop in a complex system and in an environmentally sustainable manner is a challenge. The region is dominated by tribal population and the development of agriculture and production of food grains in the region is highly dependent on the customs, cultures, and the food habits of the tribal people.

Agriculture is an important sector in the economy of the NER, with its share in state domestic product (SDP) ranging from 19 per cent to 37 per cent in different states. This contribution of agricultural sector in SDP has declined during the past three decades. Though this is considered a sign of development, the percentage of population dependent on agriculture remains very high.

As a result, agriculture in the region has not been able to generate surpluses for investment and augment purchasing power, not to speak of employment generation. Moreover, factors such as natural calamities, large number of smallholders, low-intensity agri-inputs, and negligible seed/variety replacement are also threatening the livelihood sustainability in the region.

7.2.1 Land–Man Ratio

Land is a critical resource, and availability and management of land for agricultural activities are essential for raising agricultural production and productivity. Table 7.1 presents the geographical land to man ratio of the different NE states as in 2011. The NER's agricultural system is predominantly traditional. The overall geographical land to man ratio for the NER (0.58 ha/person) is much higher

than the national average (0.27 ha/person). Among the NE states, the geographical land to man ratio is highest in Arunachal Pradesh (6.05 ha/person) and lowest in Assam (0.25 ha/person).

7.2.2 Land Use Classification

A summarized version of the land use pattern in the NE India is presented in Table 7.2. It is evident from the table that the region has maintained the forest cover during the period 2008–9 to 2012–13. Area not available for cultivation is almost stagnant or slightly declined in all the states of the NER except Meghalaya and Tripura. This might be due to the rapid urbanization and shifting of agricultural land towards non-agricultural uses. Net area sown has also shown an increasing trend over the years. Cropping intensity is as low as 106 per cent for Mizoram

Table 7.1 Geographical Land to Man Ratio (Hectares/Person) as on 2011

State	Geographical Area (Lakh ha)	2001 Census		2011 Census	
		Population (in Lakhs)	Ratio	Population (in Lakhs)	Ratio
Arunachal Pradesh	83.74	10.98	7.63	13.84	6.05
Assam	78.44	266.55	0.29	312.06	0.25
Manipur	22.33	21.67	1.03	25.70	0.87
Meghalaya	22.43	23.19	0.97	29.67	0.76
Mizoram	21.08	8.89	2.37	10.97	1.92
Nagaland	16.58	19.90	0.83	19.78	0.84
Sikkim	7.10	5.41	1.31	6.11	1.16
Tripura	10.49	31.99	0.33	36.74	0.29
All NE	**262.19**	**388.58**	**0.67**	**454.87**	**0.58**
All India	**3,287.26**	**10,286.10**	**0.32**	**12,101.93**	**0.27**

Source: Census Report 2001 and 2011, Government of India.

Table 7.2 Land Use Classification in the NER during 2008–9 to 2012–13 (in Thousand Hectares)

States	Forest Area		Area Not Available for Cultivation		Net Area Sown		Cropping Intensity (%)	
	2008–9	2012–13	2008–9	2012–13	2008–9	2012–13	2008–9	2012–13
Arunachal Pradesh	5,154	5,154	64	64	211	216	133.4	133
Assam	1,853	1,853	2,626	2,620	2,753	2,811	134.5	135
Manipur	1,693	1,742	27	27	236	309	100.0	149
Meghalaya	948	946	226	239	284	285	121.9	120
Mizoram	1,594	1,585	133	95	95	116	100.0	106
Nagaland	863	863	98	95	316	380	125.2	114
Sikkim	319	584	250	11	107	77	109.8	117
Tripura	606	629	134	141	280	256	106.6	186
All India	69,635	70,007	43,324	43,738	141,364	139,932	135.9	130

Source: www.databank.nedfi.com.

and as high as 186 per cent in Tripura. At the national level, cropping intensity was found to be 130 per cent.

7.2.3 Size of Holding

About 80 per cent of the farmers in the NER belong to the small and marginal categories. Moreover, with increase in population, the average size of holding is gradually reducing over the years. Table 7.3 presents the average size of holding in NE states during 1990–1 and 2010–11. The average size of holding was found to be the highest in

Nagaland: it was 6.92 ha in 1990–1, which has reduced to 6.02 during 2010–11. Almost in all the states the average size of holding is significantly higher than the national average (1.15 ha), except Tripura (0.49 ha), during 2010–11.

Table 7.4 presents the number of small and marginal holdings during the year 2009–10, in the NER. It is evident from the table that small and marginal holdings together constitute about 81.98 per cent of the total holding in the region. This is primarily because hilly terrain constitutes nearly two-thirds of the region's geographical area, and large-sized holdings are not feasible. The average

Table 7.3   Average Size of Holding during 1990–1 to 2010–11 (in Hectares)

State		Marginal	Small	Semi-medium	Medium	Large	Average Holding Size
Arunachal Pradesh	1990–1	0.60	1.50	2.81	5.76	18.43	3.62
	2010–11	0.55	1.34	2.76	5.54	14.90	3.51
Assam	1990–1	0.41	1.39	2.70	5.23	74.17	1.31
	2010–11	0.42	1.38	2.69	5.15	68.11	1.10
Manipur	1990–1	0.55	1.37	2.56	5.01	12.16	1.24
	2010–11	0.52	1.28	2.48	4.86	11.00	1.14
Meghalaya	1990–1	0.54	1.38	2.54	5.46	13.00	1.81
	2010–11	0.45	1.33	2.79	5.67	16.48	1.37
Mizoram	1990–1	0.62	1.57	2.78	4.00	0.00	1.34
	2010–11	0.60	1.27	2.42	5.13	15.09	1.14
Nagaland	1990–1	0.69	1.43	2.92	6.34	16.85	6.92
	2010–11	0.51	1.13	2.58	6.17	17.57	6.02
Sikkim	1990–1	0.41	1.40	2.71	5.87	24.21	1.85
	2010–11	0.37	1.20	2.49	5.44	15.77	1.42
Tripura	1990–1	0.40	1.53	2.69	5.14	12.15	0.97
	2010–11	0.28	1.38	2.52	5.07	14.29	0.49
All India	1990–1	0.40	1.44	2.76	5.90	17.30	1.57
	2010–11	0.39	1.42	2.71	5.76	17.38	1.15

Source: Basic Statistics of North Eastern Region 2015, Published by NEC Secretariat, Shillong.

Table 7.4   Number of Small and Marginal Operational Holdings in North Eastern States, 2009–10 (in Thousands)

Sl. No.	State	No. of Operational Holdings (Total)	No. of Operational Holdings (Small and Marginal)	Proportion (in %)
1	Arunachal Pradesh	109	40	36.70
2	Assam	2,720	2,328	85.59
3	Manipur	151	126	83.44
4	Meghalaya	210	161	76.67
5	Mizoram	92	80	86.96
6	Nagaland	178	26	14.61
7	Sikkim	75	57	76.00
8	Tripura	578	554	95.85
9	North East	4,113	3,372	81.98
10	All India	138,348	117,605	85.01

Source: Agricultural Census, 2010–11.

plot size is too small for mechanization of agriculture and adoption of modern farming practices. Subsistence farming, therefore, is predominant in the NER and there is hardly any commercial surplus.

Total operational land in the NER is 53.4 lakh ha. The highest operated area of 31.6 lakh ha is in Assam and the lowest (0.8 lakh ha) is in Mizoram. Nagaland has the unique characteristic of the highest size of operational holding at 6.02 ha, much higher than the average of the region (1.49 ha) and all India (1.15 ha).

7.2.4 Characteristics of North East Farmers

Farmers in the region can be classified into the following three major categories:

- The first category includes small- and multiple-job holders who work as agricultural labourers and also do some farming on leased land.

- The second category includes small- to medium-starter farmers who cultivate owned and leased lands with little off-farm income (cafeteria approach).
- The third category includes medium- to large-scale farmers with high level of farm production, income, and expenditure.

7.2.5 Changes in Foodgrain Production

Almost 90 per cent of the region's rural population is dependent on agriculture. Table 7.5 presents the progress of agriculture in terms of foodgrains in the NE states during the period from 2001–2 to 2013–14. Almost all the NE states have recorded a significant increase in the foodgrain production except Mizoram. The increase in production has come from both area expansion and productivity improvements. The performance of the NE agricultural sector is quite good, comparable to the all-India level (Buragohain 2007).

Table 7.5   Progress of Agriculture (Foodgrains) in the North East

State	Factors	2001–2	2009–10	2013–14
Arunachal Pradesh	Area (thousand ha)	188.4	193.9	214.4
	Prod (thousand tonnes)	217.4	303.4	384.6
	Yield (kg/ha)	1,154	1,565	1,794
Assam	Area (thousand ha)	2,755	2,695.6	2,660
	Prod (thousand tonnes)	4,023	4,481.2	5,096.8
	Yield (kg/ha)	1,460	1,662	1,916
Manipur	Area (thousand ha)	173.7	188.7	281.1
	Prod (thousand tonnes)	400.5	338.9	490.6
	Yield (kg/ha)	2,306	1,796	1,745
Meghalaya	Area (thousand ha)	134.8	132.2	134.1
	Prod (thousand tonnes)	224.7	239.2	320.0
	Yield (kg/ha)	1,667	1,809	2,387
Mizoram	Area (thousand ha)	65.9	59.6	48.4
	Prod (thousand tonnes)	126.3	62.3	72.8
	Yield (kg/ha)	1,917	1,045	1,506
Nagaland	Area (thousand ha)	257.5	264.5	309.5
	Prod (thousand tonnes)	355.4	333.9	624.6
	Yield (kg/ha)	1,380	1,262	2,018
Tripura	Area (thousand ha)	258.5	254.6	271.1
	Prod (thousand tonnes)	597.5	647.9	726.7
	Yield (kg/ha)	2,209	2,545	2,680
All India	Area (thousand ha)	122,779.6	121,333.6	125,042.0
	Prod (thousand tonnes)	212,851.2	218,097.7	265,043.2
	Yield (kg/ha)	1,734	1,798	2,120

Source: *Agriculture Statistics at a Glance 2015* (e-book), Ministry of Agriculture and Farmers Welfare, Government of India, available at www.agricoop.nic.in, last accessed on 5 January 2018.

It is also evident from the table that during 2009–10, states like Manipur, Mizoram, and Nagaland could not maintain the pace of improvements in agriculture of the Indian agricultural scenario. Since then, due to the implementation of many central government–sponsored schemes, the agricultural sector in almost all the states of the region has gained momentum. During 2013–14, the yield performance of foodgrain production is found to be very satisfactory. Even the productivity in Meghalaya (2,387 kg/ha) and Tripura (2,680 kg/ha) was much higher than the national average (2,120 kg/ha), while in other states it was much lower than the national average.

7.2.6 Production of High-Value Crops in the North East

The NER possesses immense potential for the production of high-value crops. Table 7.6 presents production of fruit and vegetables in the region for the period from 2001–2 to 2013–14. It is seen from the table that in almost all the NE states, the production of fruit and vegetables has increased manifold. It may be concluded that in recent years, diversification of NE agriculture is taking place towards high-value agriculture.

The agro-climatic and altitudinal advantage accompanied by the tradition of growing fruit and vegetables should help enhance the productivity and output by formulating state-specific programmes on selected fruit and vegetables, linking with, among others, supply of planting material, inputs, processing facilities, and marketing network. On a priority basis, small farmers' horticulture estates (SFHEs) can be established by forming fruit-grower self-help groups (SHGs), training farmers to upgrade their technical and managerial skills, and providing credit support. A system has to be put in place that ensures post-harvest handling, assembly, storage, transport packing, processing, credit, and modern marketing system for horticulture products in the public–private–partnership mode. Floriculture potential available in Arunachal Pradesh, Meghalaya, Mizoram, Nagaland, and Sikkim can be exploited on a commercial scale through preparing feasibility studies and an action plan. It will be pertinent to mention the names of the two organizations Agricultural & Processed Food Products Export Development Authority (APEDA) and North Eastern Regional Agricultural Marketing Corporation Limited (NERAMAC) that have formulated and implemented many policies for the procuring, processing, semi processing, packaging, and exporting of perishable horticultural commodities from this region in recent years. Declaring agro-export zones for ginger and pineapple has also added another significant milestone in the cultivation development of these two crops.

The region also possesses a high potential for production of spices. Table 7.7 presents the area, production, and productivity of major spices in the NE states for the period from 2009–10 to 2013–14. It is seen from the table that in almost all the NE states, the area under spices has increased significantly. The production also increased in almost all the states except Mizoram, where the yield rate has decreased during the period. The increase in production is due to increase in both area and yield.

7.2.7 Shifting Cultivation

Shifting cultivation (jhum cultivation) is a common practice in the hills. Recently, terrace cultivation has been encouraged through state government initiatives. The annual area under shifting cultivation is 3.87 lakh ha; minimum area under shifting cultivation at one time is 14.66 lakh ha and 4.43 lakh families are practising it

Table 7.6   Production of Fruit and Vegetables in North East India (in Thousand MT)

States	Fruit			Vegetables		
	2001–2	2009–10	2013–14	2001–2	2009–10	2013–14
Arunachal Pradesh	41.6	57.6	321.26	83.9	110.0	35.00
Assam	110.80	138.46	2,007.80	2,935.20	2,916.70	3,031.90
Manipur	26.10	42.40	515.69	66.10	174.30	271.04
Meghalaya	24.00	32.95	348.00	265.90	415.80	515.34
Mizoram	19.00	34.50	343.90	44.10	114.40	254.14
Nagaland	25.00	18.16	411.00	286.00	78.30	492.37
Sikkim	12.30	12.19	24.05	60.00	98.00	134.53
Tripura	28.30	31.31	786.35	353.20	294.70	780.52

Source: Indian Horticultural Database, 2009, 2013, and *Horticultural Statistics at a Glance 2015*, National Horticulture Board.

Table 7.7   Area, Production, and Productivity of Major Spices in North East India

States	Area (in Thousand ha)		Production (in Thousand MT)		Productivity (MT/ha)	
	2009–10	2013–14	2009–10	2013–14	2009–10	2013–14
Arunachal Pradesh	7.63	10.17	43.34	64.27	5.68	6.32
Assam	27.37	93.08	18.55	279.14	0.68	2.99
Manipur	8.98	10.47	7.84	24.14	0.87	2.31
Meghalaya	17.41	17.50	72.01	83.88	4.14	4.79
Mizoram	22.67	22.47	80.63	59.62	3.56	2.65
Nagaland	7.22	9.77	38.62	39.16	5.35	4.01
Sikkim	26.58	32.06	41.73	55.80	1.57	1.74
Tripura	3.96	5.69	12.10	18.04	3.06	3.17

Source: Indian Horticultural Database, 2009, 2013, and *Horticultural Statistics at a Glance 2015*, National Horticulture Board.

Table 7.8   Status of Shifting (Jhum) Cultivation in North East India, 2008

State	Annual Area under Shifting Cultivation (Thousand ha)	Fallow Period (Years)	Minimum Area under Jhum at a Given Time (Thousand ha)	Number of Jhumia Families (in Thousands)	Jhum Land/ Family (ha)
Arunachal Pradesh	70.00	3–10	210	54	1.29
Assam	69.60	2–10	139	58	1.20
Manipur	90.00	4–7	360	70	1.29
Meghalaya	53.00	5–7	265	52	1.01
Nagaland	19.00	5–8	191	116	0.16
Tripura	22.30	5–9	112	43	0.51
Sikkim	NA	NA	NA	NA	NA
Mizoram	63.00	3–4	189	50	1.26

Source: Report of the Inter-Ministerial National Task Force on Rehabilitation of Shifting Cultivation areas, 2008.

(Table 7.8). The jhum cycle varies from 2 to 10 years and due to the pressure of population the jhum cycles comes down to 2–3 years. Jhum land per family ranges from 0.16 ha in Nagaland to 1.29 ha in Arunachal Pradesh and Manipur. Shifting cultivation has its own danger of soil erosion, soil degradation, loss of valuable forest products, and flooding in the river valley below. All these cause ecological imbalance. Settled cultivation is encouraged through various programmes such as permanent settlement of *jhumia* cultivators (those who practice jhum cultivation) through development of plantation crops in Karbi Anglong and NC hills of Assam, providing 2 ha of terrace land to each jhumia family along with inputs and financial help for permanent cultivation in Meghalaya, pilot projects in selected villages, land reclamation, minor irrigation, land improvement, provision of seeds, fertilizers, and development of horticulture and cash crops in Mizoram, and pilot projects in Nagaland

to induce farmers to give up jhum cultivation and adopt terrace cultivation.

Efforts need to address the social and human aspects of jhuming and offer alternatives acceptable to the farmers in consultation with the local farming communities. The Nagaland Environment Protection and Economic Development (NEPED) project, which raises cash crops and carries out horticulture using the forest as alternative to jhuming in Nagaland, has proved to be a promising model demonstrating environmental soundness and profitability. This can be replicated in other jhuming areas also. This alternative promises success in minimizing jhuming by involving farming communities and integrating with timely provision of quality planting material and production inputs, and efficient extension and marketing services. This would also need adequate financial resources to sustain field operations including maintenance for the initial five years. Besides, tea, cardamom, and rubber plantations can be tried successfully on a pilot basis.

7.2.8 Changes in Cropping Pattern

Rice is the main crop in the NER covering around 61 per cent of gross cropped area. Maize is the next important crop for all the hill states except Tripura and Assam, followed by oilseed. In recent years, changes in cropping pattern have been observed. The new economic reforms brought about several changes in the economy. The opening up of trade has also influenced the cropping pattern in the region. Table 7.9 presents the changes in area under major crops across the NE states during 2009–10 to 2013–14.

The region is slowly and steadily moving towards commercial agriculture through the cultivation of high-value crops such as fruit and vegetables. In the NER the main changes were as follows.

1. Rice continued to remain as the major crop in all the states. However, the area declined in Assam and Mizoram, remained stable in Sikkim and Meghalaya, but increased in Arunachal Pradesh, Manipur, Nagaland, and Tripura. The productivity increase contributed significantly towards increase in foodgrain production.

2. Oilseeds are the next important crop covering around 6–8 per cent of area except in Mizoram and Tripura. Rape and mustard were the only oilseed crops till the 1970s, but after that new oilseed crops such as linseed, castor, sunflower, and groundnut have entered into the cropping pattern.

3. Wheat is grown mainly in Assam, and saw tremendous area expansion in the late 1970s due to the Green Revolution. But since 1985–6, wheat area is declining due to lack of irrigation facilities, problem of pre-harvest sprouting in the event of early showers and the problem of post-harvest processing. Wheat is newly introduced in all the NE states except Mizoram.

4. Pulse area is increasing only in Assam. In other states, pulse area is decreasing or remains stagnant due to the problem of soil moisture stress in the sowing season, poor management, disease and pest, and so on.

5. Jute and sugarcane are the two important cash crops of the region. Due to problem of retting, processing, and marketing the jute area is declining. Rice is substituting jute area.

6. Potato is gaining priority in all the states except Mizoram.

Table 7.9   Changes in Cropping Pattern in North Eastern States (Area in Lakh Hectares)

Crops	Period	Arunachal Pradesh	Assam	Manipur	Nagaland	Tripura	Mizoram	Meghalaya	Sikkim
Rice	2009–10	1.22	24.96	1.69	1.69	2.46	0.47	1.08	0.13
	2013–14	1.32	24.49	2.23	1.89	2.54	0.39	1.10	0.11
Wheat	2009–10	0.03	0.58	–	0.02	0.07	–	0.04	0.52
	2013–14	0.03	0.31	0.02	0.03	0.02	–	0.04	0.04
Maize	2009–10	0.44	0.20	0.04	0.68	0.02	0.09	0.17	0.40
	2013–14	0.47	0.24	0.26	0.69	0.05	0.05	0.18	0.40
Total pulses	2009–10	0.09	1.15	0.14	0.33	0.06	0.04	0.04	0.13
	2013–14	0.10	1.50	0.30	0.38	0.12	0.04	0.03	0.06
Total oilseeds	2009–10	0.31	2.75	0.09	1.01	0.03	0.03	0.10	0.09
	2013–14	0.33	3.05	0.37	0.65	0.06	0.02	0.14	0.08
Jute	2009–10	–	0.85	–	–	0.01	–	0.04	–
	2013–14	–	0.70	–	0.02	0.08	–	0.04	–
Sugarcane	2009–10	–	0.36	0.01	0.04	0.02	0.01	0.0001	–
	2013–14	–	0.34	–	0.01	0.02	–	0.002	–
Potato	2009–10	0.05	0.68	0.04	0.02	0.04	0.005	0.18	–
	2013–14	–	0.27	–	–	0.03	0.01	0.16	–
Cotton	2009–10	–	0.02	0.001	–	0.02	0.01	0.08	–
	2013–14	–	0.02	–	–	0.01	–	0.07	–

Source: Directorate of Economics & Statistics, Department of Agriculture, Co-operation & Farmers' Welfare, Government of India.

7. Area and production under fruit and vegetables increased significantly in all the NE states.
8. Mizoram recorded significant increase in spice cultivation.

7.3 FISHERY SECTOR IN THE NORTH EASTERN REGION OF INDIA

The aquatic bodies of the region harbour a rich diversity of ichthyofauna with 274 fish species belonging to 114 genera, available in water resources with long riverine stretches; a large number of beels, ponds, water reservoirs, rivulets, streams, lakes, and other waterbodies with perennial flow of water in the region shows potential for development of the fishery sector in NE India. This region is considered as one of the hot spots of freshwater fish diversity in the world. Apart from this, varied soil and climatic conditions offer a conducive environment for rearing and developing high-value ornamental fish species. Farmers of this region have rich indigenous technical knowledge of rearing and capturing of local fishes and other fishery activities, and so on. Fish Ecotourism/Angling sports can play a major role in boosting the NE Indian economy as many scenic areas and landscapes prevail within the NER. The state-wise inland fish production in NE states during 2006–7 to 2012–13 is presented in Table 7.10.

Production and productivity of all existing fish species can be increased to a sizeable amount since almost all fish farmers are practising traditional fish farming. High-value, export-oriented, ornamental fish species can be identified, cultured, and promoted. Modern and scientific fish farming presents another aspect that to be popularized thereby attracting the rural youth to the fish-farming sector. International markets can be explored for various high-value ornamental fish species (Chetia and Das 2015).

7.4 LIVESTOCK AND POULTRY SECTOR IN THE NORTH EASTERN REGION

Many indigenous breeds of livestock and birds are available in the region. The demand for animal protein, milk, milk products, and eggs are increasing at a very fast rate. This sector also provides ample avenues for employment for the educated unemployed youth of the region. The farmers have indigenous technical knowledge for rearing a number of animals and birds, and the participation of women is also found to be very high (Chakraborty and Sarma 2015). The total number of livestock and poultry as per livestock census 2012 is presented in Table 7.11.

Production of milk, meat, and eggs and productivity of all existing breeds of cattle, pigs, and birds can be increased considerably by using crossbreeds and following modern farming practices. The high-value indigenous birds of the region need to be identified, developed, and promoted for the better performance of this sector. One or two high-capacity milk and meat processing factories can be established in the region. There is a need to develop a favourable attitude towards commercial livestock and poultry production among the rural unemployed youth.

The major weaknesses of this sector is the lack of availability of quality animals, breeding boar, poor availability and accessibility to quality feed, inadequate veterinary services, poor slaughter house facilities and value addition, lack of awareness about improved management practices, and so on.

Table 7.10   State-wise Inland Fish Production in the NER, 2005–6 to 2012–13 (in Tonnes)

States	2005–6	2006–7	2007–8	2008–9	2009–10	2010–11	2011–12	2012–13
Arunachal Pradesh	275	2,770	2,830	2,880	2,650	3,150	3,300	3,710
Assam	18,801	181,479	190,320	206,150	218,822	227,242	228,621	254,270
Manipur	1,822	18,614	18,600	18,800	19,200	20,200	22,219	24,502
Meghalaya	412	5,487	4,000	3,959	4,332	4,557	4,768	5,417
Mizoram	375	3,760	3,760	2,891	3,246	2,901	2,928	5,430
Nagaland	550	5,800	5,800	6,175	6,360	6,585	6,840	7,130
Sikkim	15	150	175	168	168	180	280	490
Tripura	2,387	28,634	36,245	36,000	42,285	49,231	53,335	57,460
North Eastern Region	24,637	246,694	261,730	277,023	297,063	314,046	322,291	358,409
All India	375,558	3,844,889	4,207,346	4,637,896	4,894,141	4,981,253	5,294,704	5,444,057

Source: Department of Animal Husbandry, Dairying and Fisheries, Ministry of Agriculture, Government of India.

Table 7.11   Total Number of Livestock and Poultry as Per Livestock Census 2012 (in Lakhs)

States	Rural		Urban		Total (Rural + Urban)	
	Livestock	Poultry	Livestock	Poultry	Livestock	Poultry
Arunachal Pradesh	13.66	21.89	0.46	0.55	14.13	22.44
Assam	188.47	268.38	2.35	3.79	190.82	272.16
Manipur	6.11	19.21	0.85	5.79	6.96	24.99
Meghalaya	19.52	33.80	0.06	0.20	19.58	34.00
Mizoram	2.01	8.51	1.11	4.21	3.12	12.71
Nagaland	8.06	18.39	1.05	3.40	9.11	21.78
Sikkim	2.89	4.46	0.03	0.06	2.92	4.52
Tripura	18.89	40.92	0.47	1.80	19.36	42.73
North Eastern Region	**259.61**	**415.56**	**6.39**	**19.80**	**266.00**	**435.33**
All India	**4,916.86**	**6,978.95**	**203.71**	**313.14**	**5120.57**	**7,292.09**

Source: Nineteenth Livestock Census 2012.

A strategy for development of rural economy and employment in the region must be outlined in what follows:

- a well thought out plan to develop the rural infrastructure
- development of agro-based, horticulture-based, forest-based small-scale industries
- development of floriculture and mushroom culture
- use of the export development fund for setting up marketing infrastructure
- train the educated manpower for entrepreneurial activities

At present, rural development attracts some 5–6 per cent of the plan allocation. Sceptics would always apprehend that all the state government machineries would be neither capable of nor free from corruption in implementing the projects/schemes drawing resources from the centre. Moreover, it is necessary that before the implementation of any strategy for rural development, evaluation be made so as to choose one among the various alternative strategies, the one yielding best possible results.

7.6 FOODGRAIN PRODUCTION AND REQUIREMENT

An attempt was made to see the production and requirement of foodgrains in various NE states in near future. The result is presented in Table 7.12. The production/supply of foodgrain was estimated using the compounded growth rate (CGR) of foodgrains for the states. It was assumed that the growth rate will continue at the same rate for another 10 years. Similarly, the requirement/demand

Table 7.12   Foodgrain Production and Requirement (in Thousand Tonnes)

States	CGR	Production		Requirement		Gap	
		2015	2025	2015	2025	2015	2025
Arunachal Pradesh	1.3	246	280	276	348	(−)30	(−)68
Assam	2.58	6,105	7,876	6,214	7,377	(−)109	(+)499
Manipur	1.96	505	613	630	817	(−)125	(−)204
Meghalaya	1.19	243	273	608	787	(−)365	(−)514
Nagaland	6.57	720	1,360	720	1,169	0	(+)191
Tripura	2.25	730	911	717	829	(+)13	(+)82
All NER	–	8,549	11,315	9,165	11,326	(−)616	(−)11

Source: Hazarika (2014).

was calculated by projected population multiplied by the ICMR rate of requirement of foodgrains/person/day. It was seen from the table that Assam, Nagaland, and Tripura will be able to bridge the demand–supply gap in 2025 provided the same growth trend continues. These three states will be surplus in foodgrain production by 2015. On the other hand, Arunachal Pradesh, Manipur, and Meghalaya, whose production growth rate is 1.30, 1.96, and 1.19 respectively, have to work hard and evolve suitable policy for attaining foodgrain self-sufficiency or else they should concentrate more on other high-value commodities having comparative advantage. Otherwise they will remain as foodgrain deficit states in the near future.

The table also reveals that the scenario for the NER as a whole is not very depressing, as it is evident from the table that by the year 2025, the whole region will be deficit by only 11,000 tonnes if the same growth rate continues. With a little effort the region can very well be self-sufficient in foodgrain production by 2025. Information for Mizoram and Sikkim could not be compiled because of unavailability of required information.

7.7 SWOT ANALYSIS

SWOT analysis was carried out to know the strengths, weaknesses, opportunities, and threats for the agricultural sector in the NER. The results are presented in Table 7.13.

Table 7.13 SWOT Analysis

Strength	Weakness
1. Mega biodiversity hot spot areas	1. Inaccessibility, marginality, and fragility
2. Abundant natural resources	2. Improper land use
3. Indigenous germplasm	3. Shifting cultivation
4. Border trade	4. Poor infrastructure
	5. Social unrest
	6. Lack of database
	7. Subsistence farming

Opportunities	Threats
1. Agro-ecological zone specific farming system	1. Extinction of bio-resources
2. Organic farming	2. Area being degraded due to shifting cultivation.
3. Mechanization	3. Replacement of ecosystem people by ecological refugees.
4. Rainwater harvesting	4. Germplasm piracy
5. Post-harvest and domestic market tapping	5. Competition from other countries
6. Agri export zone	6. Fragile ecology
7. Contract farming	
8. Agripreneurship	

The NER is constrained by various environmental, technical, and physical factors. The major environmental constraints are soil acidity, high rainfall and humidity, shifting cultivation, and land tenure system. Technical factors include lack of quality seeds and planting material, pest and disease management, mechanization, and so on; physical constraints include infrastructure and undulating topography.

The strength of NE agriculture lies in the fact that it is one of the 18 mega bio-diversity hot spots of the world. The region has 171.08 lakh ha of forest area, 39.08 lakh ha of agricultural land, besides waterbodies, and a sizeable population of livestock and poultry. The NER has approximately 4,500 indigenous crop germplasm. The region is rich in water resources and receives high amount of precipitation as rainfall. Available river, rivulet, streams, lake, reservoir, tank, pond, and other water bodies with perennial flow of water in the region show potential for irrigation, fishery, electricity generation, and so on. Women participation in agriculture in this region is also very high. Farmers are also rich in indigenous technical knowledge. Agro-tourism can also play a major role. This region shows a very high potential for rainbow revolution.

The weaknesses include inaccessibility, marginality, and fragility of the area. Overexploitation of forest for fuel, timber, and fodder also poses a major problem in the region. By and large, all crops, livestock and poultry, and fishery show lower yield as compared to the national average owing to the traditional and subsistence nature of cultivation practices. Shifting cultivation also proves to be unproductive due to shorter cycles. Undulating land, hill, terrain of region also hinders optimum agricultural production. Lack of availability of modern inputs, poor marketing facilities, lack of infrastructures such as cold storage, irrigation, regulated market, electricity, and so on, compel the rural youth to migrate to urban areas for livelihood. Lack of proper database is another problem of the region. Above all, social unrest really hampers the growth process in the region.

There are many opportunities for NE agriculture. The region is organic by default. In the near future, export may play a crucial role for the development of the region's agrarian economy (Bujarbaruah 2004). There is an urgent need to formulate research proposals to evaluate the comparative advantages of various agricultural and allied commodities for promoting exports including fruit, vegetables, processed products, meat, and so on in the Asian markets in near future. Production and productivity of all existing crops can be increased considerably using modern methods of cultivation. Water resources can easily be used for fishery and irrigation. A positive attitude towards commercial agriculture needs to be developed through contract farming and farm mechanization. The possibility of developing agri-input and food processing industry is very bright as raw materials are available and there are a high post-harvest losses.

There is a threat that the valuable bio resources may undergo extinction. There are some evil effects of shifting cultivation also. The competition from neighbouring countries under the new economic regime can never be ignored. Ecologically fragile regions hinder sustainable agricultural production. Flood and drought damage significant crop area, livestock, and so on every year. Owing to heavy rainfall, nutrient loss, soil erosion, and landslides are common phenomena in the region. In addition, it also attracts more pests and diseases.

Agricultural development strategy has to be evolved depending on resources, conditions, and people's needs and priorities. Private-sector participation can provide additional resources and create necessary environment to generate job opportunities, better utilization of resources and enhance credit flow impacting directly on farm-sector development. With appropriately defined targets, clear outcomes, strategies, and coordinated planning, the NER can become increasingly self-reliant in food output. Effective computer-based monitoring and management information system can facilitate timely implementation of programmes with improved quality and service delivery that can avoid cost and time overruns and yield envisioned results.

7.8. STRATEGIES FOR AGRICULTURAL DEVELOPMENT

From the preceding discussion, a few strategies for agricultural development may be drawn. These include the following:

- Intensive farming with yield-improvement strategies, crop diversification, development of cash crops and high-value crops.
- Extensive cultivation of prospective crops—expansion of area under summer rice, oilseeds, pulses, horticultural crops, development of medicinal and aromatic plants.
- Infrastructure development—storage, processing, marketing, irrigation, rural development and communication, input delivery, and credit supply.

- Technology development for different agro-ecological situations—upland, hill areas, and flood affected areas.
- Strengthening training and demonstration, on farm trials.

Above all, there is an urgent need for investment in the agricultural sector in the NER. For this purpose, the main agenda should be to attract new investors to this region. In this context, it is imperative to popularize the avenues and opportunities for investment in the NER (Ram et al. 2012).

7.8.1 Why Invest in North Eastern India?

- Fertile stretches of land
- Abundant forest resources
- Rich mineral resources
- Plentiful energy sources—Brahmaputra and its tributaries, forming the largest perennial water system in India, has immense potential for energy, irrigation, and transportation
- Storehouse of horticultural products/plantation, crops/vegetables/spices, and rare forest products
- Diverse tourist attractions
- Reasonably priced and easily available labour as well as growth centres, total tax free zones
- Subsidies on transport, capital investment, and interest on working capital are available for industries in the NER
- Proximity to countries that are members of South Asian Association for Regional Cooperation (SAARC)
- South East Asia is one of the fastest growing potential markets. The NER is close to Myanmar, the gateway to the ASEAN countries.

North East India's location advantage and rich natural resources provide a backdrop to its development as a base for foreign investors.

7.8.2 Prioritization and Policy Perspectives

- Agriculture in this region is mostly rain fed and under such a scenario cropping intensity is very difficult to increase. Development of irrigation facilities and promotion of water-harvesting methods for assured water supply particularly in the rabi season shall not only improve the cropping intensity but also help in increasing crop productivity.

- Establishment of agri-clinics near the production centre with single-window input delivery system.
- Technology showcasing at farmers' fields, technology back-stopping, farmer-participatory interaction programme on a continuous basis.
- Identification of need-based programmes for overcoming technology gaps through extensive field surveys under diverse agro ecological and socio-economic situations.
- Programmes to promote the development of cash crops such as jute, sugarcane, maize, horticultural crops, and so on.
- Creating storage facilities, particularly cold storage for perishable commodities.
- Introduction of value-addition to agricultural produce through research and development activities.
- Agricultural development programmes must take care of cropping pattern in the pre- and post-flood situations, particularly in flood-affected areas including development of allied agricultural activities.
- Improved crop cultivation practices for jhumming in hill areas.
- Financial support for creation of agricultural infrastructure such as strengthening irrigation facilities, farm machineries, processing and storage facilities, rural roads and communication.
- The Krishi Vigyan Kendra (KVK) should act as a change agent to transfer technology, extension services, market-information, and impart skill and management up-gradation training, and be the agent for social mobilization.
- Enabling product- and area-specific rural infrastructure should be created to add value to horticultural products, namely, Assam lemon, ginger, pineapple in Assam, passion fruits cultivated in Senapati district of Manipur, Anthurium in Aizawl district, Mizoram, strawberry cultivated under horticulture mission in RiBhoi district of Meghalaya, apple cultivated in Arunachal Pradesh.
- Marketing infrastructure to be created at the primary markets in rural areas.

7.9 CONCLUSION

NE India has a large untapped production reservoir. The progress of agricultural productivity and the economic and ecological well-being of farm families are inextricably linked. Resources are necessary but not panacea for tackling poverty, disparities, and backwardness. The determining factor is the institutional capacities to formulate viable need-based schemes/projects with efficient delivery systems to utilize optimally the available resources. Establishment of regional consultative and monitoring bodies would help to speed up the process.

The rich resource base in the region could be a potential source of agricultural and economic development of the NE India. However, due to lack of appropriate strategies for development of natural resources, absence of coordination in programme implementation, weak geographical links, and poor infrastructure facilities, the region is handicapped in catching up with the agricultural developmental pathways in tune with the national ethos. Slow agricultural development widens the disparities across the states. In this circumstance, agricultural sector needs prioritization of development perspectives for enhancing the adoption of recommended technologies through extension programmes, input supply, support of financial institutions, and marketing functionaries.

REFERENCES

Anon. 2014. *All India Report on Number and Area of Operation Holdings. Agricultural Census 2010–11.* DAC, Ministry of Agriculture, GOI.

Bagchi, K.K. 2008. *Agricultural Development in North East India, Issues and Options.* New Delhi, India: Abhijeet Publications.

Basic Statistics for North Eastern Region. 2015. *Various Issues of Basic Statistics for North Eastern Region.* Shillong: Published by NEC, Shillong NER data bank website.

Bujarbaruah, K.M. 2004. 'Organic Farming: Opportunities and Challenges in North Eastern Region of India'. In Souvenir. *International Conference on Organic Food 14–17 February, 2004.* Umiam, Meghalaya: ICAR Research Complex for NEH Region.

Buragohain, T. 2007. 'Agricultural Development and Sources of Growth of Output: An Analysis of Major Crops in India'. *Agricultural Situation in India* 64(6): 231–42.

Chakraborty, A. and K.K. Sarma, eds. 2015. *Status and Strategies for Improvement of Livestock and Poultry in Assam, Agriculture in Assam.* Jorhat: Assam Agricultural University.

Chand, Ramesh. 2004. 'Indian National Agricultural Policy: A Critique'. Working Paper No. 85, Institute of Economic Growth, Delhi.

Chetia, B.C. and S.K. Da, eds. 2015. *Fisheries Resources in Assam—Problems and Prospects, Agriculture in Assam.* Jorhat: Assam Agricultural University.

Das, A., D. Kalita, and S. Banik, eds. 2015. *Piggery Sector in Assam—Status and Way Forward, Agriculture in Assam*. Jorhat: Assam Agricultural University.

Das, S. 2016. 'Agriculture and Allied Sectors: Quantum Jump through New Initiative'. *Kurukhetra* 64(5): 5–8.

Hazarika, C. 2006. *Status of Agricultural Sector in North-East India: Problems and Prospects*. In Changing Agricultural Scenario in North East India. New Delhi: Published by Concept Publishing Company.

———. 2014. 'North East Agriculture: Dynamics and Perspectives'. In *Agriculture in North East India—Its Problems and Prospects*. Guwahati: Published by EBH Publishers (India).

National Horticultural Board Publications. 2014. Available at www.nhb.gov.in.

Ram, D., M.K. Singh, and A. Prasad. 2012. 'Prospects of Agriculture and Allied Entrepreneurship Development in North-East India'. *Indian Journal of Extension Education* Special Issue (II): 66–72.

8

Rural Economy

An Overview

*J. Dennis Rajakumar**

ABSTRACT

This chapter provides an overview of India's rural sector. Availability of data has facilitated a comparison of emerging rural scenario, on several axes, under economic reforms with the preceding two decades, as well as with their urban counterparts. Since the early 1990s, the rural sector has been witnessing structural transformation. Rural activities have become broad based with the farm sector's share in rural income declining and that of industry rising. Mirroring this, rural employment has become diversified, but the increased proportion of contract jobs pose a challenge to sustainable and guaranteed livelihood. Though registered manufacturing has increasingly become rural centric, the wage share in rural areas has been on the decline and also lower than their urban counterparts. Rural share in total bank deposits and credit show a marked rise in the 1970s and 1980s and in bank deposits only since then. The Credit Deposit (CD) ratio of rural areas remained far lower than that of urban areas since the 1990s and also compared to the preceding two decades despite the demand for financial services showing a marked rise. The consumption pattern in the rural sector has converged to that of urban sector, but the rate at which rural per capita consumption expenditure grew is lesser than that of urban. Although the terms of trade had favoured agriculture during the last two decades or so, the rural rich benefited the most given the skewed distribution of land holding. Reduction in urban poverty is faster than in rural poverty and the rural poor continue to account for about 81 per cent of the poor in the country. The findings indicate how India's growth is lopsided with a bias in favour of the urban sector. This reinforces the idea of achieving balanced rural and urban growth by appropriate policy interventions.

JEL Classification: J11, J21, J31, O16, O19, R10, R11, R12

Keywords: Indian economy, rural economy, rural employment, rural industrialization, rural banking and finance, rural well-being, rural–urban gap

* Director, EPW Research Foundation, Mumbai, India. The author wishes to thank S.L. Shetty, Gyanendra Mani, and the anonymous reviewer for their comments on the earlier draft of the paper.

8.1 INTRODUCTION

Rural versus urban sector is a defining dualistic character of the Indian economy. Rural development has been central to several policies pursued, be it under the state-controlled regime till about the early 1990s or later under the reforms regime. In the early era of planning, industrialization programmes focused on urban centres with the intent of reducing disguised unemployment featuring rural economy. Development strategies pursued in the 1970s and 1980s promoted industries in rural areas with an objective to alleviate poverty. In the post-reform era too, the state continues to focus on rural development by a number of policy measures.[1] Undeniably, state intervention has been the hallmark of rural development in the country during the last few decades, although forms of such intervention have changed from time to time.

This chapter provides an overview of the rural economy of India as discerned on several dimensions such as demographic profiles, vital health indicators, economic activities, factory characteristics, employment performance, financial intermediation and inclusiveness, consumption expenditure (CE), relative prices, and poverty. Besides analysing trends in these indicators, it also examines the rural–urban gap. While we recognize the profound influence of traditional social factors in rural India, we confine the analysis to these identified economic indicators.

This chapter relies on diverse sources of data published by several government agencies—time series, as well as census and sample surveys periodically conducted. For rural and urban classification, most of these data sources rely on the definition of a unit of habitation as followed by the Census of India. In Appendix 8.1, we provide how urban centres have been defined in different censuses and the balance of areas is taken as 'rural'.

[1] For more details, see Radhakrishna and Rao (2006).

8.2 RURAL DEMOGRAPHY

To begin with, we mapped the distribution of India's population between rural and urban centres (see Table 8.1). A notable feature of post-Independence development is the steady fall in the percentage of population living in rural areas—from 82.7 per cent in 1951 to 68.8 per cent in 2011. Between 2001 and 2011, the rate of decline was of a high order of 3.4 per cent, as in the decade of 1981–91. The ratio of rural to urban population was 4.78 in the census year 1951 and this has steadily gone down to 2.21 in 2011 (Figure 8.1), which suggests an increased urbanization in the country with nearly one-third of Indian population now residing in urban centres.

The compounded annual growth rate (CAGR)[2] of rural population not only indicated a declining trend but also remained lower than that of urban population. Rural population grew at a decelerating annual rate of 1.84 per cent during 1981–91, at 1.68 per cent during 1991–2001, and at 1.16 per cent during 2001–11. The CAGR of urban population during the last two decades has remained at 2.78 per cent and 2.8 per cent during 1991–2001 and 2001–11 respectively, which has generally been lower than that registered during previous decades, but higher than that of rural population. At 1.64 per cent, during 2001–11, the CAGR of total population was the lowest in comparison with previous periods. The observed declining growth in rural population has thus been a major factor responsible for contributing to the fall in the population growth in the country.

Literacy rate[3] has considerably improved in the country over the years (Table 8.2). Although literacy

[2] The formula is: $T = I (1 + r)^n$, where 'T' is terminal value, 'I' is initial value, 'n' is number of years and 'r' is CAGR. In India, census years are years ending with 01.

[3] Literacy rate refers to literate population in the population aged five years till 1991 and then seven years and above.

Table 8.1   Rural–Urban Distribution of Population: All India

Census	Rural			Urban			All-India	
	(in Millions)	CAGR %	% Share	(in Millions)	CAGR %	% Share	(in Millions)	CAGR %
1951	299	0.85	82.7	62	3.53	17.3	361	1.26
1961	360	1.90	82.0	79	2.37	18.0	439	1.98
1971	439	2.00	80.1	109	3.29	19.9	548	2.24
1981	524	1.78	76.7	159	3.87	23.3	683	2.23
1991	629	1.84	74.3	218	3.16	25.7	846	2.16
2001	743	1.68	72.2	286	2.78	27.8	1,029	1.97
2011	833	1.16	68.8	377	2.80	31.2	1,210	1.64

Source: Office of the Registrar General of India, Ministry of Home Affairs (Census documents).

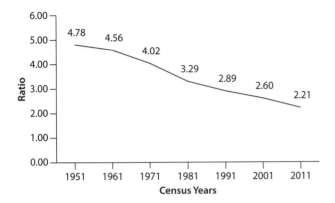

Figure 8.1   Rural Population to Urban Population

rate in rural areas has increased from 12.1 per cent in 1951 to 68.9 per cent in 2011, it continues to remain less when compared to urban. While the rural–urban gap in literacy rate widened till the 1970s, the gap has lowered thereafter, more prominently between 1991 and 2011 when the total increase in rural literacy rate was significant at 24.2 per cent, against 11.9 per cent in urban literacy rate. Thus, about one-fourth of the rural population has become literate during the last two decades. Such a scale of rise in rural literacy rate has reflected in the country's overall literacy rate, which has improved by 21.8 percentage points between 1991 and 2011. Given the overwhelming share of rural population in the total, rise in rural literacy influences literacy rate achieved at the country level. However, a disquieting trend is that one-third of the rural population still remains illiterate, against 15 per cent in urban centres.

Sex ratio, that is, the number of females per 1,000 males, continues to remain in favour of males in the country as well as in rural and urban areas (Table 8.2). Sex ratio fared better in rural areas than in urban areas but has steadily declined from 968 in 1951 to 938 in

1991, but then rose to 947 in 2011. On the other hand, sex ratio of urban centres has gradually risen from 860 in 1951 to 926 in 2011. Between 1951 and 1991, sex ratio of rural areas dropped by 27 but of urban areas rose by 34. During 1991–2011, the sex ratio increased by 9 and 32 respectively in rural and urban areas, thus helping the country's overall sex ratio to go up by 13.

Furthermore, several health indicators such as crude birth rate, crude death rate, infant mortality rate, and total fertility rate have been declining over the years in both rural and urban areas (Table 8.3). On these health indicators, the urban sector is found to be performing better than the rural sector; however, the rural–urban gap in these indicators has reduced noticeably.

The social sector indicators of rural areas have improved phenomenally over years—literacy rate rising, sex ratio improving in favour of females, and health indicators showing signs of a better healthy society. More importantly, the rural–urban gap in these indicators has also been reducing. In particular, the improvement noticed in the post-1991 census is noteworthy. This shows that with rising urbanization, the character of rural India has also been changing. Population growth has implications for labour supply and so lower rural population growth would mean a possible reduction in rural labour force in future. At the same time, demand for quality employment may be expected to go up with improved literacy rate and female participation in labour force may be expected to increase with better sex ratio.

8.3 STRUCTURE OF THE RURAL ECONOMY IN INDIA

We propose to understand the structure of rural economy by examining (a) relative share of rural income by sectors and (b) sectoral composition of rural income. For the purpose of analysis, we have relied on sector-wise

Table 8.2   Rural–Urban Gap in Literacy Rate and Sex Ratio

Census	Literacy Rate				Sex Ratio			
	All India	Urban	Rural	Rural–Urban Gap	All India	Urban	Rural	Rural–Urban Gap
1951	18.3	34.6	12.1	−22.5	946	860	965	105.4
1961	28.3	47.0	19.1	−27.9	941	845	963	118.1
1971	34.5	52.4	23.7	−28.7	930	858	949	91.1
1981	43.6	67.3	36.1	−31.3	934	879	951	71.8
1991	52.2	73.1	44.7	−28.4	927	894	938	44.4
2001	64.8	79.9	58.7	−21.2	933	901	946	45.2
2011	74.0	85.0	68.9	−16.1	940	926	947	21.0

Source: Office of the Registrar General of India, Ministry of Home Affairs (Census documents).

Table 8.3   Health Indicators: All India, Rural, and Urban

	1971	1981	1991	2001	2011
Crude Birth Rate					
All India	36.9	33.9	29.5	25.4	21.8
Rural	38.9	35.6	30.9	27.1	23.3
Urban	30.1	27	34.3	20.3	17.6
Rural Urban Gap	8.8	8.6	-3.4	6.8	5.7
Crude Death Rate					
All India	14.9	12.5	9.8	8.4	7.1
Rural	16.4	13.7	10.6	9.1	7.6
Urban	9.7	7.8	7.1	6.3	5.7
Rural Urban Gap	6.7	5.9	3.5	2.8	1.9
Infant Mortality Rate					
All India	129	110	80	66	44
Rural	138	119	87	72	48
Urban	82	62	53	42	29
Rural Urban Gap	56	57	34	30	19
Total Fertility Rate					
All India	5.2	4.5	3.6	3.1	2.4
Rural	5.4	4.8	3.9	3.4	2.7
Urban	4.1	3.3	2.7	2.3	1.9
Rural Urban Gap	1.3	1.5	1.2	1.1	0.8

Source: Office of the Registrar General of India, Ministry of Home Affairs (Census documents).

national domestic product (NDP) at factor cost made available by Central Statistics Office (CSO) separately for rural and urban areas. Unlike other major economic statistics given in National Accounts Statistics (NAS), the rural and urban NDP data are available only for base years[4] starting from 1970–1.

Rural income, as percentage of economy-wide NDP, has been on the declining trend from 62.4 per cent in 1970–1 to 47.4 per cent in 2011–12—a fall of 15 percentage points. This was also a period when the percentage of rural population registered a decline of 11.5 percentage points. The rate of decline in the share of rural in total income is more than that of its population share, and this suggests that the rural sector did not perform as well as its urban counterparts. Such overall trend is reflected even if the entire period is divided into two segments, namely, 1970–1 to 1993–4 (period 1) and 1993–4 to 2011–12 (period 2). During period 1, share of rural income declined by 8.6 percentage points, whereas of rural population declined by 6.7 points. During period 2, the decline was in the order of 6.3 and 4.8 percentage points, respectively. Rural per capita NDP as percentage of country's per capita NDP also went down by 8.8 percentage points between 1970–1 and 2011–12 (Figure 8.2). Rural per capita NDP as percentage to all India remained lesser during period 2; but within this period, it marginally improved from 66.6 per cent in 1999–2000 to 69 per cent in 2011–12. Urban per capita thus outnumbered rural per capita.

[4] Base years for which sector-wise NDP by rural and urban are available include 1970–1, 1980–1, 1993–4, 1999–2000, 2004–5, and 2011–12.

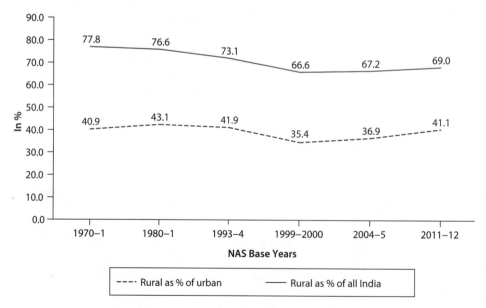

Figure 8.2   Rural Per Capita as % of Urban and All India

Source: Author's calculation based on CSO, NAS (1999, 2006, 2009, and 2016).

Table 8.4   Sectoral Rural NDP as % of Total (All India)

Sl No.	Sectors	1970–1	1980–1	1993–4	1999–2000	2004–5	2011–12
1	Agriculture, forestry, and fishing	96.2	94.9	93.9	93.2	94.0	94.5
2	Mining and quarrying	61.0	54.7	65.9	42.4	66.3	53.4
3	Manufacturing	25.8	31.8	29.8	41.5	42.5	51.2
3.1	Registered	23.7	20.4	30.1	39.9	41.9	
3.2	Unregistered	28.1	45.2	29.3	44.3	43.4	
4	Electricity, gas, and water supply	39.8	40.0	37.9	45.4	33.2	33.2
5	Construction	43.2	45.6	45.1	43.3	45.5	46.9
6	Trade, hotels, and restaurants	18.2	30.3	31.0	27.1	40.9	27.9
6.1	Trade			31.3	26.3	41.0	27.9
6.2	Hotels and restaurants			25.6	35.9	39.5	28.2
7	Transport, storage, and communication	22.8	23.0	34.7	29.3	33.4	29.8
7.1	Transport	20.4	20.0	33.4	28.9	37.4	36.6
7.2	Storage		16.7	31.0	31.2	14.0	39.6
7.3	Communication	35.8	38.7	41.6	30.8	17.0	6.8
8	Banking and insurance	19.3	15.7	16.4	14.5	14.8	13.1
9	Real estate, ownership of dwelling, and business services	48.4	50.0	40.2	32.1	35.8	36.4
10	Public administration and defence	42.2	34.3	40.3	19.9	16.1	18.9
11	Other services	37.9	42.9	42.2	36.3	36.3	31.3
12	Total: Net domestic product	62.4	58.9	53.7	48.3	48.0	47.4
	By Farm and Non-farm Activities						
A	Farm	96.2	94.9	93.9	93.2	94.0	94.5
B	Non-farm	32.4	35.0	34.8	31.8	36.8	36.0
	By Broad Sectors						
I	Agriculture	96.2	94.9	93.9	93.2	94.0	94.5
II	Industry	31.9	36.3	36.9	42.4	45.6	49.0
III	Services	32.8	34.0	33.6	27.1	32.7	27.7
	By Per Capita						
12	Population (in million)	80.2	76.9	73.5	72.5	71.4	68.7
13	Per capita NDP	77.8	76.6	73.1	66.6	67.2	69.0

Note: A and I represent 1; non-farm represents all non-agriculture activities; industry includes 2, 3, 4, and 5; services includes 6, 7, 8, 9, and 10.
Sources: CSO, *NAS* (1999, 2006, 2009, and 2016).

We have grouped economic activities broadly into farm and non-farm. Agriculture and allied activities consisting of crop, forestry, fishing, and livestock are considered farm activities, and others belonging to industry and services as non-farm activities.[5] According

to Census classification, urban centres are defined as towns with at least 75 per cent of the male population engaged in non-agricultural activities, while rural areas are villages. Thus, a large concentration of farm activities may be expected in rural areas and non-farm activities in urban centres (Table 8.4). This has been mirrored in the relatively higher contribution of rural areas to the

[5] It is worth mentioning here that the NDP of farm sector mentioned here is not same as that of income of farmers. The farm sectoral income has to be shared by farmers as well as hired workers. For further discussion, see Chand et al. (2015). The principal source of income of agricultural households is diversified. An estimate by Chandrasekhar and Mehrotra (2016), based on NSSO's Situation Assessment Survey of Agricultural Households

2013, shows that as much as 31.8 per cent of total agricultural households have principal source of income other than agricultural activities per se; non-agricultural enterprises (4.7 per cent of total), wage/salaried employment (22 per cent), pension (1.1 per cent), remittances (3.3 per cent), and others (0.7 per cent).

country's farm income—at as high as 94 per cent, and a little over one-third of non-farm income. Although rural share in total income has gone down over the years, its share in farm income has remained nearly the same and in non-farm income marginally has gone up from 32.4 per cent in 1970–1 to 36.0 per cent in 2011–12, with a dip to 31.8 per cent in 1999–2000. During the last decade, there has been a rise in the rural sector's contribution to non-farm income, but, at the same time, its share in the country's NDP marginally reduced.

A major structural shift is taking place with rural India emerging as the manufacturing hub of the country. Back in 1970–1, the share of rural area in manufacturing NDP was about one-fourth and this has steadily doubled by 2011–12, contributing a little over one-half of the manufacturing income. A steady rise in the registered manufacturing NDP of rural areas is also seen between 1970–1 and 2004–5. But rural contribution to NDP of electricity, gas, and water supply shows a gradual decline from 39.8 per cent in 1970–1 to 33.2 per cent in 2011–12, except a spike in 1999–2000 to 45.4 per cent. Comparing two time points, that is 1970–1 and 2011–12, one can see a small rise in the share of rural areas in its share in the NDP of sectors such as construction, trade, hotel and restaurants, and transport; but a noticeable decline is seen in its share in the NDP of sectors such as mining and quarrying, communication, banking and insurance, real estate and ownership of dwelling, public administration, and other services. Among non-farm sectors, the share of rural areas in industry NDP has simultaneously gone up from 31.9 per cent in 1970–1 to 49 per cent in 2011–12, whereas in services NDP, its share has declined from 32.8 per cent to 27.7 per cent during the same period with some fluctuations in between. This shows that the share of urban centres in non-farm activities has gradually declined largely due to declining share in manufacturing NDP and this has also reduced its share in industry as a whole.

8.3.1 Structural Changes within the Rural Economy

In order to gauge the structure of the rural economy, sectoral composition of rural NDP has been worked out (Table 8.5). The importance of a sector can be reckoned by its relative contribution to total NDP of rural sector, and changes in the relative importance of a sector would imply structural change taking place. A major transformation has taken place within the rural economy with a sharp decline in the role of agriculture in it. Viewed thus, it is seen that the farm sector has been losing its significance in the rural areas with its contribution to

rural NDP falling from 72.4 per cent in 1970–1 to 39 per cent in 2011–12, although this has been arrested, though fractionally, since 2004–5. Simultaneously, considerable diversification has occurred in the rural economy, which is being reflected in a rise in the relative contributions from other sectors, although in varying degrees.

Particularly, the manufacturing sector's contribution to rural NDP has gone up from 5.9 per cent in 1970–1 to 17.2 per cent in 2011–12, up by 11.3 percentage points. Contribution of construction sector to rural NDP has also gone up by 6.7 percentage points from 3.5 per cent in 1970–1 to 10.2 per cent in 2011–12. The share of trade, hotels, and restaurants also shows a rise by 4.2 percentage points during the same period. A close look, however, reveals that one half of the rise in the share of manufacturing or by 5.3 percentage points from 11.9 per cent of rural NDP to 17.2 per cent has taken place in just about half a decade during 2004–5 to 2011–12, with the share of trade in rural NDP falling correspondingly from 13.7 per cent in 2004–5 to 6.2 per cent in 2011–2. Such a sharp decline is noticeable at the all-India level as well. This has been due to corrections made in the estimates of gross value added (GVA) from trade when NAS was rebased to 2011–12.[6]

8.3.2 Services Dominate the Urban Areas

Urban economic activities are dominated by services; more than two-thirds of urban NDP originates from the services sector. Farm activities not only have a small contribution (about 5 per cent in the 1970s and 1980s), but it has also further shrunk (to about 2 per cent in 2011–12). Industry's contribution to urban NDP has also come down over the years, although a marginal rise is seen in 2011–12. Within industry, manufacturing's share has nearly halved from 28 per cent in the early 1970s to

[6] The GVA of unorganized trade for 2004–5 was based on the results of the Enterprise Survey (ES) and Employment and Unemployment Survey (EUS) of NSS 55th Round in 1999–2000. In 2004–5, this was moved forward by using Gross Trading Income (GTI) Index, which was a volume indicator, assuming a strong correlation between volume and value added. In the survey of the unincorporated sector in 2010–11 (NSS 67th Round), trade was included and estimates obtained from this survey were observed to be at variance with previous estimates of the GVA of trade sector. On observing overstated GVA of unorganized trade sector under previous estimate, the CSO carried out necessary correction under the NAS new series (2011–12). This gave rise to a fall in the relative share of trade in the country's overall GVA as well (Central Statistics Office, 2015). A part of the trading activity is now being covered under manufacturing, which is partly responsible for the rise in that sector's share.

Table 8.5 Sectoral Shares in Respective Years Total

Sl No.	Sectors	Rural						Urban						All India					
		1970–1	1980–1	1993–4	1999–2000	2004–5	2011–12	1970–1	1980–1	1993–4	1999–2000	2004–5	2011–12	1970–1	1980–1	1993–4	1999–2000	2004–5	2011–12
1	Agriculture, forestry and fishing	72.4	64.4	56.1	51.8	38.3	39.0	4.7	5.0	4.2	3.5	2.2	2.1	46.9	40.0	32.1	26.9	19.6	19.6
2	Mining and quarrying	0.8	1.2	2.5	1.8	3.7	3.6	0.9	1.5	1.5	2.3	1.7	2.8	0.9	1.3	2.0	2.1	2.7	3.2
3	Manufacturing	5.9	9.2	8.1	10.9	11.9	17.2	28.0	28.1	22.3	14.4	14.8	14.8	14.2	16.9	14.7	12.7	13.4	16.0
3.1	Registered	2.9	3.1	5.2	6.6	7.0		15.3	17.7	14.2	9.3	9.0		7.6	9.1	9.4	8.0	8.1	
3.2	Unregistered	3.0	6.0	2.9	4.3	4.8	1.2	12.6	10.5	8.2	5.1	5.8	2.2	6.6	7.8	5.3	4.7	5.3	1.7
4	Electricity, gas, and water supply	0.4	0.6	0.8	1.4	0.7	1.2	0.9	1.2	1.6	1.6	1.2	2.2	0.6	0.8	1.2	1.5	1.0	1.7
5	Construction	3.5	4.1	4.5	5.7	7.9	10.2	7.6	6.9	6.4	7.0	8.8	10.4	5.0	5.2	5.4	6.4	8.4	10.3
6	Trade, hotels and restaurants	2.7	6.7	8.7	8.6	15.0	6.9	20.3	22.0	22.5	21.8	20.0	16.0	9.3	13.0	15.1	15.4	17.6	11.7
6.1	Trade			8.4	7.7	13.7	6.2			21.5	20.2	18.2	14.4			14.5	14.2	16.1	10.5
6.2	Hotels and restaurants			0.3	0.9	1.3	0.7			1.0	1.6	1.8	1.6			0.6	1.3	1.5	1.1
7	Transport, storage, and communication	1.3	1.3	4.0	4.0	5.8	3.9	7.1	6.3	8.8	9.0	10.7	8.2	3.4	3.4	6.2	6.6	8.4	6.2
7.1	Transport	0.9	0.9	3.2	3.0	5.2	3.6	6.1	5.3	7.3	7.0	8.1	5.6	2.9	2.7	5.1	5.1	6.7	4.7
7.2	Storage	0.0	0.0	0.0	0.1	0.0	0.1	0.0	0.2	0.1	0.1	0.1	0.1	0.1	0.1	0.1	0.1	0.1	0.1

(Contd)

Table 8.5 (*Cont'd*)

Sl No.	Sectors	Rural						Urban						All India					
		1970–1	198–1	1993–4	1999–2000	2004–5	2011–12	1970–1	1980–1	1993–4	1999–2000	2004–5	2011–12	1970–1	1980–1	1993–4	1999–2000	2004–5	2011–12
7.3	Communication	0.3	0.4	0.8	0.9	0.6	0.2	0.9	0.8	1.3	1.9	2.5	2.5	0.5	0.6	1.0	1.4	1.6	1.4
8	Banking and insurance	0.5	0.8	1.7	1.9	2.0	1.8	3.7	6.2	10.1	10.6	10.4	10.9	1.7	3.0	5.6	6.4	6.3	6.6
9	Real estate, ownership of dwelling, and business services	6.2	4.6	4.2	4.6	6.5	9.6	10.9	6.5	7.2	9.0	10.7	15.1	8.0	5.4	5.6	6.9	8.6	12.5
10	Public administration and defence	3.0	2.8	4.1	2.7	1.9	2.2	6.8	7.7	7.0	10.3	9.2	8.7	4.4	4.8	5.5	6.7	5.7	5.6
11	Other services	3.4	4.5	5.2	6.4	6.4	4.5	9.1	8.5	8.3	10.5	10.4	8.8	5.5	6.1	6.6	8.5	8.5	6.8
11	Net domestic product	100.0	100.0	100.0	100.0	100.0	100.0	100.0	100.0	100.0	100.0	100.0	100.0	100.0	100.0	100.0	100.0	100.0	100.0
	By Farm and Nonfarm activities																		
A	Farm	72.4	64.4	56.1	51.8	38.3	39.0	4.7	5.0	4.2	3.5	2.2	2.1	46.9	40.0	32.1	26.9	19.6	19.6
B	Non-farm	27.6	35.6	43.9	48.2	61.7	61.0	95.3	95.0	95.8	96.5	97.8	97.9	53.1	60.0	67.9	73.1	80.4	80.4
	Net domestic product	100.0	100.0	100.0	100.0	100.0	100.0	100.0	100.0	100.0	100.0	100.0	100.0	100.0	100.0	100.0	100.0	100.0	100.0
	By broad sectors																		
I	Agriculture	72.4	64.4	56.1	51.8	38.3	39.0	4.7	5.0	4.2	3.5	2.2	2.1	46.9	40.0	32.1	26.9	19.6	19.6
II	Industry	10.6	15.0	16.0	19.9	24.1	32.2	37.4	37.7	31.8	25.3	26.5	30.2	20.7	24.3	23.3	22.7	25.4	31.1
III	Services	17.1	20.6	27.9	28.3	37.5	28.8	57.9	57.3	64.0	71.2	71.2	67.8	32.5	35.7	44.6	50.5	55.1	49.3
	Net domestic product	100.0	100.0	100.0	100.0	100.0	100.0	100.0	100.0	100.0	100.0	100.0	100.0	100.0	100.0	100.0	100.0	100.0	100.0

Note: A and I represent 1; Non-farm represent all non-agriculture activities; Industry includes 2, 3, 4, and 5; Services includes 6, 7, 8, 9, and 10.
Sources: CSO, *NAS* (1999, 2006, 2009, and 2016).

about 14.8 per cent in 2011–12. A marginal rise is seen in the share of construction that helped to improve the overall share of industry in urban NDP in the latest years. The rising prominence of services sector in urban areas is largely due to the boom in banking and insurance activities, which contributed 10.9 per cent to urban NDP in 2011–12 compared to 3.7 per cent in 1970–1, and also due to the increased contribution of real estate, ownership of dwelling and business services increased from 10.9 per cent to 15.1 per cent during the same period.

While rural NDP has the dominance of agriculture and industry, the services sector has considerable share in urban and all-India NDP. In 1970–1, industry used to contribute 10.6 per cent to rural NDP, compared to 37.4 per cent of urban NDP and 20.7 per cent of the country's NDP. This has gradually changed and in 2011–12, the sector's contribution remained in the order of 32.2 per cent, 30.2 per cent, and 31.1 per cent respectively of rural, urban, and the country's NDP. Rise in the share of industry in rural NDP has been aided by manufacturing activities that constitute a relatively higher share in rural NDP compared to that in urban NDP. Rural activities thus have increasingly become broad-based. The reduction in its reliance on farm (agriculture-based) activities is a fact of considerable importance, and it is fast being replaced by industry, particularly manufacturing. We will examine this later in some details.

8.4 EMPLOYMENT PERFORMANCE

Employment generation has been central to the country's development policies, particularly with regard to improving the rural economy. Examining employment situation is thus germane to an understanding of the rural economy. We have relied on the estimates presented in various rounds of Employment and Unemployment Surveys (EUS) of National Sample Survey Office (NSSO) with different reference periods.[7]

To begin with, we have examined labour force and their participation rate.[8]

8.4.1 Labour Force Participation Rates

The total labour force[9] in the country, as per NSSO's estimates, had gone up from 240.2 million in 1973–4 to 483.7 million in 2011–12 (Table 8.6). Rural labour force has accounted for a major chunk of the total labour force, 199.6 million and 342.4 million respectively, during these years.[10] Thus, as a percentage of total labour force, rural labour force has come down from 83.1 per cent in 1973–4 to 70.8 per cent in 2011–12, which is also reflected in lower CAGR of rural labour force compared to the total. Both in terms of absolute size and as percentage to total, urban labour force has gone up. While percentage of male labour force has increased in rural areas, that of female labour force has gone up in urban centres. The CAGR of male and female labour force in rural areas remained relatively low compared to that of urban centres. During the period 2004–5 to 2011–12, female labour force in rural areas has sharply fallen by (–)2.8 per cent and total labour force increased marginally by 0.4 per cent. The decelerated annual growth in total labour force between 2004–5 and 2011–12 is mostly due to the sharp fall in rural labour force, particularly the female labour force, which in turn is explained by the qualitative changes in the nature of labour force participation in rural areas.

The labour force participation rate (LFPR)[11] remained higher throughout in rural areas compared to urban centres. But the LFPR has been gradually declining in rural areas and rising in urban centres and consequently the rural-urban gap narrowed down from 9.4 percentage points in 1973–4 to 3.9 points in 2011–2. The LFPR represents willingness to work (basically labour supply in relation to total population) and so, a falling LIFR suggests rising withdrawal symptom of labour force in rural sector. The LFPR of rural females remained well above

---

[7] The concepts and definitions recommended by an Expert Committee on Unemployment Estimates have been uniformly used in surveys starting from NSS 27th round (October 1972–September 1973). Since then eight quinquennial surveys had been conducted such as 32nd round (July 1977–June 1978), 38th round (January–December 1983), 43rd round (July 1987–June 1988), 50th round (July 1993–June 1994), 55th round (July 1999–June 2000), 61st round (July 2004–June 2005), 66th round (July 2009–June 2010), and 68th round (July 2011–June 2012). For further details, see NSSO 2014a, chapter 1.

Though estimates are available in these successive NSS rounds, we propose to consider only those years either falling close to or overlapping with NAS base years. Thus, we have avoided 32nd round (1977–8), 43rd round (1987–88), and 66th round (2009–2010).

[8] To capture employment situations, NSSO used to have three reference periods, namely, one year, one week, and each day of the reference week. Here, we have taken into account the reference period of one year, which is captured through principal status (ps) and subsidiary status (ss)—collectively they are known as usual status (ps + ss). For further details, see NSSO 2014a, chapter 1.

[9] This includes number of persons employed and number of persons unemployed.

[10] For regional dimension, see Himanshu (2015).

[11] Labour force participation rate represents size of labour force (number of persons employed + number of persons unemployed) as per cent of total population.

Table 8.6   Labour and Workforce Participation Rate by Usual Status (PS + SS) (%)

Reference Year	Labour Force (in Million)						Labour Force Participation Rate (%)		
	Rural		Urban		All India		Rural	Urban	All India
Persons									
1972–3	199.6		40.6		240.2		43.9	34.5	42.0
1983	247.2	(2.0)	63.2	(4.1)	310.4	(2.4)	45.2	36.2	43.0
1993–4	293.0	(1.7)	85.7	(3.1)	378.7	(2.0)	44.9	36.3	42.7
1999–2000	305.2	(0.7)	100.7	(2.7)	405.9	(1.2)	42.3	35.4	40.4
2004–5	348.7	(2.7)	120.3	(3.6)	469.0	(2.9)	44.6	38.2	43.0
2011–12	342.4	–(0.3)	141.3	(2.3)	483.7	(0.4)	40.6	36.7	39.5
Male									
1972–3	128.7		32.9		161.6		55.1	52.1	54.5
1983	155.9	(1.8)	50.2	(3.9)	206.1	(2.2)	55.5	54.0	55.1
1993–4	189.3	(2.0)	67.3	(3.0)	256.6	(2.2)	56.1	54.3	55.6
1999–2000	200.2	(0.9)	80.7	(3.1)	280.8	(1.5)	54.0	54.2	54.1
2004–5	222.5	(2.1)	93.9	(3.1)	316.4	(2.4)	55.5	57.0	55.9
2011–12	238.8	(1.0)	112.5	(2.6)	351.3	(1.5)	55.3	56.3	55.6
Female									
1972–3	70.9		7.7		78.6		32.1	14.2	28.6
1983	91.3	(2.3)	13.0	(4.9)	104.3	(2.6)	34.2	15.9	29.9
1993–4	104.7	(1.4)	18.4	(3.5)	123.1	(1.7)	33.0	16.5	28.7
1999–00	105.0	(0.0)	20.0	(1.4)	125.1	(0.3)	30.2	14.7	25.8
2004–5	126.2	(3.7)	26.4	(5.7)	152.6	(4.1)	33.3	17.8	29.4
2011–12	103.6	–(2.8)	28.8	(1.3)	132.4	–(2.0)	25.3	14.7	22.5

Note: Figures in brackets are growth rates (CAGR) over the previous reference period; Data relate to usual status of individuals. Usual Status = Principal Status (PS) + Subsidiary Status (SS); Labour force covers those involved in gainful activity regularly, those involved in gainful activity occasionally and those unemployed; Labour force participation rate represents size of labour force as per cent of population.
Source: National Sample Survey Office (NSSO), various reports.

their urban counterparts throughout; the rural–urban gap in female LFPR had come down over the years from 17.9 percentage points in 1973–4 to 10.6 in 2011–12. Thus, rural females are more in supply in the job market in comparison to urban females, but in a declining trend. In terms of absolute size, as per NSSO estimates, urban female labours used to be about 10.7 per cent of rural female labours in 1973–4 and this has gradually risen to 27.8 per cent in 2011–12. No doubt, urban females' participation is on the rise.

The LFPR of rural females continues to be lower than that of their male counterparts. There is a preponderance of supply of rural male labourers in the country's labour market. The LFPR of rural male labours had virtually stagnated. The LFPR for urban males accounted for 25.7% of LFPR for rural males in 1973–4 and this has gradually risen to 47.1 per cent in 2011–12. The LFPR of rural males remained marginally higher than that of urban males

between 1973–4 and 1993–4, but thereafter LFPR of urban males remained higher. LFPR among rural females is relatively higher compared to their urban counterparts; but lower compared to male counterparts. The observed marginal fall in the overall LFPR could be attributed to a virtual stagnation in the LFPR of rural males and of urban females, and decline in LFPR of rural females.

8.4.2 Workforce Participation Rates

A similar trend is also noticed in respect of workforce and workforce participation rate (WFPR) (Table 8.7). By definition, a workforce comprises those who are actually employed either on principal status or subsidiary status. According to NSSO estimates, the size of rural workforce increased gradually from 197.8 million in 1972–3, to 290.3 million in 1993–4 and further to 342.9 million in 2004–5, but it declined to 336.4 million in 2011–12.

Table 8.7 Workforce Participation Rate by Usual Status (PS + SS) (%)

Reference Year	Workforce (in Million)						Workforce Participation Rate (%)		
	Rural		Urban		All India	All India	Rural	Urban	All India
Persons									
1972–3	197.8		38.5		236.3		43.5	32.7	
1983	243.1	(1.9)	59.6	(4.1)	302.7	(2.3)	44.5	34.0	42.0
1993–4	290.3	(1.8)	81.8	(3.2)	372.1	(2.1)	44.4	34.7	42.0
1999–2000	300.8	(0.6)	96.0	(2.7)	396.8	(1.1)	41.7	33.7	39.7
2004–5	342.9	(2.7)	115.0	(3.7)	457.9	(2.9)	43.9	36.5	42.0
2011–12	336.4	–(0.3)	136.5	(2.5)	472.9	(0.5)	39.9	35.5	38.6
Male									
1972–73	127.2		31.8		159.0		54.5	50.1	
1983	152.7	(1.7)	47.3	(3.7)	200.0	(2.1)	54.7	51.2	53.8
1993–4	186.6	(2.0)	64.5	(3.2)	251.1	(2.3)	55.3	52.1	54.5
1999–2000	196.8	(0.9)	77.1	(3.0)	273.9	(1.5)	53.1	51.8	52.7
2004–05	201.7	(0.5)	70.7	–(1.7)	272.4	–(0.1)	54.6	54.9	54.7
2011–12	234.6	(2.2)	109.2	(6.4)	343.8	(3.4)	54.3	54.6	54.4
Female									
1972–73	70.6		7.2		77.8		31.8	13.4	
1983	90.4	(2.3)	12.3	(5.0)	102.7	(2.6)	34.0	15.1	21.6
1993–94	103.7	(1.4)	17.3	(3.5)	121.0	(1.7)	32.8	15.5	28.6
1999–2000	104.0	(0.0)	18.9	(1.5)	122.9	(0.3)	29.9	13.9	25.9
2004–5	116.1	(2.2)	19.7	(0.8)	135.8	(2.0)	32.7	16.6	28.7
2011–12	101.8	–(1.9)	27.3	(4.8)	129.1	–(0.7)	24.8	14.7	21.9

Note: Figures in brackets are the CAGR over previous reference period. Data relate to usual status of individuals. Usual Status = Principal Status (PS) + Subsidiary Status (SS); Workforce covers those involved in gainful activity regularly and those involved in gainful activity occasionally; Workforce participation rate represents size of workforce as per cent of population.
Source: National Sample Survey Office (NSSO), various reports.

The rural workforce has been dominated by males, whose proportionate share remained at about 65 per cent between 1972–3 and 1999–2000. Though this went down to 58.8 per cent in 2004–5, it subsequently rose to 70 per cent in 2011–12. There is a surge in female work participation in the rural sector in 2004–5 and this was reduced in 2011–12 to a level lower than what prevailed in the preceding decades. The annual rate of increase in rural female workforce was negative at (–)1.9 per cent, compared to 4.8 per cent of urban female workforce, and 0.5 per cent of total workforce during 2004–5 to 2011–12. Rural workforce used to be 5.1 times more than urban workforce in 1972–3, which gradually declined to 3.5 per cent in 1993–4 and further to 2.5 per cent in 2011–12. The WFPR of rural males remained constant at 54 per cent in all survey years, whereas of rural females shows a decline. In sharp contrast, WFPR of urban males and females shows an upward trend. This shows that employment in rural sector has stagnated for rural males, contracted for females, and improved for urban males and females.

Scholars have tried to assess quality of employment by taking into account if labour force has been self-employed, employed on regular basis, or on contract basis (Papola and Sahu 2012). Given the regularity of income and security of job, a higher proportion of employment on regular basis indicates better quality of employment and the opposite holds if casual labour dominates. Self-employment remains neutral as welfare would vary depending upon the fortune of the enterprise.

8.4.3 Rising Proportion of Casualization

As for rural segments, the percentage of self-employed, of both males and females, have come down; the fall is more prominent in the case of males (Table 8.8).

Table 8.8   Percentage Distribution of Employees by Status

	Self-Employed		Regular Employees		Casual Labour		Index of Casualization	
	Male	Female	Male	Female	Male	Female	Male	Female
Rural + Urban								
1972–3	60.6	63.0	19.7	6.3	19.7	30.7	100.0	487.3
1983	55.9	60.0	18.2	5.6	25.9	34.4	142.3	614.3
1993–4	53.7	56.8	16.7	6.2	29.6	37.0	177.2	596.8
1999–2000	51.5	55.8	17.2	7.1	31.3	37.1	182.0	522.5
2004–5	54.7	61.4	17.2	8.3	28.1	30.3	163.4	365.1
2011–12	50.7	56.1	19.8	12.7	29.4	31.2	148.5	245.7
Rural								
1972–3	65.9	64.5	12.1	4.1	22.0	31.4	181.8	765.9
1983	60.5	61.9	10.3	2.8	29.2	35.3	283.5	1260.7
1993–4	57.7	58.6	8.5	2.7	33.8	38.7	397.6	1433.3
1999–2000	55.0	57.3	8.8	3.1	36.2	39.6	411.4	1277.4
2004–5	58.1	63.7	9.0	3.7	32.9	32.6	365.6	881.1
2011–12	54.5	59.3	10.0	5.6	35.5	35.1	355.0	626.8
Urban								
1972–3	39.2	48.4	50.7	27.9	10.1	23.7	19.9	84.9
1983	40.9	45.8	43.7	25.8	15.4	28.4	35.2	110.1
1993–4	41.7	44.8	42	29.2	16.3	26.1	38.8	89.4
1999–2000	41.5	45.3	41.7	33.3	16.8	21.4	40.3	64.3
2004–5	44.8	47.7	40.6	35.6	14.6	16.7	36.0	46.9
2011–12	41.7	42.8	43.4	42.8	14.9	14.3	34.3	33.4

Source: National Sample Survey Office (NSSO), various reports.

The percentage of regular employees has also been on a downward trend though a reversal happened marginally in 2011–12. Concomitantly, the percentage of casual labour has gone up. Rural female labour was increasingly engaged in casual jobs until 1999–2000. The point differences between percentage of males and females doing contract job has been closing down in the last decade due to increased male employment in casual jobs. In the recent years, more than one-third of rural males, like females, are employed on contract basis. In sharp contrast, an overwhelming percentage of males and females have been employed on regular basis in urban areas; the percentage of male regular employees has come down over the years, whereas that of female employees accelerated. The percentage of male casual labour went up in the 1970s but of female casual labour has come down. We have worked out an index of casualization, by expressing casual jobs as percentage to regular jobs. This shows an accelerated trend in the casualization of labour force, noticeably of rural males and females. Urban females

taking up regular jobs have also gone up. More so, decline in the self-employed males and females in rural segment is prominent compared to urban areas. Rural economy is thus not only featured by falling LFPR/WFPR, but also by questionable quality of the employment opportunities. Not only have the employment in urban segments moved up, but also the quality of urban employment appears to be better.

8.4.4 Employment Diversification

A conjecture based on the observed rise in casualization of labour is that most of the employment would have occurred in the farm sector (agriculture), which does not offer regular jobs. On the whole, agriculture continues to be the main economic activity accounting for a sizeable proportion of employment (Table 8.9). However, in rural areas, its importance has come down, with the percentage of workers employed in agriculture sector falling from 85.6 per cent in 1972–3 to about 64.1 per cent

Table 8.9   Sectoral Distribution of Workers (in Terms of Usual Status [PS + SS]) by Residence

	Agriculture	Industry					Services			
		Sub-total	Mining and Quarrying	Manufacturing	Electricity, Gas, and Water	Construction	Sub-total	Trade	Transport and Storage	Other Services
India—Persons										
1972–3	73.9	11.3	0.4	8.8	0.2	1.9	14.8	5.1	1.8	7.9
1983	68.6	13.8	0.6	10.7	0.3	2.2	17.6	6.2	2.5	8.9
1993–4	64.7	14.8	0.7	10.5	0.4	3.2	20.5	7.4	2.8	10.3
1999–2000	60.3	16.3	0.6	11.0	0.3	4.4	23.4	10.3	3.6	9.5
2004–5	58.5	18.2	0.6	11.7	0.3	5.6	23.3	9.0	3.8	10.5
2011–12	48.9	29.1	5.4	12.6	0.5	10.6	22.0	10.6	5.7	5.7
Rural—Persons										
1972–3	85.6	7.2	0.3	5.4	0.1	1.4	7.2	2.5	0.6	4.1
1983	81.5	9.0	0.5	6.8	0.1	1.6	9.4	3.4	1.1	4.9
1993–4	78.2	10.2	0.6	7.1	0.2	2.3	11.5	4.3	1.4	5.8
1999–2000	76.3	11.4	0.5	7.4	0.2	3.3	12.4	5.1	2.1	5.2
2004–5	72.5	13.7	0.5	8.1	0.2	4.9	13.6	6.1	2.5	5.0
2011–12	64.1	20.4	0.5	8.6	0.2	11.1	15.5	5.6	2.9	7.0
Urban—Persons										
1972–3	14.8	32.2	1.0	26.3	0.8	4.1	53.0	18.2	7.7	27.1
1983	14.8	33.9	1.2	27.0	0.9	4.8	51.3	17.8	8.2	25.3
1993–4	12.3	32.2	1.2	23.7	1.0	6.3	55.5	19.5	8.0	28.0
1999–2000	7.9	32.3	0.8	22.6	0.7	8.2	59.8	27.0	9.0	23.8
2004–5	8.8	32.2	0.8	22.7	0.7	8.0	59.2	26.9	8.7	23.6
2011–12	6.7	35.0	0.8	23.6	1.3	9.3	58.3	19.6	11.2	27.5

Source: National Sample Survey Office (NSSO), various reports.

in 2011–12. Industry has absorbed more workers; proportion of workers in manufacturing has gradually gone up from 5.4 per cent in 1972–3 to 8.6 per cent in 2011–12, and in construction sector it was up from 1.4 per cent in 1972–3 to 4.9 per cent in 2004–5, further to 11.1 per cent in 2011–12. In urban centres, services sector leads in employment generation. In 2011–12, about 15 per cent of labour is employed in service sector compared to 58.3 per cent in rural areas. And, about one-fifth of rural labourers are employed in industry against a little over one-third in urban areas. Manufacturing sector is losing its importance as the employer in urban centres with percentage of persons employed by this sector is falling from 26.3 per cent in 1972–3 to 23.6 per cent in 2011–12; whereas the same sector is gaining some importance in rural areas with the same percentage going up from 5.4 per cent to 8.6 per cent during the same period. The increased employment opportunities in the construction sector and manufacturing sector in

rural areas have been mostly on account of contract jobs leading to casualization.

8.4.5 Unemployment Rates

Does the fall in LFPR imply a simultaneous increase in the unemployment rate in rural sector? The unemployment rate[12] at the best has been arrested in rural sector, whereas the same in urban centres has come down (Table 8.10). Various changes made in the policy regime particularly since the early 1990s has reduced unemployment rate in both rural and urban areas. The unemployment rate used to be 0.9 per cent in 1972–3 in rural areas compared to 5.2 per cent in urban centres with a rural–urban gap of 4.3 percentage points; and this

---

[12] Unemployment rate is the number of unemployed persons as percentage of labour force (number of persons employed and number of persons unemployed).

Table 8.10   Estimates of Unemployment Rate (%)

	Rural	Urban	All India
1972–3	0.9	5.2	1.6
1983	1.7	5.7	2.5
1993–4	1.6	5.6	2.5
1999–2000	1.4	3.8	2.0
2004–5	1.7	4.5	2.3
2011–12	1.7	3.4	2.2

Note: Unemployment rate is the number of unemployed as percentage of labour force.
Source: National Sample Survey Office (NSSO), various reports.

stood at 2.9 per cent in 1987–88 in rural areas against 6.5 per cent in urban centres with a rural–urban gap of 3.6 points. The same remained at 3.4 per cent in urban centres in 2011–12 exceeding by 1.7 points over rural areas which recorded an unemployment rate of 1.7 per cent. Following unemployment rate in urban areas remaining higher than in rural areas, the efforts to improve employment opportunities appear to be more urban-centric as evinced by the sharp reduction in rural–urban gap in unemployment rate. While appreciable efforts have been made to reduce overall unemployment rate, rural areas appear to have gained only little with unemployment rate remaining virtually around 1.7 per cent during the last two decades,[13] when quality of rural employment also deteriorated. On the contrary, not only has the unemployment rate come down in urban areas, but employment quality has relatively remained better in these areas.

8.5 REGISTERED MANUFACTURING AND RURAL–URBAN DISPARITY

Earlier analysis showed that the rural sector is fast emerging as a centre of manufacturing, which in itself has also become a major sector in rural areas both in terms of contributing to rural NDP and also absorbing rural labour force. A question here is: whether this observed trend gets reflected on the spread of factories between rural and urban centres and the accompanying welfare implication for rural factory employees vis-à-vis their urban counterparts.

[13] Using data for 1999–2000, Radhakrishnan and Rao (2006) observed that unemployment rates in rural areas was very high among educated females; twice that of their male counterparts.

In this section, we make an attempt to examine the characteristics of registered manufacturing sector in rural areas as they may be discerned through the Annual Survey of Industries (ASI), which is the principal database for studies on Indian industry. The ASI covers all factories (that is, registered establishments under Indian Factories Act 1948) employing 10 or more workers with power and 20 or more workers without power. It is important to note that ASI follows establishment approach, as opposed to the concept of a company that follows enterprise approach. Establishments are essentially factories within a physical boundary in a particular location, whereas a company may have several establishments spread across rural and urban centres. If we rely on enterprise approach, we may not be able to capture rural dynamics, as most of the enterprises would be headquartered in urban areas and, therefore, not be counted as rural enterprises. The use of ASI data helps in better understanding the characteristics of factories distributed among rural and urban areas as opposed to the data from the corporate sector. Although ASI was canvassed more systematically since 1972–3, data for rural and urban factories are available from 1987–8 onwards.

In Table 8.11, we have presented the relative share of rural sector in selected characteristics of manufacturing. A distinct feature that emerges from these data is that contrary to the general perception, the sizes of factories

Table 8.11   Percentage Share of Rural Sector in Selected Characteristics of Registered Manufacturing

Year	Number of Factories	Total Persons Engaged	Total Emoluments	Value of Gross Output	Gross Value Added
1987–8	26.4	24.6	17.3	23.0	22.2
1993–4	29.2	27.3	20.3	29.7	28.2
1999–2000	35.0	36.7	30.4	40.8	39.9
2004–5	39.0	40.4	34.6	42.7	43.3
2005–6	39.5	41.4	35.4	42.9	45.8
2006–7	40.7	44.4	37.0	45.2	51.1
2007–8	41.3	44.3	37.8	48.9	51.8
2008–9	42.0	47.0	41.2	50.4	54.8
2009–10	37.4	40.8	36.1	45.6	49.0
2010–11	36.9	42.2	36.5	46.6	51.3
2011–12	37.2	42.6	37.7	47.8	53.3
2012–13	38.3	43.3	38.5	46.7	51.5
2013–14	38.4	43.3	39.2	49.3	52.3

Source: Author's estimates based on data extracted from *EPWRF India Time Series*.

in rural areas are not relatively small as compared with the sizes of factories in urban areas. This is reflected in higher proportions of personnel employed, value of gross output (GVO), and GVA than the proportions of the numbers of factories for rural areas except for emoluments. As for the spread of factories, rural areas have attracted more number over the years, and so its share has steadily risen from 26.4 per cent of total in 1987–8 to 35 per cent in 1999–2000 and further to 42 per cent in 2008–9. This has come down to 38.4 per cent in 2013–4. When seen in terms of a long-term series, an increased presence of factories in rural areas is seen (Figure 8.3). Such a rise has, indeed, been accompanied by a rise in the proportion of employment in rural centres as well. Factories in rural areas used to employ nearly one-fourth of total persons engaged by all factories in 1987–8 and this has gone up to 36.7 per cent in 1999–2000 and further to 47 per cent in 2008–9. This has, however, declined to 43.9 per cent in 2013–14. Overall, there is a rise in the share of employment of registered manufacturing in rural areas. Although the proportionate share of rural areas in number of factories remained higher than employment in 1987–8, the share of employment has become higher since 1998–9. A similar trend is also noticed with respect to total emoluments; however, employment share remained disproportionately larger than emoluments' share. Thus while employment share of urban centres have fallen, their share in emoluments have remained higher. At the same time, rural–urban gap in employment and emoluments has narrowed down over the years—4.1 percentage points in 2013–14 against 7.3 percentage points in 1987–8.

Rural areas' share in GVO and GVA have phenomenally gone up over the years; from being about one-fourth in 1987–8 to around half in 2013–14. In fact, the proportion of GVO remained higher than that of GVA till the late 1990s and thereafter GVA has been marginally higher than its relative share in GVO—signifying more efficiency being achieved by factories with their increased presence in rural areas. Does this mean that productivity of labour in rural areas has gone up and their emoluments have increased simultaneously?

In fact, rural areas have a disproportionately larger share in employment compared to GVO and GVA; this indicates rural workers are more productive. Rural areas' share in GVA exceeded its share in total emoluments by 4.9 percentage points in 1987–8 and this has gradually increased to 13.1 percentage points in 2013–14. This shows that rural workers have benefited in terms of employment with factories spreading into rural areas but not in terms of emoluments.

We further examined some important technical coefficients such as output per employee, GVA per employee, GVA to output, employee per factory, emoluments per employee, and emoluments to GVA. Except the number of factories and employment, all other indicators

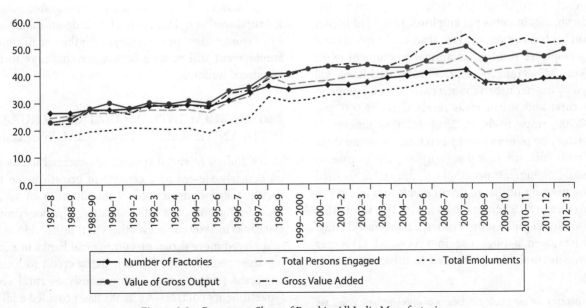

Figure 8.3 Percentage Share of Rural in All India Manufacturing

Source: Author's estimates based on data extracted from *EPWRF India Time Series*.

are expressed in terms of their current monetary value, which render them incomparable over the years. We had deflated each of these variables by applying suitable deflators such as Wholesale Price Index for Manufactured Products (WPI-MP) (Base year = 2004–5) for GVO and GVA, and CPI for industrial workers (CPI–IW base year = 2001–2) for deflating emoluments.[14] For comparison purpose, we have indexed CPI–IW to 2004–5 year.

The increased presence of registered manufacturing is also mirrored in these technical coefficients (Table 8.12). In rural areas, the GVO per employee (at 2004–5 prices) had gone up nearly 6.8 times, from Rs 532,000 in 1987–8 to Rs 363,500 in 2013–14, and GVA per employee (2004–5 = 100) was up by 5.4 times from Rs 116,000 to Rs 627,000 during the same period. At the same time, GVO and GVA per employee in urban areas have gone up by 4.9 and 3.3 times respectively. A steady rise in labour productivity in rural areas is also noticed in comparison to urban centres. For instance, the GVO per employee in rural areas used to be 91.6 per cent of that in urban areas in 1987–8 and this rose to 127.0 per cent in 2013–14. Similarly the GVA per employee in rural areas also rose from 87.6 per cent of those in urban centres to 143.3 per cent in 2013–14.

Number of employees per factory in rural centres used to account for 71.7 employees per factory in 1987–8, lower than the 78.9 in urban centres. Although employment per factory has been going down over the years, such decline is more prominent in urban centres. As a result, factories in rural areas employed 67.9 employees per factory in 2013–14, compared to 55.5 in urban centres. Although per factory employment has gone down, emoluments per employee remained higher in urban centres compared to rural areas. A typical rural factory employee received an annual emolument of Rs 43,700 in 1987–8 (at 2004–5 price) compared Rs 68,200 received by his/her urban counterparts. Factory employees in rural and urban areas received Rs 86,600 and Rs 102,700, respectively, in 2013–14. Emoluments of rural factory employees rose by two times between these two time points, whereas that of urban centres rose by 1.5 times. Emoluments per employee in rural areas used to be 64 per cent of that of urban employees in 1987–8 and this rose to 84.3 per cent in 2013–14. This shows that the rural–urban gap in industrial wage rate is fast closing.

We had seen a huge rise in GVO and GVA per employee in rural areas compared to urban areas with a simultaneous reduction in rural–urban gap in wage rate. Does this mean that the wage share, representing bargaining power of employees, in rural areas had been any better? A sharp decline in wage share (percentage of total emoluments in total GVA) is noticed throughout, but that may hold well for rural and urban areas and, therefore, at the all-India level. However, what is more noteworthy is the observation that such a fall in wage share is more pronounced in rural centres in comparison with urban centres. In rural areas, total emoluments used to account for 31.6 per cent of GVA in 1987–8 and this has fallen to 13.9 per cent in 2007–8, and thereafter rose to 19.2 per cent in 2013–4. Although wage share in urban centres remained higher than rural areas throughout, it also registered a fluctuation as well—43.3 per cent of GVA in 1987–8, 24.6 per cent in 2007–8 and 32.6 per cent in 2013–14. The wage share in rural areas used to account for 73.1 per cent of wage share of urban areas and this has steadily fallen to 56.6 per cent in 2007–8, and thereafter marginally rose to 58.8 per cent in 2013–14. While it is important to recognize the falling wage share irrespective of rural or urban areas, what is more revealing is the widening of the rural–urban gap in the wage share.

While registered manufacturing activities have penetrated more into rural areas, there has not been any discernible improvement in wage share of rural workers, and this performs poorly in comparison with their urban counterparts. It was earlier observed that registered manufacturing contributed more to rural NDP; however, what remains a moot point from wage share point of view is, has such an increased spread of manufacturing activities in rural areas created any favourable outcome for rural workers? This coupled with deteriorating quality of employment in rural areas with the rise in contract employment still poses a far greater challenge to rural labourers' welfare.

8.6 FINANCIAL INTERMEDIATION IN RURAL INDIA AND ISSUES OF FINANCIAL INCLUSION

In the Indian financial system, commercial banks were particularly viewed as a catalyst of growth given their widely acknowledged role in mobilization of savings. More importantly, the nationalization of major commercial banks in 1969 and a few others in 1980 heralded an era that placed more thrust on commercial banks in achieving balanced growth by channelizing credit to hitherto neglected sectors—read synonymously as rural sector. Government's control over banks had provided a fillip to the presence of commercial banks in rural areas, thus, enhancing their role as a catalyst of rural development.

---

[14] Wherever we used index numbers of different base years, we followed splicing method so as to convert different series into a single base year series.

Table 8.12 Structural Ratios and Technical Coefficients of Manufacturing, Rural versus Urban

Years	GVO per Employee				GVA per Employee				Emoluments per Employee				No. of Employees per Factory				Emoluments as % of GVA			
	Rural	Urban	All India	Rural as % of Urban	Rural	Urban	All India	Rural as % of Urban	Rural	Urban	All India	Rural as % of Urban	Rural	Urban	All India	Rural as % of Urban	Rural	Urban	All India	Rural as % of Urban
1987–8	532	581	569	92	115	132	128	88	44	68	62	64	72	79	77	91	32	43	41	73
1988–9	597	636	626	94	126	147	142	86	45	70	64	64	72	77	76	94	30	40	38	75
1989–90	711	655	670	108	157	149	151	105	50	73	67	68	73	78	76	94	25	39	35	65
1990–1	825	687	723	120	172	162	165	106	51	73	67	70	72	76	75	94	24	37	33	67
1991–2	754	701	715	108	154	160	158	96	47	65	60	73	71	75	74	94	26	34	32	76
1992–3	820	721	748	114	187	169	174	111	50	73	67	69	71	75	74	94	22	36	32	62
1993–4	869	775	801	112	204	195	197	105	48	72	65	68	68	75	73	91	20	30	27	65
1994–5	931	793	831	117	219	198	204	110	53	77	70	69	71	77	75	92	19	31	28	62
1995–6	1010	853	895	118	229	213	218	107	52	81	73	65	70	78	76	89	19	31	28	60
1996–7	1073	890	945	121	258	222	233	116	55	81	73	68	71	73	73	97	19	32	28	58
1997–8	1186	1018	1072	116	261	236	244	111	55	82	73	67	71	75	74	94	19	32	27	61
1998–9	1162	1119	1136	104	245	256	252	96	53	73	65	72	72	62	65	116	21	28	26	75
1999–2000	1481	1245	1332	119	304	266	280	115	59	78	71	75	65	60	62	108	19	29	25	66
2000–1	1541	1254	1362	123	297	241	262	123	62	82	74	75	64	59	61	108	21	34	28	61
2001–2	1629	1309	1431	124	310	249	272	125	64	80	74	79	63	59	60	108	21	33	28	63
2002–3	1738	1510	1600	115	340	279	303	122	63	83	75	76	67	59	62	113	19	31	26	62
2003–4	1903	1628	1738	117	366	314	335	117	64	86	77	75	65	58	61	112	18	28	24	65
2004–5	2090	1903	1979	110	392	349	366	113	65	84	76	78	64	61	62	106	17	24	21	69
2005–6	2119	1992	2045	106	432	362	391	119	67	86	78	77	68	63	65	108	16	24	20	65
2006–7	2195	2123	2155	103	473	362	412	131	64	87	77	74	78	67	71	116	14	25	19	56
2007–8	2583	2150	2342	120	545	404	466	135	73	95	85	76	77	68	71	113	14	25	19	57
2008–9	2577	2244	2400	115	523	382	448	137	78	98	88	79	82	67	73	122	16	28	21	58
2009–10	2873	2365	2573	121	577	414	480	140	76	93	86	82	81	70	74	115	16	26	21	59
2010–11	3132	2615	2833	120	613	424	504	145	78	99	90	79	69	55	60	125	16	29	22	54
2011–12	3466	2800	3084	124	653	424	521	154	82	100	92	82	71	56	62	125	16	29	22	53
2012–13	3418	2971	3164	115	629	452	529	139	85	104	96	82	66	54	58	123	18	30	24	59
2013–14	3635	2862	3197	127	627	437	519	143	87	103	96	84	68	56	60	122	19	33	26	59

Source: Author's estimates based on data extracted from *EPWRF India Time Series.*

Major banking sector reforms initiated since the early 1990s changed the terrain in which commercial banks had to operate; competition and efficiency became the guiding principles. Consequently, commercial banks now operate in a different environment; so much so that their focus on rural areas is also expected to vary if their rural presence is not driven by profit motive.

The role of intermediation of banks can be examined using several indicators, of which credit to deposit (CD) ratio assumes cardinal importance. In terms of banks' efforts such as opening offices and deploying credit, there has been a marked rise in the rural share over the years but with some fluctuations (Figure 8.4).[15] The share of rural deposits in total bank deposits went up from 7.1 per cent in 1973 to as high as 15.5 per cent in 1991 (Table 8.13). Since then, a gradual reduction to 10.3 per cent in 2015 is seen in rural deposits' share, despite the number of deposit account holders going up from 30.7 per cent of number of total deposits to 34.3 per cent in 2015. In respect of credit share, rural areas accounted for 4.6 per cent

of total credit in 1973 and this rose to 15 per cent in 1991 but gradually fell to 8.7 per cent by 2015. Unlike the number of deposit accounts, number of credit accounts in rural areas witnessed a sharp fall from 52.1 per cent of total bank credit accounts in 1991 to 34.6 per cent in 2015. Further, percentage share in the number of rural bank offices rose from 36 per cent in 1973 to 56.9 per cent in 1991 and then dropped to 37.2 per cent in 2015. This shows that banking sector reforms had relatively favoured urban segment; perhaps due to lacklustre demand for banking services in rural areas or rural operations not being lucrative for banks. Either way, this only suggests that the competition featuring commercial banks' operation under the reform period has made the differences; what is more significant is the fall in CD ratio of rural areas as percentage of that of urban areas, particularly since the early 1990s. Although a reversal has taken place since March 2002, CD ratio of rural areas still remains far lower than their urban counterparts and lower than the level achieved in the 1980s (Figure 8.5). This indicates a downward trend in the intermediation role of banks and their role as a catalyst of rural development.

In part, this may be explained by the reduced thrust on priority sector lending (PSL), which has become a nebulous concept (EPW Research Foundation 2014). Though commercial banks have been contributing towards the shortfall in meeting PSL target to rural infrastructure fund, the direct intervention by banks is missing in

[15] The Reserve Bank of India publishes these banking variables in its annual publication known as *Basic Statistical Returns (BSR)*, wherein annual data are available as at end June of every year till 1989 and thereafter as at end March. Analysis here has been done using the time series BSR data extracted from EPW Research Foundation's online database, *EPWRF India Time Series*, accessed at www.epwrf.in

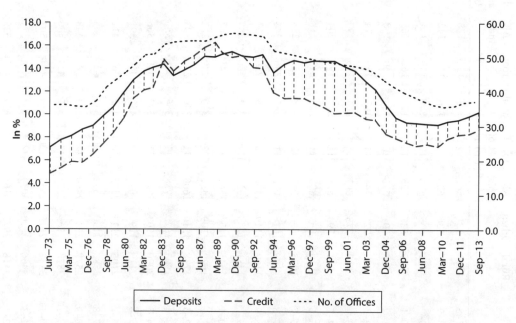

Figure 8.4   Percentage of Rural Share in Bank Credit, Deposit, and Offices

Source: Author's estimates based on data extracted from *EPWRF India Time Series*.

Table 8.13   Rural Share in Vital Banking Indicators (in %)

As at End	Deposits		Credit		CD Ratio (%)				No. of Offices
	No. of Accounts	Amount (Rupees in Lakh)*	No. of Accounts	Amount (Rupees in Lakh)*	Rural	Urban	All India	Rural as % of Urban	
Jun-1973		7.1		4.8	47.2	71.3	69.6	66.2	36.0
Jun-1980		11.9		9.7	54.5	68.9	67.2	79.1	45.7
Mar-1991	30.7	15.5	52.1	15.0	60.0	62.3	61.9	96.3	56.9
Mar-2000	30.5	14.7	46.1	10.6	40.4	58.7	56.0	68.9	48.7
Mar-2005	30.4	12.2	37.7	9.5	51.6	68.0	66.0	75.9	45.7
Mar-2006	28.8	10.8	33.4	8.3	55.8	74.4	72.4	75.0	43.2
Mar-2007	28.8	9.7	32.3	8.0	61.2	76.5	75.0	80.1	41.5
Mar-2008	28.9	9.3	30.6	7.6	60.3	75.8	74.4	79.6	39.8
Mar-2009	30.2	9.3	30.3	7.3	57.1	74.2	72.6	77.0	38.6
Mar-2010	30.5	9.2	30.5	7.5	59.3	74.8	73.3	79.3	37.2
Mar-2011	30.9	9.2	32.4	7.3	60.0	77.2	75.6	77.7	36.2
Mar-2012	31.3	9.4	31.4	7.9	66.4	80.3	79.0	82.6	35.6
Mar-2013	32.1	9.6	34.3	8.3	68.1	79.9	78.8	85.2	35.9
Mar-2014	33.1	9.9	34.5	8.4	66.6	80.3	79.0	83.0	36.9
Mar-2015	34.3	10.3	34.6	8.7	65.3	78.4	77.1	83.3	37.2

Note: *1 lakh = 100,000.

Up to June 1983, classification is based on 1971 Census; December 1983 to March 1994 classification is based on 1981 Census; March 1995 to March 2005 classification is based on 1991 Census; March 1995 to March 2005 classification is based on 1991 Census; March 2006 to March 2009 the classification is based on 2001 Census.

Source: Author's estimates based on data extracted from *EPWRF India Time Series*.

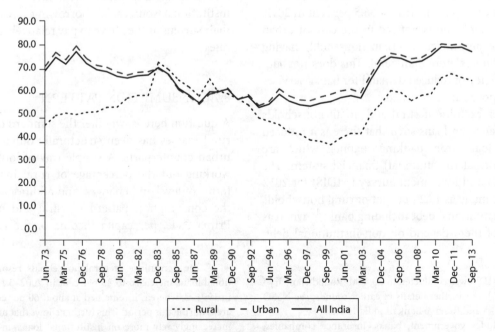

Figure 8.5   Credit to Deposit Ratio of Rural, Urban, and All India

Source: Author's estimates based on data extracted from *EPWRF India Time Series*.

rural areas. Does the reduced importance of rural areas for commercial banks imply any corresponding decline in the demand for their services? This is discerned by examining rural households' reliance on various sources of funds, including banks.

We propose to examine households' debt-related estimates presented in All India Debt and Investment Survey (AIDIS), conducted by the NSSO almost every decade. It may be noted that the AIDIS is the principle source of assets and liability and capital expenditure of households in the country belonging to both rural and urban sectors (NSSO 2016).[16]

First, we have examined the incidence of indebtedness (IOI) among households (Table 8.14). According to NSS 26th Round, 42.8 per cent of rural households were indebted in 1971. Subsequent surveys have placed IOI of household debt on the lower side. As much as 20 per cent of rural households were indebted in 1981 and this had gradually risen to 31.4 per cent by 2013. In comparison, the percentage of indebted urban households, though on a rising trend since 1981, had remained lower than that of rural sector. Debt to asset ratio (DAR) of rural households showed a fall till 1991, but rose thereafter. Except in 2002, DAR of rural households remained lower than that of their urban counterparts. The share of deposit in total assets of rural households, though increased from 1.3 per cent in 1991 to 2.3 per cent in 2002, declined to 1.7 per cent in 2012. This is far lower than that of urban households. More so, number of households having deposits as an asset item has also drastically reduced from 87.8 per cent in rural areas to 66.5 per cent in 2012. Though a similar trend is noticed in the case of urban segments, the percentage of urban households having deposit accounts is more than rural. This does not suggest any tendency of reduced demand for banks services so long as deposits are concerned.

We further examine if rural and urban households have less reliance on loans such that there is a reduced demand for loans from banking channels which are part of the formal (institutional) financial system. The All India Debt and Investment Survey (AIDIS) for 2012 shows that as many as 17.2 per cent of rural households depend on institutional debt including banks,[17] whereas 19 per cent of them depend on non-institutional debt.

Thus, relatively more rural households depend considerably on non-institutional loans. On the contrary, not only a lesser percentage of urban households depend on loans but their reliance on institutional sources is higher than non-institutional sources.[18] Non-institutional loans usually carry exorbitant interest rates. For instance, about 90 per cent of loans taken from institutional sources carry interest rates of 15 per cent or less in both rural and urban sectors; compared to 74.2 per cent of loans taken from non-institutional in rural and 62.3 per cent of urban areas with unduly higher interest rate of more than 15 per cent (see NSSO, 2016: Statement 3.10, p. 22). The rural households that have relatively higher reliance on non-institutional sources for loans also end up paying huge interest rates. Had institutional loans such as from banks been available, rural households would not have preferred non-institutional loans.

An inevitable conclusion from the analysis of AIDIS results is that there is no dearth of demand for services rendered by formal financial institutions among rural households in order to reduce their reliance on institutional sources. The declining CD ratio of banks in the rural segment is, therefore, a matter of serious concern. We concede that the AIDIS considers households as a unit of respondent, which may be different from formal bank credit provided to sectors such as manufacturing in rural areas. To that extent, the analysis may become incomparable. Notwithstanding this limitation, one can still venture to conclude that rural India is being less served financially which, with their recourse to non-institutional sources for borrowing, creates a dent in their surplus as they have to pay relatively higher interest rates.

8.7 CONSUMPTION PATTERN

A question here is, whether the standard of living of the rural masses has been structurally different from their urban counterparts. A simple way of looking at this is working out the percentage of rural income, both in terms of level and changes, and additionally comparing the consumption pattern of rural and urban masses. Prima facie, per capita income of the rural sector as

---

[16] The last AIDIS was conducted in the 70th Round (January–December 2013). For further details of earlier rounds, see NSSO 1998, 2005, 2014a and Reserve Bank of India 1987.

[17] This includes government, banks, insurance companies, provident funds, financial companies, self-help groups, and so on. For details, see NSSO 2014a, 19.

[18] The percentage of rural households resorting to institutional loans increased to 83 per cent in 2002–3 from 70 per cent in 1991–2, whereas it remained at about 60 per cent in the urban areas during this period. This further shows that urban households increasingly rely more on institutional loans and more of rural households on non-institutional sources. For details see, Bisaliah et al. (2014, 75, Tables 4.2 and 4.3).

Table 8.14 Indicators of Household Indebtedness, Rural and Urban

NSS Round	Year	Rural					Urban					Rural to Urban (Actual Ratio)				
		Incidence of Indebtedness (%)	Average Value of Debt per Household (in Rs)	Debt-Asset Ratio	Households Having Deposits and so on as Assets	Share of Deposits and so on in Total Assets (%)	Incidence of Indebtedness (%)	Average Value of Debt Per Household (Rs)	Debt-Asset Ratio	Households Having Deposits and so on as Assets	Share of Deposits and so on in Total Assets (%)	Incidence of Indebtedness (%)	Average Value of Debt Per Household (Rs)	Debt-Asset Ratio	Households Having Deposits and so on as Assets	Share of Deposits and so on in Total Assets (%)
26	1971	42.8	500	4.42												
37	1981	20	661	1.83			17.36	1030	2.54			1.15	0.64	0.72		
48	1991	23.4	1906	1.78	15.1	1.3	19.3	3618	2.51	42.8	7.9	1.21	0.53	0.71	0.35	0.16
59	2002	26.5	7539	2.84	87.8	2.3	17.8	11771	2.82	92.5	9.7	1.49	0.64	1.01	0.95	0.24
70	2012	31.4	32522	3.23	66.5	1.7	22.4	84625	3.7	75.9	4.3	1.40	0.38	0.87	0.88	0.40

Sources: Reserve Bank of India (1987) and NSSO (1998, 2005, 2014b, 2015).

percentage of urban sector has practically remained nearly the same at about 42 per cent, though a drastic reduction is noticed to about 36 per cent in the 1990–2000 and 2004–5 base years. This persisting disparity between rural and urban per capita income has been the feature of India's growth.

In what follows, we further examine if the level of living of rural population, as captured through consumption pattern, shows any perceptible differences over the years, more so under the reform period since the early 1990s as well as how they compare with urban sectors. For this purpose, we have relied on NSS Consumer Expenditure Survey (NSS CES),[19] which provides estimates of households' monthly per capita consumption expenditure (MPCE). The analysis has been done at two levels: one, by working out MPCE under different commodity groups of the rural sector as percentage of urban sector and the other, by distribution of their monthly spending across consumption items. While intra-group disparity will exist within the rural sector, we do not make an attempt of that kind.

Both rural and urban centres have been witnessing structural changes in their consumption pattern, as shown by various NSS CESs. Overall, there is a decline in expenditure on food items as percentage of total expenditure (Table 8.15). Rural population on an average used to spend 72.9 per cent on food items in 1972–3 and this has gradually declined to 48.6 per cent in 2011–12. Cereals are the major food items consumed. Among non-food items, spending on services including education and medical care have shot up over the years. Spending on durable goods also shows an upward trend.

A near similar trend is also noticeable in the consumption pattern of urban sector as well. Their spending on food accounts for 38.5 per cent in 2011–12 compared to 64.5 per cent in 1972–3. Urban mass spend relatively a higher amount on non-food items, mostly due to accelerated rise in expenses associated with miscellaneous goods and services, which account for 39.7 per cent of total expenditure in 2011–12, marginally higher than that spent on food item. Services such as education, medical care, consumer services, conveyance, and rent have contributed to such a rise in non-food spending of urban sector. A comparison reveals that rural sector is also catching up with the consumption pattern of urban segment, with these service components showing a rising trend.

A related question is whether rural spending on each of these items shows any marked difference from urban spending. To understand this, we have worked out spending by rural population on each consumption item as a percentage of their urban counterparts' spending on the same items (Table 8.16). Rural population spends increasingly lesser amount on most of the consumption items compared to urban population, with an exception of items such as milk and its products, edible oil, egg, fish and meat, fruit and nuts, sugar, and beverages. Rural spending on food items as a whole has come down; percentage of spending on food by rural sector used to be 78.9 per cent that of urban sector in 1972–3, and this has gradually come down to 65.6 per cent in 2011–12. Similarly, rural spending on non-food items has also come down in comparison with urban spending—from 53.3 per cent of urban sector in 1972–3 to 43.4 per cent in 2011–12. So is the case with durable goods. However, their spending on miscellaneous goods and services shows a marginal rise, from 31.6 per cent of urban spending on these goods in 1972–3 to 34.2 per cent in 2011–12. A continuous drop in rural consumption as a whole is discernible in comparison with urban consumption of these commodities and this suggests a rising disparity.[20]

We further examine growth in CE. As CE is collected at different points of time and at the price prevailing during different reference periods, we have to adjust for price changes. For this, we have used consumer price index (CPI) given for both rural and urban sectors, in various NSS Reports for two base (= 100) years, 1972–3 and 1987–8. By applying the splicing method, we arrived at a single price series with 1987–8 = 100. Having separately converted total CE of rural and urban sectors using their respective CPI to a common year base prices, we worked out CAGR between two successive NSS rounds.

Rural population continues to spend relatively less than their urban counterparts. In nominal values, rural total CE spending accounts for 69.8 per cent of urban CE in 1972–3, which prominently dips to 52 per cent in 2011–12, and a mixed trend is seen when they are expressed in terms of 1987–8 prices (Table 8.17). This

---

[19] These surveys were conducted in the same round of employment surveys as noted earlier (see NSSO 1993 and 2013). In order to maintain consistency, we have, therefore, not considered three rounds covering reference periods 1977–8, 1987–88, and 2009–10.

[20] Using NSS CES results, several studies have attempted to examine the question of inequality in India. For more details, see Basole and Basu (2015).

Table 8.15 Trends in Percentage Composition of Consumer Expenditure (%)

Item Group	Rural						Urban					
	1972–3	1983	1993–4	1999–2000	2004–5	2011–12	1972–3	1983	1993–4	1999–2000	2004–5	2011–12
Cereals	40.6	32.3	24.2	22.2	18.0	12.0	23.3	19.4	14.0	12.4	10.1	7.3
Gram	0.6	0.3	0.2	0.1	0.1	0.2	0.3	0.2	0.2	0.1	0.1	0.1
Cereal substitutes	0.5	0.2	0.1	0.1	0.1	0.1	0.1	0.1	0.1	0.0	0.0	0.1
Pulses and their products	4.3	3.5	3.8	3.8	3.1	3.1	3.4	3.2	3.0	2.8	2.1	2.1
Milk and its products	7.3	7.5	9.5	8.8	8.5	9.1	9.3	9.2	9.8	8.7	7.9	7.8
Edible oil	3.5	4	4.4	3.7	4.6	3.8	4.9	4.8	4.4	3.1	3.5	2.7
Egg, fish, and meat	2.5	3	3.3	3.3	3.3	3.6	3.3	3.6	3.4	3.1	2.7	2.8
Vegetables	3.6	4.7	6.0	6.2	6.1	4.8	4.4	5.0	5.5	5.1	4.5	3.4
Fruit and nuts	1.1	1.4	1.7	1.7	1.9	1.9	2.0	2.1	2.7	2.4	2.2	2.3
Sugar	3.8	2.8	3.1	2.4	2.4	1.8	3.6	2.5	2.4	1.6	1.5	1.2
Salt and spices	2.8	2.5	2.7	3.0	2.5	2.4	2.3	2.1	2.0	2.2	1.7	1.7
Beverages and so on	2.4	3.3	4.2	4.2	4.5	5.8	7.6	6.8	7.2	6.4	6.2	7.1
Food total	72.9	65.6	63.2	59.4	55.0	48.6	64.5	59.1	54.7	48.1	42.5	38.5
Pan, tobacco, and intoxicants	3.1	3	3.2	2.9	2.7	2.4	2.8	2.4	2.3	1.9	1.6	1.4
Fuel and light	5.6	7	7.4	7.5	10.2	9.2	5.6	6.9	6.6	7.8	9.9	7.6
Clothing and bedding	7	8.6	5.4	6.9	4.5	6.3	5.3	7.6	4.7	6.1	4.0	5.3
Footwear	0.5	1	0.9	1.1	0.8	1.3	0.4	1.1	0.9	1.2	0.7	1.2
Education					2.7	3.1					5	5.7
Medical care					6.6	6.9					5.2	5.5
Entertainment					0.6	1.1					1.9	1.8
Toilet articles					2.7	2.4					2.6	2.4
Other household consumables					2.3	2.2					2.2	2
Consumer services excluding conveyance					3.8	4.5					7	6.5
Conveyance					3.8	4.8					6.5	7.5
Minor durable-type goods					0.2	0.3					0.2	0.4
Rent					0.5	0.5					5.6	7
Taxes and cesses					0.2	0.3					0.8	0.9
Misc. Goods and services#	8.7	12.5	17.3	19.6	23.4	26.1	19.2	20.5	27.5	31.3	37.2	39.7
Durable goods	2.2	2.3	2.7	2.6	3.4	6.1	2.2	2.3	3.3	3.6	4.1	6.3
Non-food total	27.1	34.4	36.8	40.6	45	51.4	35.5	40.9	45.3	51.9	57.5	61.5
Total expenditure	100	100	100	100	100	100	100	100	100	100	100	100

Note: #Includes education and medical care.

Source: Author's estimates based on data extracted from NSSO (1996 and 2013).

Table 8.16   Consumption Spending of Rural as % of Urban

Items Group	1972–3	1983	1993–4	1999–2000	2004–5	2011–12
Cereals	121.7	114.2	106.5	101.8	93.4	85.4
Gram	139.7	102.9	61.6	56.9	52.4	103.9
Cereal substitutes	349.1	137.2	61.6			52.0
Pulses and their products	88.3	75.0	78.1	77.2	77.4	76.7
Milk and its products	54.8	55.9	59.7	57.5	56.4	60.6
Edible oil	49.9	57.2	61.6	67.9	68.9	73.1
Egg, fish, and meat	52.9	57.2	59.8	60.5	64.1	66.8
Vegetables	57.1	64.5	67.2	69.1	71.1	73.4
Fruit and nuts	38.4	45.7	38.8	40.3	45.3	42.9
Sugar	73.7	76.8	79.6	85.3	83.9	77.9
Salt and spices	85.0	81.7	83.2	77.5	77.1	73.4
Beverages and so on	22.1	33.3	35.9	37.3	38.1	42.4
Food total	78.9	76.1	71.2	70.2	67.9	65.6
Pan, tobacco, and intoxicants	77.3	85.7	85.7	86.8	88.5	89.1
Fuel and light	69.8	69.6	69.1	54.7	54.0	62.9
Clothing and bedding	92.2	77.6	70.8	64.3	59.0	61.8
Footwear	87.3	62.4	61.6	52.1	59.9	56.3
Education					28.3	28.3
Medical care					66.5	65.2
Entertainment					16.6	31.8
Toilet articles					54.4	52.0
Other household consumables					54.8	57.2
Consumer services excluding conveyance					28.5	36.0
Conveyance					30.7	33.3
Minor durable-type goods					52.4	39.0
Rent					4.7	3.7
Taxes and cesses					13.1	17.3
Misc. goods & services[#]	31.6	41.8	38.8	35.6	33.0	34.2
Durable goods	69.8	68.6	50.4	41.1	43.5	50.3
Non-food total	53.3	57.7	50.1	44.5	41.0	43.4
Total expenditure	69.8	68.6	61.6	56.9	52.4	52.0

Note: [#]Includes education and medical care.
Source: Author's estimates based on data extracted from NSSO (1996 and 2013).

Table 8.17   Trends in Rural and Urban Monthly Per Capita Consumption Expenditure (in Rs)

Reference Period	At Current Prices			At Constant Prices (1987–8 = 100)				
	Rural	Urban	Rural as % of Urban	Rural	CAGR	Urban	CAGR	Rural as % of Urban
1972–3	44	63	69.8	128		230		55.4
1983	113	164	68.6	143	(1.0)	231	(0.0)	61.9
1993–4	286	464	61.6	163	(1.3)	268	(1.5)	60.6
1999–2000	486	855	56.9	179	(1.7)	306	(2.2)	58.5
2004–5	579	1105	52.4	182	(0.2)	327	(1.3)	55.6
2011–12	1287	2477	52.0	222	(2.9)	414	(3.4)	53.7

Source: Author's estimates based on data extracted from NSSO (1996 and 2013).

had gone up from 55.4 per cent in 1972–3 to 60.6 per cent in 1993–4, but thereafter has markedly declined to 53.7 per cent in 2011–12. The total CE of rural masses grew relatively at lesser rate than that of urban CE. Thus, the consumption divide between rural and urban is rising.

The observed widening disparity between rural and urban sectors, both in terms of spending on individual items as well as total spending is a notable feature of growth of Indian economy, particularly during the last two decades or so. We further present below evidences as to how such widening has also been felt with respect to rural poor as well.

8.8 RELATIVE PRICES

Normally, inflation has been considered either good or bad depending upon the nature of economic agents. Higher prices reduce consumers' surplus and it increases producers' surplus. Rural sector is a producer and a consumer simultaneously. So much so that movements in relative prices, that is, the price rural sector pays in relation to the price they receive, determine how favourably or unfavourably their surplus (well-being) have been impacted. Traditionally, this has been understood by inter-sectoral terms of trade, whereby agriculture prices (purportedly representing rural sector) have been expressed as percentage of manufactured prices and/or services. This assumes that rural sector is the producer of agriculture produce and consumer of other goods and services.

In order to understand if they pay higher prices in comparison with their urban counterparts, we have also worked out rural and urban inflation rates using rate of change in CPI for Agriculture Labour (CPI–AL) and CPI–IW respectively. Both CPI–AL and CPI–IW were available for different base years and we have converted them first to a single year base by applying splicing method, and then indexed them to 2004–5. Rural inflation rate in most of the years in the 1970s and 1980s used to be lower than urban inflation rate (Figure 8.6). Though differences between these two continue to persist thereafter, their magnitude has been relatively lesser. This signifies a convergence in rural and urban inflation rate.[21]

[21] The standard deviation of point differences between rural and urban inflation rates used to be 4.1 during 1971–2 to 1991–2 and 2.0 during 1992–3 to 2015–16. If we consider the higher growth phase of 2004–5 to 2015–16, the standard deviation remained at 1.0 (author's calculation based on data extracted from *EPWRF India Time Series*, available at www.epwrfits.in).

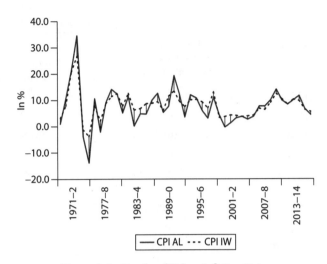

Figure 8.6 Rural and Urban Inflation Rates

Source: Author's estimates based on data extracted from *EPWRF India Time Series*.

Thus, one cannot say that rural is paying more compared to urban counterparts.

To undertake the exercise of inter-sectoral terms of trade, we have relied on multiple indicators such as WPI of agricultural products (food and non-food combined using their respective weights) as percentage of WPI of manufactured products and implicit agriculture GDP deflator to that of manufacturing GDP, of services GDP, and of combined manufacturing and services GDP.

By and large, the analysis shows that terms of trade favoured non-agriculture products for a very long time till the mid-1990s, since when it remained in favour of agriculture (Table 8.18). Krishnaswamy and Rajakumar (2014) observed a rise in terms of trade due to a whopping rise in minimum support price (MSP). Such favourable terms of trade may be said to have influenced rural income to move upwards. Given the skewed distribution of land-holding with a fraction of rural population holding a disproportionately larger share of land, successive hikes in MSP had favoured large farmers. Krishnaswamy and Rajakumar (2014) noticed a rise in inequality in rural areas with the rate of increase in consumption of bottom income deciles remaining lower than that of top ones. It can thus be gainsaid that accelerated movements in agriculture prices had impacted rural sector more favourably. Although rural masses may not be paying too high prices for consumption goods compared to their urban counterparts, terms of trade intended to favour rural sector as a whole have benefited a very few

Table 8.18   Trends in Terms of Trade (in %)

Years	WPI Agriculture Products to WPI Manufactured Products (2004-5 = 100)	Implicit GDP Deflators (Base Year = 2004-5)			
		Agriculture to Manufacturing	Agriculture to Industry	Agriculture to Services	Agriculture to Non-Agriculture
1971-2	93.2	90.7	112.4	90.7	88.6
1972-3	91.9	98.2	122.3	98.2	96.2
1973-4	101.4	104.2	130.3	104.2	106.6
1974-5	102.2	92.9	117.3	92.9	99.8
1975-6	93.4	80.0	100.4	80.0	82.6
1976-7	91.9	85.3	104.2	85.3	85.5
1977-8	99.1	87.0	106.3	87.0	87.5
1978-9	97.3	85.3	101.5	85.3	85.9
1979-80	88.8	85.5	103.6	85.5	92.6
1980-1	83.1	85.5	104.7	85.5	93.5
1981-2	79.8	84.7	100.6	84.7	89.5
1982-3	82.7	86.6	98.5	86.6	90.2
1983-4	88.2	87.3	98.3	87.3	89.9
1984-5	87.7	86.0	95.4	86.0	88.0
1985-6	82.7	85.5	94.8	85.5	88.0
1986-7	91.3	87.9	96.2	87.9	89.4
1987-8	93.2	92.4	101.1	92.4	93.7
1988-9	90.0	90.8	99.2	90.8	91.6
1989-90	82.3	89.5	99.0	89.5	93.5
1990-1	86.6	91.8	102.5	91.8	94.7
1991-2	92.9	98.3	110.8	98.3	100.6
1992-3	90.4	92.0	103.3	92.0	96.9
1993-4	89.1	96.7	106.4	96.7	99.7
1994-5	92.1	95.4	105.6	95.4	100.5
1995-6	92.1	96.4	105.9	96.4	101.2
1996-7	97.7	101.4	109.1	101.4	102.6
1997-8	97.6	106.2	111.9	106.2	105.9
1998-9	104.8	108.4	112.1	108.4	105.7
1999-2000	103.3	108.7	112.2	108.7	105.6
2000-1	102.9	104.5	108.4	104.5	102.8
2001-2	104.6	104.9	108.3	104.9	101.0
2002-3	105.4	106.7	107.6	106.7	102.0
2003-04	104.1	104.1	106.8	104.1	100.9
2004-5	100.0	100.0	100.0	100.0	100.0
2005-6	100.9	102.6	102.4	102.6	104.3
2006-7	103.9	104.9	104.6	104.9	107.5
2007-8	107.1	109.6	107.5	109.6	112.2
2008-9	110.9	115.4	112.2	115.4	117.4
2009-10	122.7	129.8	123.4	129.8	126.9
2010-11	135.8	136.3	128.3	136.3	131.2
2011-12	136.5	137.4	128.9	137.4	130.0

2012–13	142.5	140.7	130.7	140.7	131.2
2013–14	153.8	151.3	137.7	151.3	137.2
2014–15	157.2				
2015–16	164.5				

Note: Non-agriculture includes industry and services combined.

Source: Author's estimates based on data extracted from *EPWRF India Time Series*.

and thus contributed to a rise in inequality within rural sector.

8.9 RURAL POOR IS THE MAJORITY OF THE COUNTRY'S POOR

That poverty alleviation was a driving objective of government policies in the post-Independence period is widely known and acclaimed; the progress achieved has also been commendable. The erstwhile Planning Commission used to regularly provide estimates of poverty level using head count ratio, which is the percentage of population whose consumption falls below the defined poverty level. As per the estimates for 2004–5, 28.3 per cent of rural population and 25.7 per cent of urban population still live below poverty line (Table 8.19).[22] Between 1973–4 and 1993–4, the percentage of rural and urban poor went down by 19.1 and 16.6 percentage points respectively; but between 1993–4 and 2004–5, the respective reduction was in the order of 9.0 and 6.7 percentage points. Even if we consider estimates based on Tendulkar Expert Group 2009, a vast reduction in poverty is seen in both rural and urban sectors. According to the new estimates, about one-fourth of rural population lived under poverty in 2011–12 compared to almost half of that segment in 1993–4. The reduction in rural poverty during this period has been lesser than that featuring urban poverty; rural poverty as percentage of

urban poverty moved up from 157.5 per cent in 1993–4 to 187.6 per cent in 2011–12.

Rural India constitutes the bulk of poor in India. In terms of absolute number, there is a reduction in rural poor from 261.3 million in 1973–4 to 244 million in 1993–4, and further down to 220.9 million in 2004–5. It accounted for 73.2 per cent of total population under poverty line in 2004–5, as against 81.3 per cent in 1973–4. The rate of decline in the proportion of rural poor was 5.2 per cent between 1973–4 and 1993–4; but only 2.9 per cent between 1993–4 and 2004–5. As per the new estimates, rural poor numbered 328.6 million in 1993–4, 326.3 million in 2004–5, and 216.5 million by 2011–12. A drastic reduction in the number of rural poor has occurred during the period between 2004–5 and 2011–12, which had witnessed a relatively a higher GDP growth. There is, however, no marked differences in the percentage of rural poor; throughout, about 80 per

[22] This is based on Uniform Recall Period (URP) consumption, whereby consumer expenditure data have been collected using 30 days of recall period. Planning Commission also collects data on the basis of Mixed Recall Period (MRP) consumption, wherein they used 365 days as recall period for the purpose of collecting expenditure for five non-food items. According to MRP method, there is hardly any difference between the respective urban and rural poverty ratios, which stands at 21.8 per cent for rural and 21.7 per cent for urban. Even by MRP consumption method, as many as 71.4 percent of people living under poverty line live in rural areas. See Planning Commission 2013.

Table 8.19   Percentage of Poor in India, 1973–4 to 2011–12

Year	Poverty Ratio			Rural as % of Urban	Rural Poor as % of Total Poor
	Rural	Urban	Total		
1973–4	56.4	49	54.9	115.1	81.3
1977–8	53.1	45.2	51.3	117.5	80.4
1983	45.6	40.8	44.5	111.8	78.0
1987–8	39.1	38.2	38.9	102.4	75.5
1993–4	37.3	32.4	36	115.1	76.2
1999–2000	27.1	23.6	26.1	114.8	74.3
2004–5*	28.3	25.7	27.5	110.1	73.2
2004–5#	21.8	21.7	21.8	100.5	71.4
Expert Group 2009 (Tendulkar Methodology)					
1993–4	50.1	31.8	45.3	157.5	81.5
2004–5	41.8	25.7	37.2	162.6	80.2
2011–12	25.7	13.7	21.9	187.6	80.4

Notes: *Comparable with 1993–4 estimates; #Comparable with 1999–2000 estimates.

Source: Planning Commission (2013).

cent of the total poor in the country belonged to the rural areas.[23]

Rural poverty ratio to urban poverty ratio had gone up implying that urban poverty is falling faster than rural poverty. And also, percentage of rural poor in the county's total poor remains steadier, particularly during the period marked by a stupendous growth. This suggests that while rural sector has gained absolutely, the gain at the margin is not as much as what urban segments have achieved.

8.10 LOPSIDED TENDENCIES: WIDENING RURAL–URBAN GAP

About 25 years ago, the country launched a major change in respect of economic policies, with liberal milieu replacing a hitherto state-controlled regime. An assessment carried out in this chapter provides an opportunity to understand the performance of rural sector on various dimensions. Multiple data availability facilitated a comparison of rural scenario of last two decades with the preceding two decades, as well as with their urban counterparts. Based on the analysis, characters featuring rural India may be summed up as follows:

1. Share of rural income in the country's NDP has been on the declining trend. Contribution of farm sector to rural NDP has come down, whereas that of manufacturing has gone up. During the last two decades, economic activities in rural sector has become more broad based with both agriculture and industry having a share of about 38 per cent each, compared to urban sector with preponderance of services.

2. Employment share of farm sector shows a decline over the years, whereas shares of manufacturing and construction sectors show a rise in rural areas. The incidence of contract jobs has increased, and this suggests that employment in these emerging sectors may fail to provide a sustainable and guaranteed livelihood, thus, raising concerns over quality of rural employment from the point view of well-being, although employment opportunities would have increased in the last two decades.

3. Unemployment rate in rural areas remained stagnant at about 1.7 per cent during the last two decades. Although this is half of what has been observed in urban centres, quality of rural employment generated to check unemployment rate raises concerns because of the increased share in casual segment of labour force compared to urban centres where regular jobs have increasingly featured in employment.

4. Rural areas have been witnessing increased presence of registered manufacturing, but wage share in rural areas has been on the decline, more particularly in comparison with their urban counterparts.

5. Deposits and credit of rural areas in total bank deposits and credit showed a marked rise from the early 1970s to the early 1990s, since when they had drastically come down. Although the number of deposit accounts of rural areas witnessed a marginal rise since the early 1990s, the number of credit accounts shows a dramatic fall. During the same period, the CD ratio of rural areas remained far lower than that of urban areas and also compared to the preceding two decades of 1970s and 1980s.

6. Rural households increasingly rely on non-institutional debt availed at exorbitantly higher interest rates compared to their urban counterparts.

7. While consumption patterns in both rural and urban areas have changed drastically since the early 1990s, spending on services such as medical care, education, conveyance, and rent show an upward trend, and food expenditure as a percentage to total has come down. Rural population displays a tendency of catching up with the consumption pattern of its urban counterpart. The rate at which rural CE grew is lesser than that of urban; and also, rural consumption spending as percentage of urban spending has also reduced.

8. Significant progress has been achieved in reducing rural poverty; however, in comparison to urban poverty, rural sector is yet to catch up. Reduction in urban poverty is faster than that of rural poverty and rural poor continue to account for about 81 per cent of the poor of the country. This is not to undermine strides made in alleviating poverty in the country; rather this indicates failings in reducing rural poverty compared to the success achieved in combating urban poverty.

[23] Radhakrishna (2015) observed that for the year 2011–12, the households of Scheduled Tribe (ST) constituted 17.4 per cent of the poor in the country against their share of 8.9 per cent in total population, and Scheduled Caste (SC) accounted for 25.4 per cent of the poor compared to 19 per cent of their share in total population. Thus, disparity exists across social groups.

The widening of the rural–urban gap in several vital indicators inevitably suggests that India's growth has been lopsided, particularly after economic reforms were initiated.[24] Rural areas have witnessed (or are witnessing) structural transformation with increased opportunities coming from manufacturing, but it remains a moot question if such transformation would lead to enhancing of rural well-being in the long run as well as for bridging the rural–urban divide. This reinforces the need of achieving a balanced rural and urban growth, and creating an equalitarian rural India by appropriate policy interventions.

APPENDIX

Rural–Urban Areas under Census of India

Generally Census of India classifies 'town' as urban areas and 'village' as rural areas.

In the Census of India 2001, the definition of urban area adopted is as follows:

(a) All statutory places with a municipality, corporation, cantonment board, or notified town area committee, and so on.
(b) A place satisfying the following three criteria simultaneously:
   (i) a minimum population of 5,000 (formerly 4,000 and above under 1991 census);
   (ii) at least 75 per cent of male working population engaged in non-agricultural pursuits; and
   (iii) a density of population of at least 400 per sq km (1,000 per sq mile).
   The balance of the administrative units is considered as 'rural'.
   To work out the proportion of male working population referred earlier, the data relating to main workers were taken into account.
   An Urban Agglomeration is a continuous urban spread constituting a town and its adjoining urban outgrowths (OGs) or two or more physically contiguous towns together and any adjoining urban OGs of such towns. Examples of OGs are railway colonies, university campuses, port areas, and so on, that may come up near a city or statutory town outside its statutory limits

but within the revenue limits of a village or villages contiguous to the town or city. Each such individual area by itself may not satisfy the minimum population limit to qualify it to be treated as an independent urban unit but may deserve to be clubbed with the town as a continuous urban spread.

For the purpose of delineation of Urban Agglomerations during Census of India 2001, following criteria are taken as pre-requisites:

(a) The core town or at least one of the constituent towns of an urban agglomeration should necessarily be a statutory town; and
(b) The total population of all the constituents (that is, towns and OGs) of an Urban Agglomeration should not be less than 20,000 (as per the 1991 Census).

With these two basic criteria having been met, the following are the possible different situations in which Urban Agglomerations would be constituted:

   (i) a city or town with one or more contiguous OGs;
   (ii) two or more adjoining towns with their OGs; and
   (iii) a city and one or more adjoining towns with their OGs all of which form a continuous spread.

Source: Reproduced from Registrar of Census, available at www.censusindia.gov.in/metadata/metada.htm, accessed on 10 January 2018

REFERENCES

Anand, I. and A. Thampi. 2016. 'Recent Trends in Wealth Inequality in India'. *Economic & Political Weekly* 51(50): 59–67.

Basole, A. and D. Basu. 2015. 'Non-Food Expenditures and Consumption Inequality in India'. *Economic & Political Weekly* 50(36): 43–53.

Bisaliah, S., S.M. Dev, S. Saifullah, and D. Sarkar. 2014. *Asset and Liability Portfolio of Farmers: Micro Evidences from India*. New Delhi: Academic Foundation.

Central Statistics Office. 2015. *Understanding the New Series of National Accounts: Frequently Asked Questions*. Available at http://www.mospi.gov.in/sites/default/files/press_releases_statements/Understanding_New_GDP.pdf, accessed on 10 January 2018.

Chand, R., R. Saxena, and S. Rana. 2015. 'Estimates and Analysis of Farm Income in India, 1983–84 to 2011–12'. *Economic & Political Weekly* 50(22): 139–45.

[24] Anand and Thampi (2016) have observed that rise in wealth and consumption inequality has been more pronounced in urban areas than in rural areas between 1992 and 2012.

Chandrasekhar, S. and N. Mehrotra. 2016. 'Doubling Farmers' Incomes by 2022: What Would It Take?' *Economic & Political Weekly* 51(18): 10–13.

EPW Research Foundation. *EPWRF India Time Series.* Accessed at the www.epwrf.in

———. 2014. *Agricultural Credit in India: Trends, Regional Spreads and Database Issues.* Occasional Paper 58. Mumbai, India: National Bank for Agriculture and Rural Development.

Himanshu. 2015. 'Rural Non-farm Employment in India, Trends, Patterns and Regional Dimension'. In *India Rural Development Report 2013/14.* New Delhi, India: Orient Blackswan.

Krishnaswamy, R. and J.D. Rajakumar. 2015. 'Recent Trends in Inter-Sectoral Terms of Trade'. *Economic & Political Weekly* 50(5): 82–4.

National Sample Survey Office. 1996. *Level and Pattern of Consumer Expenditure NSS 50th Round 1993–94.* Report No. 402. Government of India, New Delhi.

———. 1998. *Household Assets and Liabilities as on 30.06.1991, Debt and Investment Survey NSS 47th Round January–December 1992.* Report No. 419. Government of India, New Delhi.

———. 2000. *Employment and Unemployment Situation in India 1999–2000 Key Results NSS 55th Round July 1999–June 2000.* Report No. 455 (55/10/1). Government of India, New Delhi.

———. 2005. *Household Indebtedness in India as on 30.06.2002, All India Debt and Investment Survey NSS 59th Round (January–December 2003).* Report No. 501 (59/18.2/2). Government of India, New Delhi, December.

———. 2011. *Key Indicators of Employment and Unemployment in India 2009–2010 NSS 66th Round July 2009–June 2010.* Report No. KI (66/10). Government of India, New Delhi.

———. 2013. *Key Indicators of Household Consumer Expenditure in India 2011–12 NSS 68th Round July 2011–June 2012.* Report No. KI (68/1.0). Government of India, New Delhi.

———. 2014a. *Employment and Unemployment Situation in India NSS 68th Round July 2011–June 2012.* Report No. 554 (68/10/1). Government of India, New Delhi.

———. 2014b. *Key Indicators of Debt and Investment in India NSS 70th Round January–December 2013.* Report No. NSS KI (70/18.2). Government of India, New Delhi.

———. 2016. *Household Assets and Liabilities NSS 70th Round (January–December 2013).* Report No. 570 (70/18.2//1). Government of India, New Delhi, January.

Papola, T.S. and P.P. Sahu. 2012. *Growth and Structure of Employment in India Long-Term and Post-Reform Performance and the Emerging Challenge.* ISID Occasional Paper Series 2012/01. New Delhi, India: Institute for Studies in Industrial Development.

Planning Commission. 2013. *Data Table.* Available at http://planningcommission.nic.in/data/datatable/index.php?data=datatab, accessed on 11 May 2013.

Radhakrishna, R. 2015. 'Well-Being, Inequality, Poverty and Pathways Out of Poverty in India'. *Economic & Political Weekly* 50(41): 59–71.

Radhakrishna, R. and K.H. Rao. 2006. 'Poverty, Unemployment and Public Intervention'. *India Social Development Report.* New Delhi: Oxford University Press.

Reserve Bank of India. 1987. *All-India Debt and Investment Survey 1981–82: Assets and Liabilities of Households as on 30th June 1981.* Mumbai: RBI.

9

Rural Development in India
Opportunities for Reform

Jugal Mohapatra* and Santhosh Mathew**

ABSTRACT

Rural development policies in India continue to focus on mitigating the effects of poverty and unequal growth without adequately addressing issues of market and governance failures particularly salient in impeding long-term pro-poor growth in rural areas. Through a historical overview of rural development programmes and policies and an analysis of trends in expenditure, this chapter demonstrates the emphasis on alleviation through social protection and livelihoods promotion without adequately addressing the conditions that make rural areas particularly vulnerable to market and governance failures. Finally, the authors propose key opportunities for market- and governance-oriented reform, including using the lens of behavioural economics to re-examine the conventional wisdom that currently dictates programme design; exploring the potential of big data analytics for improving financial inclusion; leveraging information and communications technologies (ICTs) such as geo-tagging, remote sensing, and crowd sourcing for better monitoring and programme management; improving audit quality; separating front office and back office processes to curb corruption in public service delivery; and, most urgently, reforming the existing fund flow process, which continues to hinder even the most effective implementers.

JEL Classification: H410, H500, H530, I300, R110

Keywords: rural development, pro-poor growth, market failure, governance reforms, public service delivery

* Former Secretary, Department of Rural Development (DoRD), Government of India.

** Former Joint Secretary, Department of Rural Development (DoRD), Government of India.

All views and errors are solely those of the authors and this chapter does not represent the views of DoRD or any part of the Government of India.

9.1 OVERVIEW

9.1.1 The Economic Rationale for State Intervention in Rural Development

By and large, India's growth story since liberalization in the 1990s has been characterized by its distributional unevenness (Chaudhuri and Ravallion 2006). Although absolute levels of poverty have declined in both rural and urban India, a considerable body of literature has highlighted rising inequality and regional disparity since 1991 (Ravallion 2000; Deaton and Dreze 2002; Sen and Himanshu 2004; Banerjee and Piketty 2005; Datt and Ravallion 2011). This raises serious questions about the inclusiveness of this growth. Therefore, the extent to which India's poor have benefited from the growing economy remains a prime policy concern. This is also important in terms of the viability of India's continued economic growth.[1]

Central to these concerns is the role of the state in promoting pro-poor and inclusive growth. In tracing the factors responsible for increasing inequality in the post-reform period, some scholars have pointed towards the retreat of the *dirigiste* state, which had previously kept demand constraints at bay by actively protecting and promoting the rural sector (Pal and Ghosh 2007; Patnaik 2015). Pal and Ghosh (2007), for example, highlight the role of several macroeconomic policies which saw a reduction in government expenditure on the rural sector, a decline in priority sector lending,[2] and the sectoral and geographical concentration of foreign and domestic investment as possible reasons for increasing inequality and the persistence of poverty in the post-reform period. The resulting trends in increased consumption disparity between rural and urban India (Sen and Himanshu 2005), the steady increase in the casualization of labour

(Harriss-White and Gooptu 2009), decline in agricultural employment (Ramaswamy and Agrawal 2012), and increase in the size of the unorganized or informal economy (Harriss-White and Gooptu 2009) have underscored the insufficiency of growth alone in reducing poverty through the trickle-down effect.

Much of this scholarship positions rural growth as the main driver of poverty reduction. However, more recent work on the impact of economic growth and structural transformation on the incidence of poverty continues to add fuel to existing debates. Using data spanning nearly six decades, Datt et al. (2016) argue that post-1991, urban growth has displaced rural growth as the primary driver of poverty reduction, suggesting that urban growth has improved rural living standards. Datt and Ravallion (2011) observe that this is likely due to the growth in the non-farm sectors such as trade, construction, and the unorganized sector, which use unskilled labour more intensively. They hypothesize that the rural poor have benefited from urban economic growth, particularly through employment in and remittances from the non-farm sectors (Datt and Ravallion 2011).

Whether the nature of economic growth thus far has been pro-poor or not remains undecided. However, these discourses on growth have important implications for the role of the state in managing the persistence of inequality. Chaudhuri and Ravallion (2006) provide an insightful interjection by distinguishing between good and bad inequalities and the prioritization of the latter in policy prescriptions. Good inequalities, they argue, foster innovation, entrepreneurship, and growth, whereas bad inequalities such as geographic poverty traps, structures of social exclusion, lack of access to credit, corruption, and so on fuel inequality and prevent individuals from rising out of poverty. Therefore, the focus of policymaking, while looking at social protection, infrastructure, and livelihood promotion, should also address issues in market, coordination, and governance failures (particularly salient in rural areas) that promote bad inequalities and impede long-term pro-poor growth (Chaudhuri and Ravallion 2006).

9.1.2 State Intervention in Rural Development—The State of Play

The Indian state has historically played a very visible role in managing socio-economic inequalities. Unlike Western democracies where universal franchise followed industrialization, a newly independent India was still largely poor when universal adult franchise was enshrined. As a consequence, 'inclusiveness has played

---

[1] Growing inequality across the world has prompted a new look at its economic costs. A recent study released by the International Monetary Fund (IMF) argues that governments should be especially concerned about the consequences of growing inequality on economic growth. The study estimates that 'if the income share of the top 20 per cent increases by 1 percentage point, GDP growth is actually 0.08 percentage points *lower* in the following five years, suggesting that the benefits do not trickle down. Instead, a similar increase in the income share of the bottom 20 per cent (the poor) is associated with 0.38 percentage point *higher* growth' (Dabla-Norris et al. 2015, 7).

[2] While priority sector lending has increased in absolute terms, the rate of growth has slowed down from an average of 18.4 per cent between FY 1994–5 and 2003–4 to 16.3% between FY 2010–11 and 2015–16 (Annual Report of the RBI, 1998–2010; RBI Draft Technical Paper on Priority Sector Lending, 2005).

a more significant role in Indian policy making than was generally true at a comparable level of development elsewhere' (Ahmed and Varshney 2008, 17–18).

Since Independence, democratic norms and practices have been embraced by more and more people, including those at the bottom of India's socio-economic ladder (Kohli 2001). Scholars of Indian democracy have observed consistently high voter turnout at national elections (Jaffrelot 2008) and particularly among the poor (Yadav 1996, 2000; Palshikar and Kumar 2004; Kumar 2009; Yadav and Palishkar 2009). The National Election Survey (2014) found that Scheduled Castes, Scheduled Tribes, and Other Backward Classes account for 71 per cent of voters.

Studies of a more ethnographic nature have contributed various explanations for the high level of electoral participation in India. Some have highlighted the image of the instrumental voter (Chandra 2007; Witsoe 2013), while others have emphasized the ritualistic dimensions that permeate elections and the act of voting (Banerjee 2007). Moving away from singular explanations, Ahuja and Chhibber (2012) have argued that different social groups are fuelled by different motivations, which are in turn shaped by the nature of their relationship with the state. Unlike the non-poor, who vote because they expect benefits or because of a sense of civic duty, the poor 'view voting as a valued right, one that gives them a rare chance to associate with those who govern as equals' (Ahuja and Chhibber 2012, 389).

Consequently, the need to respond to the demands of the poor majority has been a key feature of Indian politics. In fact, it has been argued that the persistence of democracy in a heterogeneous society marked by caste-based hierarchies, low levels of basic education, and widespread poverty, can be attributed to the ability of the Indian state to balance the demands of various politicized social groups (Kohli 2001). The success of Indian democracy, Kohli argues, can be partly attributed to the state's ability to serve the interests of the powerful without fully excluding those at the margins (Kohli 2001).

The Indian state has a long history of efforts to combat poverty, particularly in rural India, where a majority of the poor continue to reside. The post-Independence emphasis on industrialization saw the continuation of limited provision of basic public goods by the state (Banerjee and Somanathan 2007). As a result, rural development policies were still nascent in their scope and reach. Early efforts drew from experiments in Etawah and Nilokheri, which took place immediately after Independence and centred on community development through participatory planning, building, and strengthening of village institutions and provisioning of extension services. During this phase, the state experimented with panchayats as a public service delivery system and focused on technology transfer for food self-sufficiency in rural India (Vijayanand 2014).

It was not until the 1970s that the removal of poverty became central to political rhetoric. What followed was 'the direct attack on poverty' articulated as *garibi hatao*—the centrepiece of the Fifth Five Year Plan. A number of poverty alleviation programmes were introduced during this period which largely centred on two main sets of interventions for (a) employment and (b) livelihoods promotion. Different schemes were launched aimed at specific groups within the purview of the above two categories.

There have been several employment generation programmes like the National Rural Employment Programme (NREP) initiated in 1980 and the Jawahar Rozgar Yojana (JRY) initiated in 1989, which have been undertaken to provide the rural poor with supplementary wage employment, particularly during the lean agricultural season through public works such as construction of village roads, ponds, irrigation wells, and school buildings in an around their villages. In 1985 Indira Awaas Yojana (IAY) was launched as a sub-scheme of JRY for helping rural poor households to build *pucca* (brick and mortar) houses. In 1996 it was made a separate scheme and in 2015 it was converted to Pradhan Mantri Awas Yojana (PMAY) with the goal of providing housing for all by 2022. The year 2000 was a major departure in the strategy for rural development in India because for the first time a dedicated scheme for rural infrastructure in the form of Pradhan Mantri Gram Sadak Yojana (PMGSY) was launched. It aimed to provide all-weather rural connectivity to all habitations by 2022. In 2015 the target completion date was brought forward to 2019. Many state governments have also launched their own versions of the scheme often called MMGSY or Mukhya Mantri Gram Sadak Yojana.

A key state-level employment programme was the Maharashtra Employment Guarantee Scheme (MEGS), which started in 1965 and served as a precursor to the Mahatma Gandhi National Rural Employment Guarantee Scheme (MGNREGS) in 2005. MEGS was based on the principle of right to work for all adults in the rural areas and had the twin aims of guaranteeing employment and improving rural infrastructure (Papadimitriou 2008). Although drawing on the experiences of a number of rural wage employment programmes of the state and central governments, MGNREGS drew largely from MEGS and signalled a shift from allocation-based programmes to a rights-based one (Vijayanand 2014).

Livelihoods-based interventions emerged with the introduction of the Integrated Rural Development Programme (IRDP), which was launched throughout the country in 1978 with the aim of enabling poor households to engage in economically gainful self-employment. The focus of IRDP was on the provision of subsidized credit to enable the poor to build productive assets and raise their income levels. With its emphasis on skill building through Training of Rural Youth for Self-Employment (TRYSEM) and building market linkages, the IRDP represented a paradigm shift in the approach to livelihoods programmes in rural India (Vijayanand 2014).

In 1999 the IRDP and allied programmes were merged into the Swarnajayanti Gram Swarojgar Yojana (SGSY). Under this new avatar, beneficiaries were organized into Self Help Groups (SHGs), which were then extended financial support through subsidized institutionalized bank credit. Small organized income generating enterprises were thus given an opportunity to get established. A component for skilling and placement of rural poor youth was also launched called SGSY (Special Projects).

Following the recognition that credit alone may not be enough, SGSY was restructured into the National Rural Livelihood Mission (NRLM). NRLM went beyond self-employment to livelihood promotion and took away interest subsidy and replaced it with interest subvention in those cases where the repayment had been prompt (Vijayanand 2014). The skills and placement component was redesigned in 2013 and launched as Aajeevika Skills. In 2014 it was upgraded and announced as Deen Dayal Upadhyay Grammen Kaushalya Yojana (DDU-GKY).

To summarize, since the launch of the direct attack on poverty in the 1970s, the state's poverty alleviation attempts have undergone many changes but the broad pattern of pursuing wage employment through works programmes and self-employment thorough capacity development and credit has persisted. The addition of housing and rural roads has also sustained and gathered steam since their launch in 1985 and 2000 respectively (Vijayanand 2013). Despite these shifts, rural development efforts continue to focus on mitigating the effects rather than addressing the structural causes of rural poverty, even though it is widely understood that lack of employment and livelihoods form only a part of a set of conditions—including lack of infrastructure, information asymmetries, and high transaction costs—that coalesce to make the rural poor particularly vulnerable to market failure (Kydd and Dorward 2004).

The deepening of democracy in India has come with its own set of concerns. According to Bardhan (2001), the equity-centric mass political culture in India has hampered economic growth, as the more the government seeks to satisfy the numerous interest groups that clamour for a share of public resources, the less it has available to undertake crucial long-term investments in social and economic infrastructure. Rural development initiatives in India have, by and large, evolved within the context of this 'equity-politics'. Banerjee and Somanathan (2007), for example find empirical support for the role of political mobilization on the allocation of public goods over the 1970s and 1980s in rural India, particularly for historically disadvantaged social groups. Similarly, Pande (2003) shows evidence of political preference for targeted spending. She finds that while political reservation increased the transfers of government resources to disadvantaged groups, such increases largely took the form of access to government jobs and targeted welfare transfers at the expense of general redistributive programmes and social services necessary to overcome the market failures that exacerbate poverty (Pande 2003). Future attempts to enable pro-poor growth and reduce inequality, particularly in rural India, must, therefore, look beyond mitigation and address the market and governance failures that have hitherto been overlooked.

9.2 THE SIZE OF THE RURAL DEVELOPMENT CAKE[3]

In the earlier section we highlighted the inadequacy of current rural development policies to address market and governance failure. In this section we look at the expenditure on rural development from 2011–12 to 2016–17 to elaborate further. To understand government investment in rural India, we need to look beyond budget allocations to the Department of Rural Development (DoRD). Several ministries such as Drinking Water and Sanitation, Agriculture, and Health also spend on rural programmes (see Table 9A.1 in the Appendix for a breakdown of ministry-wise spending).

As Figure 9.1 demonstrates, the size of the rural development cake is much larger when we take into consideration spending across all other ministries investing in rural programmes.[4] Furthermore, DoRD spending does not make up the majority of investment in rural India. In fact, as Figure 9.1 indicates, average allocations to DoRD have consistently hovered around 18–23 per cent of total spending in rural areas. In fact, it is interesting to note

[3] The authors of the chapter thank the Centre for Budget and Governance Accountability (CBGA) and the Accountability Initiative for assistance in collating data for the analysis in this section.

[4] The schemes used in this analysis are listed in Table 9A.1 in the Appendix.

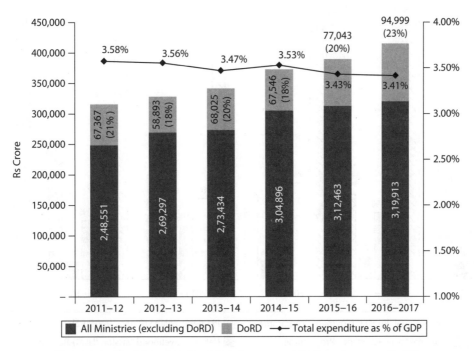

Figure 9.1   Total Spend on Rural Development—All Ministries versus DoRD

Note: Figures are revised estimates (RE), except for FY 2011–12, which are actuals. GDP figure for 2016–17 is an advance estimate.
Source: Compiled from expenditure budgets of various ministries of Government of India (www.indiabudget.nic.in). GDP figures for 2011–12 have been obtained from the *Economic Survey* of 2014–15. Estimates for years onwards have been obtained from the *Economic Survey* of 2015–16.

that over this period, budget allocations for fertilizer subsidies (which include the subsidy on decontrolled fertilizers, imported fertilizers, and to fertilizer industries) have hovered close to the total DoRD budget despite the pernicious effects of overuse on soil health and the general price imbalances in the fertilizer market (Gulati and Banerjee 2015; Himanshu 2015).

Furthermore, trends in allocation for different schemes support our earlier claim that rural development efforts within the ministry have focused predominantly on social safety net programmes and done little to address market and governance failures more directly. As Figure 9.2 indicates, in any given year between 2011–12 and 2016–17, 70–80 per cent of the DoRD budget has been allocated towards three key social safety nets: Pradhan Mantri Awas Yojana (PMAY), Rural, National Social Assistance Programme (NSAP), and Mahatma Gandhi National Rural Employment Guarantee Scheme (MGNREGS).

Turning our attention to the effectiveness of ministries in spending their budget allocation we find that between FY 2012–13 and 2014–15, DoRD spent, on an average, less than 80 per cent of allocated funds. In comparison, all other ministries combined were able to utilize close to 97 per cent of their allocated funds (Figure 9.3). We hypothesize that the underutilization of allocated funds

may have been due to the decentralization of spending, which slows down the system of fund flow as utilization certificates necessary for the release of funds have to be aggregated at the panchayat level and sent up the administrative chain via a files-based system. The improvement in DoRD's fund utilization in 2015–16 can be attributed to the streamlining of fund release through just-in-time financing initiated in 2015.

While the early post-Independence years were marked by the prioritization of investment in the rural sector,[5] the percentage share of expenditure on the rural economy[6] in Union and state government budgets has markedly declined since the 1990s (Jha and Acharya 2011). With the added increase in input prices, vulnerability to price fluctuations in the world market, and weakening of the rural credit system particularly for small and marginal farmers, the period from the early 1990s till the present

---

[5] The plan allocation for agriculture, irrigation, and flood control as a share of total plan expenditure in the first five-year plan amounted to 37 per cent, the highest among all five-year plans and annual plans till date (Jha and Acharya 2011, 137).

[6] Jha and Acharya take into account the combined budgetary allocation made towards the rural economy by the union and state governments under agriculture and allied activities, rural development, fertilizer subsidy, irrigation, and cooperation.

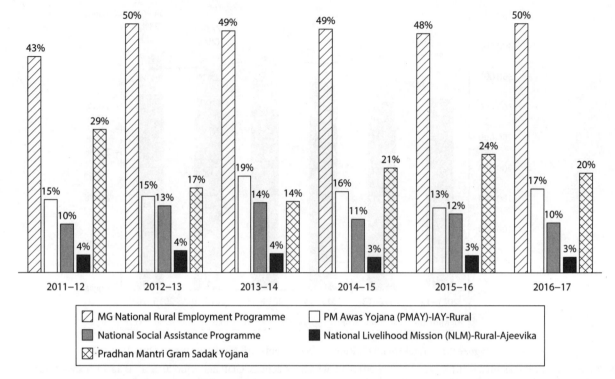

Figure 9.2 Proportion of Spending on Various Rural Development Schemes (DoRD)

Note: Based on REs, except for 2011–12, which are based on actuals.
Source: Compiled from Expenditure Budget, vol. II, MoRD (www.indiabudget.nic.in).

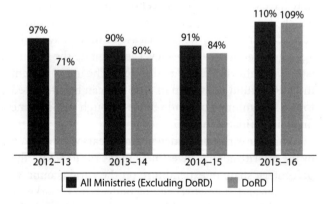

Figure 9.3 Expenditure as a Proportion of Funds Allocated—
All Ministries versus DoRD

Note: Figures are actuals as a percentage of BE.
Source: Compiled from expenditure budgets of various ministries of Government of India (www.indiabudget.nic.in).

is also one of sustained agrarian crisis (Jha and Acharya 2011). Given the decline in percentage share there is an urgent need to utilize public expenditure more effectively and maximize its impact on rural development. This will require greater interdepartmental coordination, changes in the way the rural development spend is administered

as well as efforts to ameliorate market and governance failures. In the following section we outline a few opportunities in this direction.

9.3 OPPORTUNITIES FOR REFORM

9.3.1 Behavioural Economics: The Power of a Well-Timed Nudge

9.3.1.1 Improving Agricultural Productivity: Lessons from Behavioural Economics

Agriculture is the main source of income and employment in rural India and yet agricultural productivity has declined over the years (Fan et al. 2008). This is often attributed to the low adoption of improved agricultural practices and crop varieties as well as inputs such as fertilizers—which have the potential to increase yields and reduce spoilage and risk when used appropriately.[7]

As farmers are credit constrained and lack information, policymakers have relied largely on input subsidies

[7] Critics of fertilizer subsidies argue that it promotes overuse, which leads to environment damage thereby ultimately reducing productivity in the long run.

and extension services to boost agricultural productivity (World Development Report 2015). While these assumptions may indeed capture important relationships between monetary incentives and investment in enhancing agricultural productivity, behavioural economics has shown cognitive, psychological, and social barriers which are more difficult to observe, could also be playing a role in limiting farmer productivity (World Development Report 2015) (see Box 9.1).

9.3.1.2 Nudges to Increase Health-Promoting Behaviours

Despite large levels of public spending, demand for preventative health services remains limited due to barriers such as distance, inconvenience, procrastination, and so on. Standard health models assume that individuals will 'carefully weigh the benefits and barriers to adoption against their susceptibility to, and the likely severity of, bad outcomes if they do not adopt' (World Development Report 2015 149). However, studies have consistently found that people consider benefits and barriers over susceptibility and severity (World Development Report

2015, 149). How then can people be induced to seek more preventative health care? (See Box 9.2.)

Rational choice theory assumes that individuals consider all possible costs and benefits when faced with a decision or choice. In such a world, farmers will invest in high-yielding seeds and families will use chlorine to disinfect their drinking water because the benefits of doing so outweigh the costs. This thinking has driven many policy prescriptions aimed at improving outcomes for the poor. Yet, we know that human beings do not always make decisions in this way (Glennerster and Kremer 2011).

In recent decades, the burgeoning field of behavioural economics has offered an alternative set of assumptions

---

Box 9.1   Nudging Farmers to Use Fertilizer: Experimental Evidence from Kenya

Lack of money may not be the main barrier in the low adoption of fertilizers. An alternate view rooted in behavioural economics points to issues of timing and impatience. Fluctuations in farm income may mean that farmers do not have the money to buy fertilizers when they are most needed or that the effort required to procure inputs such as fertilizers leads them to procrastinate.

A randomized evaluation in Kenya tested whether a 'nudge' in the form of small time-limited offer for advanced fertilizer purchase could increase fertilizer adoption. The study found that when farmers were offered a small incentive (free delivery) and the opportunity to pre-purchase fertilizer at the time of harvest, adoption increased by 64 per cent. This impact was comparable to that of a 50 per cent subsidy offered later in the season when fertilizer was needed.

POLICY INSIGHTS

- Commitment devices can help farmers overcome time-inconsistent preferences.
- A small well-timed nudge can be as effective as a heavy subsidy for improving farming investments—and may even be a better policy.

Sources: Duflo et al. (2011) and J-PAL Policy Briefcase 2011.

Box 9.2   Chlorine Dispensers for Safe Water in Kenya

In 2012, 11 per cent of the global population did not have access to improved sources of drinking water (Millennium Development Goals Report 2012). Safe drinking water could prevent 1.4 million child deaths from diarrhoea and 860,000 deaths from malnutrition annually (World Health Organization 2016). Improving access to clean water was largely thought of as an engineering problem that could be addressed by digging more wells; however, this does little to address the issue of water contamination. Chlorine is a cheap and easy solution to disinfect drinking water, yet information and marketing campaigns have not improved uptake.

Using insights from behavioural economics, researchers at Innovations for Poverty Action (IPA) tested a range of interventions to improve access to clean water in Kenya. They first tried to improve water quality by protecting spring water from runoff, which proved fruitless since the water often became contaminated by the time it was consumed. They then tested the impact of free home distribution of chlorine, which increased initial take-up but failed to generate sustained results. Behavioural insights from these attempts led to the design of a point-of-collection chlorine dispenser system that provided a free supply of chlorine at local water sources. This proved to be the most cost-effective method for increasing use of chlorine for a number of reasons: it made water treatment convenient and salient, provided a visual reminder, and encouraged peer learning and habit formation by making the decision to use chlorine public.

Policy insights:

- Take-up of preventative health products, such as chlorine, is highly sensitive to price, convenience, and social context.
- Nudges can be a highly cost-effective way of promoting take-up of preventative health products.

Source: Kremer et al. (2011).

underlying decision-making in the context of poverty. In the field of health and education, a large body of behavioural studies across different contexts has shown that small inconveniences and charges can prevent people from making important upfront investments, even when nominal (Glennerster and Kremer 2011). The empirical evidence suggests that 'both poor people and people who are not poor are affected in the same fundamental way by certain cognitive, psychological, and social constraints on decision making. However it is the context of poverty that modifies decision making in important ways' (World Development Report 2015, 81). For those who are impoverished, the cognitive burden of living hand to mouth can lead to sub-optimal economic decisions—such as saving too little or under-investing in

health and education—which further entrench them in poverty (World Development Report 2015, 81).

Understanding how people make decisions in the context of poverty can help improve the design and implementation of policies and programmes targeted towards them. As demonstrated by the studies in Boxes 9.1 and 9.2, nudges are one example of a highly cost-effective behavioural intervention, which can help narrow down the intention–action divide that often discourages the take-up of programmes with proven efficacy. The application of behavioural insights to catalyse behaviour change is not just limited to the poor. Increasingly, these insights are helping design interventions that can make public officials more efficient in delivering public services (see Boxes 9.3a and 9.3b).

Box 9.3a Can Visualized MGNREGS Report Cards Nudge Administrators and Political Leaders towards Improving Programme Implementation?

The MGNREGS Management Information System (MIS) now contains over 30 terabytes of open data that it collected and entered on a quasi-real-time basis, making it extremely useful for implementers and policymakers.

However, as with many government programmes, this data remains under-utilized.

The Ministry of Rural Development has teamed up with Evidence for Policy Design (EPoD), a research network based at the Harvard Kennedy School, to understand how data visualizations of performance at all administrative levels via the MGNREGS Report Dashboard can nudge block- and district-level officials to improve MGNREGS implementation.

Source: Dodge (2015).

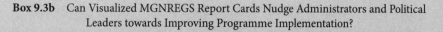

Box 9.3b Can Visualized MGNREGS Report Cards Nudge Administrators and Political Leaders towards Improving Programme Implementation?

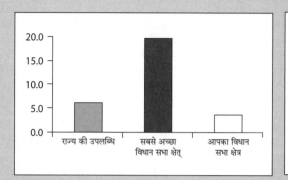

इस रिपोर्ट कार्ड को आप अपने विधान सभा क्षेत्र अंतर्गत मनरेगा कार्यक्रम की स्थिति की जानकारी प्राप्त करने के लिए उपयोग कर सकते है। मनरेगा अंतर्गत पंचायत वारश्रम बजट तैयार किया गया है एवं उसके अनुरूप SOW भी तैयार किया गया है। हर पंचायत को श्रम बजट के आधार पर हर सप्ताह में श्रम बजट को बांट कर संसूचित सके। काम की मांग के आलोक में ही योजना लिया जाना है। विदित हो कि राशि की कोई सीमा नहीं है। आप मनरेगा के प्रगति का मुल्यांकन करने के क्रम में अन्य विधानसभा क्षेत्रों के तुलनात्मक स्थिति, कौन प्रखंड/पंचायत पिछड रहे है, किन बिन्दुओं पर ध्यान देना है, क्या आंकड़े वस्तुस्थिति का सही प्रतिबिम्ब है अन्यथा नहीं इत्यादि बिन्दुओं पर जिला कार्यक्रम समंवयक (जिला पदाधिकारी) से समीक्षा कर एवं सहयोग कर योजना के सफल कार्यान्वयन में अपना बहुमुल्य योगदान दे सकते हैं ।

In 2012–13 the Government of Bihar's Rural Development Department distributed report cards summarizing constituency-wise MGNREGS performance to members of the Bihar legislative assembly. The report cards were designed to nudge MLAs to improve the implementation of MGNREGS in their constituency by providing them with information on the performance of panchayats within their constituency as compared to the state average and the best performing constituency. MLAs were also given small pocket cards with a calendar specifying the process flow of the MNREGS muster-cycle (that is, the steps between completion of work and the payment of wages within a weekly or fortnightly work cycle) to ensure that each step from submission of muster rolls to measurement of work to uploading of wage slip is done on time and delays in the payment process averted.

Around the world governments and policy-makers are already recognizing the relevance of behavioural insights for improving social programmes. In 2010, the UK government established the Behavioural Insights Team (BIT) to apply insights from behavioural economics and psychology to public policy design. They have since been spun out as a social purpose company jointly owned by the UK government, Nesta (an innovation foundation), and employees. Likewise, an executive order to use behavioural science insights was issued by the president of the United States in 2015 with a policy directive for departments and agencies to identify policies and programmes where behavioural science insights can be applied to improve outcomes and cost effectiveness and strengthen relationships with research communities to better utilize findings from rigorous research in the field (Rao and Tagat 2016).

Efforts to institutionalize behavioural insights into policy-making are similarly underway in India. The NITI Aayog has recently moved towards setting up a 'Nudge Unit' to bring behavioural insights to bear on the implementation of key government flagship programmes such as Swachh Bharat and Jan Dhan Yojana (Seth Sharma and Tiwari 2016). If such a unit is armed with the appropriate expertise and the necessary resources, it could hold very promising potential for increasing the efficacy of social sector spending in India.

9.3.2 Harnessing the Potential of Big Data

In 2014, as an outbreak of Ebola in West Africa grew into a global health crisis, emergency response teams and humanitarian agencies began exploring ways of using big data technologies to contain the spread of the virus. In Senegal, one mobile phone carrier provided access to anonymized voice and text data to a group of researchers who utilized it to create detailed maps of typical population movements in the region, offering clues as to where to focus resources and containment efforts (Richards 2014). The US Centres for Disease Control and Prevention (CDC) went one step further and used mobile phone tower activity data to map the origin of calls to Ebola helplines, giving responders a real-time picture and researchers data to model the spread of the disease (Wall 2014).

Characterized by three 'V's—volume, variety, and velocity—big data refers to datasets whose size is beyond the ability of typical software programmes to capture, manage, and analyse (Mani 2016). Big data can be obtained from a variety of sources including mobile phones, social media content, global positioning system (GPS) satellite identifications, and so on (Mani 2016). Big data analytics, in turn, refer to the methodologies and tools through which large quantities of this raw data can be transformed into interpretable data

Box 9.4   Spotlight: Using Big Data to Improve Skilling Outcomes for Rural Youth

Despite considerable investments in skill development—Rs 18.04 billion in the 2016–17 budget and the establishment of a separate ministry for skill development—there remains considerable room for improvement in closing the widening skills gap in India. At present, the skills sector suffers from high drop-out rates and low retention rates in jobs post-placement. While government and industry unanimously agree on the need to improve youth employability, there is a lack of consensus on how to best achieve this. How can skilling and placement outcomes be improved to transform India's demographic surplus into a demographic dividend?

The Ministry of Rural Development with the help of Interglobe Foundation is utilizing big data analytics to address this skills gap in the context of DDU-GKY and its goal to skill and employ more than 1.05 million rural youth by 2017. Big data analytics are being used to identify predictors of success (defined as enrollment in the mobilization phase, training completion, and job take-up in the training and pre-placement phase, and job retention in the post-placement phase) at different stages, monitor predictors, and prescribe actions and interventions to prevent shortfall. The use of predictive analytics is supplying the programme with insights into characteristics of successful candidates, risk profiles of each candidate, and the risk of drop-out at each stage—insights that will ultimately help identify the right interventions to increase the likelihood of success for candidates.

Source: DDU-GKY (2015).

(Mani 2016). Around the world, governments and organizations are starting to use big data to address critical problems from containing the spread of Ebola to predicting food shortages.

Although big data is beginning to take root in India, many of its applications are still nascent (see Box 9.4). At an institutional level, initiatives have been taken by the Department of Science and Technology and the Ministry of Electronics and Information Technology (MeitY) to set up a 'big data division' and underscore its importance in a draft Internet of Things (IoT) policy. The National Association of Software and Services Companies (NASSCOM), an industry body, is in the process of setting up centres of excellence for building big data analytics capacity in the country. Central government projects such as the unique identification (UID) project and Digital India are also envisioning the use of big data technologies to improve public service delivery (Srivastava 2015).

9.3.3 Future Potential—Leveraging Digital Exhaust for Financial Inclusion

One key area of potential application for big data analytics in India lies in leveraging digital exhaust for financial inclusion. Defined as the digital footprint left behind by individuals' digital activities, digital exhaust is a key input in the emerging space of credit scoring via advanced analytics on non-traditional and big data sources (Deb 2014). Social enterprises such as *Cignifi*[8] and *First Access*[9] are leveraging mobile data to

enable their lending and insurance partners to identify and assess the creditworthiness of underserved and unbanked populations without credit histories (Naef et al. 2014). Similarly, solutions like *DemystData*[10] are utilizing big data analytics to create customer profiles that can be used by financial institutions to verify the identity of 'thin-file' or no-file individuals—a process that banks and other financial service providers spend significant time and energy conducting for traditionally underserved populations (Breloff and Hookey 2014).

While digital data on the lives of the poor has thus far been scant, the proliferation of mobile phones has now brought into the fold billions who were previously digitally invisible (Gupta 2014). India currently ranks second in the world with over 1 billion mobile phone subscriptions, of which approximately 240 million are smartphone users (Shah et al. 2016). The number of smartphone users, India-wide, is projected to reach 520 million by 2020. Rural India is following suit in terms of 3G and 4G penetration. According to a KPMG-IAMAI report (2015), the Active Internet User base in rural India stands at 6.7 per cent of the overall rural population or 61 million users, of whom nearly 50 per cent access the internet via mobile phones. A more recent report by BCG pegs the percentage of mobile internet users in rural India at 70 per cent (2016). This level of mobile phone penetration and internet usage is significant for rural India where, despite various attempts to bring people into the formal banking system, most continue to rely on cash, physical assets such as jewellery and livestock, and informal providers such as moneylenders to meet their financial

[8] http://cignifi.com/.
[9] http://www.firstaccessmarket.com/.

[10] See http://demyst.com/.

needs. Furthermore, due to little or no record of past borrowing behaviour and volatile income and expenditure patterns, the rural poor are often excluded from accessing formal financial services such as savings products and credit (Naef et al. 2014). Therefore, mobile proliferation, particularly among the poor, and the associated developments in big data analytics to use mobile data to create alterative financial profiles hold a lot of promise for furthering the aim of financial inclusion in rural India.

With increased mobile penetration, the availability of anonymized call detail records (CDRs) also opens up opportunities to use big data analytics to construct new socio-economic proxy indicators that can help researchers and governments better understand and measure growth (Šćepanović et al. 2015). For example, a study in the UK used mobile and census socio-economic data to validate a previously untestable assumption that greater diversity of social networks provides individuals with greater access to economic opportunities (World Bank Report 2014).

The utilization of big data requires the availability of several capabilities, including hardware and software for storing and processing data and human capabilities to analyse big data and make their insights actionable. As such it is an endeavour that governments in India need to undertake, but only if it can make possible meaningful cooperation and collaboration between scientists, subject experts, and policy-makers.

9.3.4 Leveraging ICT for Effective Monitoring

Effective monitoring structures are an important element in ensuring that public service delivery is not weakened by leakages and corruption. Despite the scope and reach of public services in India, they continue to be plagued by implementation bottlenecks that impede the government's ability to achieve desired social outcomes. Take the PMGSY for example. As India's flagship rural road construction programme, the PMGSY accounts for a large share of Government of India's budget for rural infrastructure development. As of June 2016, PMGSY has connected more than 120,000 villages or habitations through more than 460,000 km of roads at a cost of Rs 1.4 trillion and rising (Lehne et al. 2016a). In a recent study assessing political influence on the allocation of PMGSY road contracts, Lehne et al. (2016b) find evidence of local politicians influencing the tendering process in favour of members of their caste/kinship networks. Additionally they find that preferential allocation was associated with significant increase in the initial cost of road construction, adverse road quality, and increases in the likelihood of 'missing' roads.

Lehne et al.'s study suggests that existing monitoring and quality assurance provisions intended to check undue corruption under PMGSY may not be enough to curb 'subtler mechanisms by which caste or kinship networks facilitate corrupt exchange' (2016b, 4). The insufficiency of existing monitoring structures in PMGSY is also well-documented in a recent comptroller and auditor general (CAG) report which found irregularities in state-level monitoring of projects and deficiencies in the operationalization of the Online Management, Monitoring and Accounting System (OMMAS) (PRS 2016). While entrenched corruption may be more difficult to measure and tackle, improving existing monitoring and audit systems through technology is a low-hanging fruit that can help dis-incentivize misreporting.

9.3.5 Geo-Informatics for Better Planning and Management

Monitoring the implementation of government projects in rural areas presents its own set of challenges. For one, government projects are often large in scale and geographically spread out. Furthermore, rural areas are often difficult to access and, therefore, require more manpower and resources. However, with advances in the field of geo-informatics and the ubiquity of GPS-enabled devices, innovative applications of technologies such as geo-tagging and remote sensing are offering up new ways through which projects in remote locations can be easily and accurately located and managed.

Geo-tagging involves adding geographical identification metadata such as geographical coordinates to various media such as photographs, videos, and even SMS messages. Since it requires little beyond a GPS-enabled phone and an internet connection to upload the multimedia onto a platform or web-based application, geo-tagging can be a low-cost solution to improving the quality of project monitoring. For large infrastructure projects that involve the creation of assets—for example, roads under PMGSY or community assets under MGNREGS—missing or fictitious assets are of key concern. For such projects, geo-tags can function as UID tags so as to avoid duplication and curb false reporting of assets.

While the monitoring guidelines of PMGSY already require the submission of digital photographs, compliance is often an issue as photographs of assets are not uniformly available across all sites or updated regularly to document progress. Where they are available, their authenticity may be suspect, given that there is no further verification of this monitoring data. Making the up-loading of geo-tagged photographs onto the public

---

Box 9.5 Spotlight: GSM-Enabled Remote Monitoring of Rural Hand Pumps

Reliable water service remains an unrealized goal in rural Africa where one-third of the community managed groundwater hand pumps—the primary source of water supply for over 200 million people—remain non-functional. This is further exacerbated by long repair times and weak payment systems which further contribute to service delivery failure.

Researchers at Oxford University took advantage of mobile network expansion in rural areas to design a water-point data transmitter (WDT) capable of providing real-time data on hand pump usage for better monitoring and maintenance response. The WDT is attached to the handle of the water pump and uses a low-cost integrated-circuit-based accelerometer to monitor the number of strokes made in operating a hand pump and transmits this information over the global system for mobile communications (GSM) network. The data generated by the WDT is capable of showing daily to seasonal demand levels, including under-or-over usage information.

To test the impact of this technology, 66 hand pumps servicing a catchment area of roughly 20,000 households were fitted with WDTs. The aggregation of this real-time usage data enabled maintenance teams to track hand pump functionality and respond to maintenance needs immediately. At the end of one year, the smart hand pumps decreased pump downtime from 37 days to two days and increased willingness to pay for continued maintenance service from 29 per cent to 91 per cent.

Source: Thomson et al. (2012); Koehler et al. (2015).

---

domain a precondition for payment and instituting a systematic process of periodical back-checks of scientifically chosen random samples by both independent forensic auditors and national- and state-level Business Processing Outsourcing (BPO) units can dis-incentivize monitors from falsifying or neglecting to update the required monitoring data to some extent.

Geo-tagging of assets built via public funds is already underway in the energy sector, where the Ministry of New and Renewable Energy (MNRE) has mandated all entrepreneurial and public sector units and other agencies implementing solar rooftop projects to geo-tag executed and planned projects to ensure better monitoring (Aggarwal 2016). Similar initiatives have been taken by the Ministry of Rural Development, which in June 2016 signed an agreement with the Indian Space Research Organisation (ISRO) to geo-tag the nearly 3 million assets created annually under MGNREGS (Aggarwal 2016).

Geo-informatics are also being utilized for planning, monitoring, and managing the implementation of PMGSY, where the Ministry of Rural Development is using remote sensing to detect the variance between progress reported manually/electronically by the states and independently ascertained progress through satellite imagery. A study covering 10 districts across five states[11] was conducted using remote sensing, and the results

cross-verified against the progress reported on OMMAS, which is the MIS of the PMGSY. Of the 124 roads analysed, the study found that the length of 31 per cent of the roads varied from that reported in the MIS. The study also detected variation in habitat connectivity in 18 per cent of the roads and culverts and causeway road lengths in 12 per cent of the roads (C-GARD Report 2016). The application of remote sensing can go beyond just detecting variation in official reporting. Remote sensing can also contribute towards improving the planning process by helping determine the least costly route and ease land acquisition bottlenecks which continue to hamper programme implementation in many states (see Box 9.5).[12]

9.3.6 Bridging the Accountability Gap through Crowdsourcing

Programme or scheme monitoring is an expensive undertaking in rural areas where the lack of infrastructure can hinder the collection and transmission of high-quality monitoring data. Even where collection and transmission structures are in place, the quality of data collected may be suspect, particularly when those responsible for monitoring public service delivery are themselves subject to little or no oversight. As a response there has been a recent shift towards involving beneficiaries in

---

[11] The study was the result of a collaboration between the Centre for Geo-Informatics Application in Rural Development (CGARD) at the National Institute of Rural Development (NIRD), the National Remote Sensing Centre (NSRC), and the Ministry of Rural Development, Government of India.

[12] A CAG report recently tabled in parliament found many discrepancies in the planning, implementation, and management of funds for PMGSY. The report found non-availability of land to be a major roadblock for states—11 states abandoned plans to construct 372 roads due to land disputes or non-availability of land (Roche 2016).

monitoring public service delivery and making service providers accountable to users.

Randomized evaluations testing the impact of increasing community participation in the monitoring process, however, find mixed results. In Uttar Pradesh an evaluation testing the effectiveness of increasing community oversight and participation in monitoring local schools found that it did not increase participation in school governance or improve education outcomes (Banerjee et al. 2008). In Indonesia, Olken (2005) tested the impact of encouraging community participation in monitoring road construction, and found that community participation reduced corruption, only when the process was designed to prevent elite capture and only in corruption that villagers had individual stake in reducing. On the other hand, Björkman and Svensson (2009) find that community monitoring of health worker performance in Uganda led to better quality and more frequently utilized health services. Similarly, Duflo et al. (2015) find evidence that parental involvement in school management improved teaching quality and learning outcomes in western Kenya. Despite mixed results, these studies highlight a key lesson for policy-makers: community participation in monitoring may not be effective if community members are not given a clear avenue through which to effect change (J-PAL Policy Briefcase 2015).

Emerging ICTs are involving local communities in the process of monitoring public service delivery in novel ways. Civil society organizations such as the Janaagraha Centre for Citizenship and Democracy are using crowdsourcing platforms[13] to engage citizens in reporting issues of common civic concern in their local neighbourhood and connecting them with the appropriate local authorities to demand action. A similar e-governance initiative in the province of Punjab in Pakistan is bridging the trust deficit between citizens and the state by proactively collecting feedback from citizens availing public services at government offices. The Citizen Feedback Monitoring Programme (CFMP),[14] a joint venture of the Government of Punjab and the Punjab Information Technology Board (PITB), reaches out to citizens interacting with government offices and collects their feedback via robo-call, SMS, or agent calls. The feedback is then compiled, analysed, and made available to relevant authorities for alleviating public service delivery gaps in real time. Since its inception in 2009, CFMP has contacted 6.3 million citizens for feedback regarding 17 public services across 36 districts and its model is now being scaled up in Albania and Romania.

While crowdsourcing has been applied in various contexts towards various ends—such as crisis mapping during natural disasters, citizen reporting during elections, and addressing information asymmetries in rural agricultural markets—it holds particular promise for enhancing the internal monitoring of government public service delivery. The mobile application 'Meri Sadak',[15] for example, allows citizens to take photographs of PMGSY works and submit feedback on the pace and quality to the nodal departments in the state government or the National Rural Roads Development Agency (NRRDA). The application then interfaces users with state quality coordinators (SQCs) of the nodal implementing department to ensure that user feedback is addressed. Till February 2018 the application had been downloaded by over 939,567 users. Similar applications can be made for schemes that involve the creation of rural assets—for example, the Pradhan Mantri Awaas Yojana–Gramin (PMAY–G), which aims to build 10 million pucca houses in rural areas by 2019.

Monitoring road quality under PMGSY should not stop once construction is complete. However, regular manual inspections are a costly and time-consuming endeavour. Crowdsourcing road quality data via mobile phones can drastically lower the labour and time costs associated with monitoring road quality in rural India. Applications such as RoadScan[16] are taking advantage of the sensors in smartphones to aggregate large amounts of acceleration and location data in real time. Again, such technologies will have to enable clear pathways for accountability in order to be of value to citizens.

The use of crowdsourcing technology can allow programme administrators to not only deploy monitoring resources more efficiently but also realign incentives for monitors by increasing the cost of false reporting. Most importantly, crowdsourcing platforms can allow citizens to bypass 'the "long route" of accountability where citizens must influence policymakers to improve service provision … by increasing citizens' direct power over government agents' (Rezaee et al. 2015, 3).

9.3.7 Future Potential: Crowdsourcing for Data Accuracy and Timeliness

Reliable and timely data is a key tool for better governance. However, key government databases such as the

[13] See http://www.ichangemycity.com/.
[14] See http://cfmp.punjab.gov.pk/.

[15] See https://play.google.com/store/apps/details?id=com.cdac.pmgsy.citizen&hl=en.
[16] See https://www.changemakers.com/saferoads/entries/smartphones-road-surface-monitoring.

Socio Economic and Caste Census (SECC)[17] face many constraints in this regard. Since it is self-disclosed, there are currently no strong checks on the SECC data. Furthermore, the error rate in the database is not known. The frequency with which the data can be updated is also severely limited by feasibility and resource availability constraints. Given the objective of the SECC as an input in beneficiary identification, the updating of this data is crucial. In the case of the public distribution system, for example, the lack of up-to-date data on household size has resulted in the exclusion of eligible members such as persons who may have joined a household through marriage post-2011 when the SECC data was collected (Shaw 2015). Furthermore, the updating of household level SECC data is contingent on the willingness of local administrators who act as gatekeepers (Shaw 2015). In this context, crowdsourcing can be a highly practical solution for strengthening the credibility and usefulness of SECC data.

Many mapping sites utilize crowdsourcing for greater information accuracy. Google Maps, for example, is using crowdsourcing to verify suggested edits and conflicting details on mapped locations by prompting users to confirm or edit location details during navigation or via the Google Map Maker interface. Similarly, existing SECC data can be validated by prompting local communities to verify panchayat-level data. Currently, SECC data is only subject to verification back-checks if citizens file an official objection during the time period before it is finalized. If we imagine a spectrum where on the one end is the ideal case scenario where every household is back-checked and on the other end is the worst case scenario where no back-checks are conducted to verify data quality, the current system falls somewhere in between.

By opening up the current system to allow individuals to participate in the process of verifying the SECC data in their Panchayat on a continuing basis, we can move closer towards the ideal case scenario. Instead of having teams of back-checkers go to the field to verify the SECC data, a certain percentage of the crowd sourced data can be back-checked for accuracy. Over time users with high truth percentages can be phased out of the back-check routine and resources can be diverted towards screening the accuracy of newer users.

[17] The Socio Economic and Caste Census (SECC) 2011 was carried out to provide a more comprehensive picture of the socio-economic status of various sections of the Indian population. Furthermore, the SECC was intended to improve beneficiary identification and targeting for various government schemes. Results from the SECC 2011 can be accessed at http://www.secc.gov.in.

9.3.8 Effective Auditing

In 1984, then Prime Minister Rajiv Gandhi famously commented that out of every one rupee released for anti-poverty programmes only 15 paise reaches the real beneficiary (Farazmand and Pinkowski 2006). The issue of leakage in the Indian public service delivery system is no less salient today. In one of the first systematic attempts to measure leakages in the implementation of MGNREGS, Niehaus and Sukhtankar (2013) surveyed a sample of households reported to have worked on the programme in Odisha and Andhra Pradesh and compared household reports of work done and payments received with officials' reports on nrega.nic.in—the public database on MGN-REGS. Of the 1,328 households in which they completed the survey, they found only 821 individuals both existed and confirmed having worked on an MGNREGS project during the period in question (Niehaus and Sukhtankar 2013). Likewise, Imbert and Papp (2011) compared administrative data on the implementation of MGN-REGS with public works employment data collected by the National Sample Survey Office (NSSO) between 2007 and 2008. They found that the independent survey data was able to confirm only 51 per cent of reported MGN-REGS employment (Imbert and Papp 2011).

Over the last few years, considerable progress has been made in curbing leakages and corruption in the system, largely due to reforms in the payment of MGNREGS wages (Drèze 2014; Muralidharan et al. 2014; Banerjee et al. 2016). Compared to estimates from 2007–8 (prior to the introduction of bank/post office account payments of MGNREGS wages), NSSO data from 2011–12 reflected 68–78 per cent of official MGNREGS person-days (Drèze 2014). However, crucial gaps still remain. A recent CAG report on the functioning of social audits (a key transparency and accountability mechanism enshrined in MGN-REGS) found that a majority of states had non-existent or under-resourced social audit units often staffed by departmental officers rather than independent organizations as required by the law (The Financial Express 2016). Out of 234,594 Gram Panchayats (GPs) to be covered for social audit in 25 states during 2014–15, only 120,841 GPs (51 per cent) were covered (The Financial Express 2016). As the key monitoring and accountability mechanism established to cross-verify government records of expenditure, the shortfall in independently conducted social audits is indicative of the limitations of a solely bottom-up approach to monitor public service delivery at the last mile.

MGNREGS is exemplary in its response towards curbing corruption and leakages endemic in the system. In addition to being the first government programme to incorporate 'social audits' to provide a platform for beneficiaries to participate in governance and demand accountability from the state, MGNREGS guidelines also mandate proactive disclosure of information by all levels of government (Aiyar and Samji 2006). The MGNREGS MIS—nrega.nic.in—is 'the first transaction-based real-time system for any public works programme in the country that is available in the public domain' (Dhorajiwala and Narayanan 2016). The ongoing digitization of all MGNREGS transactions is a laudable undertaking, yet its potential for strengthening government monitoring remains underutilized. The MGNREGS MIS is a repository of implementation data on around 250,000 gram panchayats, allowing the Ministry of Rural Development to implement a systematic audit process whereby a random sample of MGNREGS projects can be drawn centrally rather than the ad hoc manner in which they are currently selected for *jaanch* (checks) in most states. The checks done in this manner can also be randomly crossed-checked for integrity.

Effective audit systems must be designed to incentivize accurate reporting. A randomized evaluation conducted by Duflo et al. (2013) found that altering auditors' incentives to mitigate conflict of interest led auditors to report more truthfully. Duflo et al.'s study focused on the regulation of air and water pollution from industrial plants in Gujarat, which are required by the Gujarat Pollution Control Board and where third-party auditors have to be hired to check and report the plants' pollution levels three times annually. Since auditors are hired by the firms they are to audit, conflict of interest

may incentivize auditors to distort or falsify their reports in order to maintain relations with firms (J-PAL Policy Briefcase 2013). So for a randomly selected subset of firms, auditors were randomly assigned, paid a fixed fee from a common pool, monitored for accuracy, and paid a bonus for accurate reports (see Figure 9.4) (J-PAL Policy Briefcase 2013).

The study found striking results: altering the rules of the audit system caused auditors to report more truthfully. Auditors under the new system were 80 per cent less likely to report false pollution readings in compliance with the regulatory standard (Duflo et al. 2013). More significantly, industrial plants facing the new audit system significantly reduced their emissions of air and water pollution (Duflo et al. 2013). While directly relevant to third-party audit markets, the study has broader relevance for audit reforms in other sectors as well. In the case of MGNREGS and other big ticket government programmes, the audit process can itself become a source of corruption and extortion if it is not subject to back-checks or if the choice of what is to be checked is not undertaken through statistically valid random sampling.

In 2013, the Rural Development Department (RDD) of the Government of Bihar launched MGNREGS Divas as a special initiative to improve the implementation of the programme. As part of MGNREGS Divas, district administrators were charged with sending independent teams to one panchayat per block in the district every week to assess the status of public works, audit muster rolls, and generally report back on the situation on the

	STATUS QUO AUDIT SYSTEM	NEW AUDIT SYSTEM
AUDITOR SECTION	Plants selected and paid their own auditors.	Auditors were randomly assigned to the plants that they would monitor.
AUDITOR FEES	Plants paid auditors directly and negotiated the price of the audit.	Auditors were paid a fixed fee of Rs 45,000 per audit from a common pool.
MONITORING	Auditors' reports were not verified for accuracy.	Of the auditor pollution readings, 20 per cent were randomly selected to be back-checked by the technical staff of independent engineering colleges. Auditors were aware that they might be back-checked, but were not told when.
ACCURACY INCENTIVE	None	In year two, auditors were also given incentive payments for accurate reports.

Figure 9.4 Truth-Telling in Third-Party Audits—Study Design

Source: J-PAL Policy Briefcase (2013).

ground. A process evaluation of this initiative conducted by IDInsight found low level of compliance with the instructions of the RDD in relation to the number of visits that were to be conducted as well as the processes to be followed during them. A key objective of the initiative was to capture irregularities in the implementation of the programme; however, the study found that the teams may have systematically selected higher-quality sites for their visits. Furthermore, when their reports were compared to an independent survey conducted by the process evaluation team, they found that MGNREGS Divas teams tended to under-report irregularities and wage discrepancies at the work sites (IDinsight 2013). Ultimately, as the process evaluation states, irregularities in the implementation of MGNREGS divas failed to send a 'strong message of transparency and high quality accountability' (IDinsight 2013, 10). One of the big impediments to quality audit of MGNREGS works is the failure to insist that before workers are assigned to work sites, detailed estimates for the proposed work along with engineering drawings, showing the pre-existing and proposed levels and geo-tagged photos of the proposed work site, have to be uploaded on the public domain via narega.nic.in. In the absence of this it is virtually impossible to detect whether the work done has been overbooked in the measurement books.

In the absence of a well-functioning social audit structure, the wealth of implementation data available on national portals can be better utilized for systematically auditing and back-checking the veracity of reporting. This could potentially help reduce leakages and shortcomings in the timeliness and accuracy of data being fed into the MIS programme.

9.3.9 Separating Front-Office and Back-Office Processes

Between 2004 and 2005, Bertrand et al. (2008) studied a seemingly innocuous bureaucratic process—obtaining a driving licence in Delhi—to better understand the mechanics of petty corruption. The study found that on average individuals who succeeded in getting their licences paid about 2.5 times the official fee, close to 60 per cent of licence getters did not take the licensing exam, and 54 per cent were unqualified to drive at the time they obtained their licence. The study uncovers the large social costs of corruption. In the case of obtaining licences, corruption went beyond simple redistribution from citizens to bureaucrats, as many who support an efficiency view of corruption would argue, and resulted in a misallocation of public services, with many

unqualified drivers obtaining licences (Bertrand et al. 2008).

A similar reality holds true for the process of securing below poverty line (BPL) ration cards which entitle eligible households to subsidized food under the public distribution system (PDS). A large-scale survey conducted in rural Karnataka found that 75 per cent of households reported paying a bribe in the process of obtaining a BPL ration card (Niehaus et al. 2013). As in the case of drivers licences, there is a high social cost associated with this type of petty corruption. The survey found that 70 per cent of ineligible households had a card and 13 per cent of eligible households did not, leading to a serious misallocation of public resources (Niehaus et al. 2013). This type of routine corruption, what Sukhtankar and Vaishav (2015) refer to as 'facilitative corruption', is familiar to the majority of Indians who have attempted to access routine government services and documents such as ration cards, passports, business licences, and so on.

Among the broad set of policy responses available to combat facilitative corruption and the monopolization of access to basic public services, technological interventions are showing promise particularly when used to bypass middlemen (Sukhtankar and Vaishnav 2015). In India, the use of ICTs for simplifying government processes began with the computerization of the Indian railways' passenger reservation system. The ease with which anyone with a computer or smartphone and an internet connection can now buy a railway ticket online was not always the norm. Prior to the introduction of the eTicketing system, passengers had to stand in queues at railway stations or pay travel agents to secure railway tickets. The eTicketing system significantly increased the efficiency of the reservation process and reduced corruption in the system by instituting a predictable rule-based process for purchasing tickets (Heeks 2000).

In the mid-1990s, many state governments also began experimenting with computerization by building one-stop service centres where citizens could access basic services such as payments of taxes, land records, driving licence, registration of births, deaths and marriages, payments of water, telephone, and electricity bills, and so on. As Bussell (2012) notes, in theory these reforms went beyond just the computerization of government processes: 'By instituting computer-based monitoring and queuing systems, automated document transfer, and databases of citizen information, these centres can help limit the degree of discretion that bureaucrats hold over who received services and when they receive them' (Bussell 2012, 67). In an ideal system, computerized service delivery separates the 'front office' from the 'back office'. When a citizen goes to a centre to avail a government service, the centre operator who receives the application (that is, the front office) and pushes it along the pipeline to an authorizing official (that is, the back office) has to process the application and associated documents via an IT system such that the individual at the front office has no discretionary power over verification of the application. An IT-driven workflow, where applications and supporting documents are verified by an IT system rather than an individual, can break the monopoly that the 'front office' has over access to the 'back office' through the withholding of files.

Although the IRCTC model has been extended to many other spheres including passport sewa and e-visas, in practice, however, the proliferation of service centres and the extent of services offered remain highly varied. In 1999, Andhra Pradesh for example, 'launched an aggressive policy that resulted in the provision of more than forty services to citizens in urban areas', whereas 'West Bengal, a state with similar levels of economic development, did not launch a policy until 2003 and neglected to develop a range of government service to offer in the centers' (Bussell 2012, 69). Similarly, the neighbouring low-income states of Odisha and Chhattisgarh also vary in the extent of government services offered via such service centres, with Chhattisgarh offering nearly 40 government services as compared to Odisha, which offers less than ten (Bussell 2012, 69).

Common service centres (CSCs) that effectively separate front-office and back-office processes via IT-driven platforms can go a long way towards curbing corruption and overcoming inclusion and exclusion errors in the provision of public services. However, the variation in proliferation of such centres as well as the kinds of services provided limits the potential that such IT-driven government initiatives can have. Where these reforms have already been initiated, second-generation innovations need to be made so that services are delivered faster and platforms are more user friendly and easier to navigate. This should be done both by allowing private providers to interact with government platforms via open application programming interfaces (APIs) and by improving the usability of government platforms themselves.

Under Digital India's goal of establishing at least one CSC for every GP in the country, those in rural areas who do not have devices are increasingly being provided access to the internet. While laudable in its scale, such initiatives for rural inclusion will only succeed if there are well-designed government platforms and they understand and address the specific constraints faced by rural populations including lack of information regarding government services and benefits and lack of literacy which inhibits their capacity to navigate complex bureaucratic procedures (which digitization does not necessarily resolve). In the meantime, social enterprises such as Haqdarshak[18] are emerging to fill the gap in rural areas by aggregating information on government programmes and eligibility criteria to screen individuals and guide them through the process of availing eligible benefits through the help of local facilitators or 'haqdarshaks'. While still nascent, platforms such as Haqdarshak are exemplary of technological solutions designed with an acute understanding of the rural context and constraints—a lesson highly relevant for government attempts to improve public service delivery through technological innovation.

In separating front-office processes from back-office processes, the government should ensure that all scheme administration and regulatory clearances at all levels move from electronic or physical files to workflow-driven IT platforms that are accessible via the internet. Furthermore, these platforms should be made accessible via one of three ways: the internet, a service provider, or a front office. Given that the rate of change in government processes is often not able to match that of technological advances, governments can pass on some of the burden to private service providers. By publishing open APIs for all government IT workflows (a practice already required by government policy[19]) and ensuring that all government platforms comply with eGov data standards,[20] private service providers can develop their own applications and help citizens get regulatory approval or public services through their own user friendly and responsive interfaces that respond on a real-time basis much like in way that you can now book rail tickets via IRCTC's own website or via portals such as Cleartrip.com.

The necessary digital infrastructure is already available via India Stack[21]—a set of open APIs[22] that provide access to proprietary software applications for Aadhaar (for authentication), e-KYC documents (a digital locker which allows documents to be stored and shared digitally), e-Sign (digital signature acceptable under law), the

---

[18] See http://www.haqdarshak.com/.

[19] See http://meity.gov.in/content/policy-open-application-programming-interfaces-government-india.

[20] See http://egovstandards.gov.in/faq.

[21] India Stack is a combined initiative of UIDAI, Controller of Certifying Authorities (CCA), Department of Electronics and Information Technology (DeitY), and National Payments Corporation IF India (NPCI).

[22] An API is a set of rules or that enables software to communicate with each other. Online travel services such as Cleartrip.com, for example, use APIs to interact with airlines systems to aggregate information on flight prices.

unified payment interface (for financial transactions), and privacy-protected data sharing within the stack. This open digital infrastructure is a base on which technology entrepreneurs can innovate and build Stack-enabled applications that can simplify the provision of key government services. Services that previously required a litany of physical documents such as identity proof, physical documents, and wet signatures (and, therefore, multiple interactions with government officials) can now be integrated seamlessly onto a single application such that an individual can access that service without ever having to step into a service centre or bank. This presence-less, paperless, and cashless ecosystem could potentially render front offices non-essential for accessing key government services (see Figure 9.5).

As India leapfrogs towards a digital economy, the open access and scalable technology infrastructure available through India Stack can be leveraged in numerous ways. For example, India Stack can serve as the backbone for tech innovations enabling greater financial inclusion by eliminating existing roadblocks such as requirement of paper-based identity proofs, lack of access to physical banks, and lack of availability of hard cash. The goods and services tax etwork (GSTN) will be using a similar architecture to provide a platform for tax data management, and reporting across all stakeholders including taxpayers, banks, and central and state governments. While still nascent, the digital ecosystem created by India Stack can, on the supply side, enable entrepreneurs to innovate and create applications and products for the Indian market and, on the demand side, make key government services easily and universally accessible.

9.3.10 Just-In-Time Financing: Reducing Inefficiencies in Government Fund Flow

In 2014–15, 70 per cent of MGNREGS workers' wages were delayed by over 15 days. Of these, 13 per cent encountered a delay of over 90 days. Delays occurred even though various levels of central, state, and local governments had unspent funds parked in bank accounts. The multiple layers of fund management prevented some panchayats from having money to pay workers and suppliers.

Unlike many low- and middle-income countries which in recent years have transitioned towards digitizing government payment systems, India continues to rely largely on a files-based system for fund flow. Within the current system, funds are allocated based on estimated spending for the coming year, rather than actual expenditure, following which they travel down in tranches from centre → state → district → block → panchayat. Each level must submit evidence of fund utilization up to a certain amount in the form of a utilization certificate (UC) before they can receive the next tranche of funds. Not only does this files-based fund management system impinge on the ability of programme administrators to focus on programme implementation by burdening them with chasing funds but it also creates loopholes for corruption as officials at each level can seek rent in

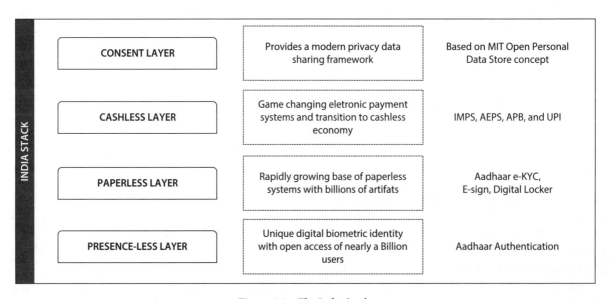

Figure 9.5   The India Stack

Source: www.indiastack.org.

exchange for file approvals. Moreover, money meant for social expenditure lies parked in various accounts, accruing interest costs and adding to the fiscal deficit until it is approved for use.

To address some of these problems in the context of MGNREGS, the Cabinet Committee on Economic Affairs, in August 2015, approved a proposal of the Ministry of Rural Development to introduce direct benefit transfer (DBT) of wages from the central pool to the bank and post office accounts of MGNREGS workers through the National Electronic Fund Management System (NeFMS). The cabinet proposal was informed by a 2012–13 evaluation by the RDD in Bihar and researchers affiliated with the Abdul Latif Jameel Poverty Action Lab (J-PAL), which found that reducing the number of intermediaries in the MGNREGS payment structure (Figure 9.6) reduced leakages of public funds by 25 per cent (Banerjee et al. 2016).

As of January 2018 NeFMS has been implemented in 24 states and 1 union territory. Preliminary assessment of data on the MGNREGS MIS shows that whenever funds have been available it has had a positive impact on reducing wage payment delays.

9.3.10.1 Expanding the Benefits of Just-in-Time to Other Schemes and Payments

The problem of layers, delays, administrative effort and corruption, however, is not the sole preserve of MGNREGS. The Government of India today spends around Rs 3 trillion each year on centrally sponsored schemes (CSS). Many CSS operate by transferring money to states and different functional levels below the state before reaching the beneficiary. Since levels below the central government are only required to spend a portion of the money they receive to become eligible for additional funding, unspent money accrues within accounts of different state and local governments over time (Dikshit et al. 2007). These unspent, parked funds, known as float, require the Central government to borrow more than is actually required to fund schemes, thereby adding to the fiscal deficit.

It is estimated that approximately 30 per cent of the total expenditure for CSS remains as float. These parked funds are forcing the central government to unnecessarily borrow in excess of Rs 1 trillion each year (Ehrbeck et al. 2010). This is significantly adding to the country's fiscal deficit. While the government has embarked on reforming the fund flow for MGNREGS, other central and state schemes are yet to undergo similar reforms. Moreover, the Government of India also makes other types of payments, for example to vendors, which are adversely affected by the current inefficiencies in fund flow, thereby increasing the burden of doing business with the government.

Just-in-time financing entails doing away with the current utilization certificate (UC) based system of fund management and adopting workflow-driven IT-based platforms for each scheme or programme. This would allow the implementation layer to pull funds directly from the centre and/or the state as and when needed, thereby reducing administrative burden and eliminating float. The use of IT platforms for fund management would also improve the quality of the audit processes since expenditure can be accounted for in real-time on a voucher-to-voucher basis. This will only improve transparency in fund flow and enable the government to overcome the current lag in reporting that hinders its

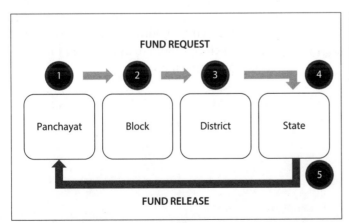
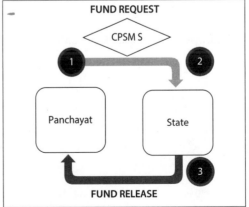

Figure 9.6   MGNREGS Fund Flow Reforms in Bihar: Old versus New

Source: Banerjee et al. (2016).

ability to create more realistic budgets based on real-time expenditure data rather than 'actual' expenditure data that is two years old.

Efforts to actualize just-in-time financing are already under way. In January 2016, the Committee of Secretaries on Innovative Budgeting and Effective Implementation in their presentation to the prime minister recommended the development of a system of 'just-in-time' budgetary releases through extensive IT platforms covering centre, states, and RBI, making UCs redundant. This recommendation was subsequently accepted and taken up for implementation under the supervision of the NITI Aayog. To actualize 'just-in-time' budgetary releases, the Ministry of Finance issued letters mandating the use of the Public Financial Management System (PFMS) to cover all transactions and payments under Central Sector (CS) schemes and Central Assistance to State Plan (CASP) schemes.[23] However, contractor/vendor payments are yet to be covered by these reforms and many government departments are yet to develop the workflow-driven internet-enabled IT platforms for the administration of all their schemes.

Largely overlooked in discussions around public service delivery failures in India, the current fund flow process is creating various problems of delays, float, leakages, inefficiency, and accountability, thereby hampering the effective implementation of government programmes. Ultimately, this broken fund flow mechanism is impeding public expenditure from achieving maximum impact for beneficiaries. Given the encouraging evidence from similar reforms for MGNREGS fund flow in Bihar, just-in-time payments—which would enable implementing agencies to pull funds from the centre or state as and when required—are a reform whose time has come. However, to be effective, such a system would have to go beyond just enabling electronic payments—the entire architecture of allocating, disbursing, and processing government expenditure must be modernized by leveraging on India's IT capabilities and infrastructure.

9.4 CONCLUDING REMARKS

The successes of India's economic reforms since the 1990s have failed to trickle down to the millions of rural Indians who continue to remain impoverished. All this despite the centrality of poverty eradication in political rhetoric and the thousands of crores spent in the name of rural development every year. A historical overview of rural development priorities shows that rural development policies, at least since the 1980s, have focused squarely on mitigating the effects of poverty through social protection and livelihoods promotion without adequately addressing the conditions that make rural areas particularly vulnerable to market failure. Deficiencies in programme design and implementation, poor systems of transparency and accountability, targeting inefficiency and leakages, which further contribute to the inability of government spending to achieve intended outcomes also remain inadequately addressed.

In this chapter we have provided an overview of opportunities for reforms that address some of these pressing market and governance failures more directly. These opportunities include using the lens of behavioural economics to re-examine the conventional wisdom that currently dictates programme design; exploring the potential of big data analytics for improving financial inclusion; leveraging ICTs such as geotagging, remote sensing, and crowdsourcing for better monitoring and programme management; improving audit quality; separating front-office and back-office processes to curb corruption in public service delivery; and most urgently, reforming the existing fund flow process which continues to hinder even the most effective of programme managers.

---

[23] Central Assistance to State Plan (CASP) includes budget allocation for CSS.

APPENDIX

Table 9A.1 Ministry-wise Spending on Rural Development

Ministry-wise Break-up of Total Spending on Rural Development (in Rs Crore)	2011–12	2012–13			2013–14			2014–15			2015–16			2016–17		2017–18
	Actual	BE	RE	Actual	BE	RE	Actual	BE	RE	Actual	BE	RE	Actual	BE	RE	BE
Ministry of Agriculture and Farmer Welfare																
1 Rashtriya Krishi Vikas Yojana	7,794	9,217	8,400	8,400	9,954	7,089	7,053	9,954	8,444	8,443	4,500	3,900	3,940.01	5,400	3,550	4,750
2 Prime Minister Krishi Sinchayee Yojna	–	–	–	–	–	–	–	–	–	–	–	–	–	–	–	–
3 Pradhan Mantri Fasal Bima Yojana/NAIS	1,053	1,136	1,550	1,549	2,151	2,551	2,551	2,541	2,588	2,598	2,589	2,955	2,983.04	5,501	13,240.04	9,000
4 National Food Security Mission	1,287	1,780	1,655	1,723	2,025	1,738	2,027	2,030	1,830	1,873	1,300	1,137	1,162.34	1,706	1,280	1,720
Total	10,134	12,133	11,605	11,672	14,130	11,378	11,630	14,525	12,862	12,914	8,389	7,991	8,085.39	12,607	18,070.04	15,470
Department of Land Resource, MoRD																
1 Integrated Watershed Management Programme (IWMP)[a]	2,312	3,050	2,904	2,891	5,387	2,284	2,275	3,500	2,319	2,319	1,530	1,530	1,527.4	1,550	1,550	2,150.47
2 NLRMP	106.3	150.5	96.0	94.8	377.5	215.9	213.2	250.0	181.0	179.3	97.3	36.0	39.9	150.0	140.6	150.0
Total	2,418.6	3,200.5	2,999.5	2,986.2	5,764.5	2,499.9	2,487.7	3,750.0	2,500.0	2,498.3	1,627.3	1,566.0	1,567.3	1,700.0	1,690.6	2,300.5
Ministry of Water Resources																
1 Accelerated Irrigation Benefit Programme and Other schemes under PMKSY in Water Resources Ministry	9,902	18,676	10,884	10,051	12,962	6,162	3,093	9,992	3,311	3,261	3,800	6,060	6,254	4,217	3,638.55	5,227
Total	9,902	18,676	10,884	10,051	12,962	6,162	3,093	9,992	3,311	3,261	3,800	6,060	6,254	4,217	3,638.55	5,227
Ministry of Human Resource Development																
1 Sarva Shiksha Abhiyan	20,841	25,555	23,645	23,873	27,258	26,608	24,802	28,258	24,380	24,097	22,000	22,015	21,661.44	22,500	22,500	23,500

(Cont'd)

[a] The Department of Land Resources has been implementing IWMP w.e.f. 2009–10. From 2015–16 the IWMP has been re-named the Watershed Development Component of Pradhan Mantri Krishi Sinchayee Yojana (PMKSY).

Table 9A.1 (*Cont'd*)

2 Rashtriya Madhyamik Shiksha Abhiyan	2,500	3,124	3,173	3,168	3,983	3,123	2,679	5,000	3,628	3,398	3,720	3,565	3,562.61	3,700	3,700	3,830
3 Midday Meal Scheme	9,891	11,937	11,500	10,849	13,215	12,189	10,918	13,215	11,051	10,523	9,236	9,236	9,144.89	9,700	9,700	10,000
Total	33,232	40,616	38,318	37,890	44,456	41,920	38,398	46,473	38,018	39,059	34,956	34,817	34,368.94	35,900	35,900	37,330
Ministry of Women and Child Development																
1 Integrated Child Development Services Scheme (ICDS)	14,266	14,250	14,250	15,704	15,912	14,648	16,254	18,195	16,581	16,562	8,336	15,484	15,433.09	14,000	14,560.6	15,245.19
Total	14,266	14,250	14,250	15,704	15,912	14,648	16,254	18,195	16,581	16,562	8,336	15,484	15,433.09	14,000	14,560.6	15,245.19
Ministry of Consumer Affairs, Food and Public Distribution																
1 Food Subsidy/National Food Security Act/Food Subsidy	72,822	75,000	85,000	85,000	90,000	92,000	92,000	115,000	117,671	122,676	124,419	139,419	139,419	134,835	135,172.96	145,338.6
Total	72,822	75,000	85,000	85,000	90,000	92,000	92,000	115,000	117,671	122,676	124,419	139,419	139,419	134,835	135,172.96	145,338.6
Ministry of Chemicals and Fertilizers																
1 Fertilizer Subsidy (All)[b]	70,792	60,974	65,974	65,613	65,971	67,972	67,339	72,970	71,076	70,967	72,969	72,438	72,415.17	70,000	70,000	70,000
Total	70,792	60,974	65,974	65,613	65,971	67,972	67,339	72,970	71,076	70,967	72,969	72,438	72,415.17	70,000	70,000	70,000
Ministry of Panchayati Raj																
1 BRGF (district)	3,917	5,050	3,734	3,720	6,500	2,800	2,800	5,900	2,837	2,837	–	–	–	–	–	–
2 RGPSA	–	45	45	43	407	590	630	1,050	526	527	50	169	184.4	655	592.95	691.9
Total	3,917	5,095	3,779	3,763	6,907	3,390	3,430	6,950	3,363	3,364	50	169	184.4	655	592.95	691.9
Ministry of Drinking Water and Sanitation																
1 Swachh Bharat (Gramin)[c]	1,500	3,500	2,500	2,474	4,260	2,300	2,244	4,260	2,841	2,850	3,625	6,525	6,703.4	9,000	10,500	13,948.27
2 NRDWP	8,493	10,500	10,500	10,490	11,000	9,700	9,691	11,000	9,243	9,250	2,611	4,373	4,369.55	5,000	6,000	6,050
Total	9,993	14,000	13,000	12,963	15,260	12,000	11,935	15,260	12,084	12,100	6,236	10,898	11,072.95	14,000	16,500	19,998.27

[b] Fertiliser Subsidy includes: Subsidy on decontrolled fertilizers, subsidy on imported fertilizers and to fertilizer industries.
[c] SBA/SBM/TSC/NBA/NGP.

(*Cont'd*)

Table 9A.1   *(Cont'd)*

Ministry of Health and Family Welfare

1 NHM	16,752	20,908	17,188	18,047	18,328	18,635	18,609	19,751	18,875	19,122	18,971.49	19,037	20,437	21,940.7
Total	16,752	20,908	17,188	18,047	18,328	18,635	18,609	19,751	18,875	19,122	18,971.49	19,037	20,437	21,941

Ministry of Power

1 Deen Dayal Upadhyaya Gram Jyoti Yojna[d]	4,323	9,661	6,300	1,373	3,138	2,939	2,886	3,374	4,500	4,500	4,500	3,000	3,350	4,814
Total	4,323	9,661	6,300	1,373	3,138	2,939	2,886	3,374	4,500	4,500	4,500	3,000	3,350	4,814

Department of Rural Development, MoRD

1 PM Awas Yojana (PMAY)-IAY-Rural	9,872	11,075	9,024	7,869	13,184	12,982	11,000	11,106	10,025	10,025	10,116.2	15,000	16,000	23,000
2 National Livelihood Mission (NLM)-Rural-Ajeevika	2,392	3,879	2,600	2,195	2,600	2,022	2,105	1,413	2,383	2,672	2,514.35	3,000	3,000	4,500
3 MG National Rural Employment Guarantee Scheme	29,215	33,000	29,387	30,274	33,000	32,993	33,000	32,977	34,699	36,967	37,340.71	38,500	47,499	48,000
4 National Social Assistance Programme	6,546	8,382	7,882	7,825	9,541	9,046	7,241	7,087	9,082	9,082	8,616.4	9,500	9,500	9,500
5 Pradhan Mantri Gram Sadak Yojana	19,342	24,000	10,000	8,884	21,700	9,700	14,200	14,188	14,294	14,391	18,289.87	19,000	19,000	19,000
Total	67,367	80,336	58,893	57,047	83,424	66,848	79,026	66,771	70,483	77,043	76,878	85,000	94,999	104,000
Total (All Ministries)	315,918	354,849	328,190	322,109	380,631	341,459	372,442	410,256	367,362	354,640	389,506	389,149	394,951	414,912	442,356

[d] The Government of India launched Deendayal Upadhyaya Gram Jyoti Yojana (DDUGJY) in 2015–16. The erstwhile RGGVY has been subsumed in DDUGJY as its rural electrification component.

REFERENCES

Aggarwal, Mayank. 2016. 'Solar Rooftop Projects to Be Geo-Tagged'. *Livemint*. Available at http://www.livemint.com/Industry/hC1QWY7KcNClzzxEv32KdI/Solar-rooftop-projects-to-be-geotagged.html, last accessed on 11 January 2018.

Ahmed, Sadiq and Ashutosh Varshney. 2008. 'Battles Half Won: The Political Economy of India's Growth and Economic Policy since Independence'. Working Paper 15. Commission on Growth and Development. Available at http://citeseerx.ist.psu.edu/viewdoc/download?doi=10.1.1.207.2478&rep=rep1&type=pdf, last accessed on 11 January 2018.

Ahuja, Amit and Pradeep Chhibber. 2012. 'Why the Poor Vote in India: "If I Don't Vote, I Am Dead to the State"'. *Studies in Comparative International Development* 47(4): 389–410. doi:10.1007/s12116-012-9115-6.

Aiyar, Yamini and Salimah Samji. 2006. 'Improving the Effectiveness of National Rural Employment Guarantee Act'. *Economic and Political Weekly* 41(4): 320–6.

Banerjee, Abhijit, Rukmini Banerji, Esther Duflo, Rachel Glennerster, and Stuti Khemani. 2008. 'Pitfalls of Participatory Programs: Evidence from a Randomized Evaluation in Education in India'. Working Paper 14311. National Bureau of Economic Research. Available at http://www.nber.org/papers/w14311, last accessed on 11 January 2018.

Banerjee, Abhijit, Esther Duflo, Clement Imbert, Rohini Pande, and Santhosh Mathew. 2016. 'Can E-Governance Reduce Capture of Public Programs? Experimental Evidence from a Financial Reform of India's Employment Guarantee'. Working Paper. Available at http://lagv2015.idep-fr.org/submission/index.php/LAGV2015/LAGV14/paper/view/1434, last accessed on 11 January 2018.

Banerjee, Abhijit and Thomas Piketty. 2005. 'Top Indian Incomes, 1922–2000'. *World Bank Economic Review* 19(1): 1–20. doi:10.1093/wber/lhi001.

Banerjee, Abhijit and Rohini Somanathan. 2007. 'The Political Economy of Public Goods: Some Evidence from India'. *Journal of Development Economics* 82(2): 287–314. doi:10.1016/j.jdeveco.2006.04.005.

Banerjee, M. 2007. 'Sacred Elections'. *Economic and Political Weekly of India* 42(17): 1556–62.

Bardhan, Pranab. 2001. 'Sharing the Spoils: Group Equity, Development and Democracy'. In *The Success of India's Democracy*, edited by A. Kohli, 226–41. Cambridge: Cambridge University Press.

Bertrand, Marianne, Simeon Djankov, Rema Hanna, and Sendhil Mullainathan. 2008. 'Corruption in Driving Licensing Process in Delhi'. *Economic and Political Weekly* 43(5): 71–6.

Björkman, Martina and Jakob Svensson. 2009. 'Power to the People: Evidence from a Randomized Field Experiment on Community-Based Monitoring in Uganda'. *The Quarterly Journal of Economics* 124(2): 735–69. doi:10.1162/qjec.2009.124.2.735.

Breloff, Paul and Mark Hookey. 2014. 'Big Data for Financial Inclusion: Is Boring Better?' *CGAP*. Available at http://www.cgap.org/blog/big-data-financial-inclusion-boring-better, last accessed on 11 January 2018.

Bussell, Jennifer. 2012. *Corruption and Reform in India: Public Services in the Digital Age*. Cambridge: Cambridge University Press.

C-GARD. 2016. 'Application of Space Technology in Rural Road Projects under PMGSY'. Report Summary. Centre for Geo-Informatics Application in Rural Development (C-GARD) at the National Institute of Rural Development (NIRD).

Chandra, Kanchan. 2007. *Why Ethnic Parties Succeed: Patronage and Ethnic Head Counts in India*. Cambridge: Cambridge University Press.

Chaudhuri, Shubham and Martin Ravallion. 2006. *Partially Awakened Giants: Uneven Growth in China and India*. Washington DC: World Bank Publications.

Dabla-Norris, Era, Kalpana Kocchar, Nujin Suphaphiphat, Frantisek Ricka, and Evridiki Tsounta. 2015. 'Causes and Consequences of Income Inequality: A Global Perspective'. International Monetary Fund. Available at https://www.imf.org/external/pubs/ft/sdn/2015/sdn1513.pdf, last accessed on 11 January 2018.

Datt, Gaurav and Martin Ravallion. (2011). 'Has India's Economic Growth Become More Pro-Poor in the Wake of Economic Reforms'. *World Bank Economic Review* 25(2): 157–89. doi:10.1093/wber/lhr002.

Datt, Gaurav, Martin Ravallion, and Rinku Murgai. 2016. 'Growth, Urbanization and Poverty Reduction in India'. Working Paper 21983. National Bureau of Economic Research. Available at http://www.nber.org/papers/w21983, last accessed on 11 January 2018.

DDU-GKY. 2015. 'Leveraging Evidence and Predictive Analytics to Improve Program Outcomes'. PowerPoint slides.

Deaton, Angus and Jean Drèze. 2002. 'Poverty and Inequality in India: A Re-Examination'. *Economic and Political Weekly* 37(36): 3729–48.

Deb, Anamitra. 2014. 'It's Time to Listen to the Voice of the Consumer'. *CGAP*. Available at http://www.cgap.org/blog/its-time-listen-voice-consumer, last accessed on 11 January 2018.

Dhorajiwala, Sakina and Rajendran Narayanan. 2016. 'All about Means and Ends'. *The Hindu*. Available at http://www.thehindu.com/opinion/op-ed/all-about-means-and-ends/article9180982.ece, last accessed on 11 January 2018.

Dodge, E. 2015. 'Promoting Data Accessibility: The Case of NREGA'. PowerPoint Slides.

Drèze, J. 2014. 'Learning from NREGA'. *The Hindu*. Available at http://www.thehindu.com/opinion/op-ed/learning-from-nrega/article6342811.ece, last accessed on 11 January 2018.

Duflo, Esther, Pascaline Dupas, and Michael Kremer. 2015. 'School Governance, Teacher Incentives, and Pupil–Teacher Ratios: Experimental Evidence from Kenyan Primary Schools'. *Journal of Public Economics* 123: 92–110. doi:10.1016/j.jpubeco.2014.11.008.

Duflo, Esther, Michael Greenstone, Rohini Pande, and Nicholas Ryan. 2013. 'Truth-Telling by Third-Party Auditors and the Response of Polluting Firms: Experimental Evidence from India'. *The Quarterly Journal of Economics* 128(4): 1499–545. doi:10.1093/qje/qjt024.

Duflo, Esther, Michael Kremer, and Jonathan Robinson. 2011. 'Nudging Farmers to Use Fertilizer: Theory and Experimental Evidence from Kenya'. *American Economic Review* 101(6): 2350–90.

Ehrbeck, Tilman, Rajiv Lochan, Supriyo Sinha, Naveen Tahilyani, and Adil Zainulbhai. 2010. *Inclusive Growth and Financial Security: The Benefits of E-Payments to Indian Society*. McKinsey & Company. Available at http://ccmrm.org/wp-content/uploads/2015/05/McKinsey-2010-inclusive-growth-report.pdf, last accessed on 11 January 2018.

Fan, Shenggen, Ashok Gulati, and Sukhadeo Thorat. 2008. 'Investment, Subsidies, and Pro-Poor Growth in Rural India'. *Agricultural Economics* 39(2): 163–70. doi:10.1111/j.1574-0862.2008.00328.x.

Farazmand, Ali, and Jack Pinkowski. 2006. *Handbook of Globalization, Governance, and Public Administration*. CRC Press.

The Financial Express. 2016. 'MGNREGA: No Annual Social Audit in Majority of States, Finds CAG'. *The Financial Express*. Available at http://www.financialexpress.com/economy/mgnrega-no-annual-social-audit-in-majority-of-states-finds-cag/245759/, last accessed on 11 January 2018.

Glennerster, Rachel, and Michael Kremer. 2011. 'Small Changes, Big Results'. *Boston Review*. Available at http://www.bostonreview.net/glennersterner-kremer-changes-big-results, last accessed on 11 January 2018.

Gulati, A. and P. Banerjee. 2015. 'Rationalising Fertiliser Subsidy in India: Key Issues and Policy Options'. Indian Council for Research on International Economic Relations Working Paper No. 307.

Gupta, Nirant. 2014. 'How Analytics Drive Innovative Financial Services for the Poor'. *CGAP*. Available at http://www.cgap.org/blog/how-analytics-drive-innovative-financial-services-poor, last accessed on 11 January 2018.

Harriss-White, Barbara and Nandini Gooptu. 2009. 'Mapping India's World of Unorganized Labour'. *Socialist Register* 37(37). Available at http://socialistregister.com/index.php/srv/article/download/5757, last accessed on 11 January 2018.

Heeks, Richard. 2000. 'The Approach of Senior Public Officials to Information Technology-related Reform: Lessons from India'. *Public Administration and Development* 20(3): 197–205. doi:10.1002/1099-162X(200008)20:3<197::AID-PAD109>3.0.CO;2-6.

Himanshu. 2015. 'India's Flawed Fertilizer Policy'. *LiveMint*. Available at http://www.livemint.com/Opinion/XCCJwEzbzwiyWFYfK1wRdO/Indias-flawed-fertilizer-policy.html, last accessed on 11 January 2018.

IDinsight. 2013. 'Auditing the Auditors: Rapid Response Process Evaluation of MGNREGA Divas for Rural Development Department, Government of Bihar'. Process Evaluation. IDinsight.

Imbert, Clement, and John Papp. 2011. 'Estimating Leakages in India's Employment Guarantee'. In *The Battle for Employment Guarantee*, edited by Reetika Khera. Oxford University Press.

India National Election Survey. 2014. 'All India Postpoll 2014'. Survey Report. Lokniti. Available at http://www.lokniti.org/pdf/All-India-Postpoll-2014-Survey-Findings.pdf, last accessed on 11 January 2018.

Jaffrelot, C. 2008. '"Why Should We Vote?" The Indian Middle Class and the Functioning of the World's Largest Democracy'. In *Patterns of Middle Class Consumption in India and China*, edited by C. Jaffrelot and P. van Der Veer, 35–54. New Delhi: SAGE.

Jha, Praveen and Nilachala Acharya. 2011. 'Expenditure on the Rural Economy in India's Budgets since the 1950s: An Assessment'. *Review of Agrarian Studies* 1(2). Available at http://ras.org.in/index.php?citation=expenditure_on_the_rural_economy_in_indias_budgets_since_the_1950s&citation_status=0, last accessed on 11 January 2018.

J-PAL Policy Briefcase. 2011. 'A Well-Timed Nudge'. Policy Briefcase. Cambridge, MA: Abdul Latif Jameel Poverty Action Lab.

———. 2013. 'Truth-Telling in Third-Party Audits'. Policy Briefcase. Cambridge, MA: Abdul Latif Jameel Poverty Action Lab.

———. 2015. 'The Power of Information in Community Monitoring'. Cambridge, MA: Abdul Latif Jameel Poverty Action Lab.

Koehler, Johanna, Patrick Thomson, and Robert Hope. 2015. 'Pump-Priming Payments for Sustainable Water Services in Rural Africa'. *World Development* 74(October): 397–411. doi:10.1016/j.worlddev.2015.05.020.

Kohli, Atul. 2001. *The Success of India's Democracy*. Cambridge: Cambridge University Press.

KPMG-IAMAI. 2015. 'India on the Go: Mobile Internet Vision 2017'. Available at http://rtn.asia/wp-content/uploads/2015/07/Report.pdf, last accessed on 11 January 2018.

Kremer, Michael, Edward Miguel, Sendhil Mullainathan, Clair Null, and Alix Zwane. 2011. 'Social Engineering: Evidence from a Suite of Take-up Experiments in Kenya'. Working Paper.

Kumar, Sanjay. 2009. 'Patterns of Political Participation: Trends and Perspective'. *Economic and Political Weekly* 44(39): 47–51.

Kydd, Jonathan and Andrew Dorward. 2004. 'Implications of Market and Coordination Failures for Rural Development in Least Developed Countries'. *Journal of International Development* 16(7): 951–70. doi:10.1002/jid.1157.

Lehne, Jonathan, Jacob Shapiro, and Oliver Vanden Eynde. 2016a. 'Building Connections: Political Corruption and Road Construction in India'. PSE Working Papers. Available at https://halshs.archives-ouvertes.fr/halshs-01349350, last accessed on 11 January 2018.

———. 2016b. 'Building Connections: Political Corruption and Road Construction in India'. *Ideas for India*. Available at http://ideasforindia.in/article.aspx?article_id=1686, last accessed on 11 January 2018.

Mani, Tanvi. 2016. 'Big Data in the Global South—An Analysis'. *The Centre for Internet and Society*. Available at http://cis-india.org/internet-governance/blog/big-data-in-the-global-south-an-analysis, last accessed on 11 January 2018.

Millennium Development Goals Report. 2012. 'Millennium Development Goals Report 2012'. Statistical material. United Nations, Department of Economics and Social Affairs. Available at http://www.un.org/en/development/desa/publications/mdg-report-2012.html, last accessed on 11 January 2018.

Muralidharan, K., Paul Niehaus, and Sandip Sukhtankar. 2014. 'Payments Infrastructure and the Performance of Public Programs: Evidence from Biometric Smartcards in India'. NBER Working Paper. Available at http://www.nber.org/papers/w19999.pdf, last accessed on 11 January 2018.

Naef, E., P. Raza, S. Frederick, R. Kendall, and N. Gupta. 2014. 'Using Mobile Data for Development'. Cartesian. Available at https://docs.gatesfoundation.org/Documents/Using%20Mobile%20Data%20for%20Development.pdf, last accessed on 11 January 2018.

Niehaus, Paul, Antonia Atanassova, Marianne Bertrand, and Sendhil Mullainathan. 2013. 'Targeting with Agents'. *American Economic Journal: Economic Policy* 5(1): 206–38. doi:10.1257/pol.5.1.206.

Niehaus, Paul and Sandip Sukhtankar. 2013. 'Corruption Dynamics: The Golden Goose Effect'. *American Economic Journal: Economic Policy* 5(4): 230–69. doi:10.1257/pol.5.4.230.

Olken, Benjamin A. 2005. 'Monitoring Corruption: Evidence from a Field Experiment in Indonesia'. Working Paper 11753. National Bureau of Economic Research. Available at http://www.nber.org/papers/w11753, last accessed on 11 January 2018.

Pal, Parthapratim and Jayati Ghosh. 2007. 'Inequality in India: A Survey of Recent Trends'. Working Paper 45. United Nations, Department of Economics and Social Affairs. Available at https://ideas.repec.org/p/une/wpaper/45.html, last accessed on 11 January 2018.

Palshikar, Suhas and Sanjay Kumar. 2004. 'Participatory Norm: How Broad-Based Is It?' *Economic and Political Weekly* 39(51): 5412–17.

Pande, Rohini. 2003. 'Can Mandated Political Representation Increase Policy Influence for Disadvantaged Minorities?

Theory and Evidence from India'. *The American Economic Review* 93(4):1132–51.doi:10.1257/000282803769206232.

Papadimitriou, Dimitri B. 2008. 'Promoting Equality through an Employment of Last Resort Policy'. SSRN Scholarly Paper ID 1281476. Rochester, NY: Social Science Research Network. Available at http://papers.ssrn.com/abstract=1281476, last accessed on 11 January 2018.

Patnaik, Prabhat. 2015. 'Economic Liberalisation and the Working Poor'. *Economic and Political Weekly* 51(29): 47–51.

PRS. 2016. 'PRS Report Summaries: CAG Audit of Pradhan Mantri Gram Sadak Yojana'. Report Summary. PRS Legislative Research. Available at http://www.prsindia.org/parliamenttrack/report-summaries/cag-audit-of-pradhan-mantri-gram-sadak-yojana-4414/, last accessed on 11 January 2018.

Ramaswamy, K.V. and Tushar Agrawal. 2012. 'Services-Led Growth, Employment and Job Quality: A Study of Manufacturing and Service-Sector in Urban India'. Indira Gandhi Institute of Development Research (IGIDR) Working Paper 2012–007. IGIDR, Mumbai, India. Available at https://ideas.repec.org/p/ind/igiwpp/2012-007.html, last accessed on 11 January 2018.

Rao, Sowmya and Anirudh Tagat. 2016. 'India's Nudge Unit: An Idea Whose Time Has Come'. *LiveMint*. Available at http://www.livemint.com/Opinion/DAzJfdnfgHFOXdKWPI68QM/Indias-nudge-unit-An-idea-whose-time-has-come.html, last accessed on 11 January 2018.

Ravallion, Martin. 2000. 'What Is Needed for a More Pro-Poor Growth Process in India?' *Economic and Political Weekly* 35(13): 1089–93.

Rezaee, Arman, Ali Hasanain, and Yasir Khan. 2015. 'Crowdsourcing Government Accountability: Experimental Evidence from Pakistan'. Unpublished Manuscript.

Richards, David. 2014. 'How Big Data Could Help Stop the Ebola Outbreak'. *CNBC*. Available at http://www.cnbc.com/2014/10/01/how-big-data-could-help-stop-the-ebola-outbreakcommentary.html, last accessed on 11 January 2018.

Roche, Elizabeth. 2016. '11 States Abandon Rural Road Projects under PMGSY for Want of Land'. *LiveMint*. Available at http://www.livemint.com/Politics/CqoHXE5cyoUACngAkkNQLI/11-states-abandon-rural-road-projects-under-PMGSY-for-want-o.html, last accessed on 11 January 2018.

Šćepanović, Sanja, Igor Mishkovski, Pan Hui, Jukka K. Nurminen, and Antti Ylä-Jääski. 2015. 'Mobile Phone Call Data as a Regional Socio-Economic Proxy Indicator'. *PLoS ONE* 10(4). doi:10.1371/journal.pone.0124160, last accessed on 11 January 2018.

Sen, Abhijit, and Himanshu. 2004. 'Poverty and Inequality in India: II: Widening Disparities during the 1990s'. *Economic and Political Weekly* 39(39): 4361–75.

———. 2005. 'Poverty and Inequality in India: Getting Closer to the Truth'. In *Data and Dogma: The Great Indian*

Poverty Debate, edited by Angus Deaton and Valerie Kozel, 306–70. New Delhi: Macmillan.

Seth Sharma, Yogima Seth, and Dheeraj Tiwari. 2016. 'NITI Aayog Plans "Nudge Unit" to Help Push Government's Flagship Schemes'. *The Economic Times*. Available at http://economictimes.indiatimes.com/news/economy/policy/niti-aayog-plans-nudge-unit-to-help-push-governments-flagship-schemes/articleshow/54041144.cms, last accessed on 11 January 2018.

Shah, Alpesh, Prateek Roongta, Chilman Jain, Vibha Kaushik, and Abhishek Awadhiya. 2016. 'Digital Payments 2020: The Making of A $500 Billion Ecosystem in India'. Boston Consulting Group. Available at http://image-src.bcg.com/BCG_COM/BCG-Google%20Digital%20Payments%202020-July%202016_tcm21-39245.pdf, last accessed on 11 January 2018.

Shaw, Abhishek. 2015. 'Research as If People Matter'. *Economic and Political Weekly* 51(41): 7–8.

Srivastava, Moulishree. 2015. 'Govt May Turn to Supercomputing for Better Use of Aadhaar Database'. *LiveMint*. Available at http://www.livemint.com/Politics/PYN4cIu1tiRL5BCuTUoXBO/Govt-may-turn-to-supercomputing-for-better-use-of-Aadhaar-da.html, last accessed on 11 January 2018.

Sukhtankar, Sandip and Milan Vaishnav. 2015. 'What Do We Know about Corruption in India?' *Ideas for India*. Available at http://www.ideasforindia.in/article.aspx?article_id=1503, last accessed on 11 January 2018.

Thomson, Patrick, Rob Hope, and Tim Foster. 2012. 'GSM-Enabled Remote Monitoring of Rural Handpumps: A Proof-of-Concept Study'. *Journal of Hydroinformatics* 14(4): 829–39. doi:10.2166/hydro.2012.183.

Vijayanand, S.M. 2013. 'Rural Development in India: Challenges and Policy Responses'. PowerPoint slides.

———. 2014. 'Rural Development Policies and Programmes: Historical Analysis'. PowerPoint slides.

Wall, Matthew. 2014. 'Ebola: Can Big Data Analytics Help Contain Its Spread?' *BBC News*. Business. Available at http://www.bbc.com/news/business-29617831, last accessed on 11 January 2018.

Witsoe, Jeffrey. 2013. *Democracy against Development: Lower-Caste Politics and Political Modernity in Postcolonial India*. University of Chicago Press.

World Bank Report. 2014. 'Big Data in Action for Development'. The World Bank. Available at http://live.worldbank.org/sites/default/files/Big Data for Development Report_final version.pdf, last accessed on 11 January 2018.

World Development Report. 2015. 'World Development Report 2015: Mind, Society, and Behavior'. World Bank. Available at http://www.worldbank.org/en/publication/wdr2015, last accessed on 11 January 2018.

World Health Organization. 2016. 'WHO | Poor Sanitation Threatens Public Health'. Available at http://www.who.int/mediacentre/news/releases/2008/pr08/en/, last accessed on 11 January 2018.

Yadav, Yogendra. 1996. 'Reconfiguration in Indian Politics: State Assembly Elections, 1993–95'. *Economic and Political Weekly* 31(2/3): 95–104.

———. 2000. 'Understanding the Second Democratic Upsurge: Trends of Bahujan Participation in Electoral Politics in the 1990s'. In *Transforming India: Social and Political Dynamics of Democracy*, edited by F.R. Frankel, Z. Hasan, R. Bhargava, and B. Arora, pp. 120–45. New Delhi: Oxford University Press.

Yadav, Yogendra and Suhas Palishkar. 2009. 'Between Fortuna and Virtu: Explaining the Congress' Ambiguous Victory in 2009'. *Economic and Political Weekly* 44(39): 33–46.

10

Issues in Rural Infrastructure Development

*G. Raghuram**

ABSTRACT

The development of the rural economy, which contributes to 48 per cent of the gross domestic product with nearly 70 per cent of the population, is critical to India's overall development. In this context, rural infrastructure is a very important facilitator. The chapter addresses issues in rural infrastructure development by first examining the profile of rural India using various data sources like the Census, National Sample Survey, Socio Economic Caste Census, National Nutrition Monitoring Bureau, and Labour Bureau. It then looks at the budgetary allocation towards rural infrastructure. During the years 2000–12, key infrastructure sectors, namely, roads, drinking water and sanitation, housing, irrigation, electrification, and information and communication technology were among the top six in terms of central government spending. A brief profile of each of the sectors is presented along with the summary of the achievements with regard to various central government schemes. Based on this, the article then highlights key issues related to overall rural infrastructure development like non-farm rural economy, access and mobility, maintenance of infrastructure, co-ordination, and finally, the role that the National Bank for Agriculture and Rural Development can play.

JEL Classification: O18, R11

Keywords: rural infrastructure, rural development and rural economy

10.1 PROFILE OF RURAL INDIA

As per the provisional data released on 3 July 2015, based on the Socio Economic Caste Census (SECC) (Department of Rural Development, Ministry of Rural Development 2015) carried out in India during 2011–12, there were 17.9 crore (73.4 per cent) rural households out of a total of 24.4 crore households. As per the 2011 census, the rural population was 83.3 crore, implying a share of 68.8 per cent. The growth rate of this rural population has declined to 1.2 per cent during 2001–11 from 1.7 per cent per year during 1991–2001. Urban population growth was about 2.8 per cent per year during

* Director, Indian Institute of Management Bangalore, India.

Box 10.1   Socio Economic Caste Census 2011

Of the rural households, 71.1 per cent had a mobile phone each and an additional 1 per cent had only landline connectivity. Land was owned by 55.3 per cent, of which less than 50 per cent had irrigated land. Two-wheelers were owned by 17.4 per cent. Some form of motorized transport was owned by 20.7 per cent. There was a high variance in such ownership across the states and union territories. The high performers were Goa, Punjab, Chandigarh, and the National Capital Territory of Delhi. The low performers were Chhattisgarh, Odisha, and Madhya Pradesh.

Of the total number of households, 7.97 crore (44.5 per cent) lived in *kuccha* type houses, of which 2.37 crore (13.3 per cent) of the total households lived in one-room kuccha type houses.

Of the rural households, 30.1 per cent had their primary source of income from land and 51.1 per cent from manual/casual labour. Non-agricultural enterprises were owned by 1.6 per cent. There was a household member holding a salaried job in 9.7 per cent of cases.

There are concerns in the data. For example, the rural population share is less than rural household share, reflecting lower (than urban) household size. The two wheeler ownership reflects a lower number than the stock of two wheelers (11.5 crore in 2012). If we account for a possible 100 per cent ownership per urban household, this would result in a 28 per cent ownership rate for rural households. Further, two-wheeler ownership and mobile phone subscriptions have gone up significantly in recent years. As of 30 April 2015, the rural teledensity was 48.37. At a household size of 5, would this imply over 200 per cent rural household connectivity?

both periods as stated in the IDFC (2012) report (IDFC Limited 2013).

One of the issues while studying rural contexts is data integrity. We present some discrepancies based on the SECC data in Box 10.1. That the SECC data does not match with National Sample Survey (NSS) data for similar parameters is highlighted in a *Financial Express* article dated 23 July 2015 (Bhalla 2015).

There were 16,78,26,730 households, 16,66,075 habitations (Department of Drinking Water & Sanitation, Ministry of Rural Develoment 2016), 6,40,867 villages (Ministry of Health & Family Welfare, 2010), and 2,38,617 gram panchayats (GPs) (Ministry of Panchayati Raj 2013) in rural India as per the 2011 census. The Indian government defines rural areas as 'areas which are not urban'.[1] The rural economy experienced a shift in composition in the last few decades, from being primarily agricultural in the post-Independence era to achieving a more balanced share of agriculture, industry, and services today. In 2011–12, rural areas accounted for 48 per cent of the country's GDP. While the sectoral split of

the country's GDP was 14 per cent for agriculture, 28 per cent for industry, and 58 per cent for services, the sectoral split of the rural GDP was 27 per cent for agriculture, 33 per cent for industry, and 40 per cent for services.

Between 1999–2000 and 2009–10, the rural employment share of agriculture decreased from 76.2 per cent to 67.9 per cent, while for industries, it increased from 11.4 per cent to 17.4 per cent and for services from 12.4 per cent to 14.7 per cent (IDFC Limited 2013). Table 10.1 provides the sector-wise share in rural GDP and change in share of rural employment.

A National Sample Survey Office (NSSO) survey in 2014 showed that despite the large percentage of population employed in the sector, only 39.5 per cent of rural households actually depended on agriculture as a primary source of income (National Sample Survey Office 2016). This is also in line with SECC 2011.

Rural wages in India had registered an average annual growth of 3.8 per cent in November 2014, the lowest since July 2005, according to Labour Bureau data. The 3.8 per cent year-on-year increase is a significant drop relative to the two-digit growth rates prevailing until June 2014, and the peak 20 per cent-plus levels of 2011 (Figure 10.1). (Harish and Surabhi 2015)

Rural consumption is also experiencing changes: the percentage of income spent on food continues to decline, while spending on durables and services continues to rise. The share of consumer expenditure on food reduced from 63.2 per cent in 1993–4 to 48.6 per cent in 2011–12 (Table 10.2). Even within food, the profile of expenditure has changed. During the same period the share of food expenditure on cereals has reduced from 38.29 per cent

---

[1] The definition of an urban area (Census of India 2016) is as follows:
- All statutory places with a municipality, corporation, cantonment board or notified town area committee, and so on (that is, a statutory town).
- All other places which satisfy the following criteria simultaneously (a census town):
  - a minimum population of 5,000;
  - at least 75 per cent of male working population engaged in non-agricultural pursuits; and
  - A density of population of at least 400 per square kilometre (1,000 per square mile).

Table 10.1   Rural Sectors

Sector	Estimated Share in Rural GDP* (%)	Share in Rural Employment (%)		
	2011–12	1999–2000	2004–5	2009–10
Agriculture	27.0	76.2	72.7	67.9
Industry	40.0	11.4	13.7	17.4
Services	33.0	12.4	13.6	14.7

Note: *Credit Suisse (2012).
Source: IDFC Limited (2013).

Table 10.2   Rural Percentage Composition of Consumer Expenditure

	1993–4		2011–12	
	% of Total	% of Food	% of Total	% of Food
Cereals	24.20	38.29	12.00	24.69
Milk and products	9.50	15.03	9.10	18.72
Vegetables	6.00	9.49	4.80	9.88
Edible oil	4.40	6.96	3.80	7.82
Beverages, refreshment, processed food*	4.20	6.65	5.80	11.93
Pulses and products	3.80	6.01	3.10	6.38
Egg, fish, and meat	3.30	5.22	3.60	7.41
Others	7.80	12.34	6.40	13.17
Food Total	**63.20**	**100.00**	**48.60**	**100.00**
Non-food Total	**36.80**		**51.40**	

Note: *Includes purchased cooked meals.
Source: NSSO (2013).

to 24.69 per cent. The biggest growth has been in 'beverages, refreshments, processed food' from 6.65 per cent to 11.93 per cent. Studies note that this change in consumption trend marks a shift to a more urban consumption pattern as consumer spending increases.

Taking this further to actual consumption, with the focus on nutrition, we draw upon the National Nutrition Monitoring Bureau (NNMB) survey, last carried out in 2011–12. The NNMB carried out longitudinal studies in rural areas to assess the diet and nutritional consumption patterns. The first survey was carried out in 1975–9, followed by surveys in 1988–90, 1996–7, and 2011–12. These studies have been carried out in the same 11,095 villages spread across 10 states of Kerala, Tamil Nadu, Karnataka, Andhra Pradesh, Maharashtra, Gujarat, Madhya Pradesh, Odisha, West Bengal, and Uttar Pradesh. The latest survey covered 86,898 individuals from 23,889 households. The time trends reflect a disturbing trend of an overall reduction in per capita intake over four decades.

The average daily per capita intake of cereals and millets has declined by about 137 g, energy by about 500 Kcal and protein by 13 g. The trend is even more disturbing since there is a variance across states (National Institute of Nutrition 2012).

The overall picture of the rural citizen is one who has aspiration to move into higher-income employment and spend a higher share on non-food consumables and

durables, even at the cost of lower food and nutrition intake. This would increase the demand for agricultural efficiency, non-agricultural employment, health, education and skilling, and being 'connected' with the rest of society in terms of entertainment, information, and physical mobility.

10.2 GOVERNMENT SPENDING ON RURAL INFRASTRUCTURE

As per the India Rural Development Report 2012–13

government spending on rural infrastructure quadrupled between 2000–01 and 2010–11. Since 2005, with the launch of Bharat Nirman, the central government's flagship rural infrastructure programme that includes roads, electricity, drinking water supply, telecom, irrigation and housing, investment in rural infrastructure has shot up. The Eleventh Five Year Plan (2007–12), which had a major focus on infrastructure, had projected rural infrastructure investment at Rupees (Rs) 4.35 lakh crore (in 2006–07 prices), equivalent to 30 per cent of total infrastructure investment. It is estimated that 90 per cent of the rural infrastructure investment has been realised, with over 40 per cent from the Centre. To supplement these budgetary allocations, debt financing has been obtained from several sources, such as National Bank for Agriculture and Rural Development (NABARD), Rural Infrastructure Development Fund, National Cooperative Development Corporation, Housing and Urban Development Corporation, Small Industries Development Bank of India, public sector banks and multilateral development banks. (IDFC Limited 2013)

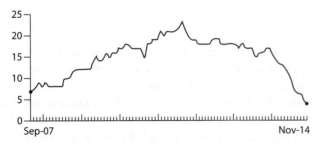

Figure 10.1   Annual Rural Wage Growth (%)
Source: Harish and Surabhi (2015).

In the Union Budget 2016–17, of the Rs 19.78 lakh crore, Rs 87,765 cr was allocated to the rural sector, including Rs 38,500 crore for the Mahatma Gandhi National Rural Employment Guarantee Scheme (MGNREGS). In addition, Rs 19,000 crore was allocated to Pradhan Mantri Gram Sadak Yojana (PMGSY) (Ministry of Finance 2016).

The central government's spending on rural infrastructure during 2000–12 was over Rs 3 lakh crore, of which rural roads had the highest share at 29.8 per cent (Table 10.3).

The role of rural infrastructure is critical as India's rural economy transitions from an agriculture-led to a non-farm economy. Indeed, government spending on infrastructure has a more significant and lasting impact on poverty reduction than government outlay on fuel, food and other subsidies. (IDFC Limited 2013)

The rest of the chapter addresses issues in rural infrastructure and development, focusing on the infrastructure segments with a high spend. These are roads, drinking water and sanitation, housing, irrigation, electrification, and telecommunication.

10.2.1 Roads

India has possibly the largest rural road network in the world, at over 3 million (mn) kilometres (km), out of a total road length of over 5 mn km. Rural Roads include Village Roads and Other District Roads of the Indian Roads Congress (IRC) classification (NRRDA 2014a).

All weather road access to rural areas is critical since they provide access to markets, employment opportunities, schools, and health care. They help reduce goods transportation cost and increase household surplus. The following two histograms (Figure 10.2) provide a perspective on this:

PMGSY was launched in 2000 for the development of all-weather rural roads. It has played a big role in increasing rural connectivity. The criterion of accessibility for a habitation to be deemed connected by a rural road is the permissible maximum distance of the habitation from an all-weather road. This distance has been defined as 500 m for the plains and 1.5 km in case of hills and special areas (NRRDA 2005). Connectivity is to be provided to habitations of population more than 500 in plains and 250 in the rest of the country.

The percentage of habitations unconnected by road has reduced from 43 per cent in 2000 to 31 per cent in August 2013 by connecting nearly 130,000 habitations (IDFC Limited 2013). The figures are slightly different if we do an assessment based on the Online Management, Monitoring and Accounting System (OMMAS) (NRRDA 2014b) of the National Rural Road Development Agency (NRRDA), the institution that is responsible for PMGSY. As per OMMAS, out of about 10 lakh habitations as per the 2001 census, 524,807 were eligible for all weather connectivity. Of these, 207,208 habitations were unconnected as on 1 April 2000. Of these unconnected eligible

Table 10.3 Central Government Spending on Rural Infrastructure (2000–12) (2006–7 prices)

	Expenditure (in Rs cr)	Share (%)
Roads	90,517	29.8
Drinking Water and Sanitation	62,432	20.5
Housing	48,551	16.0
Irrigation	48,184	15.9
Electrification	24,100	7.9
Telecommunication	13,851	4.6
Watershed	10,557	3.5
Storage	1,972	0.6
PURA	206	0.1
Integrated Action Plan (IAP)	3,654	1.2
Total Expenditure on Rural Infrastructure	303,894	100

Source: IDFC Limited (2013).

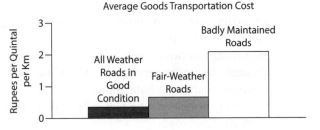

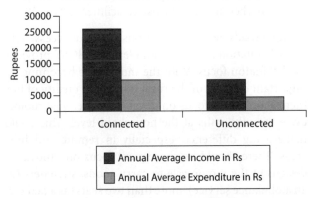

Figure 10.2 Road Access, Cost, and Surplus

Source: IDFC Limited (2007).

habitations, 133,836 have been connected until end August 2016. While connecting these, 45,918 habitations with a lower population have also got connected.

In November 2015, the government brought forward the target date for completion of PMGSY from 2022 to 2019 (Press Information Bureau 2015), with increased budgetary allocations. The allocation under PMGSY increased to Rs 19,000 crore in 2016–17 from Rs 15,100 crore in 2015–16 (*Business Standard* 2016). PMGSY has been executed in two phases. In the first 11 years from 2001–2 to 2011–12, the focus of PMGSY I was on new connectivity with 100 per cent central funding. In PMGSY II, the focus is on new connectivity (to achieve 100 per cent connectivity of the remaining 2001 census eligible habitations, upgradation of the poor-quality rural roads to the earlier connected habitations, and development of a maintenance framework. The central funding is only partial, to the extent of 75 per cent in the plains states and 90 per cent in the eight North Eastern and three Himalayan states.

As a way forward, it is important to devise the contours of the future rural road connectivity schemes. The priorities would be as follows:

1. Connectivity to habitations with a population of 500 persons and above in plain areas, and 250 persons and above in special category states that have emerged in Census 2011
2. Re-layering of early PMGSY roads and other rural roads
3. Ensuring periodic maintenance of rural roads based on vehicle profiling
4. Improving network reliability and enabling through transport services by providing two-sided connectivity to habitations
5. Removing bottlenecks on higher-level roads that serve the rural roads.
6. Influencing service providers including transport, marketing, agri-extension facilities (IIMA, 2016).

Rural roads need a stronger push towards access, both at the habitation and household levels. PMGSY provides the habitation focus. With the motorcycle becoming an important element of the rural household quality of life, there should be a focus on developing even just motorcycle friendly paths at the household level. This could make a big difference, especially in remote and hilly areas. There should be consequent focus on innovative designs of the motorcycle to carry goods, stretchers (as an ambulance service), more than two seats (as a taxi service), and of course, support services like maintenance, fuelling, and so on.

Rural road pavement design also needs a quality focus, keeping in view the traffic conditions. One of the major causes of road deterioration are cuts made on the road due to irrigation pipes (primarily by individual farmers, and, sometimes, even by government departments). This needs to be built into the road design by incorporating pipes under the road surface at frequent intervals, for farmers to pass through their irrigation pipes. Similarly, there need to be well-designed speed breakers near schools and other habitation areas, rather than leaving it to informal channels.

10.2.2 Drinking Water and Sanitation

The government has increased its spending on household infrastructure such as drinking water, sanitation, and housing. However, these areas are still lagging. While showing an improvement over the levels in 2000, the number of households with drinking water within the premises was 35 per cent and the percentage of rural households with latrine facility stood at 31 per cent in 2011 (IDFC Limited 2013).

Water and sanitation are inextricably linked and must be considered together. Without water, sanitation cannot be hygienic, and unsafe sanitation is a leading cause of water contamination and disease. Studies indicate that by positively affecting health, clean water supply allows for greater productivity in the long term. Beyond direct health impacts, poor sanitation also negatively affects girl school attendance. (WSP 2011; IDFC Limited 2007)

Schemes like the Swachh Bharat Mission now have provisions to reduce open defecation through the development of more latrines (public and household), and the creation of awareness on the importance of proper hygiene. Swachh Bharat Mission is India's biggest drive to improve sanitation and cleanliness, especially in rural India. The 2016–17 central budget provided Rs 9,000 crore for the Swachh Bharat Abhiyan. In order to continue this momentum, priority allocation from Centrally Sponsored Schemes will be made to reward villages that have become free from open defecation (Khanna 2016).

The NSSO carried out Swachh Survekshan 2016, commissioned by the Ministry of Drinking Water and Sanitation (MODWS), to rank states based on percentage of households that have access to sanitary toilets. The variance between the top-performing and the poor-performing states seems to be explained largely by literacy, followed by per capita income (Table 10.4). Size of the state could be another explanatory variable.

MoDWS also carried out a survey, Swachh Survekshan 2016—Gramin, through the Quality Council of India to

Table 10.4   Top and Poor Performers on Sanitation

State	Households Having Access to Sanitary Toilets (2016)	Literacy (2011 Census) (Rank Excludes UTs)		Per Capita Income (at Current Prices, 2013–14)	
	Rank	%	Rank	Rs	Rank
	1	2	3	4	5
Top Performers					
Sikkim	1	82.20	7	176,491	3
Kerala	2	93.91	1	103,820	11
Mizoram	3	91.58	2	76,120	20
Himachal	4	83.78	5	92,300	15
Nagaland	5	80.11	9	77,529	19
National Average		**74.04**		**74,380**	
Poor Performers					
Uttar Pradesh	22	69.72	29	36,250	32
Madhya Pradesh	23	70.63	28	51,798	28
Odisha	24	73.45	25	52,559	27
Chhattisgarh	25	71.04	27	58,547	26
Jharkhand	26	67.63	31	46,131	29

Sources: Express News Service (2016) for column 1; Census 2011, accessed on 9 September 2016 for columns 2 and 3; and Indian states by GDP per capita based on the last update from MoSPI (2015) for columns 4 and 5.

rank districts. Each district has been judged on four distinct parameters (MoDWS 2016):

- Households having access to safe toilets and using them (toilet usage, water accessibility, safe disposal of waste) (40 per cent)
- Households having no litter around (30 per cent)
- Public places with no litter in the surrounding (10 per cent)
- Households having no stagnant wastewater around (20 per cent)

Many of the hill districts performed well. Sindhudurg in Maharashtra, followed by Nadia in West Bengal performed as top among the plains districts (Press Information Bureau 2016).

Beyond just providing infrastructure, the need for change in behaviour, especially in the context of open defecation has come out as an important parameter. We provide an example of a study done on the Open Defecation Free (ODF) initiative of the Rotary Club of Madras (RCM) in Box 10.2 (Parmar and Raghuram 2015).

10.2.3 Housing

The share of rural households facing a housing shortage had increased from 18 per cent in 2001 to 26 per cent in 2012.

The Working Group on Rural Housing for the Twelfth Five Year Plan estimated a total rural housing shortage of 44 mn units in 2012 (Planning Commission 2011a). The 15 per cent that are homeless or live in temporary housing face the most acute problems, being exposed to natural calamities and severe weather conditions (IDFC Limited 2013).

Schemes such as the Indira Awaas Yojana (IAY) and various state government–driven initiatives have targeted the rural poor, though significant numbers have yet to be covered. For the year 2014–15, a total of Rs 19,512.97 crore was allocated under IAY out of which Rs 14,396.26 crore was utilized and 1,764,574 houses were built against the annual target of 2,445,143 houses. During 2015–16, a total of Rs 15,519.27 crore was allocated, out of which Rs 13,751.83 crore was utilized, and 1,330,005 houses were built against the annual target of 2,120,228 houses (Ministry of Rural Development 2015). In pursuance of the goal of housing for all by 2022, the rural housing scheme IAY was renamed and revamped to Pradhan Mantri Awaas Yojana—Gramin, and approved during March 2016.

10.2.4 Irrigation

With an annual demand of 688 billion cubic metres (bcm) out of a total of 813 bcm in 2010, irrigation requires by far the most water among various applications in the rural

---

Box 10.2   ODF Initiative of RCM

The RCM, Chennai, had achieved the successful execution of the ODF Communities project in Amarampedu village in Gummidi-poondi block, in the state of Tamil Nadu in 2015. Under this project, all 108 households in the village had constructed toilets. They attributed the success of this project primarily to the critical factor of bringing about behavioural change in toilet usage rather than just toilet construction. For selection of a partner for this project, three organizations were considered.

- Sulabh, a non-profit voluntary social organization, which uses environmentally friendly two-pit, pour-flush compost toilet known as Sulabh Shauchalaya, for community toilets rather than household toilets.
- World Toilet Organisation, a global non-profit organization, which focuses on providing technology for building toilets and em-powering individuals through education, training, and building local marketplace opportunities to advocate for clean and safe sanitation facilities in their communities.
- Community-Led Total Sanitation (CLTS) Foundation headed by Dr Kamal Kar, which focuses on behavioural change using 'trig-gers' such as disgust and shame to make communities change their behaviour in a sustainable manner. They have been successful in dozens of countries around the world, including parts of India, in ending open defecation.

Finally, CLTS was chosen for this project. Thereafter, construction of toilets was community led, not imposed by an outsider, be it the government or any other agency. Shaming and participative techniques were employed to bring about the transformation and this led to a behavioural change among the participants and imbibed a sense of responsibility within them.

---

areas (Table 10.5). While overall water availability is not an issue for India, there are major imbalances across the country's geography. Irrigation enables multi-cropping and has a direct impact on increased agricultural productivity and farm incomes.

10.2.5 Electrification

Electricity is another essential element of infrastructure. It enables increased productivity in agriculture and labour, and improvement in the delivery of social services such as health and education. Other services such as telecom, broadband, and television depend on the availability of electricity.

As per the Ministry of Power's letter dated 5 February 2004, a village would be considered electrified if:

1. Basic infrastructure such as distribution transformer and distribution lines are provided in the inhabited

locality as well as the Dalit Basti hamlet where it exists.
2. Electricity is provided to public places like schools, panchayat office, health centres, dispensaries, community centres, and so on.
3. The number of households electrified should be at least 10 per cent of the total number of households in the village.

The Rajiv Gandhi Gram Vidyutikaran Yojana (RGGVY), launched in 2005, played an important part of the electrification of rural areas nationwide.

While 98.7 per cent of villages are now considered 'electrified', only 63.99 per cent of households in India are electrified (see Table 10.6) (Rural Electrification Corporation Limited 2016).

Rural electrification programmes have focused primarily on extending the grid. But ensuring electricity supply to areas where the grid has been extended remains a challenge. Many households in electrified villages in fact choose not to connect to the grid because of the insufficient and poor quality of electricity supply. An overemphasis on grid extension thus can merely lead to wasteful and stranded investment. (IDFC Limited 2013).

Impact assessments of Gujarat's Jyotigram Yojana, which successfully provided 24-hour three-phase quality power supply to rural areas of the state, found that the constant supply of electricity had tremendous socio-economic benefits, increasing time spent on income generating activities, average employment levels, and even reducing migration from rural areas (Devaiah 2010).

Table 10.5   Annual Rural Water Demand (in bcm)

Sector	2010 (Projected)	2025 (Projected)
Irrigation	688	910
Drinking (including livestock)	56	73
Industrial	12	23
Energy	5	15
Others (Forestry, Pisciculture, Tourism, Navigation, and so on)	52	72
Total	813	1,093

Source: IDFC Limited (2007).

Table 10.6   Electricity Access (as on 31 July 2016)

State	Households Unelectrified (in Lakhs)	Households with Access to Electricity (%)	Villages Electrified (%)
Top Performers			
Gujarat	–	100	100
Punjab	–	100	100
Sikkim	0.14	84.78	100
Tamil Nadu	0.15	99.85	100
Andhra Pradesh	2.09	97.68	100
National Average	**602.87 (Total)**	**63.99**	**98.7**
Poor Performers			
Assam	35.35	34.22	95.3
Odisha	42.63	47.65	96.9
Madhya Pradesh	46.84	57.89	99.8
Bihar	145.86	13.82	97.9
Uttar Pradesh	181.16	28.89	99.9

Source: Rural Electrification Corporation Limited (2016).

As of July 2016, 10 states claim to have 100 per cent electrification at the village level. Six more states claim to have more than 99 per cent villages electrified. The poor performers were Arunachal Pradesh (76.3 per cent) and Manipur (93.1 per cent), followed by Nagaland, Assam, Meghalaya, and Jharkhand (all between 95 per cent to 96 per cent). However, at the household level, the picture is quite different. A state like Uttar Pradesh, which claims 99.9 per cent village electrification, has only 28.89 per cent households with electricity.

The RGGVY has been replaced by the Deen Dayal Upadhyay Gram Jyoti Yojana (DDUGJY), with a planned investment of Rs 75,600 crore for rural electrification.

Under DDUGJY-Rural Electrification, Ministry of Power has sanctioned 5,236 projects (including 3,709 Decentralised Distributed Generation projects) to electrify 128,432 un-electrified villages, intensive electrification of 655,247 partially electrified villages and provide free electricity connections to 420.04 lakh below poverty line (BPL) rural households. As on 31 March 2016, works in 116,144 un-electrified villages and intensive electrification of 351,233 partially electrified villages have been completed and 232.25 lakh free electricity connections have been released to BPL households. (Ministry of Power, 2016)

The obvious challenge in electrification is improving the percentage of households with electricity.

10.2.6 Information and Communication Technology

In the recent past, rural teledensity peaked at 51.75 per cent as on 31 May 2016 and marginally declined to 51.41 per cent as on 30 June 2016 (Telecom Regulatory Authority of India [TRAI] 2016). Mobile phone communication in rural areas has increased the quality of life in a variety of ways. It will be interesting to see whether the decline in June 2016 was a temporary blip or a reflection of a certain saturation.

A 50 per cent rural teledensity amounts to about 2.5 connections per household at an average of 5 persons per household. An important supply-side reason behind this is the subsidy offered by the Universal Service Obligation Fund (USOF) to the service providers and tower operators based on their bidding. The USOF is generated as a cross-subsidy from telecom usage over the national network. The total USOF disbursements, which began in 2002–3, has reached Rs 20,035 crore as of 2014–15.

Recognizing the need for broadband connectivity, the central government initiated a major project called the National Optical Fibre Network (NOFN) project. It was to be funded by the USOF, with a target of providing optical fibre–based connectivity to all GPs at an investment of Rs 20,000 crore. A special purpose vehicle called Bharat Broadband Network Limited (BBNL) was set up to execute the project through three central public sector undertakings (Bharat Sanchar Nigam Limited, RailTel, and Power Grid). While execution had begun in 2012, it is significantly delayed. Till 31 October 2015, an amount of Rs 3,054.43 crore has been released by USOF to BBNL (Aanchal 2016).

While in 2014–15, plans were afoot to execute work for 1 lakh GPs, which was later scaled down to 50,000 GPs, data up to March 2015 showed that only about 20,000 GPs had been covered under the NOFN. As on 6 December 2015, optical fibre cable laying in 32,272 GPs had been completed and 76,624 km fibre laid, according to latest government data. (Aanchal 2016)

The project has since been renamed as the BharatNet Project with increased scope, and has an allocation of Rs 72,778 crore. BharatNet proposes to develop a network with increased reliability and bandwidth, and to bring in the public–private partnership model. Various issues are still under debate.

Various studies have tried to profile the rural consumption of Information Ccommuniation Technology (ICT) usage. A recent study by the Boston Consulting Group (see Figure 10.3) segments the rural consumer across occupations and age. The internet penetrations are higher in the 18 to 30 segment, especially among those who have employment. This identifies both the opportunity and the challenge that employment is essential for

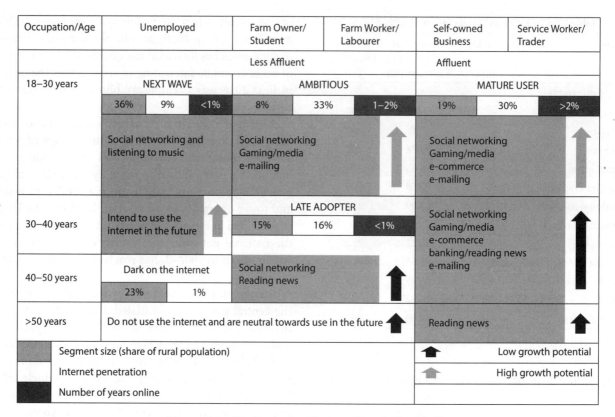

Figure 10.3   Five Segments of Internet Users in Rural India

Source: Jain and Sanghi (2016).

increasing internet penetration. Such penetration can help in improving access not only to agricultural, health, and educational services, but also entertainment and e-commerce.

China has leveraged ICT infrastructure for e-commerce. Alibaba, China's e-commerce colossus, provides a model for how companies can think about using digital channels to bring e-commerce to rural markets in a large and diverse developing country. We present this case in Box 10.3. There are lessons from this for India.

10.3 ISSUES

Given the above profile of rural India and infrastructural efforts so far, we crystallize a few issues.

10.3.1 Non-farm Rural Economy

Very often, the focus for rural infrastructure development has been viewed as 'mitigating agrarian distress and enhancing farmer income'. While this is important, the real issue is 'mitigating rural distress and enhancing

---

Box 10.3   Alibaba Moves e-Commerce into the Countryside

In October 2014, Alibaba announced it was investing $1.6 billion to set up 100,000 rural service centres all over China's countryside. It has a presence in almost 16,000 villages so far. These e-commerce outposts are equipped with computers and free internet services. The centres give villagers a place to pick up the goods they buy online from Alibaba. They can also pay their utility bills, add credit to their prepaid mobile phone plans, and book travel at these centres. Service managers are available to help first-time shoppers.

In addition, the company's 'rural partners' programme tasks internet-savvy young people who live in cities but often return to their home villages with helping people learn to buy and sell online. Some villagers have used the service centres to start their own online businesses—selling clothes made in nearby factories on Taobao, Alibaba's eBay-like online marketplace, for example.

The company's rural expansion programme is credited with helping fuel Alibaba's continued overall growth.

rural income'. Given that India is self-sufficient in food, the agrarian distress is more a phenomenon of lack of opportunity in the rural non-farm sector. Any efficiency in agriculture will result in employment demand in the rural non-farm sector.

The over Rs 200,000 crore (Dey 2014) annual subsidies offered through the minimum support price and National Food Security Act (NFSA) and for fertilizers tend to benefit the farmers with significant surplus production having access to formal grain procurement. A recent NSSO survey estimated this to be no more than 15 per cent of the farmers (NSSO 2014). The natural question is whether this money is better spent in ways other than subsidy. The same issue can be raised with respect to the National Rural Employment Guarantee Scheme, which has not only contributed to improving rural wages, but has also brought in a perceived 'entitlement' culture, resulting in lower human output.

Towards this, the most important priority for economic growth of rural India would be to increase rural income by creating opportunities for non-farm activities, which would also make room for improving agricultural productivity. This is because agricultural productivity would primarily happen through employing more capital and irrigation for multi-cropping than labour. This would also balance the phenomena of urbanization and migrant labour, and to an extent, their negative consequences.

With allocations of Rs 70,000 crore to the infrastructure sector, and Rs 25,000 crore to the Rural Infrastructure Development Fund (RIDF) in the Union Budget of 2016–17 (Ministry of Finance 2015), the new government has signalled a commitment to the development of a physical asset base for future development. The Micro Units Development and Refinance Agency (MUDRA) was launched in 2015 to provide loans at low rates to microfinance institutions and non-banking financial institutions, which then provide credit to various micro, small, and medium enterprises (MSME).

While the profile of potential non-farm income economic activities (of which agro processing would be one obvious choice) in rural areas needs to be examined for targeting priorities in rural infrastructure development, there should be no debate on the need for improving the access and quality of basic infrastructural requirements.

10.3.2 Access and Mobility

While setting targets, it is important that access parameters penetrate to the household level, and not just the habitation/village/GP level. Currently, broadband focuses at the GP level, electricity at the village level, and roads at the habitation level. Further, roads, electricity, and mobile coverage (if not, broadband) need to 'cover' the entire geography rather than just habitation areas. This would help spur developmental activities and improve disaster management. For example, we would need to target parameters like 100 per cent mobile coverage, no part of the geography being more than say 'x' km from an electricity line, or a rural road, with 'x' being reduced over the years.

10.3.3 Maintenance

Maintenance of rural infrastructure assets need focus. Given that such assets are spread out, it is important to draw in the local community both for maintenance and prevention of abusive use of infrastructure that increases the need for maintenance. An appropriate way to do this would be the inclusion of local communities in the planning and oversight of execution (to build their sense of ownership) and then maintenance of assets. This could have a major impact, for example, on roads to avoid the cuts for irrigation. It could improve health and hygiene as a consequence of behavioural change towards better sanitation habits.

10.3.4 Coordination

Infrastructure also needs to be viewed in a holistic sense, keeping in view the underlying need of the beneficiaries and scope of coordination across stakeholders including government departments. For example, road development may have to be seen in a 'network' perspective rather than a 'segment' perspective, so that better access to markets or rural tourism is enabled. Coordination across government departments, as for example between the PMGSY and the BharatNet projects, can reduce costs of laying optical fibre during road construction/upgradation works. Access to markets may imply not only physical access, but also informational access in terms of prices at various markets. Coordination between construction of roads under PMGSY and irrigation department for construction of check dams can reduce overall costs.

10.3.5 Role of NABARD

We believe that NABARD, given its mandate and mission, can play an important role in driving rural development by financing in such a manner that effective quality rural infrastructure gets created. Its mission is to promote sustainable and equitable agriculture and rural prosperity through effective credit support, related services, institution development, and other innovative initiatives. NABARD can leverage its position and expertise to bring about the much required focus on rural infrastructure, rural non-farm sector, and coordination between stakeholders.

REFERENCES

Aanchal, M. 2016. 'BharatNet Project: Despite Push, Need Right Course for "Right-of-Way"'. *The Indian Express*, 3 February.

Bhalla, S.S. 2015. '"Column: How Bad Is the SECC Data?" Very Bad'. *The Financial Express*, 23 July.

Business Standard. 2016. 'Budget 2016: Farm Sector Gets Rs 35,000 cr in Allocation'. 29 February.

Census 2011. Ranking of States and Union Territories by Literacy Rate: 2011, available at http://censusindia.gov.in/2011-provresults/data_files/india/Final_PPT_2011_chapter6.pdf

Census of India. 2016. 'Provisional Population Totals: Urban Agglomerations and Cities'. *Census India*, 30 August. Available at http://censusindia.gov.in/2011-prov-results/paper2/data_files/India2/1.%20Data%20Highlight.pdf, alst accessed 9 September 2016.

Credit Suisse. 2012. *India Market Strategy—The Great Indian Equalisation*. Hong Kong: Credit Suisse.

Department of Drinking Water & Sanitation, Ministry of Rural Develoment. 2016. 'Basic Information: Format B1—Basic Habitation Information'. National Rural Drinking Water Programme. Available at http://indiawater.gov.in/IMISReports/Reports/BasicInformation/rpt_RWS_AbstractData_S.aspx?Rep=0&RP=Y&APP=IMIS, alst accessed on 21 August 2016.

Department of Rural Development, Ministry of Rural Development. 2015. 'SECC 2011 at a Glance'. Socio Economic and Caste Census 2011. Available at http://secc.gov.in/statewiseSeccDataSummaryReport?reportType=SECC%20Data%20Summary, last accessed on 3 August 2015.

Devaiah, D. 2010. *Government of Gujarat: Jyotigram Yojana*. Erehwon Innovation Consulting Pvt. Ltd.

Dey, A. 2014. 'Fertiliser Subsidy Higher by Only 3% in 2014–15'. *The Indian Express*, 14 February.

Express News Service. 2016. 'Sikkim Tops Swachh Rural Ranking, UP among Worst'. *The Indian Express*, 9 September. Available at http://indianexpress.com/article/india/india-news-india/sikkim-tops-swachh-rural-ranking-up-among-worst-3021207/, last accessed on 12 January 2018.

Harish, D. and Surabhi. 2015. 'Rural Wage Growth Lowest in 10 Years, Signals Farm Distress, Falling Inflation'. *The Indian Express*, 7 January. Available at http://indianexpress.com/article/india/india-others/rural-wage-growth-lowest-in-10-years-signals-farm-distress-falling-inflation/, last accessed on 12 January.

IDFC Limited. 2007. *India Infrastructure Report 2007 (Rural Infrastructure)*. New Delhi: Oxford University Press.

———. 2013. *IDFC Rural Development Network*. New Delhi: Orient BlackSwan.

IIMA. 2016. *Inception Report for NRRDA*. Ahmedabad: IIM.

Jain, Nimisha and Kanishka Sanghi. 2016. 'The Rising Connected Consumer in Rural India'. Available at https://www.bcg.com/publications/2016/globalization-customer-insight-rising-connected-consumer-in-rural-india.aspx, accessed on 29 January 2018.

Khanna, P. 2016. 'Budget 2016: Swachh Bharat Abhiyan Allotted Rs 9000 Crore'. *Live Min*, 29 February. Available at http://www.livemint.com/Home-Page/Tlof7bdi5zHc78ROFpbABN/Budget-2016-Swachh-Bharat-Abhiyan-allotted-Rs9000-crore.html, last accessed on 12 January.

Ministry of Drinking Water and Sanitation. 2016. Swachh Survekshan—Gramin: 2016. Available at http://www.mdws.gov.in/sites/default/files/Swachh%20Survekshan%20Report%20Eng.PDF, last accessed on 22 February 2018.

Ministry of Finance. 2015. *Key Features of Budget 2015–2016*. New Delhi: National Informatics Centre.

———. 2016. *Key Features of Budget 2016–2017*. New Delhi: National Informatics Centre.

Ministry of Health & Family Welfare. 2010. 'Bulletin'. *Health Management Information System*, 20 March. Available at https://nrhm-mis.nic.in/RURAL%20HEALTH%20STATISTICS/(D)%20RHS%20-%202010/RHS%20Bulletin-March%202010.pdf, last accessed on 6 August 2015.

Ministry of Panchayati Raj. 2013. 'Documents'. Ministry of Panchayati Raj, Government of India, 8 March. Available at http://www.panchayat.gov.in/documents/401/0/USQ%201863.pdf, last accessed on 6 August 2015.

Ministry of Power. 2016. *Status of Rural Electrification (RE) under DDUGJY*. New Delhi: Ministry of Power, Government of India.

Ministry of Rural Development. 2015. *20011/01/2015-RH(AC);340279. Circulars*. New Delhi: Ministry of Rural Development, Government of India.

MoSPI. 2015. 'Indian States by GDP per Capita'. *Statistics Times*, 20 August. Available at http://statisticstimes.com/economy/gdp-capita-of-indian-states.php, last accessed on 9 September 2015.

National Institute of Nutrition. 2012. *Diet and Nutritional Status of Rural Population, Prevalence of Hypertension & Diabetes among Adults and Infant & Young Child Feeding Practices—Report of Third Repeat Survey*. Hyderabad: National Nutrition Monitoring Bureau.

National Sample Survey Office. 2013. 'Key Indicators of Household Consumer of Household Consumer Expenditure in India 2011–12'. Press Release, 20 June. New Delhi: MoSPI.

———. 2014. *Key Indicators of Situation of Agricultural Households in India (January–December 2013)*. New Delhi: Ministry of Statistics and Programme Implementation.

———. 2016. *Key Indicators of Household Expenditure on Services and Durable Goods (July 2014–June 2015)*. New Delhi: MoSPI.

———. 2005. *Operations Manual*. New Delhi: NRRDA.

———. 2014a. *Managing Maintenance of Rural Roads in India*. New Delhi: NRRDA.

———. 2014b. 'OMMAS'. *PMGSY*. Available at https://online.omms.nic.in/, last accessed on11 September 2016.

Parmar, A.J. and G. Raghuram. 2015. *Case. Rotary Club of Madras: Open Defecation Free Communities Project*. Ahmedabad: IIM.

Planning Commission (2011) from Working Group on Rural Housing for XII Five Year Plan. New Delhi, Ministry of Rural Development: http://planningcommission.nic.in/aboutus/committee/wrkgrp12/rd/wgrep_iay.pdf

Press Information Bureau. 2015. 'Ministry of Rural Development.' Press Information Bureau, Government of India, 24 November. Available at http://pib.nic.in/newsite/PrintRelease.aspx?relid=131846, last accessed on 16 August 2016.

———. 2016. 'Ministry of Drinking Water & Sanitation'. Press Information Bureau, Government of India, 8 September. Available at http://pib.nic.in/newsite/PrintRelease.aspx?relid=149633, last accessed 11 September 2016.

Rural Electrification Corporation Limited. 2016.. Progress Report: State-wise Summary. Available at http://www.ddugjy.gov.in/mis/portal/statewisesummary.jsp, accessed on 9 September 2016.

Telecom Regulatory Authority of India (TRAI). 2016. Available at http://www.trai.gov.in/, last accessed on 16 August 2016.

WSP. 2011. 'Economic Impact of inadequate Sanitation in India'. Available at https://www.wsp.org/sites/wsp.org/files/publications/WSP-esi-india.pdf, last accessed on 29 January 2018.

11

NABARD's Initiatives on Financial Support to Agriculture and Rural Development

Some Reflections

H.R. Dave*

ABSTRACT

Institutional rural credit in India has evolved for more than a century. The period from 1935 (establishment of RBI) to 1982 (setting up of NABARD) can be defined as phase of 'Financial Institution Development', when the financial institutions mainly focused on expanding their service base in rural and semi-urban areas as well as their clientele base. The creation of NABARD was an outcome of the realization of the need for a new organizational structure for providing undivided attention, forceful direction, and pointed focus to the credit problems arising in the pursuit of integrated rural development. The chapter discusses the sources and uses of NABARD's financial resources, followed by the performance of the four major areas where NABARD has provided significant policy as well as financial support since its establishment, namely, (*a*) short-term agricultural production credit, (*b*) long-term agricultural investment credit, (*c*) Self-Help Group–Bank Linkage Programme (SBLP), and (*d*) support to rural infrastructure projects. Some of the major policy initiatives of NABARD aimed at upscaling the flow of institutional credit to agriculture and allied activities, rural non-farm sector, and other priority sector activities have certainly contributed positively to the growth of the rural economy. The positive and significant growth in short-term agricultural credit, especially the introduction of Kisan Credit Cards (KCC) is certainly a result of various policy interventions made by NABARD for ensuring not only the special distribution but also the deeper penetration of agricultural credit across farmlands. Ground-level credit (GLC) flow to agriculture has improved substantially during the last decade, and along with the general trend, credit disbursement to small and marginal farmers has also improved. NABARD's support to state governments under the Rural Infrastructure Development Fund (RIDF) constitutes about one-fifth of the investments made by state governments in the rural infrastructure sector. NABARD also provides support to government agencies and the private sector for rural infrastructure through NABARD Infrastructure Development

*Deputy Managing Director, NABARD, India.

The author thanks Dr Gyanendra Mani, General Manager, NABARD for his assistance/inputs during preparation of this chapter.

Assistance (NIDA), Warehouse Infrastructure Fund (WIF), and Food Processing Fund (FPF). NABARD is one of the few institutions in India that has done well on all the three aspects of sustainability—the 3P's, people, profit, and planet. Although the country is now self-sufficient in food production, agricultural farming has turned non-profitable over time due to rising costs and uneconomical holdings. Phenomenal growth in terms of the size of the balance sheet speaks volumes about NABARD's success on the profit parameter. NABARD's efforts in terms of the 'people account' can be gauged from the success of its various microfinance and other interventions, namely, SBLP, joint liability groups (JLGs), and tribal development programmes, which have provided livelihood opportunity to more than 70 million families. NABARD's efforts on the 'planet account' include its various interventions relating to watershed development, climate change, and so on. Deviating from past strategies aimed at increasing the profitability of crop cultivation, the Government of India has set the target of 'doubling of farmers' income by 2022', having a direct impact on almost half of the population and aiming for a sense of income security for farmers in a time-bound manner.

JEL Classification: O180, Q140, Q180

Keywords: ground-level credit, refinance, rural infrastructure, microfinance, climate change

11.1 INTRODUCTION

The financial support in the form of *taccavi* loans from state governments to agriculturists in times of distress such as famine or flood or other widespread natural calamity may be considered as the first public intervention in rural credit in India. But, most of the times, this system could not provide the needed relief to the farmers, due to factors such as inadequacy of the loans, undue delays in sanction and disbursement of loans, and inequitable distribution of loans; the government had little consideration of the borrower's ability to repay in agriculturally bad years. The acceptance of the model of village agricultural credit societies towards the end of nineteenth century (Nicholson 1960) and its implementation under the Co-operative Societies Act of 1904 may be regarded as the next important step towards institutionalizing rural credit in the country.

The World Bank in its sector policy paper in 1975 had remarked that 'credit is often a key element in the modernization of agriculture. Not only can credit remove financial constraint but it also accelerates the adoption of new technology. Credit facilities are also an integral part of the process of commercialization of the rural economy. However, no amount of credit even at the most reasonable rates can guarantee higher productivity or income among the rural poor, as the success depends upon many factors including the availability of inputs and services, sound credit policies, well-managed institutions and appropriate delivery channels' (World Bank 1975).

Although India had already realized the above fact in the beginning of the 1930s, which resulted in the establishment of the Reserve Bank of India (RBI) in 1935, it was the setting up of the Agricultural Credit Department (ACD) simultaneously with the establishment of the RBI that marked the beginning of the present-day structure of institutional finance—both for reducing the dependency of farmers on moneylenders and for providing crop loans as well as investment credit for agriculture and allied activities. Starting with the creation of the State Bank of India (SBI) in 1955 with the specific target of opening 400 new branches in rural and semi-urban areas for extending agricultural credit; nationalization of major commercial banks in July 1969 and April 1980; establishing regional rural banks (RRBs) in 1976 to provide more focused attention to the rural areas, particularly in underdeveloped and under-banked regions; and finally setting up the National Bank for Agriculture and Rural Development (NABARD) on 12 July 1982 as an apex body for the rural credit institutions and also to undertake supervisory functions in respect of cooperative banks (other than urban/primary cooperative banks) and RRBs, India completed the process of development of the institutional framework for purveying credit support to the rural sector, more specifically to the agriculture production system in the country. Therefore, the period from 1935 (establishment of RBI) to 1982 (setting up of NABARD) can be defined as phase of 'Financial Institution Development'. During this period, the financial institutions mainly focused on expanding their service base (branch expansion) in rural and semi-urban areas as well as their clientele base.

Today, the Indian banking network comprises 149 scheduled commercial banks, including 56 RRBs with 132,587 branches (49,902 rural and 75,704 semi-urban); 1,579 Urban Co-operative Banks (UCBs); and 94,178 Rural Co-operative Credit Institutions comprising both short-term and long-term rural cooperative credit structures (March 2016). The short-term credit cooperatives (STCCs) (93,444) comprises State Cooperative Banks (StCBs) (32), District Central Co-operative Banks (DCCBs) (370), and Primary Agricultural Credit Societies (PACS) (93,042) and long-term credit institutions (734) comprises 20 State Coop Agriculture & Rural Development Banks (SCARDBs), and 714 Primary Coop Agriculture & Rural Development Banks (PCARDBs).

11.2 EMERGENCE OF NABARD

The creation of NABARD was an outcome of the realization of the need for a new organizational structure for providing undivided attention, forceful direction and pointed focus to the credit problems arising in the pursuit of integrated rural development. The present chapter, therefore, aims at discussing as to what efforts NABARD has made so far to align with its mandate and to meet the expectations of the Committee to Review Arrangements for Institutional Credit for Agriculture & Rural Development (CRAFICARD), the committee that spawned NABARD. After analysing the sources and uses of funds of NABARD, the chapter discusses in brief the performance of the four major areas where NABARD has been providing significant policy as well as financial support since its establishment. These areas are (a) short-term agricultural production credit, (b) long-term agricultural investment credit, (c) Self Help Group Bank Linkage Programme (SBLP), and (d) support to rural infrastructure projects.

National Bank for Agriculture and Rural Development (NABARD) came into existence on 12 July 1982 by an Act of Parliament (Act 61 of 1981) to function as an apex bank not only to implement effectively various credit as well as developmental/non-credit interventions in agriculture and rural development but also to carry out some regulatory works on behalf of the RBI. Some of the features stipulated in the NABARD Act, 1981, were as follows:

(i)   To provide credit for the promotion of agriculture, small-scale industries, cottage and village industries, handicrafts and other rural crafts, and other economic activities in rural areas with a view to promoting integrated rural development and securing prosperity of rural areas and for matters connected therewith or incidental thereto.

(ii) To provide refinance (and even direct loans to an institution approved for the purpose by the Government of India) of short, medium, and long durations for production as well as fixed investments in farm and non-farm sectors.

(iii) To coordinate rural credit operations; study of problems relating to agriculture and rural development; training for officials of RRBs, cooperatives, and commercial banks; research, monitoring and evaluation; and credit information.

On its establishment, NABARD took over the functions of the erstwhile Agriculture Credit Department (ACD) and Rural Planning and Credit Cell (RPCC) of the RBI and the Agricultural Refinance and Development Corporation (ARDC). As an apex development bank, NABARD (a) serves as an refinancing agency for institutions providing investment and production credit for promoting agriculture and developmental activities in rural areas; (b) takes measures towards institution building for improving the absorptive capacity of the credit delivery system, including monitoring, formulation of rehabilitation schemes, restructuring of credit institutions, training of personnel, and so on; (c) coordinates the rural financing activities of all the institutions engaged in developmental work at the field level; and (d) maintain liaison with GOI, state governments, RBI, and other national-level institutions concerned with policy formulation.

11.3 NABARD: SOURCES AND USES OF FUND

NABARD is a unique financial institution as on the one hand its credit support in the form of refinancing activity supplements the resources of rural financial institutions to cater to the credit needs of the rural population for farm and non-farm activities and, on the other hand its financial support to state governments helps in creating infrastructure in agriculture and social sectors with an aim to speed up the agricultural growth. The analysis in this section helps understand as to how NABARD has diversified its sources and fund use to justify its mandate.

11.3.1 Sources of Fund

All the assets and liabilities associated with two funds built up in RBI—the National Agricultural Credit (Long Term Operations) Fund [NAC (LTO) Fund] and the National Agricultural Credit Stabilisation Fund [NAC (Stab) Fund]—were transferred to NABARD on its formation, involving an initial transfer of Rs 1,390 crore. The authorized capital as well as paid up capital of NABARD has increased from Rs 100 crore at the time of its establishment to Rs 6,700 crore as on 31 March 2017. The ratio of contribution between the GOI and the RBI has changed from 50:50 in 1982–3 to 99.6:0.40 as on 31 March 2017.

Table 11.1   Sources of Funds of NABARD (Amount in Rs Crore)

Sl	Items	1982–3	1992–3	1995–6	2002–3	2012–13	2016–17
1	Capital	100	100	500	2,000	4,000	6,700
2	Reserves	122	654	1,738	4,319	15,234	24,771
3	NRC (LTO) Fund	1,252	7,127	8,185	12,945	14,481	14,489
4	NRC (Stab) Fund	448	833	840	1,474	1,581	1,589
5	RBI—General line of Credit for short-term credit	904	3,437	4,787	5,792	0	0
6	Deposits—STCRC Fund (2008–9)	0	0	0		25,000	45,009
7	Deposits—ST Fund-RRB (2012–13)	0	0	0	0	10,000	10,003
8	Deposits—Long Term Rural Credit Fund	0	0	0	0	0	30,000
9	Borrowings from GOI	1,216	1,463	1,294	589	43	0
10	Open Market Borrowings (>1 year)	406	832	1,045	8,702	47,666	50,537
11	Short Term Borrowings—Term Money Market/CBLO (<1 year)	0	0	0	0	2,567	34,463
12	Foreign Currency loan	0	0	70	302	463	684
13	Rural Infrastructure Development Fund	0	0	350	12,159	78,758	105,502
14	Other Liabilities/Funds	71	1,341	799	2,603	13,377	24,513
	Total	**4,519**	**15,787**	**19,608**	**50,885**	**213,170**	**348,260**

Source: NABARD, Various annual reports.

Now the authorized capital of NABARD has been raised to Rs 30,000 crore.

The analysis of the sources of the funds of NABARD (Table 11.1) shows that its resources have increased almost 77 times from Rs 4,519 crore to Rs 348,260 crore during the last 34 years. The share of 'Owned funds' capital, reserve, National Rural Credit (LTO) Fund, National Rural Credit (Stab.) Fund—which are cost free in the sense that there are no paid-out interest costs associated with their use—had grown from 42.5 per cent (Rs 1,922 crore) to 57.4 per cent of NABARD's total resources (Rs 11,263 crore) in 1995–6, but declined to 13.7 per cent (Rs 47,549 crore) during 2016–17 because of the establishment of several other funds with NABARD dedicated to diverse themes. The increase in NABARD's paid-up capital by 77 times in 34 years, from Rs 100 crore in 1982–3 to Rs 6,700 crore in 2016–17, speaks of NABARD's credibility and its contribution to the betterment of rural economy.

Among the components of owned fund, the NRC Funds (LTO & Stab. Funds) were originally built up in RBI from out of its annual surpluses, and the balance of Rs 1,025 crore to its credit was handed over to NABARD on the latter's formation in July 1982. Even after the establishment of NABARD, the RBI used to transfer annually a part of its surplus to these two Funds till 1990–1. The RBI stopped its contribution to the NRC (LTO) and NRC (Stab.) Funds in 1991–2, seemingly due to the announcement of the then finance minister in his 1992–3 budget speech stating that 'the Reserve Bank of India will also be transferring a large share of its profits', aimed at curbing its fiscal deficit. However, the RBI realized that by stopping its contribution to these two funds, it was violating section 46(A) of the RBI Act 1934 and section 42(1) of the NABARD Act 1981 and, therefore, it started contributing a token amount of Rs 1 crore each to these funds since 1992–3. From that year onwards the only contribution to the NRC (LTO) and NRC (Stab.) Funds has been out of the surpluses of NABARD itself with a view to promote private capital formation in agriculture and rural development. However, keeping the declining share of investment credit in total credit support to agriculture sector in view, the GOI has now established the 'Long Term Rural Credit Fund (LTRC)' with NABARD in 2014–15 with initial allocation of Rs 5,000 crore for refinance support to Cooperatives and RRBs for investment credit.

Further, the RBI was extending the General Line of Credit (GLC) to NABARD under Section 17 (4E) of RBI Act for providing refinance to Cooperatives as also to RRBs for their short-term credit extended to agriculture. The GLC from RBI, which reached a level of Rs 6,600 crore in 2000–1, started declining since then and came down to Rs 3,000 crore and ceased completely from 31 January 2007 (Satish 2012). This impacted adversely the short-term operations of cooperatives and RRBs as NABARD was not able to meet the credit requirement of these two institutions at concessional rate. Finally, the GOI established two separate funds with NABARD to support the short-term credit requirements of cooperatives and RRBS.

These are (i) Short Term Cooperative Rural Credit Fund (STCRC) launched in 2008–9 with an allocation of Rs 5,000 crore for short-term refinance support to Coop, and (ii) Short Term Rural Credit Fund for RRBs (STRC-RRB) launched in 2012–13 with an allocation of Rs 10,000 crore for short-term refinance support to RRBs.

The year 1995–6 is considered very significant in NABARD's journey of rural development as the 'Rural Infrastructure Development Fund (RIDF)' with an initial corpus of Rs 2,000 crore was instituted in NABARD with the sole objective of providing low-cost fund support to state governments and state-owned corporations for quick completion of ongoing projects relating to medium and minor irrigation, soil conservation, watershed management, and other forms of rural infrastructure. The utilization of RIDF has increased from Rs 350 crore (1.8 per cent of total resources) in 1995–6 to Rs 105,502 crore (30.3 per cent of total resources) in 2016–17.

In the recent past, some other very important funds have also been established in NABARD to support its effort to diversify its financial and developmental programmes. Some of these funds are (a) the 'Warehouse Infrastructure Fund' created in 2013–14 with budgetary allocation of Rs 5,000 crore for extending loan to public and private sectors for construction of warehouses, silos, cold storage, and other cold chain infrastructure for storage of agricultural commodities, and (b) the 'Food Processing Fund' created in 2014–15 with an allocation of Rs 2,000 crore for providing affordable credit to agri-processing units in designated food parks.

11.3.2 Uses of Fund

As far as the uses of resources is concerned, medium-term/long-term (MT/LT) refinance for fixed investments and short-term refinance for production and marketing credit together cornered the major share in total resources deployed by NABARD (Table 11.2). These two components accounted for about 71 per cent of total resources in 1982–3, which increased to an all time high of 81 per cent during 1995–6, and thereafter their share started declining in percentage terms after the introduction of loans out of RIDF; however they still account for 51 per cent of total resources deployed. The share of loan out of RIDF has increased from just 1 per cent in 1995–6 to 29 per cent during 2016–17.

Keeping in view the limitation of borrowing power of state governments under Article 293(3) for availing loan under RIDF, NABARD has created an additional loan product called 'NABARD Infrastructure Development Assistance (NIDA)' for providing credit support to state-owned institutions/corporations for funding rural infrastructure projects. NIDA is designed to fund state-owned institutions/corporations on both on-budget as well as off-budget for creation of rural infrastructure outside the ambit of RIDF borrowing. The assistance under NIDA is available on flexible interest terms with longer repayment period up to 15 years (2–4 years repayment holiday).

As a part of its capacity-building programme for cooperative institutions, NABARD, since the beginning, has been providing long-term loans out of NRC (LTO) Fund to state governments for contribution of share capital to

Table 11.2   Uses of Funds of NABARD (Amount in Rs Crore)

Sl No.	Items	1982–3	1992–3	1995–6	2002–3	2012–13	2016–17
1	Cash and bank balance	11	548	129	1,785	8,466	11,612
2	Government securities and other investments	267	1,688	1,298	1,355	5,464	26,450
3	Refinance (medium term and long term) for fixed investment	2,292	8,085	11,145	25,416	48,504	101,532
4	Refinance (short term) for production and marketing credit	896	3,463	4,789	6,053	65,176	73,553
5	Refinance (MT) other than 3 above for approved purposes	29	310	178	451	109	53
6	Refinance for conversion of short-term loan to medium-term loans	123	161	32	370	64	1,065
7	Rediscounting bill and call money markets/CBLO	0	42	108	0	532	1,349
8	Loan from RIDF	0	0	387	13,062	75,061	100,981
9	NIDA loan	0	0	0	0	1,281	4,978
10	Direct loan to DCCBs	0	0	0	0	1,350	2,565
11	Credit facilities to federations	0	0	0	0	0	6,961
12	Other uses/loans	756	2,038	1,671	11	3,676	13,267
13	Fixed assets and other assets	145	0	0	2,383	3,487	3,894
	Total	**4,519**	**15,787**	**19,608**	**50,885**	**213,170**	**348,260**

Source: NABARD, various annual reports.

cooperative credit institutions (state cooperative banks [StCBs], district central cooperative banks [DCCBs], state cooperative agriculture and rural development banks [SCARDBs], primary cooperative agriculture and rural development banks [PCARDBs], primary agriculture credit societies [PACS], farmers' service societies [FSS], large-size Adivasi multi-purpose societies [LAMPS]) for periods up to 12 years in order to strengthen the share capital base of these institutions and thereby increase their maximum borrowing power and enable them to undertake larger lending programmes, subject to certain conditions.

Further, the implementation of the GOI Revival Package of Short Term Co-operative Credit Structure (STCCS) in January 2006 as per Vaidyanathan Committee recommendations has now enabled the DCCBs to borrow funds directly from any financial institution regulated/approved by RBI. Keeping this in view, NABARD developed a product 'Short Term Multipurpose Credit Product' (STMPCP) to provide financial assistance to cooperative banks (StCBs/DCCBs) primarily to expand their lendable resources and also enable them to diversify business operations to improve their profitability.

NABARD has also launched a new product for extending short term credit facility (less than 12 months) to state/central government Agricultural Marketing Federations, corporations, dairy cooperatives/federations, agriculture marketing cooperatives/federations, and registered companies for meeting the working capital requirement for procurement and marketing of agricultural commodities, processing and marketing of agricultural commodities, procurement, processing, and marketing of milk, supply of agricultural inputs including animal feed, and so on.

As a part of its farm-sector interventions, NABARD has taken an initiative for supporting producer organizations, adopting a flexible approach to meet the needs of producers. In order to give a special focus, the Producers Organization Development Fund (PODF) was set up on 1 April 2011, with an initial corpus of Rs 50 crore. Any registered producers' organization, namely, producers company (as defined under Section 465 (1) of Company's Act 2013), producers' cooperatives, registered farmer federations, mutually aided cooperative society (MACS), industrial cooperative societies, other registered federations, PACS, and son on set up by producers are eligible under the fund.

11.4 BUSINESS OPERATIONS OF NABARD

The efforts of the GOI and the RBI, such as expansion of bank branches of commercial banks even in the remote areas of the country; establishment of RRBs in 1975; the RBI's directive in 1972 to allocate of a proportion of aggregate bank advances to priority sectors (40 per cent 'adjusted net bank credit' [ANBC] or the credit equivalent amount of 'off-balance sheet exposure' [OBE] as of now); and so on had already caused the financial institutions to direct their credit flow into the desired direction. The establishment of NABARD provided sufficient push to take the developmental and financial efforts in the agriculture and rural development sector to a higher plane. Some of the major policy initiatives of NABARD aimed at upscaling the flow of institutional credit to agriculture and allied activities, rural non-farm sector and other priority sector activities (both short term as well as long term) have certainly contributed positively to the growth of the rural economy. Some of such policy interventions involving NABARD are briefed as follows.

(i) Government of India introduced the Kisan Credit Card (KCC) scheme replacing old 'crop loan scheme' in 1998 as an innovative credit delivery mechanism to enable farmers to meet their production credit requirements in a timely and hassle-free manner. The KCC guidelines have undergone several changes since then and now incorporates many new features over and above the financing of crop production requirement, namely, consumption expenditure, maintenance of farm assets, term loan for agriculture and allied activities, coverage of KCC holders under Personal Accident Insurance Scheme (PAIS), and, recently, the coverage of KCC holders under Atal Pension Yojna, and so on. Today this product is considered to be one of the most convenient banking products for farmers.

(ii) As a part of its strategy to boost agricultural production, the GOI had announced the 'Doubling of Agricultural Credit' programme to double the flow of institutional credit to agriculture in three years during 2004–5 to 2006–7 over the base of 2003–4. The programme envisaged accelerated expansion of KCCs, financing of new investments, rescheduling and restructuring of loans in areas affected by natural calamities, one time settlement (OTS) for farmers in distress, and redemption of loans from informal sources. The programme of doubling of agricultural credit received an enthusiastic response from the banks and the doubling happened in less than the prescribed time frame. The programme was a great success and in fact overachieved the target.

(iii) The revival package under the Vaidyanathan Committee's recommendations aimed at reviving the STCCS and making it a well-managed and vibrant medium to serve the credit needs of rural India, especially the small and marginal farmers, was a major policy step that had been under implementation since 2006. The programme also sought to introduce legal and institutional reforms necessary for the democratic, self-reliant, and efficient functioning, taking measures to improve the quality of governance and management, and providing financial assistance to bring the system to an acceptable level of financial health. Financial assistance under the package included technical assistance to cover computerization, installation of standard accounting system and MIS, training and capacity building, in addition to covering accumulated losses in the STCCS. A World Bank assessment in four states commented positively on the implementation of the reform package in terms of amendments to the Acts, elections to three tiers, toning up the accounting systems, and a massive training effort. In terms of credit growth in these states, short-term co-operatives witnessed a 120 per cent growth in aggregate since the reform process started and an overall improvement in recovery levels (NABARD 2011).

11.4.1 Ground-Level Short-Term Credit Flow and NABARD's Support to Rural Financial Institutions

The short-term credit, which meets the working capital requirement of farm production activity, and long-term credit, which is used to create on-farm as well as off-farm agriculture sector-related assets/infrastructure, are basically complementary to each other. Short-term credit, which directly leads to the enhancement in farm productivity by way application of optimum dozes of modern farm inputs and thereby increasing the income of the farmers, may not yield the desired results unless it is supported by the suitable investments in the related agricultural and allied activities (see Table 11.3).

Table 11.3   Direct Institutional Credit (Short Term) to Agriculture and Refinance by NABARD Against That (Amount in Rs Crore)

Year	Agency-wise Short-Term Loan Issued				Short-Term Refinance by RBI/NABARD to Various Agencies			
	Cooperatives	Comm Banks	RRBs	Total	Cooperatives	Comm Banks to PACS	RRBs	Total
1970–1	515	74	–	589				
1972–3	613	177	–	790	281		0	281
1982–3	1,908	565	98	2,759	858		188	1,046
1988–9	3,594	1,765	250	5,884	1,813		241	2,054
1992–3	4,394	2,432	451	7,665	2,896		327	3,222
2002–3	23,629	16,825	4,834	45,288	5,395		1,093	6,488
2003–4	29,326	24,134	6,133	59,593	5,361		937	6,298
2004–5	31,887	29978	9,883	71,748	7,193		1,726	8,919
2005–6	35,624	45,644	12,816	94,084	7,977		2,178	10,154
2006–7	40,796	65,245	17,031	123,072	11,174		2,451	13,626
2007–8	47,390	6,8243	20,377	136,010	13,390		2,689	16,079
2008–9	48,022	107,766	22,851	178,639	13,900		2,869	16,768
2009–10	56,946	124,646	30,529	212,121	17,437		6,780	24,216
2010–11	69,038	146,063	38,560	253,661	23,697		9,703	33,400
2011–12	81,829	217,897	47,011	346,737	33,996	79	13,926	48,001
2012–13	102,592	314,951	55,957	473,500	44,492	129	20,319	64,940
2013–14	113,574	364,164	70,697	573,001	53,903	135	25,965	80,003
2014–15	130,350	415,736	89,326	635,412	59,788	213	30,003	90,004
2015–16	143,803	419,931	101,579	665,313	53,774	227	16,000	70,001
2016–17	131,880	452,576	105,001	689,457	62,610	271	10,002	72,883

Sources: Credit Issued: (a) Reserve Bank of India, *Handbook of Statistics on Indian Economy* (September 2015); (b) NABARD Occasional Paper No 59 'Agricultural Credit in India: Trends, Regional Spreads and Database Issues' by EPWRF, Mumbai; and (c) Data on agency-wise short-term loans issued from 2012–13 to 2016–17 from NABARD; Refinance Data: Department of Refinance, NABARD, Mumbai.

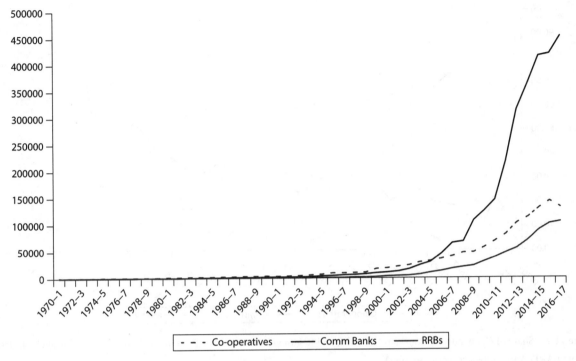

Figure 11.1   Agency-wise Short-Term Credit to Agricultre

Source: NABARD Annual Report (various issues).

The disbursement of short-term credit to agriculture sector by various agencies indicates that the cooperative sector was ahead of the other two agencies (commercial banks and RRBs) in short-term credit disbursement till 2004–5 but the commercial banks took over the lead thereafter. It can also be seen from Figure 11.1 that the rise in short-term credit disbursement is quite steep in case of commercial banks from 2004–5 onwards.

Although short-term credit (crop loan) disbursement by cooperatives increased from Rs 515 crore in 1971–2 to Rs 131,880 crore in 2016–17 in absolute terms, its share in total short-term credit disbursement by all the agencies, which was as high as 87.4 per cent in 1971–2, declined to 69.2 per cent in 2002–3, 44.4 per cent in 2004–5, and to 19.1 per cent in 2016–17. As against this performance of cooperative banks, the short-term credit disbursement by commercial banks increased from just Rs 74 crore to Rs 452,576 crore in 2016–17 in absolute terms and its share in total short-term credit disbursement by all the agencies, which was as low as 12.6 per cent in 1971–2, increased to 20.5 per cent in 2002–3, 41.8 per cent in 2004–5, and to 65.6 per cent in 2016–17 (see Figure 11.2). However, the share of RRBs, which was just 3.6 per cent in 1982–3, could reach to about 15 per cent in 2007–8, but remained below 15 per cent thereafter. The introduction of the KCC scheme and

implementation of doubling of credit programme have contributed to the increased share of RRBs in the short-term credit support by financial institutions.

As may be seen from Figure 11.1, there has been a very modest increase in short-term credit disbursement to agriculture from institutional sources till 2004–5 and it showed a respectable growth thereafter, although quite a good number of policy interventions aimed at accelerating the institutional finance to agriculture sector were already made by that time. But it was probably the 'Doubling of Agricultural Credit' programme implemented during 2004–7 that had made all the difference. The positive and significant growth in ST agricultural credit is certainly a result of various policy interventions made by NABARD for ensuring not only the special distribution but also the deeper penetration of agricultural credit across the farm lands.

11.4.2 Progress under Kisan Credit Cards Issued

The agency-wise number of KCCs issued since inception of the scheme is given in Table 11.4 and Figure 11.3 below.

Agency-wise distribution of total cards issued since inception till 31 March 2015 suggests that about 49 per cent of cumulative KCCs have been issued by commercial

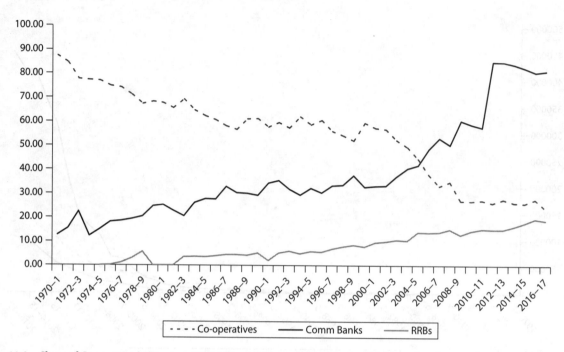

Figure 11.2   Share of Cooperatives, Commercial Banks, and Regional Rural Banks (RRBs) in Short-Term Agricultural Credit Issued
Source: NABARD Annual Report (various issues).

Table 11.4   Agency-wise Kisan Credit Cards Issued during the Year

Year	KCCs Issued (in Lakhs)				% Share in Total No. of Cards Issued		
	Coop	RRBs	Comm Banks	Total	Coop	RRBs	Comm Banks
1998–9	01.56	0.06	6.22	7.84	19.90	0.77	79.34
1999–2000	35.95	1.73	13.66	51.34	70.02	3.37	26.61
2000–1	56.14	6.48	23.90	86.52	64.89	7.49	27.62
2001–2	54.36	8.34	30.71	93.41	58.20	8.93	32.88
2002–3	45.79	9.64	27.00	82.43	55.55	11.69	32.76
2003–4	48.78	12.74	30.94	92.46	52.76	13.78	33.46
2004–5	35.56	17.29	43.95	96.8	36.74	17.86	45.40
2005–6	25.98	12.49	41.65	80.12	32.43	15.59	51.98
2006–7	22.97	14.06	48.08	85.11	26.99	16.52	56.49
2007–8	20.91	17.73	46.06	84.7	24.69	20.93	54.38
2008–9	13.44	14.14	58.30	85.88	15.65	16.46	67.89
2009–10	17.50	19.50	53.10	90.1	19.42	21.64	58.93
2010–11	28.10	17.70	55.80	101.6	27.66	17.42	54.92
2011–12	29.95	19.96	68.04	117.54	25.18	16.93	57.89
2012–13	26.79	20.30	82.43	129.52	20.68	15.67	63.65
2013–14	26.89	21.35	NA				
2014–15	17.32	24.96	NA				
Cumulative since inception	**507.99**	**238.47**	**717.52***	**1,463.98**	**34.70**	**16.29**	**49.01**

Sources: (i) EPWRF (2014); 'Agric Credit in India: Trends, Regional Spreads & Database issues', NABARD Occasional Paper No 59 for data from 1998–9 to 2011–12; (ii) *(cumulative Comm Bank) State-wise Progress of Kisan Credit Cards Issued by Commercial Banks in India (as on 31 March 2015), available at www.indiastat.com, accessed on 7 April 2016.

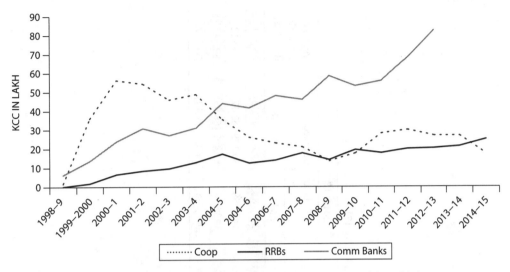

Figure 11.3   Number of Kisan Credit Cards (KCCs) Issued (in Lakhs)

Source: NABARD Annual Report (various issues).

banks followed by about 35 per cent by cooperative banks and 16 per cent by RRBs. In fact, the share of cooperative banks in total KCC issued has come down from as high as 70 per cent in 1999–2000 to 20.7 per cent during 2012–13, and that of commercial banks has gone up from 26.6 per cent to 63.7 per cent during the same period. The high share of cooperative banks (52.9 per cent) as compared to RRBs (16.7 per cent) and commercial banks (30.4 per cent) in total number of operative/live KCC (as on 31 March 2015) indicates that despite the fact that the number of cards issued by cooperative banks is continuously declining, many farmers still prefer to keep the KCC with cooperative banks alive, may be due to the advantages such as availability of good quality fertilizers, seed, and so on.

The number of operative/live KCCs at 7.41 crore as on 31 March 2015 as per cent of cumulative number of KCCs issued since inception comes to 50.6 per cent (of 14.64 crore). The analysis of state-wise total number of operative/live KCCs issued by all the agencies indicates that six big states, namely, Uttar Pradesh (15.15 per cent), Andhra Pradesh (11.02 per cent), Maharashtra (10.07 per cent), Madhya Pradesh (9.66 per cent), and Rajasthan (8.33 per cent) together account for about 55 per cent of total number of operative/live KCC cards.

11.4.3 Institutional Credit to SF/MF

Ground level credit (GLC) flow to agriculture has improved substantially during the last decade. Along with the general trend, credit disbursement to SF/MF has

also improved. During 2016–17 while 72.1 per cent of the agriculture accounts belong to SF/MF category, only 50 per cent of loans disbursed flowed to SF/MF (Table 11.5). It is observed that though all agencies are actively involved in lending to SF/MF, agency-wise differences are found to be significant in terms of share in number of accounts and amounts involved.

The comparison of the number of accounts and amounts disbursed at two points of time indicates that in terms of the loan amount disbursed, the share of SF/MF, which averaged at 35.3 per cent during 2007–8, showed an improvement during the year 2016–17 (50 per cent). The increase in the share of SF/MF in the total agriculture GLC was more evident in case of commercial banks (16.6 percentage points), followed by coop banks (15.6 percentage points), and was least in case of RRBs (7.7 percentage points). The changes in the number of accounts and loan amounts have made corresponding changes in the average loan amount of SF/MF accounts which have almost doubled during the period.

The increased GLC towards SF/MF was attained more through credit deepening than widening. This was sharper in case of commercial banks. Despite increases in the number of holdings and expanding share in total area under cultivation, there is no concomitant growth in GLC to SF/MF. Therefore, it is imperative to bring down the barriers to SF/MF lending and for the social face of banking to view SF/MF lending favourably so that timely and affordable credit to this resource-constrained group can promote inclusive growth.

Table 11.5 Share of SF/MF in Ground Level Credit Flow to Agriculture (2007–8 and 2016–17)

Agency	2007–8								2016–17							
	No. of Accounts (in Lakhs)		Loan Disbursed (in Rs Crore)		Avg. Loan Amt of SF/ MF (in Rs)				No. of Accounts (in Lakhs)		Loan Disbursed (in Rs Crore)		Avg. Loan Amt of SF/ MF (in Rs)			
	Total	SF/MF	Total	SF/MF					Total	SF/MF	Total	SF/MF				
Commercial banks	174.8	97.4 (55.8)	81,088	52,231 (28.8)	53,625				664.16	482.47 (72.64)	799,781	362,676 (45.35)	75,171			
Cooperative banks	201.8	117.9 (58.4)	48,258	22,609 (46.9)	19,176				269.54	190.10 (70.53)	142,758	89,179 (62.47)	46,912			
RRBs	62.7	42.2 (67.3)	25,312	15,019 (59.3)	35,590				136.98	98.98 (72.26)	123,216	82,497 (66.95)	83,347			
Total	439.3	257.5 (58.6)	254,658	89,859 (35.3)	34,897				1,070.68	771.55 (72.06)	1,065,756	534,351 (50.14)	69,257			

Note: Figures in parentheses refer to share in total of that agency.
Source: CPD, NABARD.

11.4.4 Refinance Support from NABARD for Short-Term Production Credit

Conceptually, refinance from NABARD is expected to supplement and not supplant, the internal lendable resources of the borrowing banks in order to augment the flow of credit to the ultimate beneficiary and direct it to desired purposes. There are a number of windows from which NABARD provides credit to eligible institutions to facilitate the growth of farm as well as non-farm sectors in the country. Occasionally, additional facilities have also been provided for ad hoc purposes for a short period. For example, a special facility was extended in 1990 to provide medium-term loans to state governments to enable them to meet their share in the write-off of loans disbursed by cooperative banks, which fell within the scope of the Government of India's ARDR Scheme, 1989. The discussion in the present section is limited to refinance support to short-term production credit only since the credit flow presented in the earlier section related to short-term production credit.

The trend in total refinance support from NABARD for production and marketing credit to StCBs and RRBs, which peaked in 1990-1 (69.3 per cent of total short-term loans issued by Coop and RRB together), showed continuous decline till 2003-4, before it took a U-turn and reached 43.4 per cent again during 2013-14 (see Figures 11.4 and 11.5). The decline in share of NABARD support from 1990-1 till 2003-4 is mainly on account of mobilization of cheaper resources by coops and rRBs (in comparison to rate

of refinance from NABARD) for their ST lending operations. Similarly, the reversal of trend in refinance support to RRBs and cooperatives in 2003-4 could be a culmination of various policy interventions like doubling of credit programme, revival package under Vaidyanathan Committee's recommendations aimed at reviving the STCCS, recapitalization of week RRBs (2010-11), and so on.

11.4.5 Ground Level Investment Credit Flow and NABARD Support to RFIs

Investment in agriculture is generally undertaken for acquiring physical assets that result in the creation of a stream of incremental income over a period of time. Capital formation through investment in agriculture helps in improving the stock of farm assets—tractor, tubewell, other equipment and tools and thereby enhances the productivity of resources employed on the farm; this, in turn, enables the farmers to use their resources, particularly land and labour, more productively.

While public sector investment is undertaken for building necessary infrastructure, private investment in agriculture is made either for augmenting productivity of natural resources or for undertaking such activities that supplement income sources of farmers. Private sector investment includes investments made by private corporates and households. The corporate sector investment includes investment by organized corporate bodies such as big private companies and unorganized entities such as sugar cooperatives and milk cooperatives.

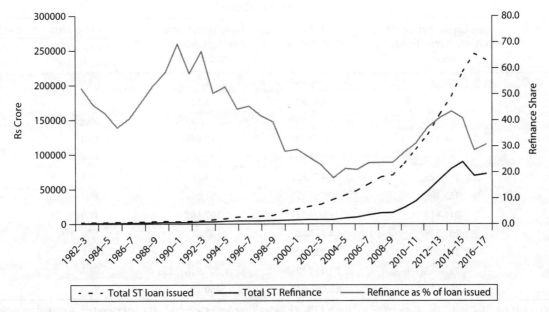

Figure 11.4   Short-term Loans and Refinance to Coop and Regional Rural Banks (RRBs) (Total)

Source: NABARD Annual Report (various issues).

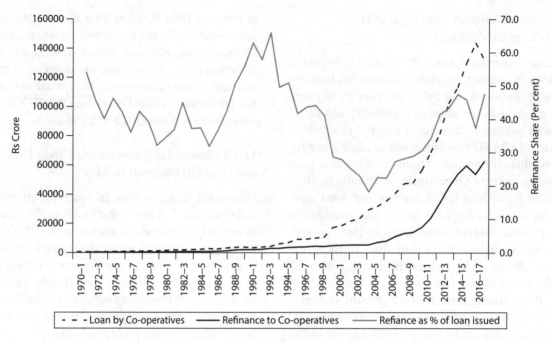

Figure 11.5   Loans Issued and Refinance Availed by Cooperatives

Source: NABARD Annual Report (various issues).

The household sector investment comprises investment in farm equipment, machinery, irrigation, land improvement, and land reclamation. It is now well established that if the term loans are utilized for asset generation at the farmer's level, it helps in accelerating capital formation.

The available evidence indicates the strong association between the term loans disbursed and private sector capital formation in agriculture (Table 11.6 and Figure 11.6). It is observed that the long-term credit is the major driver of the private sector gross capital formation (GCF)

Table 11.6   Gross Capital Formation—Private Sector and Direct Institutional Long-Term Credit to Agriculture and Allied Activities
(Amount in Rs Crore)

Year	Gross Capital Formation in Agriculture—Private Sector	GDP at Market Price	Long Term Credit to Agriculture and Allied	Long-Term Credit as % of	
				GCFA—Private Sector	GDP at Market Price
1982–3	2,488	196,644	1,593	64.0	0.81
1989–90	6,572	436,893	4,129	62.8	0.95
1994–5	13,645	1,045,590	6,841	50.1	0.65
1999–2000	48,126	2,023,130	15,968	33.2	0.79
2004–5	59,909	3,242,209	33,555	56.0	1.03
2009–10	151,325	6,477,827	74,269	49.1	1.15
2010–11	165,396	7,784,115	91,217	55.2	1.17
2011–12	214,818	9,009,722	107,162	49.9	1.19
2012–13	232,328	10,113,281	133,875	57.6	1.32
2013–14	290,008	11,233,522	181,688	62.6	1.62
2014–15	291,113	12,445,128	209,916	72.1	1.69
2015–16	274,126	13,682,035	250,197	91.3	1.83

Sources: (i) Data on GCF and GDP: Data extracted from *EPWRF India Time Series*, available at www.epwrf.in, accessed on 6 November 2017. Data from 1982–3 to 2012–13 is based on 2004–5 series at current pices and from 2013–14 to 2015–16; (ii) Long-Term Credit LT RBI from *Handbook of Statistics on Indian Economy* (up to 2011–12) and *NABARD Annual Repor*t for 2012–13 and 2013–14.

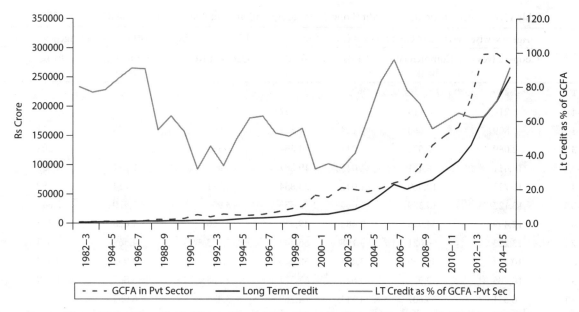

Figure 11.6   Gross Capital Formation and Long-Term Credit to Agriculture and Allied Activities

Source: NABARD Annual Report (various issues) and *Agricultural Statistics at a Glance* (various issues), Ministry of Agriculture and Farmers' Welfare, GoI.

in agriculture as reflected by its share of the private sector GCF in agriculture (Table 11.6). Thus, capital formation in agriculture is predominantly dependent on the extent of investment credit.

The agency-wise direct institutional credit (long term) indicates that loans issued by the cooperatives and commercial banks were quite comparable till 2003–4 but thereafter, the share of commercial banks in long-term loan issued to agriculture sector increased to 84.2 per cent, leaving just 5.5 per cent for cooperative banks and another 10.3 per cent for RRBs (Table 11.7 and Figure 11.7).

11.4.6 Refinance Support from NABARD for Long-Term Credit to Agriculture and Allied Sector

NABARD provides medium- and long-term refinance for fixed investment in the farm and rural non-farm sectors. The share of refinance in total long-term loan disbursed by banks, which had peaked in 1993–4 (52.2 per cent), showed continuous decline thereafter and reached its lowest point in 2013–14 with just 11.8 per cent contribution in total long-term loans issued to agriculture and allied activities (Figure 11.8). The decline in contribution of refinance by NABARD was quite steep after 2001–2, which could be on account of increased credit flow initiated by banks in response to the call by government to 'double the agricultural credit' within

three years (2004–5 to 2006–7) and NABARD preferring to maintain the same growth trajectory during that period and after (Figure 11.8).

The share of various investment purposes in total refinance disbursed by NABARD indicates that during the initial periods (1982–3), three major activities—minor irrigation (34.7 per cent), farm mechanization (20.9 per cent), and Swarnajayanti Gram Swarozgar Yojana (SGSY) (26.3 per cent)—together absorbed the major portion (81.9 per cent) of long-term refinance disbursed by the NABARD (Table 11.8).

However, there was a major shift in sectoral flow of refinance, and in 2016–17, maximum refinance was disbursed for NFS (35 per cent) and farm mechanization (20.7 per cent).

11.4.7 Credit Support to Rural Infrastructure Sector

11.4.7.1 Rural Infrastructure Development Fund (RIDF)

Recognizing the fact that adequate quality infrastructure in rural areas is necessary for increasing the productivity and efficiency of agriculture in the form of improving the credit absorbing capacity, enhancing the productivity of crops and livestock, generating employment, and increasing the farmers' income, and so on, the Government of India in 1995–6 decided to institute a dedicated fund called 'Rural Infrastructure Development Fund (RIDF)'

Table 11.7   Direct Institutional Credit (Long Term) to Agriculture and Refinance by NABARD Against That

Year	Agency-wise Investment Credit Issued (in Rs Crore)				LT Refinance by NABARD to Various Agencies (in Rs Crore)			
	Cooperatives	Commercial Banks	RRBs	Total	Cooperatives	Commercial Banks	RRBs	Total*
1970–1	229							
1973–4	214	114	0	327				
1982–3	809	660	124	1,593	597	45	61	703
1992–3	2,089	2,528	247	4,864	1,889	168	302	2,359
2002–3	10,411	8,431	1,045	19,887	4,637	1,242	1,539	7,419
2003–4	10,723	12,069	1,042	23,834	4,281	1,714	1,589	7,605
2004–5	13,122	18,389	2,043	33,555	3,954	2,570	2,049	8,577
2005–6	12,499	34,955	2,484	49,938	3,256	4,028	1,332	8,622
2006–7	13,223	50,021	3,198	66,442	2,873	4,569	1,353	8,795
2007–8	10,253	45,229	3,461	58,943	2,777	3,952	2,314	9,046
2008–9	10,765	52,924	3,648	67,337	2,788	5,867	1,879	10,535
2009–10	6,551	63,607	4,111	74,269	3,473	6,057	2,457	12,009
2010–11	9,083	76,729	5,405	912,17	3,708	7,348	2,288	13,486
2011–12	6,134	102,689	6,048	114,871	3,637	8,434	3,086	15,422
2012–13	8,611	118,372	6,892	133,875	3,812	8,709	4,754	17,674
2013–14	6,390	167,570	7,728	181,688	3,528	13,255	4,304	21,486
2014–15	8,119	188,640	13,157	209,916	6,742	13,675	10,221	31,427
2015–16	9,492	223,024	17,681	250,197	9,489	22,824	12,140	48,064
2016–17	10,878	347,205	18,215	376,298	9,832	25,834	11,370	53,506

Note: 1. Credit data up to 1990–1 pertain to the period July–June and April-March thereafter. In case of credit by SCBs, data for all the years pertain to July–June period. 2. RRBs came into existence in 1975–6. 3. Credit data for cooperatives cover only PACS as short-term loans are being provided by them. 4. Data on total loans issued includes loans issued by the state governments. 5. Refinance total includes refinance to NBFCs and NABARD subsidiaries also.

Source: (i) Credit Issued: Reserve Bank of India—*Handbook of Statistics on Indian Economy* (September 2015) for data up to 2010–11; (ii) Investment credit issued from 2011–12 to 2016–17 from NABARD; (iii) Refinance Data: Department of Refinance, NABARD, Mumbai.

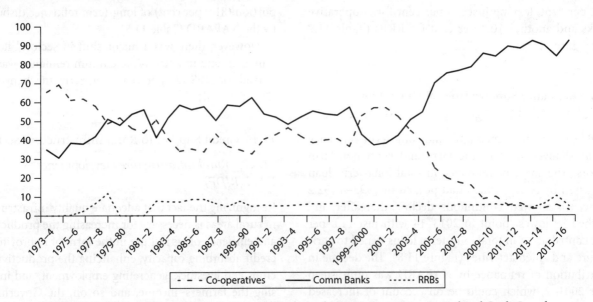

Figure 11.7   Share of Cooperatives, Commercial Banks, and RRBs in Long-Term Agricultural Credit Issued

Source: NABARD Annual Report (various issues).

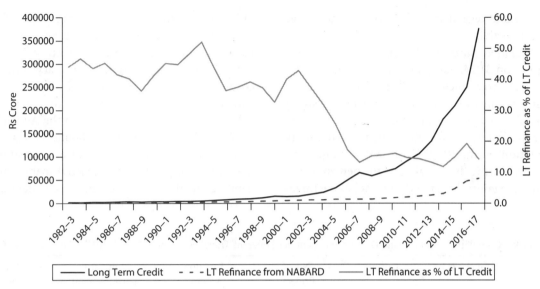

Figure 11.8   Long-term Credit Issued by Banks and Refinance Disbursed by NABARD Against That

Source: NABARD Annual Report (various issues).

Table 11.8   Purpose-wise Share in Total Refinance Disbursed by NABARD for Investment Activities (Figure in Percentage)

Year	Minor Irrigation	Land Development	Farm Mechanization	Plan/Hort	Dairy, Poultry, and SGP	Fisheries	Stock/ Market	NFS	SGSY + SHG	Others	Total (in Rs Crore)
1982–3	34.7	3.0	20.9	3.8	0.0	0.0	1.8	0.0	26.3	9.4	703
1992–3	22.2	0.5	20.5	4.2	6.5	1.2	0.6	7.3	25.7	4.7	2,523
2002–3	10.0	2.9	11.7	3.4	12.9	0.4	0.6	14.5	12.0	18.6	8,514
2012–13	3.9	4.3	12.0	7.2	6.8	0.2	1.6	27.2	21.2	8.8	18,958
2016–17	2.1	10.8	20.7	4.9	6.0	0.4	0.2	34.6	10.6	9.7	53,506

Note: 'Others' include forestry, biogas, SC/ST Action Plan, Rural Housing (2002–3 and 2003–4 only), and so on.
Source: NABARD Annual Reports.

with NABARD with the sole objective of providing low-cost fund support to state governments and state-owned corporations for quick completion of ongoing projects relating to medium and minor irrigation, soil conservation, watershed management, and other forms of rural infrastructure.

Dr Manmohan Singh, the then union finance minister, while announcing the establishment of the RIDF in his budget speech on 15 March 1995 stated:

Inadequacy of public investment in agriculture is today a matter of general concern. This is an area, which is the responsibility of States. But many States have neglected investment in infrastructure for agriculture. There are many rural infrastructure projects, which have been started but are lying incomplete for want of resources. They represent

a major loss of potential income and employment to rural population.

With an initial allocation of Rs 2,000 crore, known as tranche I, the RIDF has since been continued with annual allocation being announced in the union budget, current tranche being the XXII tranche (2016–17) with an allocation of Rs 25,000 crore. The fund is supported by deposits from scheduled commercial banks with shortfalls in lending to priority sector and/or agriculture and/or weaker sections. The importance of RIDF is that it has redirected bank credit meant for rural and priority sectors back to the rural economy. At present, 36 activities are funded under RIDF. These 36 activities are broadly classified in three categories, namely

(i) agriculture and related sector, (ii) social sectors, and (iii) rural connectivity.

The cumulative number of projects and amount sanctioned as on 31 March 2017 have reached 589,784 and Rs 287,129 crore (including Bharat Nirman Fund). As against this sanction, the total disbursement stood at Rs 215,605 crore. A special allocation of Rs 18,500 crore was made under 'Bharat Nirman' Fund for its implementation during RIDF XII to XV to fund rural road projects. During the initial years the percentage of disbursements against the phased amount has declined.

This was due to the lower phasing period for certain projects, which was later rectified and the implementation period was increased resulting in better and quicker utilization of RIDF. A summary of tranche-wise corpus, number of projects and amount sanctioned, and amount disbursed as on 31 March 2017 is given in Table 11.9 (see also Table 11A.1 in the Appendix).

Now, RIDF accounts for a significant share in public investment in rural infrastructure constituting nearly one-fifth of the pie. The share of RIDF loan to outstanding liabilities of the states has shown an increasing trend

Table 11.9   Cumulative Sanctions and Disbursements under Different Tranches (as on 31 March 2017) (Amount in Rs Crore)

Group of Tranche	Tranche No.	Corpus	No. of Projects Sanctioned	Sanction Amount	Cumulative Disbursement	Disbursement as % of Sanction (Cumulative)
Closed	I	2,000	4,168	1,906.21	1,760.86	92.38
	II	2,500	8,193	2,636.08	2,397.93	90.97
	III	2,500	14,345	2,732.69	2,453.52	89.78
	IV	3,000	6,171	2,902.55	2,477.38	85.51
	V	3,500	12,106	3,434.53	3,054.98	88.95
	VI	4,500	43,168	4,488.51	4,070.64	90.69
	VII	5,000	24,598	4,582.32	4,052.81	88.44
	VIII	5,500	20,887	5,950.2	5,148.48	86.53
	IX	5,500	19,544	5,638.26	4,916.50	87.20
	X	8,000	16,482	7,650.51	6,568.70	85.86
	XI	8,000	29,670	8,262.48	7,374.41	89.27
	XII	10,000	41,536	10,019.76	9,021.65	90.04
	XIII	12,000	36,694	12,537.79	11,253.76	89.76
	XIV	14,000	85,287	14,568.21	12,722.74	87.80
	Sub-Total	86,000	362,849	87,310.10	77,274.35	88.51
On-going	XV	14,000	37,762	15,341.72	12,893.12	84.04
	XVI	16,000	41,711	18,276.80	14,979.49	81.96
	XVII	16,000	16,719	18,751.15	14,849.27	79.19
	XVII (WH)	2,000	1,066	1,451.36	10,82.39	74.58
	XVIII	15,000	44,196	1,8426.08	14,824.57	80.45
	XVIII (WH)	5,000	2,406	1,998.89	1,380.08	69.04
	XIX	20,000	28,727	22,735.50	15,583.59	68.54
	XX	25,000	33,306	28,601.87	1,3875.34	48.51
	XXI	25,000	13,345	28,829.65	9,225.50	32.00
	XXII	25,000	17,842	27,147.61	0.00	0.00
	Sub-Total	163,000	226,935	158,618.00	98,693.34	62.22
Total		249,000	589,784	245,928.10	175,967.69	71.55
Bharat Nirman		18,500		18,500.00	18,500.00	100.00
Grand Total		267,500	589,784	287,129.00	215,605.00	73.54

Source: NABARD.

Table 11.10   Broad Purpose-wise Sanctions (I–XXII) under RIDF (Amount in Rs Crore) (as on 31 March 2017)

Purpose	Agriculture and Related Sector		Rural Connectivity		Social Sector Projects		Total
	Irrigation	Agri-related Projects	Bridges	Roads	Social Sector Schemes	Power Sector Schemes	
No. of Projects	302,356	48,299	20,869	117,878	109,678	769	599,849
% Share to Total Projects	50	8	3	20	18	0.01	100
Amount Sanctioned	81,405.39	32,303.72	30,374.06	78,835.02	43,213.09	2,498.07	268,629.35
% Share to Total Sanction	30	12	11	30	16	1	100

Source: NABARD.

from 1 per cent in 2005 to 2.91 per cent in 2014 (*NABARD Annual Report* 2015–16). The inter-state variation ranged between 1.24 per cent in Maharashtra and 7.51 per cent in Odisha during 2013–14. The fund is becoming increasingly popular among state governments in view of the cheaper cost of fund, quicker appraisal, timely disbursement by NABARD, and timely completion of projects.

The broad sector-wise classification of the number of projects sanctioned and amount sanctioned (Table 11.10) indicates that agriculture and related sector accounts for about 58 per cent (comprising irrigation projects 50 per cent and other projects 8 per cent) followed by rural connectivity comprising 23 per cent (bridges 3 per cent and roads 20 per cent) and social sector projects comprising another 18.4 per cent. As for as the share of these sectors in amount sanctioned, agriculture and related sector accounts for 42.3 per cent (comprising irrigation projects of 30.2 per cent and other projects of 12.1 per cent), followed by rural connectivity comprising 41.3 per cent (bridges 11.7 per cent and roads 29.6 per cent) and social sector projects comprising another 16.3 per cent.

Now, it is well recognized by all the stakeholders that the support to state government under RIDF is very critical for building up critical rural infrastructure in the country. As already indicated, the assistance under RIDF constitutes about one-fifth of the investments made by the various state governments in the rural infrastructure sector. Third-party evaluation of various projects indicates that there several factors, namely, timely appraisal and sanction, quick reimbursement of funds on a project-tied basis, and participative prioritization and monitoring of projects by a high-power committee chaired by the chief secretary of the state government have contributed to the successful completion of projects sanctioned under RIDF.

The RIDF investments have helped in the creation of additional irrigation potential (29.129 million hectare) and construction of a network of rural roads

(4,28,130 km) and bridges (1,037 km) for better connectivity in far-flung areas (Table 11.11). Social projects assisted under RIDF have brought improvement in quality of rural life through education, health and sanitation, drinking water supply, and other projects. In addition to the creation of these infrastructures, RIDF projects have also created employment to the tune of 18.3 million of recurring nature and additional 128.7 million of non-recurring nature.

In terms of cumulative economic benefits, RIDF has directly added about Rs 53,682 crore to the GDP and generated sizeable recurring and non-recurring employment in rural areas. Other more tangible economic benefits resulting from RIDF, and concurred by some recent studies, include diversification in cropping pattern and increase in productivity, increase in household income, creation of new assets by rural households, stability in farm income, increase in expenditure on education, increase in credit flow in command area, increase in value and use of land, and so on (NABARD Annual Report 2016–17).

Being convinced by the success of RIDF, the government of India kept instituting various other funds aimed at creating infrastructure in rural areas from time to time. 'Bharat Nirman' Fund (RIDF XII–XV) was one such which was added to finance rural road projects. This year too, the Hon'ble Union Finance Minister, during his Budget Speech 2016–17, announced the institution of a dedicated Long-Term Irrigation Fund (LTIF) in NABARD with an initial corpus of Rs 20,000 crore for fast-tracking the implementation of incomplete major and medium irrigation projects under Accelerated Irrigation Programme Benefit (AIPB) and also two national projects. A total fund requirement of Rs 91,807 crore has been estimated for the period 2016–20 to finance the identified 99 incomplete AIPB projects and two national projects by Ministry of Water Resources (MoWR), GoI.

Three other very important initiatives to support rural infrastructure involving NABARD have been put in place

Table 11.11 Anticipated Benefits on Completion of RIDF Projects (as on 17 March 2017)

Tranche No.	Irrigation				Roads and Bridges			Others
	Creation of Irrigation Potential (Thousand Ha)	Value of Production (in Rs Crore)	No. of Recurring Jobs (Thousand Numbers)	Non-Recurring Employment (Lakh Man-days)	Road Length Covered ('Thousand km)	Bridge Length Covered ('Thousand metre)	Non-recurring Employment (Lakh Man-days)	Non-recurring Employment (Lakh Man-days)
Closed Tranches (I to XIV)	14,438.26	19,413.00	7,053.47	22,524.27	272.20	501.91	29,256.96	13372.77
XV	1,159.37	2,745.00	1,063	2,119.67	19.08	78.55	3,953.29	2,649.72
XVI	880.43	1,652.29	424	1,752.84	26.61	86.85	3,268.20	2,746.45
XVII	1,964.39	6,877.16	533	1,850.49	18.22	64.80	2,310.03	2,729.75
XVIII	1,536.50	3,112.03	1,233	1,569.69	20.08	78.63	4,843.70	1,913.17
XIX	1,861.46	8,178.00	719	1,719.12	19.73	73.44	3,072.58	1,899.47
XX	4,039.60	5,865.71	6,887	2,637.60	20.15	77.00	3,745.54	3,218.27
XXI	1,612.76	3,673.47	346	8,070.78	23.86	53.92	3,234.58	3,379.80
XXII	1,635.86	2,165.30	467	91,725.78	8.19	22.29	2,329.69	8,268.28
Subtotal	14,690.35	34,268.96	11,670.75	111,445.97	155.93	535.47	26,757.61	26,804.91
Grand Total	29,128.61	53,681.96	18,724.22	133,970.24	428.13	1037.38	56,014.57	40,177.68

Source: NABARD.

to speed up the rural infrastructure in the country. They are summarized in the following sections.

11.4.7.2 NABARD Infrastructure Development Assistance

NABARD Infrastructure Development Assistance (NIDA) supports state-owned institutions and corporations for both off- and on-budget infrastructure, and companies and cooperatives in creating rural infrastructure. The scope of funding under NIDA has been broadened by covering public private partnership (PPP) and non-PPP projects executed by registered entities such as companies, cooperatives, and so on. Agriculture, roads and bridges, rural transport, renewable energy, power transmission, drinking water and sanitation, and social and commercial infrastructure in rural areas are some of the major sectors covered under NIDA. The cumulative term loans sanctioned since 2010–11 under NIDA stood at Rs 15,746.74 crore spread across 52 projects and the corresponding disbursement is Rs 6,146.32 crore as on 31 March 2017 (Table 11.12).

11.4.7.3 Warehouse Infrastructure Fund

In developed countries, inventory credit plays an important role in providing agricultural producers access to credit and it serves effectively in overcoming credit constraints. Credit extended against commodities stored in warehouses is a mainstay in developed countries, where

the prerequisites for facilitating such financial transaction (legal, enforcement, skill requirements, and the like) are met. Appropriate inventory finance contributes not only directly to an increase in access to credit of producers but also indirectly to reduce the instability of inter-seasonal commodity prices. Warehouse receipts finance constitutes an effective instrument in ensuring loan security and consequently could add to credit enhancement and transformation of poor and low-income farming households from non-creditworthy to creditworthy ones.

The major objective of the Warehouse Infrastructure Fund (WIF) was to provide credit to the public and private sectors for creation and augmentation of decentralized, modern, and scientific dry warehouses and cold chain infrastructure in the country to offer a better price discovery mechanism to farmers and producers, ensure better post-harvest liquidity, and preclude distress sale. Against a corpus of Rs 10,000 crore allowed by the Government of India, the cumulative sanctions under WIF stood at Rs 8,848 crore. A total of 9,096 projects envisaging creation of 9.97 MMT capacity of storage infrastructure have been sanctioned. Cumulatively, a loan amount of Rs 3,529 crore has been disbursed till 31 March 2017 (*NABARD Annual Report* 2016–17).

11.4.7.4 Special Fund for Food Processing

The Government of India set up a Food Processing Fund (FPF) in 2014–15 in NABARD with a corpus of Rs 2,000 crore, to make available affordable credit for

Table 11.12 Cumulative NIDA Term Loans by Activities (as on 31 March 2017)

Sector	Units	Loan Sanctioned (in Rs Crore)	Disbursement (in Rs Crore)
Bridge	1	462.60	185.00
Cyclone damage restoration	4	1,063.25	1,169.12
Drinking water	2	3,144.80	1,384.37
Road	6	3,328.55	360.00
Sewerage	1	70.69	59.48
Solar power	2	448.01	72.96
Wind power	2	225.00	203.10
Warehousing	3	220.12	206.16
Transmission	26	5,364.93	2,184.79
Market yard	1	59.97	0.00
Hydro power	1	145.74	0.00
Renewable energy	1	95.00	0.00
Irrigation	2	1,118.08	321.34
Total	**52**	**15,746.74**	**6,146.32**

Source: NABARD.

establishing designated food parks and for setting up of individual food processing units therein. This fund is being operationalized in coordination with the Ministry of Food Processing Industries (MoFPI), Government of India, and the financial assistance in the form of capital grant available under various schemes of MoFPI is dovetailed with FPF, wherever applicable. Financial assistance from FPF is available to state governments, entities promoted by state governments, joint ventures, cooperatives, federation of cooperatives, special purpose vehicles, farmers' producers organizations, corporates, companies, entrepreneurs, and so on. As on 31 March 2017, NABARD had sanctioned term loans for 10 mega food park projects and two processing units in designated food paks, involving a committed term loan of Rs 464.49 crore. The cumulative disbursement till 31 March 2017 in respect of sanctioned projects stood at Rs 144.49 crore (*NABARD Annual Report* 2016–17).

11.4.8 Credit Support to Microfinance Sector

The microfinance sector, particularly in India, has played a very significant role in achieving the objectives of (*a*) eradicating poverty and hunger, and (*b*) women's empowerment. As far as the first goal is concerned, global poverty (people living on less than $1.25 a day) has declined significantly over the past two decades from 36 per cent in 1990 to 12 per cent in 2015. However, the cause of concern for us is that nearly 60 per cent of the world's 836 million extremely poor people (those living on less than $1 a day) live in just five countries—India, Nigeria, China, Bangladesh, and the Democratic Republic of the Congo.

The microfinance sector has seen a spurt during the last two decades. The number of institutions providing microfinance services has grown many fold and the quantum of credit (outstanding) made available to the poor and financially excluded clients by the microfinance institutions (MFIs) has reached Rs 106,916 crore extended to more than 4 crore clients as on 31 March 2017 ('The Status of Microfinance in India 2016–17'). The Government of India, state governments and the RBI have created conducive policy and regulatory frameworks for MFIs to operate in the country. These factors go a long way in infusing confidence among all the stakeholders.

SHG Bank Linkage Programme (SBLP) pioneered by NABARD a little more than two decades ago from a pilot of 500 SHGs in 1992 covers about 86 lakh SHGs and nearly 10.1 crore poor families in the country as on 31 March 2017. These groups have savings deposits with banks to the tune of Rs 16,114 crore and nearly 48.48 lakh SHGs, having credit outstanding of more than Rs 61,581 crore with the formal lending institutions. During the year 2016–17, a bank loan of Rs 38,781 crore was extended to SHG under SBLP and a refinance of Rs 5,659 crore has been extended by NABARD to RFI against that bank loan amount. Cumulative disbursement of refinance by NABARD for SHG lending now stands at Rs 43,293.60 crore. Year-wise credit by bank under SBLP and refinance support from NABARD against that amount is presented in Figure 11.9.

The phenomenal growth of SBLP is the outcome of concerted efforts of various stakeholders including NGOs, self-help promoting institutions, capacity building agencies, government programmes, and others under the overall guidance and directions of MoRD, NABARD, and RBI. The SBLP has emerged as the largest microfinance movement in the world in terms of coverage. The SBLP is also the foremost tool of financial inclusion. Primarily being a savings led model, SBLP contributed to augmenting financial inclusion and financial literacy among the rural poor.

NABARD, being a pioneer in the field of SBLP, has implemented another important initiative recently by launching a pilot on the digitization of SHG records. Two pilots on digitization of books of SHGs are being implemented under project EShakti, one in Dhule district of Maharashtra and another in Ramgarh district of Jharkhand. The pilot now covers more than 24 districts across the country. The data is housed in the website https://eshakti.nabard.org being maintained by NABARD. The digitization of SHG accounts will repose the faith of bankers in the SHG programme. Digital availability of data will help in generating reports online, monitoring and credit rating of SHGs, and it will also lead to reduction in transaction cost. This can also help in financial inclusion of individual members of SHGs through various Government of India schemes such as Pradhan Mantri Jan Dhan Yojana (PMJDY), Atal Pension Yojana (APY), and so on.

Similarly NABARD has propagated another group concept under its microfinance interventions called Joint Liability Group (JLG) in 2004–5 as a pilot project in 8 states with the support of 13 RRBs with a view to developing effective credit product for mid-segment clients such as tenant farmers, share croppers, oral lessees, and farmers who do not have access to proper land records. Based on the experience of the pilot project, the concept was operationalized in 2006–7. Apart from extending 100 per cent refinance support to banks, NABARD also extends financial support for awareness creation and capacity

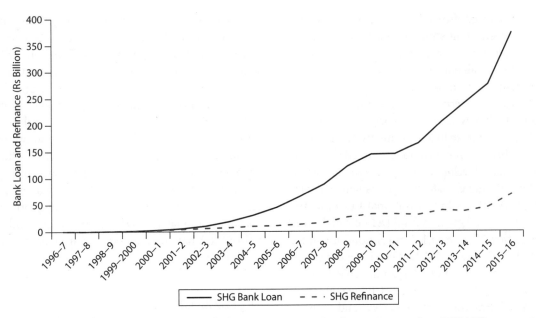

Figure 11.9   Bank Loan to Self-Help Groups (SHGs) and Refinance Support from NABARD

Source: NABARD Annual Report (various issues).

building of all stakeholders of this programme. Besides, NABARD extends grant support for the formation and nurturing of JLGs to banks and other JLG promoting agencies. As on 31 March 2017, 22.57 lakh JLGs (a jump of nearly 5.05 lakh JLGs over the previous year) have been promoted. The cumulative credit support to JLGs stood at Rs 17,337 crore as on 31 Marh 2016.

Institutional credit support, particularly though SBLP and JLG financing, has not only enabled the rural poor households to keep themselves away from the usurious informal lenders but also facilitated the underprivileged communities in less developed regions with income generating opportunities. Penetration of SHGs mitigated financial distress among the poor and contributed to stemming rural poverty. SBLP, though not basically designed as a poverty alleviation programme, was pursued as a potential platform for poverty alleviation by GoI.

11.5 FUTURE OUTLOOK

In spite of so many initiatives of the Government of India, RBI, and NABARD as discussed in the previous sections, the dream of providing easy and timely credit to 100 per cent farmers is yet to be realized. The results of the NSSO survey 'Key Indicators of Debt and Investment in India' (NSS KI [70/18.2]) show that non-institutional agencies played a major role in advancing credit to the households, particularly in rural India. The non-institutional agencies had advanced credit to 19 per cent

of rural households, while the institutional agencies had advanced credit to 17 per cent households in 2012–13.

Another major challenge Indian agriculture is facing since a long time is low productivity of major foodgrains and other crops, especially of pulses and oilseeds. Concerted efforts need to be ensured, not only from the food security point of view but also to transfer some amount of land from subsistence farming to commercial farming to make agriculture, particularly the small farms, viable with a view to retaining the agriculturists remaining in farming activity. Ensuring economic viability of the agricultural holdings and linking them to the integrated market systems is still an unfinished agenda that we need to achieve in the near future.

Although the country is now self-sufficient in food production, agricultural farming has turned non-profitable over time due to rising costs and uneconomical holdings. Deviating from past strategies aimed at increasing the profitability of crop cultivation, the Government of India has now set the target of 'doubling of farmers' income by 2022', having a direct impact on almost half of the population, aiming for a sense of income security to farmers in a time-bound manner. While scholars like Dr M.S. Swaminathan (*Financial Chronicle* 2016) and Chand (2016) have argued that doubling of farmers' income is possible, some scholars like Dr Ashok Gulati and Sweta Saini (2016) and Ashok V. Desai (2016) have expressed doubts about achieving the target by 2022. The task is very tough but a concerted effort in the right direction by all the stakeholders can help us in reaching quite close to the target. The Prime Minister himself has highlighted a seven-point strategy to achieve the target of 'doubling of farmers' income by 2022', which is serving as guiding factors to all policy planners.

Climate change has now become one of the most important areas of concern not just for India but for the entire world, which may adversely impact the net income from farming through reduced productivity of various field crops. NABARD, with its mandate aimed at sustainable and equitable development, has taken up various initiatives for building climate change resilience of rural livelihoods. NABARD is India's National Implementing Entity (NIE) for the adaptation fund (AF) created under the United Nations Framework Convention on Climate Change (UNFCCC). NABARD has also been designated as NIE for implementation of adaptation projects under National Adaptation Fund for Climate Change (NAFCC) by Ministry of Environment, Forestry and Climate Change, Government of India. Moreover, NABARD has been designated as 'Direct Access Entity' for the internatonal 'Green Climate Fund'. Through these funding mechanism, NABARD has supported 28 projects in different states of the country. In addition, a number of other projects are in the pipeline. Although these steps are in the right direction, it is just a beginning and we have to accomplish a very huge task in this regard.

11.6 SUMMING UP

NABARD is one of the few institutions in India that has done well on all the three aspects of sustainability, namely, 3Ps—people, profit, and planet (also called 'the triple bottom lines' as coined by John Elkington). Despite the fact that NABARD is a development bank,

its phenomenal growth in terms of the size of the balance sheet from Rs 4,519 crore to Rs 3.20 lakh crore in 33 years (69 times) speaks volumes about its success on the profit parameter. NABARD's efforts in terms of the 'people account' can be gauged from the success of its various microfinance and other interventions—SBLP, JLGs, financial inclusion, and tribal development programmes, which provided livelihood opportunity to more than 70 million families. NABARD's efforts on the 'planet account' include its various interventions relating to watershed development, climate change, and so on, and have been appreciated at various national as well as international fora. However, having said that what NABARD has done so far is commendable, it still has miles to go.

REFERENCES

Chand, Ramesh. 2016. 'Why Doubling Farm Income by 2022 Is Possible'. *The Indian Express*, April 15.

Desai, A.V. 2016. 'Budçget 2016: Jaitley's Promise to Double Farmers' Income in 5 Years Is Next to Impossible'. *First Post*, March 2.

Gulati, Ashok and Shweta Saini. 2016. 'PM's Agri-vision and the Harsh Reality'. *The Financial Express*, June 20.

National Bank for Agriculture and Rural Development. 2011. *Annual Report 2010–11*. Mumbai.

Nicholson, F.A. 1960. 'Report Regarding Possibility of Introducing Land and Agricultural Banks into Madras Presidency 1875'. Bombay.

Satish, P. 2012. 'Innovations in Agricultural Credit Market—Rationalisation of Policy Response'. *Indian Journal of Agricultural Economics* 67(1).

Financial Chronicle. 2016. 'How to Double Farmers' Income'. March 24. https://www.pressreader.com/india/financial-chronicle/20160324/282252369654047.

APPENDIX

Table 11A.1 State-wise/Tranche-wise Cumulative Sanctions and Disbursements (as on 31 March 2017) (Amount in Rs Crore)

Name of State	Total of All Closed Tranches (I–XIV)			Total of All On-going Tranches (XV–XXII)			Warehousing (XVII–XVIII)			Total of All Tranches		
	Amount Sanctioned	Amount Disbursed	Percentage Utilization	Amount Sanctioned	Amount Disbursed	Percentage Utilization	Amount Sanctioned	Amount Disbursed	Percentage Utilization	Amount Sanctioned	Amount Disbursed	Percentage Utilization
Andhra Pradesh/ Telangana	10,583.00	9,009.90	85.14	9,449.28	6,212.10	65.74	105.70	84.00	79.47	20,137.98	15,306.00	76.01
Arunachal Pradesh	681.63	615.63	90.32	781.3	392.36	50.22	0.00	0.00	0.00	1,462.93	1,007.99	68.90
Assam	1,546.02	1,275.74	82.52	3,546.92	1,981.68	55.87	49.46	0.00	0.00	5,142.40	3,257.42	63.34
Bihar	2,597.93	2,245.85	86.45	10,602.21	6,482.81	61.15	396.49	325.43	82.08	13,596.63	9,054.09	66.59
Chhattisgarh	1,452.52	1,263.71	87.00	5,162.29	3,299.32	63.91	140.40	110.27	78.54	6,755.21	4,673.30	69.18
Goa	179.54	151.26	84.25	1,350.57	826.83	61.22	0.00	0.00	0.00	1,530.11	978.09	63.92
Gujarat	7,251.26	6,854.69	94.53	14,831.38	10,584.63	71.37	0.00	0.00	-	22,082.64	17,439.32	78.97
Haryana	1,998.82	1,793.11	89.71	3,870.67	2,377.29	61.42	84.83	69.45	81.87	5,954.32	4,239.85	71.21
Himachal Pradesh	2,215.73	2,019.19	91.13	4,029.21	2,433.92	60.41	0.00	0.00	0.00	6,244.94	4,453.11	71.31
Jammu Kashmir	2,430.58	2,331.54	95.93	3,101.07	2,414.55	77.86	0.00	6.74	0.00	5,531.65	4,752.83	85.92
Jharkhand	1,913.67	1,550.36	81.01	7,625.71	5,209.43	68.31	0.00	0.00	0.00	9,539.38	6,759.79	70.86
Karnataka	4,895.02	4,469.35	91.30	6,902.81	4,093.18	59.30	119.19	91.42	76.70	11,917.02	8,653.95	72.62
Kerala	2,597.17	2,271.70	87.47	6,208.99	3,346.77	53.90	113.34	30.02	26.49	8,919.50	5,648.49	63.33
Madya Pradesh	6,355.71	5,616.62	88.37	13,032.47	8,468.69	64.98	408.25	268.31	65.72	19,796.43	14,353.62	72.51
Maharashtra	5,644.14	5,092.66	90.23	7,654.76	4,758.03	62.16	459.93	297.21	64.62	13,758.83	10,147.89	73.76
Manipur	53.93	24.88	46.13	478.99	326.43	68.15	0.00	0.00	0.00	532.92	351.31	65.92
Meghalaya	310.21	297.43	95.88	604.74	430.47	71.18	0.00	0.00	0.00	914.95	727.91	79.56
Mizoram	141.05	140.96	99.94	673.03	332.03	49.33	0.00	0.00	0.00	814.08	472.99	58.10

(Cont'd)

Table 11A.1 (*Cont'd*)

Name of State	Total of All Closed Tranches (I–XIV)			Total of All On-going Tranches (XV–XXII)			Warehousing (XVII–XVIII)			Total of All Tranches		
	Amount Sanctioned	Amount Disbursed	Percentage Utilization	Amount Sanctioned	Amount Disbursed	Percentage Utilization	Amount Sanctioned	Amount Disbursed	Percentage Utilization	Amount Sanctioned	Amount Disbursed	Percentage Utilization
Nagaland	327.13	239.77	73.30	366.08	274.74	75.05	0.00	0.00	0.00	693.21	514.51	74.22
Odisha	4,113.05	3560.68	86.57	13,583.97	8,763.96	64.52	0.00	0.00	0.00	17,697.02	12,324.65	69.64
Puducherry	54.58	51.94	0.00	532.04	326.42	61.35	1.53	1.48	96.73	588.15	379.84	64.58
Punjab	3,456.85	3,040.36	87.95	4,701.08	3,189.73	67.85	41.80	37.18	88.95	8,199.73	6,267.26	76.43
Rajasthan	5,269.52	4,566.33	86.66	13,704.01	9,954.69	72.64	251.32	192.51	76.60	19,224.85	14,713.53	76.53
Sikkim	219.90	214.42	97.51	332.21	238.26	71.72	0.00	0.00	0.00	552.11	452.68	81.99
Tamil Nadu	6,278.64	5,680.25	90.47	11,361.7	8,496.34	74.78	525.27	516.68	98.36	18,165.61	14,693.26	80.89
Telangana	0.00	0.00	0.00	2,835.68	914.40	32.25	0.00	0.00	0.00	2,835.68	914.40	32.25
Tripura	774.37	678.45	87.61	1,281.65	738.94	57.66	14.85	12.37	83.32	2,070.87	1,429.76	69.04
Uttar Pradesh	7,348.23	6,801.65	92.56	14,188.13	10,123.96	71.36	0.00	0.00	0.00	21,536.36	16,925.61	78.59
Uttarakhand	1,282.48	1,179.44	91.97	5,790.59	4,046.83	69.89	0.00	0.00	0.00	7,073.07	5,226.27	73.89
West Bengal	5,337.42	4,236.88	79.38	9,328.95	6,117.48	65.58	694.40	631.12	90.89	15,360.77	10,985.48	71.52
RIDF Total	87,310.10	77,274.76	88.51	177,912.49	117,156.25	65.85	3,406.76	2,674.19	78.50	268,629.35	197,105.20	73.37
Bharat Nirman	12,000.00	12,000.00	0.00	6,500.00	6,500.00	100.00	0.00	0.00	0.00	18,500.00	18,500.00	100.00
Grand Total	99,310.10	89,274.76	89.89	184,412.49	123,656.25	67.05	3,406.76	2,674.19	78.50	287,129.35	215,605.20	75.09

12

Financial Inclusion in India

A Review

R. Ramakumar[*]

ABSTRACT

This chapter is an attempt to review the status of India's financial inclusion policy, with particular focus on developments after 2004–5. The motivation behind these policies in India was two-fold. One, policies of financial liberalization in the 1990s had led to shrinking access to the public banking system. Two, millions of people were outside the ambit of the banking system even after more than four decades of state-led intervention. The financial inclusion policy was a response to these entitlement failures. However, the new policies were not a throwback to pre-1991 policy; instead, they were introduced and implemented without compromising on the commercial viability of banking operations.

The government's financial inclusion policy in the 2000s revolved around three pillars: (*a*) there was an effort to expand the supply of agricultural credit; (*b*) provision of microfinance by public banks and private microfinance institutions was encouraged; and (*c*) banks were directed to open banking outlets in unbanked centres and provide the newly included with new financial products. This chapter critically examines these three spheres of intervention. It argues that while some progress at financial inclusion was achieved between 2005 and 2016, the unfinished tasks were enormous. India's financial sector needs a more progressive policy framework that would facilitate further penetration of public banking into previously excluded regions and sections.

JEL Classification: G21, Q14

Keywords: financial inclusion, microfinance, agricultural credit, financial liberalization

12.1 INTRODUCTION

The term 'financial inclusion' is a rather new term in the discourse on finance and development. The emergence of the term followed the evolution of its opposite—'financial exclusion'. The term 'financial exclusion' origi-

nated in the early 1990s, when, globally, concerns were raised regarding large-scale closure of bank branches and

[*] NABARD Chair Professor and Dean, School of Development Studies, Tata Institute of Social Sciences, Mumbai, India.

restricted access to banking services (see Aynsley 2011). In the United Kingdom (UK), the term found mention in official reports in the late 1990s and early 2000s, and was also noted to be associated with 'social exclusion' (Cabinet Office 2001). As a result, the UK government began to target people living in 'deprived neighbourhoods' as part of a financial inclusion policy. From 2006, the United Nations also began to advocate policies of financial inclusion in the developing world (see United Nations 2006). Following global trends, India embraced policies of financial inclusion from 2005 onwards.

This chapter discusses financial inclusion policy in India, broadly documenting the evolution of the official policy related to financial inclusion, and evaluating the achievements and claims made by multiple agencies—public and private—with respect to financial inclusion.

12.2 FINANCIAL INCLUSION POLICY

Financial inclusion, if conceptualized broadly as *the expansion of access to banking services for previously unbanked sections and sectors*, has a long history in India. In this sense, the history of financial inclusion in India can be divided into two distinct phases.

12.2.1 The First Phase

The nationalization of the banking system in India after 1969 was one of the largest financial inclusion programmes in the developing world. After 1969, India had strongly pursued a policy of 'social and development banking', particularly in the rural areas. As a result, formal institutions of credit provision, mainly commercial banks, emerged as important sources of finance for agriculture, thus displacing usurious moneylenders, traders, and landlords. The policy of social and development banking was a supply-led policy; it aimed at augmenting the supply of credit to rural areas, and that too at an affordable interest rate (Ramachandran and Swaminathan 2005; Shetty 2006).

12.2.1.1 The Thrust

Three aspects of the post-1969 policy of social and development banking stood out. First, according to the new branch licensing policy, commercial banks were required to open four branches in unbanked rural areas for every branch opened in metropolitan or port areas. As a result, if there were only 1,443 rural branches of banks in 1969, there were 35,134 rural branches of banks by 1991. Second, according to the policy of priority sector lending,

40 per cent of the net bank credit was to be provided to those *sectors* of the economy (and *sections* of the society) that would not get timely and adequate credit in the absence of binding targets. These sectors were, typically, loans to farmers for agriculture and allied activities (18 per cent), micro and small enterprises, housing for poor people, education for students, and other low-income groups and weaker sections such as scheduled caste and scheduled tribe households (10 per cent). As a result, the share of credit from rural branches in total bank credit increased from 5.9 per cent in 1975 to 15 per cent in 1990. Third, according to the differential interest rate scheme of 1974, loans were provided at concessional interest rates on advances made by public banks to selected low-income groups to engage in productive and gainful activities. The differential rate of interest was fixed uniformly at 4 per cent per annum, that is, 2 per cent below the bank rate.

These regulations on banking and the promotional role of the government were premised on the recognition that rural credit markets were deeply imperfect. The social and developing banking policy consciously mopped up surplus savings as deposits from richer rural areas and diverted them as loans to savings-deficient areas (Ramachandran and Swaminathan 2005).

12.2.1.2 The Outcomes

A major outcome of bank nationalization was the expansion of access to formal credit for different *sectors* and *sections* that were previously deprived of credit. First, increased flow of credit to the rural areas and the agricultural sector stimulated rural economic growth. Data from the All India Debt and Investment Survey (AIDIS) show that in 1971, formal sources of credit contributed only 29 per cent of the total outstanding debt of rural households; the corresponding share rose to 64 per cent by 1992. For cultivator households in rural areas, the share of formal sources in total debt outstanding increased from 32 per cent in 1971 to 66 per cent in 1992. The increased availability of credit from public banks helped small and marginal farmers to adopt the costlier new technologies and farming practices that were a part of the green revolution strategy.

Second, flow of credit to weaker sections like agricultural labourer households and scheduled caste households expanded (Chavan 2007). Data from the Rural Labour Enquiry (RLE) reports show that in 1974–5, about 48 per cent of the total debt outstanding of agricultural labourer households in rural India was from private moneylenders. By 1987–8, the corresponding share had declined to 22 per cent. According to data from the

AIDIS, in 1992, if the share of formal sources in the total debt outstanding of all rural households stood at 64 per cent, the corresponding share for rural scheduled caste households stood at 61 per cent.

12.2.1.3 The New Era

The era of financial liberalization that began in 1991 witnessed a reversal of many of the achievements of nationalization (Ramakumar and Chavan 2007). By the late 1980s and early 1990s, the policy of social and development banking came to be severely criticized. First, the committee on the financial system (Narasimham Committee) made a sharp pitch for delinking monetary policy from the objective of redistribution (RBI 1991). It argued that banks should function on a commercial basis, and profitability should be the prime concern of their activities. Thus, the 4:1 norm for opening new branches under the branch licensing policy was removed and banks were permitted to 'rationalize' their branch network in rural areas. Second, the norms related to the definition of priority sector lending were broadened. Third, it was argued that banks should be given a free hand to charge rates of interest because administering interest rates would lead to 'financial repression'.[1]

After 1991, there was a weakening of the public banking network in rural India. If new sections and sectors were the beneficiaries of the post-1969 expansion of public banking, these very sections and sectors found their access to public banking restricted after 1991.

- About 922 rural bank branches were closed down between 1995 and 2005 under the policy of branch rationalization (Ramakumar and Chavan 2011).
- There was a widening of inter-state inequalities in credit provision and a fall in the proportion of bank credit directed towards regions where banking was historically underdeveloped (Chavan 2004).
- There was a fall in the growth rate of credit flow to agriculture. If agricultural credit grew at an annual rate of 8.7 per cent between 1980 and 1990, it grew at just 1.8 per cent between 1990 and 2000 (Ramakumar and Chavan 2007).

[1] Financial repression is defined as a situation where the degree of financial intermediation is weak due to negative real rates of interest on deposits and a large spread between borrowing and lending rates. As a result, it was argued, private savings and investments are discouraged in the economy.

- There was increased sidelining of small and marginal farmers in the supply of agricultural credit. The share of loan accounts in commercial banks held by marginal and small cultivators was about 73 to 74 per cent in the mid-1990s; in 2004–5, the corresponding share was 71 per cent (Ramakumar and Chavan 2007).
- A large proportion of the rural poor were shut out from the public banking system and forced to depend on informal sources such as landlords or moneylenders. According to data from the AIDIS, the share of formal sources in the total outstanding debt of rural scheduled caste households declined from 61 per cent in 1992 to 45 per cent in 2002 (Chavan 2007). Data from the RLE showed that the share of loans from moneylenders in the total debt of agricultural labour households increased from 22 per cent in 1987–8 to 44.5 per cent in 2004–5 (Chavan 2016).
- Finally, the cost of credit in rural areas increased sharply. The share of rural households that paid compounded annual interest rates of above 20 per cent increased from 15 per cent in 1992 to 34 per cent in 2002.

In other words, there was strong evidence of financial exclusion as well as rising burden of debt in rural India in the 1990s. It was in this context that the Reserve Bank of India (RBI) announced a new initiative on financial inclusion in 2005. According to the RBI, 'concerns on financial inclusion ... emanated from the results of the All India Debt and Investment Survey (AIDIS) 2002' (RBI 2008a, 194). This announcement of the RBI roughly coincided with the announcement in 2004 of a new 'comprehensive credit policy' by the union government. We may call this the beginning of the second phase of financial inclusion policy in India.

12.2.2 The Second Phase

It was in the annual 'Monetary Policy Statement' for 2005–6 that the RBI made its first announcement with regard to financial inclusion. In the statement, there was a frank admission of the enormity of financial exclusion that had set in after 1991. The statement said: 'There are legitimate concerns in regard to the banking practices that tend to exclude rather than attract vast sections of population, in particular pensioners, self-employed and those employed in unorganised sector' (RBI 2005a). It further said that banks 'should be obliged to provide banking services to all segments of the population, on equitable basis' and urged them to 'review their existing practices to align them with the objective of financial inclusion' (RBI 2005a). Writing in 2011, the governor of the RBI in 2005—Y.V. Reddy—commented, 'To the best of my knowledge, the concept of financial inclusion, as a matter of public policy, was articulated in that statement for the first time, at least in India' (Reddy 2011, 46).

12.2.2.1 Agricultural Credit

One of the conclusions that emerged from the AIDIS of 2002 was the sidelining of rural areas and agricultural credit after 1992. The 'comprehensive credit policy' of 2004 sought to address these concerns. Though the term financial inclusion was not explicitly used, the policy had elements of an inclusive intent. It included a commitment to raise agricultural credit flow by 30 per cent every year (thus, doubling the flow of agricultural credit in three years), financing of 100 farmers per branch (thus, 50 lakh[2] farmers in a year), two to three new investments in agricultural projects per branch every year and a host of debt-relief measures such as debt restructuring and one-time settlement and financial assistance to redeem loans from moneylenders (Ministry of Agriculture 2007).

12.2.2.2 Branch Expansion

In response to criticisms that pointed to large-scale closure of rural bank branches, the RBI, in 2011, replaced its branch licensing policy with a new 'branch authorization policy'. As part of the new branch authorization policy, it was mandated that at least 25 per cent of the new branches under the Annual Branch Expansion Plan (ABEP) of banks should be located in unbanked rural centres. Further, for each additional branch opened in Tiers 2 to 6 (that is, urban, semi-urban, or rural centres), the banks were offered an incentive: they could open one branch in any metropolitan centre (Tier 1 centres). Even here, the total number of branches opened in Tier 1 centres was not to exceed the total number of branches proposed to be opened in Tier 2 to 6 centres. The post-2011 branch authorization policy of the RBI was, in a sense, a return to the spirit of the post-1969 branch licensing policy.

12.2.2.3 The Thrust

Outside agricultural credit and branch expansion, the financial inclusion policy of the RBI in the early years was limited to the opening of 'no-frills' accounts to

previously unbanked households. In a circular to banks issued in December 2005, the RBI stated:

In many banks, the requirement of minimum balance and charges levied, although accompanied by a number of free facilities, deter a sizeable section of population from opening/ maintaining bank accounts. With a view to achieving greater financial inclusion, *all banks need to make available a basic banking 'no frills' account either with 'nil' or very low minimum balances* as well as charges that would make such accounts accessible to vast sections of population. (RBI 2005b, emphasis added)[3]

In 2008, the RBI appointed a 'Committee on Financial Inclusion' headed by C. Rangarajan. The Rangarajan committee recommended moving towards a new approach of 'comprehensive financial inclusion', which implied an expansion of the earlier concept of financial inclusion. It specified the constituent parts of financial inclusion as: (*a*) a basic no-frills bank account to make and receive payments; (*b*) a savings product; (*c*) money transfer facilities; (*d*) small loans and overdrafts; and (*e*) an insurance product. It also suggested that financial inclusion should be prioritized under a 'National Mission on Financial Inclusion'. The committee also provided a new 'broad working definition' for the term 'financial inclusion':

Financial inclusion may be defined as the *process of ensuring access to financial services and timely and adequate credit* where needed by vulnerable groups such as weaker sections and low income groups at an affordable cost. (RBI 2008b, 1, emphasis added)

12.2.2.4 The New Approach

There were at least three ways in which the financial inclusion policy after 2005 differed from the social and development banking policy after 1969. First, social and

---

[2] 1 lakh is equal to 100,000.

[3] Y.V. Reddy explained the RBI's intent behind the idea of opening 'no-frills' accounts thus:

We felt that many people would like to keep their money safe. For instance, many working class women would like to keep their money safe from their husbands. People who have seasonal employment prefer to keep their money safely whenever they get informal work and utilise it during the period when they do not get daily wages. Sometimes, they may require small loans to smoothen consumption. More important, many parents from rural areas have to send money to their children who may be in nearby towns in hostels. There are also migrant workers who temporarily move to different parts of the country, and who may have to send money to their dependents. The 'no-frills accounts' scheme of banks was introduced as part of this approach of financial inclusion (Reddy 2011, 46).

development banking was defined as 'the elevation of the entitlements of previously disadvantaged groups to formal credit even if this may entail a weakening of the conventional banking practices' (see Copestake et al. 1984). In other words, commercial viability was not a primary consideration in the earlier policy. The new policy, however, urged banks to approach financial inclusion not as a social task but 'as a viable business proposition' (see RBI 2011a, 85). Banks were encouraged to develop viable financial products for the poor that would concurrently 'generate revenue rather than being cost-centric' (RBI 2011). In sum, the effort in the new policy was to not deviate from the core principles of commercial banking operations laid out by the larger framework of financial liberalization.

Second, the growth of microfinance was envisaged by the new policy as 'an effective tool' for financial inclusion, which could 'raise incomes, contribute to individual and household security and change social relations for the better' (RBI 2008a, 192). There were two models of microfinance that operated in India: one, the SHG–Bank-Linkage programme initiated under the National Bank for Agriculture and Rural Development (NABARD); and two, the private microfinance institution (MFI) model initiated by private social entrepreneurs and corporate groups. In the former model, microfinance activities were treated as 'extended arms' of public bank branches, while 'parallel financial intermediaries' undertook microfinance activities in the latter model. The RBI, for a prolonged period, was in opposition to the idea of regulating private MFIs and preferred a model of 'self-regulation' (see RBI 2008a, 193; RBI 2001; Reddy 2011).[4]

Third, there was considerable reliance on 'branchless banking' through the banking correspondent (BC) model in the new policy.[5] According to Mundra (2016, 4),

'the BC model is the critical lynchpin of our financial inclusion initiative'; it was seen as an important tool to practice 'cost-effective' financial inclusion. Here, instead of opening a large number of brick-and-mortar branches in far-flung villages, BCs were appointed as intermediaries between banks and customers and were paid a salary/commission for their service. In 2006, the RBI issued special guidelines for appointing BCs. These guidelines allowed banks to appoint NGOs, non-NBFC MFIs, and other civil society organizations as BCs. In 2009, the RBI allowed the engagement of *kirana*/medical/fair price shop owners, individual public call office operators, agents of small savings schemes of government or public insurance companies, individual petrol pump owners, retired teachers, and SHG functionaries as BCs. In 2010, to make the model more attractive, the RBI permitted banks to appoint 'any individual' as BC, and added to the list 'for-profit companies' also.

These apart, the RBI initiated a few other policy measures to expand financial inclusion.

- The Know-Your-Customer (KYC) norms for opening accounts were simplified for persons belonging to low-income groups, if the account balance did not exceed Rs 50,000 and the credits did not exceed Rs 100,000 in a year.
- Banks were asked to introduce a General Purpose Credit Card (GCC), with withdrawals up to Rs 25,000 at the rural and semi-urban branches.
- As an incentive measure, banks were allowed since May 2008 to classify overdrafts of up to Rs 25,000 per account granted against no-frills accounts in rural and semi-urban areas as indirect finance to agriculture under priority sector.
- As another incentive measure, banks were allowed since May 2008 to classify the whole of their credit outstanding under GCCs as indirect finance to agriculture under priority sector.
- All state-level bankers' committees (SLBCs) were asked to identify at least one district in each state for 100 per cent financial inclusion (defined in terms of opening of no-frills accounts and issue of GCCs).
- Two funds—a Financial Inclusion Fund (FIF) and a Financial Inclusion Technology Fund (FITF)—were created in 2007–8 with contributions from the Government of India, RBI, and NABARD. The FIF and FITF were merged into a single financial inclusion fund in July 2015 with a corpus of Rs 20 billion.

[4] As laid out by Jagdish Capoor, a former deputy governor of the RBI: it is 'desirable and appropriate to support evolution of a self-regulatory mechanism for micro-finance institutions, such as NGOs (MFIs), which would prescribe codes of conduct and ground rules' (RBI 2001, 307).

[5] According to Usha Thorat (2010, 4), a former deputy governor of the RBI:

With 600,000 villages in the country, we realized that it was impossible to provide access to a bank account for every household through branch banking. At the same time, electronic banking for such a populace where cash forms the dominant payment mechanism, is unlikely to become a reality for quite some time. Keeping in view these ground realities, RBI issued the business correspondent guidelines in 2006, which paved the way for branchless banking through agents.

12.2.2.5 Two Schemes

While the initial announcement on the new financial policy initiative had taken place in 2005, concrete actions to implement began only by 2011. In January 2010, banks were asked to prepare annual financial inclusion plans (FIP) on a three-year basis. There have been two FIPs since then: 2010–13 and 2013–16.

The FIPs have, from 2010, focused on extending banking services to unbanked villages. However, such extension of banking services was not solely based on increasing the number of branches but based on a combination of new branches, the BC model, or other modes such as ATMs or mobile vans. *That is, the presence of a branch or a BC or any other mode was adequate for a village to be classified as having a 'banking outlet'.* Banks were indeed asked to open more brick-and-mortar branches, but all the new branches were not to be full-fledged branches. Instead, they could be a 'low cost intermediary kiosk with a simple structure, requiring minimum infrastructure for operating small customer transactions and supporting up to 8–10 BCs at a reasonable distance of 2–3 km' (RBI 2011a, 86).

In 2009, a high-level committee, headed by Usha Thorat, suggested that there should be at least one 'banking outlet' (that is, either a branch or a BC or any other mode) in every village having a population of more than 2,000 persons. In the first phase of FIPs starting in 2010, banks identified 74,414 villages with population of more than 2,000 persons to be covered by a banking outlet by 2013. Two years later, in 2012, the then finance minister, Pranab Mukherjee, brought the items in the first FIP (2010–13) under a scheme titled Swabhimaan, which was essentially a multimedia campaign to inform, educate, and motivate people to open bank accounts. Under Swabhimaan, there were also plans to 'extend insurance and other services to the targeted beneficiaries'.[6]

In the second FIP of banks, implemented between 2013 and 2016, the objectives in the first FIP were expanded upon. The second FIP identified 490,298 unbanked villages with a population of less than 2,000 persons; by March 2016, all these villages were to be covered with a banking outlet. In 2014, a year after the second FIP began, the Government of India announced a new scheme titled Pradhan Mantri Jan Dhan Yojana (PMJDY) into which the items in the second FIP were included with a few modifications. According to an official brochure released by the Department of Financial Services (DFS), the programme for financial inclusion under the PMJDY was to be based on 'six pillars' (GoI 2014):

1. The country will be divided into a number of sub-service areas, each with 1,000–1,500 households. One banking outlet will be established within a distance of 5 km from every SSA by August 2015;
2. One bank account will be ensured for every household by August 2015, along with a RuPay debit card and an accident cover worth Rs 100,000. If the credit history is satisfactory during the first six months, the account holder will become eligible for an overdraft worth Rs 5,000;
3. Financial literacy programmes will be expanded by August 2015 to spread awareness about financial services;
4. A Credit Guarantee Fund will be created before August 2018 to cover potential defaults in overdrafts;
5. All willing and eligible persons will be provided with micro-insurance by August 2018; and
6. Pension payments under the Swavalamban Yojana scheme for workers in the unorganized sector will be paid through bank accounts by August 2018.

To summarize, the government's efforts in the 2000s with respect to financial inclusion revolved around three pillars: (*a*) there was an effort to expand the supply of agricultural credit to farmers; (*b*) provision of microfinance by public banks and private MFIs was encouraged; and (*c*) banks were directed to deepen financial inclusion by opening banking outlets in unbanked centres and providing the newly included with new financial products in the spheres of savings and insurance. In the following sections, we shall examine the progress made under each of these.

12.3 AGRICULTURAL CREDIT

The expansion of agricultural credit has often been claimed as the key success story in the financial inclusion initiatives of different union governments after 2004. Official data on credit flow to agriculture show that if agricultural credit increased at the rate of 2.6 per cent between 1991 and 2001, it increased at the rate of 18.1 per cent between 2001 and 2015 (Table 12.1). In fact, the growth rate of agricultural credit between 2001

---

[6] See press note of the Ministry of Finance, New Delhi, available at http://pib.nic.in/newsite/erelcontent.aspx?relid=58476, last accessed on 16 January 2016.

Table 12.1   Rate of Growth of Credit to Agriculture and Total Bank Credit, at Constant Prices, India, 1972–2015, in Per Cent Per Annum

Period	Annual Growth Rates (%) in	
	Credit to Agriculture	Total Bank Credit
1972–81	16.1	8.4
1981–91	6.8	8.0
1991–2001	2.6	7.3
2001–15	18.1	11.1

Source: 'Basic Statistical Returns of Scheduled Commercial Banks in India', RBI, various issues.

Table 12.2   Selected Basic Indicators of Household Debt in Rural India, Rural and Cultivator Households, AIDIS, 1992–2013, in Number and Per Cent

Type of Household/Item	1992	2002	2013
(a) Incidence of Indebtedness (%)			
Cultivator households	25.9	29.7	35.0
All rural households	23.4	26.5	31.4
(b) Debt to Asset Ratio			
Cultivator households	1.6	2.5	2.8
All rural households	1.8	2.8	3.2
(c) Share of Institutional Sources in Total Debt (%)			
Cultivator households	66.3	61.1	58.0
All rural households	64.0	57.1	56.0
(d) Share of Commercial Banks in Total Debt (%)			
Cultivator households	35.2	26.3	27.7
All rural households	33.7	24.5	25.1
(e) Share of Non-institutional Sources in Total Debt (%)			
Cultivator households	30.6	38.9	41.6
All rural households	32.7	42.9	44.0
(f) Share of Moneylenders in Total Debt (%)			
Cultivator households	17.5	26.8	31.5
All rural households	17.5	29.6	33.2

Source: AIDIS reports, various years.

and 2015 was higher than the growth rate of total bank credit. These higher growth rates in agricultural credit were the basis for the argument that the adverse effects of the poor growth rate in agricultural credit in the 1990s were reversed in the 2000s. The question, then, is: does the Indian farmer face a more favourable credit market today than in 1992?

12.3.1 Persistent Exclusion

A careful and disaggregated analysis of data would show that the claims of revival of agricultural credit in India in the 2000s might be premature, if not wrong. New data from the AIDIS reports form the starting point for such a sceptical assessment. In brief, AIDIS data show that while there was a moderate improvement in the access of rural and cultivator households to public agricultural credit between 2002 and 2013, the debt situation of rural and cultivator households in 2013 remained worse than in 1992 (see Table 12.2).

First, a higher share of rural and cultivator households were indebted in 2013 than in 1992. The share of cultivator households indebted rose from 25.9 per cent in 1992 to 35 per cent in 2013.

Second, of course, a rise in the share of indebted households may actually show an expansion of access to credit. However, strikingly, the rise in the incidence of indebtedness occurred alongside a rise in the debt to asset ratios (which shows the extent to which debt is a drain on the value of owned assets) of households. In 1992, the debt to asset ratio for cultivator households was 1.6, which rose to 2.8 by 2013. Thus, there was an intensification of the debt burdens of cultivator households between 1992 and 2013.

Third, between 1992 and 2013, the share of debt outstanding from formal sources decreased. For cultivator households, the share of debt outstanding from the

formal sector fell from 66.3 per cent in 1992 to 61.1 per cent in 2002; between 2002 and 2013, the share of debt outstanding from the formal sector fell further to 58 per cent, which was far lower than the corresponding share in 1992. The fall of lending by commercial banks appears to be a major reason. Between 1992 and 2002, for cultivator households, the share of debt outstanding from commercial banks fell from 35.2 per cent to 26.3 per cent; the share indeed rose to 27.7 per cent in 2013 but was still about 7 percentage points lower than in 1992.

Informal sources of credit became increasingly important in the debt portfolios of farmers in the 1990s and 2000s. If we consider cultivator households, the share of debt outstanding from the informal sector rose from 30.6 per cent in 1992 to 38.9 per cent in 2002, and then fell to 41.6 per cent in 2013. Within the informal sector, it was the share of debt from moneylenders that rose most sharply.

The results from the AIDIS reports of 1992, 2002, and 2013 lead us to the conclusion that about 25 years of financial liberalization has left the cultivator households worse off. The revival of agricultural credit in the 2000s appears to have largely bypassed the farmer.

12.3.2 Where Did All the Credit Go?

There are four validating reasons to argue that much of the rise in agricultural credit in the 2000s might not have reached the farmer.

Diversion as Indirect Finance   First, a significant part of the incremental agricultural credit provided in the decade of the 2000s was *indirect finance* and not *direct finance*.

In the 1990s and 2000s, the share of indirect credit in total agricultural credit consistently rose (see Table 12.3). Between 1985 and 1990, there was actually a fall in the share of indirect credit in total agricultural credit; the share began to rise in the 1990s—particularly after 1998—to reach 23.9 per cent in 2010. Thus, while the share of indirect credit in total agricultural credit had begun to rise in the 1990s, its increase in the 2000s was considerably rapid. Of the total increase in agricultural credit between 2002 and 2010, more than one-fourth (26 per cent) was contributed by indirect credit.

The ability of banks to provide higher amounts of indirect finance was aided by a series of changes in the definition of indirect finance instituted by the RBI after 1991. These definitional changes broadly involved (*a*) the addition of new forms of financing commercial, export-oriented, and capital-intensive agriculture; (*b*) raising the credit limit of many existing forms of indirect financing; and (*c*) bringing loans given to corporates and partnership groups also into the ambit of agricultural credit (for a list of definitional changes, see Ramakumar and Chavan 2013).

As Table 12.3 shows, after 2011, there was fall in the share of indirect finance in total agricultural credit. The share of direct finance in total agricultural credit increased from 76.1 per cent in 2010 to 87.7 per cent in 2015, which was higher than the corresponding share in 1990. From here, an argument may be advanced that the flow of direct finance to the farmer has been restored in the years after 2010. However, there are reasons to be sceptical of the rise in the share of direct finance between 2010 and 2015. These relate to a set of changes in the definition of direct finance after 2007.

From 2007 onwards, the entire amount of loans given to *corporates, partnership firms*, and *institutions* for agricultural and allied activities (such as beekeeping, piggery, poultry, fishery, and dairy) up to Rs 1 crore,[7] and one-third of the loans in excess of Rs 1 crore in aggregate per borrower was considered as direct finance to agriculture (the remaining two-thirds were considered as indirect finance). From 2012 onwards, loans extended to corporates, partnership firms, and other institutions of up to Rs 2 crores were fully included under direct finance (the rest was included under indirect finance). It is possible that a significant part of the new direct finance provided in the years after 2010 were in the form of such loans to corporates and partnership firms. This is, of course, a proposition that needs further analysis with longer time series data.

Increase in Agricultural Loans of Large Sizes   Much of the increase in the *direct finance* to agriculture in the 2000s was on account of a sharp increase in the number of loans of above Rs 2 lakh and particularly above Rs 10 crore and Rs 25 crore.

Ideally, any meaningful comparison of agricultural credit across time should be attempted after deflating the credit series and dividing them into uniform size classes. However, such deflation requires account-level figures on agricultural credit, which are not available. Nevertheless, an agricultural loan of Rs 2 lakh could be safely considered as the upper limit of a farmer's loan in rural India both in the 1990s and 2000s. If we consider the example of crop loan provisions for sugarcane by credit cooperatives in Maharashtra, the maximum loan that a farmer with 5 acres could avail was fixed at Rs 1.92 lakh even

Table 12.3 Shares of Direct and Indirect Credit to Agriculture in Total Credit to Agriculture from Scheduled Commercial Banks, India, 1985 to 2015, in Per Cent

Year	Share in Total Agricultural Credit (Per Cent)		
	Direct Credit	Indirect Credit	Total
1985	83.2	16.8	100.0
1990	86.8	13.2	100.0
2000	84.5	15.5	100.0
2005	76.1	23.9	100.0
2006	72.1	27.9	100.0
2007	74.5	25.5	100.0
2008	77.5	22.5	100.0
2009	77.1	22.9	100.0
2010	76.1	23.9	100.0
2011	82.0	18.0	100.0
2012	83.4	16.6	100.0
2013	86.0	14.0	100.0
2014	84.3	15.7	100.0
2015	87.7	12.3	100.0

Source: 'Basic Statistical Returns of Scheduled Commercial Banks in India', RBI, various issues.

---

[7] 1 crore is equal to 10 million.

Table 12.4 Distribution of Amount Outstanding under Direct Agricultural Advances by Scheduled Commercial Banks, by Broad Size Classes of Credit Limit, 1985 to 2015, in Per Cent

Year	Share of Amount of Direct Advances with Credit Limit (%)					
	≤ Rs 2 Lakh	> Rs 2 Lakh	Total	≤ Rs 10 Lakh	> Rs 10 Lakh	Total
1985	NA	NA	NA	96.7	3.3	100.0
1990	92.2	7.7	100.0	95.8	4.1	100.0
1995	89.1	10.9	100.0	93.6	6.4	100.0
2000	78.5	21.4	100.0	91.3	8.6	100.0
2005	66.7	33.4	100.0	88.1	12.0	100.0
2011	48.0	52.0	100.0	76.2	23.8	100.0
2015	46.3	53.7	100.0	83.6	16.4	100.0

Source: 'Basic Statistical Returns of Scheduled Commercial Banks in India', RBI, various issues.

Table 12.5 Share of Direct Agricultural Credit Outstanding, by Population Groups, by Direct and Indirect Credit, India, 1995 to 2015, in Per Cent

Year	Share of Direct Agricultural Credit Outstanding from Branches in (%)				
	Rural	Semi-urban	Urban	Metropolitan	Total
1995	56.5	31.2	8.2	4.0	100.0
2005	52.9	31.4	10.0	5.7	100.0
2006	48.0	32.0	12.6	7.5	100.0
2011	43.2	31.2	16.5	9.1	100.0
2015	44.6	36.0	13.7	5.7	100.0

Source: 'Basic Statistical Returns of Scheduled Commercial Banks in India', RBI, various issues.

in 2014–15 (see Ramakumar and Chavan 2013). Among all crops, sugarcane had one of the highest scales of crop finance. In other words, a loan of above Rs 2 lakh could be unarguably considered a large-size agricultural loan. Hence, the construction of size classes of loans with Rs 2 lakh as the upper limit allows us to judge the changes in the shares of small and marginal farmers in total agricultural credit.

Thus, in Table 12.4, we have divided the amount of direct credit into those of up to Rs 2 lakh and above Rs 2 lakh, as well as up to Rs 10 lakh and above Rs 10 lakh. If Rs 2 lakh is taken as a cut-off as to indicate a typical agricultural loan, then data in Table show that only 46.3 per cent of the *direct* agricultural credit reached the farmers in 2015. The corresponding share for 1990 was 92.2 per cent, for 2000 was 78.5 per cent, for 2005 was 66.7 per cent, and for 2011 was 48 per cent. To provide an illustration, an amount of Rs 792,691 crore was disbursed as direct agricultural finance in 2014–15. If we consider that only loans up to Rs 2 lakh as those provided to 'farmers', only Rs 367,015 crore is likely to have reached the farmers in 2014–15, and the remaining amount of Rs 425,675 crore is likely to have reached persons other than farmers.

A similar conclusion emerges from the classification of the amount of direct credit into sizes up to Rs 10 lakh and above Rs 10 lakh also. In 1990, the amount constituted by loans of size above Rs 10 lakh was 3.3 per cent of the total amount; this share rose to 8.6 per cent in 2000, 12 per cent in 2005, 23.8 per cent in 2011, and 16.4 per cent in 2015. Further disaggregated data analysed in Ramakumar and Chavan (2013) show that there was a

sharp rise in the share of direct finances of size above Rs 10 crore and Rs 25 crore in this period.

Urbanization of Agricultural Credit There was an increased provision of agricultural credit from bank branches located in urban and metropolitan areas in the 2000s. Agriculture is primarily a rural occupation, and most agricultural loans should typically be given out from rural branches of banks. However, the share of agricultural credit outstanding from rural branches saw a fall in the 2000s.

Let us here consider direct agricultural credit alone (Table 12.5). Between 1995 and 2005, the share of direct credit to agriculture outstanding in rural branches fell from 56.5 per cent to 52.9 per cent. Between 2006 and 2015, the share of direct credit to agriculture outstanding in rural branches fell from 48 per cent to 44.6 per cent. On the other hand, the share of direct credit outstanding in urban or metropolitan branches was 20.1 per cent in 2006 and 19.4 per cent in 2015. In other words, about one-fifth of the direct agricultural credit was outstanding in urban or metropolitan branches of banks in 2015. Such a phenomenon implied a significant diversion of direct agricultural credit away from rural farmers and towards urban-based individuals, corporates, partnership firms, and joint-stock companics.

The 'March Phenomenon' Month-wise disbursement pattern of agricultural loans from commercial banks shows that most of the loans are disbursed in months with no agricultural activity. RBI does not publish data on month-wise disbursements, but a table in the 'Report of the Task Force on Credit Related Issues of Farmers'—chaired by U.C. Sarangi—provided data for one year: 2008–9 (see Table 12.6). According to the report, about one-fourth (23.4 per cent) of the annual disbursement to agriculture by the commercial banks was in the month of March; the

Table 12.6   Share of Agricultural Credit Disbursed, Commercial Banks, by Months, India, 2008–9, in Per Cent

Month	Share of Agricultural Credit Disbursed (%)
April	1.2
May	2.5
June	5.4
July	6.3
August	4.6
September	9.3
October	5.8
November	7.0
December	11.7
January	11.0
February	11.8
March	23.4
All Months	100.0

Source: Ministry of Agriculture (2010).

committee noted this as 'a matter of serious concern' as March was 'not a critical month for agricultural production' (Ministry of Agriculture 2010, 34). Another 22.7 per cent of the disbursement was in the months of January and February. Thus, together, about 46.1 per cent of all disbursements were in three months: January, February, and March.

The task force also suggested some reasons for the phenomenon. (*a*) It noted that large disbursements may have been made to 'institutions' in these months. (*b*) There might have been significant disbursement of large loans through urban branches in metropolitan regions like Delhi and Chandigarh, but 'booked as agricultural lending'. (*c*) There might have been 'window-dressing' by banks to meet the government targets for credit, deposit, and recovery. All these reasons listed by the task force corroborate the findings of this chapters as elaborated in the earlier sections. The task force's findings were striking:

The Task Force, while taking note of the doubling of agricultural credit, observed that *it did not reach large number of small and marginal farmers who form the bulk of the farming community* and are a critical contributor to the food security of the nation. Substantial loan disbursement by commercial banks takes place in March each year. It appears necessary to take a closer look at what is being termed 'agricultural' credit, especially by commercial banks. Given, too, that rather large 'agricultural' loans were being disbursed in urban centres, a closer look at who is being termed 'farmer' is also needed. (Ministry of Agriculture 2010, xviii, emphasis added)

To conclude, the most important beneficiaries of the revival of agricultural credit in the 2000s were not farmers, who are direct producers in agriculture. The major beneficiaries were corporate groups, joint-stock companies, and other organizations indirectly involved in agricultural production. Agricultural credit in the 2000s moved away from production *per se*, and into post-production functions. In the 2000s, banks increasingly financed activities that aid the growth of specific sub-sectors within agriculture, which are large-scale, commercial, capital-intensive, and export-oriented. These activities were also actively promoted by the government as part of a conscious shift in agricultural policy.

12.4 MICROFINANCE

Globally, microfinance is seen as an important component of financial inclusion. It has been claimed that microfinance could transform the lives of the poor—by raising incomes and reducing poverty—through its innovative methods of small-loan provision.[8]

The ability of microfinance to reduce income poverty is a matter of controversy in the literature. Many scholars have been hesitant to claim conclusively and confidently that microfinance can significantly reduce income poverty. The criticisms against studies that have claimed so are, in the main, methodological. As Morduch (1999, 1609) noted in a review, 'the "win-win" rhetoric promising poverty alleviation with profits has moved far ahead of the evidence, and even the most fundamental claims remain unsubstantiated'. According to these scholars, at best, microfinance can act as a weak survival strategy for the poor by contributing to the reduction of vulnerability.

On the other hand, Indian policymakers in the early stages were convinced of the potential of microfinance as an instrument to reduce income poverty. In the budget speech for 2000–1, the then finance minister, Yashwant Sinha, noted that 'microfinance has emerged as an effective tool for alleviating poverty in many countries'. At the same time, contrary to the Grameen Bank–type models in other countries, Indian banking policy innovatively attempted to involve the public banking network in the provision of microfinance through self-help groups (SHGs). Public banks adopted the approach of group lending and peer monitoring for lending to the SHGs.

---

[8] At the International Micro-credit Summit in 1997, Mohammad Yunus, the founder of the Grameen Bank in Bangladesh, declared that the 'summit [was] about creating a process that will send poverty to the museum'.

This approach, termed the SHG–Bank Linkage programme, distinguished the Indian approach to microcredit as opposed to the NGO-led approaches in other countries.[9]

12.4.1 The SHG–Bank Linkage Programme

The number of SHGs formed by public banks in India grew rapidly in the 1990s, and in particular after the second half of the 1990s. In 1992–3, India had only about 255 SHGs under the SHG–Bank Linkage programme, which rose to 4,757 SHGs in 1995–6 and 2.13 lakh SHGs by 2000–1. By 2014–15, the number of SHGs under the programme had risen to 76.9 lakh (NABARD 2015). Clearly, the Indian SHG–Bank Linkage programme is the largest microfinance programme in the world (NABARD 2008).

A limitation in assessing the impact of microfinance is the lack of reliable data. There are several methodological problems in estimating household earnings. Any such study is beset with difficulties such as under-reporting, recall bias in recording incomes from previous years, and inaccurate evaluation of earnings in kind. In the absence of properly maintained accounts of small household enterprises, the problem of income measurement becomes more acute.

Even though reliable studies on income changes are not available, a few broad statements could be made regarding the SHG–Bank Linkage programme. First, the programme has significantly expanded the access of poor rural households to bank credit, particularly in southern India. Second, access to microfinance has helped many rural households to diversify their sources of livelihood and thus reduce the extent of vulnerability. Third, the network of SHGs created by the programme serves as a useful platform to initiate broader livelihood-enriching programmes assisted by the government.

At the same time, the programme has a number of weaknesses also. (*a*) Microfinance has continued to form only a small part of the total lending portfolio of public banks even though the number of SHGs has risen rapidly. For instance, in 2015–16, the total amount of loans disbursed to all SHGs under the SHG–Bank Linkage programme was only Rs 37,286 crore (see NABARD 2015).

(*b*) A major limitation of the programme has been its inability to bring down the average interest rates at which

small loans are provided. Unfortunately, the official policy on interest rates charged by SHGs has been guided by the view that administering interest rates amounted to 'financial repression', which undermined the profitability of the model. It has been held that banks, intermediaries, and SHGs should be given a free hand to charge rates of interest. In line with such thinking, the 'Monetary and Credit Policy' of the RBI in 1999–2000 fully deregulated interest rates on microfinance.

Deregulation of interest rates was associated with a rise in the costs of credit for borrowers. Final rates of interest on microfinance have been in the range of 24 to 36 per cent per annum (for a review, see Ramakumar and Chavan 2005). Large administrative costs of delivering microfinance were the primary reason for high interest rates. Cost overruns resulted in the charging of margins by each participant in the credit chain between the bank and the borrower. Participants charged margins to cover for transaction costs, that is, the costs of information, negotiation, monitoring, and enforcement of the credit contract. In the end, the burden of margins was transferred to the borrowers as high interest rates. Thus, according to careful studies, the rise in household incomes of beneficiaries due to microfinance in India has been marginal, though positive indeed (for early review, see Chavan and Ramakumar 2002; for more recent reviews, see Bateman 2010 and Karim 2011).

There are exceptions to the charging of higher interest rates under the SHG–Bank inkage programme. An example in this genre is the Kudumbashree scheme of the Kerala government, where the internal lending rate in SHGs has been brought down to 11–12 per cent per annum. There is a further interest subsidy (amounting to 5–7 per cent per annum) provided by the state government to the SHGs so that the loans from SHGs to its members are provided at an interest rate of about 6 per cent per annum.

(*c*) NABARD itself has noted a number of infirmities in the day-to-day functioning of SHGs, which might threaten the long-term sustainability of the programme. According to Bhanwala (2014):

The increasing outreach of the microfinance programmes has brought in its own challenges. For example, the short-term goals of increasing the number of SHGs at 'any cost' has short-circuited the core principles of SHG financing called 'Pancha Sutras', namely regularity in meetings, savings, inter-loaning, repayment of credit and book-keeping. Further, the thrust on providing larger multiples of loan irrespective of maturity level of SHGs has accentuated the problems for SHGs.

---

[9] An early paper by NABARD referred to the Indian policy on microfinance as 'relationship banking' as against 'parallel banking' in other countries (Jayaraman 2001, 18).

12.4.2 The MFI Model

The SHG–Bank Linkage programme is only one, though the dominant, model of microfinance provision in India. In the late-1990s, a private MFI model of microfinance emerged in parallel. By 2010, however, the private MFI model of microfinance entered into a number of controversies.

Legally, a private MFI may be a not-for-profit society or trust or company (registered under Section 25 of the Companies Act); the activities of these not-for-profit MFIs, except Section 25 companies, are largely unregulated. An MFI could also be a for-profit non-banking financial company (NBFC), whose activities are regulated by the RBI. Typically, an MFI in India begins as a not-for-profit unit that uses grants or bank loans and then matures gradually into a for-profit NBFC.

When private MFIs began their operation in India, they largely relied on loans for funds. However, as they began to expand, they increasingly looked at the equity market for funds. There were two reasons why MFIs were encouraged to tap the equity market. First, MFIs other than rated NBFCs were not allowed by the RBI to collect deposits from group members. As a result, the option of using deposits to fund current activities was not open to them. Second, the options for non-deposit mobilization of finances became increasingly limited as MFIs grew in size. Once the portfolios of MFIs expanded beyond a threshold, banks or other specialized lenders (such as the Rashtriya Mahila Kosh and the Small Industries Development Bank of India or SIDBI) were unable to provide the required size of funds. At this point of their growth, private equity (PE) investment and later initial public offerings (IPO) were chosen by the MFIs as financing options.

Thus, by the mid-2000s, MFI-NBFCs became an attractive destination for PE investors. In particular, venture capitalists showed great interest in microfinance. Corporate interest in MFIs grew alongside an increase in potential returns. According to MFI trackers, the returns on equity in MFIs grew from 5.1 per cent in 2008 to 18.3 per cent in 2009; the compound growth rate of returns on equity was 105 per cent between 2005 and 2009 (see Ramakumar 2010). Major private MFIs in India—such as SKS Microfinance, SPANDANA, and SHARE—were recipients of PE funds.

While it appeared that the growth story of private MFIs would continue, a major crisis struck the sector in the second half of the 2000s. In states such as Andhra Pradesh, high interest rates charged by private MFIs forced many borrowers to default on repayment.

To ensure repayment, the staff of the MFIs used severe forms of harassment against borrowers and their family members. The need to repay the first loan from one MFI led many borrowers to obtain either a second loan from another MFI or a new loan from a moneylender; this led to debt cycles for households. Bhanwala (2014) has written about the 'malady' in the private MFI sector 'with rising instances of multiple financing with scant respect to the client's ability to afford the loan'.

In early 2006, there were reports that about 10 MFI borrowers had committed suicide in the Krishna district of Andhra Pradesh. In response, the Andhra Pradesh government closed down about 50 branches of MFIs for charging usurious interest rates and harassing borrowers (Ramakumar 2010). More cases of suicide emerged after 2006. In 2010, there were at least 30 reported cases of suicide by MFI borrowers. Pressured by public protests against alleged harassment by recovery agents, the state government issued the Andhra Pradesh Microfinance Institutions (Regulation of Money Lending) Ordinance seeking to regulate the practices of MFIs and cap interest rates.

The crisis of the private MFI model in India was systemic. The private equity route, and later the IPO route, had a rather straightforward problem. The only attraction for private investors to invest in MFIs was their relatively high yield rates. Given the operational and financial structure, higher yields of MFIs were sustained largely by keeping interest rates higher. Thus, higher interest rates sustained higher yields, and higher yields attracted higher PE investments and better valuations in the market. Put differently, if yields were relatively low to attract investments, MFIs could raise interest rates to improve yields. MFIs, thus, became heavily dependent on the highly volatile system of financial flows in the market. In the end, the burden was borne by the poor borrowers.

In 2011, a subcommittee of the RBI's Central Board of Directors, chaired by Y.H. Malegam, was appointed to study issues and concerns in the MFI sector. This subcommittee examined the issue of interest rates charged by MFIs and included 'unjustified high rates of interest', 'lack of transparency in interest rates and other charges', and 'coercive methods of recovery' among 'specific areas of concern' in the microfinance sector (RBI 2011b, 10). The report recommended:

Given the vulnerable nature of the borrowers, it becomes necessary to impose some form of interest rate control to prevent exploitation … [T]o prevent exploitation in individual cases, a ceiling on the rate of interest charged on individual loans is desirable.

The Indian experience with the private MFI model, thus, shows the importance of strong regulations—particularly in the sphere of interest rates—in the functioning of private MFIs. In this context, the experiences with the SHG-Bank Linkage programme of NABARD have stood in sharp contrast to the experiences with private MFIs.

12.5 EXPANSION OF OUTREACH

A major objective of the new financial inclusion policy was to expand the number of banking outlets in unbanked villages. Banking outlets included both brick-and-mortar branches as well as other modes, such as BCs, ATMs, and mobile vans.

12.5.1 Number of Bank Branches

If large-scale closure of rural bank branches was an outcome of policy till 2005, the trend was indeed reversed after 2005 (see Table 12.7). Between 2005 and 2011, the number of rural bank branches rose moderately from 30,646 to 33,967: a rise by 3,321 branches. In 2011, banks—under the new branch authorization policy—were directed to open at least 25 per cent of their new branches in unbanked centres. Thereafter, the number of rural bank branches increased from 33,967 in 2011 to 48,536 in 2015: a rise by 14,569 branches. The number of semi-urban branches also rose during this period.

Not all the new rural branches were opened in unbanked centres. Of the 3,445 new rural branches

opened in 2014–15, only 2,230 were located in unbanked centres (RBI 2015). Of the 2,259 new rural branches opened in 2015–16, only 1,670 were located in unbanked centres (RBI 2016a). Further, there is lack of clarity on how long the new branch authorization policy would continue. A recent report of the RBI has recommended that the direction to scheduled commercial banks to open at least 25 per cent of their *brick-and-mortar branches* in unbanked rural centres be replaced with a new direction to 'open at least 25 per cent of their *total "banking outlets"* opened during a year in "unbanked rural centres"' (RBI 2016b, 8; author's emphasis). The reason: 'As the business prospects in an unbanked rural centre are not commensurate with the cost of having a full-fledged "brick and mortar" branch, banks find it unviable to open these branches' (RBI 2016b, 5).

12.5.2 The BC Model and New Accounts

As mentioned, a banking outlet was defined as not just a brick-and-mortar branch, but also as the presence of a BC (also called a Bank Mitra or a BM) or any other mode. While there was progress in opening new bank branches, the record of the BC model has been far from successful.

The target set by the banks under their second FIP was to cover 490,298 villages with a banking outlet by March 2016. Data show that banks covered 450,686 villages (91.9 per cent of the target) with a banking outlet by March 2016 (RBI 2016a). Of these 450,686 villages,

Table 12.7   Changes in the Number of Bank Branches in India, by Population Group, 1991–2015

Quarter Ending	Number of Bank Offices Located in Regions				
	Rural	Semi-urban	Urban	Metropolitan	Total
March 1991	35,206	11,344	8,046	5,624	60,220
March 1994	35,329	11,890	8,745	5,839	61,803
Change, 1991–4	**123**	**546**	**699**	**215**	**1583**
March 1995	33,004	13,341	8,868	7,154	62,367
March 2005	32,082	15,403	11,500	9,370	68,355
Change, 1995–2005	**−922**	**2,062**	**2,632**	**2,216**	**5,988**
March 2005 (corrected)	30,646	15,253	12,315	11,685	69,899
March 2011	33,967	23,386	19,255	17,950	94,558
March 2015	48,536	34,131	25,149	22,666	130,482
Change, 2005–11	**3,321**	**8,133**	**6,940**	**6,265**	**24,659**
Change, 2011–15	**14,569**	**10,745**	**5,894**	**4,716**	**35,924**
Change, 2005–15	**17,890**	**18,878**	**12,834**	**10,981**	**60,583**

Note: The figures for March 2005 are based on Census data for 1991, but the corrected figures for March 2005 are based on Census data for 2001. See Ramakumar and Chavan (2011) for details.
Source: 'Basic Statistical Returns of Scheduled Commercial Banks in India,' RBI, various issues.

only 14,901 villages (or 3.3 per cent) were covered with a new bank branch; 415,207 villages (or 92.1 per cent) were covered through BCs and 20,578 villages (or 4.6 per cent) were covered through other modes, such as ATMs or mobile vans.

In Table 12.8, we have provided the progress in the different components of the new financial inclusion policies till March 2016. As on March 2016, there were 51,830 bank branches in villages, and 534,477 villages were additionally covered with a BC or an ATM or a mobile van. Thus, the total number of villages with a banking outlet rose from 67,694 in 2010 to 586,307 villages in 2016.

An important function of the new banking outlets was to facilitate the opening of 'Basic Savings Bank Deposit Accounts' (BSBDA) for unbanked customers. A BSBDA is defined as an account that does not have any minimum balance requirement, provides a debit card to the holder that is operable in ATMs, and allows unlimited number of deposits and four total withdrawals in a month. Between 2010 and 2016, about 17.8 crore BSBDAs were opened by bank branches and about 22 crore BSBDAs were opened by BCs. Together, these accounts held Rs 55 billion in 2010, which rose to Rs 638 billion in 2016.

While the increase in the number BCs and BSBDAs appears commendable, all has not been well on the operational front. These operational issues have been endogenous, and stem from systemic weaknesses in the BC model. For instance, a recent report of the RBI noted that 'the BC model has, as yet, not been successful' and

that 'the BC model is yet to scale up' (RBI 2016b, 5–25). We shall briefly mention three of these weaknesses.

First, financial viability has remained an insurmountable problem in the functioning of BCs. As RBI reports have noted, 'the average transaction per account still remains low' (RBI 2014, 68; see also RBI 2013, 81) compared to the rise in the number of banking outlets and accounts. A recent countrywide survey by Microsave showed that the average daily customer footfall for a BC outlet in 2015 was less than 19 customers for about 49 per cent of all the BCs surveyed. For about 79 per cent of the BCs surveyed, the average daily customer footfall was less than 39 customers (see Sharma et al. 2016). One BC, in a month, conducted an average of 127 cash withdrawals (worth Rs 135,657) and 173 cash deposit transactions (worth Rs 142,316). This implied a total of 300 transactions per month per BC. In another survey of BCs in Madhya Pradesh, conducted by PricewaterhouseCoopers for SIDBI in 2015, the average number of transactions per BC was estimated to be 33 (PwC 2015).

Incomes of the BCs are based on the commissions they receive on each transaction. Smaller number of transactions implies lower incomes for BCs. According to the Microsave survey, the average monthly compensation of a BC was only Rs 4,692 in 2015–16 compared to the 'average expected income' of Rs 13,303 per month (PwC 2015). The PwC survey in Madhya Pradesh also estimated a similar level of monthly income for BCs: Rs 4,008; the estimate was lower in rural areas at Rs 3,745

Table 12.8 Progress in the Financial Inclusion Plans of Banks, 2010–16

Particulars	End-March 2010	End-March 2014	End-March 2016
Banking outlets in villages, branches	33,378	46,126	51,830
Banking outlets in villages, branchless mode	34,316	337,678	534,477
Banking outlets in villages, total	67,694	383,804	586,307
BSBDA, through branches, in million	60.2	126.0	238.0
BSBDA, through branches, in Rs billion	44.3	273.3	474.0
BSBDA, through BCs, in million	13.3	116.9	231.0
BSBDA, through BCs, in Rs billion	10.7	39.0	164.0
BSBDA, total, in million	73.5	243.0	469.0
BSBDA, total, in Rs billion	55.0	312.3	638.0
GCC, total, in million	1.4	7.4	11.0
GCC, total, in Rs billion	35.1	1096.9	1493.0
ICT accounts/BC: transactions, in million	26.5	328.6	826.8
ICT accounts/BC: transactions, in Rs billion	6.9	524.4	1,686.9

Note: BSBDA: Basic Savings Bank Deposit Account; ICT: Information and Communication Technologies.
Source: RBI (2014, 2016a).

per month and higher in urban areas at Rs 5,393 per month.

Here, a caveat needs to be added. Both the Microsave and the PwC surveys were conducted when banks, under their first and second FIPs, were opening large numbers of new accounts. Banks paid a commission of Rs 10 to Rs 100 for every new account opened and such commissions formed a major share of BC incomes in the survey. As the targets fixed by the FIPs were met by March 2016, commission payments from banks to the BCs were likely to fall, leading to a fall in BC incomes. The PwC report noted that '63% of BCs interviewed were under the opinion that the business is not viable after the initial phase of account openings' (2015, 12). The report noted high attrition rate for BCs to the extent of 60 per cent; the reasons were 'low salaries and commission' (PwC 2015, 12).

In other words, unless the volume of transactions rise, it is unlikely that the BC model can be financially viable. One suggested solution—as in the Direct Benefit Transfer (DBT) scheme of the government—has been to populate the new bank accounts with multiple subsidy payments of the government by converting all cash payments into bank payments; where kind payments are involved, it is suggested to end these transfers, and to transfer a fixed amount to the bank accounts in lieu of the kind transfer.[10] An example of the latter is the public distribution system (PDS). However, the social desirability of closing down key welfare institutions like the PDS in favour of direct cash transfers has been questioned (for a note, see Ramakumar 2012).

Second, the technology platform used by the BCs has been subject to criticism by scholars. Initially, each BC was supposed to carry handheld devices that could act as smart card readers. Till 2008, the RBI considered the smart card technology as 'practical', 'robust', and 'affordable' (RBI 2008a, 1956). However, with the establishment of the Unique Identification Authority of India (UIDAI) in 2009, banks were asked to ensure that their policies 'adapt to the solutions being proposed by' the UIDAI, which meant a move from smart cards to Aadhaar-based biometric authentication (RBI 2010, 93).

A concern with Aadhaar—apart from the considerations of privacy and liberty that are currently sub judice—is related to the error rates in biometric authentication. In countries like India, where hard manual labour persists across low-paid occupations, fingerprints of a significant proportion of manual labourers are broken or eroded,

in addition to accidental damages to fingers from burns, chemicals, and other agents. Old age is another potential cause for the lack of clear fingerprints. Thus, it has been pointed out that pervasive usage of fingerprint-based authentication might lead to the exclusion of many needy from the purview of welfare schemes. In his speech delivered in August 2012, the then RBI governor, D. Subbarao, referred to Aadhaar-based biometric authentication in online transactions and noted that 'the robustness of this technology is as yet unproven' (Subbarao 2012).

Between 2012 and 2016, Aadhaar has been incorporated into the implementation of social sector schemes, such as old-age pension disbursements, wage payments of the Mahatma Gandhi National Rural Employment Guarantee Scheme (MGNREGS), and PDS grain sales at ration shops. From the pilot projects on these schemes, journalists, and researchers have documented large error rates in the centralized biometric authentication of beneficiaries as well as the presence of disruptive factors like lack of electricity and poor internet connectivity. According to the PwC survey of BCs in Madhya Pradesh, 'close to 50% of BCs mentioned that they have daily/regular issues with internet connectivity, whereas another around 36% of the BCs had issues on an irregular basis' (2015, 13). According to a study by the United Nations Development Programme (UNDP 2013) and the Ministry of Rural Development on Aadhaar linkage in MGNREGS in Jharkhand, only 4 per cent of the surveyed beneficiaries reported successful fingerprint authentication at the first attempt. About 54 per cent reported two to three attempts, 23 per cent reported four to five attempts, and 18 per cent reported more than five attempts before authentication was completed. There have also been a number of reports where beneficiaries were denied benefits because of the poor quality of their fingerprints. For the elderly beneficiaries of old-age pensions, fingerprint authentications have had the highest error rates.[11]

Third, there have been allegations of corruption against BCs. In March 2011, an internal circular of the State Bank of India noted that BCs were 'found to indulge in malpractices, such as asking for unauthorised money, over and above the bank's approved rates of charges from the customers'. The circular noted that 'gullible customers' were being 'exploited' (SBI 2011). In October 2012, *The Economic Times* reported that the Finance Ministry was investigating BCs 'demanding thousands of rupees

---

[10] As the official brochure of the PMJDY notes, the government 'proposes to channel all government benefits (from Centre/State/ local bodies) to the beneficiaries to such accounts' (GoI 2014).

[11] For examples of reports that demonstrate the fallibility of fingerprint-based authentication and the exclusion that results, see Yadav (2012, 2016).

in deposits' from account holders. A related issue identified by a survey of BCs by the RBI was that about 47 per cent of the BCs were 'untraceable' in their allotted villages (GoI 2014).

The challenges to the BC model, then, are multifarious. More recently, efforts have been made to restructure the BC model by opening more brick-and-mortar branches and increasing the remuneration to BCs. It is, however, too early to comment on the success of these initiatives.

12.6 CONCLUDING POINTS

This chapter is an attempt to review the status of India's financial inclusion policy, with particular focus on developments after 2004–5.

Like elsewhere in the world, in India too, policy focus on financial inclusion emerged after 2004–5. The motivation behind these policies in India was twofold. One, policies of financial liberalization in the 1990s had led to shrinking access of cultivators and other deprived sections to the public banking system. Two, there was recognition of the fact that millions of people were outside the ambit of the banking system even after some decades of state-led intervention in the credit markets. Financial inclusion policy, then, was a response to these entitlement failures.

However, the new policies were not a throwback to the social and development banking policy that existed after 1969. Instead, they were introduced and implemented within the larger framework of financial liberalization, that is, without compromising on the commercial viability of banking operations.

One of the major initiatives within the new framework of financial inclusion was in agricultural credit. Our disaggregated analysis shows that while the growth rate of agricultural credit sharply rose after 2004, its most important beneficiaries were not farmers, who are direct producers in agriculture. The major beneficiaries were corporate groups, joint-stock companies, and other organizations indirectly involved in agricultural production. A careful look at who are the recipients of agricultural credit and how to ensure that agricultural credit reaches the real farmer are challenges of an immediate nature for policy.

Microfinance was an important component of financial inclusion initiatives in India. This chapter discussed two models of microfinance that have existed in India: NABARD's SHG–Bank Linkage programme and the private MFI model. The SHG–Bank Linkage programme, the largest microfinance programme in the world, expanded access to credit to millions of unbanked women and contributed to a reduction in their livelihood vulnerabilities. On the other hand, the private MFI model has faced serious questions of credibility and viability. At the same time, our analysis also pointed to some infirmities in the SHG–Bank Linkage programme, such as its inability to scale up and the problem of high interest rates. These problems need special attention in India's banking policy.

After 2011, there was a rise in the number of rural bank branches, which more than reversed the impact of closure of rural bank branches between 1995 and 2005. A major challenge that India continues to face is the continued presence of unbanked rural centres. As on 31 December 2015, there were 554,064 rural centres in India that were not covered by a brick-and-mortar branch. The focus of financial inclusion policy has been to fill the gap using the BC model. However, the government and the RBI have noted lack of success in the implementation of the BC model. This chapter discussed the reasons for the failure of the BC model; the argument was that weaknesses of the model were endogenous.

More recently, the RBI has initiated steps to establish Small Finance Banks (SFB) and Payment Banks (PB); these new banks are part of a new differentiated structure for banking envisaged by the RBI. About six SFBs and two PBs—including the India Post Payments Bank (IPPB)—have started operations in early-2017. However, it is presently too early to judge the performance of these new banking units.

At its current stage of development, India needs a big push to bring the unbanked millions into the ambit of public banking. While some progress at financial inclusion was made between 2005 and 2016, the unfinished tasks are enormous. India's financial sector currently needs a policy framework that would facilitate further penetration of public banking into previously excluded regions and sections.

BIBLIOGRAPHY

Aynsley, Helen (2011. *Financial Inclusion and Financial Capability: What's in a Name?* London: Toynbee Hall.

Bateman, Milford. 2010. *Why Doesn't Microfinance Work?* London: Zed Books.

Bhanwala, Harsh Kumar. 2014. Speech at the National Microfinance Conclave 13 November, Mumbai.

Cabinet Office. 2001. *National Strategy for Neighbourhood Renewal: Policy Action Team Audit.* Report by the Social Exclusion Unit, Cabinet Office, London.

Chavan, Pallavi 2004. 'Banking Sector Liberalization and the Growth and Regional Distribution of Rural Banking'. In *Financial Liberalisation and Rural Credit in India*, edited by V.K. Ramachandran and M. Swaminathan. New Delhi: Tulika Books.

———. 2005. 'Banking Sector Reforms and Growth and Regional Distribution of Rural Banking in India'. In *Financial Liberalisation and Rural Credit in India*, edited by V.K. Ramachandran and M. Swaminathan. New Delhi: Tulika Books.

———. 2007. 'Access to Bank Credit: Implications for Rural Dalit Households'. *Economic and Political Weekly* 42(31):3219–23.

———. 2016. 'Bank Credit to Small Borrowers: An Analysis based on Supply and Demand Side Indicators'. *Reserve Bank of India Occasional Papers*, 35.

Chavan, Pallavi and R. Ramakumar. 2002. 'Micro-credit and Rural Poverty: An Analysis of Empirical Evidence'. *Economic and Political Weekly* 37(10): 955–65.

Copestake, James, John Howell, and Steve Wiggins. 1984. *The Structure and Management of Formal Rural Credit in Madurai and Ramnad Districts*, Research Report No 1, The University of Reading, UK.

Government of India. 2014. *Pradhan Mantri Jan-Dhan Yojana: A National Mission on Financial Inclusion*. New Delhi: India: Department of Financial Services, Ministry of Finance.

Jayaraman, B. 2001. 'Micro-Finance: Retrospect and Prospects'. Occasional Paper 20, National Bank for Agriculture and Rural Development, Mumbai.

Karim, Lamia. 2011. *Micro-Finance and Its Discontents: Women in Debt in Bangladesh*. Minneapolis: University of Minnesota Press.

Ministry of Agriculture. 2007. 'Agricultural Credit'. In *Annual Report: 2006–07*. New Delhi: Government of India.

———. 2010. *Report of the Task Force on Credit-Related Issues of Farmers*. Chair: U.C. Sarangi, submitted to the Ministry of Agriculture, Government of India, New Delhi.

Morduch, J. 1999. 'The Microfinance Promise'. *Journal of Economic Literature* 37:1569–614.

Mundra, S.S. 2016. 'Financial Inclusion in India: The Journey So Far and the Way Ahead'. Speech delivered at the BRICS Workshop on Financial Inclusion, Mumbai, 19 September.

NABARD. 2008. *Annual Report 2007–08*. Mumbai: National Bank for Agriculture and Rural Development.

———. *Annual Report 2014–15*. Mumbai: National Bank for Agriculture and Rural Development.

———. *Status of Microfinance in India, 2015–16*. Mumbai: National Bank for Agriculture and Rural Development.

PricewaterhouseCoopers (PwC). 2015. 'Compilation of Drill-down Case Studies of Existing Business Correspondents and Business Correspondent (BC) models in MP'. Report submitted to Small Industries Development Bank of India (SIDBI), October.

Ramachandran, V.K. and Madhura Swaminathan, eds. 2005. *Financial Liberalisation and Rural Credit in India*. New Delhi, Inida: Tulika Books.

Ramakumar, R. 2010. 'A Route to Disaster'. *Frontline* 27(24): 20 November.

———. 2012. 'Cash Evangelism'. *Frontline* 29(25): 28 December.

Ramakumar, R. and Pallavi Chavan. 2005. 'Interest Rates on Micro-credit in India: A Note'. In *Financial Liberalisation and Rural Credit in India*, edited by V.K. Ramachandran and M. Swaminathan. New Delhi: Tulika Books.

———. 2007. 'Revival of Agricultural Credit in the 2000s: An Explanation'. *Economic and Political Weekly* 42(52): 57–64.

———. 2011. 'Changes in the Number of Rural Bank Branches in India, 1991 to 2008'. *Review of Agrarian Studies* 1(1): 141–8.

———. 2013. 'Bank Credit to Agriculture in India in the 2000s: Dissecting the Revival'. *Review of Agrarian Studies* 4(1).

Reddy, Y.V. 2011. 'Microfinance Industry in India: Some Thoughts'. *Economic and Political Weekly* XLVI(41): 46–9.

Reserve Bank of India. 1991. *Report of the Committee on Financial Systems*. Chair: M. Narasimham. Mumbai.

———. 2001. 'Developmental Issues in Micro-Credit'. Speech by Jagdish Capoor. *RBI Bulletin*, March, pp. 305–9.

———. 2005a. 'Monetary Policy Statement 2005–06'. Mumbai.

———. 2005b. 'StCBs/DCCBs—Financial Inclusion'. Circular, Mumbai.

———. 2008a. *Annual Report 2007–08*. Mumbai.

———. 2008b. Report of the 'Committee on Financial Inclusion'. Chair: C. Rangarajan, Mumbai.

———. 2010. *Annual Report 2009–10*. Mumbai.

———. 2011a. *Annual Report 2010–11*. Mumbai.

———. 2011b. *Report of the Sub-Committee of the Central Board of Directors of Reserve Bank of India to Study Issues and Concerns in the MFI Sector*. Chair: Y.H. Malegam, Mumbai.

———. 2013. *Annual Report 2012–13*. Mumbai.

———. 2014. *Annual Report 2013–14*. Mumbai.

———. 2015. *Annual Report 2014–15*. Mumbai.

———. 2016a. *Annual Report 2015–16*. Mumbai.

———. 2016b. *Report of the Internal Working Group on Rationalisation of Branch Authorisation Policy*. Chair: Lily Vadera. Mumbai.

Sharma, M., A. Giri, and S. Chadha. 2016. 'Pradhan Mantri Jan Dhan Yojana (PMJDY) WAVE III Assessment'. Report for Microsave. New Delhi.

Shetty, S.L. 2006. 'Policy Responses to the Failure of Formal Banking Institutions to Expand Credit Delivery for Agriculture and Non-Farm Informal Sectors: The Ground Reality and Tasks Ahead'. Monthly Seminar Series on India's Financial Sector, ICRIER, New Delhi, 14 November.

State Bank of India. 2011. 'E-Circular'. From Chief General Manager (Rural Business), No. RB/AC/RKA/298 dated 18 March 2011.

Subbarao, D. 2012. 'Indian Payment and Settlement Systems Responsible Innovation and Regulation'. Keynote address at the IDRBT Banking Technology Awards Function, Hyderabad, 3 August.

Thorat, Usha. 2010. 'Financial Regulation and Financial Inclusion—Working Together or at Cross-Purposes'. Speech at the 10th Annual International Seminar on Policy Challenges for the Financial Sector, co-hosted by the Federal Reserve System, the International Monetary Fund, and the World Bank, Washington, June 2–4.

———. 2015. 'Inclusion and Opportunity'. *The Indian Express*, 29 May.

UNDP. 2013. *Assessing the Impact of the MGNREGS-Aadhaar Pilot in Jharkhand*. Report, United Nations Development Programme, New Delhi.

United Nations. 2006. *Building Inclusive Financial Sectors for Development*. New York.

Yadav, Anumeha. 2012. 'To Pass Biometric Identification, Apply Vaseline or Boroplus on Fingers Overnight'. Available at http://www.thehindu.com/opinion/op-ed/to-pass-biometric-identification-apply-vaseline-or-boroplus-on-fingers-overnight/article4200738.ece, accessed on 17 January 2018.

———. 2016. 'Rajasthan's Living Dead: Thousands of Pensioners without Aadhaar or Bank Accounts Struck Off Lists'. Available at http://scroll.in/article/813132/rajasthans-living-dead-thousands-of-pensioners-without-aadhaar-or-bank-accounts-struck-off-lists, accessed on 17 January 2018.

13

Rural Enterprises in India

A Review

P.M. Mathew*

ABSTRACT

The 'Fourth Industrial Revolution' that we are in today, is characterized by some major changes in economic structure around the world, and more specifically, in India. The conventional rural-urban divide has given way to a new paradigm of 'Hubanomics'. While the traditional processes of globalization are fast changing, the hegemonic role of technology still continues. Naturally, the influence of the so-called 'new economy' needs to be necessarily factored into the agenda of rural enterprise development. While, there is a general tendency of many of the rural enterprise activities becoming redundant and moving out of the market, there are also new and emerging opportunities, especially in the peri-urban centres of India. Based on the experience of Kerala's rural service enterprises, this chapter spells out a thirteen-point action strategy. The debate could be extended based on the regional specifics of the country. Naturally, the development banks also need to closely follow such debate. They need to worry about shaping innovative lending strategies in the coming days.

JEL Classification: O140, O180

Keywords: new economy, peri-urban development opportunities, rural services

13.1 INTRODUCTION

The Kuznetsian schema of economic transition, popular in the literature of development economics, is a simple way of presenting things. In the twenty-first century, the economy itself has become more complex. From the era of 'Fordism', which was inaugurated in the mid-twentieth century, the world has moved into an era dominated by micro-electronics. Micro-electronics is the common factor that brings together two distinct aspects of human progress, that is, information and communication, into a single platform, and thereon, into a single bundle called

* Senior Fellow and Director, Institute of Small Enterprises and Development, Cochin, India.

The views expressed in the chapter are of the author and not of NABARD, which extended financial support for this research work.

'information and communication technologies' (ICTs) that can further trigger structural changes in the economy. In the era of ICT, spatial distinctions have become near irrelevant. And naturally, the concepts of 'rural' and 'urban' in the development literature are becoming less relevant compared to the past. Unless these major changes are understood in a proper perspective, it is difficult to shape meaningful policies for the rural sector of the country. Against the above-mentioned background, this chapter has six tasks relating to: (*a*) outlining the conceptual framework surrounding rural economic structure; (*b*) bringing to light the key issues of the debate on structural changes in the economy; (*c*) discussing the trends in structural diversification in India, against the global experience; (*d*) bringing to light the micro- meso level processes in structural changes and entrepreneurial performance; (*e*) discussing the implications for policy and shaping of strategies; and (*f*) examining the effectiveness of institutional support regime.

13.2 UNDERSTANDING THE 'RURAL ECONOMY'

The conventional theory of economic growth assumes a tendency towards formalization as the dominant economic behaviour, though varying in degrees among economies. However, the reality is much different in many countries. In India, it is estimated that nearly half of the country's gross domestic product (GDP) and 90 per cent of employment are informal. This high share of the informal economy, which has been considered to be the highest in the world, is a structural problem as well as an opportunity. The tendency within the Indian economy is that of a slow pace of formalization, which is likely to remain slow. Such a hard reality and experience necessitates a closer understanding of this segment of the economy in terms of its structure and progression. This is important because, public policy and development strategies need to be anchored on such an understanding.

13.2.1 Manufacturing and Services: The Changing Trend

There is a wealth of global literature on the industrialization debate. In place of the old dichotomy between 'product' and 'service', there is now a *service–product continuum*. Many products are undergoing change and becoming services. For example, bakeries in rural and semi-urban areas today are largely service enterprises; the place of rural ovens have been taken by large-sized bakery units, which specialize in manufacture.

The global trend, over the past two decades, has been oriented towards the outsourcing of business-related services, such as research and development, financing, or logistics. Services have been contracted out to specialized service providers, or are provided by a newly created firm or spin-off from a manufacturing firm that can provide the services at lower cost and/higher quality. Czarnitzki and Spielkamp (2000), therefore, characterize services industries as 'bridges for innovation', not only for the services sector, but increasingly also for services-using manufacturing industries. Dathe and Schmid (2002) point to the role of regulation in the decision to outsource. If labour markets for services industries are less regulated than those for manufacturing industries, firms may wish to buy services from external providers or outsources, as this may circumvent regulations on dismissal or working time.

There are five main differences between 'services' and 'manufacturing' organizations: (*a*) the tangibility of their output; (*b*) production on demand or for inventory; (*c*) customer-specific production; (*d*) labour-intensive or automated operations; and (*e*) the need for a physical production location. However, in practice, 'services' and 'manufacturing' organizations share many characteristics. Many manufacturers offer their own service operations and both require skilled people to create a profitable business.

In India, the analytical distinction between manufacturing and services mentioned earlier has not often been used for administrative purposes. The nature and type of fixed investment forms the criterion for demarcation. Manufacturing enterprises are identified with investment in 'plant and machinery', whereas service enterprises are identified with 'equipment'. Since different sources of data and various agencies having their distinct purpose and interests deal with small enterprises, it is necessary to have a common understanding of the broad concepts used in such discussions.

The India growth story has been a subject of heated debates. A key area of debates has been related to the share of manufacturing and services and as to how manufacturing has declined over time. There are diverging perceptions on the rural–urban divide in India. According to Abhijit Sen, 'if ideas and capital move, even if people don't move, we will reach a stage where we will forget the rural–urban divide'. According to him, while there is an understanding of what 'rural' India means, there is no real definition of it. To truly understand rural India, one needs to go beyond the census yardsticks and take note of the changes that have occurred in the last ten years. Notable among these have been increased connectivity, higher enrolment in and completion of school education, and the spread of cell phones across rural India. These have, in some measure, changed the face of 'rural' India, taking it beyond the commonly held definitions. Additionally, the focus should be on connectivity and innovative ideas for rural development.

At the national level, there are several studies including the output of individual research and reports of official committees. NABARD itself has brought out several studies on the subject area and related fields. The role of the non-agricultural rural sector in reducing poverty has been an area of intensive academic debates in India. The rural non-agricultural sector in most developing countries accounts for roughly 40 per cent of rural incomes. Nearly 40 per cent of men and 50 per cent of economically active women are employed in this sector. The sector represents an important route out of poverty—poverty declines as the share of total income from non-agricultural sources rises. Recent evidences indicate that employment and earnings in the non-agricultural sector are increasingly influenced by a new set of variables. Of these, the level of education and also access to infrastructure stand out as key elements. While women are more likely to be employed in this sector than are men, their earnings for the given levels of education and other household characteristics are significantly lower. Employment opportunities in these activities are crucial determinants that explain income gains of the poor.

As agricultural transformation takes place and urbanization proceeds, consumption as well as input/output links with urban areas are strengthened. Urbanization implies changes in the tastes and preferences of the consumers as well. According to the National Sample Survey Office Survey 2011, there were 57.7 million non-corporate business units excluding the construction sector. While seven out of ten of them are unregistered, the size of this segment has almost doubled since 1998. Of these, 85 per cent are 'own account enterprises' (OAE) (or self-employment units) and the rest are 'establishments' employing wage labour. The aggregate value addition by these units is Rs 6.28 lakh crore—70 per cent of it in rural areas. Value addition, per unit, and per worker, was Rs 1.09 lakhs and Rs 58,000 respectively. Value added per hired worker is Rs 47,000, which equals the average per capita income of India in 2009–10; this is higher than the rural per capita income. These enterprises employ 108 million people (rural—53 million). These units also employ capital that is not insignificant. The value of fixed assets per unit is Rs 2 lakhs. A fourth of these units are engaged in manufacturing, and more than two-thirds in retail trade and services. Mobile phone repairing is a

typical example of a service industry that has emerged in the rural and semi-urban areas over the past one decade.

Growth of the non-farm sector in India demonstrates two broad patterns of entrepreneurships: (a) necessity-driven; and (b) and opportunity-driven. The experience of agrarian crisis and the acceleration of the 'new economy' in the mid-2000s have resulted in the growth of self-employment opportunities. However, the movement of rural labour still remains largely confined to agriculture and related works. The potentially more lucrative rural non-farm (RNF) activities are largely cornered by the really well-to-do sections in the rural areas. The challenge of public policy, therefore, is to harness the synergies of the RNF sector, and to exploit them to the best advantage of the poor.

According to the National Sample Survey Office (NSSO) Survey 2011, there were 57.7 million non-corporate business units excluding the construction sector. While seven out of ten of them are unregistered, the size of this segment has almost doubled since 1998. Of these, 85 per cent are 'own account enterprises' (OAE) (or self-employment units) and the rest are 'establishments' employing wage labour. The aggregate value addition by these units is Rs 6.28 lakh crore—70 per cent of it in rural areas. Value addition, per unit, and per worker, was Rs 1.09 lakh and Rs 58,000 respectively. Value added per hired worker is Rs 47,000, which equals the average per capita income of India in 2009–10; this is higher than the rural per capita income. They employ 108 million (rural—53 million). The units do employ capital that is not insignificant. The value of fixed assets per unit is Rs 2 lakh. A fourth of these units is engaged in manufacturing, and more than two thirds in retail trade and services.

How much does the non-farm sector's growth in India depend on agriculture? More recent studies on the Indian experience depart from the conventional understanding of non-farm sector growth and its linkages. For example, Binswanger-Mkhize (2013) note that there is a significant tendency towards autonomous growth of the RNF sector, even when agriculture remains stagnant. The finding is that India's economy has accelerated sharply since the late 1980s, but agriculture has not. The rural population and labour force continue to rise, and rural–urban migration remains slow.

The interaction between manufacturing and services industries can take various forms. Depending on the type of interaction, different conclusions may have to be drawn as regards its implications for productivity growth and employment. In the available literature there are four broad categories of interaction between manufacturing and services: They are (*a*) vertical integration; (*b*) buying-in of components; (*c*) transaction costs; and (*d*) outsourcing of service functions.

Beyond conceptual distinctions operational distinctions are crucial from the point of view of policy and shaping of strategies. There are five main operational differences between service and manufacturing organizations. They are: (*a*) tangibility of output; (*b*) production on demand or for inventory; (*c*) customer-specific production; (*d*) labour-intensive or automated operations; and (*e*) need for a physical production location. However, in practice, service and manufacturing organizations share many characteristics. Many manufacturers, as already noted, offer their own service operations, along with their core activity.

13.3 THE STRUCTURAL CHANGES DEBATE: CURRENT STATUS AND PERSPECTIVES

It is important to discuss the phenomenon of changes in economic structure in relation to its two dimensions: (*a*) global; and (*b*) national. This is because the processes are distinct; so also is the nature of the value chains. It is important that these specifics are properly understood.

13.3.1 Global Discussion on Growth

There is a rich source of international literature on economic growth and structure, which provides insights into the comparative growth experience of countries in relation to their share and role of the services sector. The international literature on the subject has come essentially from organizations such as the World Bank, the Food and Agriculture Organization of the United Nations (FAO), and the International Fund for Agricultural Development (IFAD). The *Eurostat*, in the context of the European Union, provides useful insights in addition to important methodological contributions.

Rural services, as a subset of the services sector, need to be discussed in the context of the RNF sector growth. According to Nagler and Naudé (2014), three important stages of the RNF sector transformation have been identified in literature.

The mainstream and the focal phenomenon of today is the growth of the 'new economy'. The word, 'new economy' was coined by the business press in the late 1990s, in order to mean two broad trends in the world economy which have been underway for some time (Shepard 1997). Of these, the first one is the globalization of business, which essentially means the international expansion of markets guided by trade, capital flows, and organization of work processes. The second trend is the revolution in ICT, which in turn acts as a facilitator of the expanded global operation of capital. This, in fact, is not a sudden development, but a more advanced stage of a longer process, starting from the invention of the transistor in the late 1940s, the growth of semiconductor manufacturing in the mid-1990s, and the increase in network computing. Functionally, this leads to a superior economic structure called the 'new economy'. A business firm, industry, or an economy which is able to successfully utilize these global trends would eventually outperform its rivals.

While innovation in small enterprises has been an area of active academic debates for the last several years, the actual drivers of innovation have not gained the attention that they deserve. The discussion on innovation is largely in the context of the individual firm, whereas the external changes in the economy have not been properly analysed and understood. In the modern world, these changes can be summarized under the rubric 'the new economy'. An understanding of the new economy and its influence on small enterprises is essential for planning and development of strategies.

There are some important but overlapping themes that differentiate the 'new economy' from the old. They are: (*a*) knowledge; (*b*) digitization; (*c*) virtualization; (*d*) molecularization and integration/internet working; (*e*) dis-intermediation; (*f*) convergence; (*g*) innovation; (*h*) prosumption; (*i*) immediacy; (*j*) globalization; (*k*) discordance; and (*l*) boom of self-employment.

13.3.1.1 Origin of the New Economy Wave

In India, the 'new economy' wave was kick-started with the economic reforms, with the goal of making the economy more market-oriented and expanding the role of private and foreign investment. The specific changes under the new economy wave include a reduction in import tariffs, deregulation of markets, reduction of taxes, and greater foreign investment. Liberalization has been credited by its proponents for the high economic growth recorded by the country in the 1990s and 2000s. There has been significant debate, however, around liberalization as an inclusive economic growth strategy. Available literature suggests the following broad outcomes of the above reform initiatives:

- Enhanced growth rate: The low annual growth rate of the economy of India before 1980, stagnated around 3.5 per cent from the 1950s to 1980s, while per capita income averaged 1.3 per cent. At the same time, Pakistan grew by 5 per cent, Indonesia by 9 per cent, Thailand by 9 per cent, South Korea by 10 per cent, and Taiwan by 12 per cent.

- Industrial decontrol: Only four or five licences would be given for steel, electrical power, and communications. This regime was done away with.
- Growth of the private sector: Focus on disinvestment.
- Income tax department and customs department became efficient in checking tax evasion.
- Greater focus on infrastructure: Infrastructure investment was poor because of the public sector monopoly.
- Progressive reduction of 'inspector raj' and 'license raj'.

The fruits of liberalization reached their peak in 2007, when India recorded its highest GDP growth rate of 9 per cent. With this, the country became the second fastest growing major economy in the world, next only to China. The growth rate slowed significantly in the first half of 2012. An Organisation for Economic Co-operation and Development (OECD) report states that the average growth rate of 7.5 per cent will double the average income in a decade, and more reforms would speed up the pace. The impact of these reforms may be gauged from the fact that total foreign investment (including foreign direct investment, portfolio investment, and investment raised on international capital markets) in India grew from a minuscule US$132 million in 1991–2 to US$5.3 billion in 1995–6.

As in the corporate sector, the micro-meso private sector also underwent some significant changes during the reform era. The era of size-based product reservation for manufacture was done away with. The lifting of quantitative restrictions threw away some constraints on manufacture. In India, despite its long history of micro, small, and medium enterprises (MSME) development policy, our efforts towards knowledge creation and its transmission to the context of this sector is much below global standards. Quantitative restrictions (QRs), which offered a protective framework to the MSMEs, were abandoned. However, being exposed to the open market, the sector did not get the benefit. While, a level playing ground was expected to be brought through the liberalization policy, the result was not in tune with the expectations of the sector. At the policy level, it was argued that while innovation is the mantra of sustainability of the sector, action in this regard was relatively constrained.

In a knowledge economy, the sustainability of MSMEs cannot be expected on a stand-alone basis. It needs the benefits of inter-sectoral linkages. Here, the old concepts of development dependence essentially on imported technology has a lesser role. In the 'new economy', space and time are crucial, and they need to be best used through local knowledge systems. India's track record relating to knowledge systems specific to the MSME sector needs much more improvement.

The 'new economy' phenomenon essentially touches on two critical constraints in the day-to-day functioning of an economy: (a) time; and (b) space. Just-in-time production methods facilitate an effective management of time, which reduces the production cycle, and thereby the unit cost of production. The growth of micro-electronics, and of information technology in particular, makes possible production on a global scale, which again helps to bring down unit cost of production, as also the constraints on the supply side. On the demand side, the expansion in information technology facilitates understanding of products and their market behaviour in real time, thereby making consumer choice easier than before.

13.3.1.2 Concepts, Measurement, and Policy Challenges

Some services are crucial in the development of specific technological innovations. Business services, especially knowledge-intensive services (KIS), are used as intermediate inputs in production due to their positive effects on innovation in those companies that make use of these services.

Business knowledge-intensive services have achieved an important role in modern economies and national innovation systems (Kox and Rubalcaba 2007; Windrum and Tomlinson 1999), and favour the modernization of a country's knowledge base. Traditionally, most of the discussion of the management of innovation has been in the context of manufacturing. This is not surprising because manufacturers have tangible products, the development of which normally follows a well-defined process. However, the service sector is now of major importance in many countries of the world.

13.3.1.3 The Nature of Service Products

Innovation management, in the context of services, is a complex subject. Service products are mostly intangible. Manufactured products often offer customer service as an after-sales component; interaction with customers is built into the delivery of services. Therefore, innovation in service companies is altogether a much different task than in manufacturing. Not only about 'what' is being offered has to be addressed, but also about 'how' it is being offered. While the very concept of innovation implies an addition of new knowledge and its practice, the task is again compounded (Kox and Rubalcaba 2007).

13.3.2 The Debate in India

India has a distinctive role for the rapid growth of its service sector—high-tech, communication, and business services in particular. Unlike the conventional three-stage theory of economic growth, India's shift from agriculture to the services sector has been faster. However, whether the service sector provides a route out of poverty for the masses, and thus a path to rapid growth, is a matter that needs to be closely examined.

In India, service sector growth is widespread across activities. However, the fastest growing are business services, communication, and banking, all of which belong to Group III. Business services, which include computer-related services, machinery rental, accounting, legal services, technical services, and research, of which computer services (which accounted for about four-fifths of business services in 2005–6) is the single fastest growing segment. Financial services include banking and insurance, with banking being the largest and fastest growing. Other rapidly growing sectors include hotels, restaurants, education, health (all Group II), and trade and transport (Group I). The transport sector includes road, railway, air, and water transport. The most dynamic of these is road transport, which increased six-fold between 1991–2 and 2005–6. The stagnant service sectors in India have been public administration and defence, whose growth seems to have levelled off, and miscellaneous other personal services. The share of Group I services stagnated following an early period of rapid growth. By contrast, the share of Group II continued growing steadily, while that of Group III has accelerated since 1990. On balance, then, India has been moving in the direction of higher-tech services.

The issue of looking at 'services' as the gateway to development in India has, of late, been widely debated (Agrawal 2012; Chandrasekhar 2011). While the arguments often focus on the so-called 'triple bottom line', the productivity argument has not been well articulated in the Indian context. While 'service sector boom' is a reality that is interpreted differently by the promotional agencies and the bankers, strategies need to be based on ground-level understanding of the content of the so-called 'services'. Raghuram Rajan (2011) analyses certain economies that grew through the government pressuring local industry to focus on exports, with Japan being a key case study. He points out that by propping up a small group of these firms, it actually did great harm to local innovation and local economic efficiency. Innovations by new entrants are often checkmated by existing and politically powerful guilds, which influence the government and see to it that the very competitive conditions are changed in such a way that it makes it difficult for the new start-ups to function. Typically, they cannot compete any more. This has played out in many sectors such as transport, retail, and construction, where a few incumbents monopolize what is going on, and do not allow a different kind of growth. While Raghuram Rajan's argument is contestable, it raises some important issues that demand an introspection on the nature of service sector growth at the regional and local levels, especially in relation to the role of public promotional agencies and public financial institutions.

The role of the services sector in the Indian economy has been widely debated. Most of these studies have been based on National Accounts Statistics (NAS). However, authors like, Gupta and Gordon (2001), Mattoo, Mishra and Singhal (2001), and Bosworth et al. (2007) have raised doubts about the usefulness of NAS data used to compare the growth of the relative share of sectors. Various studies on the sectoral growth behaviour in the Indian economy show an increasingly similar mix of skilled and unskilled labour. Hence, it has been argued that both modern manufacturing and modern services are constrained by lack of skilled labour. This rationalizes the official policy thrust on skill development.

13.3.2.1 Skills, Self-employment, and Rural Pegging

The concept of skills in the context of small enterprise development, has been questioned by some scholars (see, for instance, Mathew 2014 and ISED 2014). In the mainstream discussions on skill development, the focus has been on modular skills, leaving aside the crucial role of motivational skills. It is motivation that determines labour flows, though skills imparted need to be productively used. In the Indian context, this does not often happen and has implications for entrepreneurship development policy and strategies.

The three-stage theory of economic growth considers shifting of labour from agriculture to industry and then to services as a necessary sequence. Scholars have raised doubts on the need for such a transition. Why not think of a policy of 'rural pegging' by enhancing the productivity of agriculture, and rural services? This option needs to be discussed against the experience of growth and structural changes in these sectors.

13.4 STRUCTURAL CHANGES AND ENTREPRENEURIAL PERFORMANCE

The 'new economy' essentially means new rules of the game based on an altogether different kind of knowledge base. Both for the management of knowledge and for drawing from its benefits, some co-operant services are required. For example, while there is a demand for telephony, and as education and socialization grow, a larger number of people would need the opportunity of telephony. For many people, the same usage of telephony services would need to be enhanced. While telephony is a service widely used by civilized people across the world, the need for telephony gets reflected in the market in a larger number of phones than before. For example, a visitor who has landed in a new city would require to ensure that he has a mobile phone with him. He may need to change his SIM card for a prepaid connection or to reduce his telephony costs. While making an international call, he would be on the lookout for a cheaper calling facility than the usual Integrated Services Digital Network (ISDN). In the modern world, all the above facilities are available, and all such services are provided by a series of service providers, starting from the mobile phone company down to a shopkeeper who sells prepaid SIM cards.

The example, as mentioned earlier, indicates two things: First, there is an array of services available for satisfying a human want today. Second, as a particular demand is satisfied, new demands are created with much greater speed than before. In this paradigm of new types of delivery system for a particular demand, and altogether new demands, the number of new income opportunities are added on a progressive basis. These opportunities emerge from services rather than from hard-core manufacturing, as before.

According to estimates by the NSSO, carried in the report titled 'Household Consumption of Various Goods and Services in India', there has been a significant penetration of consumer goods in rural India during 2004–5 and 2011–12. Ownership of products such as cars, motorcycles, and white goods more than doubled between 2004–5 and 2011–12, but lower than in the urban markets. About 50 per cent of the rural households owned a television in 2011–12 compared with 25 per cent in 2004–5, as per the NSSO, and 9.4 per cent households

in villages possessed a refrigerator in 2011–12 against 4.4 per cent seven years ago. Spending on products such as mobiles and laptops also rose at a faster pace in the rural areas during the period. As per NSSO data, about 2 per cent of rural households owned a car in 2011–12 compared with just 0.8 per cent in 2004–5. In 2011–12, nearly 13 per cent of rural households incurred expenditure on a mobile handset, higher than 12 per cent of urban households. The data shows that the faster rise in rural incomes than in the urban areas led to a near doubling of spending in the hinterlands during the period that saw flat overall sales in various categories.

Another significant aspect revealed by the above data is that the increase in rural spending happened even against the dismal power supply situation in the country. If the power situation in the country improves, consumption in rural areas could rise at an even faster rate. The number of rural households consuming electricity went up by 36 per cent between 2004–5 and 2011–12. This contributed to the higher sales of products such as refrigerators and televisions. Rural areas contribute 25–30 per cent to the sales of white goods companies.

While agri inflation is higher than the non-agricultural inflation in the country, there has been an increased tendency for income to get transferred from urban areas to rural areas. Several flagship programmes of the government, such as, rural roads programmes, the Mahatma Gandhi National Rural Guarantee Act (MGNREGA), and microfinance have all led to a rise in rural incomes from 2004–5. Moreover, the gap between rural and urban consumption patterns and expenditures had narrowed to a large extent in the past few years, and is expected to converge over the next decade.

The higher expenditure by rural households on consumer durables is also a result of the availability of these products in the villages, besides the rise in incomes. Also, they are much cheaper compared to 20 years ago when rural households would have had to spend their entire life savings just to buy white goods.

13.4.1 'New Economy' Services

The most dynamic sector in the last decade globally has been the services sector. India is said to have outpaced a number of countries with its growth in the services sector, powered by software and business process outsourcing (BPO) services. Unni and Ravi Kiran (2011) examine whether any of India's high-productivity, high-income growth in the services sector is occurring in rural India, and if so, to what extent. Though disaggregated data on services is not adequately available in the Indian context, available studies have shown the following broad indications.

a.   Different subsectors of the services sector have changed over time (Mukherjee et al. 2014).
b.   After the economic reforms of 1990, the share of services sector in GDP has increased.
c.   Share of financing and transport have increased. Community, social, and personal services have declined.
d.   During the 1950s–1960s, transport, storage and communication services, trade, and hotel and restaurants grew faster.
e.   During 1970s–1980s, financing and business services grew faster.
f.   There is a mismatch between production structure and occupational structure. Therefore, services sector growth is essentially 'jobless'.

An analysis of these major trends in relation to growth of the new economy will help to understand how the rural services subsector moves today, as also the shape of things that are emerging. Unlike in the 1997–2002 period, declining savings rate in the corporate sector is a characteristic feature of the subsequent economic downturn in the country. Unless the rate of savings picks up, investments cannot take place at the desired level. Moreover, the economy has been reeling under the pressure of inflation. There is a significant reluctance on the part of public sector banks to enhance the flow of credit to the MSMEs, though this sector is willing to step up the level of investments. The situation, as outlined earlier, demands a major restructuring of policy. Such a policy change, at the macro level, can happen through the application of macroeconomic instruments which can enhance the level of investment. The union government, under its new leadership, seeks to address this issue through a two-pronged strategy: (*a*) promotion of FDI; and (*b*) boost to local investment promotion, including start-up, with focus on MSMEs.

The data for the past two decades indicate that in India, the corporate sector is much more sensitive to global developments than the MSME sector, which seems to be more attuned to the dynamics of the domestic economy. Despite claims by the Finance Minister that GDP growth in the coming quarters could be higher than the 5.7 per cent at which the economy expanded during April–June 2014, economists have raised doubts on the chances of corporate investment recovering in the immediate future. If so, the option, if any, is available with the

MSMEs. How is the MSME scene today in terms of its potential? Our analysis based on the Economic Census gives some important results.

India's entrepreneurial talent embedded in the so-called bottom of the pyramid is substantial. The findings of the Sixth Economic Census demonstrate this. According to the Census, the net increase in the number of non-agricultural establishments in the country is estimated to be about 8 million every 10 years. While involving an array of sizes and scope, in terms of investment and employment, the primary task of public policy needs to be to pinpoint and understand these specificities. Our failure to harness the potential of the MSMEs is an indicator of a serious policy paralysis.

13.4.2 Regional and Sub-sectoral Distribution

Over the years, the share of services in the GDP of different Indian states has increased, but there are variations across states in terms of share of the services sector in the GDP and its growth. In 2009–10, share of services in the GDP of states such as Bihar, Delhi, Kerala, Maharashtra, Mizoram, Nagaland, Tamil Nadu, Tripura, and West Bengal was higher than the all-India average, while in Chhattisgarh and Himachal Pradesh it was lower. The growth rate of services for states such as Arunachal Pradesh and Sikkim is higher than the all-India average while that of Andhra Pradesh, Karnataka, Rajasthan, Nagaland, and Tripura is lower (*Economic Survey 2011–12*). Even though the share of services sector in GDP is high for states such as Nagaland and Tripura, it is expected to fall in future because of falling growth rates. Kochhar et al. (2006) found that the share of public sector services including administration is growing in laggard states, while the share of private sector services is growing in fast-growing states. A number of fast-growing states have shown a decline in growth in manufacturing and rise in services.

An analysis of the contribution of services subsectors to India's GDP shows some interesting results. There are variations in the growth and performance of different subsectors of services. Business services (including IT), communications, and trade have grown faster than the overall services sector growth in India. Others such as real estate, legal services, transport, storage and personal administration, and defense services have grown at the same rate as the overall services sector growth (see Gordon and Gupta 2003). Existing literature shows that services such as IT, telecommunications, and financing services have contributed to the high growth of the services sector. Hansda (2001) and Joshi (2008) have pointed out that the rise in the export demand of IT has led to high services growth in India.

Following the economic reforms of the 1990s, the share of all the services subsectors in GDP has increased. Studies have also shown that the share of financing, trade, and transport sectors in total services sector has increased, while that of community, social, and personal services has declined. This 'new economy effect' needs to be understood properly from the point of view of policy and financing strategies.

The recent structural changes in the service sector demands innovations in development strategies and financing. The challenge today is to understand and appreciate entrepreneurship as a critical resource that can trigger a variety of economic activities around it. The major challenge in this regard is not simply development action by the government, but development financing. As the latest thinking of the Government of India goes, there need to be more governance than governmental interventions for development. Development banking alone can perform this role meaningfully. While the major changes in the strategic approach to banking in the country during the past few decades witnessed a major shift from development banking to universal banking, the need for a comeback has been increasingly felt. In this context, there is need for a fresh look at policy and the role of institutions and organizations.

13.4.3 Role of Institutions

Institutions are best understood as the 'rules of the game' (North 1990) which shape human behaviour in economic, social, and political life (IPPG 2012). Organizations can best be understood as the formally or informally coordinated vehicles for the promotion or protection of a mix of individual and shared ideas (IPPG 2012). They are the 'players' of the game. Strengthening institutions and organizations provides an opportunity to optimize performance and outcomes of social interventions and development projects. Such a policy approach was lost sight of in the country in recent times. For example, organizations such as NABARD have significant potential to be explored and utilized. There was no serious effort to identify a new role and relevance for agencies such as the Coir Board and the Khadi Village Industries Commission (KVIC). The rural industries, in general, did not get an integrated policy support. On the other hand, each of these institutions retained their proud place within the limited confines of their respective subsectoral constituencies.

Various studies have discussed the above issue during the past few years (Mathew 2012, 2014; ISED 2014;

Chandrasekhar 2010), in addition to the rich sources of international literature. It is important that the relationship between policy, institutions, and organizations is critically analysed on the basis of available literature. The role of NABARD deserves a special mention here.

Besides the above, the present researcher has directed several studies on the non-farm sector in the context of the 'India MSME Communication Programme', and the 'India MSME Report' Project. The 'India MSME Report' provides an annual review of the non-farm sector since 1997. The experience gained in the context of this project would be a rich source of information.

13.4.4 Informal Sector

Despite the presence of a large number of manufacturing and service enterprises in the informal sector in India, we know very little about their characteristics and evolution over time. Rajesh and Sen (2016) present some puzzles about firms in the Indian informal manufacturing sector using unit-level data from the NSSO surveys of unorganized enterprise from 2000–1 to 2010–11. There is clear evidence of a positive relationship between workers' wages and firm productivity, indicating the importance of improving firm productivity in the Indian informal sector as a means to improve the living standards of workers. This analysis also shows that there are social and economic barriers to informal enterprises increasing their productivity, which is a matter of major policy concern. There are also gender-related differences in the productivity of firms.

The question as to which of the characteristics of firms matter in explaining variations in wages paid to workers and firm productivity in the Indian informal manufacturing sector is more relevant today. Digging deeper into the Indian informal manufacturing sector through the analysis of detailed firm-level data, Rajesh and Sen find that there has been a downward shift in the size of the average informal firm in the Indian manufacturing sector over time. They find average firm size declining in both own account manufacturing enterprises (OAMEs) and non-directory manufacturing establishments (NDMEs) while remained stagnant among the Directory Manufacturing Establishments (DMEs). Moreover, they find that rural DMEs are larger in size and have experienced a faster increase in size compared to urban DMEs over the study period. In terms of labour productivity, they notice an inverted-U relationship between firm size and firm performance: productivity increases up to a certain large size before stagnating or declining. Productivity is highest among firms that operate from fixed premises, and have permanent structure, but the evidence is not decisive on the role of fixed premises and permanent structures on driving up productivity. Surprisingly, this analysis also suggests that female-owned proprietary DMEs are larger in size and more productive than their male-owned counterparts.

The attempt of Rajesh and Sen (2016) at understanding the correlates of wages and labour productivity reveals that firm size, gender and social group of the firm owner, and locations of the firm are important determinants of wages and labour productivity in the informal manufacturing sectors. The analysis clearly suggests that the most effective way to increase the wages of informal workers is to increase the productivity of the enterprises they work in, and that the larger these enterprises are, the more productive they are. However, the analysis also shows that there are social and economic barriers to informal enterprises in increasing their productivity.

13.4.5 Exclusion and Inclusive Development Strategies

Controlling for other factors, Rajesh and Sen find enterprises owned by members of disadvantaged social groups such as the SC and ST, and female-owned enterprises are less productive than those headed by the OBC and general social groups, and by males. This suggests that targeted government programmes towards these groups may help reduce the disparities in wages of workers employed in enterprises headed by these groups and the wages of workers in enterprises owned by males from the OBC and general social groups. The two researchers conclude that targeted government programmes are needed to address the issues which socially disadvantaged groups and female entrepreneurs face in the informal manufacturing sector.

13.5 NEW ECONOMY LINKAGES: EVIDENCES FROM THE FIELD

The above discussion leads us to two broad changes in the rural economic structure: (*a*) Within several critical constraints faced by the agricultural sector, structural changes are broadly in favour of a broad-based enterprise system; and (*b*) the new additions to the enterprise system are increasingly service enterprises than manufacturing.

Rural services have a great significance in an emerging economy for a variety of reasons. First, there is an angle of inclusiveness embedded in it. An unemployed person with a minimum of investible funds can enter into this sector. Second, from the point of view of employment promotion, public programmes for enterprise development target this sector. Because of these reasons, the sector has a high visibility. Therefore, from the angle of sustainability, it is important to have a policy focus on this sector. With the introduction of the MSME Development Act, 2006, a broad-based definition of MSMEs came into force, which implies a significant place for the services as well. In Kerala, the services sector has a much greater importance than elsewhere in the country.

In India, labour productivity in the services sector is the highest, and it has increased over time. However, in the era of 'jobless growth' that India has been undergoing, its employment effects are not commensurate with the GDP contribution. Besides, a large part of such employment is contributed by the rural unorganized sector. Therefore, in order to enhance employment opportunities, and to sustain them, either per-unit employment or the number of enterprises, or both, should increase. This policy question demands a deeper understanding of structural changes in the rural economy, with focus on service enterprises. This is because enterprise is the basic unit of strategy in an agenda of enterprise development.

Industry-related service and business-related enterprises with investment in fixed assets, excluding land and building, up to Rs 5 crores, irrespective of location as on 31 March 2007 are to be treated as registered services (formerly known as SSSBEs). The list of services covered under the erstwhile definition of SSSBEs will also form the part of services enterprise. While in the MSME sector, for all practical purposes, manufacturing and service activities are often intertwined, and it is quite difficult to distinguish between manufacturing and services, there are some broad patterns and leads of the growth of the sector that provide broad indications on the changes underway. Such indications are given by the results of the All India Census of MSMEs. What determines the size of a specific subsector in the economy? It is a resultant of both objective and subjective factors. The distinction between 'opportunity entrepreneurship' and 'necessity entrepreneurship' has great relevance in influencing such entrepreneurial decisions. In a case where the returns on manufacturing is felt to be much lower than the returns on services (considering transaction costs as well) entrepreneurs have a tendency to opt for the latter. But there is also a question of long-term expected returns and short-term returns. How this trade-off takes place depends both on macroeconomic and subjective factors.

13.5.1 Kerala: A Case of Rapid Transition

The above discussion leads us to the conclusion that it is the changes in the demand pattern that, to a large extent, explain the structural changes in the rural enterprise scene. The caveat applicable in this context is imports. In the context of Kerala, it is the important changes in the rural and urban consumption pattern that significantly explains the structural changes in the rural enterprises. Kerala is not a typical case of the Indian experience of rural transition. However, it gives some learnings on how improvement in quality of life can lead to a change in economic structure. In this context, the experience of Tamil Nadu is closer to that of Kerala. Given Kerala's peculiar economic geography, the rural–urban divide in consumption pattern is much less relevant compared to that of other states. It is also important to note that there has been a significant leakage from this backward linkage effect, as explained by the significant imports, especially of consumer goods, that is, the so-called 'Chinese market' phenomenon. An analysis of Kerala's changing consumption pattern, drawn from the data furnished by the NSSO, gives some important indications (Mathew 2016).

The fact that Kerala stands first in terms of the average monthly per capita consumption expenditure (MPCE) has important implications on consumer behaviour in the rural, urban, and overall settings. In fact, these distinctions are getting progressively eroded over time, as the pace of international migration and out-migration proceeds across the length and breadth of the state. Migration and outmigration set in motion a particular pattern of urbanization.

The household consumer expenditure data for Kerala, from 57th (2001–2), 59th (2003), 62nd (2005–6), 64th (2007–8), and 66th (2009–10) rounds of NSSO, indicate that it is the rural sector of the state which plays a significant role in pulling up Kerala's consumer expenditure.

Rural services are a critical subsector in Kerala. While the state is characteristically a rural–urban continuum, it is important that the goods and services in demand by the people are serviced effectively. How this role has been performed by the services sector in the state is a matter of critical importance both from the point of view of policy and practise of enterprise development. A study was specially devoted to look into the current status of the rural services sector in Kerala. The special focus on services is for the reason that in most of the self-employment programmes, which are dominant in the state, new service enterprises take shape with a significant mushrooming effect. It is also important that the growth of these enterprises is properly channelized from the point of view of their sustainability and growth. Considering the importance of the sector, a special study was conducted for the requirements of this project.

The Institute of Small Enterprises and Development (ISED)/NABARD study, while looking into the emerging trends in the rural services sector, in relation to its structural and related aspects, analysed its 'New Economy' effect. Considering the level of technology and entrepreneurship, with focus on recent changes, it examined the critical constraints in development, and suggested measures to overcome them. The research also looked into the financing pattern and requirements of the sector, to makes relevant recommendations on appropriate strategies, with critical comments on the changing role and capabilities of institutions and organizations in channelizing the potential of this vital subsector. The study was focused on a sample survey of 100 service enterprises from two districts, namely, Ernakulam and Idukki. Our detailed enquiries, on the above lines, led us to some important findings as follows.

13.5.2 Growth Experience

Unlike the national level experience, services in Kerala remain relatively less significant in terms of micro level performance indicators. The small size of the services industry, dominance of family labour, small capital base, limited growth, limited diversification, and innovation are some of the characteristic features. However, at the policy level, these internal weaknesses of Kerala have not gained proper attention. On the other hand, Kerala's growth relating to MSMEs has been projected as a success story, both by the state government and the popular media in relation to variables such as number of units registered and estimated employment and figures.

13.5.3 Skills and Entrepreneurship

Kerala's experience of entrepreneurship development, as per the evidences available to this research, can be explained in relation to a concept of a *renteer entrepreneurship ratchet*. Unlike the global experience of a clear division between 'necessity' and 'opportunity' entrepreneurship, Kerala's experience remains unique. As studies by the ISED and the ISED Small Observatory indicate, there is a disproportionate growth of 'necessity entrepreneurship'. During the early phase of accelerated industrialization effects of the early 1970's, there existed a mix of both 'necessity'- and 'opportunity'-oriented entrepreneurship; the surge in migration since the 1970s resulted in a weakening of opportunity entrepreneurship. It is important that this bias is corrected through policy measures. There is also a significant lethargy towards serious start-up initiatives, both for the unemployed people and for the state. This precarious position explains Kerala's unsatisfactory position relating to entrepreneurship, even in promising areas like IT, despite the state's natural advantages.

Regarding the medium and the corporate sector, Kerala's record today is confined to education and health services, where the private sector has come up to some extent. However, these achievements are a continuation of the legacy created by the dominant religious groups and castes who have taken up some initiatives since the mid-nineteenth century. Besides, the new private initiatives raise serious questions of quality and innovation.

Over the last five years, there have been some isolated attempts by the corporate sector in the areas of media and IT and related areas; they are still to prove to be of any significant impact. Given the huge size of the services market in Kerala, the supply response needs closer examination. Having a relatively weak base of enterprise and entrepreneurship, as demonstrated by the 'Kerala model of development', it is necessary to look into the causal relationship that explains such weak enterprise and entrepreneurship base. Our field research shows a mixed experience of entrepreneurial attributes that constrain a major transformation in favour of the huge and emerging opportunities in the services sector (Tables 13.1 to 13.3). The field research shows a significant career stigma that has been explained by some of the important responses by entrepreneurs. Consequently, growth is stalled. However, this simply does not mean lack of achievement motivation. But achievement motivation is limited to the rigidities of the business ecosystem of Kerala. These rigidities, to a large extent, are explained by sociological factors, such as the value system, role of the media, and family bondages.

13.5.4 New Economy Effect

'New economy' is the major innovation driver in the modern world. It brings in radical changes in the demand pattern within a relatively short period of time, demanding innovations on the production line as also in service delivery. While, at the national level, the changes associated with the new economy shows some broad indicators of such a change in areas like use of ICT products and services, as also in relation to access to some of the modern services, the demand for such services is indicated by the per capita consumption behaviour. It is important to examine the consumption basket for a realistic understanding of the potential of various rural services. On this count, the experience of Kerala stands out. Kerala has a remarkable position at the national level, in terms of its diversity of the consumption basket. This, alternatively, implies a big market potential for several

Table 13.1 Progression of Entrepreneurs

Career Track Types	Kunnathunadu	Pallipuram	Muttom	Adimali	Total
1. Job track unchanged	29	12	27	19	87 (36.25%)
2. Job track completely changed	16	22	20	24	82 (34.17%)
3. Job track broadly the same	15	26	13	17	71 (29.58%)
Total	**60**	**60**	**60**	**60**	**240 (100%)**

Source: Author.

Table 13.2 Skill-sets of the Entrepreneurs

Skill Domain	Kunnathunadu	Pallipuram	Muttom	Adimali	Total
1. Commercial	4	4	3	4	15 (6.25%)
2. Technical	2	4	2	1	9 (3.75%)
3. Soft	1	3	2	1	7 (2.92%)
4. 1+2+3	20	20	15	29	84 (35%)
5. 1+3	32	29	38	22	121 (50.42%)
6. 2+3	1			3	4 (1.66%)
Total	**60**	**60**	**60**	**60**	**240 (100 %)**

Source: Author.

Table 13.3   Wage Labour Ratio Analysis

Name of the Panchayath	Services Offered by the Unit	Hired Workers Per Day	Working Family Members Per Day	Total Employment	Wage Labour/Total Employment Ratio
Adimali	Full hiring services	4	1	5	80.00
	Production & marketing	8	2	10	80.00
	Sales outlet (shop)	121	46	167	72.46
	Work to order	43	11	54	79.63
Adimali total		176	60	236	74.58
Kunnathunadu	Production & marketing	32	4	36	88.89
	Sales outlet (shop)	110	47	157	70.06
	Work to order	30	11	41	73.17
Kunnathunadu total		172	62	234	73.50
Muttom	Others	1	3	4	25.00
	Production & marketing	2	2	4	50.00
	Sales outlet (shop)	87	64	151	57.62
	Work to order	28	19	47	59.57
Muttom total		118	88	206	57.28
Pallipuram	Sales outlet (shop)	50	54	104	48.08
	Work to order	22	10	32	68.75
Pallipuram total		72	64	136	52.94
Grand total		538	274	812	66.26

Source: Author.

of the services applicable both to the common man and to the upper class. The matrix of these services ensure a huge market potential for investors, especially in the rural areas, simply for the reason that the Kerala market, by nature, is highly distributed.

13.5.5 Growth and Structural Changes

Growth and structural changes necessitate an active role by the entrepreneur. Such role can best be understood in terms of the individual-level perspectives and awareness regarding the environment in which he operates. Our analysis, based on a correlation matrix, indicates that both the change-orientation attributes and change-understanding attributes, as two important sets of reflective attributes used by the study, explain a positive change orientation. However, further analysis of action by the entrepreneurs demonstrates a state of inaction. Such an 'entrepreneurship ratchet effect' is a reflection of the predominance of 'necessity entrepreneurship'.

13.5.6 Growth Linkages and Extent of the Market

The present-day stagnancy in the rural services sector in Kerala needs to be examined in relation to a subsector approach. While it is a useful analytical category, the

concept of a subsector need to be understood in terms of its important distinguishing features. These features can be broadly categorized as follows: (*a*) extent of the market; (*b*) market concentration; (*c*) technology and skill levels; and (*d*) employment effects. Each of these features are critical from the point of view of development strategy and financing. These features are likely to be completely different from one another and, therefore, both the real services and financial needs may also vary significantly. Therefore, a broad 'pattern' of assistance, as followed by the banks today, though may be operationally easy for the lender, may not satisfy the needs of the borrower. Hence, enhancing credit flow into this sector requires new strategies.

13.5.7 Technology, Diversification, and Growth

Our field evidences indicate that the majority of the entrepreneurs (70.83 per cent) have some expansion/diversification plan. However, developing such a plan into a growth strategy involves careful examination of the case and appropriate strategy development. While the services of business development service (BDS) providers can be crucial in this regard, the ground level situation remains far from satisfactory. While growth strategy is not in the public agenda of Kerala, the entrepreneurs themselves have to venture into such an attempt. MSME associations, professional agencies, and development banks have a crucial role to play in this regard.

13.5.8 Finance

While the services sector has its particular features, unlike manufacturing it has its own constraints of mobilizing credit. While, 'policy-based lending' and 'asset-based lending' are two models of credit delivery available today, the task of the lending institutions becomes complex in the case of rural service enterprises. Policy-based lending in India has so far shown significant negative results, which have got reflected in the Non-Performing Asset (NPA) levels of banks. Asset-based lending has often proved not to be in tune with the interests of the borrowers. A solution has come in the form of initiatives such as credit rating, credit guarantee, and specialized institutional efforts on small loans. However, the success of all these strategies depends upon the information base available with the financial institutions. On the one hand, is the ability of the borrowers to furnish it with a specified time and manner. The field findings available to this project show a crucial role of commercial banks as lenders (Table 13.4). However, there are serious constraints to both bankers finding business case with rural services and the borrowers finding an appropriate partner in the commercial banks. While the Reserve Bank of India tries to improve the situation by its active intervention of training bank staff and sensitizing them, available field evidences do not give hopes of any radical changes.

This leads one to the need for exploring tailored alternative lending approaches in the context of rural enterprises. A life cycle approach and a value chain approach can be proposed as alternative strategies. However, this demands strengthening the knowledge base of the banks. While collective efficiency is the keyword for productivity enhancement in industry today, this concept can fruitfully be adapted to the context of rural services enterprises as well.

13.5.8.1 Life Cycle Approach

This approach has been increasingly advocated by the Reserve Bank of India RBI). The RBI urges banks to be sensitive towards the life cycle needs of their MSME clients and develop innovative products that are suitable to their unique and seasonal requirements for working capital and capital expenditure purposes. The RBI has already taken various initiatives like Trade Receivables Discounting System (TReDS) and rehabilitation of sick MSMEs. The RBI policy on small finance banks are meant to make the financing of MSMEs more competitive in the coming days.

The concept of life cycle approach integrates existing consumption and production strategies, preventing a piecemeal approach. Life cycle approaches avoid shifting problems from one life cycle stage to another, from one geographic area to another and from one environmental medium to another. Human needs should be met by providing functions of products and services, such as food, shelter, and mobility, through optimized consumption and production systems that are contained within the capacity of the ecosystem. Life cycle management (LCM) has been developed as an integrated concept for managing the total life cycle of products and services, and thereby the life cycle of the enterprises, to move towards the goal of more sustainable consumption and production patterns.

The means of finance employed for positive net present value (NPV) projects has important implications for the firm. The cumulative effect of these discrete financing decisions results in the capital structure of the firm, the composition of which has long been a focus of research in the corporate finance discipline. Theoretical discourse on the subject originates from the irrelevance propositions of Modigliani and Miller (1958), stating that the capital structure of the firm is independent of its cost of capital, and therefore of firm value. This has spawned a substantial body of theoretical literature and empirical tests, which have focused primarily on the decision to employ debt or equity for investment projects. These studies focus on subjects of agency, signalling, and taxation, typically examining the incremental financing decision.

13.5.8.2 Value Chain Analysis Approach

In developing a growth strategy for a subsector, it is important to distinguish between product and labour

Table 13.4   Average/Total Investment Requirement for Expansion/ Diversification in Sample Villages

Average Investment (in Rs)	Kunnathunadu	Pallipuram	Muttom	Adimali
Bank loan (in Rs)	927,778	646,324	1,224,359	1,675,000
Own funds (in Rs)	416,667	292,778	333,088	820,000

Source: Author.

markets. It may not always be optimal or feasible to upgrade 'en masse'. The following different types of upgrading can be distinguished.

Process upgrading: increasing the nature of internal processes such that these are significantly better (differentiated) or more cost-efficient than those of rivals, both within individual links in the chain (for example, increased inventory turnover, lower scrap), and between the links in the chain (for example, more frequent, smaller and on-time deliveries).

Product upgrading: introducing new products or improving old products, with increased value to end-consumers, ahead of rivals. This involves changing new product development processes both within individual links in the value chain and in the relationship between different chain links.

Functional upgrading: increasing value added by changing the mix of activities conducted within the firm (for example, taking responsibility for, or outsourcing accounting, logistics and quality functions) or moving the locus of activities to different links in the value chain (for example, from manufacturing to design). Compare the family labour–wage labour components, as we see in our sample units. Can they be improved?

Channel upgrading: moving existing products into a new pathway leading to a new end-market (for example, moving from domestic markets to export markets), or at best from a limited local market to a wider regional market.

Chain upgrading: moving to a new value chain for the production of a different product.

Building an understanding of the current cash flows and credit structures at the level of each actor in the value chain, that is, before any upgrading opportunities are considered, should be an integral part of analysing the value chain structure. The various aspects of finance in the value chain can be organized in three groups. First, there is a set of issues related to finance within the firms. Second, there are supply-side finance issues which relate to the nature of the different types of financial services provision that currently exist in the value chain. Third, there are finance issues that relate to the transactions between firms and how these transactions are governed.

13.5.8.3 Other Initiatives

Beyond the usual perception of banks generally being reluctant to lend to MSMEs (which is a global phenomenon), the issues in this area need to be approached from a different angle. There is need for in-depth studies on banking and lending strategies from the point of view of a business case.

A proper stakeholder analysis needs to form the basis of any new strategy. The initiative for such basic homework has to come from the development banks. MUDRA comes as an alternative window. But, it is less successful in Kerala, though it has been reported to be relatively more successful in states such as Telangana. The reason can best be explained, again, in terms of the structural changes in the regional economy. In Kerala, the structural changes have been faster, as has been the growth of the New Economy. This implies that most of the micro enterprises, which explains the so-called 'bottom of the pyramid', demand larger unit investment, which, MUDRA, by its very specifications, cannot often offer. Moreover, the market for many of these traditional products has shrunk, which, again, explains the unviability of these types of enterprises. The Kerala experience has, therefore, great importance from two angles: (*a*) in understanding the emerging pattern of structural changes in the country; and (*b*) in critically examining the viability of MUDRA as a national programme meant for broad-based finance for small enterprises.

The experience and lessons of micro finance and JLGs in the country have been well documented. The have immensely helped to broad-base finance, as also to build up a base of social capital and for institutionalization of finance with people's participation.

13.5.9 Subsectoral Understanding and Strategies

India's initiatives on rural enterprise development, so far, were treated under the rubric 'entrepreneurship development'. In this model, it is assumed that having interventions and support services can help such enterprises to come up. But, the bigger challenge on the demand side has not gained serious attention so far. Herein lies the role of subsectors as focal points of action strategies. This research has identified four crucial subsectors demanding serious examination and development of strategies: (*a*) retailing; (*b*) textile retailing; (*c*) tailoring, stitching, and others; and (*d4*) information technology.

13.6 CRITICAL CONSTRAINTS AND THE CHANGE AGENDA

While structural changes in India's rural economy over the last one decade or so have been fast and significant, our understanding of the situation still remains partial. Pending detailed studies (the initiative for which has to come from NABARD), what best we can do now is to pick up some critical constraints, and to address them.

The detailed analysis undertaken by Mathew (2016) shows that having an overall positive orientation for the entrepreneurs in the rural services sector in Kerala does not give us adequate evidence regarding a significant translation of this orientation into action. In fact, action can take place only in a situation where the objective environment is appropriate to the context. During the course of our field research, we tried to find out the causatives for such a stagnant situation. This may be discussed under three broad heads: (a) lack of business development services; (b) rigidities relating to institutional finance; and (c) limited ease of doing business.

13.6.1 Subsectoral Fertility

How have units mushroomed in some industries and not in others? How have some subsectors performed better than others? Though an explanation in this context is not easy, from the point of view of analysis and programme implementation, it would be ideal to examine some broad causative factors. These factors may be analysed under the following heads:

13.6.1.1 Promotional Effect

Traditionally, the promotional effect has been a significant matter in shaping the direction of enterprise development in Kerala. The effect has been visible in some of the sectors such as light engineering and food processing. However, in the modern period the promotional effect is more visible in some of the sectors such as textiles and garment making. The focus on collective enterprises and clustering has played a big role.

13.6.1.2 Demonstration Effect

The demonstration effect is visible in a number of service enterprises across Kerala. For example, this is more visible in service enterprises such as hotels and restaurants. It is estimated that the number of hotels and restaurants has significantly gone up in Kerala during the past two decades. The demonstrate effect is clear in the case of hotels and restaurants, which to a large extent is explained by remittances by non-residential Indians that have got siphoned to this subsector.

13.6.1.3 Renteer Effect

The renteer effect is visible in a few of the subsectors. Activities such as the massive reclaiming of land, water supplies on tankers, a variety of services related to supplies of liquor, and so on, which often fall under the definition of 'illegal activities', form the coverage of the so-called renteer effect. While capital intensity in contributing to productivity is understandable, the focus of most entrepreneurs seeking agricultural and rural services projects has been on 'resource intensity', which facilitates enhanced access to scarce natural resources (Table 13.5).

13.6.1.4 Backward Linkage Effect

The backward linkage effect has occurred in some of the subsectors such as building materials. Kerala's construction boom in the last three decades has produced an accelerated demand for building materials of all types. However, there is extreme shortage of some of these materials as there is promotional growth of parent industries such as quarries.

13.6.1.5 Clustering and Cluster Development

Kerala has a remarkable record at the national level relating to the development of industrial clusters. While the average size of clusters is relatively small in the state, Kerala's initiatives for the promotion of the clusters remain significant. These are of two categories: created clusters and natural clusters.

Table 13.5   Output Structure of the Service Enterprises

Output	Kunnathunadu	Pallipuram	Muttom	Adimali	Total
1. Full hiring			1	2	3 (1.25%)
2. Production and marketing	3		2	2	7 (2.94%)
3. Work-to-order	12	12	17	17	58 (24.13%)
4. Sales outlet	45	48	39	39	171 (71.25%)
5. Others			1		1 (0.43%)
Total	**60**	**60**	**60**	**60**	**240 (100%)**

Source: Author.

13.7 LESSONS FOR POLICY AND STRATEGY

Public policy in a democracy represents a majority view; however it need not always be the best. Opinion on both shaping of policies as also of the impact of policies often diverges. But it is important that there should be consensus at least on the policy process. The method by which a policy consensus can be arrived at needs to be developed. This can best be done with the support of knowledge inputs that are vital both for shaping policies and for evaluating implementation. Under globalization, which is the reality today, policy needs to focus on value chains. While, in manufacturing, global value chains are all the more important, in services, it may perhaps be largely confined to the national market. Having accepted this reality, one needs to analyse the present state of particular subsectors on the basis of realistic data and evidences. While the market is the key determinant in a value chain approach, it is also necessary to estimate the extent to which the market shocks can be reduced through some form of subsidies, at least in the short run. However, subsidies cannot be the answer in the long run.

It is in the above context that there arises the need for an analytical approach, as also sound and consistent methodologies which can be continuously applied in the context of particular subsectors. For example, functional weightage can be given to each subsector, and each component of a subsector, on the basis of their contribution to employment and value addition, which are again sensitive social variables. Let policy be decided on such a methodological approach, just like cost of living index acting as the basis of wage revisions.

Innovation is a key imperative of the times. Many states of the country have come forward with innovative experiments. However, sustainable economic development can happen only by kick-starting the spirit of enterprise. Moreover, the spark that has been created needs to achieve satisfactory scale within a reasonable period of time. In a global situation where there is a lag in these two imperatives, there can be a backwash effect. The backwash effect happens either in terms of a morale shock, or in terms of an easy catch-up by competitors. In the case of Kerala, this happened to a significant extent.

A critical factor that can take forward innovation to a reasonable scale is achievement motivation. The degree of achievement motivation in entrepreneurs varies from state to state. In Kerala, despite several initiatives by the state and union governments in industrialization and enterprise creation, they have not taken momentum, essentially because of deficiencies relating to achievement motivation. Mathew (1994) has analysed the situation in terms of a 'crisis' and 'cushions' model. This model says that it is a serious crisis in the economy that often leads to hard initiatives, which can broadly be described as entrepreneurship. Historically, Kerala, unlike other states, has emerged victorious in the face of such crisis from time to time through accelerated countervailing forces, or 'cushions'.

The unsatisfactory record in manufacturing in many states is a problem. It is not advisable to further explore expansion of its manufacturing base. Even if there is a marginal opportunity, it lies in high-technology manufacturing that is less labour intensive. On that count, there is some opportunity in specific subsectors in various states.

The challenges and opportunities for the states that are backward in manufacturing are to enhance the overall growth and productivity of the services sector. Given Kerala's record of high foreign remittances, growth of the educated young population and the presence of a large number of return migrants provide some objective ground for stepping up the base of service enterprises. But there need to be entrepreneurial solutions at the forefront.

Despite such opportunities, the field research under Mathew (2016) points towards the need for a deeper analysis of the related issues. The following issues need closer examination:

1. Career stigma among existing entrepreneurs
2. Start-up inertia
3. Volatility of entrepreneurship, leading to high sickness
4. Inertia among existing entrepreneurs towards innovation
5. Lack of trust in the social system and the government
6. Non-participative behaviour relating to knowledge sharing and organization
7. Mistrust with the public financial institutions at the cost of NBFCs and money lenders
8. Stigma on product lines and lack of innovativeness
9. High business information and awareness coupled with inaction and lack of response

The broad findings, as in Tables 13.6 to 13.8, demonstrate a 'ratchet effect', from where one cannot expect a spontaneous change.

On the other hand, the lead has come essentially from the following sources:

1. Government, through its proactive policy support
2. An active role of development finance institutions at the following levels: (a) a major programme of subsectoral mapping and product development;

Table 13.6   Change Understanding Attributes: Correlation Matrix

Correlation Matrix of Awareness (Pearson)			
	Base to 2010	2010 to 2015	Base to 2015
NO	0.816	0.943	0.826
YES	0.801	0.932	0.828

Source: Author.

Table 13.7   Change Orientation of the Entrepreneurs: Coefficient of Correlation (Base Year to 2015)

Orientation	Values
Knowledge (K)	0.926967
Attitude (A)	0.937134
Practice (P)	0.925929

Source: Author.

Table 13.8   Capital Structure of Rural Service Enterprises

Sources of Finance	Kunnathunadu	Pallipuram	Muttom	Adimali	Total
1. Government grant	1			1	**2 (0.83%)**
2. Savings from business		3		2	**5 (2.08%)**
3. Personal loans	24	13	21	21	**79 (32.92%)**
4. Moneylender	4	2		2	**8 (3.33%)**
5. Bank finance	26	16	32	26	**100 (41.67%)**
6. Others	1	9	4	3	17 (7.08%)
7. Community loans and group loans	4	17	3	5	**29 (12.09%)**
8. Total	**60**	**60**	**60**	**60**	**240 (100%)**

Source: Author.

and (*b*) demand projections, which can be taken up by existing and potential entrepreneurs

3. Introduction of voluntary standards in products and services against regulations and fewer regulations

4. Encouragement to and engagement of professional institutions by the public authorities at the state and district levels as policy and strategy partners.

While these policy constraints vary from state to state, there are also such challenges for policy institutions to shape appropriate strategies.

13.7.1 Policy Institutions: Changing Role and Challenges

In any development debate, the role of institutions has a crucial place. This is because it is institutionalized action that turns public policy into strategies. In the context of rural service enterprises, India has a significant institutional network that caters to various functional areas such as business development services, finance, and promotion in general. It is necessary to examine the current role and potential of these institutions, in a context where the rural services sector is left with significant utilized potential in waiting.

The institutional framework, relevant to the context of rural service enterprises, can be broadly divided into

two: (*a*) promotional; and (*b*) financial. Promotional institutions are generally involved in non-financial developmental activities such as BDS, as also knowledge, educational, and escort services of various kinds. The financial institutions are predominantly engaged in financial services, such as banking insurance, factoring, and so on.

The entrepreneurship movement that emerged in India in the early 1970s, marks a departure from the conventional thinking on the emergence and growth of businesses. Based on this conventional thinking, businesses sprout and grow at the level of business houses. Accordingly, the early entrepreneurship theory in India was grounded on the business houses. A more scientific approach to entrepreneurship growth and development emerged from the new theories of entrepreneurship having their empirical roots in India. McClelland's 'N-achievement motivation' theory brought to the fore achievement motivation as a critical factor influencing vocational decisions of the individual. Over time, such a theoretical stream assumed an important place in labour market analysis and policy.

The Gujarat model of institutionalization of entrepreneurship development marks a significant experiment in the developing world. Following this, the Entrepreneurship Development Institute of India (EDII) was set up at the national level, followed by state-level counterparts in various states. Today, the country has a large network of entrepreneurship development institutions that are involved in the design and implementation of entrepreneurship development programmes of various kinds. Since the 1990s, with the explosion in higher education in the country, there has also been a significant growth of facilities for entrepreneurship education. Today, almost every engineering college in the country has either a separate department or business school where entrepreneurship is taught as a subject.

The above theoretical contributions had their impact at the operational plane, in the form of structured entrepreneurship development programmes, which has also taken different shapes and forms over time. The Rural Entrepreneurship Development Programme (REDP) model evolved by the EDII marked an important exercise, which was subsequently taken up by the development finance institutions of the country. Besides offering entrepreneurship as a new opportunity for educated rural people, it also facilitated the growth of several grass-root level institutions that imparted delivery of such programmes. The REDP was essentially a programme oriented towards providing new opportunities to unemployed people, and, therefore, its focus was largely on services.

Despite the mainstreaming of entrepreneurship development initiatives, there are some critical areas of concern which need to be addressed. First, many of these programmes are not demand driven. Second, there is a lack of a proper knowledge system that can support entrepreneurship development initiatives. Third, while escort services are vital for early stage start-ups, such facilities are not often offered properly. Fourth, BDS in India has not emerged significantly on a market mode. Fifth, publically funded entrepreneurship development programmes are often not based on effective entrepreneurship development models. All these demands—putting in place facilities for relevant entrepreneurship research, training facilities, and knowledge systems—can feed each other and can nourish public programmes and add to the business ecosystem. While the latest thrust of the Government of India is on start-ups, it is necessary to fine-tune the programme based on the local level reality and the needs of regional development.

KVIC: KVIC was set up on the lines of the Gandhian vision of rural development. The term *gram swaraj* implicitly assumes the existence of goods and services that are in demand in village communities. However, in the original programmes of KVIC the focus was largely on manufacture. The KVIC has, from time to time, identified a set of enterprise activities where funding support and training facilities are offered to entrepreneurs. Subsequently, with the introduction of the Prime Minister's Employment Generation Programme (PMEGP), a better scope for support to rural services, along with manufacturing, came up.

Rural Development and Self Employment Training Institutes (RUDSETIs): This is a voluntary institutionalization model developed in Karnataka where some of the leading Karnataka-based banks participated in an active role. Subsequently the model got wider acceptance with the Government of India and the RBI, such that it has now become a national-level model. RUDSETIs are institutional platforms created by the individual public sector banks of the country. The idea came as a response to the RBI's guidelines regarding earmarking of 40 per cent of its lending to the priority sectors of the economy. It was suggested that many of those potential entrepreneurs who approach the banks do not have the necessary skills and motivation. Therefore, the banks directly entered into the creation of a specialized institutional platform. While, such an institutional platform helps entrepreneurship development in general, the focus has largely been on service enterprises. However, the focus of individual RUDSETIs again depends on the priorities and orientation of the parent bank. Canara Bank, for example, has its own specialized network of a number of entrepreneurship training institutions.

Commodity Boards: The commodity boards also have a limited role of promotion of entrepreneurial activities in relation to enhancement of production and producer incomes of the commodities they are mandated with. However, of late, they have also started promotion of entrepreneurship development initiatives. For example, the Spices Board from time to time entered into varied forms of enterprise development initiatives. The Central Silk Board also has programmes for enterprise development. The Coir Board has schemes that are addressed to development of tiny units, general and gender-specific.

NABARD: NABARD by mandate is geared to the development of agriculture and the rural sector, including non-farm sector. The focus on the non-farm sector covers a wide variety of activities that are closely linked with most of the rural economic activities. The linkage is both from the supply side as well as the demand side. Naturally, from the promotional side, the bank has evolved financing developmental strategies for the sector from time to time. In fact, at the institutional level, though there has been close linkages among the various nodal departments, the off-farm development department currently takes care of planning and development of the rural services sector.

Small Industries Development Bank of India (SIDBI): SIDBI is the official nodal bank for the MSME sector in the country. However, like the usual ambivalence relating to prioritization in the policy circles, SIDBI also has an ambivalent approach to the role and relevance of the services subsector of the MSME sector. In essence, SIDBI's concern and focus on the services sector today is partial and this needs to be further improved.

MUDRA: MUDRA is a new addition to the platform of financial institutions in the country. It is yet to establish its legal existence under an act of the Parliament. The objective and mandate of MUDRA emerge from the national-level debates on the issues relating to credit delivery for the unorganized sector in the country. The debates during 2013 and 2014, in the context of the general elections in the country, and soon after, resulted in the announcement by the Union Budget 2014–15 in favour of a dedicated agency that can cater to the credit requirements of the unorganized sector. That was MUDRA. The objective of the agency is to ensure collateral-free credit to the so-called bottom of the pyramid.

At the operational level, MUDRA raises some important issues that need to be addressed in relation to the credit requirements of rural enterprises in the country. These issues may be discussed as follows:

1. MUDRA undoubtedly gives an answer to the credit requirements of tiny enterprises, which were hitherto neglected by the commercial banks. While the Credit Guarantee Fund Trust for Micro and Small Enterprises (CGTMSE) as a collateral-free credit mechanism has also proved that it has its limitations, there is need for some mechanism that can ensure the ease of credit. If the ease of credit is ensured at the prevailing interest rate of the banks, it is undoubtedly a welcome step.

2. A particular feature of MUDRA is that it brings in a number of players, and thereby a competitive environment, on the supply side of credit. For example, commercial banks, cooperative banks, Gramin banks, and other financial intermediates can give MUDRA loans. This means that on the demand side there are several options for the entrepreneurs.

3. Even when there are a large number of options on the demand side, on the supply side the main players continue to be the commercial banks, and especially the public sector banks. Therefore, the success of the programme, to a significant extent, would depend on the cooperation from the public sector banks.

4. The coverage of MUDRA loans goes up from a minimum of Rs 50,000 up to a maximum of Rs 10 lakhs. However, a collateral-free loan that is easily available—even as small an amount as Rs 50,000—may send a negative message to the borrowers, going by the experience of schemes like PMEGP.

5. The available experience so far indicates that while in states such as Andhra Pradesh and Telangana the scheme has already made some headway, in other states such as Kerala it is yet to come up.

6. The introduction of MUDRA demands innovative credit assessment methods, unlike the one practised by the public sector banks today. This demands serious research and innovation.

7. While the average size of the loan ticket is important for the lending institutions from a profitability angle, the number of loans given is also crucial. Unless trade organizations and MSME associations are involved by the financial institutions, MUDRA cannot achieve its critical minimum size and visibility.

8. In Kerala, one of the public sector banks is a negotiating with the Kerala Vyapaari Vyvasaayi Ekopana Samithi (KVVES) for extending loans to its members. However, the State Level Banker's Committee, Kerala, has given a target of 150,000 cases of MUDRA accounts in the current year, covering 6,000 bank branches in the state. The results relating to the achievement of this target, and the repayment record over the next two years will also be a pointer to the quality of entrepreneurship, especially of start-ups in Kerala.

State finance corporations (SFCs): SFCs were set up under the SFC Act of 1962. Though SFCs as a decentralized institutional platform can play a significant role in channelizing financial resources and meeting the credit requirements of enterprises at the bottom of the pyramid, their track record so far remains far from satisfactory. There are various reasons, a discussion on which would not be within the scope of this study. However, factors such as the focus of self-employment and enterprise development and the presence of multiple state level promotional agencies, along with the new roles that were visualized for public sector banks as a follow-up of bank nationalization in 1970, had their impact on the functioning of SFCs. As of today, most SFCs of the country are sick, requiring restructuring packages for their very survival. There are exceptions to this picture. The Kerala Financial Corporation (KFC) is one of the SFCs that has become important through the diversification of its activities. For example, the self-employment development programme of the corporation has been a pioneering experiment that needs to be discussed in the context of entrepreneurship promotion activities by public financial institutions in the country. According to KFC sources, the programme has brought into this stream a number of start-up entrepreneurs, making it a record in the country.

13.7.2 Success Stories in Institutional Intervention

Success stories in institutional interventions need to be documented for replication. Some of the examples are specialized network of entrepreneurship training institutions of Canara Bank, planning and development of rural services by the Off-farm Development Department of NABARD, self-employment development and start-up programme by KFC, and the voluntary funds created by the KVVES.

13.7.3 Critical Gaps in Institutionalization

The need for convergence arises out of some functional features of programmes. Most are owned by a particular department/ministry and, therefore, are confined to their limited scope. However, from the perspective of the beneficiaries, it is important that there be some minimum level of synergy in order to prevent their possible duplicative character, as also to ensure maximum end results. Gender, age, caste, and other social criteria are crucial determinants that need to be taken into account.

The need for convergence in 'gender and enterprise' policies and programmes has been increasingly felt and articulated in the country. However, there is still much confusion as to how such an idea of convergence can be taken forward. While the very purpose of the National Mission for Empowerment of Women (NMEW) is ensuring such convergence, translating this agenda into practice demands much greater clarity on strategies, modalities of implementation, and relative role of stake holders.

The very purpose of the NMEW is convergence of various national level and regional initiatives for women empowerment. This mission was launched by the Government of India in 2010 with the aim to strengthen the overall processes that promote all-round development of women. It has the mandate to strengthen the inter-sectoral convergence; facilitate the process of coordinating all women's welfare and socio-economic development programmes across ministries and departments.

The mission aims to provide a single-window service for all programmes run by the government for women under the aegis of various central ministries. The mission is meant to strengthen the processes which promote holistic development and empowerment of women, gender equality, and gender justice through inter-sectoral convergence of programmes that impact women, forge synergy among various stakeholders, and create an enabling environment conducive to social change.

The National Resource Centre for Women has been set up, which functions as a national convergence centre for all schemes and programmes for women. It acts as a central repository of knowledge, information, research, and data on all gender-related issues, and is the main body servicing the National and State Mission Authority. In accordance with its mandate, the mission has been named Mission Poorna Shakti, implying a vision for holistic empowerment of women. The Poorna Shakti Kendra (PSK) is the focal point of action on ground, through which the services to women at the grass-roots level is being facilitated. Village coordinators at the Kendras are reaching to the rural women with the motto 'HUM SUNENGE NAARI KI BAAT!' ('We shall listen to the voice of women').

13.7.3.1 Lack of Convergence

While there are a number of programmes and institutions that cater to rural enterprise development, functional convergence is a critical area of concern today. Institutions have been created in order to address particular functional problems, such as finance, marketing, technology, and so on. However, these institutions fail to have a holistic approach to enterprise development, for example, entrepreneurship development institutes, by now, have a strong network across the country. But, knowledge creation and its dissemination that should go along with training interventions are badly neglected. This critical gap can be met only if the institutions change their style of functioning. However, in the existing system of governance in the country, this cannot be expected, unless there is a major push. That big push must come through a national agenda of enterprise development, where the institutional roles are clearly defined.

13.7.3.2 Lack of an Entrepreneurial Approach

The public institutions serving enterprise and entrepreneurship development in the country are largely not tuned to function as demand-driven entities. While every public programme is largely subsidized by the governmen, and institutions are supported through government grant, there is no incentive for these institutions to assume an entrepreneurial approach in their day to day functioning. The answer lies in a major drive towards opening up these institutions and bringing them on par with private professional organizations. It is worthwhile to consider a level playing ground for entrepreneurship and media institutions, allowing both public and private agencies to work side by side. In the Netherlands, the local governments and business chambers play a key role in promotion of local enterprise development. The potential entrepreneurs and the unemployed can walk into the Municipalities and seek support for the so-called business development services (BDS) that are available from private or public institutions. The local governments play a key role in channelizing such services. The municipalities also have the role of providing guidance and support regarding further delivery outlets, such as for Entrepreneurship training, project report preparation, business development services, and so on. As such, start-up promotion, in the Netherlands, is a collective process where all major stakeholders, such as the local governments, business associations, and business development services providers, participate. India can learn a lot from such experiences.

13.7.3.3 Rigidities of the Government

While institutionalization means an important step forward on the promotional side, it is essential that these institutions work in an appropriate ecosystem of governance and development policy. In the case of many such institutions, public programmes and government grants form the main source of their income. Given such a situation, rigid public programmes, along with the constraints of institutions, mar the effective performance of the even the best designed programmes. In this context, there is need for mission mode interventions. But mission mode interventions also should mean the involvement of both public and private institutions on a level of playing ground. In the Indian context, such experiments are yet to happen in the field of enterprise development.

13.7.3.4 Lack of Subsector Approach

The best institutions and the best of programmes by themselves cannot ensure effective programme design and implementation. Programmes need to be integrated in terms of the forward and backward linkages of the constituency for which it is meant. It is in this context that the subsectoral approach becomes significant. It is important that rural services be understood, supported, and coordinated on a functional mode. In this context, issues of governance again crop up. There cannot be isolated programmes targeted to the rural sector and to the MSMEs as isolated entities. They need to focus on subsectors.

13.7.4 Present Role and Relevance of Development Banking

In the context just discussed, development banks have ever-increasing responsibility. Such responsibility arises essentially from the following seven angles:

1. The complexity of economic phenomena have significantly increased, demanding new insights on these complexities, as also innovative solutions. However, despite the multiplication of development finance institutions, there has not been a progressive effort from these institutions to sensitize the banking industry on innovative financing models. While the prudential norms are crucial for commercial banks, these norms, rather than the credit-related problems of rural enterprises, have been highlighted by the popular media. The development finance institutions have to play an important role in taking a balanced view of things, and to counter such misdirected media hype.

2. The development finance institutions are not properly equipped with knowledge systems that can support their day-to-day work. They do not also take sufficient steps to facilitate the growth of such alternative systems.

3. These institutions are also victims of the rigours of government control. It is important that they gain sufficient autonomy.

4. The allocation of business among the various development finance institutions is quite arbitrary and overlapping. This implies that as new development finance institutions are created, there arise a clash of interest among them. This situation needs to change. Ultimately, the benefit expected by the customer from the bank is cheaper credit at the appropriate time. In fact, the multiplication of institutional structures has helped to enhance the cost of credit rather than reducing it.

5. The cooperatives and the regional rural banks were expected to be closer to the rural customers in ensuring lower time and cost of credit.

But, NABARD has been constrained to exercise its effective control over these institutions. It demands radical changes in the legal and institutional structures.

6. While the concept of 'collective efficiency' has been popularized by the government and financial institutions, a collective efficiency model is yet to be shaped for the financial sector. The cost of such inefficiency goes to the customer in the form of high interest rates and insufficient service delivery.

7. The financial institutions of the country are largely averse to learning from international best practices in product development. International prudential norms alone will not help India's financial system to remain stable. Customers' confidence must not continue to be a victim.

13.8 ACTION POINTS

The policy lessons emerging from the preceding discussion are varied. But concrete action points need to be explored within several critical constraints that are faced today. We, therefore, propose some tentative action points on the following lines:

13.8.1 Focus on Skills: Skills Bridge Strategy (2016–21)

While the Government of India has recently significantly focused on skills and start-up promotion, this is an opportune time for the development banks to remodel themselves into a more integrated role. While the development banks, largely based on their mandates, conform to specific lending criteria such as rural–urban, traditional–modern, trade–manufacture, and so on, it is time to think beyond these distinctions and to evolve a strategy of skills and entrepreneurship development of a critical minimum scale.

The critical question, in the context of the states where the enterprise sector is weak is to make a major entry into the terrain of entrepreneurship. We advocate a two-pronged strategy called 'Skill Bridge Strategy', with the following components: (a) entrepreneurship preservation and (b) start-up promotion.

Under the Panchayati Raj regime, conceptualization of enterprise development should necessarily take place at the bottom, where the local government initiates the process of establishing industrial units in their geographic jurisdictions and thereby provides the required moral support, and the basic licences. The implementation support, however, has to come from the state level,

where various departments and agencies are responsible for provision of support (it includes infrastructure, incubators, and so on). While the state level departments provide the relevant knowledge support, the role of the local governments will be to ensure that such knowledge support gets translated into actual investment projects, and that the projects are sustained and nurtured on a path of growth. The paradigm of enterprise development would mean strong consensus building at the local level and enterprise at the state level.

The new economy also has the potentially dangerous effect of making the individual increasingly dependent on wage labour. In a context where inequalities in the economy are mounting, it is natural that entrepreneurial instincts at the 'bottom of the pyramid' are nipped in the bud. Reflections of the same are found in the disparities in the wage level, and the consequent unwillingness of the unemployed to opt for challenging service sector activities, such as marketing, management consultancy, and even for new economy services that are significantly field oriented. This phobia to field orientation, alternatively, would mean a significant erosion of field level exposure and real-world understanding among the youth. The causality is likely to be the potential entrepreneurial sparks. In a state such as Kerala, such an erosion of entrepreneurship base is critical for the prospects of economic development. The 'Skill Bridge Strategy' needs to be an integrated mission mode strategy meant for preserving and nurturing the entrepreneurship base of the backward states, at the fringes of their enterprise ecosystem.

13.8.2 Innovation and Standards Regime

While the role of innovation has been widely debated in the context of rural enterprises, there is significant confusion regarding the precise meaning of innovation. As the influence of the 'new economy' is on the increase, it is important to bring in a standards regime in the case of many rural enterprises. These enterprises need to be categorized into subsectors, and ideas of voluntary standards can be brought in. In a context where 'responsible business' as a concept has an emerging respectability, such an approach is relevant.

13.8.3 A New Space for Social Enterprises

In India, the opening up of the retail sector to global players is a sensitive subject. However, on the other hand, there are also consumer complaints on inefficiencies and irresponsible behaviour of the so-called *kinara* (grocery store) enterprises. This significantly creates a space for social enterprises, though it remains a largely neglected area in the country. In addition to an appropriate legislation for the sector, the development banks have to consider it as a virgin area for their activities. It is time for the development banks to develop appropriate programmes, taking into account the global developments in social enterprise. It needs going beyond the existing programmes that are meant for NGOs and self-help groups. NABARD, given its track record, needs to come out with a policy paper on the subject.

13.8.4 Need for New Financial Products

The rural service enterprises, so far, have been treated under the rubric of 'micro enterprise' and 'priority sector lending'. Going beyond these, there is need for a subsectoral approach. Besides new opportunities for financial institutions, these institutions need to think beyond their existing financial products, and should be equipped themselves to work with the rural-urban value chain. The value chain model in countries such as the USA can be a good guide for explorations in the subject area.

13.8.5 Services Finance Park

High cost of credit is a major problem cited by most of our respondents under this study. The discussions on cost of credit in India often hover around interest rates. The indirect costs, including transactions costs are often not properly considered. It is this neglect by commercial banks that has been taken advantage of by other lenders. While limited information and cumbersome procedures enhance the unit cost of credit, there needs to be an effort to bring out the cost of credit through appropriate alternative institutional mechanisms. It would be instructive to explore the concept of a service finance park, which can help to enhance the quality of credit and bring down its cost.

13.8.6 Participation in Low-Cost Funds

Traders' associations, such as the KVVES in Kerala, have set up in-house funds for meeting the small miscellaneous fund requirements of its members. While banking requires a licence from the RBI, such mutual benefit schemes can be enhanced in their scope and activities. Like the SHG–Bank Linkages programme, the opportunities for an SBMO–Bank Linkage Programme need to be explored, wherein the small business membership organizations (SBMOs) can be engaged as partners.

13.8.7 Staff Training for Banks

The staff training for banks today is largely of a generic type. The role of bankers as key decision makers needs improvements. In many cases, innovative small schemes do not catch the attention of commercial banks. Research units in the public sector banks are weak. Even the minimal research is confined to the operations side, rather than on marketing. Naturally, these banks personnel, even at the corporate office level, are least aware of the emerging trends in the economy. It is important that the bank staff are given appropriate training in dealing with rural service enterprises and issues of local economic development.

13.8.8 Restructuring of Start-up Programmes

The present-day start-up programmes are mostly outdated. There needs to be serious efforts to restructure the existing entrepreneurship development programmes (EDPs). Tailored EDPs require ground level research. The Development Financial Institutions (DFIs) need to work in tandem with professional agencies in this regard.

13.8.9 Rural Services Observatory

As pointed out by several studies, the huge size of the micro enterprises sector in India, and consequently their invisibility, is a serious problem that has to be addressed. Beyond the efforts of the Economic Census, it is necessary to identify these enterprises on the basis of a unique identification number. The learnings from the Aadhar scheme need to be explored in this context. Beyond this, there is a requirement for the services of a 'micro enterprise observatory'. Knowledge creation and dissemination on the sector is a vital necessity. ISED has set up the ISED Small Enterprise Observatory, wherein A database on rural services has also been maintained. These activities have to be strengthened in a focused manner.

13.8.10 Growth Programmes

The present study, as also, some of the earlier ones, have indicated a stagnancy of a significant number of rural enterprises that have come under the self-employment programme. It is important to identify the causes of such stagnancy, and to evolve appropriate growth programmes in order to ensure that entrepreneurship as a critical resource does not go waste for lack of policy support.

13.8.11 National Local Economic Development Fund (NLEDF)

In the paradigm of publicly oriented enterprise development programmes, the content of a specific scheme, and the associated budgetary allocations are designed by the line-ministries/departments. The programmes, in turn, are implemented at the district level, where the district collector presides over and oversees the implementation of the programme concerned. This assumes that the programme, in its content, truly reflects the aspirations and needs at the local level. Panchayati Raj, on the other hand, assumes a bottom-up approach, where the people's development aspirations are articulated and taken forward at the Panchayat level. The inconsistency between the above paradigms often results in underutilization or misutilization of funds. Even in cases of full utilization of the budgetary allocations, results regarding creation of entrepreneurial capability and enterprise are doubtful.

Given the above constraints, even the best programmes such as the Sansad Adarsh Gram Yojana (SAGY), being implemented with close supervision of a member of parliament, cannot lead to reasonable results. The mismatch between fund availability, utilization, and programme implementation can best be solved by having a clear local economic development agenda developed at the panchayat level. It also requires the setting up of the concept of a local economic development fund with the local governments. This is a state- of-the-art of practice in many advanced countries of the world today. The programmes of institutions such as MUDRA, SIDBI, Ministry of Rural Development, KVIC, and so on should be tagged to this national resource centre. The National Fund should set up state level funds for its operations down to the panchayat level. The National Fund is a corpus meant for supporting the work of the state and panchayat level fund, where the various tiers of government, as also the different promotional agencies, will be partners. The concept of such a fund goes along with the proposed focus to the micro private sector, as envisaged by the prime minister. The modalities of this fund must be worked out by NABARD.

13.8.12 Grass-roots Services Hub Model and Its Applicability

Our field evidences indicate that the limited extent of the market is both a cause and consequence of the lopsided growth of the rural services sector in Kerala. While many of the units have to depend on the fragmented market opportunities, the usual solution lies in enhanced expenditure on advertisement and publicity, which often such enterprises can ill afford. Social capital can also contribute very little to market expansion. Can the local governments, within a local economic development (LED) agenda, contribute to improve the situation? Mathew (2016) has proposed a 'Grassroots Services Hub model', the practical utility and the operational modalities of which need to be examined on the basis of detailed studies. We propose that NABARD may initiate a detailed study on the subject.

13.8.13 Broad Basing the Enterprise Demographic System

The India Micro Small and Medium Enterprise Report 2016 proposed the ways and means of broad basing 'udyog aadhar', and thereby enhancing the reach of public promotional schemes for the benefit of a larger number of entrepreneurs. Besides, having a proper KYC process for the customer is critical for the banks to expand their lending. These imperatives demand broad basing of the enterprise demographic system in a systematic manner. ISED has proposed the concept of 'Udyami Panchayath' as a new mechanism to enhance people's participation in enterprise development. The development banks can play a major role in this regard.

13.9 MAJOR IMPLICATIONS AND CONCLUSIONS

Some of the indicative issues emerging from the study are crucial. First, a high share of informal economy and slow pace of formalization is a major characterization of the Indian economy. Second, the more recent phenomenon of 'Hubanomics' provides an additional dimension to this phenomenon. Resource allocation today, is increasingly focused on 'global hubs' that offer market advantages to the corporate entities, rather than to the requirements of national policies. Against such a global trend, governments cannot do much, without adequate knowledge base and preparedness 'Hubanomics' is a state-of-the-art concept that implies the global tendency of integration of production and distribution facilities according to the needs of the global markets and marketing strategies. For example, Bangalore and Santiago are global hubs of the Information technology industry (for details, see India Micro Small & Medium Enterprise Report 2017). While formalization is necessary to create transaction history for the entrepreneur to approach banks and avail institutional loans, there are serious issues relating to economic governance in the country that constrain such formalization. Technology cannot be the ultimate solution where issues of economic governance are deep rooted. Third, the absence of structural changes of the Kuznetsian variety needs to be examined in terms of their reasons. Much of the industrialization, as we see it today, is necessity entrepreneurship. In fact, institutional interventions and public programmes have not significantly helped to change the track in favour of opportunity entrepreneurship. Unlike in many of the industrially advanced economies (for example, European Union), India does not have an effective monitoring system for the unorganized sector, though the contribution of unorganized manufacturing and services to the GDP is significantly high. On the credit front, the usage of innovative approaches, such as life cycle and value chain approach, necessitates such monitoring both at the macro and firm level.

The changes in the rural economy of India over the past one decade have been significant. The micro private sector has had a key role in this change. Unlike in the past, the role of the private sector is significant in explaining this change. However, what the micro private sector needs today is not much of the support schemes of the old variety. It is appropriate knowledge systems and continuous flow of 'real services' that can best serve the interests of these enterprises. Public–private initiatives have an important role to play in this critical area. Changes towards this direction require as its sine qua non a strong economic governance system. The primary lesson for such a governance system needs to be learnt from the first principles of LED. Despite laudable achievements relating to Panchayati Raj, the country is yet to move towards local economic governance.

SELECTED BIBLIOGRAPHY

Acharya, Shankar. 2003. 'Services Not the Real Saviour?' In Shankar Acharya (ed.), *India's Economy, Some Issues and Answers*, pp. 38–48. New Delhi, India: Academic Foundation.

Agrawal, Tushar. 2011. 'Returns to Education in India: Some Recent Evidence'. Available at https://www.iussp.org/sites/default/files/event_call_for_papers/IUSSP_1601_Tushar_Extended-Abstract.pdf, accessed on 20 February 2018.

Alejandro, Lisa, Forden Eric, Allison Gosney, Erland Herfindahl, Dennis Luther, Erick Oh, Joann Peterson, Matthew Reisman, and Isaac Wohl. 2010. *An Overview and Examination of the Indian Services Sector*. Working Paper No. ID- 26, August. Office of Industries.

Ansari, M.I. 1995. 'Explaining the Service Sector Growth: An Empirical Study of India, Pakistan, and Sri Lanka'. *Journal of Asian Economics* 6(2): 233–46.

Banga, Rashmi. 2005. *Critical Issues in India's Service-Led Growth*. ICRIER Working Paper No. 171, October.

Banga, Rashmi. 2006. 'Statistical Overview of India's Trade in Services'. In R. Chanda (ed.), *Trade in Services and India: Prospects and Strategies*. New Delhi: Wiley.

Basu, Kaushik and Annemie Maertens. 2007. *The Pattern and Causes of Economic Growth in India*. CAE Working Paper #07–08, April.

Berchert, Ingo and Aaditya Mattoo. 2009. *The Crises Resilience of Services Trade*. Working Paper 4917. World Bank Policy Research.

Bhattacharya, B.B. and Arup Mitra. 1990. 'Excess Growth of Tertiary Sector in Indian Economy: Issues and Implications'. *Economic and Political Weekly* 25 (44): 2445–50.

Bhattacharya, B.B. and S. Sakthivel. 2004. *Economic Reforms and the Jobless Growth in India in the 1990s*. Working Paper E/245/2004. Delhi: Delhi University, Institute of Economic Growth.

Bhowmik, Rita. 2004. 'A Study on Services Sector of Indian Economy during the Period 1968–69 to 1993–94'. Unpublished PhD. Thesis, Jadavpur University, Kolkata.

Binswanger-Mkhize, Hans P. 2013. 'The Stunted Structural Transformation of the Indian Economy'. *Economic and Political Weekly* 48, no. 26–7. Available at http://www.epw.in/journal/2013/26-27/review-rural-affairs-review-issues/stunted-structural-transformation-indian, accessed on 20 February 2018.

Bosworth, Barry and Susan M. Collins. 2007. 'Accounting for Growth: Comparing China and India'. NBER Working Paper Series, Working Paper No. 12943, Cambridge.

Bosworth, Barry, Susan M. Collins, and Arvind Virmani. 2007. 'Sources of Growth in the Indian Economy'. *India Policy Forum 2006–07* 3: 1–50.

———. 2007. *Sources of Growth in Indian Economy*. NBER Working Paper 12901.

Cali, Massimiliano, Karen Ellis, and Dirk Willem te Velde. 2008. *The Contribution of Services to Development: The Role of Regulation and Trade Liberalisation*. London: Overseas Development Institute.

Central Statistical Organisation. 1989. *National Accounts Statistics: Sources and Methods*. New Delhi, India: Government of India.

Central Statistical Organisation. 1999. *New Series on National Accounts Statistics (Base Year 1993–94)*. New Delhi, India: Government of India.

Chadha, G.K. 2007. 'The Rural Non-farm Sector in the Indian Economy: Growth, Challenges and Future Direction'. In A. Gulati and S. Fan (eds), *The Dragon and Elephant—Agricultural and Rural Reforms in China and India*. New Delhi: Oxford University Press.

Chadha, G.K. 2009 'Post-Reform Rural Employment Scenario in India'. In Surjit Singh V. Ratna Reddy (eds),

Changing Contours of Asian Agriculture. Acadmic Foundation.

Chanda, Rupa. 2002. *Globalization of Services: India's Opportunities and Constraints.* New Delhi: Oxford University Press.

Chandrasekhar, C.P. 2010. 'How Significant Is IT in India?' *The Hindu*, May 31.

Chandrasekhar, S. 2011. 'Estimates of Workers Commuting from Rural to Urban and Urban to Rural India: A Note'. Available at http://www.igidr.ac.in/pdf/publication/WP-2011-019.pdf, accessed on 20 February 2018.

Czarnitzki, Dirk and Alfred Spielkamp. 2000. 'Business Services in Germany: Bridges for Innovation'. ZEW Discussion Paper No. 00–52. Available at http://www.zew.de/de/publikationen/business-services-in-germany-bridges-for-innovation-1/, accessed on 20 February 2018.

Dathe, Dietmar and Günther Schmid. 2000. 'Determinants of Business and Personal Services: Evidence from West-German Regions'. WZB Discussion Paper FS I 00–20, Berlin. Available at http://citeseerx.ist.psu.edu/viewdoc/download?doi=10.1.1.198.4457&rep=rep1&type=pdf, accessed on 20 February 2018.

Datta Biswas, M. and D.P. Pal. 2010. 'Rural Non-farm Economy and India's Rural Development: An Analysis of Diversification'. *The Indian Economic Journal* (Special Issues Role of Rural non-farm sector in Rural Development) December 2010.

DIPP. 2011. *Consolidated FDI Policy (Effective from 1 April 2011).* New Delhi: Ministry of Commerce and Industry, Government of India.

Eichengreen, Barry and Poonam Gupta. 2010. *The Service Sector as India's Road to Economic Growth.* Working Paper No. 249, April. New Delhi: Indian Council for Research on International Economic Relations.

———. 2010. 'The Service Sector as India's Road to Economic Growth?' ICRIER Working Paper No. 249, April.

———. 2009. 'Two Waves of Services Growth'. NBER Working Paper no. w14968, May.

Ellis, Frank. 1999. 'Rural Livelihood Diversity in Developing Countries; Evidence and Policy Implications. Available at http://dlc.dlib.indiana.edu/dlc/bitstream/handle/10535/4486/40-rural-livelihood-diversity.pdf?sequence=1, accessed on 25 January 2018.

———. 2000. *Rural Livelihoods and Diversity in Developing Countries.* Oxford: Oxford University Press.

Freguin-Gresh, Sandrine, Eric White, and Bruno Losch. 2012. *Rural Transformation and Structural Change: Insights from Developing Countries Facing Globalization.* International Farming Systems Association 2012 Symposium.

Goldar, B.N. and B. Rashmi. 2004. 'Contribution of Services to Output Growth and Productivity in Indian Manufacturing: Pre and Post Reforms'. ICRIER Working Paper 139, July 2004.

Gordon, Jim and Poonam Gupta. 2003. 'Understanding India's Services Revolution: A Tale of Two Giants: India's and [the People's Republic of] China's Experience with Reform'. Paper prepared for the International Monetary Fund-NCAER-Conference. New Delhi. 14–16 November.

Gordon, Jim and Poonam, Gupta. 2004. 'Understanding India's Services Revolution'. IMF Working Paper WP/04/171, September 2004.

Haggblade, S., P. Hazell, and T. Reardon (eds). 2007. *Transforming the Rural Nonfarm Economy: Opportunities and Threats in the Developing World.* New Delhi: Oxford University Press.

———. 2010. 'The Rural Non-farm Economy: Prospects for Growth and Poverty Reduction'. *World Development* 38 (10): 1429–41.

Hansda, Sajay K. 2001. 'Sustainability of Services-Led Growth: An Input Output Analysis of the Indian Economy'. RBI Working Paper. Available at http://rbidocs.rbi.org.in/rdocs/Publications/PDFs/38040.pdf, accessed on 20 February 2018.

Hnatkovska, V. and A. Lahiri. 2012. 'The Rural–Urban Divide in India'. International Growth Centre Working Paper, February 2013.

Hoekman, B. and A. Mattoo. 2011. 'Services Trade Liberalization and Regulatory Reform: Re-invigorating International Cooperation'. Policy Research Working Paper Series 5517. The World Bank.

IPPG. 2012. 'Beyond Institutions: Institutions and Organisations in the Politics and Economics of Poverty Reduction—A Thematic Synthesis of Research Evidence'. DFID-funded Research Programme Consortium on Improving Institutions for Pro-Poor Growth (IPPG), September 2010. IDPM, School of Environment and Development, University of Manchester.

ISED. 2014. 'India Micro, Small and Medium Enterprise Report 2014'. Cochin: Institute of Small Enterprises and Development.

———. 2017. 'India Micro, Small and Medium Enterprise Report 2017'. Cochin: Institute of Small Enterprises and Development.

Islam, Nurul. 1997. 'The Non-Farm Sector and Rural Development'. IFPRI, Working Paper.

Jain, Sunil and T.N. Ninan. 2010. 'Servicing India's GDP Growth'. In Shankar Acharya and Rakesh Mohan (eds.), *India's Economy Performance and Challenges, Essays in Honour of Montek Singh Ahluwalia*, pp. 328–65. New Delhi: Oxford University Press.

Jha, B. n.d. 'Rural Non-Farm Employment in India: Macro Trends, Micro-Evidences and Policy Options'. Available at http://www.iegindia.org/upload/publication/Workpap/wp272.pdf, accessed on 25 January 2018.

Joshi, Seema. 2008. 'Service Sector in India's Economy: Performance, Problems and Prospects'. Country Paper Submitted for 'Study Meeting on Expansion and Development of the Services Industry in Asia', organized by Asian Productivity Organization at Seoul, Republic of Korea, 17–20 June.

Kochar, Kalpana, Utsav Kumar, Raghuram Rajan, and Arvind Subramanian. 2006. 'India's Pattern of Development: What Happened, What Follows?' Washington, D.C.: Ioannis Tokatlidis Research Department, International Monetary Fund.

Kox, Henk L.M. and Luis Rubalcaba. 2007. 'Analysing the Contribution of Business Services to European Economic Growth'. Available at https://mpra.ub.uni-muenchen.de/2003/, accessed on 20 February 2018.

Kuznets, S. 1973. 'Modern Economic Growth: Findings and Reflections (Nobel Lecture)'. *American Economic Review* 63: 247–58.

Lanjouw, Peter and Rinku Murugai. 2005. *Poverty Decline, Agricultural Wages, and Nonfarm Employment in Rural India*. Working Paper, NCAER. Available at https://openknowledge.worldbank.org/handle/10986/4054, accessed on 25 January 2018.

Lewis, A. 1954. 'Economic Development with Unlimited Supplies of Labor'. *Manchester School* 22 (2): 139–91.

Longman Wiggins, Steve and Peter Hazell. 2010. 'Access to Rural Non-farm Employment and Enterprise Development'. Background Paper for the IFAD Rural Poverty Report. Available at https://www.ifad.org/documents/10180/9946bdef-fbaa-44b5-b30a-cad26d953fd3, accessed on 25 January 2018.

Losch, B., S. Fréguin Gresh and, E.T. White. 2012. *Structural Transformation and Rural Change Revisited: Challenges for Late Developing Countries in a Globalizing World*. Washington, DC: World Bank, Agence Française de Dévelopement.

Malthus, T.R. 1798. *An Essay on the Principle of Population*. London: W. Pickering (1986).

Mathew, P.M. 1994. 'The Experience of Nonfarm Growth in India'. ISED Discussion Paper Series.

———. 2012. 'The Structural Changes Debate, a Discussion', ISED Discussion Paper Series. Cochin: Institute of Small Enterprises and Development (ISED).

———. 2014. 'Globalisation and Local Enterprise Development: The Experience of Kerala'. Cochin: ISED.

———. 2016. 'Rural Services Sector in India: Structural Changes and Implications for Policy'. NABARD Project by Institute of Small Enterprises and Development.

Mattoo A., D. Mishra, and A. Shinghal. 2001. 'Measuring Service Trade Liberalization and Its Impact on Economic Growth: An Illustration'. Available at http://econ.worldbank.org/files/2373_wps2655.pdf, accessed on 20 February 2018.

———. 2003. *Trade in Services: Access to Foreign Markets, Domestic Reform and International Negotiations*. World Bank.

McKinsey & Company. 2007. 'The "Bird of Gold": The Rise of India's Consumer Market'. McKinsey Global Institute. Available at http://www.mckinsey.com/mgi/reports/pdfs/india_consumer_market/MGI_india_consumer_full_report.pdf, accessed on 3 April2012).

Ministry of Finance. 2007. 'Strategy for India's Services Sector: Broad Contours'. Working Paper 1. Available at http://finmin.nic.in/workingpaper/1_2007_DEA.pdf, accessed on 4 May 2012.

Modigliani, Franco and Merton H. Miller. 1958. 'The Cost of Capital, Corporation Finance and the Theory of Investment'. *The American Economic Review* 48, no. 3: 261–97.

Mukherjee, A. 2012. 'Services Sector in India: Trends, Issues and Forward'. *World Economic Outlook*, 1–34.

Mukherjee, Arpita and Tanu M. Goyal. 2012. 'Employment Conditions in Organised and Unorganised Retail: Implications for FDI Policy in India'. *Journal of Business and Retail Management Research* 6(2).

Mukherjee, S., D. Chakraborty, and S. Sikdar. 2014. 'Three Decades of Human Development across Indian States: Inclusive Growth or Perpetual Disparity?' New Delhi: National Institute of Public Finance and Policy.

Nagler, P. and Naudé, W. 2014. 'Non-Farm Enterprises in Rural Africa: New Empirical Evidence'. Policy Research Working Paper No. 7066. Washington DC: The World Bank.

National Account Statistics, Government of India. 2005. New Series on National Accounts Statistics (Base Year 1999–2000). New Delhi: Government of India.

Neelkanth Mishra and Ravi Shankar. 2013. 'India Market Strategy'. Credit Suisse, Asia Pacific/India Equity Research.

North, D. 1990. 'Institutions, Institutional Change and Economic Performance. Cambridge: Cambridge University Press.

Padma, P., E.V. Ramasamy, T.V. Muralivallabhan, and A.P. Thomas. 2014. 'Changing Trend in Household Consumption Expenditure Pattern of Kerala'. November 2014.

Pal, D.P. 1981. 'Structural Interdependence in India's Economy: An Intertemporal Analysis'. PhD Dissertation, University of Kalyani.

Pal, D.P. and D. Chakroborty. 2009. 'Changes in Consumption Pattern in India'. In P. Pal (ed.), *Reforms and Structural Change in India*. New Delhi: Regal Publication.

Pal, D.P. and M. Datta Biswas. 2010. 'Diversification of Farm and Non-Farm Sectors and Structural Transformation of Rural Economy'. Available at https://www.iioa.org/conferences/19th/papers/files/586_20110504061_FarmandNon-FarmSectorsIOPaper2011(DP&MDB).pdf, accessed on 20 February 2018.

Pal, D.P. and G.P. Pal. 1981. 'Changes in Agrarian Structure and Productivity: An Entropy Analysis in India'. *Indian Journal of Agricultural Economics* 36 (4).

Panagariya, A. 2008. *India the Emerging Giant*. New York: Oxford University Press.

Pilat, D. and A. Wölfl. 2005. 'Measuring the Interaction Between Manufacturing and Services'. OECD Science, Technology and Industry Working Papers, 2005/05. OECD Publishing.

Planning Commission. 2008. 'Report by High Level Group on Service Sector'.

Planning Commission. 2011. Faster, Sustainable and More Inclusive Growth: An Approach Paper to the Twelfth Five Year Plan'. Government of India, Planning Commission, October 2011. Available at http://planningcommission.nic.in/plans/planrel/12appdrft/approach_12plan.pdf (last accessed on 27 March 2012).

Prasad, H.A.C. and R. Sathish. 2010. 'Policy for India's Services Sector'. Working Paper No. 1/2010—DEA, Department of Economic Affairs, Ministry of Finance, Government of India.

Polgreen, Lydia. 2009. 'Rural India Gets Chance at Piece of Jobs Boom'. *New York Times* (13 November): A4.

Porter, Michael. 1985. *Competitive Advantage: Creating and Sustaining Superior Performance*. New York: Free Press.

Rajan, Raghuram. 2011. 'Failed States, Vicious Cycles, and a Proposal'. CGD Working Paper 243. Washington, D.C.: Center for Global Development. Available at http://www.cgdev.org/content/publications/detail/1424879, accessed on 20 February 2018.

Rajesh, Raj S.N. and Kunal Sen. 2016. 'Out of the Shadows? The Informal Sector in Post-reform India'. Helsinki: WIDER.

Ranjan, Sharad. 2007. 'Review of Rural Non-farm Sector in India Recent Evidence'. Working Paper on Rural Employment. Available at https://ideas.repec.org/p/ess/wpaper/id1215.html, accessed on 25 January 2018.

Report of the Working Group on Workforce Estimation for Compilation of National Accounts Statistics with Base Year 1999–2000. 2004. New Delhi: Government of India.

Shepard, Stephen B. 1997. 'The New Economy: What It Really Means'. *Business Week*, November 6.

Tamil Nadu Empowerment and Poverty Reduction Project (TNEPRP). 2004: LIVELIHOOD ASSESSMENT REPORT, December.

UN. 2008. 'World Population Prospects'. *The 2008 Revision Volume III Analytical Report*. New York: United Nations Department of Economic and Social Affairs Population Division.

UNDP. 2009. 'Overcoming Barriers: Human Mobility and Development'. Human Development Report—2009, United Nations Development Programme (UNDP). Available at http://hdr.undp.org/en/media/HDR_2009_EN_Complete.pdf, accessed on 4 May 2012.

UNDP. 2011. 'Sustainability and Equity: A Better Future, Human Development Report—2011, United Nations Development Programme (UNDP)'. Available at http://hdr.undp.org/en/media/HDR_2011_EN_Summary.pdf, accessed on 13 June 2012).

Unni, Jeemol and Ravikiran Naik. 2011. 'Rural Structural Transformation: The Case of the Services Sector in India'. *Economic and Political Weekly* 46, nos 26 and 27. Available at http://www.epw.in/journal/2011/26-27/special-articles/rural-structural-transformation-case-services-sector-india.html, accessed on 20 February 2018.

Vaidyanathan, A. 1994. 'Labor Use in Rural India: A Study of Spatial and Temporal Variations'. In T.R. Sundaram (ed.), *Non-Agricultural Employment in India*. New Delhi: Sage.

———. 2010. *Agricultural Growth in India Role of Technology, Incentives and Institutions*. New Delhi: Oxford University Press. NSSO Reports No: 531 on Employment - Unemployment Situation in India & No. 532 on Education in India Economic Census Reports 1998 and 2005, CSO, India.

Visaria, Pravin and Rakesh Basant. 1994. 'Non-Agricultural Employment in India: Problems And Prospects'. In T.R. Sundaram (ed.), *Non-Agricultural Employment in India*. New Delhi: Sage.

Von Wachter, Till. 2001. 'Employment and Productivity Growth in Services and Manufacturing Sectors in France, Germany and the US'. Working Paper No. 50, European Central Bank, March 2001. Available at http://www.ecb.int/pub/pdf/scpwps/ecbwp050.pdf, accessed on 3 April 2012.

Windrum, Paul and Mark Tomlinson. 1999. Knowledge-intensive Services and International Competitiveness: A Four Country Comparison. MERIT, Maastricht Economic Research Institute on Innovation and Technology.

14

Social Sector Development

Tulsi Lingareddy*

ABSTRACT

Social sector development in India has been progressing at a significantly slower pace and in a scattered manner in rural areas compared to that in urban areas. Education, being the basis for both economic and social development, has been lagging far behind in rural areas. Although the gap between rural and urban indicators of education, health, and sanitation has reduced during the past three decades or so, it has still remained significantly large. Infrastructure facilities for education and health have remained deficient in rural areas though there has been an improvement from the mid-2000s onwards.

The most important but least developed social sector segment is sanitation and safe drinking water in rural areas. Despite government's efforts and support schemes, status of sanitation in rural areas has remained dismal in India compared to some of the least developed countries. The emerging trends have suggested that lower education levels have been associated with low health and sanitation levels in rural areas. Thus, improving education levels and creating awareness is of utmost priority to improve health conditions and sanitation in rural areas.

JEL Classification: I10, I13, I14, I15, I18, I21, I22, I24, I25, I28, I38

Keywords: education, health, sanitation, drinking water, social development indicators

14.1 INTRODUCTION

India's focus on social sector development to a significant extent has apparently begun only a decade or so ago. Despite becoming one of the fastest growing economies in the recent years, India still stood at the 130th position in the list of 188 countries on the Human Development Index (HDI) in 2014,[1] much lower than neighbouring Sri Lanka (73rd) and China (90th). Economic development facilitates social sector development through rise in income levels, but social sector development is a necessity for sustaining the economic development.

* Formerly with EPW Research Foundation, India. All views expressed are personal.

[1]A composite measure of achievements of a country in key dimensions of human development including a long and healthy life, access to knowledge, and a decent standard of living, prepared by the United Nations Development Programme (UNDP).

As the endogenous growth theorists (Paul Romer, Robert Lucas, and so on) suggest, investment in human capital, innovation, and knowledge leads to economic growth and reduces the diminishing returns to investment. The remarkable growth of East Asian economies, widely known as the 'East Asian Miracle', has been one of the extensively referred to successful examples of the endogenous growth model (Behrman 1990; World Bank 1993). The East Asian economic miracle is largely attributed, among other things, to the sustained levels of investment in human capital over a long period (Tilak 2002).

India, with around 60 per cent of its population falling in the active age group of 15–59, has a great opportunity to convert the populace into effective human capital by providing access to required education, healthcare, and better living conditions. A major section of the young potential human capital resides in rural areas of the country, and, hence, social sector development in rural areas is of utmost priority for overall development of the economy.

In this context, development of the social sector in rural areas is examined in terms of education, health, drinking water, sanitation, and social security and discussed in detail in the subsequent sections.

14.2 EDUCATION

Education is the starting point of development for any country. Although India has made significant progress in education since Independence, the progress has remained highly skewed towards urban areas while rural areas have been lagging behind due to lack of focus until recently.

Issues of social sector are interdependent, and development of education not only enhances the skills for employability of the population, but also provides awareness of healthy and better way of living. An overview of different parameters indicated that there is a definite positive influence of education, particularly of female education, on health and other social indicators in rural areas across the states.

States with higher female literacy have been in better position in terms of levels of health indicators and better access to drinking water and sanitation facilities in rural areas. States with low female literacy have high maternal mortality rate, higher infant mortality, higher under 5-year mortality, high birth rate, and low access as per the Census 2011 (Figure 14.1).

14.2.1 Current Status of Education Development

Literacy Levels Improved Variedly across Groups

The literacy (7+ years age group) levels in different parts of the country have reached about 74 per cent with wider variations across the states, gender, social groups, and locations (rural–urban). Literacy in rural areas stood at

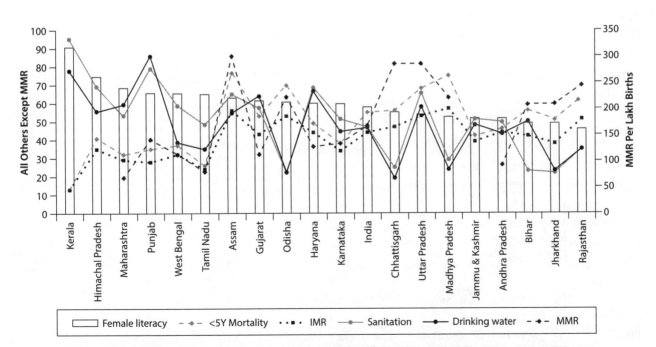

Figure 14.1 Female Literacy versus Health, Drinking Water, and Sanitation in Rural Areas

Source: Census 2011, National Health Profile 2015, *Economic Survey 2015–16.*

68 per cent, nearly 16 per cent lower than urban literacy as per the latest census in 2011. The rural–urban gap was more prominent in case of female literacy, at about 21 per cent in 2011.

The gender (male–female) gap in literacy also stood at about 16.7 per cent for the combined population but it was much wider in case of rural areas at about 20 per cent in 2011. Among social groups, literacy rates of Scheduled Castes (SC) and Scheduled Tribes (ST) population stood at 66 per cent and 59 per cent respectively, against the overall literacy of 74 per cent in 2011.

Wider Literacy Gaps across States

Although the literacy levels have increased steadily, it has not been uniform across the country. Literacy rates among states varied widely from about 61 per cent in Bihar to about 94 per cent in Kerala in 2011. The general pattern observed across the states indicated that the states

with lower literacy rates have larger rural–urban and/or gender gaps compared to that at the national level. The top 10 literate states have significantly lower gender and/or rural–urban gaps compared to the bottom 10 states, as presented in Table 14.1.

Similarly, the bottom 10 states have significantly lower SC and ST literacy rates than the top 10 states, except for Tamil Nadu, whose ST literacy is only about 54 per cent despite it being in the eighth position in terms of total literacy rate.

High Enrollment at Primary Level Is Not Sustaining at Higher Education Levels

The gross enrollment ratios (GER) at primary level have reached over 100 per cent as per the latest data provided by the Unified District Information System for Education (U-DISE) for 2013–14. But, as the education levels progressed upwards, the GER declined steadily and dipped

Table 14.1 Literacy Levels (%) of Top and Bottom 10 States Based on Census 2011

	Literacy	Rural	Rural Female	Scheduled Caste	Scheduled Tribe	Male–Female Gap	Urban–Rural Gap
All-India	74.0	67.8	57.9	66.07	58.95	16.7	16.3
Top 10 States							
Kerala	94.0	93.0	90.8	88.7	75.8	4.0	2.1
Mizoram	91.3	84.1	79.8	92.4	91.5	4.0	13.5
Goa	88.7	86.6	81.6	83.7	79.1	7.9	3.4
Tripura	87.2	84.9	79.5	89.5	79.1	8.8	8.6
Himachal Pradesh	82.8	81.9	74.6	78.9	73.6	13.6	9.2
Maharashtra	82.3	77.0	68.5	79.7	65.7	12.5	11.7
Sikkim	81.4	78.9	72.4	77.5	79.7	11.0	9.8
Tamil Nadu	80.1	73.5	65.0	73.3	54.3	13.4	13.5
Nagaland	79.6	75.3	71.5	NA	80.0	6.7	14.3
Uttarakhand	78.8	76.3	66.2	74.4	73.9	17.4	8.2
Bottom 10 States							
Assam	72.2	69.3	63.0	77.0	72.1	11.5	19.2
Chhattisgarh	70.3	66.0	55.1	70.8	59.1	20.1	18.0
Madhya Pradesh	69.3	63.9	52.4	66.2	50.6	19.5	18.9
Uttar Pradesh	67.7	65.5	53.7	60.9	55.7	20.1	9.6
Jammu and Kashmir	67.2	63.2	51.6	70.2	50.6	20.4	13.9
Andhra Pradesh*	67.0	60.4	51.5	62.3	49.2	15.8	19.7
Jharkhand	66.4	61.1	48.9	55.9	57.1	21.4	21.2
Rajasthan	66.1	61.4	45.8	59.8	52.8	27.1	18.3
Arunachal Pradesh	65.4	59.9	52.0	NA	64.6	14.9	23.0
Bihar	61.8	59.8	49.0	48.7	51.1	19.7	17.1

Note: *Includes Telangana.

Sources: Census 2011, available at www.census2011.co.in.

Table 14.2 Gross Enrollment Ratio, 2013–14

	ALL			SC			ST		
	Boys	Girls	Total	Boys	Girls	Total	Boys	Girls	Total
Primary (I–V)	98.11	100.63	99.31	110.79	112.20	111.46	111.51	108.80	110.18
Upper Primary (VI–VIII)	84.91	90.29	87.45	93.22	96.49	94.79	86.49	85.74	86.13
Elementary (I–VIII)	93.26	96.88	94.98	104.19	109.42	102.85	102.46	100.46	101.48
Secondary (IX–X)	73.48	73.66	73.56	75.96	76.24	76.09	67.51	66.72	67.13
I–X	89.37	92.35	90.78	98.62	103.02	97.62	95.88	94.23	95.07
Senior Secondary (XI–XII)	49.13	49.15	49.14	48.10	49.65	48.82	35.55	33.25	34.44
I–XII	83.31	85.94	84.55	91.13	93.35	92.18	87.49	85.98	86.75
Higher Education	22.30	19.80	21.10	16.00	14.20	15.10	12.40	9.70	11.00

Note: From 1950–1 to 1990–1, figures for Senior Secondary include Secondary Schools.
In Higher Education, stand-alone institutions have not been taken into account.
Source: Educational Statistics at a Glance (2014).

close to 20 per cent for higher education. A similar pattern was noticed in case of SC and ST students with much steeper fall to 15 per cent and 11 per cent respectively in their GER for higher education (Table 14.2).

High Dropout Rates at Higher Levels of Education

In addition to the falling GER, the dropout rates (DoR) have increased with increasing levels of education, becoming a cause for concern as it may lead to low levels of education. The DoR was around 20 per cent till the primary level, but increased to around 50 per cent at class X. Similar pattern of DoR was observed in case of SC students but the DoR of ST students were much higher at over 30 per cent till primary classes and over 60 per cent till class X.

Pupil-to-Teacher Ratio

Pupil-to-teacher ratio stood at around 28:1 for primary, 30:1 for upper primary, and 28:1 for secondary levels against the recommended ratios of 30:1 for primary and 35:1 for upper primary levels as specified by the Right to Education Act 2009.

14.2.2 Emerging Trends

Towards Universalizing Education

A steady and reasonable amount of progress has been witnessed in the country with respect to literacy levels since Independence; it has increased from less than one-fourth of literate population in 1951 to nearly three-fourth of literate population in 2011.

Following the efforts towards increasing access to primary education, enrollment rates have increased significantly in the recent decades. The significant rise in enrollment for primary schooling could be attributed to enhanced infrastructure coupled with various promotional programmes in the past three decades as listed in the subsequent sections.

Progress of education has picked up momentum, particularly in rural areas with the initiation and adoption of National Policy on Education and National Literary Mission along with a number of other programmes and schemes to promote literacy from the mid-1980s.

Subsequently, the launch of Sarva Siksha Abhiyan (SSA) or Education for All towards universalization of elementary education in 2001 has accelerated the reach of elementary education and the literacy levels in the country through narrowing the gaps of gender as well as rural–urban areas.

Slow Improvement in Rural and Female Literacy Rates

Historically, literacy levels in rural areas have always been lower than in urban areas but the gap had widened further in the early decades post-Independence and touched a high of 32.3 per cent in 1971 (see Table 14.3). Thereafter, it started moderating, particularly from the late-1980s, following the adoption of the National Policy on Education and implementation of the National Literacy Mission.

Similarly, literacy rates of rural females have been increasing, but remained significantly low. Nevertheless, following the District Primary Education Programme (DPEP) and SSA or Education for All programmes, the literacy levels of rural females have improved

Table 14.3   Trends in Literacy Rates since 1951 (%)

	Rural			Urban			Combined			Urban–Rural Gap			Gender
	Female	Male	Total	Female	Male	Total	Female	Male	Total	Female	Male	Total	Gap
1951	4.9	19.0	12.1	22.3	45.6	34.6	8.9	27.2	18.3	17.5	26.6	22.5	18.3
1961	10.1	34.3	22.5	40.5	66.0	54.4	15.4	40.4	28.3	30.4	31.7	31.9	25.1
1971	15.5	48.6	27.9	48.8	69.8	60.2	22.0	46.0	34.5	33.3	21.2	32.3	24.0
1981	21.7	49.6	36.0	56.3	76.7	67.2	29.8	56.4	43.6	34.6	27.1	31.2	26.6
1991	30.2	57.0	44.5	64.1	81.1	73.0	39.3	64.1	52.2	33.9	24.1	28.5	24.8
2001	46.7	71.4	59.4	73.2	86.7	80.3	53.7	75.3	64.8	26.5	15.3	20.9	21.6
2011	58.8	78.6	67.8	79.9	89.7	84.1	65.5	82.1	74.0	21.2	11.1	16.3	16.7

Note: 1951–71: Aged 5+, 1981–2011: Aged 7+.

Source: Census of India, various issues, and *EPWRF India Time Series* online database (www.epwrfits.in).

considerably during the 1990s and 2000s. The gender gap had widened through 1950s to 1970s and reached a high of about 26 per cent in 1981. Thereafter, the gap narrowed slowly in the 1980s and 1990s, but picked momentum in 2000s to reach about 16.7 per cent in 2011.

Impressive Increase in Gross Enrollment Ratio for Primary Level

The GER had increased over the past few decades and reached over 100 for primary (6–10 years group). (More than 100 GER could be on account of late or early enrollment or repetition, causing the enrollment to exceed the official population of that group.) In this context, studies indicated that data collected from schools may provide inflated estimates of the proportion of children regularly attending school leading to over estimation of GER (Rawal 2011 and Ramachandran et al. 1997).

The GER of upper primary (11–13 years group) had also improved but at a slower pace and reached about 87 in 2013–14 from about 12 in 1950–1 (Figure 14.2). However, the GER for higher education (18–23 years group) remained significantly lower at around 20.

A similar pattern was noticed in case of SC and ST students as well, with higher GER at primary and relatively lower GER at upper primary levels (Figure 14.3). The GER for higher education in case of SC and ST students still remained lower at around 15 and 10 respectively in 2012–13 (Table 14.4).

Steeper Fall in Dropout Rate of Girl Students across Levels and Categories

The DoRs have also come down significantly during the past five decades or so from more than 60 per cent in

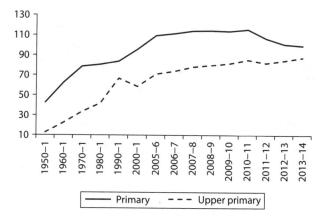

Figure 14.2   Trends in Gross Enrollment Ratio in India (%)
Source: Educational Statistics at a Glance (2014).

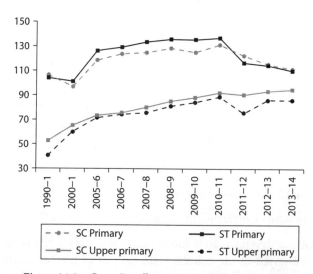

Figure 14.3   Gross Enrollment Ratio of Scheduled Caste and Scheduled Tribe Students (%)
Source: Educational Statistics at a Glance (2014).

Table 14.4   Gross Enrollment Ratio at Higher Levels of Education (%)

	All				Scheduled Caste				Scheduled Tribe			
	(IX–XII) 14–17 Years		HE 18–23 Years		(IX–XII) 14–17 Years		HE 18–23 Years		(IX–XII) 14–17 Years		HE 18–23 Years	
	Boys	Girls	Boys	Girls	Boys	Girls	Boys	Girls	Boys	Girls	Boys	Girls
2001–2	38.2	27.7	9.3	6.7	37.2	26.9	7.7	3.6	31.0	19.8	5.8	2.6
2006–7	45.0	36.8	14.5	10.0	44.0	33.3	11.5	6.9	35.9	25.3	9.5	5.5
2011–12	58.8	54.5	22.1	19.4	62.1	61.4	15.8	13.9	46.9	40.7	12.4	9.7
2012–13	56.5	56.1	22.3	19.8	58.0	58.4	16.0	14.2	48.6	46.4	12.4	9.7
2013–14	61.9	62.1	NA	NA	62.8	63.9	NA	NA	52.8	51.4	NA	NA

Note: HE refers to Higher Education.
Source: Educational Statistics at a Glance (2014).

the 1960s and 1970s to around 20 per cent after 2010 for primary (I–V). However, the DoRs have remained high at around 40 per cent and 50 per cent till the classes VIII and X. More or less similar patterns could be noticed in case of SC students but the DoR continued to be much higher for ST students at around 30 per cent, 50 per cent, and 60 per cent respectively for I–V, I–VIII, and I–X levels in 2013–14.

One interesting pattern that has been emerging in the recent years across all the educational and social groups is that the DoRs of girl students, which were earlier observed to be much higher than that of boys in all the respective categories, declined at a faster rate and stood below the boys', particularly from the late 2000s as evident from Figures 14.4–14.6.

Pupil-to-Teacher Ratio Reaching Recommended Levels

PTR used to be at much lower levels of about 20–4 per cent in 1950s as the enrollment levels were meagre at

around 10–30 per cent. As the enrollment increased, the GER has increased in the subsequent years at a faster rate than the number of teachers and schools; the PTR also increased steadily to more than 40 in 1990s. It has stayed at those levels till 2011–12. But, the efforts following the

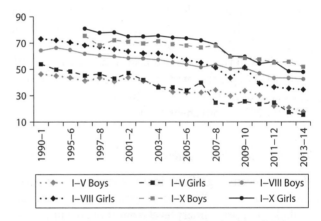

Figure 14.5   Dropout Rates in School Education (SCs) %
Source: Educational Statistics at a Glance (2014).

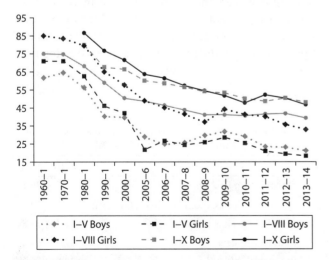

Figure 14.4   Dropout Rates in School Education (%)
Source: Educational Statistics at a Glance (2014).

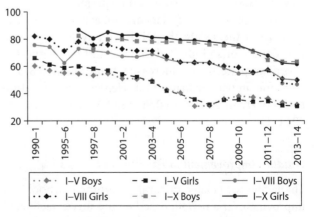

Figure 14.6   Dropout Rates in School Education (STs)
Source: Educational Statistics at a Glance (2014).

Table 14.5   Trends in Pupil–Teacher Ratio and Gender Parity Index

	Pupil–Teacher Ratio					Gender Parity Index				
	Primary	UP	Secondary	SS	HE	Primary	UP	Elementary	Secondary	HE
1950–1	24	20	NA	21	NA	0.4	0.2	0.4	NA	NA
1960–1	36	31	NA	25	NA	0.5	0.3	0.5	NA	NA
1970–1	39	32	NA	25	NA	0.6	0.5	0.6	NA	NA
1980–1	38	33	NA	27	NA	0.7	0.5	0.6	0.5	NA
1990–1	43	37	NA	31	NA	0.8	0.6	0.7	0.5	NA
2000–1	43	38	31	35	NA	0.8	0.8	0.8	0.7	0.7
2010–11	43	33	30	34	26	1.0	0.9	1.0	0.9	0.9
2012–13	30	30	30	40	23	1.0	1.1	1.0	1.0	0.9
2013–14	28	30	28	40	NA	1.0	1.1	1.0	1.0	0.9

Note: UP refers to Upper Primary, SS to Senior Secondary, and HE to Higher Education.
From 1950–1 to 1990–1, figures for Senior Secondary include Secondary Schools.
In Higher Education, Stand-alone Institutions have not been taken into account.
Source: Educational Statistics at a Glance 2014 and *EPWRF India Time Series* online database (www.epwrfits.in).

launch of Right to Education Act 2009 have brought down the PTR to recommended levels of about 30 for primary education (see Table 14.5).

The PTR in rural areas had also come down to 27–30 in 2014–15 as per the latest data released by the National University of Educational Planning and Administration (NUEPA 2015) from about 37–43 in 2004–5.

Rise in Gender Parity Index

There has been a significant increase in the gender parity index (GPI) in enrollment in elementary education, particularly at upper primary level from about 0.2 in 1950–1 to about 1.1 in 2013–14. In case of secondary education, it had doubled from 0.5 in 1980–1 to 1.0 in 2013–14, while it went up from 0.4 to 1.0 in case of overall elementary education in the corresponding period.

Although the specific data are not available for rural areas from the 1950s, the DISE data available for the past decade or so indicated that the GPI had witnessed a similar pattern and increased from about 0.8 and 0.88 for upper primary and elementary education respectively in 2004–5 to 0.96 and 0.95 respectively in 2014–15.

Gradual Improvement in Facilities at Schools

The facilities available in rural government schools are improving over a period. Based on the survey facilitated by Pratham, Annual Survey of Education Report (ASER) 2014 indicated that there is a gradual improvement in

the proportion of government schools in rural areas, with basic facilities such as drinking water, toilets, separate toilets for girls, and so on, having increased in 2014 compared to that in 2010 (ASER 2015) (see Table 14.6).

Further, proportion of schools complying with PTR norms had gone up from about 39 per cent in 2010 to over 49 per cent in 2014. However, the proportion of schools complying with classroom–teacher ratio norms has moderated to 73 per cent in 2014 from about 76 per cent in 2010.

14.2.3 Institutional Support

Government spending on education has increased from less than 1 per cent of GDP in the 1950s to more than 4 per cent in 2000–1. However, it has stagnated around 4 per cent during the recent years after recovering from a fall in the late 2000s (Figure 14.7).

Table 14.6   Proportion of Government Primary Schools in Rural Areas with Facilities (%)

	2010	2014
Complying with PTR norms	38.9	49.3
Complying with classroom–teacher ratio norms	76.2	72.8
With drinking water	72.7	75.6
With useable toilets	47.2	65.2
With useable girls' toilets	32.9	55.7

Source: ASER (2014).

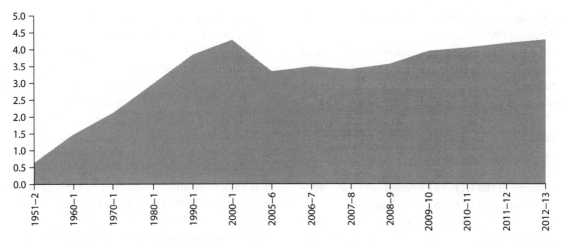

Figure 14.7   Expenditure on Education as Percentage of GDP

Source: Educational Statistics at a Glance (2014).

14.2.3.1 Important Initiatives by the Government (NUEPA 2014)

- 1986—National Policy on Education (NPE) was adopted.
- 1987—Several large centrally assisted schemes/ programmes such as 'Operation Blackboard' and the 'scheme for restructuring and reorganization of teacher education' was launched.
- 1988—National Literacy Mission (NLM) was launched.
- 1992—National Policy on Education was revised.
- 1994—DPEP was launched to universalize primary education in selected districts.
- 1995—Centrally assisted National Programme of Nutritional Support to Primary Education, popularly known as the Mid-Day Meal Scheme (MDMS) was launched.
- 1999—A separate Department of School Education and Literacy was created within the Ministry of Human Resource Development, Government of India.
- 2001—(*a*) SSA, the flagship programme for universalization of elementary education was launched; (*b*) Adoption of the National Policy on Empowerment of Women. The policy supported the provision of childcare facilities, including crèches at work places of women.
- 2002—(*a*) The Constitution (Eighty-sixth Amendment) Act, 2002, inserted Article 21-A in the Constitution of India to provide free and compulsory education for all children in the age group of six to fourteen years as a Fundamental Right; (*b*) Commitment to the provision of early childhood care and education to children below the age of six years reiterated; (*c*) The Tenth Five-Year Plan (2002–7) launched.
- 2004—(*a*) Education Cess was introduced for raising additional financial resources needed to fulfil government's commitment to universalize elementary education; (*b*) EDUSAT, a satellite exclusively dedicated to education was launched to harness modern technology for delivery of education of good quality to all, including hard-to-reach groups.
- 2005—National Curriculum Framework (NCF-2005) for school education formulated.
- 2009—(*a*) The Right of Children to Free and Compulsory Education Act, 2009, was enacted. The Act makes it incumbent on governments to provide for free and compulsory education to all children of the age of six to fourteen years; (*b*) The National Literacy Mission (NLM) was recast with a special focus on female literacy and the 'Sakshar Bharat' (Literate India) programme launched as the national adult education programme on 8 September 2009; (*c*) The revised National Curriculum Framework for teacher Education was formulated; (*d*) The Rashtriya Madhyamik Shiksha Abhiyan (RMSA) was launched in March 2009, with the vision of making secondary education of good quality available, accessible, and affordable to all young persons in the age group 15–16 years; (*e*) Revised centrally sponsored Scheme of Inclusive Education for the Disabled at Secondary Stage was approved; (*f*) The centrally sponsored scheme 'Construction & Running of Girls' Hostel

for Students of Secondary and Higher Secondary Schools' approved.

- 2010—(*a*) The Right of Children to Free and Compulsory Education (RTE) Act, 2009, came into force from 1 April 2010; (*b*) All States/Union Territories notified of state RTE Rules. Central RTE rules apply to Union Territories without legislation; (*c*) The Sarva Shiksha Abhiyan Framework was aligned to the RTE Act; The SSA is the primary vehicle for implementing the aims and objectives of the RTE; (*d*) Revised centrally sponsored scheme of ICT@ Schools approved.
- 2011—The revised centrally sponsored scheme 'Vocationalisation of Higher Secondary Education' was approved.
- 2013—(*a*) National Early Childhood Care and Education (ECCE) Policy was adopted; (*b*) The Integrated Child Development Services, the flagship programme of Government of India for ECCE was restructured and strengthened.

14.2.3.2 Growing Private Sector Involvement in Rural Education

Government institutions have been playing a predominant role in educating the rural population though the presence of private sector has also been increasing in the recent years. According to the results of the 8th All India School Education Survey (AISES), private sector schools accounted for about 14 per cent of all schools by different management in rural areas while that of government bodies account for about 71 per cent in 2009.

The contribution of privately managed schools stood at less than 10 per cent in rural areas at the primary level. However, the share of private schools increased while moving to higher levels of education as 15 per cent at upper primary level, 46 per cent at secondary level, and 64 per cent at higher secondary level in 2009.

On the other hand, results of ASER 2014 by Pratham indicated that about 30.8 per cent of all 6–14-year-old children in rural India are enrolled in private schools in 2014 compared to 29 per cent in 2013 and about 19 per cent in 2006. The report further indicated that there has been an increase in private school enrollment in almost all states in 2014 compared to that in 2013, except for Gujarat, Maharashtra, Uttarakhand, Nagaland, and Kerala.

14.2.4 International Comparison

Adult literacy (concerning the age of 15+ years) for the country stood at 69.3 per cent, while in rural areas it stood at 63 per cent, as per the 2011 census. On the other hand, as per the latest estimates of UNESCO Institute of Statistics (UIS), adult literacy for India was about 61.5 per cent in 2015 against the world's average of 85 per cent. Further, India's literacy rate stands much lower compared to other BRICS countries, namely, Brazil, Russia, China, and South Africa at 92.6 per cent, 99.7 per cent, 96.4 per cent, and 94.6 per cent respectively, in 2015.

A more or less similar pattern was observed in case of neighbouring countries such as China, Pakistan, and Sri Lanka, with a sharp reduction of GER at higher education levels (Table 14.7). However, the GER levels have remained high for all levels in the USA and declined only moderately in case of other developed countries such as UK, Germany, and Russia.

PTR in India stood higher than the neighbouring countries including China, Sri Lanka, and Nepal and much higher than the other BRICS countries and developed countries as evident from Table 14.8.

14.2.5 Challenges and Way Forward

- Education for all seems to be a long way away: Persisting wide gap of literacy rates across gender, location, and communities is a major challenge that needs to be addressed to achieve the objective of education for all. Nearly 32 per cent of the 700 million rural people are illiterate as per Census 2011.

Table 14.7   Management-wise Schools at Different Levels in 2009 (%)

	Primary	Upper Primary	Secondary	Higher Secondary	Total
Rural					
Government	75.7	82.5	51.7	36.5	71.1
Local Bodies	16.9	1.9	2.2	4.2	15.4
Private Aided	2.4	6.3	28.8	14.5	5.3
Private Unaided	5.0	9.3	17.3	44.9	8.3
Total	100.0	100.0	100.0	100.0	100.0
Urban					
Government	46.8	41.5	26.7	19.4	35.8
Local Bodies	11.1	2.8	4.0	3.2	8.7
Private Aided	9.7	10.0	24.4	15.3	14.3
Private Unaided	32.5	45.7	45.0	62.1	41.2
Total	100.0	100.0	100.0	100.0	100.0

Source: 8th AISES published in 2015 and data pertains to 2009.

Table 14.8 International Comparison on Gross Enrollment Ratio and Pupil–Teacher Ratio 2012

Countries	Gross Enrollment Ratio (GER)				Pupil–Teacher Ratio (PTR)				Govt Exp.	Adult Literacy
	(I–V)	(VI–VIII)	(IX–XII)	Tertiary	(I–V)	(VI–VIII)	(IX–XII)	Tertiary		
India	106.5	82.0	56.8	20.8	41.0	34.0	32.0	24.0	4.2	61.5
Bangladesh	111.8	70.9	40.6	13.4	NA	34.0	30.2	23.1	5.9	92.6
Brazil	103.4	99.8	91.0	45.2	20.5	17.0	14.7	20.0	NA	96.4
China	127.9	103.5	76.6	26.7	18.2	13.9	15.3	19.5	4.9	NA
Germany	100.5	99.6	104.3	61.7	11.7	11.8	14.8	7.2	3.8	72.2
Nepal	139.3	88.5	47.5	14.4	27.5	37.1	22.6	NA	NA	64.7
Pakistan	92.9	49.4	27.1	9.5	41.4	20.6	21.7	20.2	2.1	56.4
Russia	100.6	93.9	98.3	76.1	19.6	NA	NA	14.4	4.2	99.7
South Africa	101.6	111.0	96.0	18.9	29.5	NA	NA	NA	6.4	94.6
Sri Lanka	98.4	99.1	99.6	17.0	24.4	16.5	18.2	NA	1.5	92.6
UK	108.5	106.4	87.6	61.9	18.3	16.8	15.6	17.9	5.8	NA
USA	98.1	98.0	89.5	94.3	14.4	14.7	14.7	13.8	5.2	NA

Source: Educational Statistics at a Glance (2014) and online database of UNESCO Institute for Statistics (www.uis.unesco.org).

– The challenge is to ensure the equitable access to all genders, locations, communities and social groups, and so on, with specific focus on the issues associated with respective categories of population.

• **Lack of continuity in education**: Low GER and high DoR from upper primary level onwards suggests that all the students are not moving into the next levels of education. Further, students who have moved to the next level are not completing the subsequent levels of education. This may result in higher literacy rates but very low education levels.

– Access and availability to upper primary and secondary education where the GER and DoR are at discouraging levels have to be enhanced.
– Continuation of education to higher levels through economic support and incentives where needed has to be ensured.

• **Quality of education**: Although PTR has improved to the recommended levels in rural areas of majority of the states, it remained very high in states such as Bihar, Jharkhand, and Uttar Pradesh, particularly at the primary level. Hence, the focus of the new national policy on education 2016 is on improving the quality of education and restoring its credibility (MHRD 2016).

– There is a need to enhance capabilities to ensure a sufficient number of trained teachers to meet the requirements of schools.

– There is a need to improve the rural school infrastructure with the use of information and communication technology (ICT) in improving the process of education.
– Efforts have to be increased to achieve the targets for education under Sustainable Development Goals (SDGs) as specified in Box 14.1.

14.3 HEALTH

Health sector development has to be a comprehensive development covering not just improving the health status but also the readiness to deal with medical emergencies arising from both natural and accidental causes as well as preventive care towards conventional medical problems in the country.

Considerable progress has been witnessed in relation to health care in rural India, particularly during the past decade or so, with special focus brought through the launch of National Rural Health Mission in 2005, though a lot more needs to be done.

14.3.1 Health Status Indicators: Emerging Trends

Trends in various health indicators such as birth rate, fertility, death rate, infant mortality, maternal mortality, and so on suggested that there has been steady but relatively slow progress with respect to almost all the indicators, particularly in rural areas.

Box 14.1   Targets under SDGs on Education

- By 2030, ensure that all girls and boys complete free, equitable, and quality primary and secondary education leading to relevant and effective learning outcomes.
- By 2030, ensure that all girls and boys have access to quality early childhood development, care, and pre-primary education so that they are ready for primary education.
- By 2030, ensure equal access for all women and men to affordable and quality technical, vocational, and tertiary education, including university.
- By 2030, substantially increase the number of youth and adults who have relevant skills, including technical and vocational skills, for employment, decent jobs, and entrepreneurship.
- By 2030, eliminate gender disparities in education and ensure equal access to all levels of education and vocational training for the vulnerable, including persons with disabilities, indigenous peoples, and children in vulnerable situations.
- By 2030, ensure that all youth and a substantial proportion of adults, both men and women, achieve literacy and numeracy.
- Build and upgrade education facilities that are child, disability, and gender sensitive and provide safe, nonviolent, inclusive, and effective learning environments for all.

Moderation in Crude Birth Rate (CBR): As per the latest available data, CBR per 1,000 population has slowed down to 22.9 in rural areas and 17.3 in urban areas during 2013 from the corresponding 38.9 and 29.7 during 1970.

Total Fertility Rate in rural areas has come down from 173 in 1970 to 86 in 2013 and the rural–urban gap has also declined moderately from 40 to 25 (Table 14.9).

Persistent rise in the life expectancy at birth: Life expectancy at birth has increased to 66 years in 2013 from about 48 years in 1970 in rural areas and the rural–urban gap has declined from about 11 years in 1970 to about 5 years in 2013.

Significant fall in Crude Death Rate (CDR): CDR has declined significantly from 17.3 in 1970 to 7.5 in 2013 in rural areas and from 10.2 to 5.6 in urban areas based on the data generated by the Sample Registration Survey (SRS).

Reduction in maternal mortality rate (MMR): MMR, another important indicator of maternal health, has also

declined to 167 per 1 lakh births in 2011–13 from over 650 per 1 lakh births during the early 1980s (Table 14.10).

But, as per the specifications of millennium development goals (MDGs), the MMR was expected to come down from 437 in 1990 to 109 per 1 lakh births (one-third) by 2015. However, the projections based on historical trends suggested that it may reach about 140 by 2015 (GoI 2015).

Impressive fall in infant mortality rate (IMR) has also decreased steeply from about 136 in 1970 to about 44 in 2013 in rural areas while slipping to 27 from 90 in urban areas during the corresponding years. The gap between rural and urban areas has also declined significantly from 59 in 1980 to 17 in 2013 (Table 14.10). The combined IMR for the country as a whole stood at 40 in 2013.

As per the MDGs, IMR for the country needs to be brought down to 27 by 2015, one-third of 80 in 1990. However, only IMR in urban areas has reached the target; it remained significantly high at 44 till 2013 in rural areas.

Table 14.9   Trends in Major Health Indicators

	Crude Birth Rate			Total Fertility Rate			Life Expectancy at Birth (Years)		
	Rural	Urban	Gap	Rural	Urban	Gap	Rural	Urban	Gap
1970	38.9	29.7	9.2	173	133	40	48.0	58.9	10.9
1980	34.6	28.1	6.5	145	111	34	53.7	62.8	9.1
1990	31.7	24.7	7.0	133	96	37	56.1	63.4	7.3
2000	27.6	20.7	6.9	113	77	36	62.7	68.4	5.7
2010	23.7	18.0	5.7	92	64	28	64.9	69.6	4.7
2011	23.3	17.6	5.7	89	62	27	65.3	70.1	4.8
2012	23.1	17.4	5.7	88	62	26	65.8	70.6	4.8
2013	22.9	17.3	5.6	86	61	25	66.3	71.2	4.9

Source: *EPWRF India Time Series* (www.epwrfits.in) online database and Statistical Report of Sample Registration Survey (SRS).

Table 14.10 Trends in Mortality Indicators

	MMR	Crude Death Rate			Infant Mortality Rate		
	Total	Rural	Urban	Gap	Rural	Urban	Gap
1970	NA	17.3	10.2	7.1	136.0	90.0	46.0
1980	650	13.5	8.0	5.5	123.8	65.2	58.6
1990	437	10.5	6.8	3.7	86.0	50.0	36.0
2000	318	9.3	6.3	3.0	74.0	44.0	30.0
2010	NA	7.7	5.8	2.0	51.0	31.0	20.0
2011	178	7.6	5.7	1.9	48.0	29.0	19.0
2012	NA	7.6	5.6	2.0	46.0	28.0	18.0
2013	167	7.5	5.6	1.9	44.0	27.0	17.0

Source: *EPWRF India Time Series* (www.epwrfits.in) online database, Statistical Report of Sample Registration Survey (SRS) and National Health Profile various issues.

Table 14.11 Trends in Progress of Public Health Care Centres (in Numbers)

	Sub Centres	Primary Health Centres	Community Health Centres
VI Plan—1985	84,376	9,115	761
VII Plan—1990	130,165	18,671	1,910
VIII Plan—1997	136,258	22,149	2,633
IX Plan—2002	137,311	22,875	3,054
X Plan—2007	145,272	22,370	4,045
XI Plan—2012	148,366	24,049	4,833
XII Plan (as on 31 March 2015)	153,655	25,308	5,396

Source: Rural Health Statistics 2014–15.

14.3.2 Rural Health Care Infrastructure: Status and Emerging Trends

Rural health care system in India has a three-tier structure with sub centres (SCs) as the first contact points with the community, followed by primary health centres (PHCs), and community health centres (CHCs).

A significant progress has been witnessed in health infrastructure during the past three decades or so in terms of the numbers of various centres. The SCs have almost doubled while the number of PHCs has tripled during the past 30 years. Further, the number of CHCs has risen many times from 761 in 1985 to 5,396 in 2015 (Table 14.11).

Increasing government ownership of buildings: Pattern of ownership of the buildings that have been in use for various centres of rural health care system indicated that there has been a considerable shift from rented buildings to government-owned buildings, particularly in case of SCs and PHCs post launch of MHRM.

The share of government-owned buildings has risen to 67.4 per cent, 83 per cent, and 95 per cent for SCs, PHCs, and CHCs respectively in 2015 (Table 14.12). As a result, the share of rented buildings has come down to 21 per cent and 3.6 per cent in 2015 for SCs and PHCs from about 34.5 per cent and 12.2 per cent in 2005.

Further, the buildings constructed under government ownership may expand in the range of 5–7 per cent in the near future.

Infrastructure remains below the norms: Despite the significant progress witnessed in the expansion of rural infrastructure network, physical infrastructure level has not yet reached the specified norms with respect to all PHCs in rural areas. While the status of SCs and PHCs has reached closer to the general norm, the status of CHCs remained relatively far from the required norm as revealed from the latest statistics presented in Table 14.13. Hence, more emphasis is needed on expanding number of CHCs along with the other two.

Manpower Shortfall Persists in RHCs: There has been a gradual progress in the number of health care manpower in rural areas but at a significantly slow pace as evident from the near stagnant numbers of various health care professionals since 1985 presented in Table 14.14.

The increase in the number of health care manpower is much lower as compared to the rise in population. As a result, shortfall or gap between the required and actual number of health care professionals in position has been widening.

The shortfall in specialists including surgeons, obstetricians and gynaecologists, physicians, and paediatricians at CHCs has shot up to more than 80 per cent in 2015,

Table 14.12 Trends in Ownership of the Buildings of Health Care Centres (%)

	2005				2015				
	Govt	Rented	Rent Free	Total (Nos)	Govt	Rented	Rent Free	Total (Nos)	Under Construction (Nos)
SCs	43.8	34.5	9.8	146,026	67.4	21.4	11.1	153,655	10,951
PHCs	69.0	12.2	7.3	23,236	82.9	3.6	6.1	25,308	1,253
CHCs	84.3	0.1	7.6	3,346	95.1	0.6	4.2	5,396	370

Source: Rural Health Statistics 2014–15.

Table 14.13 Rural Health Care Infrastructure Norms and Present Status

	National Norms (Population)		Status (2015)
	General	Tribal/Hilly/Desert	
SCs	5,000	3,000	5,426
PHCs	30,000	20,000	32,944
CHCs	120,000	80,000	154,512
Number of SCs per PHC	6	6	6
Number of PHCs per CHC	4	4	5

Source: Rural Health Statistics 2014–15.

Table 14.14 Trends in Manpower in Rural Health Centres (in Numbers)

	Doctors at Primary Health Centres	Health Workers	Specialists at Community Health Centres
1985	18,281	179,737	NA
1991	22,013	185,773	NA
2001	25,724	208,460	3,953
2011	26,329	260,083	4,267
2014	27,355	273,225	4,091

Source: *EPWRF India Time Series* (www.epwrfits.in) online database and National Health Profile various issues.

as compared to 45 per cent in 2005 (Figure 14.8). Similarly, the shortfall in the number of doctors at PHCs has also gone up to 12 per cent in 2015 from 4.3 per cent in 2005. The shortage in pharmacists and lab technicians at PHCs and CHCs has also risen to 27 per cent and 45 per cent respectively in 2015 from the corresponding 10.8 per cent and 27 per cent a decade earlier. However, the shortfall in the number of health workers at SCs declined to 5 per cent in 2015 from about 11 per cent in 2005, while the shortfall in nursing staff at PHCs and CHCs has moderated to 21 per cent from 29 per cent in the respective years, indicating an improvement.

14.3.3 Institutional Support

Public expenditure on health in India has been dismal, particularly by the government, at around 1 per cent of GDP despite the increased focus. The expenditure by households has remained the largest contribution at about two-thirds of total health expenditure (THE) in India (Table 14.15).

The special focus on health sector with initiation of the National Rural Health Mission (NRHM) and National Health Mission (NHM) along with a number of programmes during the past decade did not raise the expenditure on health (see Box 14.2). Nevertheless, the contribution of the government to expenditure on health has gone up to about 29 per cent in 2013–14 from about 23 per cent in 2004–5. The share of firms' expenditure on health also declined to less than half between 2004–5 and 2013–14 while that of social health insurance and private health insurance nearly doubled during the same period.

Trends in Public Expenditure: Public expenditure on health has increased steadily during the XI plan period from about 0.93 per cent of GDP to about 1.09 per cent in

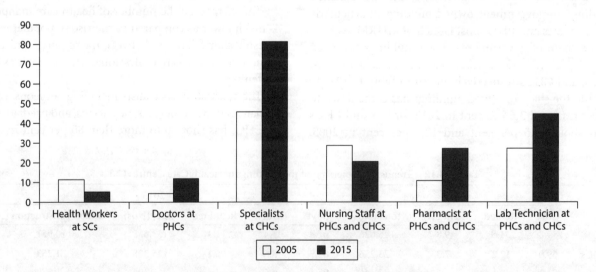

Figure 14.8 Manpower Shortfall at Rural Health Centres (%)

Source: Rural Health Statistics 2014–15.

Table 14.15 Source-wise Contribution of Funds for Health Care

	NHA 2004–5	NHA 2013–14
Total health expenditure (THE) as % of GDP	4.2	4.0
Government expenditure as % of THE	22.5	28.6
Household expenditure as % of THE	71.6	67.7
Firms as % of THE	5.7	2.4
Social health insurance expenditure as % of THE	4.2	6.0
Private health insurance as a % THE	1.6	3.4

Source: National Health Accounts Estimates for India 2013–14.

2010–11, though moderated to 1.04 per cent in 2011–12. States' contribution has remained at about 60–5 per cent in core as well as broad health expenditures (Table 14.16).

Further, the public expenditure on health care has remained significantly higher in urban areas than that in rural areas despite the two-thirds of rural coverage. As indicated by the estimates of national health accounts, health expenditure by the government on rural health services has remained below 20 while that on urban health services stood above 30 per cent of total government expenditure on health.

Immediate Requirement for Institutional Support: The required or desired density of various trained health care manpower is much higher than the available density per 1 lakh of the population in the country. The gap was more prominent with respect to physicians, nurses, and auxiliary nurse midwives (ANMs). In order to meet the desirable density through increasing the number of trained personnel in the respective categories, there is an additional requirement of 240 colleges for physicians, 500 colleges for nurses, and 970 colleges for ANMs (Table 14.17).

14.3.4 International Comparison

Health indicators in India in international comparison indicated that the status of India is well below not

---

Box 14.2 National Rural Health Mission

NRHM was launched on 12 April 2005, to provide accessible, affordable, and quality health care to the rural population, especially the vulnerable groups. In view of the wide gap between the rural and urban health indicators efforts were made to narrow the same.

MAJOR INITIATIVES

Accredited Social Health Activists (ASHAs)—the first port of call for any health-related demands of deprived sections of the population, especially women and children, who find it difficult to access health services in rural areas.

Rogi Kalyan Samiti (Patient Welfare Committee)/Hospital Management Society—This committee is a registered society whose members act as trustees to manage the affairs of the hospital and is responsible for the upkeep of the facilities.

The Untied Grants to Sub Centres (SCs) for better equipment giving more confidence to ANMs.

The Village Health Sanitation and Nutrition Committee (VHSNC)—Untied grants of Rs 10,000 are provided annually to each VHSNC under NRHM, which are utilized through involvement of Panchayati Raj representatives and other community members in many states.

Janani Suraksha Yojana (JSY) aims to reduce maternal mortality among pregnant women by encouraging them to deliver in government health facilities through providing cash assistance.

Janani Shishu Suraksha Karyakarm (JSSK) entitles all pregnant women delivering in public health institutions to absolutely no-expense delivery, including caesarean section. The free entitlements include free drugs and consumables, free diagnostics, free diet during stay in the health institutions, free provision of blood, and free transport.

Mother and Child Tracking System (MCTS): The Ministry of Health and Family Welfare (MoHFW) has introduced web-based, name-based tracking system called Mother & Child Tracking System (MCTS) across all the states and Union Territories to facilitate timely delivery of antenatal and postnatal care services to all the pregnant women and immunization to all the children.

Rashtriya Bal Swasthya Karyakram (RBSK): Launched in February 2013, this programme provides for child health screening and early intervention services through early detection and management of the 4 Ds—Defects at birth, Diseases, Deficiencies, and Development delays including disability.

Free Drugs and Free Diagnostic Service: To address the issue of high out-of-pocket expenditure, the (MoHFW) introduced an incentive to the extent of 5 per cent of the state's Resource Envelope under NRHM for those states that implemented free essential drugs scheme for all patients accessing public health facilities.

Table 14.16 Trends in Expenditure on Health Care during XI Plan Period

	Core Health Expenditure as % of GDP			Broad Health Expenditure as % of GDP		
	Centre	States	Total	Centre	States	Total
2007–8	0.32	0.61	0.93	0.71	1.17	1.89
2008–9	0.35	0.65	0.99	0.75	1.22	1.98
2009–10	0.40	0.69	1.09	0.78	1.24	2.02
2010–11	0.36	0.73	1.09	0.75	1.27	2.02
2011–12	0.34	0.70	1.04	0.74	1.19	1.94

Note: Core health includes health care expenditure of central ministries (Ministry of Health and Family Welfare, Labour on Rashtriya Swasthya Bima Yojana, and so on) on health; broad health includes drinking water and sanitation, midday meal and ICDS (plan and non-plan).
Source: Twelfth Five Year Plan (2012–17) Social Sector, vol. III, Planning Commission, GoI.

Table 14.17 Availability and Requirement of Trained Manpower in Health Care

	Available till 2011–12		Expected by 2017		Desirable Density	Colleges Required
	Number	Density	Number	Density		
Physicians	691,633	57	848,616	65	85	240
AYUSH	534,091	44	642,386	49	49	0
Dentists	88,370	7	193,797	15	15	0
Nurses/GNM	743,324	61	1,508,684	115	170	500
ANM	361,879	30	516,090	39	85	970
Pharmacist	492,923	41	918,276	70	70	0

Notes: Density is Per Lakh Population, current availability based on attrition at 25 per cent for physicians, AYUSH: Ayurveda, Yoga and Naturopathy, Unani, Siddha and Homoeopathy (), Pharmacists, and dentists and 40 per cent for nurses and ANMs.
Source: Twelfth Five Year Plan (2012–17), Social Sector, vol. III, Planning Commission, GoI.

only when compared to advanced countries but also in relation to BRICS countries. Further, India stands in a slightly lower position compared to some of the neighbouring small countries such as Sri Lanka and Nepal in terms of life expectancy and CBR. India's status in terms of maternal and child care appears to be lower compared to most of the countries as indicated by MMR and IMR (Table 14.18).

In terms of expenditure on health care, India is lagging behind most of the developing and developed countries, especially in terms of public expenditure. India's public expenditure on health care stands at a meager 1.4 per cent of GDP compared to about 6 per cent of GDP for the world (Table 14.19). India stands slightly above its neighbours, namely Pakisthan and Bangladesh. Even the public expenditure of small neighbouring countries such as Nepal and Sri Lanka stood higher than India at 2.3 per cent and 2 per cent respectively.

Per capita expenditure on health care also witnessed a similar pattern as India remained well below the world

Table 14.18 Health Indicators in Selected Countries in 2014

	CBR	Life Expectancy at Birth (Years)	CDR	MMR	IMR
Bangladesh	20.0	71.8	5.7	176.0	30.7
Brazil	14.9	75.0	6.1	44.0	14.6
China	13.3	76.1	7.2	27.0	9.2
Germany	8.5	81.0	10.6	6.0	3.1
India	**20.4**	**68.3**	**7.9**	**167.0**	**37.9**
Nepal	21.0	69.2	6.6	258.0	29.4
Pakistan	25.2	66.4	7.3	178.0	65.8
Russian Federation	11.8	70.5	14.8	25.0	8.2
South Africa	20.9	62.9	11.1	138.0	33.6
Sri Lanka	17.9	74.9	6.6	30.0	8.4
UK	12.2	81.2	8.9	9.0	3.5
USA	13.2	79.3	8.4	14.0	5.6

Source: Extracted from online databases of the World Health Organization and the World Bank.

Table 14.19   Expenditure on Health Care in Selected Countries in 2014

	Health Expenditure as % of GDP			Expenditure
	Private	Public	Total	Per capita ($PPP)
Bangladesh	2.0	0.8	2.8	88
Brazil	4.5	3.8	8.3	1,318
China	2.5	3.1	5.5	731
Germany	2.6	8.7	11.3	5,182
India	**3.3**	**1.4**	**4.7**	**267**
Nepal	3.5	2.3	5.8	137
Pakistan	1.7	0.9	2.6	129
Russian Federation	3.4	3.7	7.1	1,836
South Africa	4.6	4.2	8.8	1,148
Sri Lanka	1.5	2.0	3.5	369
UK	1.5	7.6	9.1	3,377
USA	8.9	8.3	17.1	9,403
World	**4.0**	**6.0**	**9.9**	**1,276**

Source: World Development Indicators, extracted from online database of the World Bank.

average. Per capita expenditure on health care in China is nearly three times higher than that in India. Per capita spending on health even in Sri Lanka is nearly 50 per cent higher at US$369 than the US$267 in India. Similarly, all the remaining BRICS countries spend on health care many times higher than India.

14.3.5 Challenges and Way Forward

Despite the significant progress in the recent years, major health indicators for India have remained much below the world standards, particularly in rural areas. India has missed most of the targets of MDGs related to health, at a close margin for IMR and under 5 years mortality but at a larger margin in case of MMR (Box 14.3).

The rural–urban divide is very significant in case of social sector development and more so in case of health due to inadequate reach of health care facilities in rural areas.

- Challenges in health care development are largely sourced from poor economic and educational status of the rural population and inadequate public spending.
- Poor economic conditions restrict the access to private sector health care.
- Poor education and lack of awareness is further constraining the poor population to use the scantily available public health care facilities
- Poor education and economic conditions together with poor sanitation make the rural population more vulnerable to diseases.
- Hence, there is an urgent need for raising the public expenditure on health care, particularly preventive care as the prevention or early diagnosis and treatment are the most cost-effective strategies for most diseases.

Box 14.3   Millennium Development Goals Related to Health in India

	Target (2015)	Estimated (2015)
Reduce Child Mortality (MDG 4)		
<5 Mortality (per 1,000 live births)	42	48
IMR (per 1000 live births)	27	39
Improve Maternal Health (MDG 5)		
MMR (per 100,000 live births)	109	140
Combat HIV/AIDS, Malaria, and Other Diseases (MDG 6)		
HIV among pregnant women aged 15–24 years	Halt and begin to reverse trend	Declined from 0.89% in 2005 to 0.32% in 2012–13
Annual Parasite Incidence (API) rate	Halt and begin to reverse trend	Came down from 2.12 per 1,000 in 2001 to 0.72 per 1,000 in 2013, but slightly increased to 0.88 in 2014
Tuberculosis Incidence per lakh population	Halt and begin to reverse trend	Reduced from 216 in year 1990 to 171 in 2013

Source: Millennium Development Goals India Country Report, Social Statistics Division, Ministry of Statistics and Programme Implementation, Government of India.

> **Box 14.4**   Major Targets under Sustainable Development Goals on Health
>
> - By 2030, reduce the global maternal mortality ratio to less than 70 per 100,000 live births.
> - By 2030, reduce neonatal mortality to at least as low as 12 per 1,000 live births and under-5 mortality to at least as low as 25 per 1,000 live births.
> - By 2030, end the epidemics of AIDS, tuberculosis, malaria, and neglected tropical diseases and combat hepatitis, water-borne diseases, and other communicable diseases.
> - By 2030, reduce by one-third premature mortality from non-communicable diseases through prevention and treatment and promote mental health and well-being.
> - Strengthen the prevention and treatment of substance abuse, including narcotic drug abuse and harmful use of alcohol.
> - By 2020, halve the number of global deaths and injuries from road traffic accidents.
> - By 2030, ensure universal access to sexual and reproductive health care services, including for family planning, information and education, and the integration of reproductive health into national strategies and programmes.
> - Achieve universal health coverage, including financial risk protection, access to quality essential health care services and access to safe, effective, quality, and affordable essential medicines and vaccines for all.
> - By 2030, substantially reduce the number of deaths and illnesses from hazardous chemicals and air, water, and soil pollution and contamination.
> - Substantially increase health financing and the recruitment, development, training, and retention of the health workforce.
> - Strengthen the capacity for early warning, risk reduction, and management of national and global health risks.

- Creating awareness of health care particularly of preventive care and early diagnosis for effective disease control is necessary.
- Moving ahead from the MDGs, India has taken up the SDGs in 2015 and committed to achieving the new targets by 2030 as specified in Box 14.4.

14.4 HOUSING

The rural population in India is estimated at around 83 crore as per the 2011 census accounting for about 69 per cent of total population in the country despite the growing urbanization. Yet rural housing has not progressed to the extent of urban housing owing to low income levels. Housing is one of the basic necessities and an essential component of human well-being.

14.4.1 Rural Housing Status

An overview of the latest census reports for 2011 indicated that only 46 per cent of rural houses were in good condition against 69 per cent in case of urban areas. However, ownership is predominant in rural housing pattern accounting for about 95 per cent compared to 69 per cent in urban areas. Only 3.4 per cent of rural houses are under rent whereas rent accounts for about 28 per cent in urban areas (Table 14.20).

In terms of materials used for the construction of the roofs of the houses, only 18 per cent of rural houses had concrete slab for roof against 52 per cent in urban areas. Nearly 20 per cent of rural houses had roof of

Table 14.20   Status of Rural Housing in 2011 (%)

	Ownership			Condition of House		
	Owned	Rented	Others	Good	Liveable	Dilapidated
Rural	94.7	3.4	1.9	46	47.5	6.5
Urban	69.2	27.5	3.3	68.5	28.6	2.9
Total	86.6	11.1	2.4	53.2	41.5	5.3

Source: Census 2011.

grass/thatch/bamboo/wood/mud, and so on, while another 18 per cent of rural houses were covered with handmade tiles. Thus, about 38 per cent of rural houses had non-durable/temporary or *kutcha* type of roof while it accounted for about 10 per cent in urban areas (Table 14.21).

Similarly, in terms of material used for the construction of walls of the houses, only about 54 per cent of rural houses were made of *pucca* or durable materials like burnt brick or concrete walls while about 43 per cent rural houses had walls made of non-durable materials like mud/unburnt brick (31 per cent) and grass/thatch/bamboo, so on (12 per cent).

14.4.2 Emerging Trends

The results of the latest NSSO survey also corroborated the status of rural housing in the country. Nevertheless, the results of various rounds of NSSO surveys during the past 20 years have revealed a steady progress of housing in both rural and urban areas. The results indicated that

Table 14.21   Proportion of Houses with Different Construction Materials for Walls and Roofs (%)

	Material for Roof				Material for Wall		
	Total	Rural	Urban		Total	Rural	Urban
Grass/Bamboo/Wood, and so on.	15	20	4.6	Grass/Thatch/Bamboo, and others	9	11.9	2.7
Plastic/Polythene	0.6	0.6	0.6	Plastic/Polythene	0.3	0.3	0.3
Handmade tiles	14.5	18.3	6.2	Mud/Unburnt brick	23.7	30.5	9.3
Machine-made tiles	9.3	10.4	7	Stone not packed with mortar	3.4	3.6	2.7
Burnt brick	6.6	7.2	5.4	Stone packed with mortar	10.8	10	12.3
Stone/Slate	8.6	8.9	7.9	G.I./Metal/Asbestos sheets	0.6	0.5	0.9
Galvanized Iron/Metal/Asbestos sheets	15.9	15.9	15.9	Burnt brick	47.5	40	63.5
Concrete	29	18.3	51.9	Concrete	3.5	1.7	7.2
Any other material	0.4	0.4	0.4	Any other material	1.3	1.4	1.1

Source: Census 2011.

the proportion of pucca structures has doubled from about 32 per cent in 1993 to 66 per cent in 2012 in rural areas. To that extent the proportion of semi-pucca houses has come down from 36 per cent to 25 per cent and that of kutcha structures from 32 per cent to 9 per cent in the corresponding period (Table 14.22).

Although there has been a significant progress in rural housing, the extent of pucca houses remained much lower at 66 per cent than 94 per cent in urban areas. Further, only 38 per cent of rural householders have lived in a house with good condition of the structure against 60 per cent of urban households in 2012.

14.4.3 Institutional or Government Support

In order to help rural householders own a house or improving the existing houses, the government has taken a number of initiatives since Independence, but the major one among those was Indira Awaas Yojana (IAY).

IAY was launched in 1985–6 as a sub-scheme of Rural Landless Employment Guarantee Programme (RLEGP) for construction of houses for SCs/STs and freed bonded

labourers. Subsequently, it became a sub-scheme of Jawahar Rozgar Yojana (JRY) in 1989 with an allocation of about 6 per cent of total JRY funds. The scope of IAY was extended to cover below poverty line (BPL) families in rural areas in 1993–4 with an additional allocation of 4 per cent of JRY funds. It has become an independent programme since 1 January 1996. IAY is a cash subsidy-based programme providing financial support up to 60 per cent of cost of the house (see Figure 14.9).

Schemes of states: In addition to the central government, all major states have been providing assistance for constructing rural houses with various schemes and programmes.

National Housing Bank (NHB) Schemes: NHB was set up on 9 July 1988 under the NHB Act of 1987. It is wholly owned by the Reserve Bank of India (RBI). It is the principal agency for promoting housing finance institutions at the local and regional levels. NHB provides refinance to the lending institutions such as commercial banks, housing finance companies (HFCs), and cooperative institutions that cater to the credit requirements of all segments of the population.

Table 14.22   Changing Pattern of House Structure in Rural and Urban Areas during 1993 to 2012

	Rural Households (%)				Urban Households (%)			
	49th Round (1993)	58th Round (2002)	65th Round (2008–9)	69th Round (2012)	49th Round (1993)	58th Round (2002)	65th Round (2008–9)	69th Round (2012)
Pucca structure	32.3	48.4	55.4	65.8	73.8	87.7	91.7	93.6
Semi-pucca structure	36.0	30.3	27.6	24.6	17.9	9.0	6.2	5.0
Kutcha structure	31.7	21.3	17.0	9.6	8.3	3.2	2.1	1.4
House with good condition of structure	NA	27.7	31.0	38.3	NA	47.4	54.2	60.2

Source: NSS Report No: 556 (NSS 69th round).

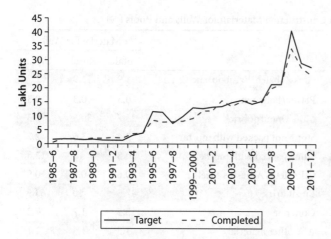

Figure 14.9   Progress under Indira Awaas Yojana

Source: Annual Reports of Ministry of Rural Development and National Housing Bank.

Golden Jubilee Rural Housing Finance Scheme (GJRHFS) was launched in 1997 to address the problem of rural housing through improved access to housing credit (see Figure 14.10). It is one of the principal instruments of NHB for financing of rural housing in the country. It aims to enable an individual to build a modest new house or to improve or add to his old dwelling in rural areas. Refinance by NHB under this scheme is provided at concessional rates of interest compared to the actual applicable rates.

Rural Housing Fund (RHF) was formulated by the NHB in 2008 for lending towards rural housing undertaken by people falling under the weaker section category, as defined in the RBI guidelines on lending

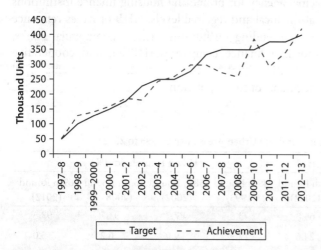

Figure 14.10   Progress under Golden Jubilee Rural Housing Finance Scheme

Source: Annual Reports of Ministry of Rural Development and National Housing Bank.

to priority sector, following the budgetary allocation of Rs 1,200 crore to enhance NHB's refinance operations in the rural housing sector.

Productive Housing in Rural Areas (PHIRA), a new scheme launched by NHB, extends refinance for a composite loan of housing and income generation with an objective to facilitate construction of houses for rural poor families and also to provide a source of sustainable income, which would develop their repayment capacity.

NABARD Rural Housing Scheme: NABARD has included rural housing as an eligible activity for providing refinance to the eligible banks from 1 April 2001. Under the scheme, refinance to a maximum amount of Rs 20 lakh for construction of new house and Rs 1 lakh for repair/renovation for a maximum period of 10 years and 7 years respectively. Financing made under GJRHFS and schemes of the Ministry of Rural Development shall also be eligible for NABARD refinance.

Progress in construction of rural houses: There has been a significant progress in the construction of rural houses under IAY as well as GJRHFS as the targets were met for majority of the years particularly in case of IAY (Figures 14.9 and 14.10).

The cumulative performance of both the programmes indicated that the IAY has completed construction of 2.87 crore rural houses against a target of 3.08 crore with about 93 per cent achievement till the end of 2011–12 from its inception. Similarly, the GJRHFS has also met its target for most of the years since its launch in 1997–8 and completed around 39 lakh rural houses against the target of 41 lakhs with about 95 per cent achievement till 2012–13.

Refinance for construction of rural houses through RHF has also witnessed a gradual increase in allocation as well as utilization since its inception in 2008 as presented in Table 14.23. The allocated funds have been largely utilized for almost all the years except for in 2013–14.

HFCs have been the major users of the funds while the share of SCBs has increased substantially since 2012–13. The scheme has supported construction of about 12.3 lakh rural houses till 2013–14 since inception.

14.4.4 Challenges and Way Forward

Land scarcity: The biggest problem or constraint in rural housing or any other housing scheme for that matter is the limited availability of land. With growing population, demand for land increases for residential, agricultural,

Table 14.23 Allocation and Utilization of Rural Housing Fund since Inception (in Rs Crore)

| | Allocation | Utilization by | | | | | | Number of Units |
		HFCs	SCBs	UCBs	RRBs	ACHFs and ARDBs	Total	
2008–9	1,778	1,545	0	15	202	0	1,761	95,577
2009–10	2,000	1,795	0	4	185	32	2,016	70,995
2010–11	2,000	1,688	182	0	134	0	2,004	42,859
2011–12	3,000	2,125	721	13	143	0	3,003	126,795
2012–13	4,000	1,940	1,802	0	285	0	4,027	356,480
2013–14	6,000	2,410	1,023	0	94	0	3,527	535,299
Total	18,778	11,502	3,729	32	1,043	32	16,339	1,228,005

Note: HFCs: Housing finance Companies, SCBS, Scheduled Commercial Banks, UCBs: Urban Cooperative Banks, ARDBs: Agriculture Rural Development Bank and ACHFs: Apex Cooperative Housing Federations.
Source: Report on Trend and Progress of Housing in India 2014.

and commercial uses. Studies have indicated that minimum level of land ownership is essential for IAY eligibility and less than the prescribed size of the plot did not receive the subsidy.

Financial constraints: Lack of affordability in rural areas due to low incomes is one of the major constraints for housing. Further, the drive of various financial institutions promoting construction of houses in urban areas through attractive loan schemes is not active in rural areas except for the specific schemes supported by the government.

Hence, enhancing access to institutional finance for housing in rural areas may help in solving the financial constraints.

Material constraints: Lack of building materials such as cement in rural areas requires transfer from nearby available areas and is adding to the costs.

Availability of skilled manpower: Due to growing urbanization and migration of skilled construction workers to urban areas, their availability in rural areas has been becoming an area of concern.

Training facilities to rural labourers to develop their skills suitable for construction activities such as masons, bar benders, plumbers, carpenters, and so on, not only increases the availability of the skilled construction workers but also enhances the employability of rural workforce.

14.5 DRINKING WATER AND SANITATION

Access to safe drinking water is a basic necessary step towards healthy human development. Constitutionally, the primary responsibility of providing safe drinking water and sanitation is the state's responsibility. However, with 73rd and 74th amendments, drinking water and sanitation are included in the list of subjects to be devolved to panchayats.

Nevertheless, the process of decentralization has not been complete and panchayati raj institutions play a limited role in drinking water supply and sanitation. As a result, states have been planning and executing drinking water supply programmes through their respective water boards or departments.

14.5.1 Status of Drinking Water and Sanitation

Limited access to safe drinking water: Despite a significant progress witnessed in other social such as education, health and housing, access to safe drinking water appears to be lagging behind in rural areas.

As revealed by the Census 2011, only 31 per cent of rural households had access to potable tap water as against nearly 71 per cent in urban areas. Moreover, only 18 per cent of rural households had access to safe treated tap water while the remaining 13 per cent of households receive tap water from untreated source (Table 14.24).

Hand pumps were the major source of drinking water in rural areas accounting for about 43.6 per cent of drinking water, catering to the needs of rural households, while they accounted for only about 12 per cent in case of urban households in 2011. The share of tap water in rural areas was 30.8 per cent. Wells were the third major source of drinking water in rural areas contributing to about 13 per cent of drinking water accessible to rural households. Other sources of drinking water contribute moderate to marginal amounts.

In this regard, the Ministry of Drinking Water and Sanitation has prepared a strategic plan for coverage of rural households with piped water to an extent of 50 per cent by 2017 and up to 90 per cent by 2022.

Table 14.24 Source-wise Accessibility of Drinking Water to Households in 2011 (%)

	Total	Rural	Urban
Access to drinking water	85.5	82.7	91.4
Tap water	43.5	30.8	70.6
Tap water from treated source	32	17.9	62
Tap water from un-treated source	11.6	13.0	8.6
Well	11	13.3	6.2
Covered well	1.6	1.5	1.7
Un-covered well	9.4	11.8	4.5
Hand pump	33.5	43.6	11.9
Tubewell/Borehole	8.5	8.3	8.9
Spring	0.5	0.7	0.2
River/Canal	0.6	0.8	0.2
Tank/Pond/Lake	0.8	1.1	0.4
Other sources	1.5	1.4	1.7

Source: Census 2011.

Sanitation is a pre-requisite for healthy human development as a number of diseases are associated with lack of proper sanitation. Lack of sanitation directly leads to a number of water- and food-borne diseases through contamination including cholera, typhoid, infectious hepatitis, ascariasis, and so on; in addition, the poor drainage system and waterlogged conditions lead to mosquito breeding further leading to the spread of other mosquito-borne diseases.

Despite several efforts and schemes with incentives announced by the government during the past three decades or so, progress has been very slow and the status of sanitation remains poor in the country as a whole, and worse in rural areas.

The data culled out from the Census 2011 indicated that only 25 per cent of rural households had bathroom facility and only 5 per cent of households had closed drainage as presented in Table 14.25. Further, the data

Table 14.25 Households Having Drainage and Bathing Facility (%)

	Drainage			Bathing Facility at Home		
	Closed	Open	None	Bathroom	Enclosure without Roof	None
Rural	5.8	31.0	63.3	25.4	19.7	55.0
Urban	44.5	37.3	18.2	77.5	9.5	13.0
Total	18.1	33.0	48.9	42.0	16.4	41.6

Source: Census 2011.

suggested that rural households with no drainage facility accounted for about 63 per cent of households, while those with no bathroom facility accounted for about 55 per cent in 2011.

Coming to availability of latrine facility, rural households with no latrine facility (open) accounted for about 67.3 per cent against 12.6 per cent in urban households as indicated by the latest Census 2011 data (Table 14.26). Moreover, although the share of rural households reported to have latrine facility within the premises accounts for over 30 per cent, the proportion of households having improved latrine facility with proper disposal system of solid waste was only 19 per cent in rural areas, compared to about 73 per cent in urban areas.

14.5.2 Emerging Trends

Slow growth in access to improved sources of drinking water: Results of NSSO surveys from 1993 to 2012 indicated that there had been a gradual increase in access to tap water from about 19 per cent in 1993 to about 31 per cent in 2012 among rural households. However, tap water has been the major source of drinking water for about 70 per cent of urban households in 2012 (Table 14.27).

The major source of drinking water remains hand pump/tubewell, and others in rural areas. Its share among rural households had increased from 45 per cent in 1993 to 55 per cent in 2008–9, though it moderated to about 52 per cent in 2012.

Table 14.26 Status of Households with Sanitation Facilities in 2011 (%)

	Total	Rural	Urban
Latrine facility within the premises	46.9	30.7	81.4
Water closet	36.4	19.4	72.6
Piped sewer system	11.9	2.2	32.7
Septic tank	22.2	14.7	38.2
Other system	2.3	2.5	1.7
Pit latrine	9.4	10.5	7.1
With slab/ventilated improved pit	7.6	8.2	6.4
Without slab/ open pit	1.8	2.3	0.7
Other latrine	1.1	0.8	1.7
Night soil disposed into open drain	0.5	0.2	1.2
Night soil removed by human	0.3	0.3	0.3
Night soil serviced by animals	0.2	0.2	0.2
No latrine within the premises	53.1	69.3	18.6
Public latrine	3.2	1.9	6.0
Open	49.8	67.3	12.6

Source: Census 2011.

Table 14.27 Trends in Principal Source of Drinking Water during 1993–2012

	Rural Households (%)				Urban Households (%)			
	49th Round (1993)	58th Round (2002)	65th Round (2008–9)	69th Round (2012)	49th Round (1993)	58th Round (2002)	65th Round (2008–9)	69th Round (2012)
Improved Source								
Bottled water	NA	NA	0.5	1.6	NA	NA	2.7	5.2
Public tap/standpipe*	18.9	27.5	30.1	31.2	70.4	73.6	74.3	69.1
Tubewell/borehole#	44.5	51.3	54.7	52.4	18.5	19.6	17.5	19.9
Unimproved Source								
Tank/pond$	0.8	0.4	0.3	0.5	0.4	0	0.1	0.1
River/dam/stream/ canal, lake, and so on	1.7	1.1	0.7	0.6	0.1	0.1	0	0

Notes: *includes 'piped water into dwelling', 'piped water to yard/plot', and 'public taps/standpipe' of NSS 69th round and 'tap' of previous NSS rounds (49th, 58th, and 65th).
#includes the source 'tubewell/hand pump' used in previous NSS rounds (49th, 58th, and 65th).
$The source 'other tank/pond' used in previous NSS rounds (49th, 58th, and 65th) is included but 'tank/pond (reserved for drinking)' is excluded.
Source: NSS Report No. 556 (NSS 69th round).

Another improved source that has become accessible to households in the recent years is bottled water. The share of households using bottled water has gone up from 0.5 per cent in 2008–9 to 1.6 per cent in 2012 in rural areas and from 2.7 per cent to 5.2 per cent in urban areas during the same period.

Use of unimproved or surface water sources had come down to less than 1 per cent of households in rural areas and was almost negligible in urban areas in 2012.

Increased proximity to principal source of drinking water: The results of the NSSO surveys have also brought out the details regarding the proximity of principal source of drinking water to the households and its changing pattern over the period.

The emerging pattern suggested that the proportion of households having the principal source of drinking water within premises had increased gradually from about 34 per cent in 1993 to 46 per cent in 2012 in rural

areas and from about 66 per cent to 77 per cent in urban areas in the corresponding period.

The proportion of households having exclusive use of principal source of drinking water had also gone up moderately to about 34 per cent in 2012 from about 21 per cent in 1993, while that of community use had declined to about 47 per cent from about 73 per cent in the corresponding period in rural areas (Table 14.28).

Sluggish Improvement in Sanitation Conditions: Trends in sanitation from the early 1990s indicated that there has been an improvement in sanitary conditions but at a significantly slow pace, particularly in rural areas compared to other social indicators, despite being an important pre-condition for health of households and community.

The proportion of rural households with bathroom facility had increased only moderately from about 13 per cent in 1993 to about 38 per cent in 2012, while it had gone up to 83 per cent from 53 per cent in urban

Table 14.28 Proximity and Use of Principal Source of Drinking Water during 1993–2012

	Rural Households (%)				Urban Households (%)			
	49th Round (1993)	58th Round (2002)	65th Round (2008–9)	69th Round (2012)	49th Round (1993)	58th Round (2002)	65th Round (2008–9)	69th Round (2012)
Within premises	34.3	37.2	40.5	46.1	66.2	70.3	74.5	76.8
Outside premises but within 0.2–0.5 km	8.1	9.0	9.2	9.3	2.5	2.9	2.0	2.9
Having exclusive use	20.6	25.4	31.1	33.7	40.2	43.8	47.0	46.8
Having community use	72.8	65.6	56.8	46.7	38.0	30.8	22.9	19.0

Source: NSS Report No. 556 (NSS 69th round).

Table 14.29   Trends in Sanitation in Rural and Urban Households during 1993–2012

	Rural Households (%)				Urban Households (%)			
	49th Round (1993)	58th Round (2002)	65th Round (2008–9)	69th Round (2012)	49th Round (1993)	58th Round (2002)	65th Round (2008–9)	69th Round (2012)
Without bathroom facility	87	76	64.4	62.3	46.5	31.5	21.5	16.7
Having attached bathroom	5.4	9.8	12.5	15.5	27.5	41.1	48	55.4
Without latrine facility	85.8	76.3	65.2	59.4	30.6	17.9	11.3	8.8
Having exclusive use of latrine	10.2	17.3	27.9	31.9	40.4	53.5	58.1	63.9

Source: NSS Report No. 556 (NSS 69th round).

areas in same period. The proportion of rural households with attached bathrooms had also increased dismally from 5 per cent to 15 per cent during 1993 to 2012 in rural areas, whereas it had improved from 41 per cent to 55 per cent in urban areas during the same period (Table 14.29).

The share of rural households having latrine facility had also increased only moderately from about 14 per cent in 1993 to about 40 per cent in 2012 against 69 per cent to 91 per cent in urban areas in the corresponding period. Further, the proportion of households having exclusive use of latrine had risen to only 32 per cent in 2012 from about 10.2 per cent in 1993 in rural areas while it stood at 64 per cent in 2012 in urban areas.

There has been a slow progress in case of construction of drainage system as well. The proportion of rural households with no drainage facility had declined moderately from about 66 per cent in 1993 to about 50 per cent in 2012. However, the proportion of households with drainage facilities in urban areas reached 87.5 per cent in 2012 from about 73 per cent in 1993 (Table 14.30).

The share of rural households with garbage disposal has also remained much lower at 32 per cent compared to 76 per cent in urban areas in 2012. However, the proportion of households with garbage disposal has declined over the period. The reason for the falling trend in urban areas was reported to be due to the process of conversion of rural areas into urban areas (NSS 2014).

14.5.3 Institutional Support

14.5.3.1 Government Support Schemes

14.5.3.1.1 RURAL DRINKING WATER

- The National Rural Drinking Water Supply Programme was launched in 1969 with technical support from UNICEF.
- The Accelerated Rural Water Supply Programme (ARWSP) was launched in 1972–3 to assist states and union territories to accelerate the pace of coverage of drinking water supply.
- 1981–91 was declared International Drinking Water Supply and Sanitation Decade. A national level apex committee was constituted to define policies to achieve the goal of providing safe water to all villages.
- The National Drinking Water Mission (NDWM) was launched in 1986.
- The first National Water Policy was drafted by the Ministry of Water Resources in 1987.
- The National Water Policy was revised in 2002, according to priority to serving villages that did not have adequate sources of safe water and to improve the level of service for villages classified as only partially covered.
- India committed to the Millennium Development Goals in 2002 to halve the proportion of people

Table 14.30   Trends in Drainage Facilities with Rural and Urban Households (%)

	Rural Households (%)				Urban Households (%)			
	49th Round (1993)	58th Round (2002)	65th Round (2008–9)	69th Round (2012)	49th Round (1993)	58th Round (2002)	65th Round (2008–9)	69th Round (2012)
With open kutcha drainage	NA	20.4	18.7	18.4	NA	8.5	5.8	5.0
With no drainage	65.5	61.8	56.7	49.9	26.8	18.5	14.8	12.5
With garbage disposal arrangement	NA	NA	24.3	32.0	NA	80.1	78.6	75.8

Source: NSS Report No. 556 (NSS 69th round).

without sustainable access to safe drinking water and basic sanitation by 2015, from 1990 levels.

- Swajaldhara was launched on 25 December 2002 to open up the reform initiatives in the rural drinking water supply sector.
- The Government of India launched the Bharat Nirman Programme in 2005 for overall development of rural areas.

14.5.3.1.2 SANITATION

- The Central Rural Sanitation Programme launched in 1986 aimed to provide sanitation facilities in rural areas. It was a high subsidy and infrastructure oriented programme. But, due to low financial allocation the programme could not achieve much.
- Total Sanitation Campaign (TSC) was initiated in 1999 to ensure sanitation facilities in rural areas and eradicate the practice of open defecation. It relied on mobilizing demand using information, education, and communication (IEC). A nominal subsidy in the form of incentive was given to rural poor households for construction of toilets. The programme also aimed to cover schools/Anganwadis in rural areas for construction of sanitation facilities and promote hygiene education and sanitary habits among students.
- Nirmal Gram Puruskar (NGP), an incentive scheme for panchayati raj institutions that achieved 100 per cent sanitation, was initiated by the government to strengthen TSC.
- TSC was renamed Nirmal Bharat Abhiyan (NBA) in 2012 with the objective of accelerating sanitation coverage in the rural areas so as to comprehensively cover the rural community through renewed strategies and saturation approach.
- The NBA was restructured as Swachh Bharat Abhiyan (SBA) and launched on 2 October 2014 with two sub-missions—Swachh Bharat Mission (Gramin) and Swachh Bharat Mission (Urban). The urban programme is under the Ministry of Urban Development (MoUD) while the rural programme works under the Ministry of Drinking Water and Sanitation (MDWS). The goal or target of the programme is to eliminate open defecation by 2019.

14.5.3.2 World Bank Support for Rural Water Supply and Sanitation Projects

The Government of India along with seven major states has been in partnership with the World Bank in implementing rural water supply and sanitation projects. The details of the projects are as follows (GoI 2012).

- Maharashtra 1 (1991–8): 1.7 million people in 1,060 villages (US$ 105 million)
- Karnataka 1 (1993–2000): 4.5 million people in 1,200 villages (US$ 118 million)
- Uttar Pradesh (Swajal, 1996–2002): 1.2 million people in 1,000 villages (US$ 70.5 million)
- Kerala 1 (2000–8): 1.1 million people in 3,700 villages (US$ 90 million)
- Karnataka 2 (2002–13): 5 million people in 2,100 villages (US$ 193 million)
- Maharashtra 2 (2003–9) 6.7 million people in 2,300 villages (US$ 287 million)
- Uttarakhand (2006–14): 1.2 million people in 3,750 villages (US$ 120 million)
- Punjab (2007–13): 1.5 million people in 1,200 villages (US$ 154 million)
- Andhra Pradesh (2009–14): 1.2 million people in 1,000 villages (US$ 150 million)

In addition, the Second Kerala RWSS project and the third Maharashtra RWSS project were also approved. Further, the World Bank has approved US$500 million for the National RWSS Project for Lagging States including Assam, Bihar, Jharkhand, and Uttar Pradesh in January 2014.

14.5.4 International Comparison

Dismal State of Rural Sanitation in India: Despite the fact that sanitation is preventive care against a number of diseases and unhealthiness, the status of sanitation in India remained at shamefully low levels, particularly in rural areas, compared to all the neighbouring developing countries and the world average. Although the government has been announcing support schemes and programmes since 1986, no significant progress has taken place in the sanitary conditions of the country in general and in rural areas in particular.

Access to improved sanitation by rural population was estimated to be around 29 per cent in 2015 as per the World Development Indicators published by the World Bank. It is a dismal figure, not only when compared to developed countries but also in comparison with neighbouring developing countries, namely, Sri Lanka (96.7 per cent), China (63.7 per cent), Bangladesh (62 per cent), Pakistan (51.1 per cent), and Nepal (44 per cent) in rural areas (Table 14.31). The gap between access to improved sanitation in rural and urban areas in India is significantly high at about 34 per cent.

Table 14.31   Access to Improved Sanitation Facilities in Selected Countries in 2015 (%)

	Rural	Urban	Total	Gap
Bangladesh	62.1	57.7	60.6	−4.4
Brazil	51.5	88.0	82.8	36.5
China	63.7	86.6	76.5	22.9
Germany	99.0	99.3	99.2	0.3
India	28.5	62.6	39.6	34.1
Nepal	43.5	56.0	45.8	12.5
Pakistan	51.1	83.1	63.5	32.0
Russian Federation	58.7	77.0	72.2	18.3
South Africa	60.5	69.6	66.4	9.1
Sri Lanka	96.7	88.1	95.1	−8.6
United Kingdom	99.6	99.1	99.2	−0.5
United States	100.0	100.0	100.0	0.0
World	50.3	82.2	67.5	31.9

Source: World Development Indicators, online database provided by World Bank.

14.5.5 Challenges and Way Forward

Despite the fast economic growth and progress in social conditions, the access to sanitation in the country remained dismal with more than 60 per cent of rural households and about 13 per cent of urban households where open defecation was still in practice. The extent of open defecation in India is much higher than the poorest African countries like Malawi, Cango, and so on, as indicated by the UNICEF–WHO Joint Monitoring Programme (JMP) data (WHO 2015).

Major constraints associated with low sanitation in rural areas as indicated by some of the field studies (Coffey et al. 2014 and O'Reilly and Louis 2014) are as follows:

- Indian rural households reported to have expressed lack of interest in low-cost affordable latrines, unlike in other developing or poor countries. But at the same time, they indicated their inability to go for expensive latrines.
- Rural households are unaware of or not concerned about the health hazards affecting the whole community as a result of widespread open defecation. Studies have reported that some of the households despite the presence of latrine within their premises, prefer open defecation as they consider it as a tradition.
- Insufficient water availability for maintaining latrines.

The government has been focusing more on economic aspects of sanitation, providing financial assistance for construction of latrines over the years. More efforts are needed to bring awareness and realization among rural households about the health hazards associated with open defecation as it affects the whole environment and the entire community, spreading infections and contamination.

Further, with a commitment to the achievement of SDGs, more efforts are needed to achieve the targets relating to water and sanitation under SDGs by 2030 as presented in Box 14.5.

14.6 SOCIAL SECURITY

Social security minimum standards were established and agreed upon worldwide, based on basic principles established by the Social Security (Minimum Standards) Convention, 1952, covering medical care, sickness benefit, unemployment benefit, old-age benefit, employment injury benefit, family benefit, maternity benefit, invalidity benefit and survivors' benefit.

There is no comprehensive social security system prevailing in India, particularly in rural areas, but, a number of social welfare schemes have been initiated over the

Box 14.5   Targets under Sustainable Development Goals on Water and Sanitation Development

- By 2030, achieve universal and equitable access to safe and affordable drinking water for all.
- By 2030, achieve access to adequate and equitable sanitation and hygiene for all and end open defecation, paying special attention to the needs of women and girls and those in vulnerable situations.
- By 2030, improve water quality by reducing pollution, eliminating dumping and minimizing release of hazardous chemicals and materials, halving the proportion of untreated wastewater, and substantially increasing recycling and safe reuse globally.
- By 2030, substantially increase water use efficiency across all sectors and ensure sustainable withdrawals and supply of freshwater to address water scarcity and substantially reduce the number of people suffering from water scarcity.
- By 2030, implement integrated water resources management at all levels, including through trans-boundary cooperation as appropriate.
- By 2020, protect and restore water-related ecosystems, including mountains, forests, wetlands, rivers, aquifers, and lakes.

past 20 years under different ministries and departments of Government of India.

The National Social Assistance Programme (NSAP) was launched on 15 August 1995 in accordance with Article 41 of the Constitution of India, which directs the state to provide public assistance to its citizens in case of unemployment, old age, sickness, and disability within the limit of its economic capacity and development. This covers both rural and urban areas.

At present, the NSAP covers the following social welfare schemes:

- Indira Gandhi National Old Age Pension Scheme (IGNOAPS): Under the scheme, BPL persons aged 60 years or above are entitled to a monthly pension of Rs. 200/- up to 79 years of age and Rs 500 thereafter.
- Indira Gandhi National Widow Pension Scheme (IGNWPS): BPL widows aged 40–59 years are entitled to a monthly pension of Rs 200.
- Indira Gandhi National Disability Pension Scheme (IGNDPS): BPL persons aged 18–59 years with severe and multiple disabilities are entitled to a monthly pension of Rs 200.
- National Family Benefit Scheme (NFBS): Under the scheme a BPL household is entitled to a lump sum amount of money on the death of the primary breadwinner, aged between 18 and 64 years. The amount of assistance is Rs 10,000.
- Annapurna: Under the scheme, 10 kg food grains per month are provided free of cost to those senior citizens who have remained uncovered under NOAPS.

The Mahatma Gandhi National Rural Employment Guarantee Act (MGNREGA) with its legal framework and rights-based approach was notified on 5 September 2005. It aims at enhancing livelihood security by providing at least one hundred days of guaranteed wage employment in a financial year to every rural household whose adult members volunteer to do unskilled manual work. It is considered as an income security to rural households. It has been generating employment of more than 200 crore days per year on average covering 4.5–5 crore rural households.

The Rashtriya Swasthya Bima Yojana (RSBY), a health insurance initiative, was launched in 2007–8 for the BPL families with the objectives to reduce out-of-pocket expenditure on health and increase access to health care. However, it has been expanded to cover other defined categories of unorganized workers in subsequent years. Initially, the scheme was launched by the Ministry of Labour and Employment but it was transferred to the Ministry of Health and Family Welfare on 1 April 2015.

The beneficiaries under RSBY need to pay only Rs 30 as registration fee for a year and are entitled to hospitalization coverage up to Rs 30,000 per annum on family floater basis, for most of the diseases that require hospitalization. In addition, transport expenses of Rs 100 per hospitalization will also be paid to the beneficiary subject to a maximum of Rs 1,000 per year per family.

The Aam Aadmi Bima Yojana (AABY) is a scheme for rural landless households and was launched on 2 October 2007 by the Ministry of Finance. The head of the family or one earning member in the family of such a household is covered under the scheme. The premium of Rs 200 per person per annum is shared equally by the central government and the state government. The member to be covered should be aged between 18 and 59 years.

14.6.1 Recently Launched Schemes

The Pradhan Mantri Suraksha Bima Yojna (PMSBY) is to ensure risk coverage in case of accidental death, or full or partial disability. The insured amount for accidental death and full disability is Rs 2 lakhs and it is Rs 1 lakh for partial disability. It has an annual premium of Rs 12 only, which will be directly auto-debited by the bank from the subscriber's account.

Pradhan Mantri Jeevan Jyoti Bima Yojana is to benefit people in case of death. It is available to people in the age group of 18 to 50, who have a bank account. People who join this scheme before completing the age of 50 can continue to have the risk of life cover up to the age of 55 years, subject to the payment of a premium. The scheme has an annual premium of Rs 330, with risk coverage of Rs 2 lakhs.

Atal Pension Yojana, a new initiative in the Union Budget proposals 2015–16, is to encourage the uninsured workers in the unorganized sector to come under the National Pension System (NPS), under the Pension Fund Regulatory and Development Authority (PFRDA).

14.6.2 Challenges and Way Forward

Providing social security is a monumental task for a country such as India where a huge population falls under the unorganized sector. However, the large-scale success of MNREGA through direct cash transfers, social audit, and so on while plugging the leakages has proven that social security programmes can be implemented in the country if there is a strong will.

Towards this, the Human Development Report 2015 published by the United Nations Development Programme (UNDP) has also indicated that the cost of setting up of such social security system with basic health care, universal pension, child benefits and employment schemes would come to about 4 per cent of GDP in India (UNDP 2015).

14.7 SUMMARY

Social sector development in India has witnessed some progress but in a scattered manner and at a slow pace, particularly in rural areas. Education in rural areas, the basis for both economic and social development, has been lagging far behind that of urban areas.

The gap between rural and urban indicators of education and health remained significantly large despite the progressive reduction over the past 50 years or so. Similarly, infrastructure facilities for education and health have remained deficient in rural areas though there has been an improvement from the mid-2000s onwards.

Further, the most important but least developed social sector segment is sanitation and safe drinking water in rural areas. Despite the implementation of government-supported schemes, the status of sanitation in rural areas has remained dismal in India compared to some of the least developed countries. Hence, more focus and strong efforts are needed to address the issue of sanitation in rural areas.

It is apparent from the emerging trends that lower education levels are associated with low health and sanitation levels in rural areas. Hence, improving education levels in rural areas is of utmost priority. There is a need to create awareness among the rural population that practising sanitation is not a choice but is obligatory to prevent a number of diseases and health hazards.

REFERENCES

ASER. 2015. *Annual Status of Education Report—ASER 2014.* Report of the ASER Survey Facilitated by Pratham, ASER Centre, January 2015.

Behrman, Jere R. 1990. *Human Resource Led Development? Review of Issues and Evidence.* International Labour Office, World Employment Programme, Asian Regional Team for Employment Promotion (ILO-ARTEP).

Diane, Coffey, Aashish Gupta, Payal Hathi, Nidhi Khurana, Dean Spears, Nikhil Srivastav, and Sangita Vyas. 2014. *Revealed Preference for Open Defecation: Evidence from a New Survey in Rural North India.* SQUAT Working Paper No. 1, June 2014.

GoI. 2012. *Review of World Bank Support to the Rural Water Supply and Sanitation Sector in India 1991–2011.* Government of India and World Bank, October 2012.

———. 2015. *Millennium Development Goals India Country Report.* Social Statistics Division, Ministry of Statistics and Programme Implementation, Government of India.

Ministry of Human Resource Development. 2016. 'National Policy on Education 2016—Report of the Committee for Evolution of the New Education Policy'. Government of India. Available at http://www.nuepa.org/New/download/NEP2016/ReportNEP.pdf, accessed on 29 January 2018.

NSS. 2014. *Drinking Water, Sanitation, Hygiene and Housing Condition in India, NSS 69th Round, NSS Report No: 556.* Ministry of Statistics and Programme Implementation, National Sample Survey Office, Government of India, July 2014.

NUEPA. 2014. *Education for All, towards Quality with Equity India, August 2014.* National University of Educational Planning and Administration, New Delhi.

———. 2015. *Elementary Education in Rural India—Where Do We Stand? Analytical Report 2014–15.* National University of Educational Planning and Administration, New Delhi.

O'Reilly, Kathleen and Elizabeth Louis. 2014. 'The Toilet Tripod: Understanding Successful Sanitation in Rural India'. *Health & Place* 29: 43–51.

Ramachandran, V.K., Vikas. Rawal, and, Madhura Swaminathan. 1997. 'Investment Gaps in Primary Education: A Statewise Study'. *Economic and Political Weekly* 32(1 and 2).

Rawal, Vikas. 2011. 'Statistics on Elementary School Education in Rural India'. *Review of Agrarian Studies* 1(2): 179–201.

Tilak, Jandhyala B.G. 2002. *Building Human Capital in East Asia: What Others Can Learn.* New Delhi: National Institute of Educational Planning and Administration.

UNDP. 2015. *Human Development Report 2015: Work for Human Development.* New York: United Nations Development Programme.

WHO. 2015. *25 Years Progress on Sanitation and Drinking Water: 2015 Update and MDG Assessment.* UNICEF and World Health Organization, 2015. Available at http://files.unicef.org/publications/files/Progress_on_Sanitation_and_Drinking_Water_2015_Update_.pdf, accessed on 2 9 January 2018.

World Bank. 1993. *The East Asian Miracle: Economic Growth and Public Policy.* A World Bank Policy Research Report, Published for World Bank. New York: Oxford University Press.

15

Sustainability Challenges in Agriculture and NABARD's Interventions

*R. Amalorpavanathan**

ABSTRACT

Achieving sustainable development will require global action to further economic and social progress with growth and employment, without impacting the environment adversely. The achievement of the UN-mandated sustainable development goals by 2030 is a major challenge for India, for which the NITI Aayog and central government ministries have been involved in developing strategies and action plans. The Government of India has taken up important initiatives to address issues related to reducing poverty, employment generation, doubling of farmers' income, diversification of livelihoods, skill development, gender equality, and so on. Developmental challenges being faced by rural India are critical for achieving sustainable development goals set up by the nation. The goals related to poverty, food–energy–water security, gender equality, ensuring education, health and sanitation, and building climate resilience are more critical for rural areas compared to urban areas. This chapter discusses the challenges related to land, water, loss of biodiversity and agricultural genetic resources, forestry, livestock, fisheries, and the impact of climate change on livelihoods. NABARD's efforts to address sustainability challenges through various policy and developmental initiatives for promoting sustainable livelihoods, namely, watershed development, tribal development, Umbrella Programme for Natural Resources Management, rural infrastructure development, farmer producer organizations, climate actions, skill development, gender equality, and agriculture risk mitigation have been presented.

JEL Classification: Q13, Q18, Q22, Q23, Q24, Q25, Q28, Q54

Keywords: sustainable development goals, poverty, agricultural sustainability, livelihoods, climate change

*Deputy Managing Director, NABARD, Mumbai, India.

15.1 INTRODUCTION

The Brundtland Commission established by United Nations Environment Programme (UNEP) Governing Council in 1983 defined sustainable development as that which helps 'to meet the needs of present without compromising the ability of future generations to meet their own needs'. Economic, social, and environmental issues are the three pillars of sustainable development.

15.2 INTERNATIONAL SCENARIO

The world is faced with challenges in all three dimensions of sustainable development—economic, social, and environmental. More than 1 billion people live in extreme poverty. Also, income inequality within and between countries is rising. Therefore, achieving sustainable development will require global action to further economic and social progress with growth and employment, without adverse impact on environment.

A set of sustainable development goals (SDGs) was firmed up by the United Nations Conference on Sustainable Development (UNCSD), popularly known as the Rio+20, convened in Rio de Janeiro, Brazil, in June 2012. On 1 January 2016, the world officially began implementation of the 2030 Agenda for sustainable development titled 'Transforming Our World: The 2030 Agenda for Sustainable Development'—the transformative plan of action based on 17 SDGs and 169 targets—to address urgent global challenges over the next 15 years. This road map was drawn up to ensure sustainable social and economic progress worldwide.

Some of the important issues that need to be reckoned with while dealing with strategies for sustainability, globally and in India, are as follows:

(i) There is a need to promote integrated and sustainable management of natural resources and ecosystems and take action for mitigation and adaptation.

(ii) Hunger and malnourishment remain persistent in many developing countries, and food and nutrition security continues to be an elusive goal.

(iii) Income inequality, particularly in developing countries, has been rising and might lead to heightened tension and social conflict.

(iv) Rapid urbanization, especially in developing countries, calls for major changes in the way urban development is designed and managed.

(v) Energy needs are likely to remain unmet for millions of households.

(vi) Long-term financing for investments remains inadequate to achieve sustainable development.

15.3 THE INDIAN CONUNDRUM

India constitutes around 17 per cent of the world's population, but accounts for about 21 per cent of the poorest and 37 per cent of the illiterates in the world. While reforms have brought about improvements in economic growth, foreign exchange, information technology (IT) revolution, export growth, and so on, inequality in income distribution has been widening. Exclusion from benefits of economic growth exists due to low level of agricultural growth, slow employment growth, concentration of poverty in certain groups, and regional inequalities (backward and resource poor regions) and inadequate development of women and children. All these factors have resulted in the widening of economic and social disparity, which is a threat to sustainable development.

Notwithstanding these issues, India has been on the path of rapid economic development, and the Indian economy registered robust gross domestic product (GDP) growth of 8.0 per cent in 2015–16,[1] followed by a decline in growth to 7.1 per cent in 2016–17, although it continued to be the fastest growing large economy in the world.

In India, the task of coordinating programmes that are expected to lead to the achievement of the UN-mandated SDGs by 2030 lies with the National Institution for Transforming India (NITI) Aayog. The Ministry of Statistics and Programme Implementation (MoSPI), Government of India, is also engaging with other ministries with a view to evolving indicators that would reflect the SDGs. The prime minister of India, Narendra Modi, has reiterated India's commitment to traversing a sustainable path to prosperity (Box 15.1).

15.4 SUSTAINABILITY CHALLENGES FOR INDIA

In order to achieve sustainable development and rapid economic growth, India needs to overcome critical challenges related to poverty, food–energy–water security, sanitation, environmental degradation, gender equality, livelihood, and employment generation.

The major challenges to achieve sustainable development include finance, technology, capacity building,

---

[1] *Economic Survey 2016–17*, vol. 2, Government of India.

Box 15.1   Excerpts from the Statement of Shri Narendra Modi, Hon'ble Prime Minister, at the United Nations Summit for the Adoption of Post-2015 Development Agenda

Mahatma Gandhi had once said, 'One must care about the world one will not see.' Just as our vision behind the Agenda 2030 is lofty, our goals are comprehensive. It gives priority to the problems that have endured through the past decades. And, it reflects our evolving understanding of the social, economic, and environmental linkages that define our lives. I am pleased that elimination of poverty in all forms everywhere is at the top of our goals. The goals recognize that economic growth, industrialization, infrastructure, and access to energy provide the foundations of development. We welcome the prominence given to environmental goals, especially climate change and sustainable consumption.

Today, much of India's development agenda is mirrored in the Sustainable Development Goals. Since Independence, we have pursued the dream of eliminating poverty from India. Our attack on poverty today includes expanded conventional schemes of development, but we have also launched a new era of inclusion and empowerment, turning distant dreams into immediate possibilities: new bank accounts for 180 million; direct transfer of benefits; funds to the unbanked; insurance within the reach of all; and, pension for everyone's sunset years.

We are focusing on the basics: housing, power, water, and sanitation for all—important not just for welfare, but also human dignity. We are making our farms more productive and better connected to markets; and, farmers less vulnerable to the whims of nature.

We are committed to a sustainable path to prosperity. It comes from the natural instinct of our tradition and culture. But, it is also rooted firmly in our commitment to the future.

Source: https://www.narendramodi.in/text-of-pm-s-statement-at-the-united-nations-summit-for-the-adoption-of-post-2015-development-agenda-332923.

defining the targets/indicators, monitoring, and reporting. Addressing the challenges with regard to social development aspects being faced by India under SDGs such as poverty reduction, food–energy–water security, sanitation, health, and so on remains critical. India's ranking in Human Development Index (HDI) was 131 (2015) out of 188 countries, according to the Human Development Report 2016 (UNDP 2016). Among the BRICS nations, India has the lowest rank with Russia at 49, Brazil at 79, China at 90, and South Africa at 119 (UNDP 2016). Further, on the Global Hunger Index (GHI) 2016, India ranks 97 out of 118 developing countries.

The Government of India has taken up important initiatives to address issues related to reducing poverty, employment generation, doubling of farmers' income, diversification of livelihoods, skill development, gender equality, and so on. These are expected to take India on an accelerated path to achieving many social sector goals.

Developmental challenges being faced by rural India are critical for achieving SDGs set up by the nation. The goals related to poverty, food–energy–water security, gender equality, ensuring education, health and sanitation, and building climate resilience are more critical for rural areas as compared to urban areas. Prevalence of subsistence agriculture, inadequate alternative sustainable livelihood opportunities in rural areas, presence of a large number of unskilled youth, and impact of inflation on rural incomes is responsible for the existence of high rural poverty (25.7 per cent), compared to urban poverty (13.7 per cent).

Major challenges and approaches towards achieving sustainable development are discussed in the following paragraphs:

(i) **Land:** Of the country's total 142 million hectares (Mha) of cultivated land, 65 Mha (45 per cent) are irrigated and the remaining 77 Mha are rain-fed. Of the total geographical area of 329 Mha, about 120 Mha are classified as degraded. Land distribution is highly skewed, with about 85 per cent of the farmers being small, marginal, and sub-marginal, together owning about 40 per cent of the total cultivated land. Increasing proportion of holdings are becoming uneconomical. Soil health is deteriorating, with widespread micro-nutrient deficiencies (hidden hunger) and fast depleting carbon content, resulting in low and decelerated growth in total food production.

(ii) **Water:** Water availability at the national level is reaching close to 1700 cubic metre (cum) per capita—the threshold line, and if things do not improve, it will drop to water scarcity line by 2025. India annually receives about 350 million hectare metre (Mham) of rain water, but almost half of it finds its way back to the sea. The per capita water storage in India is only 210 cum against 1110 cum in China and 3,145 cum in Brazil. With nearly 65 Mha of net irrigated area and irrigation using over 80 per cent of all fresh water, India ranks first in the world in irrigated acreage. There is a huge gap of 14 Mha between irrigation potential created and utilized, and irrigation intensity is only 135 per cent, which should be raised to 175 per cent or more. Besides low water use efficiency, there is high inequality in water use and irrigation development, let alone the fast receding aquifers and block after block turning 'critical' and 'over-exploited' in certain parts of the country.

(iii) **Biodiversity and agricultural genetic resources:** Rampant loss of biodiversity and agricultural genetic resources has enhanced genetic vulnerability of our agricultural systems besides losing invaluable gene pools, such as the Tharparker (breed of cattle) in western Rajasthan. The two national initiatives in this field, namely, National Biodiversity Board and Plant Variety Protection and Farmer's Rights Authority, are supposed to address this issue. Participatory breeding, integrated germplasm, and indigenous knowledge conservation and benefit sharing, particularly involving women and tribals, should be promoted. Establishment of living heritage of livestock germplasm (mostly at state farms), village gene banks, offshore quarantine centres for germplasm screening against serious diseases and pests, and maintenance and trade of pedigreed animals and elite medicinal and aromatic plant landraces by farm science graduates should be strongly supported.

(iv) **Forests:** Forests, the green cover, are the natural resource infrastructure for agriculture/primary production and rural economic growth. India harbours 16 major forest types, tropical, temperate, alpine, and so on, and is one of the 17 mega diversity centres and 2 biodiversity hotspots of the world. Per capita forest area in the country (0.064 ha) is one-tenth of that of the world's average, and 41 per cent of the country's forest cover is degraded. Despite the high importance of forests as source of food, fuel, fodder, and fibre and of linking conservation with community-based forestry, allocation to forestry subsector has been rather meagre at less than 1 per cent of the plan size. Moreover, most of the budget has to come from the state governments, which seldom meet their commitments and forests continue to suffer.

(v) **Livestock:** Livestock accounts for about 27 per cent of agricultural GDP and is egalitarian in its distribution and in ownership by women. It is also a major pillar of income, food, and employment security. Possessing the world's largest livestock population, India ranks first in milk production, fifth in egg production, and seventh in meat production. Institutional support and policy action such as livestock insurance, market and price support, livestock feed and fodder corporation, fodder banks, small holders' poultry estates, and so on are needed towards achieving rapid and inclusive growth.

(vi) **Fisheries:** Fisheries (53 per cent of the production from aquaculture) contribute significantly to food, nutrition, economic, and employment securities, and fortunately has been one of the fastest growing agricultural subsectors during the last three decades. Currently, fisheries contribute 5.08 per cent to the agricultural GDP, provide employment security to about 14 million people, and annually earn foreign exchange worth Rs 33,400 crore. The challenges in the sector include: siltation and pollution of water bodies, poor management of the production–processing–distribution chain, poor quality control of fish seed and feed, under-exploitation of available species such as cold water fishes such as trout and *mahseer* and air-breathing fishes like *mangur*. Weak infrastructure for landing and marketing and inadequate access to water bodies/tanks, multi-user conflicts, and inappropriate leasing policies are other important constraints. Suitable leasing policies, reduced duties on feed and lower power tariffs can help accelerate production of scampi (prawn) in inland saline waterlogged areas, brackish water areas, and other aquaculture systems, thus greatly contributing to employment, income, and food security.

15.5 CLIMATE CHANGE IMPACTS ON LIVELIHOODS

Climate change has become real and tangible, affecting people's lives worldwide. It is a major challenge for agriculture, food security, and rural livelihoods. As indicated in 'Intergovernmental Panel on Climate Change' (IPCC) in its Fifth Assessment Report released in March 2014, poor, marginalized, and rural communities are likely to be hit the hardest by climate impact. For these vulnerable groups, climate change acts as a 'risk multiplier', worsening existing social, economic, political, and environmental stress.

The impact of climate change is global, but countries like India are more vulnerable in view of the huge population depending on agriculture, which in turn is dependent on seasonal monsoons. As per recorded observations, India has seen an increase of 0.4 degree Centigrade, in the mean surface air temperature over the past century (1901–2000). In India, significant negative impacts have been implied with medium-term (2010–2039) climate change predicted to reduce yields of crops by 4.5 to 9 per cent, depending on the magnitude and distribution of warming (based on information from the National Initiative on Climate Resilient Agriculture [NICRA]).

Concerted and sustained efforts are required to meet the challenges resulting from climate change and its effects. Ground water conservation practices like construction of *khadin* (a construction designed to harvest surface run-off water for agriculture, popular in Maharashtra, Andhra Pradesh, Madhya Pradesh, Tamil Nadu, Karnataka, and Gujarat), check dams, farm ponds, recharge shafts, injection wells (in coastal region and to combat problems of heavily pumped out aquifers), and contour trenching, to arrest surface run-off at elevations, and similarly surface water conservation techniques, such as construction of *ooranies* (surface water collection ponds with improved catchments, commonly found in Tamil Nadu), are important measures to tackle problems of water scarcity and the decreasing groundwater table. Awareness generation and training among the masses for water conservation via rooftop rain water harvesting and threshing floors can also be implemented. Involvement of the gram panchayat/village health and sanitation committee for operation, maintenance, and surveillance of water quality, as in the National Rural Drinking Water Quality Monitoring and Surveillance Project, can have a major impact. Other measures such as recycling and reuse of water, using water-efficient household equipment such as low-volume flushing cisterns, proper metering of water, rational tariff, and the concept of a water-efficient home would reduce water demand and encourage conservation.

15.6 POVERTY ERADICATION AND SUSTAINABLE LIVELIHOODS

Environmental degradation in an agrarian economy and poverty are interlinked. Therefore, the strategy for poverty alleviation should involve improved management of natural resources while involving the rural poor, who are stakeholders in the developmental process. Climate change adaptation and improved land and water management practices should improve land and water productivity, leading to higher agricultural production.

Managing the environment, improved agricultural practices, and effective agri-value chain management through agri-marketing reforms could result in removal of poverty, hunger and malnutrition.

Sustainable development strategy involves not only managing the environment, but also creating a sustainable ecosystem which enables the creation of new and unconventional livelihood opportunities and education and skill development for the rural youth, especially, women. Livelihood opportunities need to be created in sectors allied to agriculture, namely, dairy, fisheries, beekeeping, and so on, and in off-farm/non-farm activities, including micro, small and medium enterprises (MSME) and service activities.

15.7 NABARD'S EFFORTS TO ADDRESS SUSTAINABILITY CHALLENGES

The mandate of the National Bank for Agriculture and Rural Development (NABARD) is to 'promote sustainable and equitable agriculture and rural prosperity through effective credit support, related services, institutional development and other innovative initiatives'.

As India's largest development finance institution, NABARD, since its foundation in the year 1982, has been striving for the attainment of sustainable and equitable rural prosperity. NABARD has always taken into consideration social and environmental concerns to achieve desired development results.

NABARD has taken a number of measures to promote sustainable agricultural development in the areas of watershed development, livelihood based programmes, natural resource management, agricultural technology transfer, and development of tribal farmers, enhancing resilience of agriculture against climate change, and promotion and financing of producers' organizations. Over the past 3 decades, NABARD has supported millions of small and marginal farm holders, landless labourers, women and other weaker sections, employing sustainable approaches. NABARD has been implementing several developmental projects with an objective of promoting sustainable livelihoods through natural resources management (NRM) such as watershed development, sustainable livelihood for tribal communities, Umbrella Programme for Natural Resources Management (UPNRM), climate change adaptation projects, climate proofing of watersheds, weather and crop advisory services, agriculture insurance, farmer producer organizations (FPOs), poverty eradication and sustainable livelihoods, irrigation and drinking water development, energy access, and so on. These projects have helped in building sustainable development approaches in rural communities. Some of the major initiatives by NABARD are discussed in the following paragraphs.

15.7.1 Policy Initiatives

(i) Credit planning and delivery is one of the important functions of NABARD. Every year, potential linked credit plans (PLPs) for all the districts in India are prepared, taking into account the natural resource status of a given district and existing ecosystem related to infrastructure, existing programmes, availability of financial delivery channels in tandem with government priorities. The PLPs provide estimates of credit which can be potentially absorbed at the district level, for agriculture and allied sectors, off-farm sector and other priority sectors, besides presenting a holistic view of the infrastructural facilities presently available in the district and infrastructure that needs to be created to fully harness the credit potential available in each district. Key features of this planning process are resource efficiency, effectiveness, and sustainability.

(ii) NABARD has been promoting sustainable resource management strategy for better utilization of natural resources in agriculture production systems. Prescriptions with regard to setting up technical norms for agriculture investment credit, for example, spacing norms for financing of ground water extraction structures, norms related to financing of tractors, norms for financing efficient pumpsets, organic cultivation of horticulture crops, and so on. The financial norms for various agricultural investments are accompanied with technical specifications aimed at sustainable resource management.

(iii) Environmental and Social Policy and Gender Policy of NABARD encompasses the policy framework required for many sustainable development challenges being faced in rural and agriculture sectors. The policy is aimed to apply environmental and social safeguards for various development initiatives of NABARD so that these negative externalities can be avoided.

15.7.2 Developmental Initiatives: Promoting Sustainable Livelihoods

(i) **Community involvement:** NABARD has been supporting various developmental programmes

aimed to improve natural resources management, gender equality, skill development, sanitation, and so on. A unique feature of these programmes is that they are designed and executed with close stakeholder engagement. Further, the programmes are designed keeping in view sustainability and mainstreaming as important criteria. Involvement of community based institutions (CBOs), strengthening existing and creating new CBOs, knowledge management, linking with financial institutions and convergence/dovetailing with the existing government programmes are the key features of developmental projects/programmes implemented by NABARD (see Figure 15.1).

(ii) **Watershed Development:** One of NABARD's flagship programmes is the participatory watershed development programme, being implemented since 1991. The programme is designed based on the key aspects of sustainability, including community participation, equity, resource efficiency, and environmental sustainability aimed at improved livelihoods for watershed community. More than 2000 projects covering about 1.8 Mha of watershed area, implemented by NABARD under various funding arrangements, have resulted in improved resource augmentation leading to ecological sustainability and improved livelihoods. The projects are designed, implemented, and monitored by village watershed communities (VWCs) with support from project facilitation agencies (PFAs). The watershed communities contribute voluntary labour (called Shramadan), and resource management is ensured through extensive stakeholders' consultation. The programme also integrates livelihoods for the most vulnerable sections of watershed community including the landless and women. The uniqueness of this programme is people's participation in planning, implementation of the projects, monitoring as well as financial management through CBOs. Watershed sustainability principles are presented in Figure 15.2.

The following is a summary of the impact of NABARD's watershed programmes based on an independent evaluation commissioned by NABARD.

- Increase in area under cultivation up to 35%
- Increase in crop productivity of various crops (29%–53%)
- Significant increase in groundwater recharge in watersheds

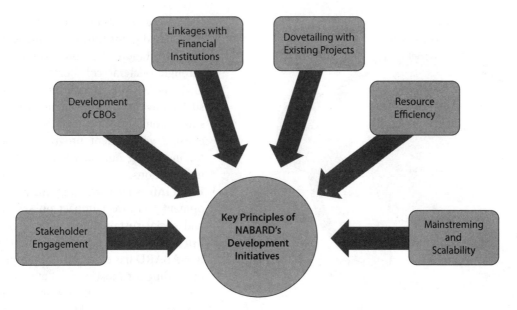

Figure 15.1   Sustainability Principles of NABARD's Development Programmes

Source: Courtesy of the author.

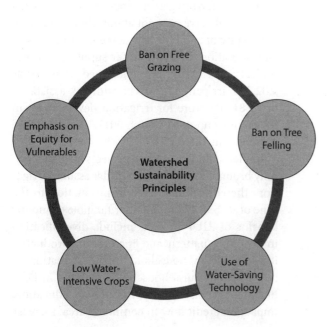

Figure 15.2   Watershed Sustainability Principles

Source: Courtesy of the author.

- Increase in net sown area (26%–35%) and irrigated area by 29%
- Generated additional employment of 24,565 man-days
- Reduction in migration due to creation of employment
- Increase in cropping intensity from 114%–133%
- Reduction in soil loss from 12 to 8 t/ha/yr

(iii) **Tribal Development:** Similarly, the Tribal Development Programme (TDP) of NABARD is one such example where the interventions for creation of livelihoods for tribal communities aim at ecological sustainability of forests and natural resources. The programme has been contributing to livelihoods of more than 5.5 lakh tribal families. The projects integrate orchard-based farming systems (known as *wadi*) as a livelihood strategy aimed at promoting the tribal livelihoods along with soil and water resources conservation. The wadi projects have been able to increase the income level of tribal families and has resulted in decreased dependence of these communities on forest resources, thereby reducing its degradation. The programme not only targets production systems but addresses the entire value chain issues around farm and non-farm livelihoods. Assistance is in the form of grant as well as soft loan for livelihood promotion is also provided. Around 0.48 million tribal families have been supported across 633 projects with a financial outlay of US$ 325 million (Rs 1952.90 crore). The programmes are supported through the Tribal Development Fund created out of NABARD's own profits as well as through bilateral collaboration with Kreditanstalt für Wiederaufbau (KfW).

(iv) **UPNRM:** UPNRM is a loan-cum-grant-based Indo-German collaborative effort, aimed to boost

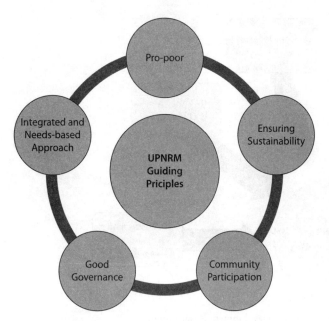

Figure 15.3   UPNRM Guiding Principles Used for Project
Appraisal

Source: Courtesy of the author.

rural livelihoods by supporting community-managed sustainable natural resource management (NRM) projects (see Figure 15.3). More than 300 projects sanctioned under this programme have successfully demonstrated NRM-based enterprise models involving vulnerable communities. UPNRM has created successful business models such as System of Rice Intensification (SRI) in Karnataka, System of Sugar Intensification in Karnataka and Maharashtra, Bt cotton initiatives with drip irrigation in Maharashtra, biogas in Sindhudurg district of Maharashtra, eco-tourism at Chamrajnagar, Karnataka, vermicomposting, organic farming, seed production, sustainable agricultural practices, medicinal plants cultivation and its primary processing, and so on. The key policy goal of UPNRM is 'supporting sustainable NRM focused initiatives to improve the livelihoods of the socially marginalized/disadvantaged groups (including poor, women, tribals)'. In addition, as a policy, UPNRM aims to promote projects that are implemented employing innovative methodologies and approaches which could be mainstreamed into the traditional NRM approach and projects that have a scope for wider replicability. 300 projects with financial outlay of US$ 94.68 million have been supported. UPNRM is an innovative model of NRM-based enterprise

financing at the community level wherein loan and need-based grant funds were blended for project implementation. The programme is supported through bilateral collaboration with KfW and GIZ. The NRM programmes are also designed in such a way that they are aligned with national and sub-national priorities and the convergence with existing government programmes are achieved for increasing outreach and effectiveness of the interventions.

(v) **Rural infrastructure:** Rural infrastructure development has direct impact on several economic and social sustainability parameters. The Rural Infrastructure Development Fund (RIDF) set up in NABARD has emerged as an important source of funding for most of the state governments for the creation of critical rural infrastructure. RIDF investments have enabled the creation of additional irrigation potential and construction of a network of rural road and bridges for better connectivity in far-flung areas. Social projects assisted under RIDF have brought about improvement in the quality of rural life through education, health and sanitation, drinking water supply, and other projects. NABARD has sanctioned as many as 3,02,356 irrigation projects with an assistance of Rs 81,405 crore for irrigation development in the country up to 31 March 2017. The details are presented in Table 15.1.

Implementation of these projects have successfully brought 291.28 lakh ha under assured irrigation, thereby adding value of production to the tune of Rs 53,147 crore. Other tangible economic benefits of RIDF projects include diversification in cropping pattern and increase in productivity, increase in household income, creation of new assets by rural households, stability in farm income, increase in expenditure on education, impact on credit flow in command area, increase

Table 15.1   Irrigation Projects Sanctioned under RIDF
(Tranches I–XXII)

Type of Projects	No. of Projects	Sanctioned Amount (In Rs Crore)
Minor	293,332	40,661
Medium	894	9,770
Major	391	27,118
Micro	7,739	3,856
Total	302,356	81,405

Source: NABARD Annual Report 2016–17.

in value and use of land, and so on. Many of these projects sanctioned have had direct impact on climate change resilience building and low emission pathways.

Projects such canal-top solar power financed by NABARD in Gujarat, under NABARD Infrastructure Development Assistance (NIDA), has innovatively integrated the low emission approaches in development planning. Under NIDA, NABARD is also financing green investments such as in solar power generation, improvement of electricity distribution networks, and so on. Further due diligence is exercised in design and appraisal of these projects to avoid negative social and environmental externalities.

Recently the Government of India has created a Long Term Irrigation Fund (LTIF) in NABARD with a corpus of Rs 40,000 crore for the funding of central and state share of major and medium irrigation projects under Pradhan Mantri Krishi Sinchai Yojana (PMKSY). The purpose is to fund and fast-track implementation of incomplete major and medium irrigation projects. This will enable creation of additional irrigation potential of 7.6 Mha.

(vi) **Farmer Producer Organizations (FPOs):** About 85 per cent of India's operational farm holdings are in the category of small and marginal holdings. The farmers' collective input and marketing management approach promoted through FPOs has been promoting better crop management practices and resources efficiency. The Government of India had created the Producer Organisation Development and Upliftment Corpus (PRODUCE) Fund of Rs 200 crore in NABARD for the promotion of 2,000 FPOs. As on March 2017, 2,157 FPOs were mobilized by producer organization promoting institutions (POPIs) for their capacity building and further development for three years.

Similarly, other developmental initiatives of NABARD are based on sustainable resource management taking into consideration community or farmers' need. The Farmers Club Programme covering 1.54 lakh farmers' clubs promotes the use of technology and credit discipline as an approach for enhancing farmers' income.

15.7.3 Ensuring Climate Resilient Rural Prosperity

As per recorded observations, India has seen an increase of 0.4 degree Centigrade, in the mean surface air temperature over the past century. It has been estimated that a 2.0 to 3.5 degree Centigrade increase in temperature and associated increase in precipitation can lower agricultural GDP by 9 to 28 per cent (12th Five Year Plan). The impact of climate change is global, but countries like India are more vulnerable due to dependence of majority of the population on agriculture and predominance of small and marginal farm holders. Significant negative impact has been projected for India in the medium-term, that is, 2010–39. It is predicted that yields will reduce by 4.5 to 9 per cent, depending on the magnitude and distribution of warming (NICRA).[2]

NABARD, in the recent past, has taken up important steps for accessing national and international funding mechanism for climate finance. NABARD has been accredited as 'National Implementing Entity (NIE)' for India under the 'Adaptation Fund' created under United Nations Framework Convention on Climate Change (UNFCCC). In the capacity of NIE, NABARD has generated a number of feasible projects on climate change adaptation in diverse agro-climatic regions and livelihood sectors. The Adaptation Fund Board (AFB) has sanctioned six projects submitted by NABARD with an outlay of US$ 9.86 million. The projects sanctioned so far by AFB represent varied agro-climatic regions and livelihood sectors, namely, mangrove fish farming in Andhra Pradesh, climate-smart agriculture in dryland areas of West Bengal, climate resilient inland fisheries in Madhya Pradesh, climate proofing of watersheds in Tamil Nadu and Rajasthan, climate resilient agriculture for the Himalayan region in Uttarakhand as well as reducing climate change-linked stress on forest biodiversity in Kanha Pench Corridor of Madhya Pradesh. These projects are designed to generate key learnings for development of adaptation projects which can be mainstreamed under existing programmes and policies.

NABARD has also been accredited as Direct Access Entity (DAE) for accessing resources under the Green Climate Fund (GCF). The resources under GCF are proposed to be utilized for creating a paradigm shift towards low-carbon pathways and climate resilient development. A project, namely, 'Ground water recharge and solar micro irrigation to ensure food security and enhance resilience in vulnerable tribal areas of Odisha', with a total outlay of US$ 166.27 million and a GCF grant of US$ 34.36 million, covering 10,000 ponds in 15 districts of Odisha, have been approved.

---

[2] http://www.nicra-icar.in/nicrarevised/index.php/component/content/article?id=69.

NABARD is also the NIE for National Adaptation Fund on Climate Change (NAFCC) set up by the Government of India. Twenty-one projects involving a total amount of Rs 442.88 crore have been sanctioned by NAFCC up to 31 March 2017.

15.7.4 Ensuring Skill Development

NABARD has been supporting rural entrepreneurship development programmes (REDPs) and skill development programmes (SDPs) for facilitating generation of self-employment and wage employment opportunities for the rural youth. Cumulatively, NABARD has supported conducting 31,022 REDPs and other Skill Development Initiatives (SDIs) imparting training to 8.02 lakh unemployed rural youth as on 31 March 2017. Further, under the Financial Inclusion Fund (FIF), NABARD provides one-time support to banks for running business and skill development centres, including rural self-employment training institutes (RSETIs) for purchase of training equipment and its maintenance.

15.7.5 Ensuring Sanitation and Habitats

Acknowledging the fact that rural people do not have access to adequate sanitation facilities, NABARD has been supporting sanitation projects through grant assistance since 2005. NABARD has also taken the the Government of India's 'Swachchh Bharat Abhiyan' forward by sanctioning sanitation projects. Further, NABARD has supported the improvement of school infrastructure, covering sanitation facilities under RIDF. As part of NABARD's mandate to bring about rural development and secure rural prosperity as also to align its policies with the Government of India's mission for providing 'Housing for All' by 2022, NABARD has been supporting the sector through a comprehensive rural housing policy.

15.7.6 Ensuring Gender Equality

The SHG–Bank Linkage Programme (SBLP), pioneered by NABARD more than two decades ago, started with a pilot of 500 self-help groups (SHGs) and now covers about 8.6 million SHGs, including 7.3 million women's SHGs, and nearly 101 million poor households in India (as on 31 March 2017). The rural poor, thought to be unbankable prior to the SBLP epoch, now constitute a staggering 4.8 million SHGs (including 4.3 women's SHGs), having credit outstanding of more than Rs 61,581 crore (Rs 56,444 crore in respect of women's SHGs) with formal lending institutions (as on 31 March 2017). The programme has

resulted in deepening and widening of access to financial services. NABARD has been enabling livelihood promotion and graduation of SHG members through a variety of programmes that focus on upgradation of skills and developing entrepreneurial abilities. With a view to creating sustainable livelihoods among SHG members and to create maximum impact of skill upgradation with hand-holding and credit linkages, the 'Livelihood and Enterprise Development Programme' (LEDP) was launched in December 2015. These programmes are implemented in small batches for a maximum of 150 SHG members on a project basis covering 15 to 30 SHGs in a cluster of contiguous villages. The programme covers agricultural and allied activities as well as rural non-farm sector activities.

15.7.7 Risk Mitigation Measures

(i) **Agriculture insurance:** The 'Pradhan Mantri Fasal Bima Yojana' (PMFBY) is a path-breaking scheme, which aims to provide insurance coverage and financial support to farmers in the event of failure of any of the notified crops as a result of natural calamities, pests, and diseases. It also aims at stabilizing income of farmers to ensure their continuance in farming. Further, it encourages farmers to adopt innovative and modern agricultural practices, to ensure flow of credit to the agriculture sector. The premium rates to be paid by farmers are very low and balance premium will be paid by the government to provide full-insured amount to the farmers against crop loss on account of natural calamities. The use of technology will be encouraged to a great extent. Smartphones will be used to capture and upload data on crop cutting to reduce the delays in claim payment to farmers. Remote sensing will be used to reduce the number of crop cutting experiments. NABARD is assisting the Government of India and state governments in the operationalization of these schemes in all the states through the banking sector.

(ii) **Weather and Crop Advisory Services:** NABARD has financed various initiatives for extending weather and crop advisory services to famers, which is an important aspect of building resilience to climate change. Under its 'Farm Sector Promotion Fund', NABARD extended weather, crop, and market advisory services through mobile phones to 55,000 farmers. Similarly information on weather and crop advisory is being delivered in collaboration with India Meteorological Department (IMD) and Krishi Vigyan Kendras (KVKs) through farmers' clubs. An approach has been developed and piloted by the Watershed Organisation Trust (WOTR), in collaboration with IMD and the State Agriculture University (MPKV) in the Climate Change Adaptation Project in Maharashtra supported by NABARD, to provide weather-based crop advisories to farmers, offer important learnings as to how to improve weather forecasting, customize crop advisories, bridge barriers, leverage institutional strengths, and accelerate adoption of on-farm adaptive responses. The key feature of this approach is that it creates a dialogue between science and technology on the one hand and field reality and the farmer on the other, with the latter being an active co-evolver of knowledge and action. This results not only in addressing immediate and emergent problems, but also the acquisition of long-term adaptive capabilities—practical knowledge that is 'owned' by the farming and scientific community alike, improved human capacities and increased resilience of farming systems. This collaborative agro-meteorology outreach project consists of the following components:

(a) Establishment of automated weather stations (AWSs) at the village level, creating weather awareness and generating a geo-referenced farmers' database;
(b) Real-time transmission of local weather data to the IMD and obtaining locale-specific short-range weather forecasts;
(c) Generation of weather-based crop- and farmer-specific advisories;
(d) Multi-channel dissemination of advisories supported by on-site capacity building and knowledge and technology transfer;
(e) Gathering feedback, actively engaging with government, public agencies, and local governance institutions.

15.8 CONCLUSION

Ensuring sustainability while following a path of rapid economic growth remains an important challenge for India. The SDGs are more ambitious than the millennium development goals, covering a broad range of interconnected issues, from economic growth to social issues to global public goods. It requires judicious prioritization, and adaption of the goals and targets in accordance with local challenges, capacities, and resources available.

Achievement of sustainable development objectives by India is closely linked to various development issues concerning rural India. The development challenges faced by rural India are very critical and require substantial resources and institutional frameworks for delivery of these development targets. Integrating these challenges with social and environmental concerns becomes more critical in case of the rural sector. With resource constraints and low institutional capacities, accelerating development would require both public and private sector investment.

The Government of India has reiterated its thrust on the farm sector by announcing 'Doubling of Farmers' Income by 2022'. Attaining the national goals and at the same time maintaining the environment gifted to us could be an insurmountable challenge that lies ahead. Further, the country, being committed to collective action to combat climate change, has to implement suitable adaptation and mitigation measures as well. These diverse and contrasting targets and commitments make the policy arena in respect of agriculture and rural development a complex one warranting a host of precise decisions.

We have to evolve a sustainable development model by taking into consideration the basic needs of our population and also preserving our natural resources for the use of coming generations. NABARD, a national entity with an intrinsic mission of promoting sustainable development has always been in the forefront of policy advocacy, which will be continued with greater vigour.

REFERENCE

UNDP. 2016. *Human Development Report, 2016 Human Development for Everyone*. New York: United Nations Development Programme.